Contemporary Human Geography

CUSTOM EDITION

Contemporary Human Geography

CUSTOM EDITION

James M. Rubenstein
MIAMI UNIVERSITY, OXFORD, OHIO

Taken from:
Contemporary Human Geography, Second Edition
by James M. Rubenstein

PEARSON

Pearson
Geography Editor: Christian Botting
Marketing Manager: Maureen McLaughlin
Project Editor: Anton Yakovlev
VP/Executive Director, Development: Carol Trueheart
Development Editors: Jonathan Cheney and Melissa Parkin
Media Producer: Ziki Dekel
Assistant Editor: Kristen Sanchez
Editorial Assistant: Bethany Sexton
Marketing Assistant: Nicola Houston
Managing Editor, Geosciences and Chemistry: Gina M. Cheselka
Project Manager, Production: Maureen Pancza
Project Manager, Full Service: Cindy Miller
Compositor: Element Thomson North America
Senior Technical Art Specialist: Connie Long
Image Lead: Maya Melenchuk
Photo Researcher: Stefanie Ramsay, Bill Smith Group
Operations Specialist: Michael Penne
Cover Photo: Front: Chicago Millennium Park. Back: Aerial view of Chicago.

Dorling Kindersley
Design Development, Page Design, and Layout: Stuart Jackman
Page Layout: Anthony Limerick
Cover Design: Stuart Jackman

Credits and acknowledgments borrowed from other sources and reproduced, with permission, in this textbook appear on the appropriate page within the text.

Taken from:
Contemporary Human Geography, Second Edition
by James M. Rubenstein
Copyright © 2013, 2010 by Pearson Education, Inc.
Published by Pearson Education, Inc.
Glenview, IL 60025

CIP data available upon request.

Pearson Learning Solutions, 501 Boylston Street, Suite 900, Boston, MA 02116
A Pearson Education Company
www.pearsoned.com

Printed in the United States of America
11 12 13 14 15 16 V011 18 17 16 15 14

0002000010271741183
NL

 ISBN 10: 1-269-22062-4
ISBN 13: 978-1-269-22062-0

Brief Contents

Contents

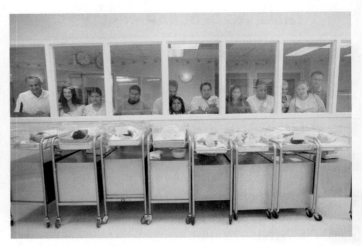

3 **MIGRATION**

4 **FOLK AND POPULAR CULTURE**

7 ETHNICITY

8 POLITICAL GEOGRAPHY

11 INDUSTRY

12 SERVICES AND SETTLEMENTS

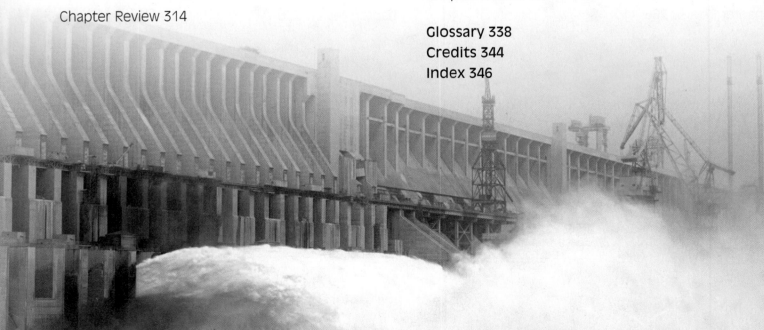

Preface

Welcome to a new kind of geography textbook! We live in a visual age, and geography is a highly visual discipline, so Pearson—the world's leading publisher of geography textbooks—invites you to study human geography as a visual subject.

This edition of *Contemporary Human Geography* builds on the strengths of the first edition, while responding to user feedback to make important changes and improvements, and incorporating innovative new features, current data, and new information.

NEW TO THIS EDITION

- **Quick Response (QR) Codes.** Each chapter opens with an introductory module that includes a QR code, enabling students on the go to link smartphones from the book to various websites relevant to each chapter, providing easy and immediate access to up-to-date information, data, and statistics from sources such as the United Nations or the U.S. Geological Survey.
- **Key Questions and Main Points.** Each chapter module is framed by conceptual "Key Questions," which ask students to take a bigger picture approach to the concept, and by two "Main Points," which students should understand after studying the module. These Key Questions and Main Points serve as an outline for the topics covered in the chapter and are revisited in the end-of-chapter Review.
- **New and Revised Cartography.** All maps have been thoroughly updated and optimized for maximum accuracy and clear presentation of current data. New projections are used with fewer distortions.
- **Integration of Photos and Text.** The best possible images have been carefully chosen to complement content and concepts. This edition features well over 400 new photos.

- **The latest science, statistics, and associated imagery.** Data sources include the 2010 U.S. Census and the 2011 Population Reference Bureau World Population Data. Also covers recent political conflicts, economic difficulties, and cultural phenomena such as Facebook and social networking.
- **MapMaster™ Interactive Maps.** These layered thematic interactive maps act as a mini-GIS, allowing students to layer different data at global and regional scales to examine the resulting spatial patterns and practice critical thinking. The interactive maps, with associated tasks and questions, are integrated into select chapter modules and into all end-of-chapter review modules, encouraging students to log in to MasteringGeography to access these exciting geospatial media to practice visual analysis and critical thinking.
- **Google Earth™ Explorations.** Images integrated into select chapter modules and at the end of the chapter pose questions to be answered through Google Earth, the leader in desktop geospatial imagery.
- **Thinking Geographically.** These critical-thinking questions are found at the end of each chapter, giving students a chance to practice higher-order thinking.
- **Looking Ahead.** Each chapter concludes with a brief preview of the next chapter and highlights connections between chapters.
- The new **MasteringGeography™** platform is linked to the Key Questions and Main Points and contains a wide range of assignable and self study resources and activities designed to reinforce basic concepts in human geography, including MapMaster interactive maps, Google Earth activities, geography videos, and more. www.MasteringGeography.com

HUMAN GEOGRAPHY IS CONTEMPORARY

The main purpose of this book is to introduce you to the study of geography as a social science by emphasizing the relevance of geographic concepts to human problems.

A central theme in this book is a tension between two important realities of the twenty-first-century world—globalization and cultural diversity. In many respects we are living in a more unified world economically, culturally, and environmentally. The actions of a particular corporation or country affect people around the world. This book argues that, after a period when globalization of the economy and culture has been a paramount concern in geographic analysis, local diversity now demands equal time. People are taking deliberate steps to retain distinctive cultural identities. They are preserving little-used languages, fighting fiercely to protect their religions, and carving out distinctive economic roles.

Recent world events lend a sense of urgency to geographic inquiry. More than a decade into the twenty-first century, we continue to face wars in unfamiliar places and experience economic struggles unprecedented in the lifetimes of students or teachers. Geography's spatial perspectives help to relate economic change to the distributions of cultural features such as languages and religions, demographic patterns such as population growth and migration, and natural resources such as energy, water quality, and food supply.

For example, geographers examine the prospects for an energy crisis by relating the distributions of energy sources and consumption. Geographers find that the users of energy are located in places with different social, economic, and political institutions than the producers of energy. Geographers seek first to describe the distribution of features such as the production and consumption of energy, and then to explain the relationships between these distributions and other human and physical phenomena.

CHAPTER ORGANIZATION

Each chapter is organized into between 9 and 12 two-page modular "spreads" that follow a consistent pattern:

- **Introductory module.** The first spread includes a short introduction to the chapter, as well as an outline of between 9 and 12 issues that will be addressed in the chapter. The key issues are grouped into several overarching Key Questions for that chapter.
- **Topic modules.** Between 9 and 12 modules cover the principal topics of the chapter. Each of these two-page spreads is self-contained and organized around the Key Questions and Main Points, making it easier for an instructor to shuffle the order of presentation. A numbering system also facilitates finding material on a particular spread.
- **Chapter Review modules.** Following the topic modules are concluding spreads that review the chapter's main concepts and key terms while providing students with opportunities to interact with media and engage in critical thinking. The Chapter Review features include:

  o **Key Questions.** The Key Questions presented on the introductory spread are repeated, along with an outline summary of Main Points made in the chapter that address the questions.

  o **On the Internet.** URLs are listed for several useful Internet sites related to the themes of the chapter.

  o **Thinking Geographically.** A thought-provoking idea is introduced, based on concepts and themes developed in the chapter, along with "essay-style" questions.

  o **Interactive Mapping.** Using Pearson's MapMaster interactive mapping media, students create maps and answer questions about spatial relationships of different data. Teachers have the option of assigning these questions in MasteringGeography.

  o **Explore.** Using Google Earth, students inspect imagery from places around the world and answer questions based on their observations. Teachers have the option of assigning these questions in MasteringGeography.

o **Key Terms.** The key terms in each chapter are indicated in bold type when they are introduced. These terms are defined both at the end of the chapter and at the end of the book.

o **Looking Ahead.** This feature provides a bridge from the chapter just concluded to the one just ahead.

HOW TO USE THIS BOOK'S MEDIA

Contemporary Human Geography features an innovative integration of media and connections to the MasteringGeography platform, giving students *and* instructors flexible self-study and assessment options to extend the book with current data, interactive mapping, and exciting geospatial tools.

- **Quick Response Codes.** Traditional books are challenged to provide students with quick and easy access to original sources and up-to-date data. *Quick Response codes* integrated into the beginning of each chapter help solve this problem, enabling students to use their mobile devices to easily and instantly access websites with current data and information related to chapter topics.

- **MapMaster™ Interactive Maps.** Maps are an important part of the geographer's toolset, but traditional print maps are limited in their ability to allow students to dynamically isolate or compare different spatial data. Available in MasteringGeography both for student self-study and for teachers as assignable and automatically gradable assessment activities, *MapMaster Interactive Maps* act as mini-GIS tools, allowing students to overlay, isolate, and examine different thematic data at regional and global scales.

  Select chapter modules and all chapter review modules from the book present MapMaster maps, along with activities and questions, encouraging students to login to the MasteringGeography Study Area on their own to explore additional map data layers to complete the activities and extend their learning beyond the book's maps.

Teachers have the option of assigning these short answer questions for credit in MasteringGeography. Teachers also have access to a separate large suite of MapMaster activities for each chapter, including hundreds of multiple-choice questions that can be customized, assigned, and automatically graded by the MasteringGeography system, for a wide range of interactive mapping assessment activity options.

- **Google Earth™.** Geobrowser technology provides unparalleled opportunity for students to get a sense of place and explore Earth's physical and cultural landscapes with mashups of various data and digital media.

  Select chapter modules and all chapter review modules present *Google Earth* imagery and activities, encouraging students to connect the print book to this exciting tool to browse the globe and explore different data, perform visual and spatial analysis tasks, and extend their learning beyond the book's photos and figures.

  Teachers have the option of assigning these short answer questions for credit, and also have access to a separate large suite of Google Earth *Encounter* activities for each chapter, including hundreds of associated multiple-choice questions that can be customized, assigned, and automatically graded by the MasteringGeography system.

  For classes not using MasteringGeography, the Google Earth *Encounter* activities are also available via a set of standalone workbooks and websites.

OUTLINE OF TOPICS

This book discusses the following main topics:

What basic concepts do geographers use?

Geographers employ several concepts to describe the distribution of people and activities across Earth, to explain reasons underlying the observed distribution, and to understand the significance of the arrangements. Chapter 1 provides an introduction to ways that geographers think about the world.

Where are people located in the world?

Why do some places on Earth contain large numbers of people or attract newcomers whereas other places are sparsely inhabited? Chapters 2 and 3 examine the distribution and growth of the world's population, as well as the movement of people from one place to another.

How are different cultural groups distributed?

Geographers look for similarities and differences in the cultural features at different places, the reasons for their distribution, and the importance of these differences for world peace. Chapters 4 through 8 analyze the distribution of different cultural traits and beliefs and the political challenges that result from those spatial patterns. Important cultural traits discussed in Chapter 4 include food, clothing, shelter, and leisure activities. Chapters 5 through 7 examine three main elements of cultural identity: language, religion, and ethnicity. Chapter 8 looks at political problems that arise from cultural diversity.

How do people earn a living in different parts of the world?

Human survival depends on acquiring an adequate food supply. One of the most significant distinctions among people globally is whether they produce their food directly from the land or buy it with money earned by performing other types of work. Chapters 9 through 12 look at the three main ways of earning a living: agriculture, manufacturing, and services. Chapter 13 discusses cities, the centers for economic and cultural activities.

What issues result from using Earth's resources?

Geographers recognize that cultural problems result from the depletion, destruction, and inefficient use of the world's natural resources. Chapter 14 is devoted to a study of issues related to the use of Earth's natural resources.

THE TEAM

At this point in the preface, an author usually goes through the motions of perfunctorily thanking many people who performed jobs that resulted in the book's production. In this case, collaborative partnership is a better way to describe the process. Let's face it, some textbooks have been slow to adapt to our visual age. This is because the steps involved in producing most textbooks haven't changed much. The book passes from one to another like a baton in a relay race; those responsible for producing a book's graphics typically start their work only after the author's words have been written, reviewed, and approved.

In contrast, this book started as a genuine partnership among the key editorial and production teams. Each two-page module was assembled in the reverse order of traditional textbooks. Instead of beginning with an author's complete manuscript, this book started with a sketch of a visual concept for each two-page module in the book. What would be the most important geographic idea presented on the spread, and what would be the most effective visual way to portray that idea? The maps and images were placed on the page first, and then the text was written around the graphics.

The traditional separation of editorial and production personnel did not occur, and in fact the lines between the two were deliberately blurred. Key members of the team included Stuart Jackman, Christian Botting, Anton Yakovlev, Melissa Parkin, Jonathan Cheney, and Cindy Miller.

Stuart Jackman, Design Director at DK Education, is the creative genius responsible for the spectacular graphics. Stuart and the DK team deserve the lion's share of the credit for giving this book the best graphics in geography.

Christian Botting, Geography Editor at Pearson Education, led the team with both the big picture and the reality checks. Christian mastered the many challenges posed by our untraditional workflow.

Anton Yakovlev, Geography Project Manager at Pearson Education, was the ringmaster. Anton kept track of what was where and who was doing what, and joined in the many discussions on design elements.

Senior Development Editor Melissa Parkin and Executive Development Editor Jonathan Cheney contributed substantially to this complex and creative project.

Cindy Miller, Vice President of Higher Education at the Element division of Thomson Digital, led the unusually complex task of managing the flow of copyediting and other production tasks for this project.

Many others have contributed to the success of this project. At DK, Anthony Limerick, Senior Designer, helped create the book's distinctive layouts. Sophie Mitchell, Publisher at DK Education, provided the strategic vision for the design team. At Spatial Graphics, Kevin Lear and Andy Green developed the maps and line art throughout the book.

At Pearson Education, Managing Editor Gina Cheselka and Production Project Manager Maureen Pancza were a major organizing force in the nonstandard production workflow. Editorial Assistant Bethany Sexton organized the substantial reviewing process for the project. Marketing Manager Maureen McLaughlin expertly created the marketing package for this unique book. Media Producer Ziki Dekel managed the production of the MasteringGeography program and senior Media Producer Angela Bernhardt managed the production of MapMaster interactive maps.

REVIEWERS

I would like to extend a special thanks to my colleagues who served as reviewers on the first and second editions, as well as on overlapping material from *Introduction to Contemporary Geography*:

Roger Balm, Rutgers University

Joby Bass, University of Southern Mississippi

Steve Bass, Mesa Community College

David C. Burton, Southmoore High School

Michelle Calvarese, California State University, Fresno

Craig S. Campbell, Youngstown State University

Edward Carr, University of South Carolina

Carolyn Coulter, Atlantic Cape Community College

Stephen Davis, University of Illinois, Chicago

Owen Dwyer, Indiana University-Purdue University, Indianapolis

Leslie Edwards, Georgia State University

Caitie Finlayson, University of Florida

Barbara E. Fredrich, San Diego State University

Piper Gaubatz, University of Massachusetts, Amherst

Daniel Hammel, University of Toledo

James Harris, Metropolitan State College of Denver

Leila Harris, University of Wisconsin

Susan Hartley, Lake Superior College

Marc Healy, Elgin Community College

Scot Hoiland, Butte College

Wilbur Hugli, University of West Florida

Anthony Ijomah, Harrisburg Area Community College

Karen Johnson-Webb, Bowling Green State University

Oren Katz, California State University, Los Angeles

Marti Klein, Saddleback College

Olaf Kuhlke, University of Minnesota, Duluth

Peter Landreth, Westmont High School

Jose López-Jiménez, Minnesota State University, Mankato

Claudia Lowe, Fullerton College

Ken Lowrey, Wright State University

Jerry Mitchell, University of South Carolina

Eric C. Neubauer, Columbus State Community College

Ray Oman, University of the District of Columbia

Lynn Patterson, Kennesaw State University

Tim Scharks, Green River Community College

Debra Sharkey, Cosumnes River College

Wendy Shaw, Southern Illinois University, Edwardsville

Laurel Smith, University of Oklahoma

James Tyner, Kent State University

Richard Tyre, Florida State University

Daniel Vara, College Board Advanced Placement Human Geography Consultant

Anne Will, Skagit Valley College

Lei Xu, California State University, Fullerton

Daisaku Yamamoto, Central Michigan University

Robert C. Ziegenfus, Kutztown University of Pennsylvania

About the Author

Dr. James M. Rubenstein received his B.A. from the University of Chicago in 1970, M.Sc. from the London School of Economics and Political Science in 1971, and Ph.D. from Johns Hopkins University in 1975. He is Professor of Geography at Miami University, where he teaches urban and human geography. Dr. Rubenstein also conducts research in the automotive industry and has published three books on the subject—*The Changing U.S. Auto Industry: A Geographical Analysis* (Routledge); *Making and Selling Cars: Innovation and Change in the U.S. Auto Industry* (The Johns Hopkins University Press); and *Who Really Made Your Car? Restructuring and Geographic Change in the Auto Industry* (W.E. Upjohn Institute, with Thomas Klier). Dr. Rubenstein is also the author of *The Cultural Landscape,* the bestselling textbook for college and high school human geography, as well as *Introduction to Contemporary Geography.* He is a semiamateur, semiprofessional painter and displays his work at galleries in Maryland and Ohio. Winston, a lab-husky mix with one brown eye and one blue eye, takes Dr. Rubenstein for long walks in the woods every day.

This book is dedicated to Bernadette Unger, Dr. Rubenstein's wife, who has been by his side through many books, as well as to the memory of his father Bernard W. Rubenstein. Dr. Rubenstein also gratefully thanks the rest of his family for their love and support.

About Our Sustainability Initiatives

Pearson recognizes the environmental challenges facing this planet, as well as acknowledges our responsibility in making a difference. This book is carefully crafted to minimize environmental impact. The -binding, cover, and paper come from facilities that minimize waste, -energy consumption, and the use of harmful chemicals. Pearson closes the loop by recycling every out-of-date text returned to our warehouse.

Along with developing and exploring digital solutions to our market's needs, Pearson has a strong commitment to achieving -carbon-neutrality. As of 2009, Pearson became the first carbon- and -climate-neutral publishing company. Since then, Pearson remains strongly committed to measuring, reducing, and offsetting our carbon footprint.

The future holds great promise for reducing our impact on Earth's environment, and Pearson is proud to be leading the way. We strive to publish the best books with the most up-to-date and accurate content, and to do so in ways that minimize our impact on Earth. To learn more about our initiatives, please visit **www.pearson.com/responsibility.**

The Teaching and Learning Package

This edition provides a complete human geography program for students and teachers.

FOR STUDENTS AND TEACHERS:
MasteringGeography with Pearson eText www.masteringgeography.com

The Mastering platform is the most effective and widely used tutorial, homework, and assessment system for the sciences. It helps instructors maximize class time with customizable, easy-to-assign, and automatically graded assessments that motivate students to learn outside of class and arrive prepared for lecture. These assessments can easily be customized and personalized for an instructor's individual teaching style. The powerful gradebook and diagnostic features provide unique insight into student and class performance even before the first test. As a result, instructors can spend class time where students need it most. The Mastering system empowers students to take charge of their learning through activities aimed at different learning styles, and engages them in learning science through practice and step-by-step guidance–at their convenience, 24/7. MasteringGeography offers:

o Assignable activities that include MapMaster interactive maps, geography videos, *Encounter Human Geography* Google Earth Explorations, Thinking Spatially and Data Analysis activities, end-of-chapter questions, reading quizzes, *Test Bank* questions, and more.
o Student study area with MapMaster interactive maps, geography videos, glossary flashcards, "In the News" RSS feeds, reference maps, an optional Pearson eText, and more.

MasteringGeography icons are integrated within the chapters of the text to highlight various online self-study media.

   MasteringGeography with Pearson eText gives students access to the text whenever and wherever they can access the Internet. The eText pages look exactly like the printed text, and include powerful interactive and annotation functions, including links to the multimedia.

Teaching College Geography: A Practical Guide for Graduate Students and Early Career Faculty (0136054471)

This two-part resource provides a starting point for becoming an effective geography teacher from the very first day of class. Divided in two parts, Part One addresses "nuts-and-bolts" teaching issues. Part Two explores being an effective teacher in the field, supporting critical thinking with GIS and mapping technologies, engaging learners in large geography classes, and promoting awareness of international perspectives and geographic issues.

Aspiring Academics: A Resource Book for Graduate Students and Early Career Faculty (0136048919)

Drawing on several years of research, this set of essays is designed to help graduate students and early career faculty start their careers in geography and related social and environmental sciences. *Aspiring Academics* stresses the interdependence of teaching, research, and service—and the importance of achieving a healthy balance of professional and personal life—while doing faculty work. Each chapter provides accessible, forward-looking advice on topics that often cause the most stress in the first years of a college or university appointment.

Practicing Geography: Careers for Enhancing Society and the Environment
(0321811151)

This book examines career opportunities for geographers and geospatial professionals in business, government, nonprofit, and educational sectors. A diverse group of academic and industry professionals share insights on career planning, networking, transitioning between employment sectors, and balancing work and home life. The book illustrates the value of geographic expertise and technologies through engaging profiles and case studies of geographers at work.

AAG Community Portal

This Web site is intended to support community-based professional development in geography and related disciplines. Here you will find activities providing extended treatment of the topics covered in both books. The activities can be used in workshops, graduate seminars, brown bags, and mentoring programs offered on campus or within an academic department. You can also use the discussion boards and contributions tool to share advice and materials with others. The Web site is found at www.personhighered.com/aag/.

FOR STUDENTS:
Goode's World Atlas, 22nd edition, by Rand McNally (0321652002)

Goode's World Atlas has been the world's premiere educational atlas since 1923, and for good reason. It features over 250 pages of maps, from definitive physical and political maps to important thematic maps that illustrate the spatial aspects of many important topics. The 22nd edition includes 160 pages of new, digitally produced reference maps, as well as new thematic maps on global climate change, sea level rise, CO_2 emissions, polar ice fluctuations, deforestation, extreme weather events, infectious diseases, water resources, and energy production.

Television for the Environment *Life* Human Geography Videos on DVD
(0132416565)

This three-DVD set is designed to enhance any human geography course. It contains 14 complete video programs covering a wide array of issues affecting people and places in the contemporary world, including international immigration, urbanization, global trade, poverty, and environmental destruction. The videos included on these DVDs are offered at the highest quality to allow for full-screen viewing on a computer and projection in large lecture classrooms.

Television for the Environment *Earth Report* Geography Videos on DVD
(0321662989)

This three-DVD set is designed to help students visualize how human decisions and behavior have affected the environment and how individuals are taking steps toward recovery. With topics ranging from the poor land management promoting the devastation of river systems in Central America to the struggles for electricity in China and Africa, these 13 videos from Television for the Environment's global *Earth Report* series recognize the efforts of individuals around the world to unite and protect the planet.

Television for the Environment *Life* World Regional Geography Videos on DVD (013159348X)

From Television for the Environment's global *Life* series, this two-DVD set brings globalization and the developing world to the attention of any world regional geography course. These 10 full-length video programs highlight matters such as the growing number of homeless children in Russia, the lives of immigrants living in the United States trying to aid family still living in their native countries, and the European conflict between commercial interests and environmental concerns.

Encounter Human Geography Workbook and Website by Jess C. Porter (0321682203)

For classes that do not use MasteringGeography, *Encounter Human Geography* provides rich, interactive explorations of human geography concepts through Google Earth. Students explore the globe through themes such as population, sexuality and gender, political geography, ethnicity, urban geography, migration, human health, and language. All chapter explorations are available in print format as well as online quizzes, accommodating different classroom needs. All worksheets are accompanied with cooresponding Google Earth media files, available for download for those who do not use MasteringGeography, from http://www.mygeoscienceplace.com.

Dire Predictions: Understanding Global Warming by Michael Mann and Lee R. Kump (0136044352)

For any science or social science course in need of a basic understanding of IPCC reports. Periodic reports from the Intergovernmental Panel on Climate Change (IPCC) evaluate the risk of climate change brought on by humans. But the sheer volume of scientific data remains inscrutable to the general public, particularly to those who may still question the validity of climate change. In just over 200 pages, this practical text presents and expands upon the essential findings in a visually stunning and undeniably powerful way to the lay reader. Scientific findings that provide validity to the implications of climate change are presented in clear-cut graphic elements, striking images, and understandable analogies.

FOR TEACHERS:

Instructor Resource DVD for Contemporary Human Geography, 2nd edition (0321819233)

The *Instructor Resource DVD* provides high-quality electronic versions of photos and illustrations form the book in JPEG, pdf, and PowerPoint formats, as well as customizable PowerPoint lecture presentations, Classroom Response System questions in PowerPoint, and the *Instructor Resource Manual* and *Test Bank* in MS. Word and TestGen formats. For easy reference and identification, all resources are organized by chapter.

Instructor Resource Manual (download only) for Contemporary Human Geography, 2nd edition, by Jacqueline McKenzie (0321819802)

New to the second edition, the *Instructor Resource Manual,* is intended as a resource for both new and experienced instructors. It includes lecture outlines, additional source materials, teaching tips, advice about how to integrate visual supplements (including the Web-based resources), and various other ideas for the classroom. http://www.pearsonhighered.com/irc.

TestGen® Computerized Test Bank (download only) for Contemporary Human Geography, 2nd edition, by Tim Scharks and Iddi Adam (0321792408)

TestGen is a computerized test generator that lets instructors view and edit *Test Bank* questions, transfer questions to tests, and print the test in a variety of customized formats. This *Test Bank* includes over 1,000 multiple choice, true/false, and short answer/essay questions. Questions are correlated to the revised U.S. National Geography Standards and Bloom's Taxonomy to help instructors better map the assessments against both broad and specific teaching and learning objectives. The *Test Bank* questions are also tagged to chapter specific learning outcomes. The *Test Bank* is available in Microsoft Word, and is importable into Blackboard. http://www.pearsonhighered.com/irc

Modular Springboard

With an innovative integration of visuals, text, active learning tools, and online media, *Contemporary Human Geography*, Second Edition is a modular and highly graphical springboard to human geography—ideal for contemporary students and learning styles.

10 Food and Agriculture

What do people eat?

What challenges does agriculture face?

How is agriculture distributed?

Every chapter is organized around conceptual **"Key Questions,"** which ask students to take a bigger picture approach to the concept, with each module framed by two unique **"Main Points,"** which students should understand after reading the module.

The book's **modular organization** consists of chapters made up of self-contained two-page spreads, a reliable presentation that offers the instructor flexibility. Each module uses integrated visuals, text, active learning tools, and online media, to effectively convey the concept at hand.

2.1 Population Concentrations

▶ Two-thirds of the world's inhabitants are clustered in four regions.
▶ Humans avoid clustering in harsh environments.

Human beings are not distributed uniformly across Earth's surface (Figure 2.1.1). Human beings avoid clustering in certain physical environments, especially those that are too dry, too wet, too cold, or too mountainous for activities such as agriculture (Figure 2.1.2).

The clustering of the world's population can be displayed on a cartogram, which depicts the size of countries according to population rather than land area, as is the case with most maps (Figure 2.1.3). Two-thirds of the world's inhabitants are clustered in four regions—East Asia, South Asia, Southeast Asia, and Europe (Figure 2.1.4).

▲ RORAIMA, BRAZIL

▶ 2.1.2 SPARSELY POPULATED REGIONS
Human beings do not live in large numbers in certain physical environments.

2.1.2A COLD LANDS
Much of the land near the North and South poles is perpetually covered with ice or the ground is permanently frozen (permafrost). The polar regions are unsuitable for planting crops, few animals can survive the extreme cold, and few human beings live there.

2.1.2B DRY LANDS
Areas too dry for farming cover approximately 20 percent of Earth's land surface. Deserts generally lack sufficient water to grow crops that could feed a large population, although some people survive there by raising animals, such as camels, that are adapted to the climate. Although dry lands are generally inhospitable to intensive agriculture, they may contain natural resources useful to people—notably, much of the world's oil reserves.

2.1.1C WET LANDS
Lands that receive very high levels of precipitation, such as near Brazil's Amazon River shown in the image, may also be sparsely inhabited. The combination of rain and heat rapidly depletes nutrients from the soil and thus hinders agriculture.

▼ 2.1.1 POPULATION DISTRIBUTION
Persons per square kilometer
● 1,000 and above   5–24
● 250–999   1–4
● 25–249   below1

▶ 2.1.4A EUROPE
Europe contains one-ninth of the world's people. The region includes four dozen countries, ranging from Monaco, with 1 square kilometer (0.7 square mile) and a population of 32,000, to Russia, the world's largest country in land area when its Asian land portion is included.

Three-fourths of Europe's inhabitants live in cities. A dense network of road and rail lines links settlements. Europe's highest population concentrations are near the major rivers and coalfields of Germany and Belgium, as well as historic capital cities like London and Paris.

The region's temperate climate permits cultivation of a variety of crops, yet Europeans do not produce enough food for themselves. Instead, they import food and other resources from elsewhere in the world. The search for additional resources was a major incentive for Europeans to explore and colonize other parts of the world during the previous six centuries. Today, Europeans turn many of these resources into manufactured products.

▼ 2.1.4 FOUR POPULATION CLUSTERS
The four regions display some similarities. Most of the people in these regions live near an ocean or near a river with easy access to an ocean, rather than in the interior of major landmasses. The four population clusters occupy generally low-lying areas, with fertile soil and temperate climate.

2.1.4B EAST ASIA
One-fifth of the world's people live in East Asia. This concentration includes the world's most populous country, the People's Republic of China. The Chinese population is clustered near the Pacific Coast and in several fertile river valleys that extend inland, such as the Huang and the Yangtze. Much of China's interior is sparsely inhabited mountains and deserts. Although China has 25 urban areas with more than 2 million inhabitants and 61 with more than 1 million, more than one-half of the people live in rural areas where they work as farmers.

In Japan and South Korea, population is not distributed uniformly either. Forty percent of the people live in three large metropolitan areas—Tokyo and Osaka in Japan, and Seoul in South Korea—that cover less than 3 percent of the two countries' land area. In sharp contrast to China, more than three-fourths of all Japanese and Koreans live in urban areas and work at industrial or service jobs.

2.1.4C SOUTHEAST ASIA
A third important Asian population cluster is in Southeast Asia. A half billion people live in Southeast Asia, mostly on a series of islands that lie between the Indian and Pacific oceans. These islands include Java, Sumatra, Borneo, Papua New Guinea, and the Philippines. The largest concentration is on the island of Java, inhabited by more than 100 million people. Indonesia, which consists of 13,677 islands, including Java, is the world's fourth most populous country.

Several islands that belong to the Philippines contain high population concentrations, and people are also clustered along several river valleys and deltas at the southeastern tip of the Asian mainland, known as Indochina. Like China and South Asia, the Southeast Asia concentration is characterized by a high percentage of people working as farmers in rural areas.

2.1.4D SOUTH ASIA
One-fifth of the world's people live in South Asia, which includes India, Pakistan, Bangladesh, and the island of Sri Lanka. The largest concentration of people within South Asia lives along a 1,500-kilometer (900-mile) corridor from Lahore, Pakistan, through India and Bangladesh to the Bay of Bengal. Much of this area's population is concentrated along the plains of the Indus and Ganges rivers. People are also heavily concentrated near India's two long coastlines—the Arabian Sea to the west and the Bay of Bengal to the east.

To an even greater extent than the Chinese, most people in South Asia are farmers living in rural areas. The region contains 18 urban areas with more than 2 million inhabitants and 46 with more than 1 million, but only one-fourth of the total population lives in an urban area.

2.1.2D HIGH LANDS
The highest mountains in the world are steep, snow covered, and sparsely settled. However, some high-altitude plateaus and mountain regions are more densely populated, especially at low latitudes (near the equator) where agriculture is possible at high elevations.

Countries with populations over 100 million are labeled.

▲ 2.1.3 POPULATION CARTOGRAM
The population cartogram displays the major population clusters of Europe, and East, South, and Southeast Asia as much larger, and Africa and the Western Hemisphere as much smaller than on a more typical equal-area map, such as the large one in the middle of these two pages.

▼ VARANASI, INDIA

Innovative End-of-Chapter Tools

Extend student learning with a rich suite of critical-thinking and media-rich activities.

Review of the Key Questions **and the associated** Main Points **from all modules in the chapter**

Thinking Geographically **critical-thinking questions**

MapMaster™ Interactive Mapping **activities**

Key Terms **definitions**

For many ethnicities, sharing space with other ethnicities is difficult, if not impossible. Grievances real and imagined, extending back hundreds of years, prevent peaceful coexistence. Even in countries like the United States, where ethnic diversity is a central feature of the shaping of the American nationality, discriminatory practices cast a long shadow over American history.

Key Questions

Where are ethnicities and races distributed?

▶ Ethnicity is identity with a group of people who share the cultural traditions of a particular homeland or hearth.

▶ Race is identity with a group of people who share a biological ancestor.

▶ Major ethnicities in the United States include African Americans, Hispanic Americans, Asian Americans, and Native Americans.

▶ Ethnic groups are clustered in regions of the country and within urban neighborhoods.

▶ African Americans have a distinctive history of forced migration for slavery.

Where are ethnicities and nationalities distributed?

▶ Nationality is identity with a group of people who share legal attachment and personal allegiance to a particular country.

▶ A nationality combines an ethnic group's language, religion, and artistic expressions with a country's particular independence movement, history, and patriotism.

Where do ethnicities face conflicts?

▶ The territory of a nationality rarely matches that inhabited by only one ethnicity.

▶ Ethnicities compete in many places to dominate territory and control the defining of a nationality.

▶ Ethnic cleansing is a process in which a more powerful ethnic group forcibly removes a less powerful one in order to create an ethnically homogeneous region.

▶ Genocide is the mass killing of a group of people in an attempt to eliminate the entire group out of existence.

On the Internet

The U.S. Bureau of the Census provides the most detailed information on the distribution by race and ethnicity in the United States at **www.census.gov**, or scan the QR at the beginning of the chapter.

Thinking Geographically

The U.S. Census permits people to identify themselves as being of more than one race, in recognition that several million American children have parents of two races.

1. What are the merits and difficulties of permitting people to choose more than one race.

Sarajevo, capital of Bosnia & Herzegovina, once contained concentrations of many ethnic groups. In retaliation for ethnic cleansing by the Serbs and Croats, the Bosnian Muslims now in control of Sarajevo have been forcing other ethnic groups to leave the city, and Sarajevo is now inhabited overwhelmingly by Bosnian Muslims (Figure 7.CR.1).

2. What are the challenges in restoring Sarajevo as a city that multiple ethnicities could inhabit?

A century ago European immigrants to the United States had much stronger ethnic ties than today, including clustering in specific neighborhoods..

3. What is the rationale for retaining strong ethnic identity in the United States as opposed to full assimilation into the American nationality?

▼ 7.CR.1 **SARAJEVO WAR GRAVES**

Interactive Mapping

ETHNICITIES AND NATIONALITIES IN SOUTHEAST ASIA

Matching the territory of a nationality to a single ethnicity is rare in the world.

Launch Mapmaster Southeast Asia in Mastering**GEOGRAPHY**

Select: *Cultural* then *Religions.* Select *Cultral* then *Languages* Select *Political* then *Countries*

Can you find an example of a nationality that almost entire encompasses a single ethnicity?

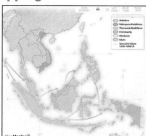

Explore

MUSEUMS IN DETROIT

Use Google Earth to explore major museums in Detroit that represent ethnic traditions.

Fly to: *Charles H. Wright Museum of African American History, Detroit*

Click 3D Buildings

Drag to: *Enter Street View* in front of the museum.

Exit *Ground Level View* and zoom out until the street and buildings one block to the west are visible.

Click on the Wright museum to see a description of its collection.

Click on the large building in the front left to see what's inside.

How would you compare the collections of the two museums?

Key Terms

Apartheid
Laws (no longer in effect) in South Africa that physically separated different races into different geographic areas.

Balkanization
Process by which a state breaks down through conflicts among its ethnicities.

Centripetal force
An attitude that tends to unify people and enhance support for a state.

Ethnic cleansing
Process in which a more powerful ethnic group forcibly removes a less powerful one from a ethnically homogeneous region.

Ethnicity
Identity with a group of people who share the cultural traditions of a particular homeland or hearth.

Genocide
The mass killing of a group of people in an attempt to eliminate the entire group from existence.

Nationalism
Loyalty and devotion to a particular nationality.

Nationality
Identity with a group of people who share legal attachment and personal allegiance to a particular place as a result of being born there.

Race
Identity with a group of people who share a biological ancestor.

Racism
Belief that race is the primary determinant of human traits and capacities and that racial differences produce an inherent superiority of a particular race.

Racist
A person who subscribes to the beliefs of racism.

Sharecropper
A person who works fields rented from a landowner and pays the rent and repays loans by turning over to the landowner a share of the crops.

Triangular slave trade
A practice, primarily during the eighteenth century, in which European ships transported slaves from Africa to Caribbean islands, molasses from the Caribbean to Europe, and trade goods from Europe to Africa.

▶ **LOOKING AHEAD**
Ethnicities aspire to political control over areas of Earth through the creation of nation-states, discussed in the next chapter.

On the Internet **web links**

Google Earth™ Explore **image analysis questions**

Looking Ahead **chapter preview section**

Current Data and Applications

The latest science, statistics, and imagery are used in the **Second Edition** for the most contemporary introduction to human geography.

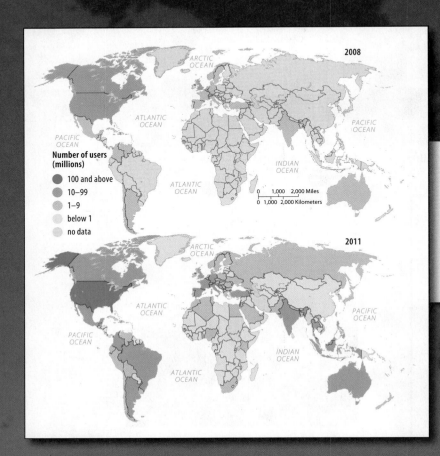

Current data incorporates the latest science, statistics, and imagery, including data from the 2010 U.S. Census, the 2011 World Population Reference Bureau World Population Data, as well as coverage of events like the 2011 "Arab Spring", the birth of South Sudan, and much more. These figures illustrate the explosive growth of Facebook.

Quick Response (QR) Codes on the chapter-opening pages enable students to use smartphones and other mobile devices to link from the book to various open source websites relevant to each chapter, providing easy and immediate access to original sources and up-to-date data.

Students simply scan the QR codes in the book with their mobile smartphones, after following a few easy steps:

1. Download a QR reader from an app store (there are many free apps available) or use the built-in code reader if the device has one.
2. Open the QR code reader app on the phone and scan the code (as shown on the left).
3. The student's device will be automatically redirected to the website. (*Note: data usage charges may apply.*)

Interactive Activities

MapMaster™ interactive map and Google Earth™ activities and questions encourage students to use exciting and engaging geospatial media to explore concepts, practice critical image and data analysis, and extend chapter learning.

MapMaster™ Layered Thematic Interactive Mapping activities are provided within select modules and at the end of each chapter in the text, linking students to the Student Study Area of MasteringGeography™. To explore additional map layers to complete the activities. Teachers have the option of assigning these questions in MasteringGeography.

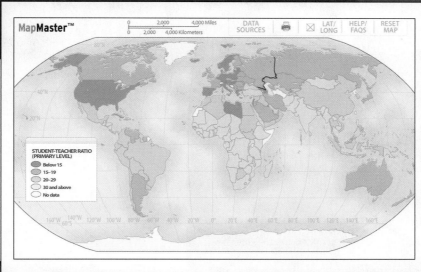

◄ 9.3.3 **PUPIL/TEACHER RATIO**

Open MapMaster World in Mastering **GEOGRAPHY**

Select: *Cultural* then *Students per teacher in primary school.*
Select: *Population* then *Percentage of population under age 15.*

Are class sizes larger or smaller in countries that have a high percentage of population under age 15?

Google Earth™ Explore image analysis questions are provided within select modules and at the end of each chapter, linking students from the print page to the dynamic geobrowsing technology of Google Earth. Teachers have the option of assigning these questions in MasteringGeography.

◄ 8.12.1 **SANCTUARY FOR TERRORISTS: BIN LADEN'S COMPOUND**

Navy SEALS killed al-Qaeda leader Osama bin Laden in this compound near the city of Abbottabad, Pakistan.

Fly to: *Osama bin Laden's hideout compound, Abbottabad, Pakistan.*

Deselect 3D Buildings. Click the time slider. Click the left arrow to go back in time.

Between which two dates was the compound constructed? How does this compare to the date of the failed U.S. attack on bin Laden in Tora Bora, Afghanistan?

Remove time slider, then click 3D Buildings. Drag to enter street view, then exit street view to get an overview of bin Laden's compound.

Mastering Geography™

This online homework and tutoring system delivers self-paced activities that provide individualized coaching, focus on your course objectives, and are responsive to each student's progress. The Mastering system helps instructors maximize class time with customizable, easy-to-assign, and automatically graded assessments that motivate students to learn outside of class and arrive prepared for lecture.

www.masteringgeography.com

Proven Results

The Mastering platform is the only online homework system with research showing that it improves student learning. A wide variety of published papers based on NSF-sponsored research and tests illustrate the benefits of the Mastering program. Results documented in scientifically valid efficacy papers are available at **www.masteringgeography.com/site/results**.

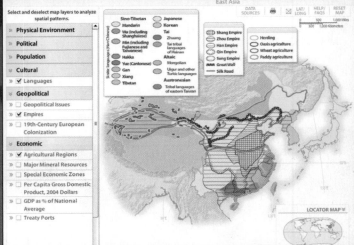

MapMaster™ Layered Thematic Interactive Map Activities

These act as a mini-GIS tool, allowing students to layer various thematic maps to analyze spatial patterns and data at regional and global scales. Multiple-choice and short-answer questions are organized around themes of Physical Environment, Population, Culture, Geopolitics, and Economy, giving instructors flexible, modular options for assessing student learning.

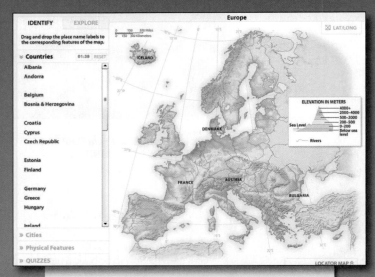

MapMaster™ Place Name Interactive Map Activities

These have students identify place names of political and physical features at regional and global scales, and explore select country data from the CIA World Factbook. Multiple-choice questions for the place name labeling activities and country data sets offer instructors flexible opportunities for summative assessment and pre- and post-testing.

Engaging Experiences

MasteringGeography provides a personalized, dynamic, and engaging experience for each student that strengthens active learning. Survey data show that the immediate feedback and tutorial assistance in MasteringGeography motivate students to do more homework. The result is that students learn more and improve their test scores.

Encounter Google Earth™ Explore Activities

Pearson's Encounter Activities provide rich, interactive explorations of human geography concepts through Google Earth™All explorations include corresponding Google Earth KMZ media files, and questions include hints and specific wrong-answer feedback to help coach students towards mastery of the concepts.

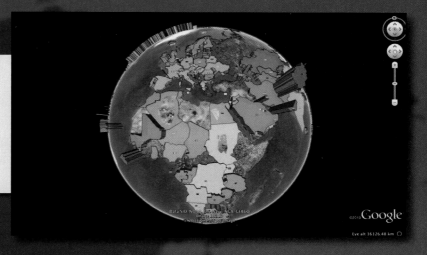

Geography Videos

A variety of short geography video activities provides students with a sense of place, helps them visualize concepts, and allows them means to explore a range of topics and places. Covering issues of economy, development, globalization, climate and climate change, culture, and more, there are 10–20 multiple choice and short answer questions for each of the 34 episodes. Students can access videos from the Study Area in MasteringGeography™, and professors can assign video questions. These video activities allow instructors to test students' understanding and application of concepts, and offer hints and specific wrong-answer feedback.

Thinking Spatially and Data Analysis

These activities help students develop spatial reasoning and critical thinking skills by identifying and labeling features from maps, illustrations, photos, graphs, and charts. Students then examine related data sets, answering multiple-choice and increasingly higher-order conceptual short-answer questions.

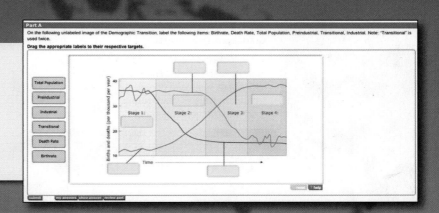

Student Study Area resources in MasteringGeography

- MapMaster™ interactive maps
- Geography videos
- Practice chapter quizzes
- "In the News" RSS feeds
- Glossary flashcards
- Optional Pearson eText and more

MasteringGeography™

www.masteringgeography.com

A Trusted Partner

The Mastering platform was developed by scientists for science students and instructors, and has a proven history with over 10 years of student use. Mastering currently has more than 1.5 million active registrations with active users in 50 states and in 41 countries.

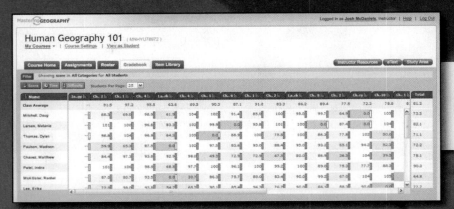

Gradebook

Every assignment is automatically graded. At a glance, shades of red highlight struggling students and challenging assignments.

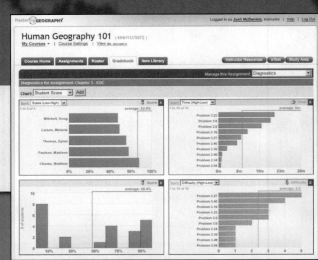

Gradebook Diagnostics

Gradebook Diagnostics provide unique insight into class and student performance. With a single click, charts summarize the most difficult problems, struggling students, grade distribution, and even score improvement over the duration of the course.

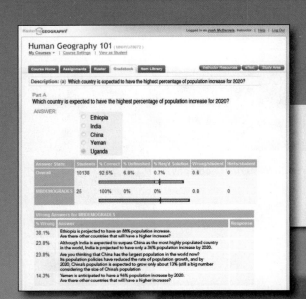

Gradebook Diagnostics

MasteringGeography provides at-a-glance statistics on your class as well as national results. Wrong-answer summaries give unique insight into your students' misconceptions and facilitate just-in-time teaching adjustments.

Learning Outcomes

MasteringGeography tracks student performance against each instructor's learning outcomes. Instructors can:

- Add their own or use the publisher-provided learning outcomes to track student performance and report it to their administrations.
- View class performance against the specified learning outcomes.
- Export results to a spreadsheet that can be customized further and/or shared with the chair, dean, administrator, or accreditation board.

Mastering offers a data-supported measure to quantify students' learning gains and to share those results quickly and easily.

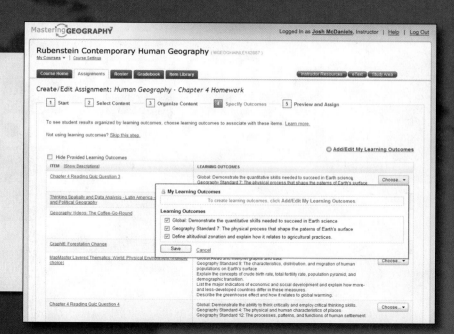

Pearson eText

Pearson eText gives students access to the text whenever and wherever they can access the Internet. The eText pages look exactly like the printed text, and include powerful interactive and customization functions. Users can create notes, highlight text in different colors, create bookmarks, zoom, click hyperlinked words and phrases to view definitions, and view as a single page or as two pages. Pearson eText also links students to associated media files, enabling them to access the media as they read the text, and offers a full text search and the ability to save and export notes.

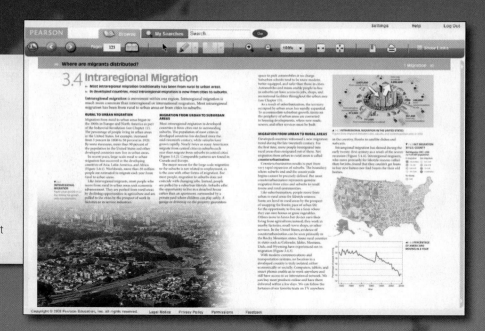

Instructor Resources in MasteringGeography

Assignable activities include:

- MapMaster™ interactive maps
- Geography videos
- Encounter Google Earth™ Explorations
- Reading quizzes
- Test Bank questions
- Thinking Spatially and Data Analysis activities
- End-of-chapter questions and more

1 Thinking Geographically

Thinking geographically is one of the oldest human activities. Perhaps the first geographer was a prehistoric human who crossed a river or climbed a hill, observed what was on the other side, returned home to tell about it, and scratched a map of the route in the dirt. Perhaps the second geographer was a friend or relative who followed the dirt map to reach the other side.

Today, geographers are still trying to understand more about the world in which we live. Geography is the study of where natural environments and human activities are found on Earth's surface and the reasons for their location. This chapter introduces basic concepts that geographers use to study Earth's people and natural environment.

Why is each point on earth unique?

How do geographers describe where things are?

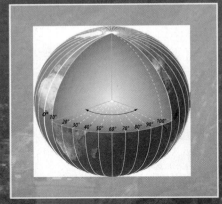

BEACH AT IPANEMA, BRAZIL

How are different locations interrelated?

SCAN TO ENTER THE WORLD OF GEOGRAPHY

How do people relate to their environment?

1.1 Welcome to Geography

► **Geography combines natural and social sciences.**
► **Geographers explain *where* things are, *why* they are there, and why their locations have *significance*.**

The word *geography* was invented by the ancient Greek scholar Eratosthenes (ca. 276–ca. 194 B.C.); it is based on two Greek words: *geo* meaning "Earth," and *graphy*, meaning "to write." Contemporary geography is more than only writing about Earth; it is a science.

GEOGRAPHY COMBINES NATURAL AND SOCIAL SCIENCE

The science of geography is divided broadly into two categories—physical geography and human geography. The beach at Ipanema, Brazil, displays features of interest to both physical and human geographers.

• Human geographers study cultural features, such as economic activities and cities (Figure 1.1.1).

• Physical geographers concentrate on the distribution of natural features, such as landforms and vegetation (Figure 1.1.2).

One of the distinctive features of geography is its use of natural science concepts to help understand human behavior, and conversely the use of social science concepts to help understand physical processes.

GEOGRAPHERS EXPLAIN *WHERE* AND *WHY*

To explain *where* things are, one of geography's most important tools is a map. Ancient and medieval geographers created maps to describe what they knew about Earth. Today, accurate maps are generated from electronic data.

Geographers study *why* every place on Earth is in some ways unique and in other ways related to other locations.

To explain why every place is unique, geographers have two basic concepts:

• A **place** is a specific point on Earth distinguished by a particular characteristic. Every place occupies a unique location, or position, on Earth's surface (Figure 1.1.3).

• A **region** is an area of Earth distinguished by a distinctive combination of cultural and physical features. (Figure 1.1.4).

To explain why different places are interrelated, geographers have three basic concepts:

• **Scale** is the relationship between the portion of Earth being studied and Earth as a whole. Geographers study every scale from the individual to the entire Earth, though increasingly they are concerned with global-scale patterns and processes (Figure 1.1.5).

• **Space** refers to the physical gap or interval between two objects. Geographers observe that many objects are distributed across space in a regular manner, for discernable reasons (Figure 1.1.6).

• **Connection** refers to relationships among people and objects across the barrier of space. Geographers are concerned with the various means by which connections occur (Figure 1.1.7).

To explain the underlying significance of observed spatial patterns, geographers examine the interrelationships between the natural environment and human behavior. Humans are influenced by nature and in turn alter natural processes.

▲ 1.1.1 **HUMAN GEOGRAPHY AT IPANEMA**
Ipanema is located in one of world's largest urban areas—Rio de Janeiro—and has an economy heavily dependent on tourism.

▲ 1.1.2 **PHYSICAL GEOGRAPHY AT IPANEMA BEACH**
Ipanema's physical landscape includes a distinctive landform, the twin peaks in the background known as Two Brothers.

▲ 1.1.3 **PLACE**
Ipanema is located along the Atlantic Ocean within the city of Rio de Janeiro, Brazil.

▲ 1.1.4 **REGION**
The climate region known by the notation Aw that includes Ipanema is warm all year round but nearly all of the year's rain falls between May and October. To be virtually guaranteed great beach weather, visit Ipanema in December. Other nearby climate regions have other patterns of temperature and rainfall.

▲ 1.1.5 **SCALE**
Geographers study trends of globalization and local diversity. For example, people in diverse locations play on sand, wearing very little clothing. At the same time, many cultures frown on public display of near-naked bodies.

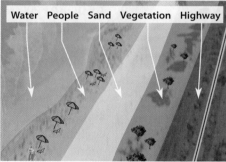

▲ 1.1.6 **SPACE**
People are not distributed randomly along Ipanema. The distribution of people follows a linear pattern parallel to the water's edge and away from the highway.

▲ 1.1.7 **CONNECTION**
Few humans live in isolation. Ipanema beach is connected with the rest of the city of Rio de Janeiro by a major highway. An airplane, such as the one in the photo, can connect Ipanema beach with the rest of the world.

1.2 Ancient and Medieval Geography

► Since ancient times, maps have helped geographers to explain where things are located.

► Accurate mapmaking revived in the Middle Ages, and developed further during the Age of Exploration

In the ancient world, geographers in Greece and neighboring Eastern Mediterranean lands, as well as in China, described and mapped Earth with increasing accuracy. A revival of geography and mapmaking occurred in Europe and Asia during the Middle Ages.

GEOGRAPHY IN THE ANCIENT WORLD

The earliest surviving maps were drawn in the Eastern Mediterranean in the seventh or sixth century B.C. (Figure 1.2.1). Major contributors to geographic thought in the Ancient Eastern Mediterranean included:

- Thales of Miletus (ca. 624–ca. 546 B.C.), who applied principles of geometry to measuring land area.
- Anaximander (610–ca. 546 B.C.), a student of Thales, who made a world map based on information from sailors, though he argued that world was shaped like a cylinder.
- Hecataeus (ca. 550–ca. 476 B.C.), who may have produced the first geography book, called *Ges Periodos*, ("Travels Around the Earth").
- Aristotle (384–322 B.C.), who was the first to demonstrate that Earth was spherical.

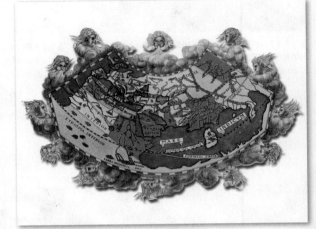

▲ 1.2.2 **WORLD MAP BY PTOLEMY, CA. 150 BC**
The map shows the known world at the height of the Roman Empire, surrounding the Mediterranean Sea and Indian Ocean.

- Eratosthenes (ca. 276–ca. 195 B.C.), the inventor of the word *geography*, who accepted that Earth was round (as few did in his day), calculated its circumference within 0.5 percent accuracy, accurately divided Earth into five climatic regions, and described the known world in one of the first geography books.
- Strabo (ca. 63 B.C–ca. A.D. 24), who described the known world in a 17-volume work *Geography*.
- Ptolemy (A.D. ca. 100–ca. 170), who wrote an eight-volume *Guide to Geography*, codified basic principles of mapmaking, and prepared numerous maps that were not improved upon for more than a thousand years (Figure 1.2.2).

Ancient Chinese geographic contributions included:

- *Yu Gong* ("Tribute of Yu"), a chapter of the book *Shu Jing* ("Classic of History"), which was the earliest surviving Chinese geographical writing, by an unknown author from the fifth century B.C., described the economic resources of the country's different provinces.
- Pei Xiu (A.D. 224–271), the "father of Chinese cartography," who produced an elaborate map of the country in A.D. 267.

▼ 1.2.1 **THE OLDEST KNOWN MAP**
A map of a plan for the town of Çatalhöyük, located in present-day Turkey, dates from approximately 6200 B.C. Archaeologists found the map on the wall of a house that was excavated in the 1960s. The map is now in the Konya Archaeology Museum. (below right) A color version of the Çatalhöyük map. A volcano rises above the buildings of the city. (below left) A 3D reconstruction of the Çatalhöyük map.

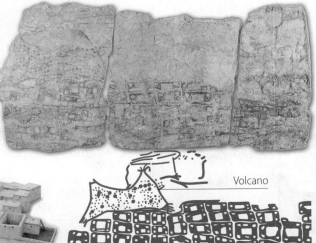

Volcano

GEOGRAPHY IN THE MIDDLE AGES

During the first millennium A.D., maps became less mathematical and more fanciful, showing Earth as a flat disk surrounded by fierce animals and monsters. Scientific mapmaking resumed during the Middle Ages, first in Asia and then in Europe. Leading medieval contributors to geography included:

- Muhammad al-Idrisi (1100–ca. 1165), a Muslim geographer who prepared a world map and geography text in 1154, building on Ptolemy's long-neglected work (Figure 1.2.3).
- Abu Abdullah Muhammad Ibn-Battuta (1304–ca. 1368), a Moroccan scholar, who wrote *Rihla* ("Travels") based on three decades of journeys covering more than 120,000 kilometers (75,000 miles) through the Muslim world of northern Africa, southern Europe, and much of Asia.

GEOGRAPHY IN THE AGE OF EXPLORATION

With the discovery of the New World and the development of printing, scientific mapmaking in Europe made rapid progress.

- Martin Waldseemuller (ca. 1470–ca. 1521), a German cartographer who was credited with producing the first map to use the label "America;" he wrote on the map (translated from Latin) "from Amerigo the discoverer . . . as if it were the land of Americus, thus 'America'" (Figure 1.2.4).
- Abraham Ortelius (1527–1598), a Flemish cartographer, created the first modern atlas, and was the first to hypothesize that the continents were once joined together before drifting apart (Figure 1.2.5).

▲ 1.2.3 **WORLD MAP BY AL-IDRISI, 1154**
Al-Idrisi built on Ptolemy's map, which had been neglected for nearly a millennium.

▲ 1.2.4 **WORLD MAP BY WALDSEEMULLER, 1507**
This was one of the first maps to depict the Western Hemisphere separated from Europe and Africa by the Atlantic Ocean, and the first to label the Western Hemisphere "America."

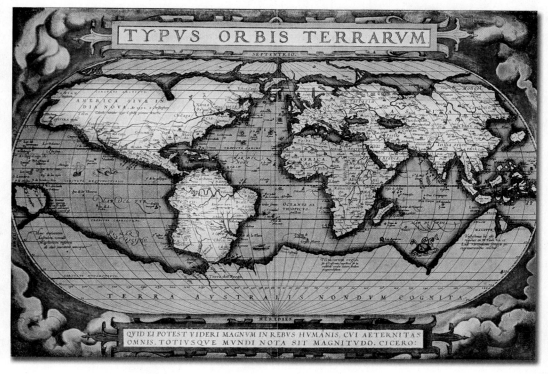

► 1.2.5 **WORLD MAP BY ORTELIUS, 1571**
This was one of the first maps to show the considerable extent of the Western Hemisphere, as well as the Antarctic land mass.

1.3 Reading Maps

► **A map is a scale model of all or a portion of Earth.**
► **A map is a flat depiction of a nearly round Earth.**

For centuries, geographers have worked to perfect the science of mapmaking, called **cartography**. A **map** is a scale model of the real world, made small enough to work with on a desk or computer. Maps serve two purposes:

- A reference tool. A map helps us to find the shortest route between two places and to avoid getting lost along the way.
- A communications tool. A map is often the best means for depicting the distribution of human activities or physical features, as well as for thinking about reasons underlying a distribution.

To make a map, a cartographer must make two decisions:

- How much of Earth's surface to depict on the map (map scale).
- How to transfer a spherical Earth to a flat map (projection).

MAP SCALE

Should the map show the entire globe, or just one continent, or a country, or a city? To make a map of the entire world, many details must be omitted because there simply is not enough space. Conversely, if a map shows only a small portion of Earth's surface, such as a street map of a city, it can provide a wealth of detail about a particular place.

The level of detail and the amount of area covered depend on the **map scale**, which is the relationship of a feature's size on a map to its actual size on Earth. Map scale is presented in three ways (Figure 1.3.1):

- A ratio or fraction.
- A written scale.
- A graphic scale.

◄ 1.3.1 **MAP SCALE**

The four images show Washington State, the Seattle metropolitan area, downtown Seattle, and Pike Place Market. These four images show map scale in three ways:

- *A ratio or fraction* shows the numerical ratio between distances on the map and Earth's surface. The Washington map has a ratio of 1:10,000,000, meaning that one unit (inch, centimeter, foot, finger length) on the map represents 10,000,000 of the same unit (inch, centimeter, foot, finger length) on the ground. The unit chosen for distance can be anything, as long as the units of measure on both the map and the ground are the same. The 1 on the left side of the ratio always refers to a unit of distance *on the map*, and the number on the right always refers to the *same unit* of distance *on Earth's surface*.
- *A written scale* describes this relation between map and Earth distances in words. For example, the statement "1 centimeter equals 10 kilometers" means that one centimeter on the map represents 10 kilometers on Earth's surface. Again, the first number always refers to map distance, and the second to distance on Earth's surface.
- *A graphic scale* usually consists of a bar line marked to show distance on Earth's surface. To use a bar line, first determine with a ruler the distance on the map in inches or centimeters. Then hold the ruler against the bar line and read the number on the bar line opposite the map distance on the ruler. The number on the bar line is the equivalent distance on Earth's surface.

1 centimeter on the map equals 100 kilometers on Earth; 1:10,000,000.

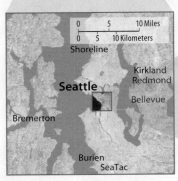

1 centimeter on the map equals 10 kilometers on Earth; 1:1,000,000.

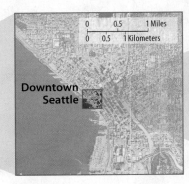

1 centimeter on the map equals 1 kilometer on Earth; 1:100,000.

1 centimeter on the map equals 100 meters on Earth; 1:10,000.

PROJECTION

Earth is very nearly a sphere and therefore accurately represented in the form of a globe. However, a globe is an extremely limited tool with which to communicate information about Earth's surface. A small globe does not have enough space to display detailed information, whereas a large globe is too bulky and cumbersome to use. And a globe is difficult to write on, photocopy, display on a computer screen, or refer to in a car.

Earth's spherical shape poses a challenge for cartographers because drawing Earth on a flat piece of paper unavoidably produces some distortion. The scientific method of transferring locations on Earth's surface to a flat map is called **projection**. Several types of projections are shown in Figure 1.3.2.

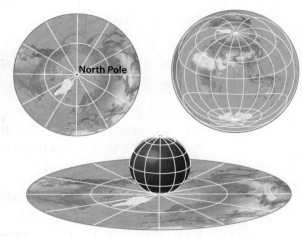

▲ 1.3.2.a **AZIMUTHAL PROJECTIONS**
Azimuthal projections are well-suited for larger areas and are used for most of the world maps.

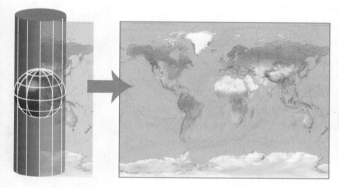

▲ 1.3.2.b **CYLINDRICAL PROJECTIONS**
Cylindrical projections are used for specialized maps. The most widely used cylindrical world map, created by Gerardus Mercator in 1569, was widely used by mariners.

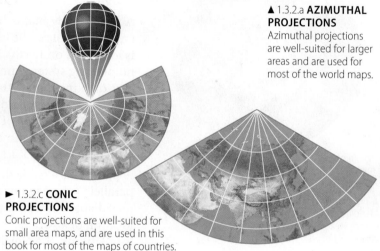

► 1.3.2.c **CONIC PROJECTIONS**
Conic projections are well-suited for small area maps, and are used in this book for most of the maps of countries.

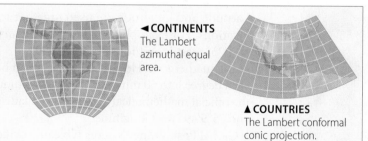

◄**WORLD MAPS**
The Winkle II pseudo–cylindrical projection.

◄**CONTINENTS**
The Lambert azimuthal equal area.

▲ **COUNTRIES**
The Lambert conformal conic projection.

1.3.2.d **PROJECTIONS USED IN THIS BOOK**

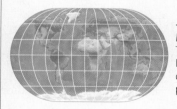

Mastering **GEOGRAPHY**
Animations
Map Projections

A projection can result in four types of distortion (Figure 1.3.3):

1. The **shape** of an area can be distorted, so that it appears more elongated or squat than in reality.

2. The **distance** between two points may become increased or decreased.

3. The **relative size** of different areas may be altered, so that one area may appear larger than another on a map but is in reality smaller.

4. The **direction** from one place to another can be distorted.

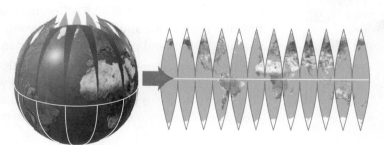

▲ 1.3.3 **DISTORTION** To make a map, the spherical Earth is divided into segments. Flattening these segments onto flat paper results in distortion.

1.4 The Geographic Grid

▶ **The geographic grid divides Earth's surface into latitudes and longitudes.**
▶ **The geographic grid is the basis for time zones.**

The **geographic grid** is a system of imaginary arcs drawn in a grid pattern on Earth's surface. The location of any place on Earth's surface can be described by these human-created arcs, known as meridians and parallels. The geographic grid plays an important role in telling time.

Lines of longitude measured in degrees from the center of Earth, are spaced more widely near the equator and converge towards the poles.

Greenwich, England

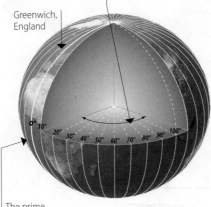

The prime meridian (0° longitude) passes through Greenwich, England

▲ 1.4.1 **LONGITUDE**
Meridians have numbers between 0° and 180° east or west longitude, depending if they are either east or west of the prime meridian.

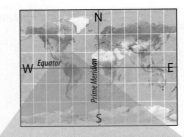

▲ 1.4.3 **HOW LATITUDE AND LONGITUDE WORK**
Philadelphia, Pennsylvania, is located near 40° north latitude and 75° west longitude.

LATITUDES AND LONGITUDES

Cartographers identify meridians and parallels through numbering systems:

- A **meridian** is an arc drawn between the North and South poles. The location of each meridian is identified on Earth's surface according to a numbering system known as **longitude**. The meridian that passes through the Royal Observatory at Greenwich, England, is 0° longitude, also called the **prime meridian**. The meridian on the opposite side of the globe from the prime meridian is 180° longitude (Figure 1.4.1).

- A **parallel** is a circle drawn around the globe parallel to the equator and at right angles to the meridians. The numbering system to indicate the location of a parallel is called **latitude**. The equator is 0° latitude, the North Pole 90° north latitude, and the South Pole 90° south latitude (Figure 1.4.2).

Latitude and longitude are used together to identify locations. For example, Philadelphia, Pennsylvania, is located at 40° north latitude and 75° west longitude (Figure 1.4.3).

The mathematical location of a place can be designated more precisely by dividing each degree into 60 minutes (′) and each minute into 60 seconds (″). For example, the official mathematical location of Philadelphia's City Hall is 39°57′8″ north latitude and 75°9′49″ west longitude.

Global Positioning Systems typically divide degrees into decimal fractions rather than minutes and seconds. The Bally Ribbon Mills factory in suburban Philadelphia, for example, is located at 40.400780° north latitude and 75.587439° west longitude.

Measuring latitude and longitude is a good example of how geography is partly a natural science and partly a study of human behavior.

- Latitudes are scientifically derived by Earth's shape and its rotation around the Sun. The equator (0° latitude) is the parallel with the largest circumference and is the place where every day has 12 hours of daylight. Even in ancient times, latitude could be accurately measured by the length of daylight and the position of the Sun and stars.

- Longitudes are a human creation. Any meridian could have been selected as 0° longitude because all have the same length and all run between the poles. The 0° longitude runs through Greenwich because England was the world's most powerful country when longitude was first accurately measured and the international agreement was made.

One degree of latitude is approximately 111 kilometers (69 miles)

0° is the equator

▲ 1.4.2 **LATITUDE**
Parallels range between 0° and 90° north or south latitude, depending if they are either north or south of the equator.

TIME ZONES

Longitude plays an important role in calculating time. Earth makes a complete rotation every 24 hours and as a sphere is divided into 360° of longitude. Therefore, traveling 15° east or west is the equivalent of traveling to a place that is 1 hour earlier or later than the starting point (360° divided by 24 hours equals 15°).

By international agreement, **Greenwich Mean Time (GMT)** or Universal Time (UT), which is the time at the prime meridian (0° longitude), is the master reference time for all points on Earth.

As Earth rotates eastward, any place to the east of you always passes "under" the Sun earlier. Thus as you travel eastward from the prime meridian, you are "catching up" with the Sun, so you must turn your clock ahead from GMT by 1 hour for each 15°. If you travel westward from the prime meridian, you are "falling behind" the Sun, so you turn your clock back from GMT by 1 hour for each 15°.

Each 15° band of longitude is assigned to a standard time zone (Figure 1.4.4). The United States and Canada share four standard time zones:

- Eastern, near 75° west, is 5 hours earlier than GMT.
- Central, near 90° west, is 6 hours earlier than GMT.
- Mountain, near 105° west, is 7 hours earlier than GMT.
- Pacific, near 120° west, is 8 hours earlier than GMT.

The United States has two additional standard time zones:

- Alaska, near 135° west, is 9 hours earlier than GMT.
- Hawaii-Aleutian, near 150° west, is 10 hours earlier than GMT.

Canada has two additional standard time zones:

- Atlantic, near 60° west, is 4 hours earlier than GMT.
- Newfoundland is 3½ hours earlier than GMT; the residents of Newfoundland assert that their island, which lies between 53° and 59° west longitude, would face dark winter afternoons if it were in the Atlantic Time Zone, and dark winter mornings if it were 3 hours earlier than GMT.

The **International Date Line** for the most part follows 180° longitude. When you cross it heading eastward toward America you move the clock back 24 hours, or one entire day. You turn the clock ahead 24 hours if you are heading westward toward Asia.

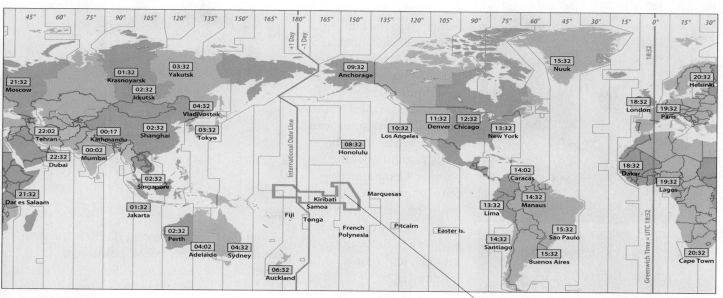

▲ 1.4.4 **TIME ZONES**

The eastern United States, which is near 75° west longitude, is therefore 5 hours earlier than GMT (the 75° difference between the prime meridian and 75° west longitude, divided by 15° per hour, equals 5 hours). Thus when the time in New York City in the winter is 1:32 PM, (or 13:32 hours, using a 24-hour clock), it is 6:32 PM (or 18:32 hours) GMT. During the summer, many places in the world, including most of North America, move the clocks ahead one hour; so in the summer when it is 6:32 PM GMT, the time in New York City is 2:32 PM.

If it is 1:32 PM, (or 13:32 hours) Sunday in New York, it is 6:32 PM Sunday in London, 7:32 PM (19:32) Sunday in Paris, 8:32 PM (20:32) Sunday in Helsinki, 9:32 PM (21:32) Sunday in Moscow, 2:32 AM Monday in Singapore, and 4:32 AM Monday in Sydney. Continuing farther east, it is 6:32 AM *Monday* in Auckland --but when you get to Honolulu, it is 8:32 AM *Sunday*, because the International Date Line lies between Auckland and Honolulu.

The International Date Line for the most part follows 180° longitude. However, in 1997, Kiribati, a collection of small islands in the Pacific Ocean, moved the International Date Line 3,000 kilometers (2,000 miles) to its eastern border near 150° west longitude. As a result, Kiribati is the first country to see each day's sunrise. Kiribati hoped that this feature would attract tourists to celebrate the start of the new millennium on January 1, 2000 (or January 1, 2001, when sticklers pointed out that the new millennium really began). But it did not.

1.5 Geography's Contemporary Analytic Tools

► Geographic study is aided by information from satellite imagery.
► Complex geographic data can be overlaid and analyzed through geographic information systems.

Having largely completed the great task of accurately mapping Earth's surface, geographers have turned to **Geographic Information Science** (GIScience), which is the development and analysis of data about Earth acquired through satellite and other electronic information technologies. GIScience helps geographers to create more accurate and complex maps and to measure changes over time in the characteristics of places.

REMOTE SENSING

The acquisition of data about Earth's surface from a satellite orbiting Earth or from other long-distance methods is known as **remote sensing**. Remote-sensing satellites scan Earth's surface and transmit images in digital form to a receiving station on Earth's surface.

At any moment a satellite sensor records the image of a tiny area called a picture element or pixel. Scanners detect the radiation being reflected from that tiny area. A map created by remote sensing is essentially a grid containing many rows of pixels. The smallest feature on Earth's surface that can be detected by a sensor is the resolution of the scanner. Geographers use remote sensing to map the changing distribution of a wide variety of features, such as agriculture, drought, and sprawl (Figure 1.5.1).

1999

2004

◄ 1.5.1 **REMOTE SENSING**
(top) Satellite image of South Dakota's Oahe Reservoir in 1999. Deep water is shown in dark blue and shallow water in light blue. (bottom) Satellite image of Oahe Reservoir in 2004. After several years of drought, the reservoir has less deep water, as shown in the reduction of the area of dark blue.

▲ 1.5.2 **GPS**
Many cars have GPS display on the instrument cluster, offering assistance in getting directions and avoiding traffic jams.

GPS

Global Positioning System (GPS) is a system that determines the precise position of something on Earth. The GPS system in use in the United States includes two dozen satellites placed in predetermined orbits, a series of tracking stations to monitor and control the satellites, and receivers that compute position, velocity, and time from the satellite signals.

GPS is commonly used in the navigation of aircraft and ships, and increasingly to provide directions for drivers of motor vehicles (Figure 1.5.2). Cell phones equipped with GPS allow individuals to share their whereabouts with friends and relatives.

GIS

A **geographic information system** (GIS) is a computer system that captures, stores, queries, analyzes, and displays geographic data. GIS can be used to produce maps (including those in this book) that are more accurate and attractive than those drawn by hand.

The position of any object on Earth can be measured and recorded with mathematical precision and then stored in a computer. A map can be created by asking the computer to retrieve a number of stored objects and combine them to form an image. Each type of information can be stored in a layer (Figure 1.5.3).

GIS enables geographers to calculate whether relationships between objects on a map are significant or merely coincidental. Layers can be compared to show relationships among different kinds of information. To protect hillsides from development, for example, a geographer may wish to compare a layer of recently built houses with a layer of steep slopes.

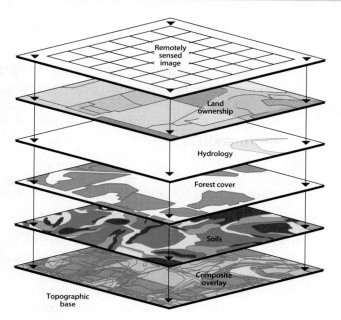

▲ 1.5.3 **GIS**

GIS involves storing information about a location in layers. Each layer represents a different piece of human or environmental information. The layers can be viewed individually or in combination.

◄ 1.5.4 **MASH-UP**
Use Google Earth to explore a mash-up of Central London and the subway ("Underground") stations near the London Eye (the Ferris wheel on the south bank of the River Thames).

Fly to: *London Eye, London, England.*

Use Google Earth's navigation tools and layer options to explore features of this area.

What is the distance from the Eye to the nearest Underground station?

MASH-UPS

Mapping services, such as Google Maps and Google Earth, give computer programmers access to the application programming interface (API), which is the language that links a database such as an address list with software such as mapping. The API for mapping software, available at such sites as www.google.com/apis/maps, enables a computer programmer to create a mash-up that places data on a map. The term mash-up refers to the practice of overlaying data from one source on top of one of the mapping services and comes from the hip-hop practice of mixing two or more songs.

Mash-ups assist in finding apartments, bars, hotels, sports facilities, and transit stops (Figure 1.5.4). Mapping software can show the precise location of commercial airplanes currently in the air, the gas stations with the cheapest prices, and current traffic tie-ups on highways and bridges.

1.6 Place: A Unique Location

▶ **Location is the position that something occupies on Earth.**
▶ **Location can be described using place names, situation, and site.**

Humans possess a strong sense of place—that is, a feeling for the features that contribute to the distinctiveness of a particular spot on Earth. Geographers think about where particular places are located and the combination of features that make each place on Earth distinct. Geographers describe a feature's place on Earth by identifying its **location**, which is the position that something occupies on Earth's surface.

PLACE NAMES

Because all inhabited places on Earth's surface—and many uninhabited places—have been named, the most straightforward way to describe a particular location is often by referring to its place name. A **toponym** is the name given to a place on Earth.

A place may be named for a person, perhaps its founder or a famous person with no connection to the community, such as George Washington. Some settlers selected place names associated with religion, such as St. Louis and St. Paul, whereas other names derive from ancient history, such as Athens, Attica, and Rome, or from earlier occupants of the place (Figure 1.6.1).

The Board of Geographical Names, operated by the U.S. Geological Survey, was established in the late nineteenth century to be the final arbiter of names on U.S. maps. In recent years the board has been especially concerned with removing offensive place names, such as those with racial or ethnic connotations.

▶ **1.6.1 LONGEST U.S. PLACE NAME**
The longest place name in the United States may be Lake Chargoggagoggman-chauggagoggchaubuna-gungamaugg, Massachusetts. The name is thought to be a combination of three phrases: "you fish on your side" (Chargog-gagogg), "I fish on my side" (Manchauggagogg), and "nobody fish in the middle" (Chaubunagungamaugg). The name is said to have been given by agreement of several Native American tribes living at opposite ends of the lake.

SITUATION

Situation is the location of a place relative to other places. Situation is a valuable way to indicate location, for two reasons:

- Situation helps us find an unfamiliar place by comparing its location with a familiar one. We give directions to people by referring to the situation of a place: "It's down past the courthouse, beside the large elm tree."

- Situation helps us understand the importance of a location. Many places are important because they are accessible to other places. For example, because of its situation, Singapore has become a center for the trading and distribution of goods for much of Southeast Asia (Figure 1.6.2).

▲ **1.6.2 SITUATION OF SINGAPORE**
The country of Singapore is situated near the Strait of Malacca, which is the major passageway for ships traveling between the South China Sea and the Indian Ocean. Some 50,000 vessels, one-fourth of the world's maritime trade, pass through the strait each year. The downtown area of the City of Singapore is situated near where the Singapore River flows into the Singapore Strait.

SITE

Geographers can describe the location of a place by **site**, which is the physical character of a place. Important site characteristics include climate, water sources, topography, soil, vegetation, latitude, and elevation. The combination of physical features gives each place a distinctive character (Figure 1.6.3).

Humans have the ability to modify the characteristics of a site. The southern portion of New York City's Manhattan Island is twice as large today as it was in 1626, when Peter Minuit bought the island from its native inhabitants for the equivalent of $23.75 worth of Dutch gold and silver coins (Figure 1.6.4).

▲ 1.6.3 **SITE OF SINGAPORE**
The site of the country of Singapore is approximately 60 islands, the largest and most populous of which is named Pulau Ujong. The site of the City of Singapore is the southern portion of Pulau Ujong.

◄ 1.6.4 **CHANGING SITE OF NEW YORK CITY**
(top) The site of Manhattan Island has been altered by building on landfill in the Hudson and East rivers. Extending the island into the rivers provided more land for offices, homes, parks, warehouses, and docks.
(left) During the late 1960s and early 1970s, the World Trade Center was built partially on landfill in the Hudson River from the colonial era. Battery Park City was built on landfill removed from the World Trade Center construction site.

Fly to: *World Trade Center, New York, NY, USA*

Click the World Trade Center site near the top of the image.

What are the plans for the site?

1.7 Region: A Unique Area

▶ **A region is an area of Earth with a unique combination of features.**

▶ **Three types of regions are functional, formal, and vernacular.**

The "sense of place" that humans possess may apply to a larger area of Earth rather than to a specific point. An area of Earth defined by one or more distinctive characteristics is a region. A region derives its unified character through the **cultural landscape**—a combination of cultural features such as language and religion, economic features such as agriculture and industry, and physical features such as climate and vegetation.

FUNCTIONAL REGION

A **functional region**, also called a nodal region, is an area organized around a node or focal point. The characteristic chosen to define a functional region dominates at a central focus or node and diminishes in importance outward. The region is tied to the central point by transportation or communications systems, or by economic or functional associations.

Geographers often use functional regions to display information about economic areas. The region's node may be a shop or service, and the boundaries of the region mark the limits of the trading area of the activity. People and activities may be attracted to the node, and information may flow from the node to the surrounding area.

Examples of functional regions include the reception area of a television station, the circulation area of a newspaper, and the trading area of a department store (Figure 1.7.1). A television station's signal is strongest at the center of its service area, becomes weaker at the edge, and eventually disappears. A department store attracts fewer customers and a newspaper fewer readers from the edge of a trading area.

New technology is breaking down traditional functional regions. Newspapers such as *USA Today*, *The Wall Street Journal*, and *The New York Times* are composed in one place, transmitted by satellite to printing machines in other places, and delivered by airplane and truck to yet other places. Television stations are broadcast to distant places by cable, satellite, or Internet. Customers can shop at distant stores by mail or Internet.

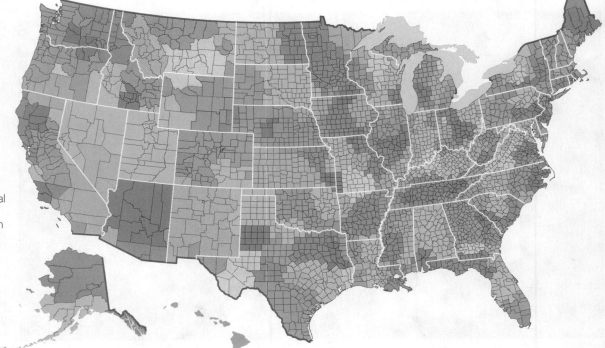

▶ 1.7.1 **FUNCTIONAL REGIONS**
The United States can be divided into functional regions based on television markets, which are groups of counties served by a collection of TV stations. Each functional region is known as a designated market areas (DMA), a term trademarked by Nielsen Media Research.

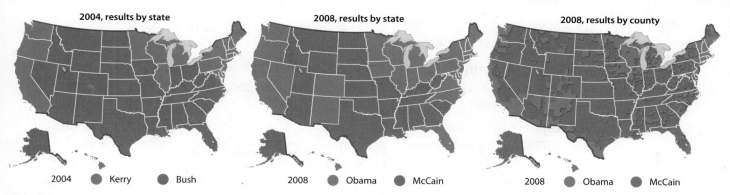

2004, results by state

2004 ● Kerry ● Bush

2008, results by state

2008 ● Obama ● McCain

2008, results by county

2008 ● Obama ● McCain

FORMAL REGION

A **formal region**, also called a uniform region or a homogeneous region, is an area within which everyone shares in common one or more distinctive characteristics. The shared feature could be a cultural value such as a common language, an economic activity such as production of a particular crop, or an environmental property such as climate. In a formal region the selected characteristic is present throughout.

Geographers typically identify formal regions to help explain broad global or national patterns, such as variations in religions and levels of economic development. The characteristic selected to distinguish a formal region often illustrates a general concept rather than a precise mathematical distribution.

Some formal regions are easy to identify, such as countries or local government units. Montana is an example of a formal region, characterized by a government that passes laws, collects taxes, and issues license plates with equal intensity throughout the state.

▲ 1.7.2 **FORMAL REGIONS**
(left) Presidential election results by state, 2004. Democrat John Kerry won the states in the Northeast, Upper Midwest, and Pacific Coast regions of the United States, while Republican George W. Bush won the remaining regions. (center) Presidential election results by state, 2008. Democrat Barack Obama won the election by capturing some states in regions that had been won entirely by the Republican four years earlier. (right) Presidential election results by county, 2008. Republican John McCain carried most of the land area of the United States, but Obama won the most votes by winning the most populous counties.

In other kinds of formal regions a characteristic may be predominant rather than universal. For example, we can distinguish formal regions within the United States characterized by a predominant voting for Republican candidates, although Republicans do not get 100 percent of the votes in these regions—nor in fact do they always win (Figure 1.7.2).

A cautionary step in identifying formal regions is the need to recognize the diversity of cultural, economic, and environmental factors, even while making a generalization. A minority of people in a region may speak a language, practice a religion, or possess resources different from those of the majority. People in a region may play distinctive roles in the economy and hold different positions in society based on their gender or ethnicity.

VERNACULAR REGION

A **vernacular region**, or perceptual region, is a place that people believe exists as part of their cultural identity. Such regions emerge from people's informal sense of place rather than from scientific models developed through geographic thought.

As an example of a vernacular region, Americans frequently refer to the South as a place with environmental, cultural, and economic features perceived to be quite distinct from the rest of the United States. Many of these features can be measured (Figure 1.7.3).

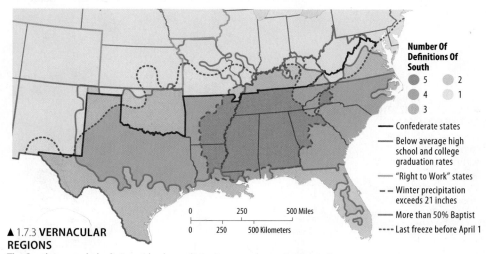

Number Of Definitions Of South
● 5   ● 2
● 4   ● 1
● 3

— Confederate states
— Below average high school and college graduation rates
— "Right to Work" states
-- Winter precipitation exceeds 21 inches
— More than 50% Baptist
---- Last freeze before April 1

▲ 1.7.3 **VERNACULAR REGIONS**
The South is popularly distinguished as a distinct vernacular region according to a number of factors.

1.8 Scale: From Global to Local

▶ **People are connected to a global economy and culture.**
▶ **Despite globalization, people play specialized economic roles and preserve cultural diversity.**

Geographers think about scale at many levels, from local to global. At the global scale, encompassing the entire world, geographers tend to see broad patterns. At a local scale, such as a neighborhood within a city, geographers tend to see unique features. Geography matters in the contemporary world because it can explain human actions at all scales, from local to global.

Scale is an increasingly important concept in geography because of **globalization**, which is a force or process that involves the entire world and results in making something world-wide in scope. Globalization means that the scale of the world is shrinking—not literally in size, of course, but in the ability of a person, object, or idea to interact with a person, object, or idea in another place. People are plugged into a global economy and culture, producing a world that is more uniform, integrated, and interdependent (Figure 1.8.1).

GLOBALIZATION OF THE ECONOMY

A few people living in very remote regions of the world may be able to provide all of their daily necessities. But most economic activities undertaken in one region are influenced by interaction with decision makers located elsewhere. The choice of crop is influenced by demand and prices set in markets elsewhere. The factory is located to facilitate bringing in raw materials and shipping out products to the markets.

Globalization of the economy has been led primarily by transnational corporations, sometimes called multinational corporations. A **transnational corporation** conducts research, operates factories, and sells products in many countries, not just where its headquarters and principal shareholders are located (Figure 1.8.2).

Every place in the world is part of the global economy, but globalization has led to more specialization at the local level. Each place plays a distinctive role, based on its local assets. A place may be near valuable minerals, or it may be inhabited by especially well-educated workers. Transnational corporations assess the particular economic assets of each place.

Modern technology provides the means to easily move money, materials, products, technology, and other economic assets around the world. Thanks to the electronic superhighway, companies can now organize economic activities at a global scale.

▲ 1.8.1 **CHAOYANG CENTRAL BUSINESS DISTRICT, BEIJING, CHINA**

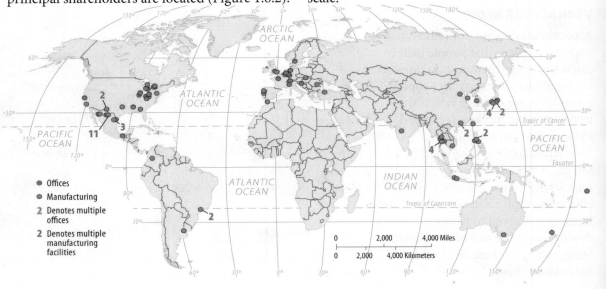

▶ 1.8.2 **GLOBALIZATION OF THE ECONOMY**
Yazaki, a transnational corporation that makes parts for cars, has factories primarily in Asia and Latin America, where labor costs are relatively low, and offices primarily in Europe, North America, and Japan, where most of the customers (carmakers) are located.

Legend:
- Offices
- Manufacturing
2 Denotes multiple offices
2 Denotes multiple manufacturing facilities

0   2,000   4,000 Miles
0   2,000   4,000 Kilometers

GLOBALIZATION OF CULTURE

Geographers observe that increasingly uniform cultural preferences produce uniform "global" landscapes of material artifacts and of cultural values. Fast-food restaurants, service stations, and retail chains deliberately create a visual appearance that varies among locations as little as possible so that customers know what to expect regardless of where in the world they happen to be (Figure 1.8.3).

The survival of a local culture's distinctive beliefs, forms, and traits is threatened by interaction with such social customs as wearing jeans and Nike shoes, consuming Coca-Cola and McDonald's hamburgers, and displaying other preferences in food, clothing, shelter, and leisure activities.

Underlying the uniform cultural landscape is globalization of cultural beliefs and forms, especially religion and language. Africans, in particular, have moved away from traditional religions and have adopted Christianity or Islam, religions shared with hundreds of millions of people throughout the world. Globalization requires a form of common communication, and the English language is increasingly playing that role.

LOCAL DIVERSITY

As more people become aware of elements of global culture and aspire to possess them, local cultural beliefs, forms, and traits are threatened with extinction. Yet despite globalization, cultural differences among places not only persist but actually flourish in many places.

Global standardization of products does not mean that everyone wants the same cultural products. The communications revolution that promotes globalization of culture also permits preservation of cultural diversity.

Television, for example, is no longer restricted to a handful of channels displaying one set of cultural values. With the distribution of programming through cable and satellite systems, people may choose from hundreds of programs. With the globalization of communications, people in two distant places can watch the same television program. At the same time, with the fragmentation of the broadcasting market, two people in the same house can watch different programs.

Although consumers in different places express increasingly similar cultural preferences,

CHINA

DUBAI

RUSSIA

THAILAND

JORDAN

JAPAN

they do not share the same access to them. And the desire of some people to retain their traditional culture in the face of increased globalization of cultural preferences, has led to political conflict and market fragmentation in some regions.

Globalization has not destroyed the uniqueness of an individual place's culture and economy. Human geographers understand that many contemporary social problems result from a tension between forces promoting global culture and economy on the one hand and preservation of local economic autonomy and cultural traditions on the other hand.

▲ 1.8.3 **GLOBALIZATION OF CULTURE**
"McDonald's" has more than 32,000 restaurants in 117 countries. To promote global uniformity of its restaurants, the company erects signs around the world that include two golden arches.

1.9 Space: Distribution of Features

▶ **Three properties of distribution are density, concentration, and pattern.**

▶ **Gender and ethnicity are important examples of how patterns in space can vary.**

Chess and computer games, require thinking about space. Pieces are arranged on the game board or screen in order to outmaneuver an opponent or form a geometric pattern. To excel at these games, a player needs spatial skills, the ability to perceive the future arrangement of pieces.

Similarly, spatial thinking is the most fundamental skill that geographers possess to understand the arrangement of objects across surfaces considerably larger than a game board. Geographers think about the arrangement of people and activities found in space and try to understand why those people and activities are distributed across space as they are.

Each human and natural object occupies space on Earth, which is the physical gap or interval between it and other objects. Geographers explain how features are arranged in space across Earth. On Earth as a whole, or within an area of Earth, features may be numerous or scarce, close together or far apart. The arrangement of a feature in space is known as its **distribution**.

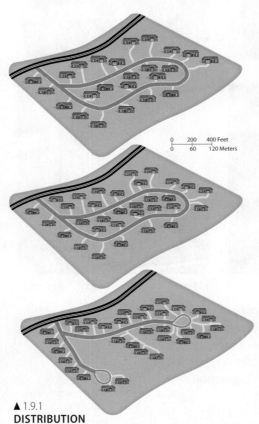

▲ 1.9.1
DISTRIBUTION
The top plan for a residential area has a lower density than the middle plan (24 houses compared to 32 houses on the same 30-acre piece of land), but both have dispersed concentrations. The middle and lower plans have the same density (32 houses on 30 acres), but the distribution of houses is more clustered in the lower plan. The lower plan has shared open space, whereas the middle plan provides a larger, private yard surrounding each house.

PROPERTIES OF DISTRIBUTION

Geographers identify three main properties of distribution across space:

- **Density.** The frequency with which something occurs in space is its density. The feature being measured could be people, houses, cars, volcanoes, or anything. The area could be measured in square kilometers, square miles, hectares, acres, or any other unit of area. A large population does not necessarily lead to a high density. Russia has a much larger population than the Netherlands, but the Netherlands has a much higher density because its land area is much smaller.

- **Concentration.** The extent of a feature's spread over space is its concentration. If the objects in an area are close together, they are clustered; if relatively far apart, they are dispersed. To compare the level of concentration most clearly, two areas need to have the same number of objects and the same size area.

- **Pattern.** The arrangement of objects in space is its pattern. Some features are organized in a geometric pattern, whereas others are distributed irregularly.

Concentration is not the same as density. Two neighborhoods could have the same density of housing but different concentrations. In a dispersed neighborhood each house has a large private yard, whereas in a clustered neighborhood the houses are close together and the open space is shared as a community park (Figure 1.9.1).

We can illustrate the difference between density and concentration at larger scales than a neighborhood. The changing distribution of baseball teams in the United States during the second half of the twentieth century resulted in a higher density of teams and a lower concentration (Figure 1.9.2).

Objects are frequently arranged in a square or rectangular pattern. Many American cities contain a regular pattern of streets, known as a grid pattern, which intersect at right angles at uniform intervals to form square or rectangular blocks. Other objects form a linear pattern, such as the arrangement of people and vegetation along the beach (refer to Figure 1.1.6).

American League
National League

1952

Mariners
Twins
Blue Jays
Brewers **Tigers** **Pirates**
Cubs **Mets**
Athletics **White Sox** **Indians** **Phillies**
Rockies **Orioles**
Giants **Royals** **Reds** **Nationals**
Dodgers **Cardinals**
Diamondbacks
Angels **Braves**
Padres **Rangers**
2012 **Astros**
Rays
Marlins

◄ 1.9.2 **DISTRIBUTION OF MAJOR LEAGUE BASEBALL TEAMS**
The changing distribution of North American baseball teams illustrates the difference between density and concentration.

These six teams moved to other cities during the 1950s and 1960s:

Braves—Boston to Milwaukee in 1953, then to Atlanta in 1966
Browns—St. Louis to Baltimore (Orioles) in 1954
Athletics—Philadelphia to Kansas City in 1955, then to Oakland in 1968
Dodgers—Brooklyn to Los Angeles in 1958
Giants—New York to San Francisco in 1958
Senators—Washington to Minneapolis (Minnesota Twins) in 1961

These 14 teams were added between the 1960s and 1990s:

Angels—Los Angeles in 1961, then to Anaheim (California) in 1965
Senators—Washington in 1961, then to Arlington (Texas) (Texas Rangers) in 1971
Mets—New York in 1962
Astros—Houston (originally Colt .45s) in 1962
Royals—Kansas City in 1969
Padres—San Diego in 1969
Expos—Montreal in 1969, then to Washington (Nationals) in 2005
Pilots—Seattle in 1969, then to Milwaukee (Brewers) in 1970
Blue Jays—Toronto in 1977
Mariners—Seattle in 1977
Marlins—Miami (originally Florida) in 1993
Rockies—Denver (Colorado) in 1993
Rays—Tampa Bay (originally Devil Rays) in 1998
Diamondbacks—Phoenix (Arizona) in 1998

As a result of these relocations and additions, the density of teams increased, and the distribution became more dispersed.

GENDER AND ETHNIC DIVERSITY IN SPACE

Patterns in space vary according to gender and ethnicity. Consider the daily patterns of an "all-American" family of mother, father, son, and daughter. Leave aside for the moment that this type of family constitutes less than one-fourth of American households.

In the morning Dad drives from home to work, where he parks the car and spends the day; then, in the late afternoon, he drives home. Meanwhile, Mom takes the children to school, drives to the supermarket, visits Grandmother, walks the dog, collects the youngsters at school, takes them to sports practice or ballet lessons, and in between organizes the several thousand square feet of space that the family calls home. Most American women are now employed at work outside the home, adding a substantial complication to an already complex pattern of moving across urban space.

The importance of gender in space is learned as a child. Which child—the boy or girl—went to play ball, and which went to ballet lessons? To which activity is substantially more land allocated in a city—ballfields or dance studios (Figure 1.9.3)?

If the above family were parented by a same-sex couple, its connections with space would change. Similarly, effects of race and ethnicity on spatial interaction can be seen across America.

▲▼ 1.9.3 **GENDER AND SPACE**
Ballfields, which are more likely to be used by boys, take up more space in a community than ballet studios, which are more likely to be used by girls.

1.10 Connection: Interaction Between Places

▶ **A characteristic spreads from one place to another through diffusion.**
▶ **Connections between places result in spatial interaction.**

Geographers increasingly think about connections among places and regions. In the past, most forms of interaction among cultural groups resulted from the slow movement of settlers, explorers, and plunderers from one location to another. Today travel by motor vehicle or airplane is much quicker. More rapid connections have reduced the distance across space between places, not literally in miles, of course, but in time. Geographers apply the term **space-time compression** to describe the reduction in the time it takes for something to reach another place. Distant places seem less remote and more accessible to us (Figure 1.10.1). We know more about what is happening elsewhere in the world, and we know sooner.

But we do not even need to travel to know about another place. We can communicate instantly with people in distant places through computers and telecommunications, and we can instantly see people in distant places on television. These and other forms of communication have made it possible for people in different places to be aware of the same cultural beliefs, forms, and traits.

▲ 1.10.1 **SPACE-TIME COMPRESSION**
Transportation improvements have shrunk the world:
- In 1492, Christopher Columbus took 37 days (nearly 900 hours) to sail across the Atlantic Ocean from the Canary Islands to San Salvador Island.
- In 1912, the Titanic was scheduled to sail from Queenstown (now Cobh), Ireland, to New York in about 5 days, although two-thirds of the way across, after 80 hours at sea, it hit an iceberg and sank.
- In 1927, Charles Lindbergh was the first person to fly nonstop across the Atlantic, taking 33.5 hours to go from New York to Paris.
- In 1962, John Glenn, the first American to orbit in space, crossed over the Atlantic in about a quarter-hour and circled the globe three times in 5 hours.

RELOCATION DIFFUSION

The process by which a characteristic spreads across space from one place to another over time is **diffusion**. The place from which an innovation originates is called a **hearth**. Something originates at a hearth or node and diffuses from there to other places. Geographers document the location of nodes and the processes by which diffusion carries things elsewhere over time.

Diffusion occurs through cultural interaction involving persons, objects, or ideas. Geographers observe two basic types of diffusion: relocation diffusion and expansion diffusion. **Relocation diffusion** is the spread of an idea through physical movement of people from one place to another. When people move, they carry with them their culture, including language, religion, and ethnicity (Figure 1.10.2).

▼ 1.10.2 **RELOCATION DIFFUSION**
Introduction of a common currency, the euro, in 12 European countries on January 1, 2002, gave scientists an unusual opportunity to measure relocation diffusion. A single set of paper money was issued, but each of the 12 countries minted its own coins in proportion to its share of the region's economy. A country's coins were initially distributed only inside its borders, although the coins could also be used in the other 11 countries. French researchers took month-to-month samples to monitor the proportion of coins from the other 11 countries. The percentage of purses containing "foreign" euro coins is a measure of the level of relocation diffusion into France. Not surprisingly, diffusion occurred earlier and in higher percentages near the borders with other countries.

% of purses containing a euro coin

0%   25%   50%   75%   100%

EXPANSION DIFFUSION

Expansion diffusion is the spread of a feature from one place to another in an additive process. This expansion may result from one of three processes:

Hierarchical diffusion is the spread of an idea from persons or nodes of authority or power to other persons or places. Hierarchical diffusion may result from the spread of ideas from political leaders, socially elite people, or other important persons to others in the community.

Contagious diffusion is the rapid, widespread diffusion of a characteristic throughout the population. As the term implies, this form of diffusion is analogous to the spread of a contagious disease, such as influenza. Ideas placed on the World Wide Web spread through contagious diffusion, because Web surfers throughout the world have access to the same material simultaneously—and quickly.

Stimulus diffusion is the spread of an underlying principle. For example, innovative features of Apple's iPhone and iPad operating systems have been adopted by competitors.

All three types of expansion diffusion occur much more rapidly in the contemporary world than in the past, because of widespread access to modern communications systems. Ideas are able to diffuse from one place to another, even if people are not actually relocating.

SPATIAL INTERACTION

When places are connected to each other through a network, geographers say there is **spatial interaction** between them. Typically, the farther away one group is from another, the less likely the two groups are to interact. Contact diminishes with increasing distance and eventually disappears. This trailing-off phenomenon is called **distance decay**.

Transportation systems form networks that facilitate relocation diffusion. Most airlines, for example, adopt a distinctive network called "hub-and-spokes" (Figure 1.10.3). Airlines fly planes from a large number of places into one hub airport within a short period of time and soon thereafter send the planes to another set of places (Figure 1.10.4).

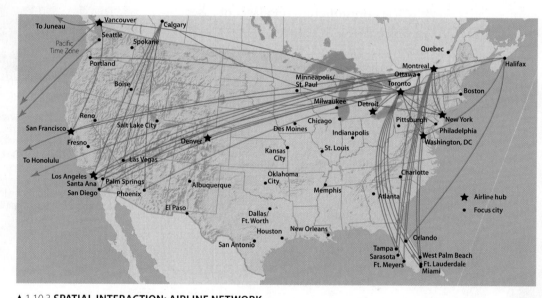

▲ 1.10.3 **SPATIAL INTERACTION: AIRLINE NETWORK**
Air Canada, like other major airlines, has configured its route network in a system known as "hub and spokes." A large percentage of Air Canada's flights originate or end at its principal hub in Toronto.

Electronic communications have removed barriers to interaction between people who are far from each other. The birth of these electronic communications was initially viewed as the "death" of geography, because they made it cheap and easy to stay in touch with people and events on the other side of the planet. In reality, geography matters even more than before. Internet access depends upon availability of electricity to either power a computer directly, or at least to recharge the battery in the computer or in a smart phone.

The Internet has also magnified the importance of geography, because when an individual is online the specific place in the world where the individual is located is known. This knowledge is valuable information for businesses that target advertisements and products to specific tastes and preferences of particular places.

▼ 1.10.4 **AIRLINE HUB**
Toronto Pearson International Airport, Air Canada's principal hub.

1.11 Earth's Physical Systems

▶ **Earth's physical environment comprises four spheres.**
▶ **The four spheres are interrelated and interact with each other.**

Geographers study natural processes in terms of four interrelated systems. These four physical systems are classified as either biotic or abiotic. A **biotic** system is composed of living organisms. An **abiotic** system is composed of nonliving or inorganic matter.

EARTH'S FOUR SYSTEMS

Three of Earth's four systems are abiotic:

- The **atmosphere**: a thin layer of gases surrounding Earth (Figure 1.11.1).
- The **hydrosphere**: all of the water on and near Earth's surface (Figure 1.11.2).
- The **lithosphere**: Earth's crust and a portion of upper mantle directly below the crust (Figure 1.11.3).

One of the four systems is biotic:

- The **biosphere**: all living organisms on Earth, including plants and animals, as well as microorganisms (Figure 1.11.4).

The names of the four spheres are derived from the Greek words for stone (litho), air (atmo), water (hydro), and life (bio).

EARTH'S ATMOSPHERE FROM SPACE SHUTTLE

▲ 1.11.1 **ATMOSPHERE**

A thin layer of gases surrounds Earth at an altitude up to 480 kilometers (300 miles). Pure dry air in the lower atmosphere contains approximately 78 percent nitrogen, 21 percent oxygen, 0.9 percent argon, 0.036 percent carbon dioxide, and 0.064 percent other gases (measured by volume). As atmospheric gases are held to Earth by gravity, pressure is created. Variations in air pressure from one location to another are responsible for producing such weather features as wind blowing, storms brewing, and rain falling.

◀ 1.11.2 **HYDROSPHERE**

Water exists in liquid form in the oceans, lakes, and rivers, as well as groundwater in soil and rock. it can also exist as water vapor in the atmosphere, and as ice in glaciers. Over 97 percent of the world's water is in the oceans. The oceans supply the atmosphere with water vapor, which returns to earth's surface as precipitation, the most important source of freshwater. Consumption of water is essential for the survival of plants and animals, and a large quantity and variety of plants and animals live in it. because water gains and loses heat relatively slowly, it also moderates seasonal temperature extremes over much of earth's surface.

▶ 1.11.3 **LITHOSPHERE**

Earth is composed of concentric spheres. The core is a dense, metallic sphere about 3,500 kilometers (2,200 miles) in radius. Surrounding the core is a mantle about 2,900 kilometers (1,800 miles) thick. The crust is a thin, brittle outer shell 8 to 40 kilometers (5 to 25 miles) thick. The lithosphere encompasses the crust, a portion of the mantle extending down to about 70 kilometers (45 miles). Powerful forces deep within earth bend and break the crust to form mountain chains and shape the crust to form continents and ocean basins.

LIGHTHOUSE REEF, TURNEFFE ATOLL, BELIZE

INTERACTIONS IN THE BIOSPHERE

An **ecosystem** is a group of living organisms and the abiotic spheres with which they interact. **Ecology** is the scientific study of ecosystems. Ecologists study interrelationships between living organisms and their environments within particular ecosystems, as well as interrelationships among various ecosystems in the biosphere.

Living organisms in the biosphere interact with each of the three abiotic systems. For example:

- The lithosphere is where most plants and animals live and where they obtain food and shelter.
- The hydrosphere provides water to drink, and physical support for aquatic life.
- The atmosphere provides the air for animals to breathe and protects them from the sun's rays.

Furthermore, the biosphere often represents the interface of the three abiotic systems with living organisms. For example, a piece of soil may comprise mineral material from the lithosphere, moisture from the hydrosphere, pockets of air from the atmosphere, and plant and insect matter from the biosphere.

Because geography is a social science as well as a natural science, geographers are especially interested in the interaction of humans with each of the four spheres (Figure 1.11.5):

- If the atmosphere's oxygen levels are reduced, or if the atmosphere contains pollutants, humans have trouble breathing.
- Without water, humans waste away and die.
- A stable lithosphere provides humans with materials for buildings and fuel for energy.
- The rest of the biosphere provides humans with food.

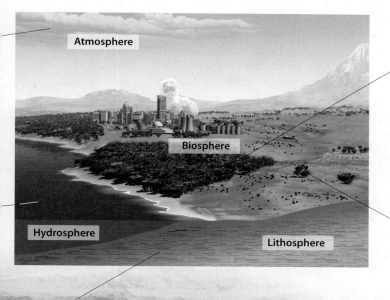

Atmosphere

Biosphere

Hydrosphere

Lithosphere

◄ 1.11.4 **BIOSPHERE**

The biosphere extends into each of Earth's abiotic systems. The biosphere encompasses all of Earth's living organisms. Because living organisms cannot exist except through interaction with the surrounding physical environment, the biosphere actually includes portions of the three abiotic systems near Earth's surface. Most of the planet's life is found within the top 3 meters (10 feet) of the lithosphere, the top 200 meters (650 feet) of the hydrosphere, and the lowest 30 meters (100 feet) of the atmosphere.

▼ 1.11.5 **ECOSYSTEMS**

Geographers are especially interested in the ecosystem of a city, because approximately half of Earth's humans live in urban areas. The lithosphere provides the ground and the materials to erect homes and businesses. The hydrosphere provides the water for urban dwellers to consume. The atmosphere is where urban dwellers emit pollutants. Some plants and other animals of the biosphere thrive along with humans in the cities, whereas others struggle.

NAMIB-NAUKLUFT PARK, NAMIBIA

IPANEMA, BRAZIL

1.12 Human–Environment Interaction

▶ The environment can limit human actions, but people adjust to the environment.

▶ Humans are able to modify the environment, not always sensitively.

Distinctive to geography is the importance given to relationships between human behavior and the natural environment. The geographic study of human–environment relationships is known as **cultural ecology**. Geographers are interested in two main types of human–environment interaction: how people adjust to their environment, and how they modify it.

POSSIBILISM: ADJUSTING TO THE ENVIRONMENT

▼▶ 1.12.1 **MODIFYING THE ENVIRONMENT IN THE NETHERLANDS**

The Zuider Zee, an arm of the north sea, once threatened the heart of the netherlands with flooding. A dike completed in 1932 caused the Zuider Zee to be converted from a saltwater sea to a freshwater lake. The newly created body of water was named the ijsselmeer, or lake ijssel, because the ijssel river now flows into it. Some of the lake has been drained to create several polders, encompassing an area of 1,600 square kilometers (620 square miles). The dutch government has reserved most of the polders for agriculture to reduce the country's dependence on imported food.

A second ambitious dike project is the Delta Plan. Flowing through the Netherlands are several important rivers, including the Rhine (Europe's busiest river), the Maas (known as the Meuse in France), and the Scheldt (known as the Schelde in Belgium). As these rivers flow into the North Sea, they split into many branches and form a low-lying delta that is vulnerable to flooding. After a devastating flood in January 1953 killed nearly 2,000 people, the Delta Plan called for the construction of several dams to close off the waterways from the North Sea. The project took 30 years to build and was completed in the mid-1980s. (below) Polder near Loosdrecht, the Netherlands

A century ago, geographers argued that the physical environment *caused* social development, an approach called **environmental determinism**. For example, according to environmental determinism the temperate climate of northwestern Europe produced greater human efficiency as measured by better health conditions, lower death rates, and higher standards of living.

To explain relationships between human activities and the physical environment, modern geographers reject environmental determinism in favor of **possibilism**. According to possibilism the physical environment may limit some human actions, but people have the ability to adjust to their environment. People can choose a course of action from many alternatives in the physical environment. For example, people learn that different crops thrive in different climates; wheat is more likely than rice to be grown successfully in colder climates. Thus, under geography's possibilism approach, people choose the crops they grow in part by considering their environment.

MODIFYING THE ENVIRONMENT

Modern technology has altered the historic relationship between people and the environment. Humans now can modify a region's physical environment to a greater extent than in the past.

Few regions have been as thoroughly modified by humans as the Netherlands and southern Louisiana. With approximately 8,000 square kilometers (3,000 square miles) of land below sea level in both regions, extensive areas would be under water today were it not for massive projects to modify the environment by holding back the sea. The modifications undertaken by the Dutch have generally been more sensitive to environmental processes.

- **Modifying the Netherlands.** The Dutch have modified their environment with two distinctive types of construction projects—polders and dikes. A **polder** is a piece of land that is created by draining water from an area. All together, the Netherlands has 6,500 square kilometers (2,600 square miles) of polders, comprising 16 percent of the country's land area (Figure 1.12.1).

  Massive dikes have been built in two major locations—the Zuider Zee project in the north and the Delta Plan project in the southwest. These dikes prevent the North Sea, an arm of the Atlantic Ocean, from flooding much of the country.

- **Modifying southern Louisiana.** In an effort to protect New Orleans and other low-lying land from flooding, government agencies have constructed a complex system of levees, dikes, seawalls, canals, and pumps. Hurricane

Katrina in 2005 showed that the efforts to control and tame all of the forces of nature in southern Louisiana and Gulf Coast regions of neighboring states were not successful.

Hurricanes such as Katrina form in the Atlantic Ocean during the late summer and autumn and gather strength over the warm waters of the Gulf of Mexico. When it passes over land, a hurricane can generate a powerful storm surge that floods low-lying areas. Human geographers were especially concerned with the uneven impact of destruction and the incompetent response to the hurricane.

Hurricane Katrina's victims were primarily poor, African American, and older individuals living in low-lying areas (Figure 1.12.2). The slow and incompetent response to the destruction by local, state, and federal emergency teams was blamed by many analysts on the victims' lack of a voice in the politics, economy, and social life of New Orleans and other impacted communities.

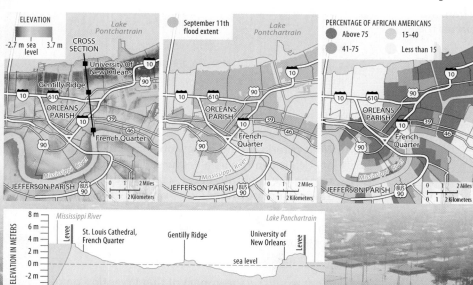

▼◄ 1.12.2 **MODIFYING THE ENVIRONMENT IN SOUTHERN LOUISIANA**
(left) Eighty percent of New Orleans is below sea level. (center and below) The day after Hurricane Katrina hit southern Louisiana, many of the levees in New Orleans broke, causing widespread flooding. (right) Neighborhoods inhabited primarily by African Americans were especially hard hit by flooding.

This chapter has introduced ways in which geographers think about the world, as well as key concepts in understanding geography.

Key Questions

How do geographers describe where things are?

► Geography describes the distribution of both natural and human phenomena.
► Geography began in ancient times as a descriptive aid for navigation and discovery.
► One of geography's most important tools since ancient times for describing the location of things on Earth has been the map.
► Satellite imagery and geographic information systems have enhanced geography's traditional ways of describing where things are.

Why is each point on Earth unique?

► Each place on Earth has distinct features of site and situation.
► Regions are areas of the world distinguished by a unique combination of features.

▼ 1.CR.1 **SATELLITE VIEW OF THE PERSIAN GULF**

"Persia" is an ancient name for present-day iran. Most countries bordering the Gulf are arab and prefer the name Arabian Gulf.

How are different locations interrelated?

► People are increasingly plugged into a global culture and economy.
► Many human and environmental features are distributed according to a regular arrangement.
► People and physical features in one place are connected to those elsewhere through processes of diffusion.

How do people relate to their environment?

► The biosphere, which comprises humans and other living things, is tied to processes in the atmosphere, hydrosphere, and lithosphere
► Human actions are influenced by the environment, and in turn humans increasingly modify the environment.

Thinking Geographically

Using geographic tools such as maps and GIS is not simply a mechanical exercise. Nor are decisions confined to scale, projection, and layers. For example, many countries believe that the Persian Gulf should be labeled the Arabian Gulf (Figure 1.CR.1). Other countries believe that Kosovo should not be shown as a country.

1. **What criteria should geographers use to decide such politically controversial features? Majority vote among the countries of the world? The U.S. government position? Other ways to decide?**

Imagine that a transportation device (perhaps the one in *Star Trek* or *Harry Potter*) would enable all humans to travel instantaneously to any location on Earth.

2. **What would be the impact of that invention on the distribution of people, activities, and physical features across Earth?**

When earthquakes, hurricanes, and other environmental disasters strike, some humans tend to "blame" nature and see themselves as the innocent victims of Earth's sometimes harsh and cruel physical environment.

3. **To what extent do environmental hazards stem from physical systems and to what extent do they originate from human actions? Should victims blame nature, other humans, or themselves for the disaster? Why?**

Interactive Mapping

ELEVATION IN NORTH AMERICA

Launch MapMaster North America in
Mastering GEOGRAPHY

Select: *Physical Features* from the *Physical Environment* menu, then select *Environmental Issues*.

What areas of North America other than Louisiana may be vulnerable to coastal flooding and groundwater depletion?

On the Internet

Useful Internet sites for learning about geography in North America are maintained by the major professional organizations, including the Association of American Geographers (**www.aag.org**, or scan the QR on the first page of this chapter), the American Geographical Society (**www.amergeog.org**), the National Council for Geographic Education (**www.ncge.org**), and the Canadian Association of Geographers (Association Canadienne des Géographes) (**www.cag-acg.ca**).

The National Geographic Society offers access to material from its magazine and television programs, as well as online mapping at **www.nationalgeographic.com.**

Explore

NEW ORLEANS

(top) Use Google Earth to explore the impact of Hurricane Katrina on New Orleans. (bottom) Desire residential area in New Orleans. Google Earth provides historical images, in this case August 30, 2005, the day after Hurricane Katrina hit. Move the timeline forward until the floodwaters have disappeared

Fly to: *Desire Neighborhood Development, New Orleans, LA, USA.*

Click icon for: *Show historical imagery.*

Move time line to: *August 30, 2005.*

What was the date, after Katrina, when the buildings were visible again?

The Physical and Political World

Key Terms

Abiotic
A system composed of nonliving or inorganic matter.

Atmosphere
The thin layer of gases surrounding Earth.

Biosphere
All living organisms on Earth.

Biotic
The system composed of living organisms.

Cartography
The science of making maps.

Concentration
The spread of something over a given area.

Connection
Relationships among people and objects across the barrier of space.

Contagious diffusion
The rapid, widespread diffusion of a feature or trend throughout a population.

Cultural ecology
The geographic study of human-environment relationships.

Cultural landscape
Fashioning of a natural landscape by a cultural group.

Density
The frequency with which something exists within a given unit of area.

Diffusion
The process of spread of a feature or trend from one place to another over time.

Distance decay
The diminishing in importance and eventual disappearance of a phenomenon with increasing distance from its origin.

Distribution
The arrangement of something across Earth's surface.

Ecology
The scientific study of ecosystems.

Ecosystem
A group of living organisms and the abiotic spheres with which they interact.

Environmental determinism
A nineteenth- and early twentieth-century approach to the study of geography that argued that the general laws sought by human geographers could be found in the physical sciences. Geography was therefore the study of how the physical environment caused human activities.

Expansion diffusion
The spread of a feature or trend among people from one area to another in an additive process.

Formal region (or uniform or homogeneous region)
An area in which everyone shares in one or more distinctive characteristics.

Functional region (or nodal region)
An area organized around a node or focal point.

Geographic grid
A system of imaginary arcs drawn in a grid pattern on Earth's surface.

Geographic Information Science (GIScience)
The development and analysis of data about Earth acquired through satellite and other electronic information technologies.

Geographic information system (GIS)
A computer system that stores, organizes, analyzes, and displays geographic data.

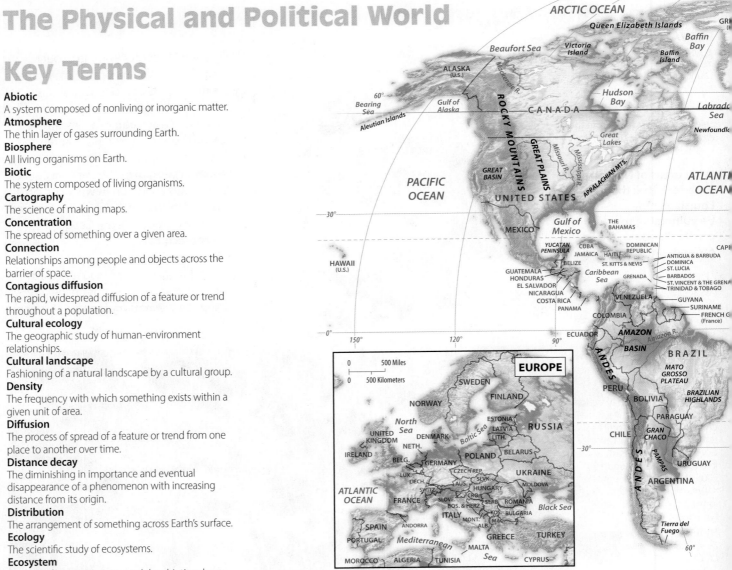

Global Positioning System (GPS)
A system that determines the precise position of something on Earth through a series of satellites, tracking stations, and receivers.

Globalization
Actions or processes that involve the entire world and result in making something worldwide in scope.

Greenwich Mean Time (GMT)
The time in that time zone encompassing the prime meridian, or 0° longitude.

Hearth
The region from which innovative ideas originate.

Hierarchical diffusion
The spread of a feature or trend from one key person or node of authority or power to other persons or places.

Hydrosphere
All of the water on and near Earth's surface.

International Date Line
A meridian that for the most part follows 180° longitude. When you cross the International Date Line heading east (toward America), the clock moves back 24 hours (one day), and when you go west (toward Asia), the calendar moves ahead one day.

Latitude
The numbering system used to indicate the location of parallels drawn on a globe and measuring distance north and south of the equator (0°).

Lithosphere
Earth's crust and a portion of the upper mantle directly below the crust.

Location
The position of anything on Earth's surface.

Longitude
The numbering system used to indicate the location of meridians drawn on a globe and measuring distance east and west of the prime meridian (0°).

Map
A two-dimensional, or flat, representation of Earth's surface or a portion of it.

Map scale
The relationship between the size of an object on a map and the size of the actual feature on Earth's surface.

Meridian
An arc drawn on a map between the North and South poles.

Parallel
A circle drawn around the globe parallel to the equator and at right angles to the meridians.

Pattern
The regular arrangement of something in a study area.

Place
A specific point on Earth distinguished by a particular characteristic.

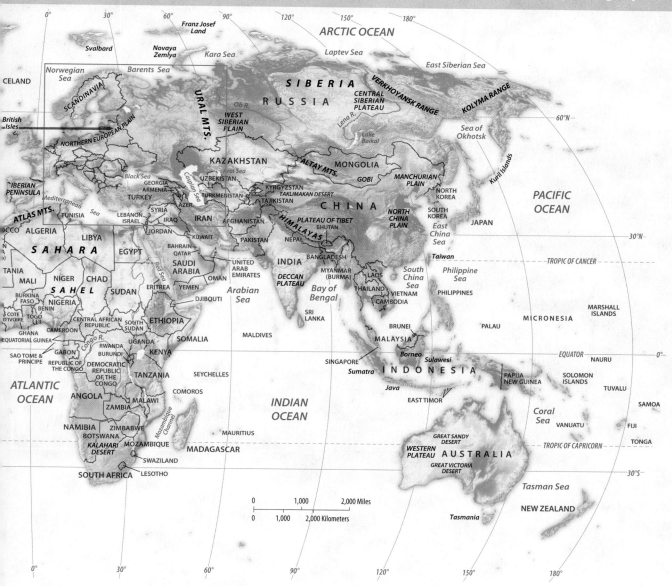

Polder
Land created by the Dutch by draining water from an area.

Possibilism
The theory that the physical environment may set limits on human actions, but people have the ability to adjust to the physical environment and choose a course of action from many alternatives.

Prime meridian
The meridian, designated as 0° longitude, that passes through the Royal Observatory at Greenwich, England.

Projection
The system used to transfer locations from Earth's surface to a flat map.

Region
An area of Earth distinguished by a distinctive combination of cultural and physical features.

Relocation diffusion
The spread of a feature or trend through bodily movement of people from one place to another.

Remote sensing
The acquisition of data about Earth's surface from a satellite orbiting the planet or other long-distance methods.

Scale
The relationship between the portion of Earth being studied and Earth as a whole.

Site
The physical character of a place.

Situation
The location of a place relative to other places.

Space
The physical gap or interval between two objects.

Space-time compression
The reduction in the time it takes to diffuse something to a distant place, as a result of improved communications and transportation systems.

Spatial interaction
The movement of physical processes, human activities, and ideas within and among regions.

Stimulus diffusion
The spread of an underlying principle, even though a specific characteristic is rejected.

Toponym
The name given to a portion of Earth's surface.

Transnational corporation
A company that conducts research, operates factories, and sells products in many countries, not just where its headquarters or shareholders are located.

Vernacular region (or perceptual region)
An area that people believe exists as part of their cultural identity.

▶ **LOOKING AHEAD**

People are not distributed uniformly across Earth. The starting point for our study of human geography is understanding where people are living in ever greater numbers, and reasons underlying the distinctive distribution of humans.

2 Population

More humans are alive at this time—about 7 billion—than at any point in Earth's long history. Most of these people live in developing countries and nearly all of the world's population growth is concentrated in developing countries.

Is the world overpopulated? Will it become so in the years ahead? Geographic approaches are well suited to address these fears. Geographers argue that overpopulation is not simply a matter of the total number of people on Earth; rather it depends on the relationship between the number of people and the availability of resources.

Overpopulation is a threat where an area's population exceeds the capacity of the environment to support it at an acceptable standard of living. The capacity of Earth as a whole to support human life may be high, but some regions have a favorable balance between people and available resources, whereas others do not. Further, the regions with the most people are not necessarily the same as the regions with an unfavorable balance between population and resources.

Where is the world's population distributed?

2.1 **Population Concentrations**

2.2 **Population Density**

NEW PARENTS
WATCH THEIR BABIES
THROUGH HOSPITAL
WINDOW

why does population growth vary among countries?

How might population change in the future?

SCAN FOR UPDATED POPULATION DATA

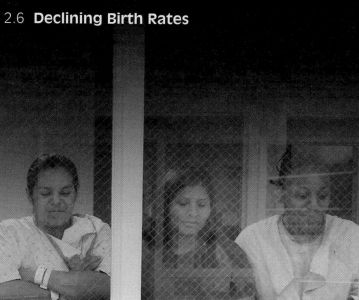

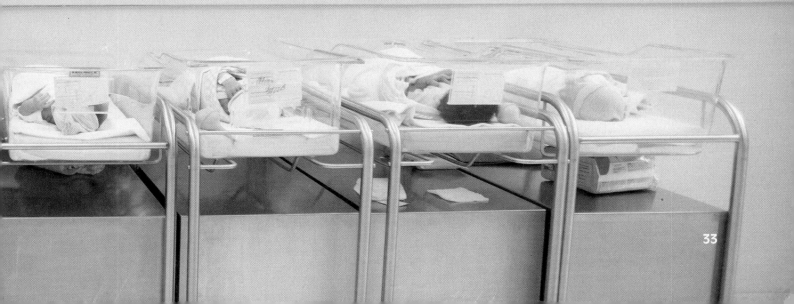

2.1 Population Concentrations

▶ **Two-thirds of the world's inhabitants are clustered in four regions.**

▶ **Humans avoid clustering in harsh environments.**

Human beings are not distributed uniformly across Earth's surface (Figure 2.1.1). Human beings avoid clustering in certain physical environments, especially those that are too dry, too wet, too cold, or too mountainous for activities such as agriculture (Figure 2.1.2).

The clustering of the world's population can be displayed on a cartogram, which depicts the size of countries according to population rather than land area, as is the case with most maps (Figure 2.1.3). Two-thirds of the world's inhabitants are clustered in four regions—East Asia, South Asia, Southeast Asia, and Europe (Figure 2.1.4).

▼ 2.1.1 **POPULATION DISTRIBUTION**

Persons per square kilometer

- 1,000 and above
- 250–999
- 25–249
- 5–2
- 1–4
- bel

▲ **RORAIMA, BRAZIL**

A 2.1.2 **SPARSELY POPULATED REGIONS**
Human beings do not live in large numbers in certain physical environments.

2.1.2A COLD LANDS
Much of the land near the North and South poles is perpetually covered with ice or the ground is permanently frozen (permafrost). The polar regions are unsuitable for planting crops, few animals can survive the extreme cold, and few human beings live there.

2.1.2B DRY LANDS
Areas too dry for farming cover approximately 20 percent of Earth's land surface. Deserts generally lack sufficient water to grow crops that could feed a large population, although some people survive there by raising animals, such as camels, that are adapted to the climate. Although dry lands are generally inhospitable to intensive agriculture, they may contain natural resources useful to people—notably, much of the world's oil reserves.

2.1.2C WET LANDS
Lands that receive very high levels of precipitation, such as near Brazil's Amazon River shown in the image, may also be sparsely inhabited. The combination of rain and heat rapidly depletes nutrients from the soil and thus hinders agriculture.

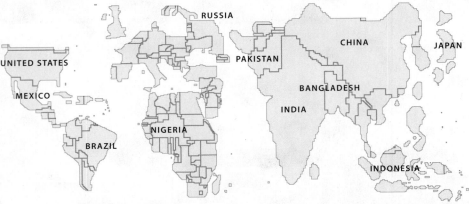

Countries with populations over 100 million are labeled.

▲ 2.1.3 **POPULATION CARTOGRAM**
The population cartogram displays the major population clusters of Europe, and East, South, and Southeast Asia as much larger, and Africa and the Western Hemisphere as much smaller than on a more typical equal-area map, such as the large one in the middle of these two pages.

2.1.2D HIGH LANDS
The highest mountains in the world are steep, snow covered, and sparsely settled. However, some high-altitude plateaus and mountain regions are more densely populated, especially at low latitudes (near the equator) where agriculture is possible at high elevations

2.1.4A EUROPE

Europe contains one-ninth of the world's people. The region includes four dozen countries, ranging from Monaco, with 1 square kilometer (0.7 square mile) and a population of 32,000, to Russia, the world's largest country in land area when its Asian land portion is included.

Three-fourths of Europe's inhabitants live in cities. A dense network of road and rail lines links settlements. Europe's highest population concentrations are near the major rivers and coalfields of Germany and Belgium, as well as historic capital cities like London and Paris.

The region's temperate climate permits cultivation of a variety of crops, yet Europeans do not produce enough food for themselves. Instead, they import food and other resources from elsewhere in the world. The search for additional resources was a major incentive for Europeans to explore and colonize other parts of the world during the previous six centuries. Today, Europeans turn many of these resources into manufactured products.

▼ 2.1.4 FOUR POPULATION CLUSTERS

The four regions display some similarities. Most of the people in these regions live near an ocean or near a river with easy access to an ocean, rather than in the interior of major landmasses. The four population clusters occupy generally low-lying areas, with fertile soil and temperate climate.

2.1.4B EAST ASIA

One-fifth of the world's people live in East Asia. This concentration includes the world's most populous country, the People's Republic of China. The Chinese population is clustered near the Pacific Coast and in several fertile river valleys that extend inland, such as the Huang and the Yangtze. Much of China's interior is sparsely inhabited mountains and deserts. Although China has 25 urban areas with more than 2 million inhabitants and 61 with more than 1 million, more than one-half of the people live in rural areas where they work as farmers.

In Japan and South Korea, population is not distributed uniformly either. Forty percent of the people live in three large metropolitan areas—Tokyo and Osaka in Japan, and Seoul in South Korea—that cover less than 3 percent of the two countries' land area. In sharp contrast to China, more than three-fourths of all Japanese and Koreans live in urban areas and work at industrial or service jobs.

2.1.2C SOUTHEAST ASIA

A third important Asian population cluster is in Southeast Asia. A half billion people live in Southeast Asia, mostly on a series of islands that lie between the Indian and Pacific oceans. These islands include Java, Sumatra, Borneo, Papua New Guinea, and the Philippines. The largest concentration is on the island of Java, inhabited by more than 100 million people. Indonesia, which consists of 13,677 islands, including Java, is the world's fourth most populous country.

Several islands that belong to the Philippines contain high population concentrations, and people are also clustered along several river valleys and deltas at the southeastern tip of the Asian mainland, known as Indochina. Like China and South Asia, the Southeast Asia concentration is characterized by a high percentage of people working as farmers in rural areas.

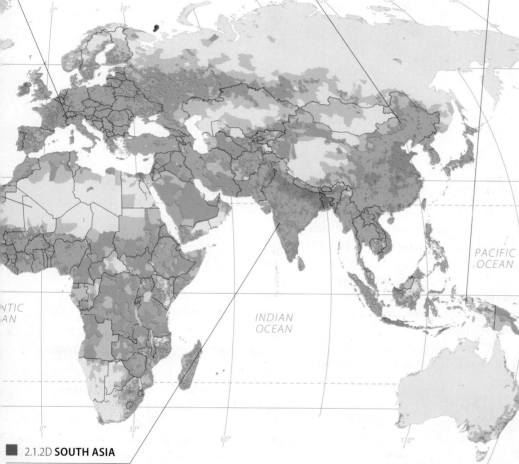

PACIFIC OCEAN

INDIAN OCEAN

2.1.2D SOUTH ASIA

One-fifth of the world's people live in South Asia, which includes India, Pakistan, Bangladesh, and the island of Sri Lanka. The largest concentration of people within South Asia lives along a 1,500-kilometer (900-mile) corridor from Lahore, Pakistan, through India and Bangladesh to the Bay of Bengal. Much of this area's population is concentrated along the plains of the Indus and Ganges rivers. People are also heavily concentrated near India's two long coastlines—the Arabian Sea to the west and the Bay of Bengal to the east.

To an even greater extent than the Chinese, most people in South Asia are farmers living in rural areas. The region contains 18 urban areas with more than 2 million inhabitants and 46 with more than 1 million, but only one-fourth of the total population lives in an urban area.

▼ VARANASI, INDIA

2.2 Population Density

▶ Arithmetic density measures the total number of people living in an area.

▶ Physiological density and agricultural density show spatial relationships between people and resources.

Density, defined in Chapter 1 as the number of people occupying an area of land, can be computed in several ways, including arithmetic density, physiological density, and agricultural density. These measures of density help geographers to describe the distribution of people in comparison to available resources.

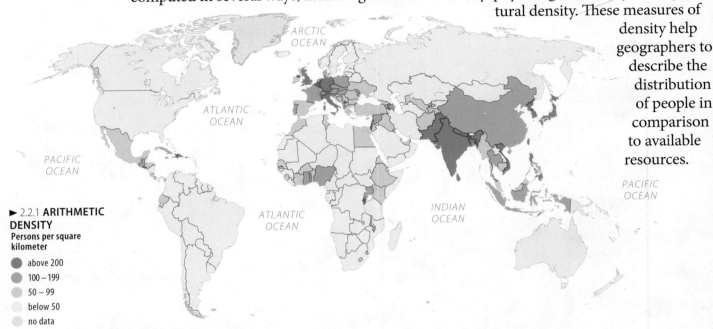

▶ 2.2.1 **ARITHMETIC DENSITY**
Persons per square kilometer

- above 200
- 100 – 199
- 50 – 99
- below 50
- no data

ARITHMETIC DENSITY

Geographers most frequently use **arithmetic density**, which is the total number of people divided by total land area (Figure 2.2.1). Geographers rely on the arithmetic density (also known as *population density*) to compare conditions in different countries because the two pieces of information needed to calculate the measure—total population and total land area—are easy to obtain.

To compute arithmetic density, divide the population by the land area. Figure 2.2.2 shows several examples.

	ARITHMETIC DENSITY (population per square kilometer)	POPULATION 2010 (million people)	LAND AREA (million square kilometers)
Canada	3	34	10.0
United States	32	310	9.6
Netherlands	400	17	0.04
Egypt	80	80	1.0

▲ 2.2.2 **ARITHMETIC DENSITY OF FOUR COUNTRIES**

Compared to the United States, the arithmetic density is much higher in the Netherlands and Egypt and much lower in Canada.

Arithmetic density enables geographers to compare the number of people trying to live on a given piece of land in different regions of the world. Thus, arithmetic density addresses the "where" question. However, to explain why people are not uniformly distributed across Earth's surface, other density measures are more useful (Figure 2.2.3).

◀ 2.2.3 **HIGH PHYSIOLOGICAL AND AGRICULTURAL DENSITY: EGYPT**
Weekly market at Qutur, Egypt.

PHYSIOLOGICAL DENSITY

A more meaningful population measure is afforded by looking at the number of people per area of **arable land**, which is land suited for agriculture. The number of people supported by a unit area of arable land is called the **physiological density** (Figure 2.2.4). The higher the physiological density, the greater the pressure that people may place on the land to produce enough food.

Physiological density provides insights into the relationship between the size of a population and the availability of resources in a region (Figure 2.2.5). The relatively large physiological densities of Egypt and the Netherlands demonstrate that crops grown on a hectare of land in these two countries must feed far more people than in the United States or Canada, which have much lower physiological densities.

Comparing physiological and arithmetic densities helps geographers to understand the capacity of the land to yield enough food for the needs of the people. In Egypt, for example, the large difference between the physiological density and arithmetic density indicates that

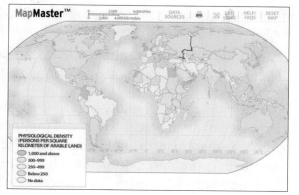

most of the country's land is unsuitable for intensive agriculture. In fact, all but 5 percent of Egyptians live in the Nile River valley and delta, because it is the only area in the country that receives enough moisture (by irrigation from the river) to allow intensive cultivation of crops.

◄ 2.2.4 **PHYSIOLOGICAL DENSITY**
Open MapMaster World in
Mastering **GEOGRAPHY**

Select: *Population* then *Physiological Density.*

What countries other than Egypt and the Netherlands have very high physiological densities?

	PHYSIOLOGICAL DENSITY (population per square kilometer of arable land)	ARABLE LAND (million square kilometers)
Canada	65	0.5
United States	175	1.7
Netherlands	1,748	0.01
Egypt	2,296	0.03

◄ 2.2.5 **PHYSIOLOGICAL DENSITY OF FOUR COUNTRIES**

AGRICULTURAL DENSITY

Two countries can have similar physiological densities, but they may produce significantly different amounts of food because of different economic conditions. **Agricultural density** is the ratio of the number of farmers to the amount of arable land (Figure 2.2.6).

Measuring agricultural density helps account for economic differences. Egypt has a much higher agricultural density than do Canada, the United States, and the Netherlands (Figure 2.2.7). Developed countries have lower agricultural densities because technology and finance allow a few people to farm extensive land areas and feed many people. This frees most of the population in developed countries to work in factories, offices, or shops rather than in the fields.

To understand relationships between population and resources in a country, geographers examine a country's physiological and agricultural densities together. For example, the physiological densities of both Egypt and the Netherlands are high, but the Dutch have a much lower agricultural density than the Egyptians. Geographers conclude that both the Dutch and Egyptians put heavy pressure on the land to produce food, but the more efficient Dutch agricultural system requires fewer farmers than does the Egyptian system.

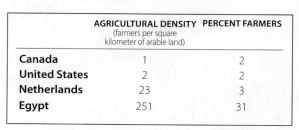

▲ 2.2.6 **AGRICULTURAL DENSITY**
Farmers per square kilometer of arable land

- above 100
- 50 – 99
- 25 – 49
- below 25
- no data

	AGRICULTURAL DENSITY (farmers per square kilometer of arable land)	PERCENT FARMERS
Canada	1	2
United States	2	2
Netherlands	23	3
Egypt	251	31

▲ 2.2.7 **AGRICULTURAL DENSITY OF FOUR COUNTRIES**

2.3 Components of Change

▶ **Geographers most frequently measure population change through three indicators.**

▶ **Indicators of population change vary widely among regions.**

Population increases rapidly in places where many more people are born than die, increases slowly in places where the number of births exceeds the number of deaths by only a small margin, and declines in places where deaths outnumber births. Geographers measure population change in a country or the world as a whole through three measures—crude birth rate, crude death rate, and natural increase rate.

The population of a place also increases when people move in and decreases when people move out. This element of population change—migration—is discussed the next chapter.

NATURAL INCREASE RATE

The **natural increase rate (NIR)** is the percentage by which a population grows in a year. The term natural means that a country's growth rate excludes migration. The world NIR during the early twenty-first century has been 1.2, meaning that the population of the world has been growing each year by 1.2 percent.

About 82 million people are being added to the population of the world annually. That number represents a slight decline from the historic high of 87 million in 1989. The world NIR, though, is considerably lower today than its historic peak of 2.2 percent in 1963. The number of people added each year has declined much more slowly than the NIR because the population base is much higher now than in the past. World population reached 1 billion around 1800. The time needed to add each additional billion has declined (Figure 2.3.1).

The rate of natural increase affects the **doubling time**, which is the number of years

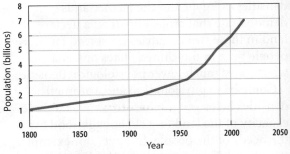

▲ 2.3.1 **WORLD POPULATION GROWTH**

needed to double a population, assuming a constant rate of natural increase. At the early twenty-first-century NIR rate of 1.2 percent per year, world population would double in about 54 years. Should the same NIR continue through the twenty-first century, global population in the year 2100 would reach 24 billion. Should the NIR immediately decline to 1.0, doubling time would stretch out to 70 years, and world population in 2100 would be only 15 billion.

More than 97 percent of the natural increase is clustered in developing countries (Figure 2.3.2). The NIR exceeds 2.0 percent in most countries of sub-Saharan Africa and Southwest Asia & North Africa, whereas it is negative in Europe, meaning that in the absence of immigrants, population actually is declining. About one-third of the world's population growth during the past decade has been in South Asia, one-fourth in sub-Saharan Africa, and the remainder divided about equally among East Asia, Southeast Asia, Latin America, Southwest Asia & North Africa. Regional differences in NIRs show that most of the world's additional people live in the countries that are least able to maintain them.

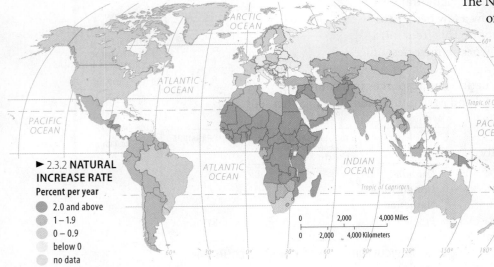

▶ 2.3.2 **NATURAL INCREASE RATE**
Percent per year

- 2.0 and above
- 1 – 1.9
- 0 – 0.9
- below 0
- no data

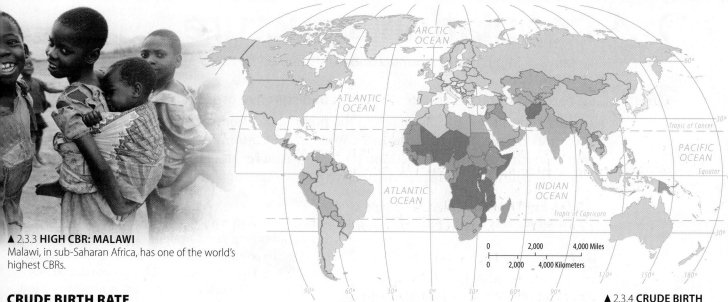

▲ 2.3.3 **HIGH CBR: MALAWI**
Malawi, in sub-Saharan Africa, has one of the world's highest CBRs.

CRUDE BIRTH RATE

The **crude birth rate (CBR)** is the total number of live births in a year for every 1,000 people alive in the society. A CBR of 20 means that for every 1,000 people in a country, 20 babies are born over a 1-year period.

The world map of CBRs mirrors the distribution of NIRs. As was the case with NIRs, the highest CBRs are in sub-Saharan Africa, and the lowest are in Europe (Figure 2.3.3). Many sub-Saharan African countries have a CBR over 40, whereas many European countries have a CBR below 10 (Figure 2.3.4).

▲ 2.3.4 **CRUDE BIRTH RATE**

Per 1,000 persons
- 40 and above
- 30 – 39
- 20 – 29
- 10 – 19
- below 10
- no data

CRUDE DEATH RATE

The **crude death rate** (CDR) is the total number of deaths in a year for every 1,000 people alive in the society. Comparable to the CBR, the CDR is expressed as the annual number of deaths per 1,000 population.

The NIR is computed by subtracting CDR from CBR, after first converting the two measures from numbers per 1,000 to percentages (numbers per 100). Thus if the CBR is 20 and the CDR is 5 (both per 1,000), then the NIR is 15 per 1,000, or 1.5 percent.

The CDR does not display the same regional pattern as the NIR and CBR (Figure 2.3.5). The combined CDR for all developing countries is lower than the combined rate for all developed countries. Furthermore, the variation between the world's highest and lowest CDRs is much less extreme than the variation in CBRs. The highest CDR in the world is 17 per 1,000, and the lowest is 1—a difference of 16—whereas CBRs for individual countries range from 7 per 1,000 to 52, a spread of 45.

Why does Denmark, one of the world's wealthiest countries, have a higher CDR than Cape Verde, one of the poorest? Why does the United States, with its extensive system of hospitals and physicians, have a higher CDR than Mexico and every country in Central America? The answer is that the populations of different countries are at various stages in an important process known as the demographic transition (see section 2.5).

▼ 2.3.5 **CRUDE DEATH RATE**

Per 1,000 persons
- 15 – 19
- 10 – 14
- 5 – 9
- below 5
- no data

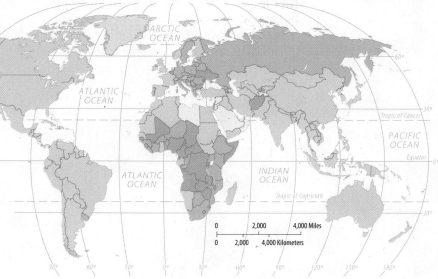

2.4 Population Structure

► **Change in a country's population is influenced by rates of fertility and infant mortality.**

► **Patterns of births and deaths result in distinctive ratios of young and old.**

In addition to the CBR discussed in the previous section, total fertility rate also measures the number of births in a country. In addition to the CDR, the infant mortality rate is another measure of a country's deaths. As a result of a combination of births and deaths, a country will display distinctive percentages of young and old people.

TOTAL FERTILITY RATE

The **total fertility rate (TFR)** is the average number of children a woman will have throughout her childbearing years (roughly ages 15 through 49). To compute the TFR, scientists must assume that a woman reaching a particular age in the future will be just as likely to have a child as are women of that age today.

The TFR for the world as a whole is 2.5; it exceeds 5 in many countries of sub-Saharan Africa, compared to 2 or less in nearly all European countries (Figure 2.4.1). The TFR attempts to predict the future behavior of individual women in a world of rapid cultural change, whereas the CBR provides a picture of a society as a whole in a given year.

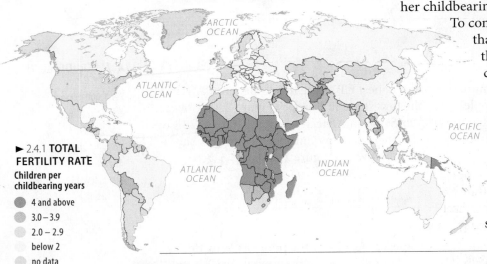

► **2.4.1 TOTAL FERTILITY RATE**
Children per childbearing years

- 4 and above
- 3.0 – 3.9
- 2.0 – 2.9
- below 2
- no data

INFANT MORTALITY RATE

The **infant mortality rate (IMR)** is the annual number of deaths of infants under 1 year of age for every 1,000 live births. As was the case with the CBR and CDR, the IMR is usually expressed as the number of deaths among infants per 1,000 births rather than as a percentage (per 100).

The highest IMRs are in the poorer countries of sub-Saharan Africa, whereas the lowest rates are in Europe (Figure 2.4.2). IMRs exceed 80 through sub-Saharan Africa, compared to less than 5 in Europe. Otherwise stated, more than 1 in 12 babies die before reaching their first birthday in sub-Saharan Africa, compared to less than 1 in 200 in Europe.

In general, the IMR reflects a country's health-care system. Lower IMRs are found in countries with well-trained doctors and nurses, modern hospitals, and large supplies of medicine. Although the United States is well endowed with medical facilities, it suffers from a higher IMR than Canada and every country in Europe. African Americans and other minorities in the United States have IMRs that are twice as high as the national average, comparable to levels in Latin America and Asia. Some health experts attribute this to the fact that many poor people in the United States, especially minorities, cannot afford good health care during pregnancy, or for their infants.

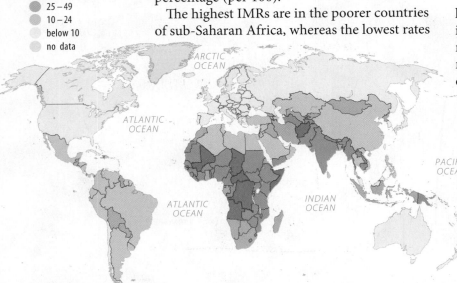

▼ **2.4.2 INFANT MORTALITY RATE**
Per 1,000 live births

- 100 and above
- 50 – 99
- 25 – 49
- 10 – 24
- below 10
- no data

LIFE EXPECTANCY

Life expectancy at birth measures the average number of years a newborn infant can expect to live, assuming current mortality levels. Life expectancy is most favorable in the wealthy countries of Europe and least favorable in the poor countries of sub-Saharan Africa. Babies born today can expect to live into their 80s in much of Europe but only into their 40s in much of sub-Saharan Africa (Figure 2.4.3).

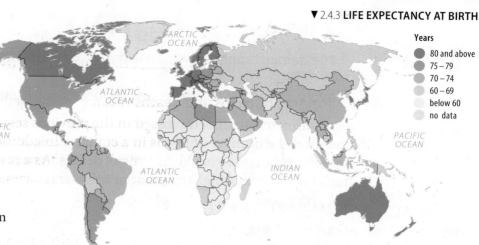

▼ 2.4.3 **LIFE EXPECTANCY AT BIRTH**

Years
- 80 and above
- 75–79
- 70–74
- 60–69
- below 60
- no data

YOUNG AND OLD

One-third of the people in the developing countries are under age 15, compared to only one-sixth in developed countries (Figure 2.4.4). The large percentage of children in developing countries strains their ability to provide needed services such as schools, hospitals, and day-care centers. When children reach the age of leaving school, jobs must be found for them, but the government must continue to allocate scarce resources to meet the needs of the still growing number of young people.

In contrast, developed countries face increasing percentages of older people, who must receive adequate levels of income and medical care after they retire from their jobs. The "graying" of the population places a burden on European and North American governments to meet these needs. More than one-fourth of all government expenditures in the United States, Canada, Japan, and many European countries go to Social Security, health care, and other programs for the older population.

The **dependency ratio** is the number of people who are too young or too old to work, compared to the number of people in their productive years. The larger the percentage of dependents, the greater the financial burden on those who are working to support those who cannot. People who are 0–14 years of age and 65-plus are normally classified as dependents.

A **population pyramid** is a bar graph that displays the percentage of a place's population for each age and gender (Figure 2.4.5). The shape of a country's pyramid is determined primarily by the CBR. A country with a high CBR has a relatively large number of young children, making the base of the pyramid very broad, whereas a country with a relatively large number of older people has a graph with a wider top that looks more like a rectangle than a pyramid. A variety of population pyramids appear on the next page.

▲ 2.4.4 **POPULATION UNDER AGE 15**
Percent
- 40 and above
- 30–39
- 20–29
- below 20
- no data

► 2.4.5 **POPULATION PYRAMID OF THE UNITED STATES**

A population pyramid shows the percentage of the total population in 5-year age groups, with the youngest (0 to 4 years old) at the base of the pyramid and the oldest at the top. The length of the bar represents the percentage of the total population contained in that group. By convention, males are usually shown on the left side of the pyramid and females on the right.

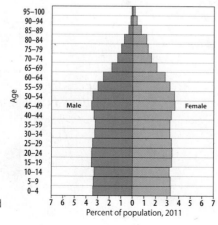

2.5 The Demographic Transition

▶ **The demographic transition is the process of change of a country's population structure.**

▶ **Every country is in one of four stages of the demographic transition.**

All countries have experienced some changes in natural increase, fertility, and mortality rates, but at different times and at different rates. Although rates vary among countries, a similar process of change in a society's population, known as the demographic transition, is operating. The **demographic transition** is a process with several stages, and every country is in one of them.

FOUR STAGES OF DEMOGRAPHIC TRANSITION

The demographic transition is a process with several stages. Countries move from one stage to the next. At a given moment, we can identify the stage that each country is in.

STAGE 1
- **Very high CBR**
- **Very high CDR**
- **Very low NIR**

The stage for most of human history, because of unpredictable food supply, as well as war and disease.

During most of stage 1, people depended on hunting and gathering for food. A region's population increased when food was easily obtained and declined when it was not. No country remains in stage 1 today.

STAGE 2
- **Still high CBR**
- **Rapidly declining CDR**
- **Very high NIR**

In developed countries 200 years ago, because the Industrial Revolution generated wealth and technology, some of which was used to make communities healthier places to live.

In developing countries 50 years ago, because transfer of penicillin, vaccines, insecticides, and other medicines from developed countries controlled infectious diseases such as malaria and tuberculosis (Figure 2.5.1).

STAGE 3
- **Rapidly declining CBR**
- **Moderately declining CDR**
- **Moderate NIR**

In developed countries 100 years ago. People choosing to have fewer children, in part a delayed reaction to the decline in mortality in stage 2, and in part because a large family is no longer an economic asset when families move from farms to cities.

Some developing countries have moved into stage 3 in recent years, especially where government policies strongly discourage large families.

STAGE 4
- **Very low CBR**
- **Low, slightly increasing CDR**
- **0 or negative NIR**

In some developed countries in recent years. Increased access to birth control methods, as well as increased number of women working in the labor force outside the home, induce families to choose to have fewer children.

As fewer women remain at home as full-time homemakers, they are less likely to be available for full-time care of young children. People who have access to a wider variety of birth-control methods are more likely to use some of them.

▼ 2.5.1 **STAGE 2: SIERRA LEONE**

A country that has passed through all four stages of the demographic transition has completed a process from little or no natural increase in stage 1, to little or no natural increase in stage 4 (Figure 2.5.2). Two crucial differences:

1. CBR and CDR are high in stage 1 and low in stage 4.

2. Total population is much higher in stage 4 than in stage 1.

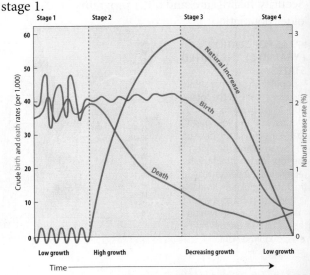

▲ 2.5.2 **DEMOGRAPHIC TRANSITION**

STAGE 2 (HIGH GROWTH): CAPE VERDE

Cape Verde, a collection of 12 small islands in the Atlantic Ocean off the western coast of Africa, moved from stage 1 to stage 2 about 1950 (Figure 2.5.3). Cape Verde was a colony of Portugal until it became independent in 1975, and the Portuguese administrators left better records of births and deaths than are typical for a colony in stage 1.

Cape Verde's population actually declined during the first half of the twentieth century because of several severe famines, an indication that the country was still in stage 1. Suddenly, in 1950, Cape Verde moved to stage 2. The reason: an anti-malarial campaign launched that year caused the CDR to sharply decline.

Cape Verde's population pyramid shows a large number of females nearing their prime childbearing years. For Cape Verde to enter stage 3, these females must bear considerably fewer children than did their mothers.

STAGE 3 (MODERATE GROWTH): CHILE

Chile's CDR declined sharply in the 1930s, moving the country into stage 2 of the demographic transition. As elsewhere in Latin America, Chile's CDR was lowered by the infusion of medical technology from MDCs such as the United States.

Chile has been in stage 3 of the demographic transition since the 1960s. It moved to stage 3 of the demographic transition primarily because of a vigorous government family-planning policy, initiated in 1966.

Chile's government reversed its policy and renounced support for family planning during the 1970s. Further reduction in the CBR is also hindered by the fact that most Chileans belong to the Roman Catholic Church, which opposes the use of what it calls artificial birth-control techniques. Therefore, the country is unlikely to move into stage 4 of the demographic transition in the near future.

STAGE 4 (LOW GROWTH): DENMARK

Denmark, like most European countries, has reached stage 4 of the demographic transition. The country entered stage 2 of the demographic transition in the nineteenth century, when the CDR began its permanent decline. The CBR then dropped in the late nineteenth century, and the country moved on to stage 3.

Since the 1970s, Denmark has been in stage 4, with roughly equal CBR and CDR. Denmark's CDR has actually increased somewhat in recent years because of the increasing percentage of elderly people. The CDR is unlikely to decline unless another medical revolution, such as a cure for cancer, keeps older elderly people alive much longer.

Denmark's population pyramid shows the impact of the demographic transition. Instead of a classic pyramid shape, Denmark has a column, demonstrating that the percentages of young and elderly people are nearly the same.

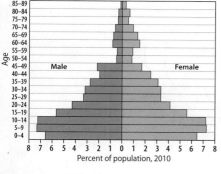

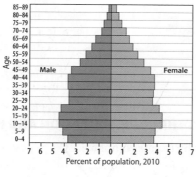

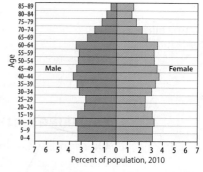

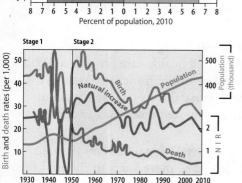

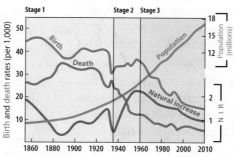

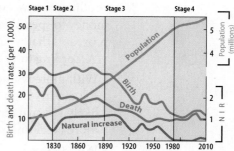

▲ 2.5.3 **POPULATION PYRAMID AND DEMOGRAPHIC TRANSITION FOR CAPE VERDE (left), CHILE (center), DENMARK (right)**

2.6 Declining Birth Rates

► **Some developing countries have lowered birth rates through improved education and health care.**

► **In other developing countries, distribution of contraceptives has reduced birth rates.**

Population has been increasing at a much slower rate since the mid-twentieth century. After hitting a peak around 1970, the world NIR has been declining steadily through the late twentieth century and the early twenty-first. The NIR declined beginning in the 1960s in developed countries and beginning in the 1970s in developing ones (Figure 2.6.1).

In most countries, the decline in the NIR has occurred because of lower birth rates (Figure 2.6.2). Between 1980 and 2010, the CBR declined in every country except for three in Northern Europe—Denmark, Norway, and Sweden—where the CBR increased by only 1.

Two strategies have been successful in reducing birth rates. One alternative emphasizes reliance on education and health care, the other on distribution of contraceptives. Because of varied economic and cultural conditions, the most effective method varies among countries.

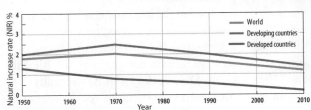

▲ 2.6.1 **NIR 1950–2010**

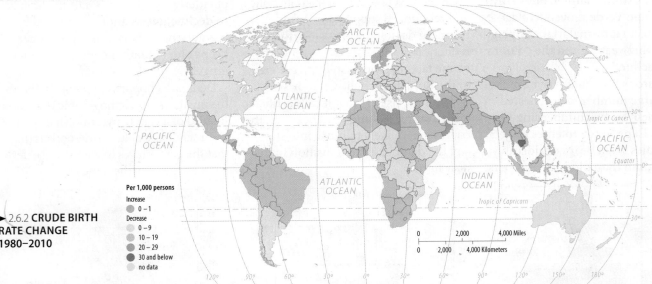

► 2.6.2 **CRUDE BIRTH RATE CHANGE 1980–2010**

Per 1,000 persons

Increase
● 0 – 1

Decrease
● 0 – 9
● 10 – 19
● 20 – 29
● 30 and below
○ no data

LOWERING BIRTH RATES THROUGH EDUCATION AND HEALTH CARE

One approach to lowering birth rates emphasizes the importance of improving local economic conditions. A wealthier community has more money to spend on education and health-care programs that would promote lower birth rates. According to this approach:

• With more women able to attend school and to remain in school longer, they would be more likely to learn employment skills and gain more economic control over their lives.

• With better education, women would better understand their reproductive rights,

make more informed reproductive choices, and select more effective methods of contraception.

• With improved health-care programs, IMRs would decline through such programs as improved prenatal care, counseling about sexually transmitted diseases, and child immunization.

• With the survival of more infants ensured, women would be more likely to choose to make more effective use of contraceptives to limit the number of children.

LOWERING BIRTH RATES THROUGH CONTRACEPTION

The other approach to lowering birth rates emphasizes the importance of rapid diffusion of modern contraceptive methods. Economic development may promote lower birth rates in the long run, but according to this approach the world cannot wait around for that alternative to take effect. Putting resources into family-planning programs can reduce birth rates much more rapidly.

In developing countries, demand for contraceptive devices is greater than the available supply. Therefore, the most effective way to increase their use is to distribute more of them, cheaply and quickly. According to this approach, contraceptives are the best method for lowering the birth rate.

- Bangladesh is an example of a country that has had little improvement in the wealth and literacy of its people, but 56 percent of the women in the country used contraceptives in 2010 compared to 6 percent two decades earlier. Similar growth in the use of contraceptives has occurred in other developing countries, including Colombia, Morocco, and Thailand.

- The percentage of women using contraceptives is especially low in Africa, so the alternative of distributing contraceptives could have an especially strong impact there (Figure 2.6.3). About one-fourth of African women employ

▼ 2.6.4 **PROMOTING FEWER CHILDREN**
China's government has erected billboards around the country to encourage families to have fewer children.

contraceptives, compared to three-fourths in Latin America and two-thirds in Asia (Figures 2.6.4 and Figure 2.6.5). The reason for this is partly economics, religion, and education.

- Very high birth rates in Africa and southwestern Asia also reflect the relatively low status of women there. In societies where women receive less formal education and hold fewer legal rights than do men, having a large family is expected of women, and men regard it as a sign of their own virility.

Regardless of which alternative is more successful, many oppose birth-control programs for religious and political reasons. Adherents of several religions, including Roman Catholics, fundamentalist Protestants, Muslims, and Hindus, have religious convictions that prevent them from using some or all birth-control devices. Opposition is strong within the United States to terminating pregnancy by abortion, and the U.S. government has at times withheld aid to countries and family-planning organizations that advise abortion, even when such advice is only a small part of the overall aid program.

▲ 2.6.3 **WOMEN USING FAMILY PLANNING**
Percent
- 75 and above
- 50 – 74
- 25 – 49
- below 25
- no data

▼ 2.6.5 **FAMILY PLANNING METHODS**
- Pill
- IUD
- Condom
- Female sterilization
- Male sterilization
- Periodic abstinence and withdrawal
- Other
- Not using a method

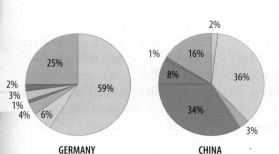

GERMANY: 59%, 25%, 2%, 3%, 1%, 4%, 6%, 2%

CHINA: 36%, 16%, 1%, 8%, 34%, 3%, 2%

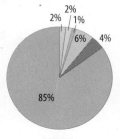

NIGERIA: 85%, 4%, 6%, 1%, 2%, 2%

2.7 Population Futures

▶ **World population will still increase but at a slower rate than in the past.**

▶ **Some developed countries may move into a possible stage 5 of the demographic transition.**

Though NIR is forecast to be much slower in twenty-first century than in the twentieth, world population with continue to grow. Virtually all growth will be in developing countries. The size of the world's population in the twenty-first century depends heavily on what happens in China and India, the two most populous countries.

COMPONENTS OF FUTURE POPULATION GROWTH

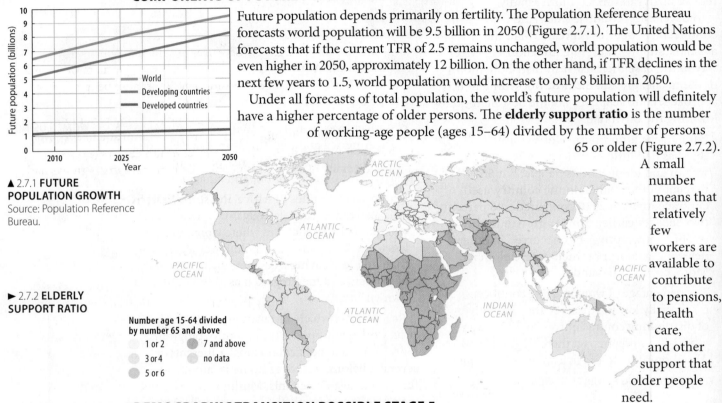

▲ 2.7.1 **FUTURE POPULATION GROWTH**
Source: Population Reference Bureau.

▶ 2.7.2 **ELDERLY SUPPORT RATIO**

Number age 15-64 divided by number 65 and above
- 1 or 2
- 3 or 4
- 5 or 6
- 7 and above
- no data

Future population depends primarily on fertility. The Population Reference Bureau forecasts world population will be 9.5 billion in 2050 (Figure 2.7.1). The United Nations forecasts that if the current TFR of 2.5 remains unchanged, world population would be even higher in 2050, approximately 12 billion. On the other hand, if TFR declines in the next few years to 1.5, world population would increase to only 8 billion in 2050.

Under all forecasts of total population, the world's future population will definitely have a higher percentage of older persons. The **elderly support ratio** is the number of working-age people (ages 15–64) divided by the number of persons 65 or older (Figure 2.7.2). A small number means that relatively few workers are available to contribute to pensions, health care, and other support that older people need.

DEMOGRAPHIC TRANSITION POSSIBLE STAGE 5

A possible stage 5 of the demographic transition is predicted by demographers for some developed countries in the twenty-first century. With more elderly people than children, many developed countries will experience population declines during the twenty-first century. Death rates will increase because of high mortality among the relatively large percentage of elderly people.

Meanwhile, after several decades of very low birth rates during the late twentieth century, stage 5 countries will have fewer young women who will eventually bear children. As many of the women within this smaller population choose to have fewer children, birth rates will continue to fall even lower than in stage 4 (Figure 2.7.3).

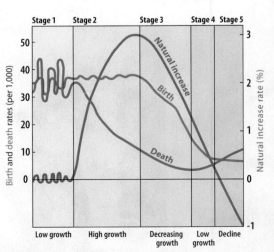

▲ 2.7.3 **POSSIBLE STAGE 5 OF DEMOGRAPHIC TRANSITION**

STAGE 5 (DECLINE): JAPAN

- **Very low CBR**
- **Increasing CDR**
- **Negative NIR**

If the demographic transition is to include a stage 5, Japan is one of the world's first countries to have reached it. Japan's population is expected to decline from an all-time peak of 128 million in 2006 to 119 million in 2025 and 95 million in 2050. With the population decline will come an increasing percentage of elderly people, as reflected in its changing population pyramid (Figure 2.7.4). Japan is forecast to be the first country to have an elderly support ratio of only 1, that is an equal number of workers and retirees.

Japan faces a severe shortage of workers. Rather than increasing immigration, Japan is addressing its labor force shortage primarily by encouraging more Japanese people to work. Programs make it more attractive for older people to continue working, to receive more health-care services at home instead of in hospitals, and to borrow against the value of their homes to pay for health care.

Rather than combine work with child rearing, Japanese women are expected to make a stark choice: either marry and raise children or remain single and work. According to the Japan's most recent census, the majority has chosen to work: More than half of women in the prime childbearing years of 20 to 34 are not married.

INDIA'S VERSUS CHINA'S POPULATION FEATURES

The world's two most populous countries, China and India, will heavily influence future prospects for global overpopulation. These two countries—together encompassing more than one-third of the world's population—have adopted different family-planning programs.

INDIA'S POPULATION POLICIES

India was one of the first countries to embark on a national family-planning program, in 1952. Birth-control devices have been distributed for free or at subsidized prices. Abortions, legalized in 1972, have been performed at a rate of several million per year.

▲ 2.7.5 **FAMILY PLANNING OFFICE IN KOLKATA (FORMERLY CALCUTTA) INDIA**

India's most controversial family-planning program was the establishment of camps in 1971 to perform sterilizations, surgical procedures by which people were made incapable of reproduction. A sterilized person was paid the equivalent of roughly one month's salary in India. But public opposition grew, because people feared that they would be forcibly sterilized. The government no longer regards birth control as a top policy priority. Government-sponsored family-planning programs have instead emphasized education, including ads on national radio and television networks and information distributed through local health centers (Figure 2.7.5). Given the cultural diversity of the Indian people, the national campaign has had only limited success.

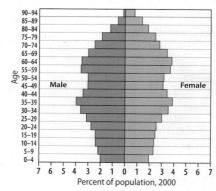

▲ 2.7.6 **POSTER IN SHANGHAI, CHINA, PROMOTES ONE-CHILD POLICY**

CHINA'S POPULATION POLICIES

China has made substantial progress in reducing its rate of growth. The core of the Chinese government's family-planning program has been the One Child Policy, adopted in 1980 (Figure 2.7.6). Couples receive financial subsidies, a long maternity leave, better housing, and (in rural areas) more land if they agree to have just one child. To further discourage births, people receive free contraceptives, abortions, and sterilizations.

As China moves toward a market economy and Chinese families become wealthier, the One Child Policy has been relaxed, especially in urban areas. Clinics provide counseling on a wider range of family-planning options. Instead of fines, Chinese couples wishing a second child pay a "family-planning fee" to cover the cost to the government of supporting the additional person.

Fears that relaxing the One Child Policy would produce a large increase in the birth rate have been unfounded.

▼ 2.7.4 **JAPAN'S POPULATION PYRAMIDS**
1950 (left), 2000 (center), and forecast for 2050 (right).

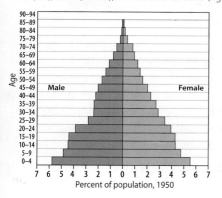

2.8 Malthus's Grim Forecast

► **Malthus predicted that population would increase faster than resources.**

► **Contemporary geographers are divided on the validity of Malthus's thesis.**

English economist Thomas Malthus (1766–1834) was one of the first to argue that the world's rate of population increase was far outrunning the development of food supplies. In *An Essay on the Principle of Population*, published in 1798, Malthus claimed that the population was growing much more rapidly than Earth's food supply because population increased *geometrically*, whereas food supply increased *arithmetically*. Malthus's views remain influential today (Figure 2.8.1).

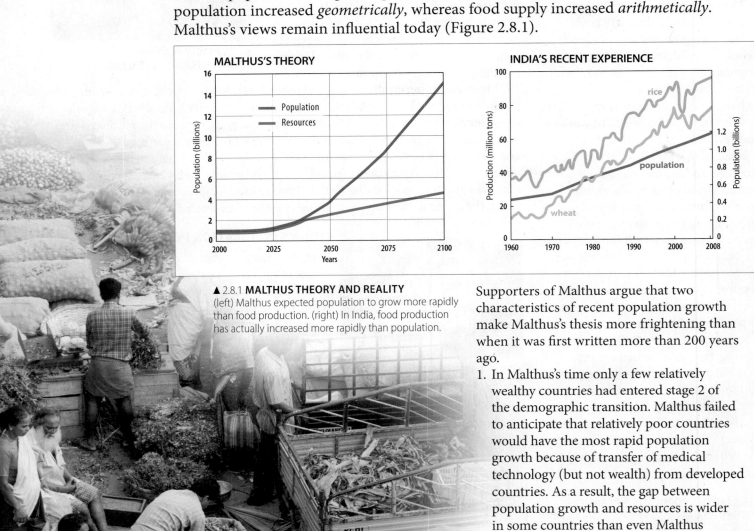

▲ 2.8.1 **MALTHUS THEORY AND REALITY**
(left) Malthus expected population to grow more rapidly than food production. (right) In India, food production has actually increased more rapidly than population.

Supporters of Malthus argue that two characteristics of recent population growth make Malthus's thesis more frightening than when it was first written more than 200 years ago.

1. In Malthus's time only a few relatively wealthy countries had entered stage 2 of the demographic transition. Malthus failed to anticipate that relatively poor countries would have the most rapid population growth because of transfer of medical technology (but not wealth) from developed countries. As a result, the gap between population growth and resources is wider in some countries than even Malthus anticipated.

2. World population growth is outstripping a wide variety of resources, not just food production. According to contemporary supporters of Malthus, wars and civil violence will increase in the coming years because of scarcities of clean water and air, suitable farmland, and fuel, as well as of food.

◄ 2.8.2 **FOOD AVAILABILITY IN INDIA**
Market in Kerala.

MALTHUS'S CRITICS

Many geographers criticize Malthus's theory that population growth depletes resources. To the contrary, a larger population could stimulate economic growth and, therefore, production of more food. Population growth could generate more customers and more ideas for improving technology.

Some theorists maintain that poverty, hunger, and other social welfare problems associated with lack of economic development are a result of unjust social and economic institutions, not population growth. The world possesses sufficient resources to eliminate global hunger and poverty, if only these resources were shared equally.

Some political leaders, especially in Africa, argue that high population growth is good for a country because more people will result in greater power. Population growth is desired in order to increase the supply of young men who could serve in the armed forces. At the same time, developed countries are viewed as pushing for lower population growth as a means of preventing further expansion in the percentage of the world's population living in poorer countries.

MALTHUS'S THEORY AND REALITY

On a global scale, conditions during the past half-century have not supported Malthus's theory. Even though the human population has grown at its most rapid rate ever, world food production has grown at a faster rate than the NIR since 1950, according to geographer Vaclav Smil. Malthus was close to the mark on food production but much too pessimistic on population growth.

Food production increased during the last half of the twentieth century somewhat more rapidly than Malthus would have predicted (Figure 2.8.2). Better growing techniques, higher-yielding seeds, and cultivation of more land all contributed to the expansion in food supply (Figure 2.8.3). Many people in the world cannot afford to buy food or do not have access to sources of food, but these are problems of unequal distribution of wealth rather than an insufficient global production of food, as Malthus theorized.

Following Malthus's model, world population should have quadrupled between 1950 and 2000, from 2.5 billion to 10 billion people, but world population actually grew during this period to only 6 billion. Malthus did not foresee critical cultural, economic, and technological changes that would induce societies sooner or later to move on to stages 3 and 4 of the demographic transition.

▲ 2.8.3 **FOOD AVAILABILITY IN INDIA** Farming potatoes near Bangalore.

2.9 The Epidemiologic Transition

▶ Each stage of the demographic transition has distinctive causes of death.

▶ The leading causes of death shift through the demographic transition.

Medical researchers have identified an **epidemiologic transition** that focuses on distinctive causes of death in each stage of the demographic transition. Epidemiologists rely heavily on geographic concepts such as scale and connection, because measures to control and prevent an epidemic derive from understanding its distinctive distribution and method of diffusion.

The term epidemiologic transition comes from **epidemiology**, which is the branch of medical science concerned with the incidence, distribution, and control of diseases that affect large numbers of people.

STAGE 1: PESTILENCE AND FAMINE (HIGH CDR)

Stage 1 of the epidemiologic transition was titled the stage of pestilence and famine by epidemiologist Abdel Omran in 1971. Infectious and parasitic diseases were the principal causes of human deaths, along with accidents and attacks by animals and other humans. Malthus called these causes of deaths "natural checks" on the growth of the human population in stage 1 of the demographic transition.

History's most violent stage 1 epidemic was the Black Plague (bubonic plague), which was probably transmitted to humans by fleas attached to migrating infected rats:

• The Black Plague originated among Tatars in present-day Kyrgyzstan.

• It diffused to present-day Ukraine when the Tatar army attacked an Italian trading post on the Black Sea.

• Italians fleeing the Black Sea trading post carried the infected rats on ships west to the major coastal cities of southeastern Europe in 1347.

• The plague diffused from the coast to inland towns and then to rural areas.

• It reached western Europe in 1348 and northern Europe in 1349.

About 25 million Europeans—more than half of the continent's population—died between 1347 and 1350. The Black Plague also diffused east to China, where 13 million died in a single year, 1380.

The plague wiped out entire villages and families, leaving farms with no workers and estates with no heirs. Churches were left without priests and parishioners, schools without teachers and students. Ships drifted aimlessly at sea after entire crews succumbed to the plague.

STAGE 2: RECEDING PANDEMICS (RAPIDLY DECLINING CDR)

Stage 2 of the epidemiologic transition is known as the stage of receding pandemics. A **pandemic** is disease that occurs over a wide geographic area and affects a very high proportion of the population.

In stage 2, improved sanitation, nutrition, and medicine during the Industrial Revolution reduced the spread of infectious diseases (Figure 2.9.1). But death rates did not decline immediately and universally. Poor people crowded into rapidly growing industrial cities had especially high death rates during the Industrial Revolution.

Construction of water and sewer systems were thought to have eradicated cholera by the late nineteenth century. However, cholera reappeared a century later in rapidly growing cities of developing countries as they moved into stage 2 of the demographic transition.

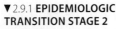

▼ 2.9.1 **EPIDEMIOLOGIC TRANSITION STAGE 2** Cholera, a stage 2 disease, has been a threat in Iraq, such as this location in the Baghdad suburb of Fdailiyah, where drinking water is being drawn from a water pipe crosses a canal carrying raw sewage.

STAGE 3: DEGENERATIVE DISEASES (MODERATELY DECLINING CDR)

Stage 3 is characterized by a decrease in deaths from infectious diseases and an increase in chronic disorders associated with aging. The two especially important chronic disorders in stage 3 are cardiovascular diseases, such as heart attacks, and various forms of cancer.

The decline in infectious diseases such as polio and measles has been rapid in stage 3 countries. Effective vaccines were responsible for these declines (Figure 2.9.2).

STAGE 4: DELAYED DEGENERATIVE DISEASES (LOW BUT INCREASING CDR)

The epidemiologic transition was extended by S. Jay Olshansky and Brian Ault to stage 4, the stage of delayed degenerative diseases. The major degenerative causes of death—cardiovascular diseases and cancers—linger, but the life expectancy of older people is extended through medical advances.

Through medicine, cancers spread more slowly or are removed altogether. Operations such as bypasses repair deficiencies in the cardiovascular system. Also improving health are behavior changes such as better diet, reduced use of tobacco and alcohol, and exercise.

▼ 2.9.2 **EPIDEMIOLOGIC TRANSITION STAGE 3**
Mother holding child receiving vaccination by injection in Zimbabwe.

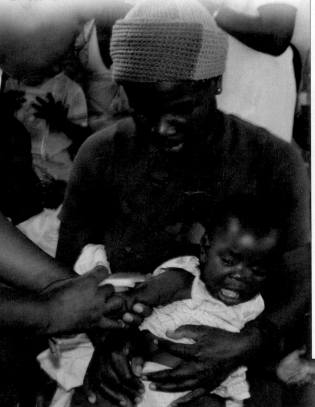

EARLY "GIS" MAPPED CHOLERA DISTRIBUTION

Dr. John Snow (1813–1858) was a British physician not a geographer. To fight one of the worst nineteenth century pandemics, cholera, Snow created a handmade GIS in 1854. On a map of London's Soho neighborhood, Snow overlaid two other maps, one showing the addresses of cholera victims and the other the location of water pumps—for the poor residents of Soho the principal source of water for drinking, cleaning, and cooking (Figure 2.9.3).

The overlay map showed that cholera victims were not distributed uniformly through Soho. Dr. Snow showed that a large percentage of cholera victims were clustered around one pump, on Broad Street (today known as Broadwick Street). Tests at the Broad Street pump subsequently proved that the water there was contaminated. Further investigation revealed that sewage was contaminating the water supply near the pump.

Before Dr. Snow's geographic analysis, many believed that epidemic victims were being punished for sinful behavior and that most victims were poor because poverty was considered a sin. Now we understand that cholera affects the poor because they are more likely to have to use contaminated water.

KEY
■ Water pump
• Cholera victims

▶ 2.9.3 **BIRTH OF GIS**
(top) Dr. John Snow's map of the distribution of cholera in Soho, London, 1854. (bottom) Use Google Earth to see memories of Dr. Snow and the cholera epidemic in modern-day London.

Fly to: *39 Broadwick Street, London, England.*
Drag to: *street view at 39 Broadwick Street.*
Move the compass: *so that south faces top (north faces bottom).*
Move *the compass so that east faces top (north faces left).*
Click on icons: *for the Broad Street pump and the Soho Cholera Epidemic.*

1. **What is the current use of the building at 39 Broadwick Street bearing John Snow's name?**
2. **What other evidence of the cholera epidemic can be seen in Broadwick Street?**

2.10 Global Reemergence of Infectious Diseases

▶ **Some infectious diseases have returned and new ones have emerged.**
▶ **The most lethal global-scale epidemic has been AIDS.**

Recall that in the possible stage 5 of the demographic transition, CDR rises because more of the population is elderly. Some medical researchers think there is also a stage 5 of the epidemiologic transition, brought about by a reermegence of infectious and parasitic diseases. A consequence of stage 5 would be higher CDRs. Other epidemiologists dismiss recent trends as a temporary setback in a long process of controlling infectious diseases.

In a possible stage 5, infectious diseases thought to have been eradicated or controlled have returned, and new ones have emerged. Three reasons help to explain the possible emergence of a stage 5 of the epidemiologic transition: poverty, evolution, and increased connections.

REASONS FOR POSSIBLE STAGE 5: POVERTY

Infectious diseases are more prevalent in poor areas because:

- Unsanitary conditions may persist.
- Most people can't afford the drugs needed for treatment.

Tuberculosis (TB) is an example of an infectious disease that has been largely controlled in developed countries like the United States but remains a major cause of death in developing countries. An airborne disease often called "consumption," TB spreads principally through coughing and sneezing, damaging lungs.

The death rate from TB declined in the United States from 200 per 100,000 in 1900 to 60 in 1940 and 0.5 today. However, in developing countries, the TB rate is more than ten times higher than in developed countries, and nearly 2 million worldwide die from it annually (Figure 2.10.1).

REASONS FOR POSSIBLE STAGE 5: EVOLUTION

Infectious disease microbes continuously evolve and change in response to environmental pressures by developing resistance to drugs and insecticides. Antibiotics and genetic engineering contribute to the emergence of new strains of viruses and bacteria.

Malaria was nearly eradicated in the mid-twentieth century by spraying DDT in areas infested with the mosquito that carried the parasite. For example, new malaria cases in Sri Lanka fell from 1 million in 1955 to 18 in 1963. The disease returned after 1963, however, and now causes more than 1 million deaths worldwide annually. A major reason was the evolution of DDT-resistant mosquitoes.

▼ 2.10.1
TUBERCULOSIS (TB) DEATHS, 2009

ARCTIC OCEAN

ATLANTIC OCEAN

PACIFIC OCEAN

ATLANTIC OCEAN

INDIAN OCEAN

Tuberculosis death rate per 100,000
- above 50
- 10 – 49
- 3 – 9
- below 3
- no data

IMPROVED TRAVEL AND AIDS IN THE UNITED STATES

Airports in New York, California, and Florida are the major ports of entry for visitors arriving in the United States (Figure 2.10.2). Consequently, residents of these states are exposed first to infectious diseases that have reemerged in an age of improved travel.

Not by coincidence, New York, California, and Florida were the nodes of origin for AIDS within the United States during the early 1980s (Figure 2.10.3, left). Though AIDS diffused to every state during the 1980s, these three states, plus Texas (also a major port of entry), accounted for half of the nation's new AIDS cases in the peak year of 1993 (Figure 2.10.3, right). The rapid decline in new cases thereafter resulted from rapid diffusion of preventive methods and medicines such as AZT.

▲ 2.10.2 **INTERNATIONAL PASSENGER ARRIVALS**
International passenger arrivals to U.S. airports (excluding passengers coming from Canada), 2007 (million passengers)

REASONS FOR POSSIBLE STAGE 5: INCREASED CONNECTIONS

As they travel, people carry diseases with them and are exposed to the diseases of others. Motor vehicles allow rural residents to easily reach urban areas and urban residents to reach rural areas. Airplanes allow residents of one country to easily reach another.

The most lethal epidemic in recent years has been AIDS (acquired immunodeficiency syndrome). Worldwide, 25 million people died of AIDS as of 2007. Another 33 million were living with HIV (human immunodeficiency virus, the cause of AIDS).

The impact of AIDS has been felt most strongly in sub-Saharan Africa. With one-tenth of the world's population, sub-Saharan Africa had two-thirds of the world's total HIV-positive population and nine-tenths of the world's infected children (Figure 2.10.4).

NEW CASES IN 1981 **NEW CASES IN 1993**

▲ 2.10.3 **DIFFUSION OF AIDS IN THE UNITED STATES**

New AIDS cases per 100,000 population: 60 and above, 40–59, 20–39, 10–19, 1–9, below 1

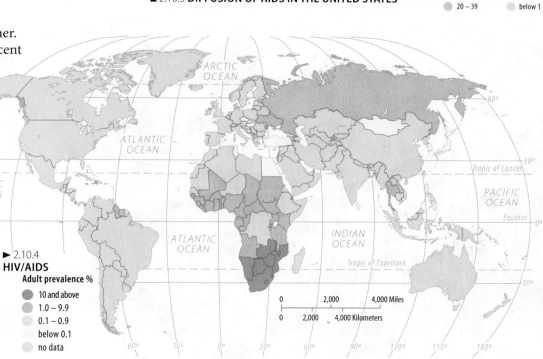

► 2.10.4 **HIV/AIDS**
Adult prevalence %: 10 and above, 1.0–9.9, 0.1–0.9, below 0.1, no data

This chapter has introduced ways in which geographers think about the world, as well as key concepts in understanding geography.

Key Questions

Where is the world's population distributed?

► Global population is highly concentrated; two-thirds of the world's people live in four clusters (Europe, East Asia, Southeast Asia, and South Asia).

► Population density varies around the world partly in response to resources.

Why does population growth vary among countries?

► A population increases because of fertility and decreases because of mortality.

► The demographic transition is a process of change in a country's population from a condition of high birth and death rates, with little population growth, to a condition of low birth and death rates, with low population growth.

► More than 200 years ago, Thomas Malthus argued that population was increasing more rapidly than the food supply; some contemporary analysts believe that Malthus's prediction is accurate in some regions.

How might population change in the future?

► Most countries in Europe and North America face slow or even declining population in the future.

► World population growth is slowing in part because birth rates are declining.

► Meanwhile, death rates are increasing in some countries because of chronic disorders associated with aging and in some developing countries because of infectious diseases.

▼ 2.CR.1 **VERY HIGH ARITHMETIC DENSITY: MARKET, DARAW, EGYPT**
What is the evidence that human behavior is affected by a high population density?

Thinking Geographically

The U.S. Census Bureau is allowed to utilize statistical sampling to determine much of the information about the people of the United States, such as age and gender. However, for determining the total population of each state and Congressional District, the Census Bureau is required to count only the people for whom a census form was completed.

1. **What are the advantages of using each of the two approaches to counting the population?**

Some humans live at very high density (Figure 2.CR.1). Scientists disagree about the effects of high density on human behavior. Some laboratory tests have shown that rats display evidence of increased aggressiveness, competition, and violence when very large numbers of them are placed in a box.

2. **Is there any evidence that high density might cause humans to behave especially violently or less aggressively?**

Members of the baby-boom generation — people born between 1946 and 1964 — constitute nearly one-third of the U.S. population.

3. **As they grow older, what impact will baby boomers have on the entire American population in the years ahead?**

On the Internet

The Population Reference Bureau (PRB) provides authoritative demographic information for every country and world region at its website **www.prb.org.**

The Population Division of the United Nations Department of Economic and Social Affairs provides tables on population, births, and deaths for every country, at **http://esa.un.org/unpd/wpp/unpp/panel_population.htm**, or scan the QR code at the beginning of the chapter.

Interactive Mapping

POPULATION DISTRIBUTION IN SOUTHWEST ASIA & NORTH AFRICA

Population is highly clustered within Southwest Asia and Northern Africa.

Open: MapMaster Southeast Asia & North Africa in Mastering**GEOGRAPHY**

Select: *Population* Density from the *Population* menu, adjust opacity to 60%, then select *Physical Features* from the *Physical Environment* menu.

Most people live near what type of physical feature?

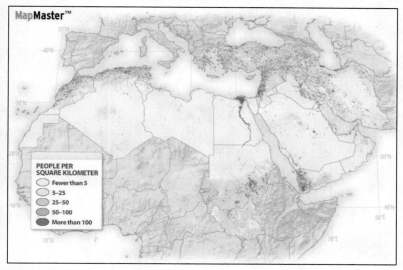

Explore

MAHĀMĪD, EGYPT

Use Google Earth to explore Mahāmīd, a town of 45,000 near the banks of the Nile River.

Fly to: *Mahāmīd, Luxor, Egypt.* Zoom in.

1. **What color is most of the land immediately in and around the town? Does this indicate that the land is used for agriculture or is it desert?**

Zoom out until you see the entire band of green surrounded by tan.

2. **How wide is the green strip? What does the tan color represent? What feature is in the middle of the green strip?**

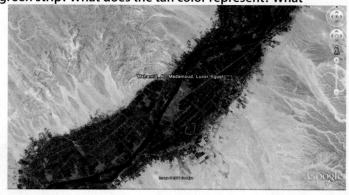

Key Terms

Agricultural density
The ratio of the number of farmers to the total amount of land suitable for agriculture.

Arable land
Land suited for agriculture.

Arithmetic density
The total number of people divided by the total land area.

Crude birth rate (CBR)
The total number of live births in a year for every 1,000 people alive in the society.

Crude death rate (CDR)
The total number of deaths in a year for every 1,000 people alive in the society.

Demographic transition
The process of change in a society's population from a condition of high crude birth and death rates and low rate of natural increase to a condition of low crude birth and death rates, low rate of natural increase, and a higher total population.

Dependency ratio
The number of people who are considered too young or too old to work (under age 15 or over age 64), compared to the number of people in their productive years.

Doubling time
The number of years needed to double a population, assuming a constant rate of natural increase.

Elderly support ratio
The number of working-age people (ages 15–64) divided by the number of persons 65 or older.

Epidemiologic transition
Distinctive causes of death in each stage of the demographic transition.

Epidemiology
Branch of medical science concerned with the incidence, distribution, and control of diseases that affect large numbers of people.

Infant mortality rate (IMR)
The total number of deaths in a year among infants under 1 year old for every 1,000 live births in a society.

Life expectancy
The average number of years an individual can be expected to live, given current social, economic, and medical conditions. Life expectancy at birth is the average number of years a newborn infant can expect to live.

Natural increase rate (NIR)
The percentage growth of a population in a year, computed as the crude birth rate minus the crude death rate.

Overpopulation
The number of people in an area exceeds the capacity of the environment to support life at a decent standard of living.

Pandemic
Disease that occurs over a wide geographic area and affects a very high proportion of the population.

Physiological density
The number of people per unit of area of arable land, which is land suitable for agriculture.

Population pyramid
A bar graph that displays the percentage of a place's population for each age and gender.

Total fertility rate (TFR)
The average number of children a woman will have throughout her childbearing years.

▶ LOOKING AHEAD

Population increases because of births and decreases because of deaths. The population of a place also increases when people move in and decreases when people move out. This element of population change—migration—is discussed in the next chapter.

How many times has your family moved? In the United States, the average family moves once every seven years. Was your last move traumatic or exciting? The loss of old friends and familiar settings can hurt, but the experiences awaiting you at a new location can be stimulating. Think about the multitude of Americans—maybe including yourself—who have migrated from other countries. Imagine the feelings of people migrating from another country when they arrive in a new land without a job, friends, or—for many—the ability to speak the local language.

Why would people make a perilous journey across thousands of kilometers of ocean? Why did the pioneers cross the Great Plains, the Rocky Mountains, or the Mojave Desert to reach the American West? Why do people continue to migrate by the millions today? The hazards that many migrants have faced are a measure of the strong lure of new locations and the desperate conditions in their former homelands. Most people migrate in search of three objectives: economic opportunity, cultural freedom, and environmental comfort. This chapter will study the reasons why people migrate.

Where are migrants distributed?

3.1 **Global Migration Patterns**

3.2 **Changing Origin of U.S. Immigrants**

3.3 **Interregional Migration**

3.4 **Intraregional Migration**

MIGRANTS, BEIJING, CHINA.

Why do people migrate?

What obstacles do immigrants face?

SCAN HERE FOR U.S. AND WORLD MIGRATION DATA

3.1 Global Migration Patterns

► Most international migration is from developing countries to developed countries.

► The United States is the leading destination for international migrants.

Migration is a permanent move to a new location. It is a form of relocation diffusion, which was defined in Chapter 1 as the spread of a characteristic through the bodily movement of people from one place to another.

Emigration is migration *from* a location; **immigration** (or in-migration) is migration *to* a location. The difference between the number of immigrants and the number of emigrants is the **net migration.**

Geography has no comprehensive theory of migration, although a nineteenth-century outline of 11 migration "laws" written by E. G. Ravenstein is the basis for contemporary geographic migration studies. To understand where and why migration occurs, Ravenstein's "laws" can be organized into three groups: the distance that migrants typically move, the reasons why they move, and their characteristics.

Ravenstein made two main points about the distance that migrants travel to their new homes:

- Most migrants relocate a short distance and remain within the same country (see sections 3.3 and 3.4).

- Long-distance migrants to other countries head for major centers of economic activity (Figure 3.1.1).

▼ 3.1.1 **MIGRATION FROM ASIA TO NORTH AMERICA**
Chinese men waiting outside an employment office in Chinatown, New York, where immigrants seek employment.

► 3.1.2 **INTERNATIONAL MIGRATION**
The width of the arrows shows the amount of net migration between regions of the world. Countries with net in-migration are in red, and those with net out-migration are in blue.

Average annual net migration 2000–2005 (thousands)

Gain	Loss
● above 100	● 0 to 20
● 20 to 100	● 20 to 100
● 0 to 20	● above 100

Annual net migration flows between regions

➤ 500,000 people

➤ 100,000 people

→ 10,000 people

MIGRATION TRANSITION

Geographer Wilbur Zelinsky identified a **migration transition**, which consists of changes in a society comparable to those in the demographic transition:

• Stage 1: High daily or seasonal mobility in search of food.

• Stage 2: International migration (Figure 3.1.2) and migration within countries from rural to urban areas.

• Stages 3 and 4: Migration within countries between cities and suburbs.

Consistent with the distance-decay principle presented in Chapter 1 (section 1.10), the farther away a place is located, the less likely that people will migrate to it. Thus, international migrants are much less numerous than internal migrants. The leading sources of international migrants in the world today are from Asia to North America and to Europe (Figure 3.1.3), as well as from Latin America to North America.

Immigrants cluster in communities where people from the same country previously settled. **Chain migration** is the migration of people to a specific location, because relatives or members of the same nationality previously migrated there.

▲ 3.1.3 **MIGRATION FROM ASIA TO EUROPE** Immigrants from India in London.

3.2 Changing Origin of U.S. Immigrants

► **The United States has had three main eras of immigration.**

► **The principal source of migrants has changed in each era.**

During three main eras of immigration, the United States drew migrants from different parts of the world (Figure 3.2.1):

- Seventeenth and eighteenth centuries—United Kingdom and Africa (Figure 3.2.2)
- Mid-nineteenth to early twentieth century—Europe (Figure 3.2.3)
- Late-twentieth to early twenty-first century—Latin America and Asia (Figure 3.2.4)

▼ 3.2.1 MIGRATION TO THE UNITED STATES BY REGION OF ORIGIN

Europeans comprised more than 90 percent of immigrants to the United States during the nineteenth century, and even as recently as the early 1960s, still accounted for more than 50 percent. Latin America and Asia are now the dominant sources of immigrants to the United States.

- Western Europe
- Eastern Europe
- Canada
- Asia
- Latin America
- Africa
- Oceania

3.2.3 U.S. IMMIGRATION: MID-NINETEENTH TO EARLY TWENTIETH CENTURY

More than 95 percent of nineteenth-century U.S. immigrants came from Europe, but the principal sources within Europe changed during the century.

- 1840s and 1850s: Primarily from Ireland and Germany.
- 1880s and 1890s: Primarily from northern and western Europe, including Norway and Sweden, as well as Germany and Ireland
- 1900–1910s: Primarily from southern and eastern Europe, including Italy and Russia.

Frequent boundary changes in Europe make precise national counts impossible. For example, most Poles came to the United States when Poland did not exist as an independent country, so they were included in the totals for Germany, Russia, or Austria. (above right) Immigrants from southern and eastern Europe line up for entry into the United States.

3.2.2 U.S. IMMIGRATION: SEVENTEENTH AND EIGHTEENTH CENTURIES

The two main sources of early immigrants to the American colonies and the newly independent United States were the United Kingdom and Africa. About 2 million Britons came to America prior to 1840, accounting for 90 percent of all European immigrants during that period. About 400,000 Africans were shipped as slaves to the 13 colonies (below). Although the importation of Africans as slaves was made illegal in 1808, another 250,000 Africans were brought to the United States during the early nineteenth century.

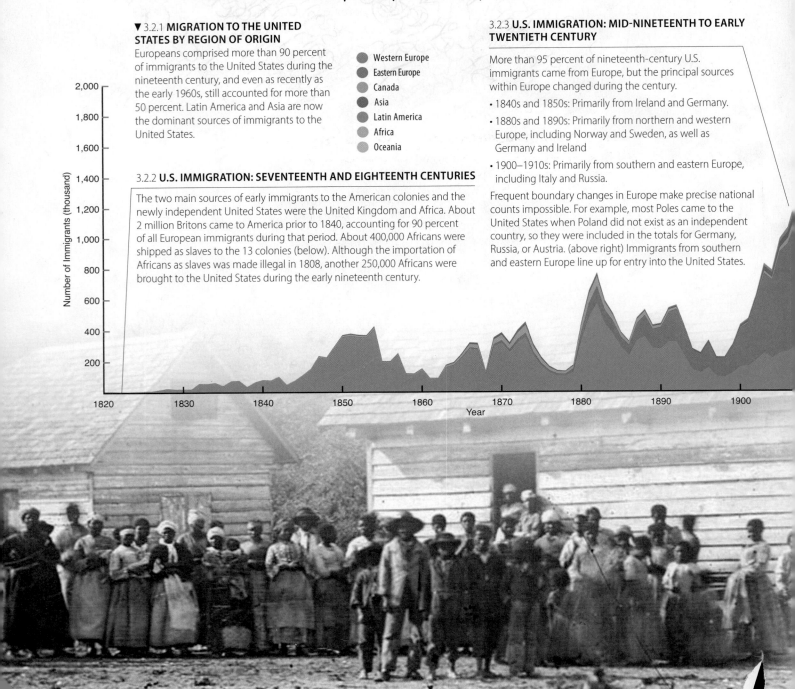

3.2.4 **U.S. IMMIGRATION: LATE TWENTIETH TO EARLY TWENTY-FIRST CENTURY**

The two leading sources of immigrants since the late twentieth century have been Latin America and Asia. About 13 million Latin Americans and 7 million Asians have migrated to the United States in the past half-century, compared to only 2 million and 1 million respectively in the two preceding centuries. Officially, Mexico passed Germany in 2006 as the country that has sent to the United States the most immigrants ever. The four leading sources of U.S. immigrants from Asia are China (including Hong Kong), the Philippines, India, and Vietnam. (below center) A family from Mexico City ready to leave. (below right) A Chinese family in New York City's Chinatown.

| 1920 | 1930 | 1940 | 1950 | 1960 | 1970 | 1980 | 1990 | 2000 | 2010 |

3.3 Interregional Migration

► **Long-distance migration can open regions for development.**
► **Long-distance migrants settled the western United States.**

International migration is permanent movement from one country to another, whereas **internal migration** is permanent movement within the same country. Most people find internal migration less traumatic than international migration because they find familiar language, foods, broadcasts, literature, music, and other social customs after they move.

Moves within a country also generally involve shorter distances than those in international migration. However, internal migration can involve long-distance moves in large countries, such as in the United States and Russia.

In the past, people migrated from one region of a country to another in search of better farmland. Lack of farmland pushed many people from the more densely settled regions of the country and lured them to the frontier, where land was abundant. Today, the principal type of interregional migration is from rural to urban areas. Most jobs, especially in the service sector, are clustered in urban areas (see Chapter 12).

MIGRATION BETWEEN REGIONS OF THE UNITED STATES

Interregional migration is movement from one region of a country to another. The most famous example of interregional migration is the opening the American West. Two hundred years ago, the United States consisted of a collection of settlements concentrated on the Atlantic Coast. Through mass interregional migration, the rest of the continent was settled and developed.

The U.S. Census Bureau computes the country's population center at the time of each census. The changing location of the center of the U.S. population graphically demonstrates the interregional migration of the American people westward across the North American continent over the past 200 years (Figure 3.3.1).

1800–1840
During this period, transportation improvements, especially canals, made land accessible for development between the Appalachians and the Mississippi River.

1790
This location reflects the fact that virtually all colonial-era settlements were near the Atlantic Coast. Few colonists ventured inland because they depended on shipping links with Europe. The Appalachian Mountains blocked western development.

► 3.3.1 **CHANGING CENTER OF POPULATION IN THE UNITED STATES**
The population center is the average location of everyone in the country, the "center of population gravity." If the United States were a flat plane placed on top of a pin, and each individual weighed the same, the population center would be the point where the population distribution causes the flat plane to balance on the pin.

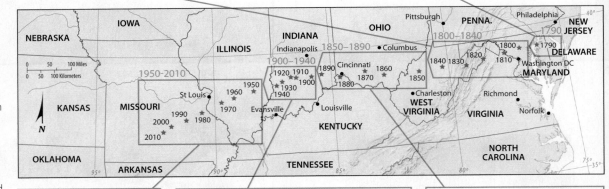

1950–2010
The population center moved westward more vigorously during this period. It also started to move southward. Americans migrated to the South primarily for better job opportunities and attractive environmental conditions.

1900–1940
Westward movement of the U.S. population center slowed during this period, because immigrants began to fill in the area between the 98th meridian and California that earlier generations had bypassed. The region's dry climate, lack of trees, and tough grassland sod convinced early explorers that the region was unfit for farming. Advances in agricultural technology enabled people to cultivate the Great Plains.

1850–1890
The population center shifted more rapidly during mid-nineteenth century. Rather than continuing to expand agriculture into the next available westward land, mid-nineteenth century pioneers kept going all the way to California, beginning with the Gold Rush of the late 1840s.

In the twenty-first century, interregional migration has slowed in the United States (Figure 3.3.2). The severe recession of the early twenty-first century has reduced prospects of finding jobs in other regions of the country.

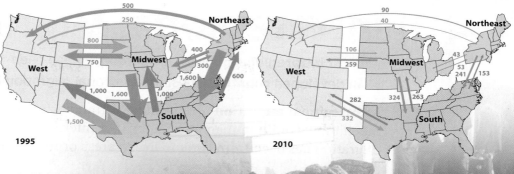

▶ 3.3.2 **U.S INTERREGIONAL MIGRATION**
Figures show average annual migration in thousands. The maps show a decrease in total interregional migration in the United States.

INTERREGIONAL MIGRATION IN OTHER COUNTRIES

Long-distance interregional migration has opened new regions for development in large countries other than the United States.

- **China.** An estimated 100 million people have migrated from rural areas in the interior of the country to urban areas along the east coast, where jobs are most plentiful, especially in factories. The government once severely limited the ability of Chinese people to make interregional moves, but restrictions have been lifted in recent years (Figure 3.3.3).

- **Russia.** Migration has been encouraged to remote resource-rich regions in Asia through construction of mines, steel mills, power plants, and other industrial enterprises. When controlled by the former Soviet Union, some of the migration was forced.

- **Brazil.** Migration has been encouraged from the large cities along the Atlantic coast to the sparsely settled tropical interior. In 1960, Brazil's capital was moved from the coastal city of Rio de Janeiro to Brasília, a newly constructed city in the interior (Figure 3.3.4).

- **Indonesia.** Since 1969, the Indonesian government has paid for the migration of more than 5 million people, primarily from the island of Java, where nearly two-thirds of its people live, to less populated islands.

- **India.** A number of governments limit the ability of people to migrate from one region to another. For example, to migrate to India's State of Assam, Indians are required to obtain a permit. Outsiders are limited in order to protect the ethnic identity of Assamese.

▲ 3.3.3 **INTERREGIONAL MIGRATION IN CHINA**
People who migrated from the countryside to Bejing for jobs are sleeping in the Bejing train station while waiting for a train.

▼ 3.3.4 **INTERREGIONAL MIGRATION IN BRAZIL**
When Brasilia became Brazil's capital in 1960, high-rise apartment buildings were constructed to house immigrants from other regions.

3.4 Intraregional Migration

▶ **Most intraregional migration traditionally has been from rural to urban areas.**

▶ **In developed countries, most intraregional migration is now from cities to suburbs.**

Intraregional migration is movement within one region. Intraregional migration is much more common than interregional or international migration. Most intraregional migration has been from rural to urban areas or from cities to suburbs.

RURAL TO URBAN MIGRATION

Migration from rural to urban areas began in the 1800s in Europe and North America as part of the Industrial Revolution (see Chapter 11). The percentage of people living in urban areas in the United States, for example, increased from 5 percent in 1800 to 50 percent in 1920. By some measures, more than 90 percent of the population in the United States and other developed countries now live in urban areas.

In recent years, large-scale rural to urban migration has occurred in the developing countries of Asia, Latin America, and Africa (Figure 3.4.1). Worldwide, more than 20 million people are estimated to migrate each year from rural to urban areas.

Like interregional migrants, most people who move from rural to urban areas seek economic advancement. They are pushed from rural areas by declining opportunities in agriculture and are pulled to the cities by the prospect of work in factories or in service industries.

MIGRATION FROM URBAN TO SUBURBAN AREAS

Most intraregional migration in developed countries is from cities out to surrounding suburbs. The population of most cities in developed countries has declined since the mid-twentieth century, while suburbs have grown rapidly. Nearly twice as many Americans migrate from central cities to suburbs each year than migrate from suburbs to central cities (Figure 3.4.2). Comparable patterns are found in Canada and Europe.

The major reason for the large-scale migration to the suburbs is not related to employment, as is the case with other forms of migration. For most people, migration to suburbs does not coincide with changing jobs. Instead, people are pulled by a suburban lifestyle. Suburbs offer the opportunity to live in a detached house rather than an apartment, surrounded by a private yard where children can play safely. A garage or driveway on the property guarantees

▼ 3.4.1
INTRAREGIONAL MIGRATION
Rapid urban growth in La Paz, Bolivia, has spread onto mountainsides.

space to park automobiles at no charge. Suburban schools tend to be more modern, better equipped, and safer than those in cities. Automobiles and trains enable people to live in suburbs yet have access to jobs, shops, and recreational facilities throughout the urban area (see Chapter 13).

As a result of suburbanization, the territory occupied by urban areas has rapidly expanded. To accommodate suburban growth, farms on the periphery of urban areas are converted to housing developments, where new roads, sewers, and other services must be built.

MIGRATION FROM URBAN TO RURAL AREAS

Developed countries witnessed a new migration trend during the late twentieth century. For the first time, more people immigrated into rural areas than emigrated out of them. Net migration from urban to rural areas is called **counterurbanization**.

Counterurbanization results in part from very rapid expansion of suburbs. The boundary where suburbs end and the countryside begins cannot be precisely defined. But most counterurbanization represents genuine migration from cities and suburbs to small towns and rural communities.

Like suburbanization, people move from urban to rural areas for lifestyle reasons. Some are lured to rural areas by the prospect of swapping the frantic pace of urban life for the opportunity to live on a farm where they can own horses or grow vegetables. Others move to farms but do not earn their living from agriculture; instead, they work in nearby factories, small-town shops, or other services. In the United States, evidence of counterurbanization can be seen primarily in the Rocky Mountain states. Some rural counties in states such as Colorado, Idaho, Montana, Utah, and Wyoming have experienced net in-migration (Figure 3.4.3).

With modern communications and transportation systems, no location in a developed country is truly isolated, either economically or socially. Computers, tablets, and smart phones enable us to work anywhere and still have access to an international network. We can buy most products online and have them delivered within a few days. We can follow the fortunes of our favorite team on TV anywhere

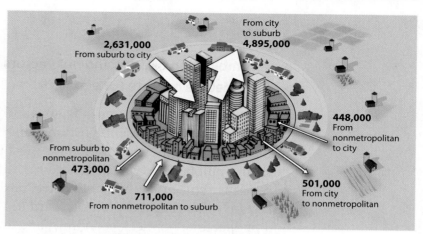

▲ 3.4.2 **INTRAREGIONAL MIGRATION IN THE UNITED STATES**
Figures show migration between cities, suburbs, and nonmetropolitan areas in 2010.

in the country, thanks to satellite dishes and webcasts.

Intraregional migration has slowed during the early twenty-first century as a result of the severe recession (Figure 3.4.4). Intraregional migrants, who move primarily for lifestyle reasons rather than for jobs, found that they couldn't get loans to buy new homes nor find buyers for their old homes.

▼ 3.4.3 **NET MIGRATION BY U.S. COUNTY**

Net Migration 2007–2008 (as % of 2007 population)

In-migration		Out-migration	
2.0 and above		0.01–0.49	
1.0–1.99		0.50–0.99	
0.50–0.99		1.0–1.99	
0.01–0.49		2.0 and below	

No change
0.00

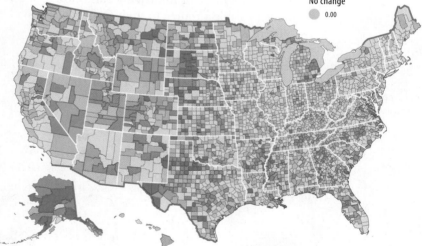

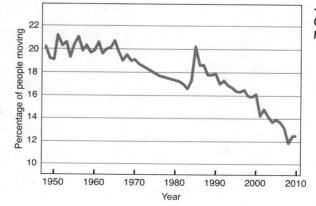

◀ 3.4.4 **PERCENTAGE OF AMERICANS MOVING IN A YEAR**

3.5 Reasons to Migrate

▶ **A combination of push and pull factors influences migration decisions.**

▶ **Most people migrate for economic reasons.**

People migrate because of push factors and pull factors. A **push factor** induces people to move out of their present location, whereas a **pull factor** induces people to move into a new location. As migration for most people is a major step not taken lightly, both push and pull factors typically play a role. To migrate, people view their current place of residence so negatively that they feel pushed away, and they view another place so attractively that they feel pulled toward it. We can identify three major kinds of push and pull factors: political, economic, and environmental.

POLITICAL PUSH AND PULL FACTORS

According to the United Nations, **refugees** are people who have been forced to migrate from their homes and cannot return for fear of persecution because of their race, religion, nationality, membership in a social group, or political opinion. The United Nations High Commissioner for Refugees counted 11 million refugees in 2010 (Figure 3.5.1). Refugees have no home until another country agrees to allow them in, or improving conditions make possible a return to their former home (Figure 3.5.2).

During the eighteenth and early nineteenth centuries, millions of people were shipped to other countries as slaves or as prisoners, especially from Africa to the Western

Hemisphere (see Chapter 7). During the twentieth and twenty-first centuries, wars have forced large-scale migration of ethnic groups, especially in Europe and Africa.

▲ 3.5.2 **POLITICAL MIGRATION: REFUGEES**
Refugees from Sudan in Chad look at a board set up by the Red Cross with pictures of missing children.

▼ 3.5.1 **POLITICAL MIGRATION: REFUGEES**

International refugees
Origin
- ● 1,000,000 and above
- ○ 100,000 – 999,999

Destination
- ● 1,000,000 and above
- ○ 100,000 – 999,999

Origin and Destination
- 100,000 – 999,999

ECONOMIC PUSH AND PULL FACTORS

Most international and interregional migration is for economic reasons. People think about emigrating from places that have few job opportunities, and they immigrate to places where the jobs seem to be available. Because of economic restructuring, job prospects often vary from one country to another and within regions of the same country.

The United States and Canada have been especially prominent destinations for economic migrants. Many European immigrants to North America in the nineteenth century truly expected to find streets paved with gold. While not literally so gilded, the United States and Canada did offer Europeans prospects for economic advancement. This same perception of economic plenty now lures people to the United States and Canada from Latin America and Asia.

The relative attractiveness of a region can shift with economic change. Ireland was a place of net

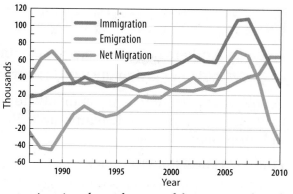

◀ 3.5.3 **ECONOMIC MIGRATION: IRELAND**
With few job prospects, Ireland had net out-migration historically until the 1990s. The severe recession of the early twenty-first century brought net out-migration back to Ireland.

out-migration through most of the nineteenth and twentieth centuries. Dire economic conditions produced net outmigration in excess of 200,000 a year during the 1850s. The historical pattern reversed during the 1990s, as economic prosperity made Ireland a destination for immigrants, especially from eastern Europe (Figure 3.5.3). However, the collapse of Ireland's economy as part of the severe global recession starting in 2008 brought a return to net out-migration.

ENVIRONMENTAL PUSH AND PULL FACTORS

People are pulled toward physically attractive regions and pushed from hazardous ones. Attractive environments for migrants include mountains, seasides, and warm climates (Figure 3.5.4).

Migrants are pushed from their homes by adverse physical conditions. Water—either too much or too little—poses the most common environmental threat. Many people are forced to move by water-related disasters because they live in an area prone to flooding (Figure 3.5.5). A lack of water pushes others from their land. Hundreds of thousands have been forced to move from the Sahel region of northern Africa because of drought conditions.

▼ 3.5.5 **ENVIRONMENTAL MIGRATION: PUSH FACTOR**
Leaving New Orleans after Katrina.

◀ 3.5.4 **ENVIRONMENTAL MIGRATION: PULL FACTOR**
Living in the sun, Florida.

3.6 Migrating to Find Work

► **Guest workers migrate from developing countries to Europe and the Middle East.**

► **They hold low-paying unskilled jobs that local citizens don't want.**

People unable to migrate permanently to a new country for employment opportunities may be allowed to migrate temporarily. Prominent forms of temporary work are found in Europe and Southwest Asia.

EUROPE'S MIGRANT WORKERS

Of the world's sixteen countries with the highest per capita income, fourteen are in northern and western Europe. As a result, the region attracts immigrants from poorer regions to the south and east (Figure 3.6.1). These immigrants serve a useful role in Europe, because they take low-status and low-skilled jobs that local residents won't accept. In cities such as Berlin, Brussels, Paris, and Zurich, immigrants provide essential services, such as driving buses, collecting garbage, repairing streets, and washing dishes (Figure 3.6.2).

Although relatively low paid by European standards, immigrants earn far more than they would at home. By letting their people work elsewhere, poorer countries reduce their own unemployment problems. Immigrants also help their native countries by sending a large percentage of their earnings back home to their families. The injection of foreign currency then stimulates the local economy.

Germany and other wealthy European countries operated a **guest worker** program mainly during the 1960s and 1970s.

Immigrants from poorer countries were allowed to immigrate temporarily to obtain jobs. They were protected by minimum-wage laws, labor union contracts, and other support programs. The guest worker program was intended to be temporary. After a few years, the guest workers were expected to return home.

The first guest worker programs involved emigration from southern European countries such as Italy, Portugal, and Spain. Northern European countries were then much wealthier and more economically developed and offered many more job opportunities. Turkey and North Africa replaced southern Europe as the leading sources. Today, most immigrants in search of work in Europe come from eastern Europe, such as Poland and Romania.

► 3.6.1 **IMMIGRATION IN EUROPE**
The largest flows in recent years have been from Poland to Germany and from Romania to Italy and Spain.

◄ 3.6.2 **MIGRANT WORKERS IN EUROPE**
North African cleaner in Paris, France.

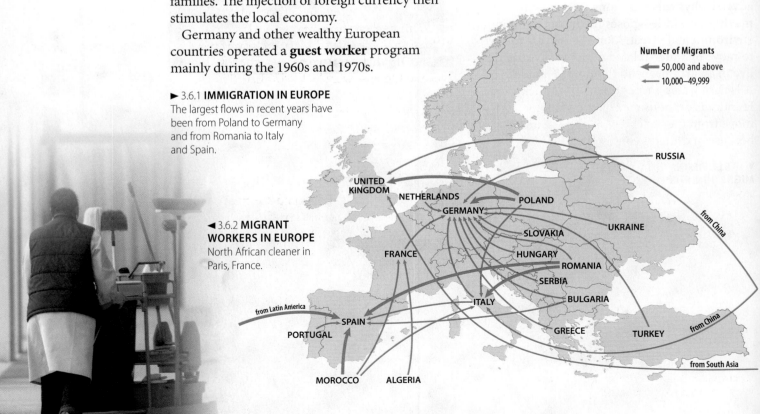

Number of Migrants
← 50,000 and above
← 10,000–49,999

RUSSIA · UNITED KINGDOM · NETHERLANDS · POLAND · GERMANY · UKRAINE · SLOVAKIA · FRANCE · HUNGARY · ROMANIA · SERBIA · BULGARIA · ITALY · GREECE · TURKEY · SPAIN · PORTUGAL · MOROCCO · ALGERIA

from China · from China · from Latin America · from South Asia

The term guest worker is no longer used in Europe. The government programs no longer exist. Many immigrants who arrived originally under the guest worker program have remained permanently. They, along with their children and grandchildren, have become citizens of the host country. The foreign-born population exceeds 40 percent in Luxembourg and 20 percent in Switzerland (Figure 3.6.3). Among the most populous European countries, Spain has the highest share of foreign-born population. Turks comprise the largest foreign-born group in Germany, and North Africans in France and Spain. In Europe as a whole, though, the percentage of foreign-born residents is only one-half that of North America.

▼ 3.6.3 **PERCENT IMMIGRANTS IN EUROPE**

Percent foreign born
- 10.0 and above
- 5.0–9.9
- Below 5.0
- no data

ASIA'S MIGRANT WORKERS

Asia is both a major source and a major destination for migrants in search of work.

- **China.** Approximately 40 million Chinese currently live in other countries, including 30 million in Southeast Asia, 5 million in North America, and 2 million in Europe. Chinese comprise three-fourths of the population in Singapore and one-fourth in Malaysia. Most migrants came from southeastern China (Figure 3.6.4). China's booming economy is now attracting immigrants from neighboring countries, especially Vietnamese, who are willing to work in China's rapidly expanding factories. However, immigration from abroad pales in comparison to internal migration within China, as discussed in Section 3.3 (Figure 3.6.5).

- **Southwest Asia.** The wealthy oil-producing countries of Southwest Asia have been major destinations for people from poorer countries in the region, such as Egypt and Yemen. During the late twentieth century, most immigrants arrived from South and Southeast Asia, including India, Pakistan, the Philippines, and Thailand. Working conditions for immigrants have been considered poor in some of these countries. The Philippine government determined in 2011 that only two countries in Southwest Asia—Israel and Oman—were "safe" for their Filipino migrants, because the others lacked adequate protection for workers' rights. For their part, oil-producing countries fear that the increasing numbers of guest workers will spark political unrest and abandonment of traditional Islamic customs.

The severe recession of the early twenty-first century suddenly disrupted global migration patterns. With the disappearance of jobs in the recession, fewer migrants have set off in search of opportunities, and unemployed migrants have returned home.

▲ 3.6.4 **EMIGRATION FROM CHINA**
Various ethnic Chinese have distinctive streams of migration to other Asian countries.

▼ 3.6.5 **INTERNAL MIGRATION IN CHINA**
Migrant workers from China's western provinces wait at the Shanghai train station to return home for holidays.

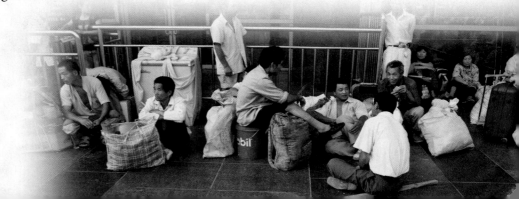

3.7 Gender and Family

► **Most migrants were traditionally males.**
► **Families with children comprise an increasing share of migrants.**

A century ago, Ravenstein noted distinctive gender and family-status patterns in his migration laws:

- Most long-distance migrants were male.
- Most long-distance migrants were adult individuals rather than families with children.

Since the late twentieth century, these characteristics have changed. Women now constitute a majority of migrants.

GENDER OF MIGRANTS

Males historically accounted for most migrants because most people migrate for economic reasons, and men once constituted the overwhelming majority of the labor force (Figure 3.7.1). During the nineteenth and much of the twentieth centuries, for example, about 55 percent of immigrants to the United States were male. But the gender pattern reversed in the 1990s, and women now constitute about 55 percent of U.S. immigrants (Figure 3.7.2). Similarly, immigrants to Europe from Africa were once predominantly male guest workers, but now an increasing number of them are women and children.

Mexicans who come to the United States without proper immigration documents—currently the largest group of U.S. immigrants—show similar gender changes. As recently as the late 1980s, males constituted 85 percent of the

▲ 3.7.2 **FEMALE IMMIGRANTS FROM MEXICO**
Mexican immigrant picks watermelons at a Michigan farm.

▼ 3.7.1 **MIGRANT WORKERS FROM MEXICO**
Mexican workers harvest iceberg lettuce near Yuma, Arizona.

◀ 3.7.3 **EMIGRATION FROM LATIN AMERICA** Children and adults display the Mexican flag at a Latinos Unidos parade in Brooklyn, New York.

Mexican migrants arriving in the United States without proper documents, according to U.S. census and immigration service estimates. But since the 1990s, women have accounted for about half of the undocumented immigrants from Mexico.

AGE AND EDUCATION OF MIGRANTS

The increased female migration to the United States partly reflects the changing role of women in Mexican society: in the past, rural Mexican women were obliged to marry at a young age and to remain in the village to care for children. Now some Mexican women are migrating to the United States to join husbands or brothers already in the United States, but most are seeking jobs. At the same time, women also feel increased pressure to get a job in the United States because of poor economic conditions in Mexico. Immigrants from Latin America and other regions often retain cultural attachment to their home country (Figure 3.7.3). But migrants also adjust to life in America (Figure 3.7.4).

Ravenstein also stated that most long-distance migrants were young adults seeking work, rather than children or elderly people. For the most part, this pattern continues for the United States.

• About 40 percent of immigrants are between the ages of 25 and 39, compared to only 23 percent of the entire U.S. population.

• Only 5 percent of immigrants are over age 65, compared to 12 percent of the entire U.S. population.

• Children under age 15 comprise 16 percent of immigrants, compared to 21 percent for the total U.S. population. However, with the increase in women migrating to the United States, more children are coming with their mothers.

• Recent immigrants to the United States have attended school for fewer years and are less likely to have high school diplomas than are U.S. citizens. The typical undocumented Mexican immigrant has attended school for 4 years, less than the average American but a year more than the average Mexican.

▼ 3.7.4 **FAMILIES OF IMMIGRANTS** Hispanic children at the Wesley Community Center after school program in Phoenix, Arizona.

3.8 Undocumented U.S. Immigrants

▶ Push and pull factors entice some immigrants to live in the United States without proper authorization.

▶ Enforcement of immigration laws is difficult along the U.S.-Mexico border.

The number of people allowed to immigrate into the United States is at a historically high level, yet the number who wish to come is even higher. Many who cannot legally enter the United States immigrate illegally. Those who do so are entering without proper documents and thus are called **unauthorized (or undocumented) immigrants**. People enter or remain in the United States without authorization primarily because they wish to work but do not have permission to do so from the government.

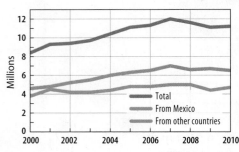

▲ 3.8.1
UNDOCUMENTED IMMIGRANTS IN THE UNITED STATES

The Pew Hispanic Center estimated that there were 11.2 million unauthorized immigrants living in the United States in 2010. The number increased rapidly during the first years of the twenty-first century (Figure 3.8.1). After hitting a peak in 2007, the figure declined because the severe recession starting in 2008 reduced job opportunities in the United States.

Other information about undocumented immigrants, according to Pew Hispanic Center:

- **Source country.** Approximately 60 percent come from Mexico. The remainder are about evenly divided between other Latin American countries and other regions of the world.

- **Children.** The 11.2 million undocumented immigrants included 1 million children. In addition, while living in the United States undocumented immigrants have given birth to approximately 4.5 million babies, who are legal citizens of the United States.

- **Labor force.** Approximately 8 million undocumented immigrants are employed in the United States, accounting for around 5 percent of the total U.S. civilian labor force. Unauthorized immigrants were much more likely than the average American to be employed in construction and hospitality (food service and lodging) jobs and less likely to be in white-collar jobs such as education, health care, and finance.

- **Distribution.** California and Texas have the largest number of undocumented immigrants (Figure 3.8.2). Nevada has the largest percentage.

▲ 3.8.2 **UNDOCUMENTED IMMIGRANTS IN THE UNITED STATES**

Individual U.S. states attract immigrants from different countries.

Launch MapMaster North America in Mastering **GEOGRAPHY**

Select: *Political* then *Countries, States, and Provinces*

Select: *Population* then *Destination of Unauthorized Immigrants.* Adjust layer opacity to 50%.

Select: *Population* then *Distribution of African Americans.*

Deselect *African Americans* and select *Hispanic Americans.*

Deselect *Hispanic Americans* and select *Asian Americans.*

Which of the three groups matches most closely with the distribution of states that have the most undocumented immigrants?

▲ 3.8.3 **BORDER CROSSING BETWEEN SAN DIEGO AND TIJUANA**

CROSSING THE BORDER

The U.S.-Mexico border is 3,141 kilometers (1,951 miles) long. Guards heavily patrol border crossings in urban areas such as El Paso, Texas, and San Diego, California, or along highways (Figure 3.8.3). Rural areas are guarded by only a handful of agents (Figure 3.8.4). Crossing the border on foot legally is possible in several places (Figure 3.8.5). Elsewhere, the border runs mostly through sparsely inhabited regions (Figure 3.8.6). The United States has constructed a barrier covering approximately one-fourth of the border (Figure 3.8.7).

Actually locating the border is difficult in some remote areas. A joint U.S.–Mexican International Boundary and Water Commission is responsible for keeping official maps, on the basis of a series of nineteenth-century treaties. The commission is also responsible for marking the border by maintaining 276 six-foot-tall iron monuments erected in the late nineteenth century, as well as 440 fifteen-inch-tall markers added in the 1970s.

◄ 3.8.4 **BORDER BETWEEN CALEXICO AND MEXICALI**
The border looks different in urban areas
Fly to *Mexicali, Mexico.*

1. **In which country are the green rectangles on the north side of the image?**

2. **What are the green rectangles?**

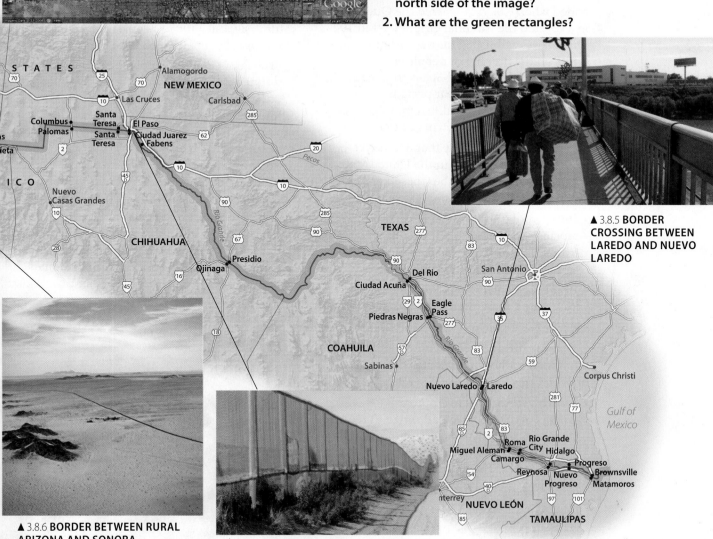

▲ 3.8.5 **BORDER CROSSING BETWEEN LAREDO AND NUEVO LAREDO**

▲ 3.8.6 **BORDER BETWEEN RURAL ARIZONA AND SONORA**

▲ 3.8.7 **BORDER BETWEEN EL PASO AND JUAREZ**

3.9 Attitudes Towards Immigrants

▶ **Quota laws restrict immigration to the United States.**
▶ **Attitudes towards immigrants are ambivalent.**

The principal obstacle traditionally faced by migrants to other countries was environmental: the long, arduous, and expensive passage over land or by sea. Today, most immigrants can arrive speedily and reasonably comfortably by motor vehicle or airplane. Instead, they face these challenges:

• Gaining permission to enter the new country.
• Hostile attitudes of citizens already living in the new country.

PERMISSION TO ENTER

The United States prides itself as a nation of immigrants (Figure 3.9.1). But the era of unrestricted immigration to the United States ended when Congress passed the Quota Act in 1921 and the National Origins Act in 1924. These laws established **quotas**, or maximum limits on the number of people who could immigrate to the United States from each country during a one-year period.

Quotas have been modified many times. Among the more significant changes:

• **1924:** For each country that had native-born persons already living in the United States, 2 percent of their number (based on the 1910 census) could immigrate each year.

• **1965:** Quotas for individual countries were replaced with hemisphere quotas (170,000 from the Eastern Hemisphere and 120,000 from the Western Hemisphere).

• **1978:** A global quota of 290,000 was set, including a maximum of 20,000 per country.

• **1990:** The global quota was raised to 700,000.

Because the number of applicants for admission to the United States far exceeds the quotas, Congress has set preferences.

• **Family reunification.** Approximately three-fourths of the quota are admitted to reunify families, primarily spouses or unmarried children of non-citizens legally residing in the United States. The typical wait for a spouse to gain entry is about five years.

• **Skilled workers.** Exceptionally talented professionals comprise most of the remainder of the quota.

• **Diversity.** A few are admitted by lottery under a diversity category for people from countries that historically sent few people to the United States.

The quota does not apply to refugees, who are admitted if they are judged genuine refugees. Also admitted without limit are spouses, children, and parents of U.S. citizens. The number of immigrants can vary sharply from year to year, primarily because numbers in these two groups are unpredictable.

Other countries charge that by giving preference to skilled workers, immigration policies in the United States and Europe contribute to a **brain drain**, which is a large-scale emigration by talented people. Scientists, researchers, doctors, and other professionals migrate to countries where they can earn higher income with their abilities.

▶ 3.9.1 **PRO-IMMIGRANT RALLY, WASHINGTON**

ATTITUDES OF U.S. CITIZENS TOWARDS IMMIGRANTS

During the nineteenth century, when immigration was at its peak, many Americans regarded new arrivals with suspicion but tempered their dislike during the nineteenth century because immigrants helped to settle the frontier and extend U.S. control across the continent. By the early twentieth century, most Americans saw the frontier as closed and thus thought that entry into the country should be closed as well. Opposition to immigration also intensified into the twentieth century when the majority of immigrants no longer came from northern and western Europe.

More recently, public support for tighter immigration controls increased after the September 11, 2001, attacks on the World Trade Center and Pentagon (Figure 3.9.2). Most controversial has been Arizona's Support Our Law Enforcement and Safe Neighborhoods Act of 2010, which authorized state law enforcement officials to enforce federal law requiring non-American citizens to carry documentation of their legal status. Whether children of undocumented immigrants should be entitled to attend school and receive social services is much debated.

Since undocumented immigrants accept low-wage jobs that most U.S. citizens are unwilling to fill, a majority of citizens would support some type of work-related program to make them legal. At the same time, most U.S. citizens would like more effective border patrols so that fewer undocumented immigrants can get into the country.

▲ 3.9.3 **IMMIGRANTS IN A SUBURB OF STOCKHOLM, SWEDEN**

ATTITUDES OF EUROPEANS TOWARDS IMMIGRANTS

In Europe, many immigrants suffer from poor social conditions. They are often relegated to high-rise apartment buildings in the suburbs of cities in neighborhoods with few services (Figure 3.9.3).

Many Europeans dislike the recent immigrants and oppose government programs to improve their living conditions. Political parties that support restrictions on immigration have gained support in France, Germany, and other European countries, and attacks by local citizens on immigrants have increased (Figure 3.9.4). Underlying anti-immigrant attitudes in Europe is the region's low natural increase rate. With most countries in the region in stage 4 of the demographic transition, the size of the future population depends primarily on the number of immigrants.

▼ 3.9.4 **ANTI-IMMIGRANT RALLY, LONDON**

▶ 3.9.2 **PROTESTING UNDOCUMENTED IMMIGRATION, NEW YORK**

Most people migrate for economic reasons, involving a combination of push factors and pull factors. Poor economic conditions at home push people to consider migration, and promising job prospects pull them to other locations. For many potential migrants, push factors are as strong as ever in the twenty-first century. But the pull factor has changed. Places offering job opportunities have been hard to find in the wake of the severe global recession. As a result, all types of migration have declined in recent years.

Key Questions

Where are migrants distributed?

▶ The United States has been the leading destination for international migrants.

▶ The principal source of immigrants to the United States has varied over time, but the principal reason for migrating to the United States has remained economic.

▶ Interregional migration (migration between regions within a country) was especially important historically in settling the frontier of large countries such as the United States, Russia, and Brazil.

▶ The most important intraregional migration (migration within a region of a country) is from rural to urban areas within developing countries and from cities to suburbs within developed countries.

Why do people migrate?

▶ Immigration involves a combination of push factors that induce them to leave a place and pull factors that attract them to a new location.

▶ Three types of push and pull factors are economic, environmental, and political.

▶ Most international and interregional migration is for economic reasons. People emigrate from places with few job opportunities and immigrate to places where jobs seem abundant.

▶ Most migrants are young males, but increasing percentages are women and children.

What obstacles do immigrants face?

▶ Undocumented or unauthorized immigrants are in the United States primarily to hold jobs that pay more than at home.

▶ Quotas restrict the number of legal immigrants to the United States.

Thinking Geographically

According to the concept of chain migration, current migrants tend to follow the paths of relatives and friends who have moved earlier (Figure 3.CR.1).

1. Can you find evidence of chain migration in your community?
The United States gives preference to immigrants with family already in the country, or with special job skills.

2. Which of these two reasons should be given a higher priority? Should a higher percentage of immigrants be selected by lottery rather than for one of these two reasons? Why or why not?
Migrants make a strong impact on the landscape of the place where they arrive

3. What is the impact of emigration on the places from which migrants depart?

On the Internet

A central clearinghouse of data on migration can be accessed at **www.migrationinformation.org** or scan the QR at the beginning of the chapter.

The Office of Immigration Statistics in the U.S. Department of Homeland Security publishes statistics by country of origin extending back to 1820 at **http://www.dhs.gov/files/statistics/data/**.

The Pew Hispanic Center reports on undocumented immigrants at **http://pewhispanic.org/reports/**.

Information on refugees can be found at **www.refugees.org** and at **refugeesinternational.org**.

▶ 3.CR.1 **BRIGHTON BEACH, NEW YORK**

Interactive Mapping

WEALTH, DEMOGRAPHY, AND IMMIGRATION IN EUROPE

Europe's wealth and demographic patterns play a major role in the region's importance as a destination for migrants.

Launch MapMaster World in *Mastering*GEOGRAPHY

Select: *Political* then *Continents and Country Boundaries*

Select: *Economic* then *Gross National Income Per Capita at Purchasing Power Parity*

1. How does income in Europe compare to that in neighboring regions?

Select: *Population* then *Population Growth Rise*

2. How does the population growth rate in Europe compare to that in neighboring regions?

3. How do Europe's differences with its neighbors in income and population growth impact its attraction as a destination for migrants from neighboring regions?

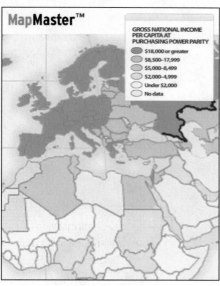

MapMaster™

GROSS NATIONAL INCOME PER CAPITA AT PURCHASING POWER PARITY
- $18,000 or greater
- $8,500–17,999
- $5,000–8,499
- $2,000–4,999
- Under $2,000
- No data

Explore

MEXICO'S OTHER BORDER

Use Google Earth to explore Mexico's border, not with the United States, as in section 3.8, but its southern one with Guatemala.

Fly to: *La Mesia, Guatemala*

Now fly to: *Ciudad Cuauhtémoc, Mexico*

Zoom out until both La Mesia and Ciudad Cuauhtémoc are visible.

1. What is the distance between the two cities?

2. The International border between Guatemala and Mexico runs between the two cities; do you see any evidence of the border, such as a fence or passport control facility?

3. How would you explain any differences between this border and the U.S.-Mexico border?

Key Terms

Brain drain
Large-scale emigration by talented people.

Chain migration
Migration of people to a specific location because relatives or members of the same nationality previously migrated there.

Counterurbanization
Net migration from urban to rural areas in more developed countries.

Emigration
Migration from a location.

Forced migration
Permanent movement compelled usually by cultural factors.

Guest worker
A term once used for a worker who migrated to the developed countries of northern and western Europe, usually from southern and eastern Europe or from North Africa, in search of higher-paying jobs.

Immigration
Migration to a new location.

Internal migration
Permanent movement within a particular country.

International migration
Permanent movement from one country to another.

Interregional migration
Permanent movement from one region of a country to another.

Intraregional migration
Permanent movement within one region of a country.

Migration
Form of relocation diffusion involving a permanent move to a new location.

Migration transition
Change in the migration pattern in a society that results from industrialization, population growth, and other social and economic changes that also produce the demographic transition.

Net migration
The difference between the level of immigration and the level of emigration.

Pull factor
Factor that induces people to move to a new location.

Push factor
Factor that induces people to leave old residences.

Quotas
In reference to migration, laws that place maximum limits on the number of people who can immigrate to a country each year.

Refugees
People who are forced to migrate from their home country and cannot return for fear of persecution because of their race, religion, nationality, membership in a social group, or political opinion.

Unauthorized (or undocumented) immigrants
People who enter a country without proper documents. Permanent movement undertaken by choice.

▶ **LOOKING AHEAD**

Migration results in the distribution of cultural features, as discussed in the next chapter.

4 Folk and Popular Culture

In everyday language we think of culture as novels, paintings, symphonies, and other works created by talented individuals. A person with a taste for these items is said to be "cultured." Culture also refers to small living organisms, such as those found under a microscope or in yogurt. Agriculture is a term for the growing of living material at a much larger scale than in a test tube.

The origin of the word culture is the Latin cultus, which means "to care for." Culture is a complex concept because "to care for" something has two very different meanings:

- To care about—to adore or worship something, as in the modern word cult.
- To take care of—to nurse or look after something, as in the modern word cultivate.

When geographers think about culture, they may be referring to either one of the two main meanings of the concept. This chapter, as well as Chapters 5 through 8, examine what people care about (their ideas, beliefs, values, and customs). Chapters 9 through 14 emphasize what people take care of (their ways of earning a living and obtaining food, clothing, and shelter.

BOYS PLAYING CRICKET NEAR THE TAJ MAHAL, AGRA, INDIA

How are folk and popular culture distributed?

How is the landscape altered by folk and popular culture?

4.1 Elements of Folk and Popular Culture

▶ **Two elements of material culture are survival activities and leisure activities.**
▶ **Material culture can be divided into folk culture and popular culture.**

Culture is the body of material traits, customary beliefs, and social forms that together constitute the distinct tradition of a group of people. This chapter focuses on the first part of this definition (material traits), the next two chapters on the second part (customary beliefs), and Chapters 7 and 8 on the third part (social forms).

Culture follows logically from the discussion of migration in Chapter 3. Two locations have similar cultural traits, beliefs, and social forms because people bring along their culture when they migrate. Differences emerge when two groups have limited interaction.

Geographers focus on two aspects of where material traits are located in space:

- Each cultural activity, like wearing jeans, has a distinctive spatial distribution. Geographers study the origin and diffusion (or lack of diffusion) of these traits.

- Geographers study the relation between material culture and the physical environment. Each cultural group takes particular elements from the environment into its culture and in turn constructs landscapes (what geographers call "built environments") that modify nature in distinctive ways.

DAILY NECESSITIES AND LEISURE

Two facets of material culture are examined in this chapter:

- Material culture deriving from the necessities of daily life—food, clothing, and shelter. All people must consume food, wear clothing, and build shelter, but different cultural groups do so in distinctive ways (Figure 4.1.1).

- Culture involving leisure activities—the arts and recreation. Each cultural group has its own definition of meaningful art and stimulating recreation (Figure 4.1.2).

Geographers search for where these various elements of culture are found in the world and for reasons why the observed distributions occur.

Culture can be distinguished from a **habit** (a repetitive act that a particular individual performs) or a **custom** (a repetitive act of a group). Unlike custom, habit does not imply that the act has been adopted by most of the society's population. A custom is therefore a habit that has been widely adopted by a group of people (Figure 4.1.3).

A collection of social customs produces a group's material culture—jeans typically represent American informality and a badge of youth. In this chapter, custom may be used to denote a specific element of material culture, such as wearing jeans, whereas culture refers to a group's entire collection of customs.

▼ 4.1.1 **CULTURE: DAILY NECESSITIES**
Traditional tea, Kyoto, Japan.

▲ 4.1.2 **CULTURE: LEISURE**
Bullfighting, Seville, Spain.

▶ 4.1.3 **HABIT AND CUSTOM**
As CEO of Fiat and Chrysler, Sergio Marchionne had a habit of wearing black sweaters, even when meeting other executives who adhered to the custom of wearing suits and ties.

CHARACTERISTICS OF FOLK CULTURE

Material culture falls into two basic categories that differ according to scale—folk and popular. **Folk culture** is traditionally practiced primarily by small, homogeneous groups living in isolated rural areas.

An element of folk culture typically has an anonymous hearth (a center of innovation), originating from anonymous sources, at unknown dates, through unidentified originators. It may also have multiple hearths, originating independently in isolated locations.

Relocation diffusion was defined in Chapter 1 as the spread of a characteristic through bodily movement of people from one place to another. This is the principal way that folk culture diffuses—slowly and on a small scale, primarily through migration (Figure 4.1.4).

Even groups living in proximity may generate a distinct collection of folk customs, because of limited communication. A group develops distinctive customs from experiencing local social and physical conditions in a place that is isolated from other groups. Landscapes dominated by a collection of folk customs tend to change relatively little over time.

▲ 4.1.4 **FOLK CULTURE: DISTRIBUTION OF THE AMISH**
Amish folk culture has been diffused across 19 U.S. states through relocation diffusion (migration). Amish communities are relatively isolated from each other but share cultural traditions distinct from those of other Americans, such as travel by horse and buggy.

Percent Old Order Amish
- 5 and above
- 1.0–4.9
- 0.05–0.99
- below 0.05

CHARACTERISTICS OF POPULAR CULTURE

Popular culture is found in large, heterogeneous societies that share certain customs (such as wearing jeans) despite differences in other personal characteristics. The amount of territory covered by a popular culture is typically much larger than that covered by a folk culture.

In contrast to folk customs, popular culture is most often a product of developed regions (Figure 4.1.5), especially North America and Europe. Popular music and fast food are good examples. They arise from a combination of advances in industrial technology and increased leisure time.

Popular culture is based on rapid simultaneous global connections through communications systems, transportation networks, and other modern technology. Rapid diffusion facilitates frequent changes in popular customs. Thus, folk culture is more likely to vary from place to place at a given time, whereas popular culture is more likely to vary from time to time at a given place.

Industrial technology permits the uniform reproduction of objects in large quantities (CDs, T-shirts, pizzas). Many of these objects help people enjoy leisure time, which has increased as a result of the widespread change in the labor force from predominantly agricultural work to predominantly service and manufacturing jobs.

▼ 4.1.5 **POPULAR CULTURE: DISTRIBUTION OF BASEBALL**
Baseball, once confined to North America, became popular in Japan after it was introduced by American soldiers who occupied the country after World War II. These Little League players are in Okinawa, site of a major U.S. base.

4.2 Origin and Diffusion of Music

▶ **Folk music has unknown origins derived from local environmental conditions.**
▶ **Popular music is created by an individual to sell.**

Every culture in human history has had some tradition of music, argues music researcher Daniel Levitan. As music is a part of both folk and popular culture traditions, it can be used to illustrate differences in the origins and diffusion of folk and popular culture.

FOLK MUSIC

Folk songs are usually composed anonymously and transmitted orally. A song may be modified from one generation to the next as conditions change, but the content is most often derived from events in daily life that are familiar to the majority of the people. As people migrate, folk music travels with them as part of the diffusion of folk culture.

Folk songs tell a story or convey information about daily activities such as farming, life-cycle events (birth, death, and marriage), or mysterious events such as storms and earthquakes (Figure 4.2.1). In Vietnam, for example, where most people are farmers,

information about agricultural technology is conveyed through folk songs, such as this one (Figure 4.2.2):

Ma chiêm ba tháng không già
Ma mùa tháng rưỡi ắt la'không non*

This song can be translated as follows:

While seedlings for the summer crop are not old when they are three months of age
Seedlings for the winter crop are certainly not young when they are one-and-a-half months old

The song hardly sounds lyrical to a Western ear. But when English-language folk songs appear in cold print, similar themes emerge, even if the specific information conveyed about the environment differs.

◀ 4.2.1 **GULLAH FOLK MUSIC**
Folk songs of the Gullah people of South Carolina's Low Country are influenced by their cultural heritage as descendents of slaves forcibly transported from Africa in the eighteenth century.

▲ 4.2.2 **VIETNAMESE FOLK MUSIC**
Singers perform Quan Ho folk songs as part of the annual Lim Festival.

*From John Blacking and Joann W. Kealiinohomoku, eds., The Performing Arts: Music and Dance (The Hague: Mouton, 1979), 144. Reprinted by permission of the publisher.

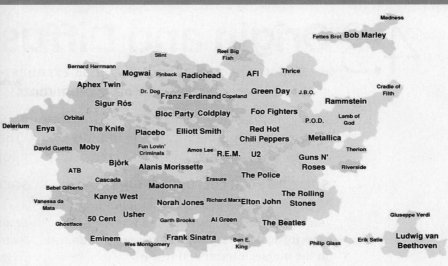

▲ 4.2.3 **POPULAR MUSIC PERFORMANCES**
Chinese punk rock band performs in Beijing, China.

▲ 4.2.4 **THE LANDSCAPE OF MUSIC**
Related musicians are situated near each other. Types of music are represented as "countries." Google "The Music Map: The Landscape of Music" to see the latest version of the map, and to zoom in for more artists in the individual "countries."

POPULAR MUSIC

Popular music is written by specific individuals for the purpose of being sold to a large number of people (Figure 4.2.3). It displays a high degree of technical skill and is frequently capable of being performed only in a studio with electronic equipment.

Popular music as we know it today originated around 1900. At that time, the main popular musical entertainment in North America and Europe was the variety show, called the music hall in the United Kingdom and vaudeville in the United States.

To provide songs for music halls and vaudeville, a music industry clustered in New York, in a district that became known as Tin Pan Alley. The name derived from the sound of pianos being furiously pounded by people called song pluggers, who were demonstrating tunes to publishers. Tin Pan Alley was home to songwriters, music publishers, orchestrators, and arrangers. Companies in Tin Pan Alley originally tried to sell as many printed songsheets as possible. After World War II, Tin Pan Alley disappeared as recorded music became more important than printed songsheets.

As with other elements of popular culture, popular musicians have more connections with performers of similar styles elsewhere in the world than they do with nearby performers of different styles (Figure 4.2.4). American popular music diffused to other countries during World War II, when the Armed Forces Radio Network broadcast music to places where American forces were stationed or fighting. Local citizens were also able to listen, and they started to perform American popular music in English. After the demise of Tin Pan Alley, New York and other large cities remained the centers of popular music production, because musicians and recording studios continued to cluster there. However, in the twenty-first century, Nashville, originally a center for country music, has become the leading center for recording many styles of popular music. Several Canadian cities have also become leading recording centers (Figure 4.2.5).

◄ 4.2.5 **POPULAR MUSIC CLUSTERS**
Nashville has by far the highest concentration of popular musicians and recording studios in North America. Three Canadian cities rank among the top five.

4.3 Origin and Diffusion of Sports

▶ **Modern spectator sports are good examples of popular culture.**
▶ **Some sports retain their folk custom roots.**

Many sports originated as isolated folk customs and were diffused like other folk culture, through the migration of individuals. The contemporary diffusion of organized sports, however, displays the characteristics of popular culture.

SOCCER'S FOLK CULTURE ORIGINS

Soccer originated as a folk custom in England during the eleventh century and was transformed into a part of global popular culture in the nineteenth century.

The origin of soccer (called football outside North America) is obscure. According to football historians, the earliest contest took place after Denmark invaded England between 1018 and 1042. Workers excavating a building site encountered a Danish soldier's skull, which they began to kick. "Kick the Dane's head" was imitated by boys, one of whom got the idea of using an inflated cow bladder.

Several British football clubs formed the Football Association in 1863 to standardize the rules and to organize professional leagues. Association was shortened to assoc, which ultimately became twisted around into the word soccer. The clubs had been formed, often by churches, to provide factory workers with organized recreation during leisure hours. Organization of the sport into a formal structure in the United Kingdom marks the transition of football from folk custom to popular culture.

SOCCER AS POPULAR CULTURE

Association football diffused from England first to continental Europe in the late 1800s and then to other countries in the twentieth century (Figure 4.3.1):

• Football was first played in continental Europe in the late 1870s by Dutch students who had been in Britain.

• Football got to Spain via English engineers working in Bilbao in 1893 and was quickly adopted by local miners.

• British citizens further diffused the game throughout the worldwide British Empire.

• Soccer diffused to Russia when the English manager of a textile factory near Moscow organized a team at the factory in 1887 and advertised in London for workers who could play football. After the Russian Revolution in 1917, both the factory and its football team were absorbed into the Soviet Electric Trade Union. The team, renamed the Moscow Dynamo, became the country's most famous.

• The global popularity of soccer is seen in the World Cup, in which national soccer teams compete every four years, including in South Africa in 2010 and Brazil in 2014. Thanks to television, each final match breaks the record for the most spectators of any event in world history (Figure 4.3.2).

▲▼ 4.3.1 **FOOTBALL PLAYED AROUND THE WORLD**
(above) Guayaquil, Ecuador, (below) Cambodia, (bottom) Cape Town, South Africa.

▼ 4.3.2 **WORLD CUP**
Most countries in Europe and Latin America have qualified for the World Cup finals. As soccer diffuses worldwide, qualification has increased in other regions.

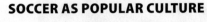
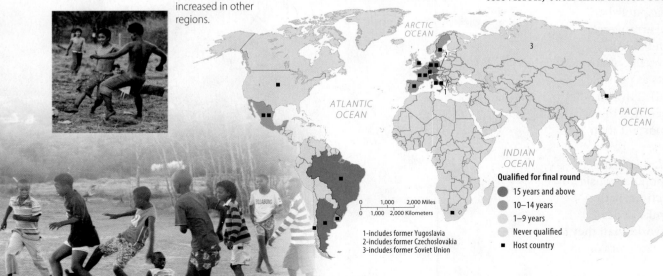

ARCTIC OCEAN

ATLANTIC OCEAN

PACIFIC OCEAN

INDIAN OCEAN

Qualified for final round
- 15 years and above
- 10–14 years
- 1–9 years
- Never qualified
- ■ Host country

0   1,000   2,000 Miles
0   1,000 2,000 Kilometers

1-includes former Yugoslavia
2-includes former Czechoslovakia
3-includes former Soviet Union

SURVIVING FOLK SPORTS

Cultural groups still have their own preferred sports, which are often unintelligible to people elsewhere:

- Cricket is popular primarily in the United Kingdom and former British colonies.

- Ice hockey prevails, logically, in colder climates, especially in Canada, the northern United States, northern Europe, and Russia (Figure 4.3.3).

- China's most popular sports include martial arts, known as wushu, which combines forms such as kicking and jumping with combat such as striking and wrestling.

- Baseball, once confined to North America, became popular in Japan after it was introduced by American soldiers who occupied the country after World War II.

- The first college "football" game played in the United States, between Princeton and Rutgers in 1869, was really soccer, and officials of several colleges met 4 years later to adopt rules consistent with those of British soccer. But Harvard's representatives successfully argued for adoption of rugby rules instead. Rugby was so thoroughly modified by U.S. colleges that an entirely new game—American football—emerged. A distinctive form of football also developed in the nineteenth century in Australia (Figure 4.3.4).

- Seventeenth-century European explorers observed the Iroquois nation playing lacrosse, known in their language as guhchigwaha, which means "bump hips." European colonists in Canada picked up the game from the Iroquois and diffused it to a handful of U.S. communities, especially in Maryland, upstate New York, and Long Island. In recent years, lacrosse has fostered cultural identity among the Iroquois Confederation of Six Nations (Cayugas, Mohawks, Oneidas, Onondagas, Senecas, and Tuscaroras), because they have been invited by the International Lacrosse Federation to participate in the Lacrosse World Championships, along with teams from sovereign states, such as Australia, Canada, and the United States (Figure 4.3.5).

Despite the diversity in the distribution of sports across Earth's surface and the anonymous origin of some games, organized spectator sports today are part of popular culture. The common element in professional sports is the willingness of people throughout the world to pay for the privilege of viewing, in person or on TV, events played by professional athletes.

► 4.3.3 **ICE HOCKEY IN CANADA**

◄ 4.3.4 **AUSTRALIAN RULES FOOTBALL**

▼ 4.3.5 **LACROSSE PLAYED BY THE MOHAWK TRIBE**

4.4 Folk and Popular House Styles

▶ **Folk housing styles varied according to migration patterns.**

▶ **Popular housing styles vary according to changing preferences.**

A key difference between folk culture and popular culture is that folk culture is more likely to vary by place whereas popular culture is more likely to vary by time. Housing in the United States is a good example of this difference.

- Folk-culture traditions are reflected in eighteenth and early nineteenth century housing in the United States. The housing built at a time period varied among communities.

- Popular culture influences are seen in housing built in the United States since the 1940s. At a particular point in time, similar-looking houses were being built across the country.

FOLK HOUSING

When families migrated westward in the 1700s and 1800s, they cut trees to clear fields for planting and used the wood to build houses, barns, and fences. The style of pioneer homes reflected whatever upscale style was prevailing at the place on the East Coast from which they migrated.

Three major hearths or nodes of folk housing formed in the Eastern United States, according to geographer Fred Kniffen (Figure 4.4.1).

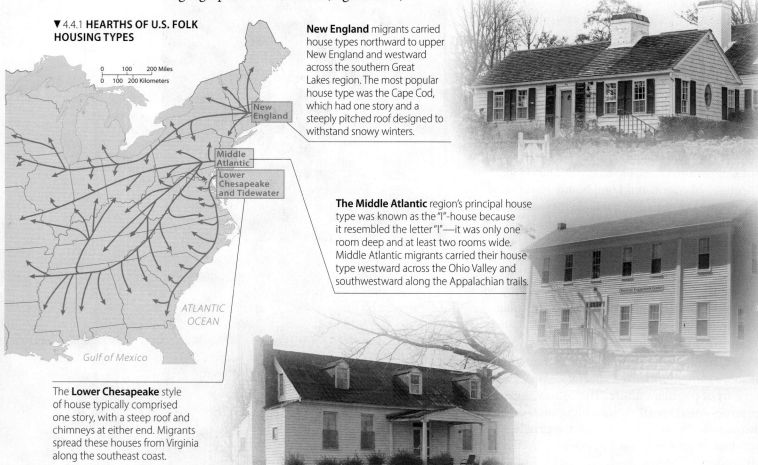

▼ 4.4.1 **HEARTHS OF U.S. FOLK HOUSING TYPES**

New England migrants carried house types northward to upper New England and westward across the southern Great Lakes region. The most popular house type was the Cape Cod, which had one story and a steeply pitched roof designed to withstand snowy winters.

The Middle Atlantic region's principal house type was known as the "I"-house because it resembled the letter "I"—it was only one room deep and at least two rooms wide. Middle Atlantic migrants carried their house type westward across the Ohio Valley and southwestward along the Appalachian trails.

The **Lower Chesapeake** style of house typically comprised one story, with a steep roof and chimneys at either end. Migrants spread these houses from Virginia along the southeast coast.

POPULAR HOUSING

Houses built in the United States during the twentieth and twenty-first centuries display popular culture influences. In contrast with eighteenth- and nineteenth-century folk housing characteristic of the early 1800s, newer housing in the United States has been built to reflect rapidly changing fashion concerning the most suitable house form.

The degree of regional distinctiveness in housing style has diminished because rapid communication and transportation systems provide people throughout the country with knowledge of alternative styles. Furthermore, most people do not build the houses in which they live. Instead, houses are usually mass-produced by construction companies and show the influence of shapes, materials, detailing, and other features of architectural style in vogue at a point in time.

In the years immediately after World War II, which ended in 1945, most U.S. houses were built in a modern style (Figure 4.4.2). Specific types of modern-style houses were popular at different times:

- Minimal traditional: Small, modest houses designed to house young families and veterans returning from World War II, they were usually one story, with a dominant front gable and few decorative details.

- Ranch house: One story, they were usually situated with the long side parallel to the street.

- Split-level: The lower level contained the garage and the newly invented "family" room, where the television set was placed; the kitchen and formal living and dining rooms were placed on the intermediate level, and the bedrooms on the top level above the family room and garage.

- Contemporary: They frequently had flat or low-pitched roofs and were especially popular for architect-designed houses.

- Shed: Popular in the late 1960s; characterized by high-pitched shed roofs, giving the house the appearance of a series of geometric forms.

Styles that architects call neo-eclectic became popular in the 1960s, and by the 1970s had surpassed modern styles in vogue:

- Mansard: The shingle-covered second-story walls sloped slightly inward and merged into the roofline.

- Neo-Tudor: The style was characterized by dominant, steep-pitched front-facing gables and half-timbered detailing.

- Neo-French: It featured dormer windows, usually with rounded tops, and high-hipped roofs.

- Neo-colonial: A large central "great room" has replaced separate family and living rooms, which were located in different wings or floors of ranch and split-level houses.

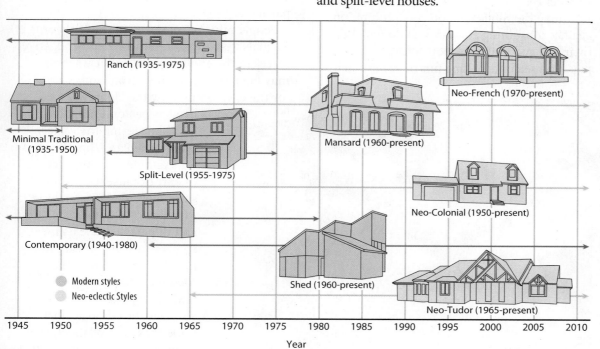

◄ 4.4.2 POPULAR HOUSING TYPES Popular housing types in the United States changed several times during the second half of the twentieth century.

Ranch (1935-1975)

Minimal Traditional (1935-1950)

Split-Level (1955-1975)

Contemporary (1940-1980)

Neo-French (1970-present)

Mansard (1960-present)

Neo-Colonial (1950-present)

Shed (1960-present)

Neo-Tudor (1965-present)

Modern styles
Neo-eclectic Styles

1945 1950 1955 1960 1965 1970 1975 1980 1985 1990 1995 2000 2005 2010

Year

4.5 Folk and Popular Food Preferences

► **People embrace or avoid specific foods for cultural reasons.**
► **Food preferences are influenced in part by environmental factors.**

Cultural preferences and environmental features influence choice of foods to consume in both folk and popular cultures.

FOOD TABOOS

A restriction on behavior imposed by social custom is a **taboo**. Taboos are especially strong in the area of food. Relatively well-known taboos against consumption of certain foods can be found in the Bible and Quran. The Biblical taboos were developed through oral tradition and by rabbis into the kosher laws observed today by some Jews.

The Biblical food taboos were established in part to set the Hebrew people apart from others. That Christians ignore the Biblical food injunctions reflects their desire to distinguish themselves from Jews beginning 2,000 years ago. Furthermore, as a universalizing religion, Christianity was less tied to taboos that originated in the Middle East (see Chapter 6).

Among the Biblical taboos is a prohibition against consuming animals that do not chew their cud and that have cloven feet, such as pigs, and seafood lacking fins or scales, such as lobsters (Figure 4.5.1). Muslims share the taboo against consuming pork.

As a result of taboos against consuming pork, the number of pigs raised in different regions of the world varies sharply. Pigs are especially scarce in predominantly Muslim regions, such as Southwest Asia and North Africa (Figure 4.5.2). On the other hand, China, where consumption of pork is embraced, has nearly one-half of the world's pig stock.

ENVIRONMENTAL INFLUENCES

Traditional food preferences are embedded especially strongly in the physical environment. Humans eat mostly plants and animals—living things that spring from the soil and water of a region. Inhabitants of a region must consider the soil, climate, terrain, vegetation, and other environmental features in deciding to produce particular foods.

People refuse to eat particular plants or animals that are thought to embody negative forces in the environment. Biblical taboos may have arisen partially from concern for the environment by the Hebrews, who lived as pastoral nomads in lands bordering the eastern Mediterranean. The pig, for example, is prohibited in part because it is more suited to sedentary farming than pastoral nomadism and in part because its meat spoils relatively quickly in hot climates, such as the Mediterranean.

Muslims, like Jews, embrace the taboo against pork. Pigs offer relatively few compensating benefits, such as being able to pull a plow, carry

▲ 4.5.1 **KOSHER PIZZA, PARIS**
Pizza is prepared here in accordance with Jewish dietary laws, including a taboo against pork products.

► 4.5.2 **SWINE STOCK**
- 500 million and above
- 10–499 million
- 1–9 million
- 100,000–999,999
- Below 100,000
- no data

ARCTIC OCEAN

PACIFIC OCEAN

ATLANTIC OCEAN

PACIFIC OCEAN

INDIAN OCEAN

ATLANTIC OCEAN

0   1,000   2,000 Miles
0 1,000 2,000 Kilometers

loads, or provide milk and wool. Widespread raising of pigs would be an ecological disaster in Islam's hearth.

In India, Hindu sanctions against consuming cows are explained in part by the need to maintain a large supply of oxen (castrated male cows), the traditional choice for pulling plows as well as carts. A large supply of oxen must be maintained in India, because every field has to be plowed at approximately the same time—when the monsoon rains arrive.

Environmental features also influence food preferences as well as avoidances:

- In Asia, soybeans are widely grown, but raw they are toxic and indigestible. Lengthy cooking renders them edible, but in Asia fuel is scarce. Asians have adapted to this environmental dilemma by deriving foods from soybeans that do not require extensive cooking. These include bean sprouts (germinated seeds), soy sauce (fermented soybeans), and bean curd (steamed soybeans).

- In Europe, traditional preferences for quick-frying foods resulted in part from fuel shortages in Italy. In northern Europe, an abundant wood supply may have encouraged the slow stewing and roasting of foods over fires, which also provided home heat in the colder climate.

FOOD AND PLACE: THE CONCEPT OF TERROIR

The environment not only influences folk food preferences, but also contributes to the characteristics of foods traditionally produced in a particular area. The contribution of a location's distinctive physical features to the way food tastes is known by the French term **terroir**. The word comes from the same root as terre (French for land or earth), but terroir does not translate precisely into English; it has a similar meaning to the English expressions "grounded" or "sense of place." Terroir is the sum of the effects of the local environment on a particular food item.

Terroir is frequently used to refer to the combination of soil, climate, and other physical features that contribute to the distinctive taste of a wine:

- Climate. Vineyards are best cultivated in temperate climates of moderately cold, rainy winters and fairly long, hot summers (Figure 4.5.3). Hot, sunny weather is necessary in the summer for the fruit to mature properly, whereas winter is the preferred season for rain. Dry summers are preferred, because plant diseases that cause the fruit to rot would be more active if summers were humid.

- Landforms. Vineyards are planted on hillsides, if possible, to maximize exposure to sunlight and to facilitate drainage. A site near a lake or river is also desirable because water can moderate extremes of temperature (Figure 4.5.4).

- Soil. Grapes can be grown in a variety of soils, but the best wine tends to be produced from grapes grown in soil that is coarse and well drained—a soil not necessarily fertile for other crops. For example, in France, the soil is generally sandy and gravelly in the Burgundy wine region, chalky in Champagne country, and of a slate composition in the Moselle Valley.

The distinctive character of each region's wine is especially influenced by the unique combination of trace elements, such as boron, manganese, and zinc, in the rock or soil. In large quantities these elements could destroy the plants, but in small quantities they lend a unique taste to the grapes.

▼ 4.5.3 **WINE PRODUCTION**

Metric tons
- 500,000 and above
- 100,000–499,999
- 10,000–99,999
- below 10,000

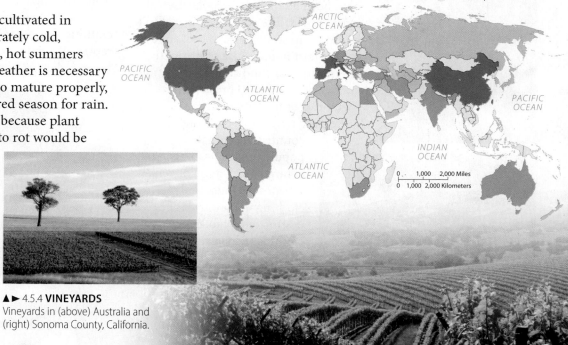

▲ ▶ 4.5.4 **VINEYARDS**
Vineyards in (above) Australia and (right) Sonoma County, California.

4.6 Folk and Popular Clothing Preferences

▶ **People adopt folk clothing customs in part because of environmental conditions.**
▶ **Some popular clothing preferences have been adopted by people around the world.**

Features of the landscape have traditionally played a central role in the provision of food, clothing, and shelter in folk culture. On the other hand, individual food, clothing, and shelter preferences reveal how popular culture can be distributed across the landscape with little regard for distinctive physical features.

FOLK CLOTHING TRADITIONS

People living in folk cultures have traditionally worn clothing in part in response to distinctive agricultural practices and climatic conditions (Figure 4.6.1). In arctic climates, fur-lined boots protect against the cold, and snowshoes permit walking on soft, deep snow without sinking in. People living in warm and humid climates may not need any footwear if heavy rainfall and time spent in water discourage such use.

Increased travel and the diffusion of media have exposed North Americans and Europeans to other forms of dress, just as people in other parts of the world have come into contact with Western dress. The poncho from South America, the dashiki of the Yoruba people of Nigeria, and the Aleut parka have been adopted by people elsewhere in the world. The continued use of folk costumes in some parts of the globe may persist not because of distinctive environmental conditions or traditional cultural values but to preserve past memories or to attract tourists.

Wearing traditional clothing in countries dominated by popular culture can be controversial, and conversely so can wearing popular clothing in countries dominated by folk-style clothing. Especially

difficult has been coexistence of loose-fitting combination body covering, head covering, and veil traditionally worn by women in Southwest Asia and North Africa, with casual Western-style popular women's clothing, such as open-necked blouses, tight-fitting slacks, and revealing skirts.

The loose-fitting combination garment, known by a variety of names, including burqa and chador, is typically worn by women following traditional folk customs in Southwest Asia and North Africa. Women in these countries are discouraged from adopting Western-style blouses, skirts, and slacks. Meanwhile, men in the region may prefer to wear Western-style suits, especially if they occupy positions of leadership in business or government.

On the other hand, European countries, including France and Belgium, prohibit women from wearing the burqa in public. Some leaders in these countries have argued that traditional clothing that completely hides the face and body represents unacceptable treatment of women as second-class citizens (Figure 4.6.2).

▲ 4.6.1 **FOLK CLOTHING TRADITIONS**
(top) Israel, (middle) Kenya, (above) Peru.

▶ 4.6.2 **CONTROVERSIAL FOLK CLOTHING**
France banned women from wearing the burqa. This woman attracted news media attention because she was wearing a burqa in France before the ban went into effect in 2011.

CLOTHING OF POPULAR CULTURE

In popular culture, clothing preferences generally reflect occupations rather than particular environments. A lawyer in Michigan is more likely to dress like a lawyer in New York than like a factory worker in Michigan. Wealth also influences popular clothing preferences. For social purposes, people with sufficient income may update their wardrobe frequently with the latest fashions.

Improved communications have permitted the rapid diffusion of popular clothing styles from one region of Earth to another. Original designs for women's dresses, created in Paris, Milan, London, or New York, are reproduced in large quantities at factories in Asia and sold for relatively low prices in North American and European chain stores. Speed is essential in manufacturing copies of designer dresses because fashion tastes change quickly.

An important symbol of the diffusion of Western popular culture is jeans, which became a prized possession for young people throughout the world (Figure 4.6.3). In the late 1960s, jeans acquired an image of youthful independence in the United States as young people adopted a style of clothing previously associated with low-status manual laborers and farmers.

Locally made denim trousers are available throughout Europe and Asia for under $10, but "genuine" jeans made by Levi Strauss, priced at $50 to $100, are preferred as a status symbol. Millions of second-hand Levi's are sold each year in Asia, especially in Japan and Thailand, priced between $100 and $1,000.

Ironically, as access to Levi's increased around the world, American consumers turned away from the brand and towards other brands. Sales plummeted from $7 billion in 1996 to $4 billion in 2004, the year Levi's closed its last U.S. factory. To reclaim lost consumers in the United States, Levi's has tried to market jeans with electronic features and other tactics to access the premium jeans market.

► 4.6.3 **JEANS**
(top) South Africa, (middle) Libya, (bottom) China.

4.7 Diffusion of Popular Media

▶ **TV diffused from the United States to other regions during the twentieth century.**

▶ **The distribution of the Internet and Facebook has followed the earlier pattern of TV.**

Media are means of mass communication. The viewing of media is an especially significant element of popular culture for two reasons.

- Viewing of media is the most popular leisure activity in much of the world.
- Viewing of media is the most important mechanism by which knowledge of popular culture is transmitted.

During the twentieth century, broadcast media were especially influential, first radio and then TV. Into the twenty-first century, electronic media have grown rapidly in importance.

DIFFUSION OF TV

The U.S. public first saw television in the 1930s, but its diffusion was blocked for a number of years when broadcasting was curtailed or suspended entirely during World War II. With the end of World War II, the number of television sets increased rapidly in the United States, from 10,000 in 1945 to 1 million in 1949, 10 million in 1951, and 50 million in 1959.

In 1954, the first year that the United Nations published data on the subject, the United States had 86 percent of the world's 37 million TV sets, the United Kingdom 9 percent, and the Soviet Union and Canada 2 percent each. The United States had approximately 200 TV sets per 1,000 inhabitants in 1954, and the rest of the world had approximately 2 per 1,000 (Figure 4.7.1).

In 1970, the United States still had far more TV sets per capita than any other country except Canada. However, rapid growth of ownership in Europe meant that the share of the world's sets in the United States had declined to one-fourth. Still, in 1970, half of the countries in the world, including most of those in Africa and Asia, had little if any TV broadcasting.

In the twenty-first century, differences in TV ownership have diminished, although they have not disappeared altogether. Ownership rates have climbed especially sharply in Asia and Latin America.

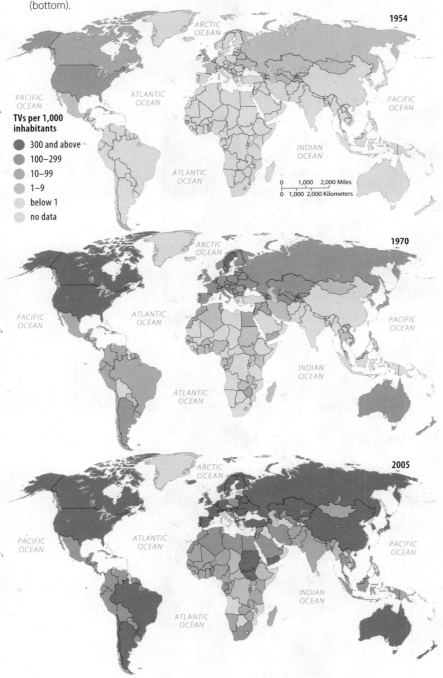

▼ 4.7.1 **DIFFUSION OF TV**
TVs per 1,000 inhabitants in 1954 (top), in 1970 (middle), and in 2005 (bottom).

TVs per 1,000 inhabitants
- 300 and above
- 100–299
- 10–99
- 1–9
- below 1
- no data

1954

1970

2005

DIFFUSION OF THE INTERNET

The diffusion of Internet service follows the pattern established by television a generation earlier, but at a more rapid pace (Figure 4.7.2). There were 40 million Internet users worldwide in 1995, including 25 million in the United States, and Internet service had not yet reached most countries (Figure 4.7.3).

Between 1995 and 2011, Internet usage increased rapidly in the United States, from 25 million to 239 million. But the increase was much greater in the rest of the world, from 40 million Internet users in 1995 to 2.2 billion in 2011. As Internet usage diffused rapidly, the U.S. share declined from 62 percent of the world total in 1995 to 10 percent in 2011.

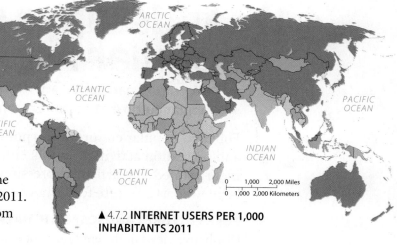

▲ 4.7.2 **INTERNET USERS PER 1,000 INHABITANTS 2011**

300 and above
100–299
10–99
1–9
below 1
no data

INTERNET HOSTS PER 1,000 POPULATION, 1995
100–299
10–99
1–9
Below 1

◄ 4.7.3 **DIFFUSION OF THE INTERNET:**
Compare the diffusion of the Internet: with the diffusion of TV and Facebook

Launch MapMaster World in Mastering**GEOGRAPHY**™

Select: *Diffusion of the Internet 1995* from the *Cultural menu.*

Then select: *Diffusion of the Internet 2000* from the *Cultural menu.*

Slide layer opacity for the map to 60%,

Check *300 and above* only.

1. **What countries achieved Internet usage of 300 hosts per 1,000 inhabitants between 1995 and 2000?**

2. **Does the speed of diffusion of the Internet appear to be more rapid or slower than TV? Than Facebook?**

DIFFUSION OF FACEBOOK

Facebook, founded in 2004 by Harvard University students, has begun to diffuse rapidly (Figure 4.7.4). As with the first few years of TV and the Internet, once again the United States at first had far more Facebook users than any other country. In 2008, four years after Facebook's founding, the United States had one-third of all users worldwide. As Facebook diffuses to other countries, the share of users in the United States has declined, to one-fifth of the worldwide total in 2011.

The diffusion of TV from the United States to the rest of the world took a half-century, whereas the diffusion of Facebook has taken only a few years. In the years ahead, Facebook is likely to either diffuse to other parts of the world, or it will be overtaken by other electronic social networking programs and be relegated to a footnote in the continuous repeating pattern of diffusing electronic communications. If Facebook does survive, the United States' share of total users will continue to decline, as people in other countries sign onto it.

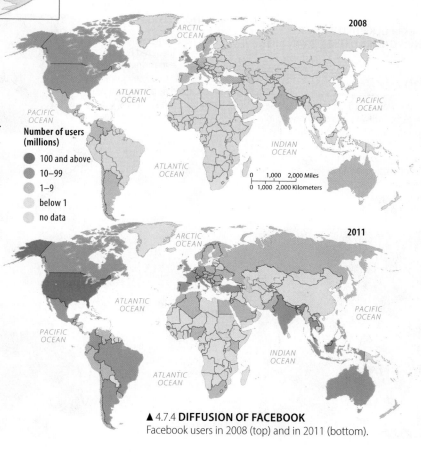

Number of users (millions)
100 and above
10–99
1–9
below 1
no data

2008

2011

▲ 4.7.4 **DIFFUSION OF FACEBOOK**
Facebook users in 2008 (top) and in 2011 (bottom).

4.8 Landscapes of Folk and Popular Art and Leisure

- **Folk culture can derive artistic meaning from the local environment.**
- **Popular culture can alter the landscape for leisure activities.**

Folk and popular cultures incorporate environmental features differently in their leisure and recreation activities. In folk culture distinctive local environmental features may be incorporated into artistic expression, whereas in popular culture the environment may be viewed as a feature to be modified.

FOLK CULTURE LANDSCAPES: HIMALAYAN ART

Distinctive views of the environment emerge among four neighboring folk culture groups in the Himalaya Mountains, according to geographers P. Karan and Cotton Mather (Figure 4.8.1). The study area was a narrow corridor of 2,500 kilometers (1,500 miles) in the Himalaya Mountains of Bhutan, Nepal, northern India, and southern Tibet (China).

Despite their spatial proximity, limited interaction among these groups produces distinctive folk customs. Through their choices of subjects of paintings, each group reveals how their folk culture mirrors their views of their environment.

The distribution of artistic subjects in the Himalayas shows how folk culture is influenced primarily by environmental processes such as climate, landforms, and vegetation, but also by cultural values such as religion. These groups also display similar uniqueness in their dance, music, architecture, and crafts. A group's unique folk culture develops through centuries of relative isolation from customs practiced by other cultural groups. As a result, the folk culture observed at a point in time can vary widely from one place to another, even among nearby places.

► 4.8.1 **FOLK CULTURE IN THE ENVIRONMENT: HIMALAYAN ART**

► **BUDDHIST**

To the north, folk art is inspired by idealized Buddhist figures, such as monks and saints. Some of these figures are depicted as bizarre or terrifying, perhaps reflecting the inhospitable environment.

▼ **ISLAMIC**

To the west, folk art is inspired by the area's beautiful plants and flowers. In contrast with the paintings from the Buddhist and Hindu regions, these paintings do not depict harsh climatic conditions. Animate objects are rarely depicted, because the practice is discouraged in Islam, the faith of most of the people in the area.

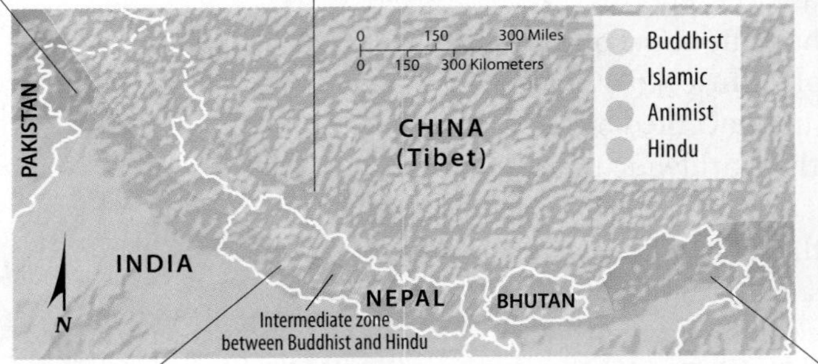
0
150
300 Miles
0
150
300 Kilometers
Buddhist
Islamic
Animist
Hindu
CHINA
(Tibet)
PAKISTAN
INDIA
N
NEPAL
BHUTAN
Intermediate zone
between Buddhist and Hindu

► **HINDU**

To the south, folk art is inspired by everyday life and familiar local scenes. Paintings sometimes portray a Hindu deity in a domestic scene and frequently represent the region's violent and extreme climatic conditions.

▲ **ANIMIST**

To the east, folk art is inspired by geometric designs and symbols that have meaning in the animist religions practiced by many of the people in the area. Local environment does not play an important role in the group's art, because many migrated from places further east, outside the study area.

POPULAR CULTURE LANDSCAPES: GOLF COURSES

Popular culture can significantly modify or control the environment. It may be imposed on the environment rather than spring forth from it, as with folk culture. In popular culture, the environment may be something to modify for a leisure activity or to promote for the sale of a product. Even if the resulting built environment looks "natural," it may actually be the deliberate creation of people in pursuit of popular social customs.

Golf courses, because of their large size (80 hectares, or 200 acres), provide a prominent example of imposing popular culture on the environment. A surge in popularity spawned construction of roughly 200 golf courses in the United States during the late twentieth century. Geographer John Rooney attributes this to increased income and leisure time, especially among recently retired older people and younger people with flexible working hours.

The provision of golf courses is not uniform across the United States. Although perceived as a warm-weather sport, the number of golf courses per person is actually greatest in the north (Figure 4.8.2). According to Rooney, people in the area have a long tradition of playing golf, and social clubs with golf courses are important institutions in the fabric of the area's popular culture.

The modern game originated as a folk custom in Scotland in the fifteenth century or earlier and diffused to other countries during the nineteenth century. In this respect, the history of golf is not unlike that of soccer described earlier in this chapter. Early Scottish golf courses were primarily laid out on sand dunes adjacent to bodies of water (Figure 4.8.3). Largely because of its origin as a local folk custom, golf courses in Scotland do not modify the environment to the same extent as those constructed in more recent years elsewhere in the world, where hills, sand, and grass are imported, often with little regard for local environmental conditions (Figure 4.8.4).

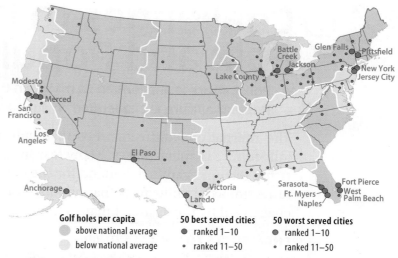

Golf holes per capita
- above national average
- below national average

50 best served cities
- ranked 1–10
- ranked 11–50

50 worst served cities
- ranked 1–10
- ranked 11–50

▲ 4.8.2 **POPULAR CULTURE IN THE ENVIRONMENT: GOLF COURSES**

▲ 4.8.3 **FOLK CULTURE OR POPULAR CULTURE? GOLF IN SCOTLAND**

Fly to: *16 Craigend Rd, Troon, Scotland,* to see one of Scotland's most famous golf courses, Royal Troon, founded in 1878.

Drag to enter street view at the square for 16 Craigend Rd.

Click Exit Street View and increase Eye alt to approximately 2,000 ft.

In what ways does this Scottish golf course appear different from typical ones in North America? Does the landscape appear more or less altered at Royal Troon than at golf courses in the United States?

If you would like to look at a U.S. golf course, fly to 8500 River Road, Bethesda, Maryland, to see the one at the Congressional Country Club.

▶ 4.8.4 **GOLF IN THE UNITED STATES**
Westin Mission Hills Resort and Spa in Rancho Mirage near Palm Springs, California.

4.9 Challenges to Landscapes of Folk and Popular Culture

▶ Folk culture is challenged to maintain traditional values.
▶ Popular culture is challenged to encourage local diversity.

The international diffusion of popular culture may threaten the survival of traditional folk culture in many places. Many fear the loss of folk culture, especially because rising incomes can fuel demand for the possessions typical of popular culture. At the same time, the uniformity that popular culture has imposed on the landscape is being challenged by the desire of many people to respect and embrace more local diversity.

CHALLENGES TO FOLK CULTURE

The survival of folk culture is threatened in two principal ways:

1. **Loss of traditional values.** When people turn from folk to popular culture, they may also turn away from the society's traditional values. Especially threatened is the subservient role of women to men in some, though not all, folk cultures. Women may have been traditionally relegated to performing household chores, such as cooking and cleaning, and to bearing and raising large numbers of children (Figure 4.9.1).

2. **Imposition of popular culture through diffusion of media.** Exposure to popular culture through the media may stimulate desire to embrace popular culture. Most broadcasting, print, and electronic media emanate from countries where popular culture predominates. Media presents values and behaviors characteristic of popular culture, such as upward social mobility, relative freedom for women, glorification of youth, and stylized violence. A large percentage of the world's countries limit individual freedom to use the Internet, primarily through blocking web and social network sites (Figure 4.9.2).

▼ 4.9.1 **TRADITIONAL FOLK CLOTHING JAPAN**
Most Japanese wear clothing from popular culture, such as jeans and T-shirts. Traditional clothing is reserved mainly for ceremonies and special occasions.

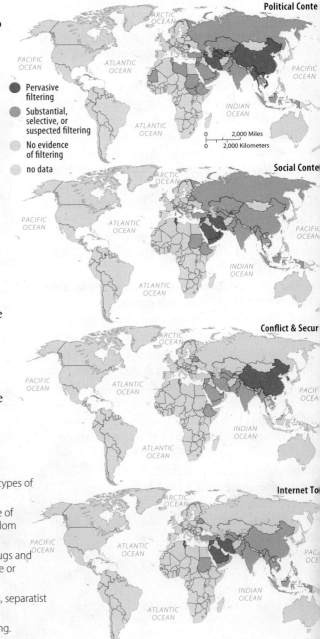

Political Conte

PACIFIC OCEAN   ARCTIC OCEAN   ATLANTIC OCEAN   PACIFIC OCEAN

INDIAN OCEAN

ATLANTIC OCEAN

● Pervasive filtering
● Substantial, selective, or suspected filtering
○ No evidence of filtering
○ no data

0   2,000 Miles
0   2,000 Kilometers

Social Conte

Conflict & Secur

Internet To

▶ 4.9.2 **LIMITING FREEDOM ON THE INTERNET**
According to OpenNet Initiative, countries limit access to four types of Internet content:

a) Political content that expresses views in opposition to those of the current government, or is related to human rights, freedom of expression, minority rights, and religious movements.

b) Social content related to sexuality, gambling, and illegal drugs and alcohol, as well as other topics that may be socially sensitive or perceived as offensive.

c) Security content related to armed conflicts, border disputes, separatist movements, and militant groups.

d) Internet tools, such as e-mail, Internet hosting, and searching.

▲ 4.9.3 **UNIFORM LANDSCAPE**
A British company emulates American-style fried chicken restaurants, including this one in Swindon, England.

CHALLENGES TO POPULAR CULTURE

The diffusion of popular culture around the world tends to produce more uniform landscapes. The spatial expression of a popular custom in one location will be similar to another. In fact, promoters of popular culture want a uniform appearance to generate product recognition and greater consumption.

Uniformity: Fast Food

The diffusion of fast-food restaurants is a good example of such uniformity. Such restaurants are usually organized as franchises (Figure 4.9.3). The franchise agreement lets the local outlet use the company's name, symbols, trademarks, methods, and architectural styles. To both local residents and travelers, the building and sign are immediately recognizable as part of a national or multinational company.

Uniformity: Gas, Food, and Lodging

Uniformity in the appearance of the landscape is promoted in North America by gas stations, supermarkets, and motels, among other buildings (Figure 4.9.4). These structures are designed so that both local residents and visitors immediately recognize the purpose of the building, even if not the name of the company. American motels and fast-food chains have diffused to other countries. These establishments appeal to North American travelers, yet most customers are local residents who wish to sample American customs they have seen on TV or the Internet.

Diffusion in the Global Marketplace

With faster communications and transportation, customs from any place on Earth can rapidly diffuse elsewhere. Japanese vehicles and electronics, for example, have diffused in recent years to the rest of the world, including North America. Until the 1970s, vehicles produced in North America, Europe, and Japan differed substantially in appearance and size, but in recent years styling has become more uniform, largely because of consumer preference around the world for Japanese vehicles. Carmakers such as General Motors, Ford, Toyota, and Honda now manufacture similar models in North and South America, Europe, and Asia, instead of separately designed models for each continent.

Local Cultures and Globalization

Though globalization has produced a uniform landscape of popular culture, diverse customs survive even in places dominated by popular culture. Even McDonald's, which has come to symbolize uniform popular culture in food service, has increased its recognition of diverse food preferences. The company offers the McMollete in Mexico (English muffin topped with beans, cheese, and salsa) and the McArabia in the Middle East (meat on a pita). In India, where most people are Hindus and avoid consumption of beef, McDonald's serves the McVeggie (rice, bean, and vegetables). The company's "We Buy Local" advertisement campaign has highlighted local sources of produce, such as eggs in Michigan and potatoes in Washington State (Figure 4.9.5).

◀ 4.9.4 **UNIFORM LANDSCAPE**
Billboard jungle along Route 66.

▼ 4.9.5 **ADVERTISING LOCALLY GROWN**
McDonald's, Seattle.

Material culture can be divided into two types—folk and popular. Folk culture is especially interesting to geographers, because it provides a unique identity to each group of people who occupy a specific region of Earth's surface. Popular culture is important, too, because it derives from the high levels of material wealth characteristic of societies that are economically developed. As societies seek to improve their economic level, they may abandon traditional folk culture and embrace popular culture.

Key Questions

How are folk and popular culture distributed?

▶ Differences between folk culture and popular culture can be seen in distinctive forms of leisure.

▶ Folk culture is more likely to have an anonymous origin and to diffuse slowly through migration.

▶ Popular culture is more likely to be invented and diffused rapidly with the use of modern communications.

How are needs of daily life met in folk and popular culture?

▶ Differences between folk and popular culture can be seen in provision of daily necessities, such as food, clothing, and shelter.

▶ Unique regions of folk customs arise because of lack of interaction among groups, even those living nearby.

▶ Popular culture diffuses rapidly; differences in popular culture are more likely to be observed in one place at different points in time than among different places at one point in time.

How is the landscape altered by folk and popular culture?

▶ Rapid diffusion of popular culture has been facilitated by modern communications, especially TV in the twentieth century and the Internet in the twenty-first century.

▶ Folk culture responds to local environmental conditions, whereas popular culture is more likely to alter the landscape.

▶ The diffusion of popular culture can produce uniform landscapes and loss of distinctive local folk customs.

Thinking Geographically

The Amish struggle to maintain their folk culture in the midst of popular culture.

1. **Can you give other examples of groups, or isolated individuals, who continue to practice folk culture in a country dominated by popular culture, such as the United States?**

Reality TV shows are often set in specific places (4.CR.1).

2. **What sorts of folk and popular customs are depicted in reality shows? Are these cultural depictions accurate reflections of the place?**

Tourist information is designed to encourage people to visit a particular place.

3. **What images of folk and popular culture do countries depict in campaigns to promote tourism? To what extent do these images accurately reflect the countries' culture?**

Key Terms

Culture
The body of customary beliefs, social forms, and material traits that together constitute a group of people's distinct tradition.

Custom
The frequent repetition of an act, to the extent that it becomes characteristic of the group of people performing the act.

Folk culture
Culture traditionally practiced by a small, homogeneous, rural group living in relative isolation from other groups.

Habit
A repetitive act performed by a particular individual.

Popular culture
Culture found in a large, heterogeneous society that shares certain habits despite differences in other personal characteristics.

Taboo
A restriction on behavior imposed by social custom.

Terroir
The contribution of a location's distinctive physical features to the way food tastes.

▼ 4.CR.1 *SURVIVOR:* SEASON 3
Shaba National Reserve, Kenya.

On the Internet

Up-do-date information on country-by-country usages of the Internet and Facebook can be found at **www.internetworldstats.com**, or scan the QR at the beginning of the chapter.

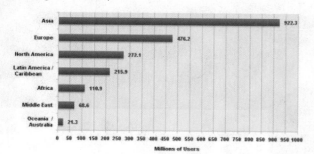

OpenNet Initiative monitors filtering, surveillance, and other activities by countries in order to limit their citizens' access to the Internet and other electronic media. Maps and findings are posted at **opennet.net**.

The Atlas of Cyberspaces (**www.cybergeography.org**) contains "maps" that are actually diagrams or graphic representations, such as frequency of visits to web sites or chat rooms, as well as other versions of the popular music "map" in section 4.1. The site has not been updated since 2007, but still has fun stuff.

Interactive Mapping

MOBILE PHONES IN AFRICA

Mobile phones have become common in sub-Saharan Africa, but their use is far from universal.

Open MapMaster Sub-Saharan Africa in in

Select: *Political,* then *Countries*

Select: *Economic,* then *Mobile Phone Network*

Select: *Population,* then *Population Density*

1. **What densely populated country has a well-developed mobile phone network? What densely populated country lacks such a network?**

2. **How do you think daily life would be different in te country that lacks a widespread phone network?**

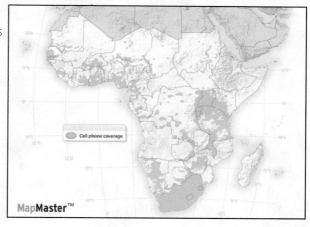

Explore

BEIJING OLYMPIC VILLAGE

Large-scale sports facilities are an aspect of global popular culture that have transformed the landscape of cities around the world. An especially prominent example is cities that host the Olympic Games, such as Bejing, China, in 2008.

Fly to: *National Stadium of China, Beijing, China*

To see facilities built for the Beijing Olympics, select 3-D Buildings from the Layers menu and drag the Street View icon to the road west of the stadium.

Deselect 3-D Buildings and exit Street View. Zoom out until the entire Olympic zone is visible.

Select: *Show Historical Imagery*

Move the date to 8/17/2005. Then click ahead to the present.

1. **How has the land been transformed since 2005?**

2. **How many years before the Olympics were held in 2008 did the transformation of the land begin?**

▶ LOOKING AHEAD

This chapter has displayed one of the key elements of cultural diversity among the world's peoples. The next chapter looks at a second key feature, language.

How many languages do you speak? If you are Dutch, you were required to learn at least two foreign languages in high school. For those of you who do not happen to be Dutch, the number is probably a bit lower.

In fact, most people in the United States know only English. Fewer than one-half of American high school students have studied a foreign language. In contrast, nearly two-thirds of graduates from Dutch high schools have learned at least three foreign languages.

Earth's collection of languages is one of the most obvious examples of cultural diversity. Language is like luggage: People carry it with them when they move from place to place. They incorporate new words into their own language when they reach new places, and they contribute words brought with them to the existing language at the new location. Thus, the geography of language follows logically from a study of migration and culture.

How are languages classified?

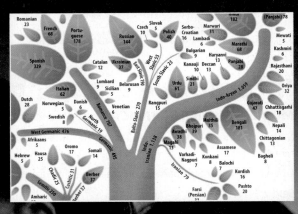

5.1 **Classifying Languages**

5.2 **Distribution of Languages**

5.3 **Indo-European Languages**

SPEECH AND HEARING IMPAIRED STUDENTS USE SIGN LANGUAGE TO ANSWER THEIR TEACHER'S QUESTION AT XA DAN SCHOOL, HANOI, VIETNAM

How are languages distributed?

How do languages share space?

5.1 Classifying Languages

▶ **The world's 6,000-plus languages can be classified into families, branches, and groups.**

▶ **Only around 100 of these languages are used by more than 5 million people.**

Language is a system of communication through speech. It is a collection of sounds that a group of people understands to have the same meaning. An **official language** is one that is used by the government for conducting business and publishing documents. Many languages also have a **literary tradition**, or a system of written communication. Approximately 85 languages are spoken by at least 10 million people, and approximately 300 languages by between 1 million and 10 million people.

The world's languages can be organized into families, branches, and groups:

- **Language family:** a collection of languages related through a common ancestral language that existed long before recorded history (Figure 5.1.1).

- **Language branch:** a collection of languages within a family related through a common ancestral language that existed several thousand years ago; differences are not as extensive or as old as between language families, and archaeological evidence can confirm that the branches derived from the same family.

- **Language group:** a collection of languages within a branch that share a common origin in the relatively recent past and display many similarities in grammar and vocabulary.

Figure 5.1.2 attempts to depict relationships among language families, branches, and groups:

- Language families form the trunks of the trees.

- Some trunks divide into several branches, which logically represent language branches, as well as groups.

- Individual languages are displayed as leaves.

The larger the trunks and leaves are, the greater the number of speakers of those families and languages.

Numbers on the tree are in millions of **native speakers**. Native speakers are people for whom the language is their first language. The totals exclude those who use the languages as second languages.

Figure 5.1.2 displays each language family as a separate tree at ground level, because differences among families predate recorded history. Linguists speculate that language families were joined together as a handful of superfamilies tens of thousands of years ago. Superfamilies are shown as roots below the surface, because their existence is speculative.

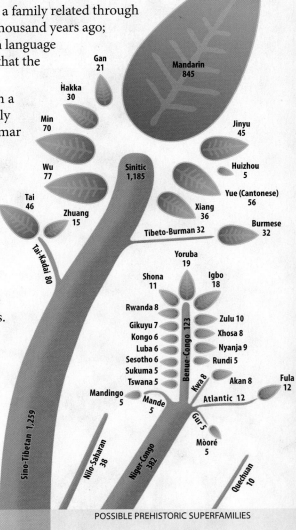

POSSIBLE PREHISTORIC SUPERFAMILIES

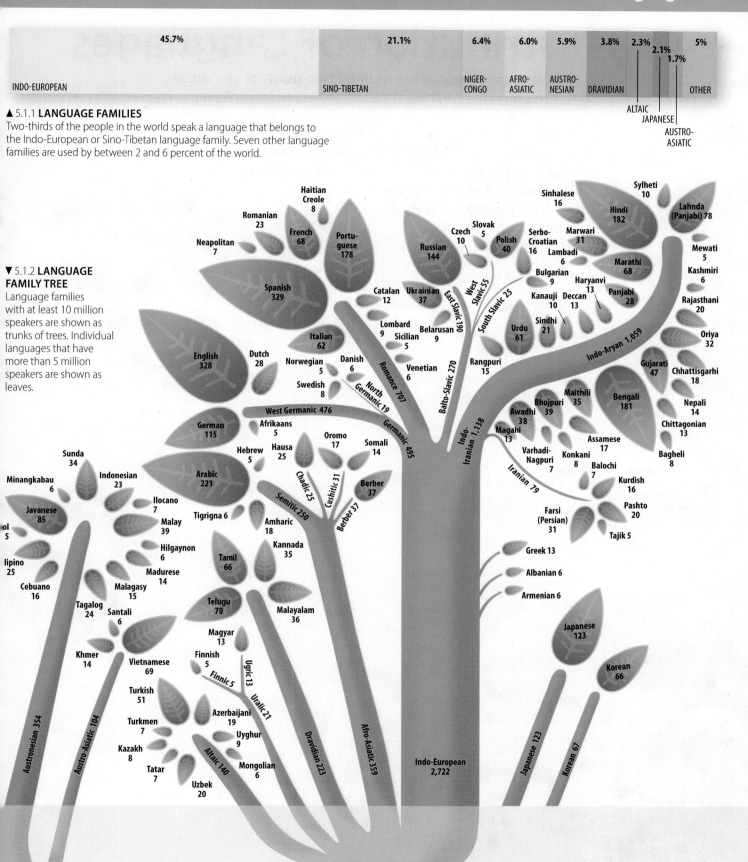

| INDO-EUROPEAN 45.7% | SINO-TIBETAN 21.1% | NIGER-CONGO 6.4% | AFRO-ASIATIC 6.0% | AUSTRO-NESIAN 5.9% | DRAVIDIAN 3.8% | ALTAIC 2.3% | JAPANESE 2.1% | AUSTRO-ASIATIC 1.7% | OTHER 5% |

▲ 5.1.1 **LANGUAGE FAMILIES**
Two-thirds of the people in the world speak a language that belongs to the Indo-European or Sino-Tibetan language family. Seven other language families are used by between 2 and 6 percent of the world.

▼ 5.1.2 **LANGUAGE FAMILY TREE**
Language families with at least 10 million speakers are shown as trunks of trees. Individual languages that have more than 5 million speakers are shown as leaves.

5.2 Distribution of Languages

▶ **Two language families are used by two-thirds of the world.**
▶ **Seven language families are used by most of the remainder.**

Language families with at least 10 million native speakers are shown on Figure 5.2.1. Paragraphs placed around Figure 5.2.1 identify the nine families with at least 100 million native speakers. The two language families with the most speakers are the Indo-European and the Sino-Tibetan (Figure 5.2.2).

▶ **5.2.1 LANGUAGE FAMILIES**
At least 10 million speakers

- Afro-Asiatic
- Altaic
- Austro-Asiatic
- Austronesian
- Dravidian
- Indo-European
- Japanese
- Korean
- Niger-Congo
- Nilo-Saharan
- Quechuan
- Sino-Tibetan
- Uralic
- Other
- Sparsely inhabited

SPANISH
Languages with more than 100 million speakers

French
Languages with 50–100 million speakers

▼ **5.2.2 TWO LARGEST LANGUAGE FAMILIES**
Hong Kong, China, has street signs in both Chinese (a Sino-Tibetan language) and in English (an Indo-European language). English is a legacy of the city's status as a colony of the United Kingdom until 1997.

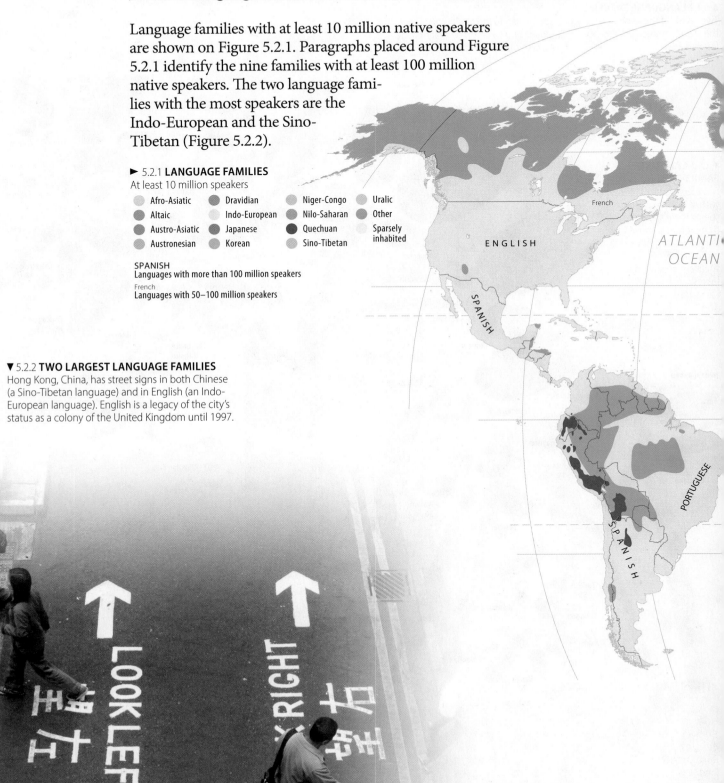

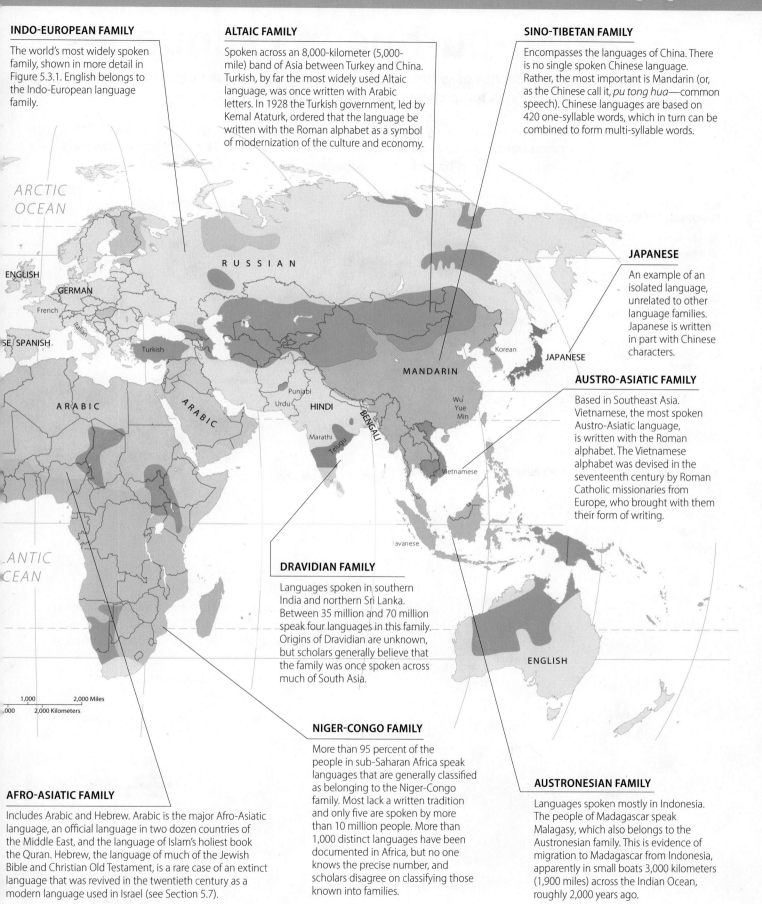

INDO-EUROPEAN FAMILY

The world's most widely spoken family, shown in more detail in Figure 5.3.1. English belongs to the Indo-European language family.

ALTAIC FAMILY

Spoken across an 8,000-kilometer (5,000-mile) band of Asia between Turkey and China. Turkish, by far the most widely used Altaic language, was once written with Arabic letters. In 1928 the Turkish government, led by Kemal Ataturk, ordered that the language be written with the Roman alphabet as a symbol of modernization of the culture and economy.

SINO-TIBETAN FAMILY

Encompasses the languages of China. There is no single spoken Chinese language. Rather, the most important is Mandarin (or, as the Chinese call it, *pu tong hua*—common speech). Chinese languages are based on 420 one-syllable words, which in turn can be combined to form multi-syllable words.

JAPANESE

An example of an isolated language, unrelated to other language families. Japanese is written in part with Chinese characters.

AUSTRO-ASIATIC FAMILY

Based in Southeast Asia. Vietnamese, the most spoken Austro-Asiatic language, is written with the Roman alphabet. The Vietnamese alphabet was devised in the seventeenth century by Roman Catholic missionaries from Europe, who brought with them their form of writing.

DRAVIDIAN FAMILY

Languages spoken in southern India and northern Sri Lanka. Between 35 million and 70 million speak four languages in this family. Origins of Dravidian are unknown, but scholars generally believe that the family was once spoken across much of South Asia.

AFRO-ASIATIC FAMILY

Includes Arabic and Hebrew. Arabic is the major Afro-Asiatic language, an official language in two dozen countries of the Middle East, and the language of Islam's holiest book the Quran. Hebrew, the language of much of the Jewish Bible and Christian Old Testament, is a rare case of an extinct language that was revived in the twentieth century as a modern language used in Israel (see Section 5.7).

NIGER-CONGO FAMILY

More than 95 percent of the people in sub-Saharan Africa speak languages that are generally classified as belonging to the Niger-Congo family. Most lack a written tradition and only five are spoken by more than 10 million people. More than 1,000 distinct languages have been documented in Africa, but no one knows the precise number, and scholars disagree on classifying those known into families.

AUSTRONESIAN FAMILY

Languages spoken mostly in Indonesia. The people of Madagascar speak Malagasy, which also belongs to the Austronesian family. This is evidence of migration to Madagascar from Indonesia, apparently in small boats 3,000 kilometers (1,900 miles) across the Indian Ocean, roughly 2,000 years ago.

Map labels: ARCTIC OCEAN, RUSSIAN, ENGLISH, GERMAN, French, Italian, SE SPANISH, Turkish, ARABIC, ARABIC, Punjabi, Urdu, HINDI, Marathi, Telugu, BENGALI, Korean, JAPANESE, MANDARIN, Wu, Yue, Min, Vietnamese, Javanese, ENGLISH, ATLANTIC OCEAN

Scale: 1,000 / 2,000 Miles; 1,000 / 2,000 Kilometers

5.3 Indo-European Languages

▶ **Four branches of Indo-European have relatively large numbers of speakers.**
▶ **Each branch has a distinctive spatial distribution.**

Indo-European is divided into eight branches (Figure 5.3.1). The four branches described below are spoken by large numbers of people. The four less extensively used Indo-European branches are Albanian, Armenian, Greek, and Celtic.

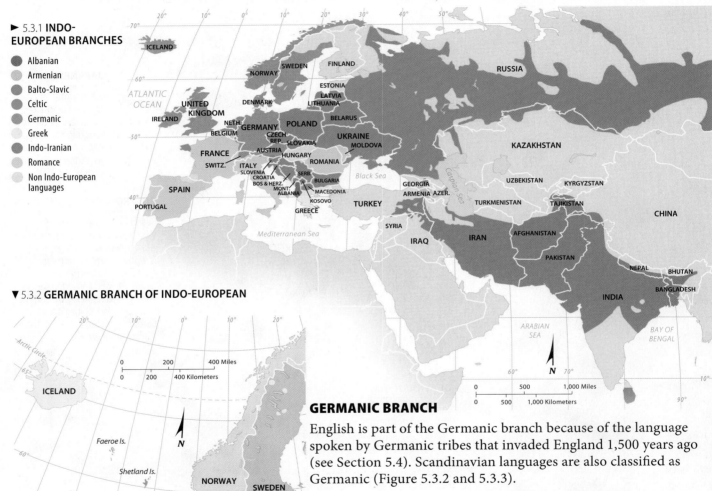

▶ **5.3.1 INDO-EUROPEAN BRANCHES**

- Albanian
- Armenian
- Balto-Slavic
- Celtic
- Germanic
- Greek
- Indo-Iranian
- Romance
- Non Indo-European languages

▼ **5.3.2 GERMANIC BRANCH OF INDO-EUROPEAN**

GERMANIC BRANCH

English is part of the Germanic branch because of the language spoken by Germanic tribes that invaded England 1,500 years ago (see Section 5.4). Scandinavian languages are also classified as Germanic (Figure 5.3.2 and 5.3.3).

▼ 5.3.3 **GERMANIC LANGUAGE GROUPS**
The Germanic branch of Indo-European is divided into the West Germanic group (including English) and the North Germanic group (including Icelandic, shown on the sign below).

North Germanic
- Danish
- Faeroese
- Icelandic
- Norwegian
- Swedish

West Germanic
- English
- Frisian
- German
- Netherlandish (Dutch)
- Mixed with non-Germanic

SLYSAHÆTTA
Heitir hverir undir yfirborði vatns
Böðun stranglega bönnuð

DANGER
Hot spots under water surface
Bathing strictly forbidden

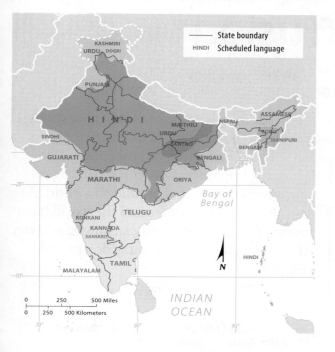

INDO-IRANIAN BRANCH

The branch of Indo-European with the most speakers, including the most widely used languages in South Asia, is Indo-Iranian (Figure 5.3.4). The official language of India is Hindi, which is an Indo-European language.

India also recognizes 22 so-called scheduled languages, including 15 Indo-European, four Dravidian, two Sino-Tibetan, and one Austro-Asiatic. The government of India is obligated to encourage the use of these languages.

Hindi is spoken many different ways—and therefore could be regarded as a collection of many individual languages. But there is only one official way to write Hindi. Pakistan's principal language Urdu is spoken much like Hindi but uses the Arabic alphabet. The two languages are sometimes considered a single one known as Hindustani.

Indo-European
● Hindi
● Other Indo-European language

Other language families
● Austro-Asiatic
Dravidian
● Sino-Tibetan

◄ 5.3.4 **LANGUAGES OF INDIA**

ROMANCE BRANCH

Romance languages evolved from Latin spoken by the Romans 2,000 years ago. As the conquering Roman armies occupied the provinces of their vast empire, they brought the Latin language with them.

Following the collapse of the Roman Empire in the fifth century, communication among the former provinces declined, creating regional

◄ 5.3.5 **ROMANCE BRANCH OF INDO-EUROPEAN**

● Portuguese
● Galician
● Spanish
● Catalán
● French/Langue d'oïl
● French/Langue d'òc (Occitan)
● Italian
● Piemontese
● Lombard
● Venetian
● Ligurian
● Napoletano-Calabrese
● Sicilian
● Sardinian
● Corsican
● Romansh
● Ladin
● Friulian
● Romanian
Not Romance languages

variations in spoken Latin. After several hundred years of isolation from each other, residents of various parts of the former empire spoke distinct languages, including Spanish, Portuguese, French, Italian, and Romanian (Figure 5.3.5). Spanish and Portuguese have achieved worldwide importance because of the colonial activities of their European speakers in Latin America.

BALTO-SLAVIC BRANCH

Balto-Slavic is the predominant branch in Russia and Central Europe (refer to Figure 5.3.1). Slavic was once a single language, but differences developed in the seventh century A.D. when several groups of Slavs migrated from Asia to different areas of Eastern Europe and thereafter lived in isolation from one other.

The most widely used Slavic language is Russian. The importance of Russian increased in the twentieth century with the Soviet Union's rise to power. Soviet officials forced native speakers of other languages to learn Russian as a way of fostering cultural unity among the country's diverse peoples. With the demise of the Soviet Union, the newly independent republics adopted official languages other than Russian.

5.4 Origin and Diffusion

▶ **Languages diffuse from their place of origin through migration.**
▶ **Dialects within languages also emerge through migration and isolation.**

A language originates at a particular place and traditionally diffuses to other locations through the migration of its speakers (Figure 5.4.1). The location of English-language speakers serves as a case study for understanding the process by which languages have been distributed around the world. A number of countries around the world have adopted English as an official language, even if most people in the country don't speak English.

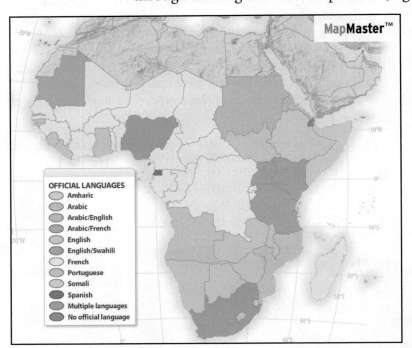

OFFICIAL LANGUAGES
- Amharic
- Arabic
- Arabic/English
- Arabic/French
- English
- English/Swahili
- French
- Portuguese
- Somali
- Spanish
- Multiple languages
- No official language

◀ 5.4.1 **OFFICIAL LANGUAGES IN SUB-SAHARAN AFRICA**
Open MapMaster Sub-Saharan Africa In

Mastering**GEOGRAPHY**

Select: *Cultural* then *Official Languages*
Select: *Geopolitical* then *European Colonization in 1923*
Select: *Political* then *Countries*

What are the English-speaking countries in sub-Saharan Africa, and what European country colonized each one?

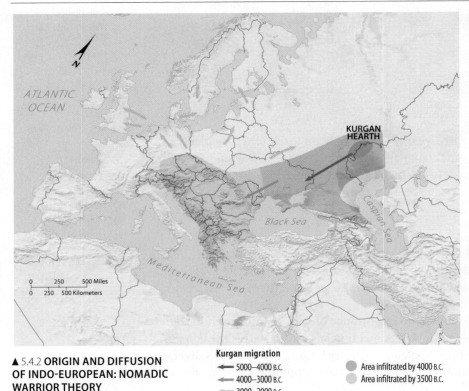

▲ 5.4.2 **ORIGIN AND DIFFUSION OF INDO-EUROPEAN: NOMADIC WARRIOR THEORY**

Kurgan migration
- ← 5000–4000 B.C.
- ← 4000–3000 B.C.
- ← 3000–2000 B.C.
- ● Area infiltrated by 4000 B.C.
- ● Area infiltrated by 3500 B.C.

ORIGIN AND DIFFUSION OF INDO-EUROPEAN: "WAR" HYPOTHESIS

The origin and early diffusion of language families predate recorded history. Linguists and anthropologists disagree on when and where Indo-European originated and the process and routes by which it diffused.

The first Indo-European speakers may have been the Kurgan people, who lived near the border of present-day Russia and Kazakhstan (Figure 5.4.2). The Kurgans were nomads, among the first to domesticate horses and cattle around 5,000 years ago. In search of grasslands for their animals, Kurgan warriors conquered much of Europe and South Asia, using their domesticated horses as weapons. According to an influential hypothesis by Marija Gimbutas, Indo-European language spread with the Kurgan migration.

Anatolian migration

← 6000–5000 B.C.

← 5000–4000 B.C.

← 4000–3000 B.C.

ORIGIN AND DIFFUSION OF INDO-EUROPEAN: "PEACE" HYPOTHESIS

Archaeologist Colin Renfrew argues that the first Indo-European speakers lived 2,000 years before the Kurgans, in eastern Anatolia, part of present-day Turkey (Figure 5.4.3). Renfrew believes that Indo-European migrated into Europe and South Asia along with agricultural practices rather than by military conquest. The language triumphed because its speakers became more numerous and prosperous by growing their own food instead of relying on hunting.

Regardless of how Indo-European diffused, communication was poor among the people, whether warriors or farmers. After many generations of complete isolation, these migrants evolved into speaking increasingly distinct branches, groups, and individual languages.

ORIGIN AND DIFFUSION OF ENGLISH

English is the language of England because of migration to Britain from various parts of Europe (Figure 5.4.4):

- **Celtic tribes around 2000 B.C.** The Celts spoke languages classified as Celtic. We know nothing of earlier languages spoken in Britain.

- **Angles, Saxons, and Jutes around A.D. 450.** These tribes from northern Germany and southern Denmark pushed the Celtic tribes to remote northern and western parts of Britain, including Cornwall and the highlands of Scotland and Wales. The name England comes from Angles' land, and English people are often called Anglo-Saxons.

- **Vikings between 787 and 1171.** Vikings from present-day Norway landed on the northeast coast of England and raided several settlements there. Although unable to conquer Britain, Vikings remaining in the country contributed words from their language.

- **The Normans in 1066.** The Normans, from present-day Normandy in France, conquered England in 1066 and established French as the official language for the next 300 years.

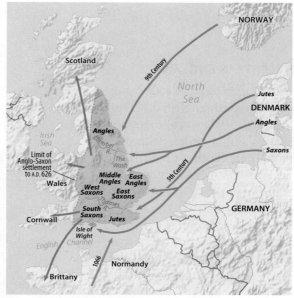

▲ 5.4.4 **INVASIONS OF ENGLAND**

The British Parliament enacted the Statute of Pleading in 1362 to change the official language of court business from French to English, though Parliament itself continued to conduct business in French until 1489.

5.5 Dialects

▶ Dialects are regional variations of languages.
▶ American and British dialects differ in vocabulary, spelling, and pronunciation.

A **dialect** is a regional variation of a language distinguished by distinctive vocabulary, spelling, and pronunciation. Generally, speakers of one dialect can understand speakers of another dialect. Geographers are especially interested in differences in dialects, because they reflect distinctive features of the environments in which groups live.

When speakers of a language migrate to other locations, various dialects of that language may develop. This was the case with the migration of English speakers to North America several hundred years ago. Because of its large number of speakers and widespread distribution, English has an especially large number of dialects.

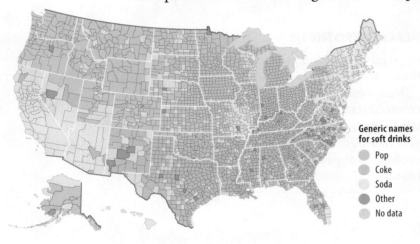

Generic names
for soft drinks

● Pop
● Coke
● Soda
● Other
● No data

ISOGLOSSES

The distribution of dialects is documented through the study of particular words. Every word that is not used nationally has some geographic extent within the country and therefore has boundaries. A word-usage boundary, known as an **isogloss** can be constructed for each word. Isoglosses are determined by collecting data directly from people, who are shown pictures to identify an object, such as a soft drink can (Figure 5.5.1).

◀ 5.5.1 **SOFT-DRINK DIALECTS IN THE UNITED STATES**
The most commonly used word for a soft drink—pop, Coke, or soda—varies by region within the United States.

DIALECTS IN ENGLAND

North Americans are well aware that they speak English differently than the British, not to mention people living in India, Pakistan, Australia, and other English-speaking countries. Further, English varies by regions within individual countries. In both the United States and England, northerners sound different from southerners.

Dialects in England can be grouped into three main ones—Northern, Midland, and Southern. The division originated with the invading Germanic tribes who settled in different parts of England. The language each spoke was the basis of distinct regional dialects (Figure 5.5.2).

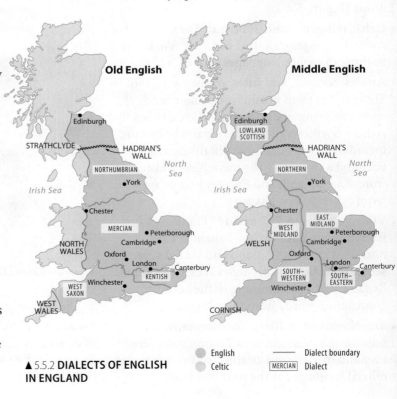

▲ 5.5.2 **DIALECTS OF ENGLISH IN ENGLAND**

● English
● Celtic

—— Dialect boundary
MERCIAN Dialect

DIFFERENCES BETWEEN BRITISH AND AMERICAN ENGLISH

The English language was brought to the North American continent by colonists from England who settled along the Atlantic Coast beginning in the seventeenth century. The early colonists naturally spoke the language used in England at the time and established seventeenth-century English as the dominant form of European speech in colonial America.

Why is the English language in the United States so different now from that in England? As is so often the case with languages, the answer is isolation.

Separated by the Atlantic Ocean, English in the United States and England evolved independently during the eighteenth and nineteenth centuries, with little influence on one another. Few residents of one country could visit the other, and the means to transmit the human voice over long distances would not become available until the twentieth century.

U.S. English differs from that of England in three significant ways:

- **Vocabulary**. The vocabulary is different in part because settlers in America encountered unfamiliar things, such as canyons and moose. In the nineteenth century, Americans and British applied different words to inventions, such as elevator (lift in England) and flashlight (torch in England [Figure 5.5.3]).

- **Spelling**. American spelling diverged from the British standard because of a strong national feeling in the United States for an independent identity. Noah Webster, the creator of the first comprehensive American dictionary and grammar books, either ignored or was unaware of recently created rules of grammar and spelling developed in England.

- **Pronunciation**. From the time of their arrival in North America, colonists began to pronounce words differently from the British. Such divergence was to be expected when interaction between the two groups was largely through printed matter rather than direct speech.

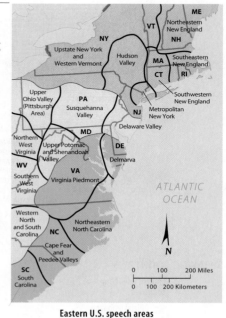

► 5.5.3 **AMERICAN AND BRITISH ENGLISH DIALECTS**
Differences in car and motoring words
(British words are listed first in CAPITAL letters)

PETROL Gas
LORRY Truck
SLEEPING POLICEMAN Speed Bump
CAR PARK Parking Lot
CAR JOURNEY Road Trip
ZEBRA CROSSING Crosswalk
MOTORWAY Freeway
SALOON Sedan
Petrol STATION Gas Station
BONNET Hood

WINDSCREEN Windshield
BOOT Trunk
REVERSING LIGHTS Back-up Lights
EXHAUST PIPE Tail Pipe
DUAL CARRIAGEWAY Divided Highway
NUMBER PLATE License Plate
FLYOVER Overpass
MULTI-STOREY CAR PARK Parking Garage

CAT'S EYE RAISED Pavement Marker
CARAVAN/CAMPERVAN RV
PAVEMENT Sidewalk
ESTATE CAR Station Wagon
MANUAL CAR Stickshift Car
GEAR STICK Stick
INDICATORS Turn Signal
TRAFFIC LIGHTS Stoplight
AMBER LIGHT (TRAFFIC LIGHTS) Yellow Light

DIALECTS IN THE UNITED STATES

Major differences in U.S. dialects originated because of differences in dialects among the original settlers (Figure 5.5.4). The settlements can be grouped into three areas:

- **Northern.** These colonies were established and inhabited almost entirely by settlers from England. Two-thirds of the New England colonists were Puritans from East Anglia in southeastern England, and only a few came from the north of England.

- **Southern.** About half came from southeast England, although they represented a diversity of social-class backgrounds, including deported prisoners, indentured servants, and political and religious refugees.

- **Midlands.** These immigrants were more diverse. The early settlers of Pennsylvania were predominantly Quakers from the north of England. Scots and Irish also went to Pennsylvania, as well as to New Jersey and Delaware. The Middle Atlantic colonies also attracted many German, Dutch, and Swedish immigrants who learned their English from the English-speaking settlers in the area.

The English dialects now spoken in the U.S. Southeast and New England are easily recognizable. Current distinctions result from the establishment of independent and isolated colonies in the seventeenth century. The dialect spoken in the Middle Atlantic colonies differ significantly from those spoken farther north and south, because most of the settlers came from the north rather than the south of England or from other countries.

Eastern U.S. speech areas
● Northern ○ Midlands ● Southern

▲ 5.5.4 **DIALECTS IN EASTERN UNITED STATES**

5.6 Global Dominance of English

▶ **English is the world's leading lingua franca.**

▶ **English is increasingly being combined with other languages.**

Increasingly in the modern world, the language of international communication is English. A Polish airline pilot who flies over France, for example, speaks to the traffic controller on the ground in English.

LINGUA FRANCA

A language of international communication, such as English, is known as a **lingua franca**. Other contemporary lingua franca languages include Swahili in East Africa, Hindi in South Asia, Indonesian in Southeast Asia, and Russian in the former Soviet Union. Some may speak a **pidgin language**, which mixes a simplified grammar and limited vocabulary of a lingua franca with another language.

In the past, a lingua franca achieved widespread distribution through relocation diffusion, in other words migration and conquest. The recent dominance of English is a result of expansion diffusion, the spread of a trait through the snowballing effect of an idea rather than through the relocation of people. Diffusion of English-language popular culture, as well as global communications such as TV

and the Internet, has made English increasingly familiar to speakers of other languages.

GLOBAL DISTRIBUTION OF ENGLISH

English is an official language in 55 countries, more than any other language, and is the predominant language in Australia, United Kingdom, and United States (Figure 5.6.1). Two billion people live in a country where English is an official language, even if they cannot speak it.

The contemporary distribution of English speakers around the world exists because the people of England migrated with their language when they established colonies during the past four centuries. English first diffused west from England to North American colonies in the seventeenth century. More recently, the United States has been responsible for diffusing English to other places.

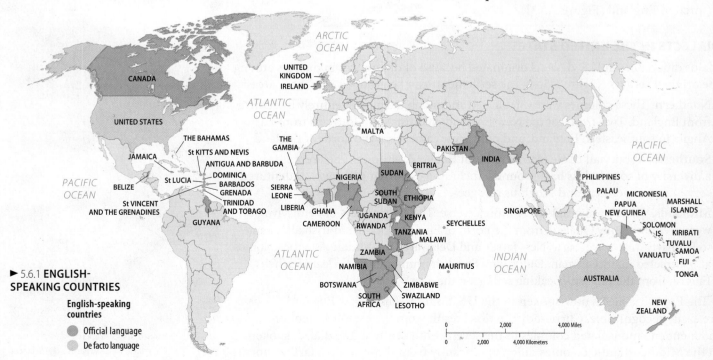

▶ 5.6.1 **ENGLISH-SPEAKING COUNTRIES**

English-speaking countries

● Official language

● De facto language

ENGLISH ON THE INTERNET

English has been the leading language of the Internet since its inception. During the 1990s, three-fourths of the people online and three-fourths of websites used English (Figure 5.6.2). In recent years, Chinese has been catching up to English and may become the leading language of online users by 2020 (Figure 5.6.3).

▲ 5.6.2 LANGUAGES OF ONLINE USERS
English is the most widely used language on the internet, but Chinese is growing more rapidly.

▼ 5.6.3 **INTERNET CAFE, CHINA**

Legend for chart:
- Chinese
- Japanese
- Korean
- Arabic
- Russian
- Portuguese
- French
- German
- Spanish
- English
- Other

5.7 Isolated, Endangered, and Extinct Languages

▶ **Many languages have become extinct.**
▶ **Some endangered languages are being preserved by governments.**

The distribution of a language is a measure of the fate of an ethnic group. A language may no longer be used, as its speakers adopt the language of a more dominant cultural group. Or a language may survive as its speakers live in relative isolation.

ISOLATED LANGUAGES

An **isolated language** is a language unrelated to any other and therefore not attached to any language family. The best example in Europe is Basque, spoken by 660,000 people in the Pyrenees Mountains of northern Spain and southwestern France (refer to Figure 5.3.5, the gray area in northern Spain).

Basque is apparently the only language currently spoken in Europe that survives from the period before the arrival of Indo-European speakers. No attempt to link Basque

to the common origin of the other European languages has been successful. Basque may have once been spoken over a wider area but was abandoned where its speakers came in contact with Indo-Europeans.

Basque's lack of connection to other languages reflects the isolation of the Basque people in their mountainous homeland (Figure 5.7.1). This isolation has helped them preserve their language in the face of the wide diffusion of Indo-European languages.

▼ 5.7.1 **ISOLATED LANGUAGE: BASQUE** The sign painted on the wall of a building in Bayonne, France, depicts the Basque flag and says in Basque "The people must live."

HERRIIK BIZI BEHAR

EXTINCT LANGUAGES

Thousands of languages are **extinct languages**, once in use—even in the recent past—but no longer spoken or read in daily activities by anyone in the world. *Ethnologue* lists 108 languages that went extinct as recently as the twentieth century and five in the first decade of the twenty-first century. For example, Aka-Bo, a language of the Andamanese family, once spoken in India's Andaman Islands, became extinct in 2010 with the death of its last known speaker.

Hebrew is a rare case of an extinct language that has been revived. A language of daily activity in biblical times, Hebrew diminished in use in the fourth century B.C. and was thereafter retained only for Jewish religious services. At the time of Jesus, people in present-day Israel generally spoke Aramaic, which in turn was replaced by Arabic.

When Israel was established as an independent country in 1948, Hebrew became one of the new country's two official languages, along with Arabic. Hebrew was chosen because the Jewish population of Israel consisted of refugees and migrants from many countries who spoke many languages. Because Hebrew was still used in Jewish prayers, no other language could so symbolically unify the disparate cultural groups in the new country (Figure 5.7.2).

▲ 5.7.2 **REVIVAL OF AN EXTINCT LANGUAGE: HEBREW** Grocery store, Jerusalem.

PRESERVING ENDANGERED LANGUAGES

Ethnologue considers approximately 500 languages in danger of becoming extinct, but some are being preserved. The European Union has established the European Bureau for Lesser Used Languages (EBLUL), based in Dublin, Ireland, to provide financial support for the preservation of endangered languages, including several belonging to the Celtic family (Figure 5.7.3):

- **Irish Gaelic.** An official language of the Republic of Ireland, along with English; Ireland's government requires publications be in Irish as well as English.

- **Scottish Gaelic.** Most speakers live in remote highlands and islands of northern Scotland.

- **Welsh.** In Wales, teaching Welsh in schools is compulsory, road signs are bilingual, Welsh-language coins circulate, and a television and radio station broadcast in Welsh.

- **Cornish.** Became extinct in 1777, with the death of the language's last known native speaker; a standard written form of Cornish was established in 2008.

- **Breton.** Concentrated in France's Brittany region; Breton differs from the other Celtic languages in that it has more French words.

The survival of any language depends on the political and military strength of its speakers. The Celtic languages declined because the Celts lost most of the territory they once controlled to speakers of other languages.

▼ 5.7.3 **ENDANGERED LANGUAGE: WELSH** Bilingual parking sign outside The Celtic Manor Resort, Newport, Wales, site of the 2010 Ryder Cup golf tournament.

5.8 French and Spanish in North America

▶ **French and Spanish are increasingly used in North America.**
▶ **Languages can mix to form new ones.**

North America is dominated by English speakers. Yet other languages, especially French in Canada and Spanish in the United States, are becoming increasingly prominent. At the same time, French, Spanish, English, and other languages are mixing to form new languages.

▲ 5.8.1 **FRENCH IN CANADA: "HELLO"**

FRENCH IN CANADA

French is one of Canada's two official languages, along with English (Figure 5.8.1). French speakers comprise one-fourth of the country's population. Most are clustered in Québec, where they comprise more than three-fourths of the province's speakers (Figure 5.8.2).

Until recently, Québec was one of Canada's poorest and least developed provinces. Its economic and political activities were dominated by an English-speaking minority, and the province suffered from cultural isolation and a lack of French-speaking leaders.

The Québec government has made the use of French mandatory in many daily activities. Québec's Commission de Toponyme is renaming towns, rivers, and mountains that have names with English-language origins. The word *Stop* has been replaced by *Arrêt* on the red octagonal road signs, even though *Stop* is used throughout the world, even in France and other French-speaking countries. French must be the predominant language on all commercial signs, and the legislature passed a law banning non-French outdoor signs altogether (later ruled unconstitutional by the Canadian Supreme Court).

Many Québécois favored total separation of the province from Canada as the only way to preserve their cultural heritage. Voters in Québec have thus far rejected separation from Canada, but by a slim majority. Alarmed at these pro-French policies, many English speakers and major corporations moved from Montréal, Québec's largest city, to English-speaking Toronto, Ontario.

Confrontation during the 1970s and 1980s has been replaced in Québec by increased cooperation between French and English speakers. Montréal's neighborhoods, once highly segregated between French-speaking residents on the east and English-speaking residents on the west, have become more linguistically mixed.

Although French dominates over English, Québec faces a fresh challenge of integrating a large number of immigrants from Europe, Asia, and Latin America who don't speak French. Many immigrants would prefer to use English rather than French as their lingua franca but are strongly discouraged from doing so by the Québec government.

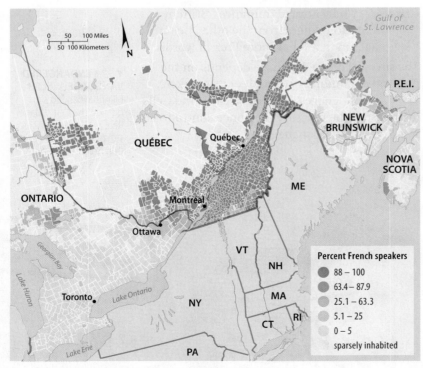

▲ 5.8.2 **FRENCH/ENGLISH LANGUAGE BOUNDARY IN CANADA**

Percent French speakers
- 88 – 100
- 63.4 – 87.9
- 25.1 – 63.3
- 5.1 – 25
- 0 – 5
- sparsely inhabited

SPANISH IN THE UNITED STATES

Spanish has become an increasingly important language in the United States because of large-scale immigration from Latin America, as discussed in Chapter 3 (Figure 5.8.3). In some communities, government documents and advertisements are printed in Spanish. Several hundred Spanish-language newspapers and radio and TV stations operate in the United States, especially in southern Florida, the Southwest, and large northern cities (Figure 5.8.4).

Linguistic unity is an apparent feature of the United States, a nation of immigrants who learn English to become U.S. citizens. However, the diversity of languages in the United States is greater than it first appears.

In 2008, a language other than English was spoken at home by 56 million Americans over age 5, 20 percent of the population. Spanish was spoken at home by 35 million people in the United States. More than 2 million spoke Chinese; at least 1 million each spoke French, German, Korean, Tagalog, and Vietnamese. In reaction against the increasing use of Spanish in the United States, 27 states and a number of localities have laws making English the official language.

Americans have debated whether schools should offer bilingual education. Some people want Spanish-speaking children to be educated in Spanish, because they think that children will learn more effectively if taught in their native

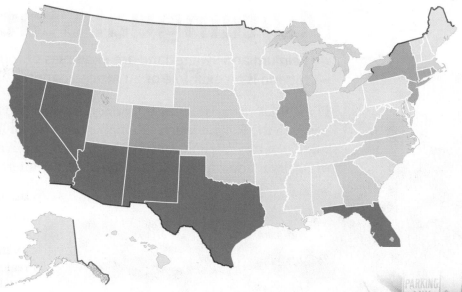

▲ 5.8.3 **DISTRIBUTION OF SPANISH BY U.S. STATES**

Percent of population that speak Spanish at home

- above 15.0
- 9.1 – 15.0
- 5.1 – 9.0
- 1.0 – 5.0

language and that this will also preserve their own cultural heritage. Others argue that learning in Spanish creates a handicap for people in the United States when they look for jobs, virtually all of which require knowledge of English.

Promoting the use of English symbolizes that language is the chief cultural bond in the United States in an otherwise heterogeneous society. With the growing dominance of the English language in the global economy and culture, knowledge of English is important for people around the world, not just inside the United States.

▲ 5.8.4 **SPANISH IN THE UNITED STATES** Little Havana, Miami, Florida.

CREOLIZED LANGUAGES

A **creole** or **creolized language** is defined as a language that results from the mixing of the colonizer's language with the indigenous language of the people being dominated (Figure 5.8.5). The word *creole* derives from a word in several Romance languages for a slave who is born in the master's house.

A creolized language forms when the colonized group adopts the language of the dominant group but makes some changes, such as simplifying the grammar and adding words from their former language. Creolized language examples include French Creole in Haiti, Papiamento (creolized Spanish) in Netherlands Antilles (West Indies), and Portuguese Creole in the Cape Verde Islands off the African coast.

English has diffused through integration of vocabulary with other languages. The widespread use of English in French is called **Franglais**, in Spanish **Spanglish**, and in German **Denglish**.

▼ 5.8.5 **BISLAMA, A CREOLE LANGUAGE OF VANUATU** Public health campaign warning sign about AIDS.

5.9 Multilingual States

▶ **Belgium and Switzerland are examples of multilingual states within Europe.**
▶ **Nigeria is an example of an African country with significant language diversity.**

Difficulties can arise at the boundary between two languages. Note that the boundary between the Romance and Germanic branches of Indo-European runs through the middle of two small European countries, Belgium and Switzerland. Belgium has had more difficulty than Switzerland in reconciling the interests of the different language speakers.

BELGIUM

Motorists in Belgium see the language diversity on expressways (Figure 5.9.1). Belgium's language boundary sharply divides the country into two regions. Southern Belgians (known as Walloons) speak French, whereas northern Belgians (known as Flemings) speak a dialect of the Germanic language of Dutch, called Flemish (Figure 5.9.2).

Antagonism between the Flemings and Walloons is aggravated by economic and political differences. Historically, the Walloons dominated Belgium's economy and politics, and French was the official state language. More recently, the Flemings have been better off economically.

In response to pressure from Flemish speakers, Belgium was divided into two independent regions, Flanders and Wallonia. Each elects an assembly that controls cultural affairs, public health, road construction, and urban development in its region.

▲ 5.9.1 **LANGUAGE DIVERSITY IN BELGIUM** Interchange sign in French (first) and Flemish.

◀ 5.9.2 **LANGUAGES IN BELGIUM**
French is the principal language in Wallonia and Flemish (a dialect of Dutch) in Flanders.

Ethnicities
- Flemings (speaking dialects)
- Walloons (speaking
- Germans
- Flemings and Wallo (legally bilingual)

Protected Minorities
- Walloons in Flande
- Flemings in Wallon
- Germans in Walloni

SWITZERLAND

Switzerland peacefully exists with multiple languages (Figure 5.9.3). The key is a decentralized government in which local authorities hold most of the power and decisions are frequently made by voter referenda. Switzerland has four official languages—German (used by 64 percent of the population), French (20 percent), Italian (7 percent), and Romansh (1 percent). Swiss voters made Romansh an official language in a 1978 referendum, despite the small percentage of people who use the language (Figure 5.9.4).

▼ 5.9.4 **LANGUAGES IN SWITZERLAND**

Languages
German   Italian
French   Romansh

▲ 5.9.3 **LANGUAGE DIVERSITY IN SWITZERLAND**
Switzerland has four official languages, shown on the sign above: German (top left), French (top right), Italian (lower left), and Romansh (lower right). The sign prevents hikers, vehicles, and horses from entering the forest because of timber cutting.

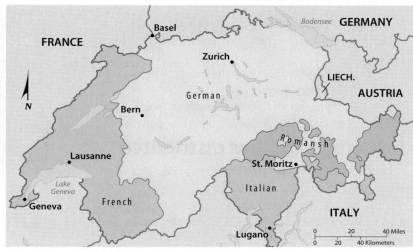

NIGERIA

Africa's most populous country, Nigeria, displays problems that can arise from the presence of many speakers of many languages. Nigeria has 527 distinct languages, according to *Ethnologue*, only three of which have widespread use—Hausa, Yoruba, and Igbo—each spoken by one-eighth of the population (Figure 5.9.5).

Groups living in different regions of Nigeria have often battled. The southern Igbos attempted to secede from Nigeria during the 1960s, and northerners have repeatedly claimed that the Yorubas discriminate against them. To reduce

▼ 5.9.5 **LANGUAGE DIVERSITY IN NIGERIA**
The Bible in Hausa.

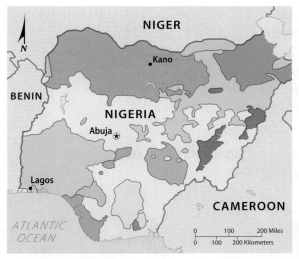

◄ 5.9.6 **LANGUAGES IN NIGERIA**
All languages with over 1 million speakers

Niger-Congo Family
Adamawa Fulfulde
Anaang
Ebira
Edo
Ibibio
Igbo
Izon
Nigerian Fulfulde
Tiv
Yoruba
other peoples

Afro-Asiatic Family
Hausa
other peoples

Nilo-Saharan Family
Kanuri
other peoples

these regional tensions, the government has moved the capital from Lagos in the Yoruba-dominated southwest to Abuja in the center of Nigeria (Figure 5.9.6).

Nigeria reflects the problems that can arise when great cultural diversity—and therefore language diversity—is packed into a relatively small region. Nigeria also illustrates the importance of language in identifying distinct cultural groups at a local scale. Speakers of one language are unlikely to understand any of the others in the same language family, let alone languages from other families.

In view of the global dominance of English, many U.S. citizens do not recognize the importance of learning other languages. One of the best ways to learn about people in other regions is to learn their language. The inability to speak other languages is a handicap for Americans who try to conduct international business.

Key Questions

How are languages classified?

▶ Languages can be classified into families, branches, and groups.

▶ The two language families with the most speakers are Indo-European and Sino-Tibetan.

▶ English is a language of the West Germanic group of the Germanic branch of the Indo-European language family.

How are languages distributed?

▶ Language families originated before recorded history, and they have diffused through migration.

▶ Through migration and conquest, some languages have become more widespread, whereas others have become less widely used.

▶ Many languages have become extinct and others are being rescued from extinction by government action.

How do languages share space?

▶ Though English dominates North America, French and Spanish have become more widely used.

▶ Some countries face conflicts among speakers of different languages, whereas other countries peacefully embrace language diversity.

▼ 5.CR.1 **DEMONSTRATION FOR INDEPENDENCE OF QUÉBEC**

Thinking Geographically

Twenty-seven U.S. states have passed laws mandating English as the language of all government functions.

1. **What are the benefits and the drawbacks for cultural integration and diversity resulting from this English-only mandate?**

Canada's French-speaking province of Québec has debated declaring independence from Canada (Figure 5.CR.1)

2. **What would be the impact of Québec's independence on the remainder of Canada, and on the United States?**

Wallonia (the southern portion of Belgium) suffers from higher rates of unemployment, industrial decline, and other poor economic conditions compared to Flanders.

3. **How do differences in language exacerbate Belgium's regional economic differences?**

On the Internet

Detailed information for every language of the world is provided at **www.ethnologue.com** or scan the QR on the first page of this chapter. Areas of greatest diversity of languages appear in red on *Ethnologue's* world map.

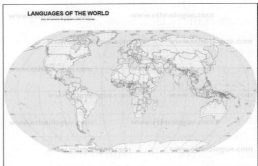

LANGUAGES OF THE WORLD

Interactive Mapping

LANGUAGE AND MIGRATION IN LATIN AMERICA

Launch Mapmaster Latin America in **Mastering**GEOGRAPHY

Select: *Cultural* then *Language*

Select: *Political* then *Countries*

Select: *Population* then *Major Migration Flows*

1. International migration flows to destinations outside Latin American (primarily to the United States) originate from speakers of which official language?

2. The speakers of which official languages show no evidence of any interregional or international migration?

Explore

SAN FRANCISCO, CA, USA

Use Google Earth to explore language diversity in the United States.

Fly to: *400 Grant Ave, San Francisco, CA, USA*

Drag to: *Enter Street View*

Use mouse to continue north along Grant Ave.

1. What languages other than English do you see on the business signs?

2. What name might be given to this section of San Francisco?

Key Terms

Creole or creolized language
A language that results from the mixing of a colonizer's language with the indigenous language of the people being dominated.

Denglish
Combination of German and English.

Dialect
A regional variety of a language distinguished by vocabulary, spelling, and pronunciation.

Extinct language
A language that was once used by people in daily activities but is no longer used.

Franglais
A term used by the French for English words that have entered the French language; a combination of *français* and *anglais* the French words for "French" and "English," respectively.

Isogloss
Geographical boundary of a language feature.

Isolated language
A language that is unrelated to any other languages and therefore not attached to any language family.

Language
A system of communication through the use of speech, a collection of sounds understood by a group of people to have the same meaning.

Language branch
A collection of languages related through a common ancestor that existed several thousand years ago. Differences are not as extensive or as old as with language families, and archaeological evidence can confirm that the branches derived from the same family.

Language family
A collection of languages related to each other through a common ancestor long before recorded history.

Language group
A collection of languages within a branch that share a common origin in the relatively recent past and display many similarities in grammar and vocabulary.

Lingua franca
A language mutually understood and commonly used in trade by people who have different native languages.

Literary tradition
A language that is written as well as spoken.

Native speakers
People for whom a particular language is their first language.

Official language
The language adopted for use by the government for the conduct of business and publication of documents.

Pidgin language
A language that mixes a simplified grammar and limited vocabulary of a lingua franca with another language.

Spanglish
Combination of Spanish and English, spoken by Hispanic Americans.

▶ LOOKING AHEAD

This chapter has displayed one of the key elements of cultural diversity among the world's peoples. The next chapter looks at a second key feature, religion.

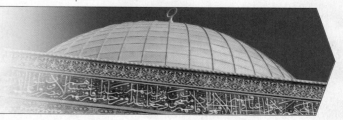

6 Religion

Religion interests geographers because it is essential for understanding how humans occupy Earth. People care deeply about their religion and draw from religion their core values and beliefs, an essential element of culture. Unfortunately, intense identification with one religion can lead adherents into conflict with followers of other religions.

Geographers, though, are not theologians, so they stay focused on those elements of religions that are geographically significant. Some religions are designed to appeal to people throughout the world, whereas other religions are designed to appeal primarily to people in geographically limited areas. Like language, migrants take their religion with them to new locations, but although migrants typically learn the language of the new location, they retain their religion.

Religious values are also important in understanding the meaningful ways that people organize the landscape. As a major facet of culture, religion leaves a strong imprint on the physical environment.

Where are religions distributed?

6.1 **Distribution of Religions**

6.2 **Geographic Branches of Religions**

6.3 **Diversity of Universalizing Religions**

6.4 **Origin of Religions**

6.5 **Diffusion of Universalizing Religions**

DOME OF THE ROCK,
JERUSALEM

How do religions shape landscapes?

Where are territorial conflicts between religions?

6.1 Distribution of Religions

▶ **Geographers distinguish between universalizing and ethnic religions.**

▶ **The two types of religions have different distributions.**

Geographers distinguish between two types of religions:

- A **universalizing religion** attempts to be global, to appeal to all people wherever they may live in the world.
- An **ethnic religion** appeals primarily to one group of people living in one place.

▶ 6.1.1 **ADHERENTS OF WORLD RELIGIONS**

Universalizing Religions
Christianity
- Roman Catholic 14.1%
- Protestant 5.8%
- Orthodox 3.2%
- Other Christian 7.5%
Islam
- Sunni 13.7%
- Shiite 1.7%
- Other Islam 6.4%
- Buddhism 5.5%
Ethnic Religions
- Hinduism 13.1%
- Chinese ethnic 5.7%
- African ethnic 5.9%
- Other religions 1.4%
- Nonreligious 16.0%

▶ 6.1.2 **DISTRIBUTION OF RELIGIONS**

Universalizing Religions

Christianity
- Roman Catholic
- Protestant
- Eastern Orthodox
- Other

Islam
- Sunni
- Shiite

Other Universalizing Religions
- Buddhism
- Sikhism

Ethnic Religions
- Hinduism
- Judaism
- African
- Mixed with universalizing

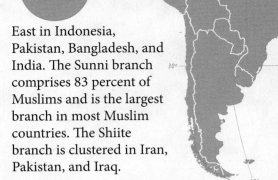

NORTH AMERICA
- 22% Catholic
- 3% Other religions
- 25% Nonreligious
- 2% Sunni Muslim
- 2% Jewish
- 28% Other Christian
- 18% Protestant

LATIN AMERICA
- 3% Nonreligious
- 4% Other religions
- 9% Protestant
- 84% Catholic

UNIVERSALIZING RELIGIONS

The three universalizing religions with the largest number of adherents are Christianity, Islam, and Buddhism (Figure 6.1.1). Each has a different distribution (Figure 6.1.2).

- **Christianity.** With more than 2 billion adherents, the predominant religion in North America, South America, Europe, and Australia (Figure 6.1.3). Within Europe, Roman Catholicism is the dominant Christian branch in the southwest and east, Protestantism in the northwest, and Eastern Orthodoxy in the east and southeast. In the Western Hemisphere, Roman Catholicism predominates in Latin America and Protestantism in North America.

- **Islam.** The religion of 1.3 billion people, and the predominant religion of the Middle East from North Africa to Central Asia (Figure 6.1.4). One-half of the world's Muslims (adherents of Islam) live outside the Middle East in Indonesia, Pakistan, Bangladesh, and India. The Sunni branch comprises 83 percent of Muslims and is the largest branch in most Muslim countries. The Shiite branch is clustered in Iran, Pakistan, and Iraq.

- **Buddhism.** With nearly 400 million adherents, mainly in China and Southeast Asia. Mahayanists account for about 56 percent of Buddhists, primarily in China, Japan, and Korea. Theravadists comprise about 38 percent of Buddhists, especially in Cambodia, Laos, Myanmar, Sri Lanka, and Thailand. The remaining 6 percent are Tantrayanists, found primarily in Tibet and Mongolia.

▲ 6.1.3 **CHRISTIANITY IN SWEDEN**

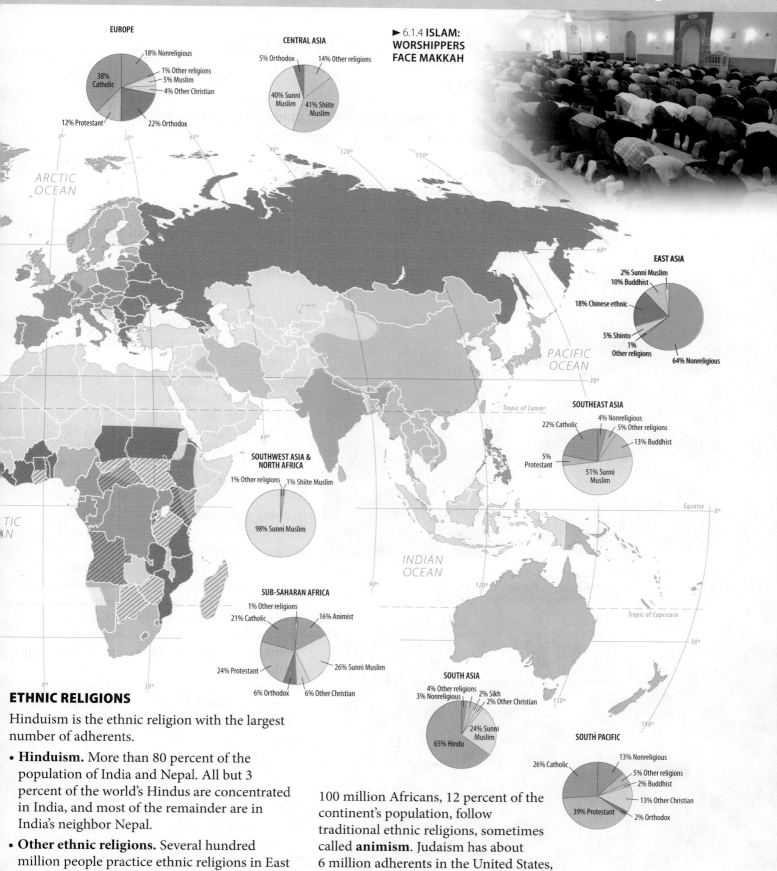

EUROPE
- 18% Nonreligious
- 1% Other religions
- 5% Muslim
- 4% Other Christian
- 38% Catholic
- 22% Orthodox
- 12% Protestant

CENTRAL ASIA
- 5% Orthodox
- 14% Other religions
- 40% Sunni Muslim
- 41% Shiite Muslim

► 6.1.4 **ISLAM: WORSHIPPERS FACE MAKKAH**

EAST ASIA
- 2% Sunni Muslim
- 10% Buddhist
- 18% Chinese ethnic
- 5% Shinto
- 1% Other religions
- 64% Nonreligious

SOUTHWEST ASIA & NORTH AFRICA
- 1% Other religions
- 1% Shiite Muslim
- 98% Sunni Muslim

SOUTHEAST ASIA
- 22% Catholic
- 4% Nonreligious
- 5% Other religions
- 13% Buddhist
- 5% Protestant
- 51% Sunni Muslim

SUB-SAHARAN AFRICA
- 1% Other religions
- 16% Animist
- 21% Catholic
- 26% Sunni Muslim
- 24% Protestant
- 6% Orthodox
- 6% Other Christian

SOUTH ASIA
- 4% Other religions
- 2% Sikh
- 3% Nonreligious
- 2% Other Christian
- 24% Sunni Muslim
- 65% Hindu

SOUTH PACIFIC
- 26% Catholic
- 13% Nonreligious
- 5% Other religions
- 2% Buddhist
- 13% Other Christian
- 39% Protestant
- 2% Orthodox

ETHNIC RELIGIONS

Hinduism is the ethnic religion with the largest number of adherents.

- **Hinduism.** More than 80 percent of the population of India and Nepal. All but 3 percent of the world's Hindus are concentrated in India, and most of the remainder are in India's neighbor Nepal.

- **Other ethnic religions.** Several hundred million people practice ethnic religions in East Asia, especially Confucianism and Daoism in China and Shintoism in Japan. Approximately 100 million Africans, 12 percent of the continent's population, follow traditional ethnic religions, sometimes called **animism**. Judaism has about 6 million adherents in the United States, 5 million in Israel, 2 million in Europe, and 1 million each in Asia and Latin America.

6.2 Geographic Branches of Religions

▶ **The three largest universalizing religions have different branches.**
▶ **Branches have distinctive regional distributions.**

Each of the three largest universalizing religions is subdivided into branches, denominations, and sects.

- A **branch** is a large and fundamental division within a religion.
- A **denomination** is a division of a branch that unites a number of local congregations in a single legal and administrative body.
- A **sect** is a relatively small group that has broken away from an established denomination.

▼ ▲ 6.2.1 **CHRISTIAN PLACES OF WORSHIP**
(top left) Protestant church in Edgartown, Massachusetts (top right) Roman Catholic Cathedral in Pisa, Italy. (below) Eastern Orthodox church in Gifhorn, Germany.

BRANCHES OF CHRISTIANITY

Christianity has three major branches (Figure 6.2.1):

- **Roman Catholicism.** "Catholic," from the Greek word for *universal*, was first applied to the Christian Church in the second century. The Roman Catholic Church is headed by the Pope, who is also the Bishop of Rome. Bishops are considered the successors to Jesus's twelve original Apostles. Roman Catholics believe that the Pope possesses a universal primacy or authority, and that the Church is infallible in resolving theological disputes.

- **Eastern Orthodoxy.** A collection of 14 self-governing churches derive from the faith and practices in the Eastern part of the Roman Empire. The split between the Roman and Eastern churches dates to the fifth century and became final in 1054. The Russian Orthodox Church has more than 40 percent of all Eastern Orthodox Christians, the Romanian Church 20 percent, the Bulgarian, Greek, and Serbian Orthodox churches approximately 10 percent each, and nine others the remaining 10 percent.

- **Protestantism.** The Protestant Reformation movement is regarded as beginning when Martin Luther posted 95 theses on the door of the church at Wittenberg on October 31, 1517. According to Luther, individuals had primary responsibility for achieving personal salvation through direct communication with God. Grace is achieved through faith rather than through sacraments performed by the Church.

▲ 6.2.2 **BUDDHIST MONKS**
(left) Theravada Buddhist at Tooth Temple in Kandy, Sri Lanka. (right) Mahayana Buddhist at Great Buddha statue in Kamakura, Japan.

BRANCHES OF BUDDHISM

The two largest branches of Buddhism are Theravada and Mahayana (Figure 6.2.2).

- **Theravada,** which means "the way of the elders," emphasizes Buddha's life of wisdom, self-help, and solitary introspection.
- **Mahayana** ("the bigger ferry" or "raft"), which split from Theravada Buddhism about 2,000 years ago, emphasizes Buddha's life of teaching, compassion, and helping others.

DEITIES IN HINDUISM

Hinduism does not have a central authority or a single holy book, so each individual selects suitable rituals (Figure 6.2.3). The average Hindu has allegiance to a particular god or concept within a broad range of possibilities:

- The manifestation of God with the largest number of adherents—an estimated 68 percent—is Vaishnavism, which worships the god Vishnu, a loving god incarnated as Krishna.
- An estimated 27 percent adhere to Sivaism, dedicated to Siva, a protective and destructive god.
- Shaktism is a form of worship dedicated to the female consorts of Vishnu and Siva.

Some geographic concentration of support for these deities exists: Siva and Shakti in the north, Shakti and Vishnu in the east, Vishnu in the west, Siva and some Vishnu in the south. However, holy places for Siva and Vishnu are dispersed throughout India.

► 6.2.3 **HINDUISM**
Bathing in the Ganges River at Varanasi, India.

BRANCHES OF ISLAM

The word *Islam* in Arabic means "submission to the will of God," and it has a similar root to the Arabic word for *peace*. An adherent of the religion of Islam is known as a Muslim, which in Arabic means "one who surrenders to God." Islam is divided into two important branches:

- **Sunni.** From the Arabic word for "orthodox," Sunnis comprise two-thirds of Muslims and are the largest branch in most Muslim countries in the Middle East and Asia.
- **Shiite.** From the Arabic word for "sectarian," Shiites (sometimes written *Shia*), comprise nearly 90 percent of the population in Iran and a substantial share in neighboring countries.

Differences between the two main branches go back to the earliest days of Islam and reflect disagreement over the line of succession in Islamic leadership after the Prophet Muhammad, who had no surviving son, nor a follower of comparable leadership ability (Figure 6.2.4).

◄ ▲ 6.2.4 **MUSLIM PLACES OF WORSHIP**
(above) Sunni mosque in Manama, Bahrain.
(left) Shiite mosque in Samarra, Iraq, which was destroyed in 2006.

6.3 Diversity of Universalizing Religions

▶ **Other universalizing religions include Sikhism and Bahá'í.**
▶ **The United States has strong regional differences in the distribution of religions.**

Christianity, Islam, and Buddhism are the three universalizing religions with the largest number of adherents, and Roman Catholicism, Protestantism, and Eastern Orthodoxy are the three largest branches within Christianity. Other universalizing religions and other Christian churches have flourished in addition to the largest ones.

OTHER UNIVERSALIZING RELIGIONS

Sikhism and Bahá'í are the two universalizing religions other than Christianity, Islam, and Buddhism with the largest numbers of adherents.

- **Sikhism.** God was revealed to Sikhism's first guru (religious teacher or enlightener) Nanak (1469–1538) as The One Supreme Being, or Creator, who rules the universe by divine will. Sikhism's most important ceremony, introduced by the tenth guru, Gobind Singh (1666–1708), is the Amrit (or Baptism), in which Sikhs declare they will uphold the principles of the faith. Gobind Singh also introduced the practice of men wearing turbans on their heads and never cutting their beards or hair. Wearing a uniform gave Sikhs a disciplined outlook and a sense of unity of purpose.

- **Bahá'í.** Siyyid 'Ali Muhammad, known as the Báb (Persian for "gateway"), founded the Bábi faith in Shíráz, Iran, in 1844. Bahá'ís believe that one of the Báb's disciples Husayn 'Ali Nuri, known as Bahá'u'lláh (Arabic for "Glory of God"), was the prophet and messenger of God. Bahá'u'lláh's function was to overcome the disunity of religions and establish a universal faith through abolition of racial, class, and religious prejudices.

OTHER CHRISTIAN CHURCHES

Several Christian churches developed independent of the three main branches of Christianity.

- The Coptic Church of Egypt and the Ethiopian Church are two small Christian churches in northeast Africa.

- The Armenian Church originated in Antioch, Syria, and was important in diffusing Christianity to South and East Asia between the seventh and thirteenth centuries.

- Maronites are clustered in Lebanon, which has suffered through a long civil war fought among religious groups.

- The Church of Jesus Christ of Latter-day Saints (Mormons) regards its church as a branch of Christianity separate from other branches (Figure 6.3.1). About 3 percent of Americans are members of the Latter-day Saints, a large percentage clustered in Utah and surrounding states.

◀ 6.3.1 **SALT LAKE TEMPLE**
The largest LDS (Mormon) temple, located in Salt Lake City, Utah.

DISTRIBUTION OF U.S. RELIGIONS

The United States displays regional variations in adherence to religions (Figure 6.3.2). The distribution result from the patterns of immigration to the United States, especially from Europe and Latin America. Among Protestant denominations, Baptists are most numerous in the southeast and Lutherans in the upper Midwest (Figure 6.3.3). The United States also has an estimated 12 million adherents of religions other than Christianity (Figure 6.3.4).

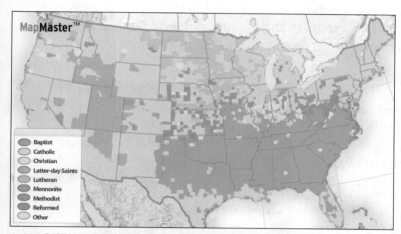

▲ 6.3.3 **DISTRIBUTION OF CHRISTIANS IN THE UNITED STATES**
The distribution of Christian branches and Protestant denominations in North America is influenced by patterns of migration.

Launch MapMaster North America in   Mastering**GEOGRAPHY**™

Select: *Distribution of Christian Denominations* from the *Cultural* menu

1. **What is the predominant religion in southwestern United States?**
2. **What pattern of immigration in the United States accounts for this distribution of religion?**

▲ 6.3.4 **MUSLIM MOSQUE, BOWLING GREEN, OHIO**

▼ 6.3.2 **RELIGIONS OF THE UNITED STATES**

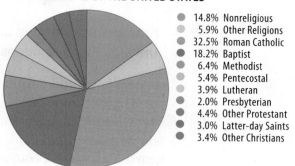

- 14.8% Nonreligious
- 5.9% Other Religions
- 32.5% Roman Catholic
- 18.2% Baptist
- 6.4% Methodist
- 5.4% Pentecostal
- 3.9% Lutheran
- 2.0% Presbyterian
- 4.4% Other Protestant
- 3.0% Latter-day Saints
- 3.4% Other Christians

30 million nonreligious or atheist
1 million Buddhists
1 million Hindus
3 million Jews
1 million Muslims
6 million other faiths
161 million Christians
  66 million Roman Catholics
  3 million Orthodox
    2 million a church of the Greek Orthodox Archdiocese of America
    1 million another Orthodox church
  82 million Protestants
    37 million a Baptist church
      17 million a Southern Baptist Convention church
      8 million a National Baptist Convention, U.S.A., church
      4 million a National Baptist Convention of America church
      3 million a National Missionary Baptist Convention of America church
      3 million a Progressive National Baptist Convention church
      2 million an American Baptist Church, U.S.A.
      3 million another Baptist church
    13 million a Methodist church
      8 million a United Methodist church
      4 million an African Methodist Episcopal or Episcopal Zion church
    11 million a Pentecostal church
      6 million a Church of God in Christ
      3 million one of the Assemblies of God churches
      2 million one of the Pentecostal Assemblies of the world churches
    8 million a Lutheran church
      5 million an Evangelical Lutheran Church in America
      3 million one of the Lutheran Church Missouri Synod churches
    4 million a Presbyterian Church U.S.A.
    2 million a Reformed church
      1 million a United Church of Christ
      1 million another Reformed Church
    2 million an Episcopal church
    3 million one of the Churches of Christ
    1 million a Christian Church (Disciples of Christ)
    1 million a Seventh Day Adventist church
  10 million other Christians
    6 million a Church of Jesus Christ of Latter-day Saints
    1 million a Jehovah's Witness church
    3 million other Christians

6.4 Origins of Religions

▶ **Ethnic religions have unknown origins.**

▶ **Universalizing religions have precise places of origin.**

Universalizing and ethnic religions typically have different geographic origins:

- An ethnic religion, such as Hinduism, has unknown or unclear origins, not tied to single historical individuals.
- A universalizing religion, such as Christianity, Islam, and Buddhism, has a precise hearth, or place of origin, based on events in the life of an individual. The hearths where the largest universalizing religions originated are all in Asia.

HINDUISM

Hinduism existed prior to recorded history (Figure 6.4.1). The earliest surviving Hindu documents were written around 1500 B.C. Aryan tribes from Central Asia invaded India around 1400 B.C. and brought with them Indo-European languages, as discussed in Chapter 5. In addition to their language, the Aryans brought their religion. Archaeological explorations have unearthed Hindu objects relating to the religion from 2500 B.C. The word Hinduism originated in the sixth century B.C. to refer to people living in what is now India.

▲ 6.4.2 **ORIGIN OF CHRISTIANITY: CHURCH OF THE HOLY SEPULCHRE, JERUSALEM**
Most Christians believe that the church was constructed on the site of Jesus's crucifixion, burial, and Resurrecti

CHRISTIANITY

Christianity was founded upon the teachings of Jesus, who was born in Bethlehem between 8 and 4 B.C. and died on a cross in Jerusalem about A.D. 30 (Figure 6.4.2). Raised as a Jew, Jesus gathered a small band of disciples and preached the coming of the Kingdom of God. He was referred to as *Christ,* from the Greek word for the Hebrew word *messiah,* which means "anointed."

In the third year of his mission, he was betrayed to the authorities by one of his companions, Judas Iscariot. After sharing the Last Supper (the Jewish Passover seder) with his disciples in Jerusalem, Jesus was arrested and put to death as an agitator. On the third day after his death, his tomb was found empty. Christians believe that Jesus died to atone for human sins, that he was raised from the dead by God, and that his Resurrection from death provides people with hope for salvation.

▼ 6.4.1 **HINDUISM'S UNKNOWN ORIGINS: MOUNT KAILĀS**
It is not known when or why people started making pilgrimages to the base of Mount Kailās. Because of its importance as a place of eternal bliss in Hinduism, as well as several other religions, no human in recorded history has ever climbed to the summit of Mount Kailās. Hindus believe that this mountain is home of Lord Siva, who is the destroyer of evil and sorrow.

BUDDHISM

The founder of Buddhism, Siddharta Gautama, was born about 563 B.C. in Lumbinī, in present-day Nepal. The son of a lord, Gautama led a privileged life, with a beautiful wife, palaces, and servants.

According to Buddhist legend, Gautama's life changed after a series of four trips. He encountered a decrepit old man on the first trip, a disease-ridden man on the second trip, and a corpse on the third trip. After witnessing these scenes of pain and suffering, Gautama began to feel he could no longer enjoy his life of comfort and security.

On a fourth trip, Gautama saw a monk, who taught him about withdrawal from the world. Gautama lived under a Bodhi (or bo) tree in a forest for seven weeks, thinking and experimenting with forms of meditation (Figure 6.4.3). He emerged as the Buddha, the "awakened or enlightened one."

◄ 6.4.3 **ORIGIN OF BUDDHISM: MAHABODHI TEMPLE, BODH GAYA**
Buddha reached perfect wisdom sitting under a Bodhi tree. This temple has stood on the site since the third century B.C., and part of the current structure was built in the first century A.D.

◄ 6.4.4 **ORIGIN OF ISLAM: AL-MASJID AL-NABAWI (MOSQUE OF THE PROPHET), MADINAH, SAUDI ARABIA**
Muhammad is buried in this mosque, built on the site of his house. The mosque is the second holiest site in Islam and the second largest mosque in the world.

ISLAM

The Prophet Muhammad was born in Makkah about 570. Muhammad was a descendant of Ishmael, who was the son of Abraham and Hagar. Jews and Christians trace their history through Abraham's wife Sarah and their son Isaac. Sarah prevailed upon Abraham to banish Hagar and Ishmael, who wandered through the Arabian desert, eventually reaching Makkah.

Muslims believe that Muhammad received his first revelation from God, through the Angel Gabriel, at age 40 while he was engaged in a meditative retreat. The Quran, the holiest book in Islam, is a record of God's words, as revealed to the Prophet Muhammad through Gabriel.

As he began to preach the truth that God had revealed to him, Muhammad suffered persecution, and in 622 he was commanded by God to emigrate to the city of Yathrib (renamed Madinah, from the Arabic for "the City of the Prophet"), an event known as the Hijra (from the Arabic for "migration," sometimes spelled *hegira*). When he died in 632, Muhammad was buried in Madinah (Figure 6.4.4).

OTHER UNIVERSALIZING RELIGIONS

Other universalizing religions, with fewer adherents, also trace their origins to single individuals. For example:

- **Sikhism** was founded by Guru Nanak (1469–1539), who traveled widely through South Asia preaching his new faith. Many people became his Sikhs (a Hindi term for "disciples").

- **Bahá'í** was founded during the nineteenth century by Husayn 'Ali Nuri, known as Bahá'u'lláh (Arabic for "Glory of God"). Bahá'u'lláh was a disciple of Siyyid 'Alí Muhammad Shírází (1819–1850), known as the Báb (Persian for "gateway"). As the prophet and messenger of God, Bahá'u'lláh sought to overcome the disunity of religions and establish a universal faith.

6.5 Diffusion of Universalizing Religions

▶ **Universalizing religions have diffused beyond their places of origin.**

▶ **Missionaries and military conquests have been important methods of diffusing universalizing religions.**

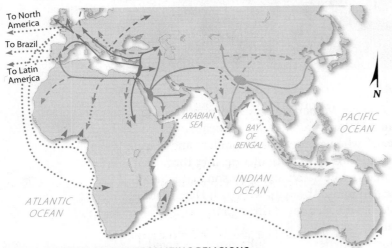

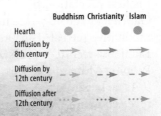

	Buddhism	Christianity	Islam
Hearth	●	●	●
Diffusion by 8th century	→	→	→
Diffusion by 12th century	⇢	⇢	⇢
Diffusion after 12th century	⋯▸	⋯▸	⋯▸

▲ 6.5.1 **DIFFUSION OF UNIVERSALIZING RELIGIONS**
Christianity diffused from present-day Israel primarily west towards Europe. Buddhism diffused from present-day Nepal primarily east towards East and Southeast Asia. Islam diffused from present-day Saudi Arabia primarily west across North Africa and east to Southwest, South, and Central Asia.

The three main universalizing religions diffused from specific hearths to other regions of the world. Followers transmitted the messages preached in the hearths to people elsewhere, diffusing them across Earth's surface along distinctive paths (Figure 6.5.1).

DIFFUSION OF CHRISTIANITY

Christianity's diffusion has been rather clearly recorded since Jesus first set forth its tenets in the Roman province of Palestine. In Chapter 1 we distinguished between relocation diffusion (through migration) and expansion diffusion (additive effect). Christianity diffused through a combination of both forms of diffusion.

Christianity first diffused from its hearth in Southwest Asia through migration. **Missionaries**—individuals who help to transmit a universalizing religion through relocation diffusion—carried the teachings of Jesus along the Roman Empire's protected sea routes and excellent road network to people in other locations (Figure 6.5.2). Migration and missionary activity by Europeans since the year 1500 has extended Christianity to other regions of the world.

Christianity spread widely within the Roman Empire through two forms of expansion diffusion:

- **Contagious diffusion:** daily contact between believers in the towns and nonbelievers in the surrounding countryside.

- **Hierarchical diffusion:** acceptance of the religion by the empire's key elite figure, the emperor; Emperor Constantine encouraged the spread of Christianity by embracing it in 313, and Emperor Theodosius proclaimed it the empire's official religion in 380.

◀ 6.5.2 **DIFFUSION OF CHRISTIANITY**
Saint Thaddeus Monastery, also known as the Black Church, near Maku, Iran, is one of the oldest Christian churches in the world. Portions of the church were originally built in A.D. 66.

DIFFUSION OF BUDDHISM

Buddhism did not diffuse rapidly from its point of origin in northeastern India (Figure 6.5.3). Most responsible for its diffusion was Asoka, emperor of the Magadhan Empire from about 273 to 232 B.C. Around 257 B.C., at the height of the Magadhan Empire's power, Asoka became a Buddhist and thereafter attempted to put into practice Buddha's social principles.

Emperor Asoka's son, Mahinda, led a mission to the island of Ceylon (now Sri Lanka), where the king and his subjects were converted to Buddhism. As a result, Sri Lanka is the country that claims the longest continuous tradition of practicing Buddhism. Missionaries were also sent in the third century B.C. to Kashmir, the Himalayas, Burma (Myanmar), and elsewhere in India.

In the first century A.D., merchants along the trading routes from northeastern India introduced Buddhism to China. Chinese rulers allowed their people to become Buddhist monks during the fourth century A.D., and in the following centuries Buddhism turned into a genuinely Chinese religion. Buddhism further diffused from China to Korea in the fourth century and from Korea to Japan two centuries later. During the same era, Buddhism lost its original base of support in India.

▲ 6.5.3 **DIFFUSION OF BUDDHISM**
Use Google Earth to explore one of the shrines constructed as Buddhism diffused across Asia.

Fly to: *Deer Park, Sarnath, India*

Select Wikipedia from the More menu.

Drag to enter street view on top of the brown structure at the bottom of the image.

Use arrows to look around inside the structure.

Click on the W icon to open the Wikipedia information box.

1. What is the name of this structure?

2. How is the structure significant to the diffusion of Buddhism?

DIFFUSION OF ISLAM

Muhammad's successors organized followers into armies that extended the region of Muslim control over an extensive area of Africa, Asia, and Europe. Within a century of Muhammad's death, Muslim armies conquered Palestine, the Persian Empire, and much of India, resulting in the conversion of many non-Arabs to Islam, often through intermarriage.

To the west, Muslims captured North Africa, crossed the Strait of Gibraltar, and retained part of western Europe, particularly much of present-day Spain, until 1492 (Figure 6.5.4). During the same century during which the Christians regained all of western Europe, Muslims took control of much of southeastern Europe and Turkey.

As was the case with Christianity, Islam, as a universalizing religion, diffused well beyond its hearth in Southwest Asia through relocation diffusion of missionaries to portions of sub-Saharan Africa and Southeast Asia. Although it is spatially isolated from the Islamic core region in Southwest Asia, Indonesia, the world's fourth most populous country, is predominantly Muslim, because Arab traders brought the religion there in the thirteenth century.

DIFFUSION OF OTHER UNIVERSALIZING RELIGIONS

- **Bahá'í** diffused to other regions during the late nineteenth century, under the leadership of 'Abdu'l-Bahá, son of the prophet Bahá'u'lláh. During the twentieth century, Bahá'ís constructed a temple on every continent.

- **Sikhism** remained relatively clustered in South Asia, where the religion originated. When India and Pakistan became independent states in 1947, the Punjab region where most Sikhs lived was divided between the two countries.

▼ 6.5.4 **DIFFUSION OF ISLAM**
Mezquita de Cordoba, Spain. This was the second largest mosque in the world, until 1236 when the Muslims were expelled from this part of Spain, and the structure was reconsecrated as a cathedral.

6.6 Holy Places in Universalizing Religions

▶ **Universalizing religions honor holy places associated with the founder's life.**
▶ **Structures play distinctive roles in each of the universalizing religions.**

Religions elevate particular places to a holy position. A universalizing religion endows with holiness cities and sacred structures associated with the founder's life. Its holy places are not related to any particular feature of the physical environment.

CHRISTIAN CHURCHES

The church plays a more critical role in Christianity than buildings in other religions, because the structure is an expression of religious principles, an environment in the image of God. The word *church* derives from a Greek term meaning lord, master, and power. In many communities, the church is the largest and tallest building and has been placed at a prominent location.

Early churches were rectangular-shaped, modeled after Roman buildings for public assembly, known as basilicas. A raised altar, where the priest conducted the service, symbolized the hill of Calvary, where Jesus was crucified.

Since Christianity split into many branches and denominations, no single style of church construction has dominated (Figure 6.6.1). Eastern Orthodox churches follow an ornate architectural style that developed in the Byzantine Empire during the fifth century. Many Protestant churches in North America are austere, with little ornamentation, a reflection of the Protestant conception of a church as an assembly hall for the congregation.

▲ 6.6.2 **HOLY PLACES IN ISLAM**
Al-Masjid al-Ḥarām (Sacred Mosque) Makkah, Saudi Arabia.

MUSLIM HOLY CITIES

The holiest places in Islam are in cities associated with the life of the Prophet Muhammad. The holiest city for Muslims is Makkah, the birthplace of Muhammad. Every healthy Muslim who has adequate financial resources is expected to undertake a hajj to Makkah. A hajj is form of a **pilgrimage**, which is a journey to a place considered sacred for religious purposes.

The holiest object in the Islamic landscape, al-Ka'ba, a cubelike structure encased in silk, stands at the center of Makkah's Sacred Mosque, al-Masjid al-Ḥarām (Figure 6.6.2). The second most holy geographic location is Madinah, where Muhammad received his first support and where he is buried (see Figure 6.4.4).

Muslims consider the mosque as a space for community assembly, but it is not a sanctified place like the Christian church. The mosque is organized around a central courtyard. The pulpit is placed at the end of the courtyard facing Makkah, the direction toward which all Muslims pray. A minaret or tower is where a man known as a *muzzan* summons people to worship.

▼ 6.6.1 **HOLY PLACES IN CHRISTIANITY**
Basilica of St. Boniface, Munich, Germany.

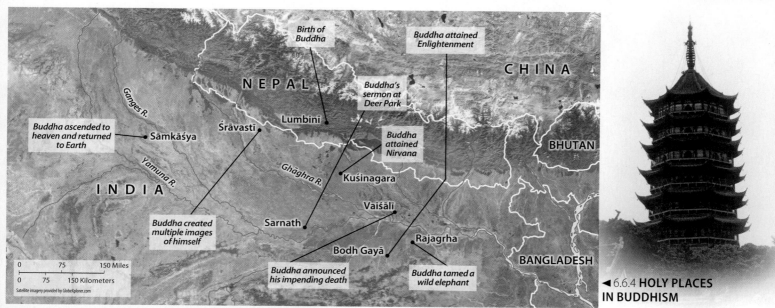

◀ 6.6.4 **HOLY PLACES IN BUDDHISM**

▲ 6.6.3 **HOLY PLACES IN BAHA'I**
House of Worship, Delhi, India.

HOLY PLACES IN BAHÁ'Í

Bahá'ìs have built Houses of Worship in every continent to dramatize that Bahá'ì is a universalizing religion with adherents all over the world. Sites include Wilmette, Illinois, in 1953; Sydney, Australia, and Kampala, Uganda, both in 1961; Lagenhain, near Frankfurt, Germany, in 1964; Panama City, Panama, in 1972; Tiapapata, near Apia, Samoa, in 1984; and New Delhi, India, in 1986 (Figure 6.6.3).

Additional Houses of Worship are planned in Tehran, Iran; Santiago, Chile; and Haifa, Israel. The first Bahá'ì House of Worship, built in 1908 in Ashgabat, Russia, now the capital of Turkmenistan, was turned into a museum by the Soviet Union and demolished in 1962 after a severe earthquake.

BUDDHIST HOLY PLACES

Eight places are holy to Buddhists because they were the locations of important events in Buddha's life. The four most important of the eight places are concentrated in a small area of northeastern India and southern Nepal (Figure 6.6.4).

The pagoda is a prominent and visually attractive element of the Buddhist landscape. Pagodas contain relics that Buddhists believe to be a portion of Buddha's body or clothing. Pagodas are not designed for congregational worship. Individual prayer or meditation is more likely to be undertaken at an adjacent temple, a remote monastery, or in a home.

HOLY PLACES IN SIKHISM

Sikhism's most holy structure, the Darbar Sahib (Golden Temple) was built at Amritsar during the seventh century (Figure 6.6.5). Sikhs seeking autonomy from India used the Golden Temple as a base to attack the Indian army. In 1984, the Indian army attacked a thousand Sikh separatists who sought sanctuary in the Temple. India's Prime Minister Indira Gandhi in turn was assassinated later that year by two of her guards, who were Sikhs.

▼ 6.6.5 **HOLY PLACES IN SIKHISM**
Darbar Sahib (Golden Temple) at Amritsar, India.

6.7 Ethnic Religions and the Landscape

▶ In ethnic religions, the calendar and beliefs in the origin of the universe are grounded in the physical environment.

▶ Ethnic religions are tied to the physical environment of a particular place.

Ethnic religions differ from universalizing religions in their understanding of relationships between human beings and nature. A variety of events in the physical environment are more likely to be incorporated into the principles of an ethnic religion.

THE CALENDAR IN JUDAISM

Calendars in ethnic religions are based upon the changing of the seasons because of the necessities of agricultural cycles. Prayers are offered in hope of favorable environmental conditions or to give thanks for past success.

Judaism is classified as an ethnic, rather than a universalizing, religion in part because its major holidays are based on events in the agricultural calendar of the religion's homeland in present-day Israel (Figure 6.7.1). The name *Judaism* derives from *Judah*, one of the patriarch Jacob's 12 sons; *Israel* is another biblical name for Jacob.

Israel—the only country where Jews are in the majority—uses a lunar rather than a solar calendar. The lunar month is only about 29 days long, so a lunar year of about 350 days quickly becomes out of step with the agricultural seasons. The Jewish calendar solves the problem by adding an extra month seven out of every 19 years, so that its principal holidays are celebrated in the same season every year.

Fundamental to Judaism is belief in one all-powerful God. It was the first recorded religion to espouse **monotheism**, the belief that there is only one God. Judaism offered a sharp contrast to the **polytheism** practiced by neighboring people, who worshipped a collection of gods.

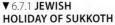

▼ 6.7.1 **JEWISH HOLIDAY OF SUKKOTH** On the holiday of Sukkoth, Jews carry branches of date palm, myrtle, and willow to symbolize gratitude for the many agricultural bounties offered by God.

COSMOGONY IN CHINESE ETHNIC RELIGIONS

Cosmogony is a set of religious beliefs concerning the origin of the universe. The cosmogony underlying Chinese ethnic religions, such as Confucianism and Daoism, is that the universe is made up of two forces, yin and yang, which exist in everything. The force of yin (earth, darkness, female, cold, depth, passivity, and death) interacts with the force of yang (heaven, light, male, heat, height, activity, and life) to achieve balance and harmony. An imbalance results in disorder and chaos.

Confucianism, based on the sayings of the philosopher and teacher Confucius (551–479 B.C.) emphasizes the importance of the ancient Chinese tradition of *li*, which can be translated roughly as "propriety" or "correct behavior," such as following traditions, fulfilling obligations, and treating others with sympathy and respect (Figure 6.7.2).

▲ 6.7.2 **CONFUCIUS TEMPLE** Nanjing, China.

Daoism, organized by a government administrator Lao-Zi (604–ca. 531 B.C.), emphasizes the mystical and magical aspects of life. Daoists seek *dao* (or *tao*), which means the "way" or "path." Dao cannot be comprehended by reason and knowledge, because not everything is subject to rational analysis, so myths and legends develop to explain events.

SPIRITS IN INANIMATE OBJECTS

To animists, the powers of the universe are mystical, and only a few people on Earth can harness these powers for medical or other purposes (Figure 6.7.3). Spirits or gods can be placated, however, through prayer and sacrifice. Rather than attempting to transform the environment, animists accept environmental hazards as normal and unavoidable.

Animists believe that such inanimate objects as plants and stones, or such natural events as thunderstorms and earthquakes, are "animated," or have discrete spirits and conscious life. Many African animist religions are apparently based on monotheistic concepts, although below the supreme god there is a hierarchy of divinities. These divinities may be assistants to the supreme god or personifications of natural phenomena, such as trees or rivers.

As recently as 1980, some 200 million Africans—half the population of the region

at the time—were classified as animists. Some atlases and textbooks persist in classifying Africa as predominantly animist, even though the actual percentage is small and declining. The rapid decline in animism in Africa has been caused by diffusion of the two largest universalizing religions, Christianity and Islam.

◀ 6.7.3 AFRICAN ANIMIST RELIGIONS
The character and form of the Odo-Kuta have evolved from the animistic origins of this once hunter-gatherer people. The circular design of the mask represents a model of the world and the individual's place in it. The masks' power to enforce this model of order is considered absolute, since mask wisdom comes from beyond the human realm and renders their authority beyond the questioning of humans.

SACRED SPACE IN HINDUISM

Unlike universalizing religions, Hindus generally practice cremation rather than burial. The body is washed with water from the Ganges River and then burned with a slow fire on a funeral pyre (Figure 6.7.4). Burial is reserved for children, ascetics, and people with certain diseases. Cremation is considered an act of purification, although it tends to strain India's wood supply.

Motivation for cremation may have originated from unwillingness on the part of nomads to leave their dead behind, possibly because of fear that the body could be attacked by wild beasts or evil spirits, or even return to life. Cremation

could also free the soul from the body for departure to the afterworld and provide warmth and comfort for the soul as it embarked on the journey to the afterworld.

▼ 6.7.4 SACRED SPACE IN HINDUISM
The most common form of disposal of bodies in India is cremation. In middle-class families, bodies are more likely to be cremated in an electric oven at a crematorium. A poor person may be cremated in an open fire, such as this one on the banks of the River Ganges. High-ranking officials and strong believers in traditional religious practices may also be cremated on an outdoor fire.

6.8 Religious Conflicts: Ireland

► **Northern Ireland and the City of Belfast are divided between Roman Catholics and Protestants.**

► **Conflicts between the two religious groups have flared periodically in Northern Ireland.**

The attempt by intense adherents of one religion to organize Earth can conflict with the spatial expression of other religious or nonreligious ideas. Contributing to more intense religious conflict has been a resurgence of religious **fundamentalism**, which is a literal interpretation and a strict and intense adherence to basic principles of a religion. A group convinced that its religious view is the correct one may spatially intrude upon the territory controlled by others.

► 6.8.1 **DISTRIBUTION OF PROTESTANTS IN IRELAND, 1911**
Long a colony of England, Ireland became a self-governing dominion within the British Empire in 1921. In 1937, it became a completely independent country, but 26 districts in the north of Ireland chose to remain part of the United Kingdom. The Republic of Ireland today is more than 95 percent Roman Catholic, whereas Northern Ireland has a Protestant majority. The boundary between Roman Catholics and Protestants does not coincide precisely with the international border, so Northern Ireland includes some communities that are predominantly Roman Catholic. This is the root of a religious conflict that continues today.

▼ 6.8.2 **IRISH INDEPENDENCE**
The words painted on the wall were the conclusion of a funeral oration by Patrick Pearse in 1915, considered one of the most important speeches in Ireland's successful revolution from England. "Fenian" refers to organizations dedicated to independence for Ireland.

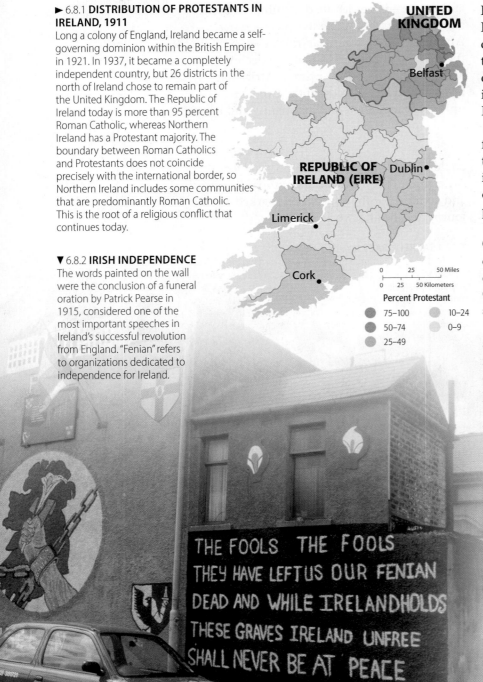

UNITED
KINGDOM

Belfast

REPUBLIC OF   Dublin●
IRELAND (EIRE)

Limerick
●

Cork
●

0   25   50 Miles
0   25   50 Kilometers

Percent Protestant
- 75–100
- 50–74
- 25–49
- 10–24
- 0–9

THE FOOLS   THE FOOLS
THEY HAVE LEFT US OUR FENIAN
DEAD AND WHILE IRELAND HOLDS
THESE GRAVES IRELAND UNFREE
SHALL NEVER BE AT PEACE

P.H. PEARSE

CHARLES HURST Body Shop

The most troublesome religious boundary in Europe lies on the island of Eire (Ireland). The Republic of Ireland, which occupies five-sixths of the island, is 92 percent Roman Catholic, but the island's northern one-sixth, which is part of the United Kingdom rather than Ireland, is about 58 percent Protestant and 42 percent Roman Catholic (Figure 6.8.1).

The entire island was an English colony for many centuries and was made part of the United Kingdom in 1801. Agitation for independence from Britain increased in Ireland during the nineteenth century, especially after poor economic conditions and famine in the 1840s led to mass emigration, as described in Chapter 3. Following a succession of bloody confrontations, Ireland became a self-governing dominion within the British Empire in 1921. Complete independence was declared in 1937, and a republic was created in 1949.

When most of Ireland became independent, a majority in six northern counties voted to remain in the United Kingdom. Protestants, who comprised the majority in Northern Ireland, preferred to be part of the predominantly Protestant United Kingdom rather than join the predominantly Roman Catholic Republic of Ireland.

A small number of Roman Catholics in both Northern Ireland and the Republic of Ireland joined the Irish Republican Army (IRA), a militant organization dedicated to achieving Irish national unity by whatever means available, including violence (Figure 6.8.2). Similarly, a scattering of Protestants created extremist organizations to fight the IRA, including the Ulster Defense Force (UDF).

Roman Catholics in Northern Ireland have been victimized by discriminatory practices,

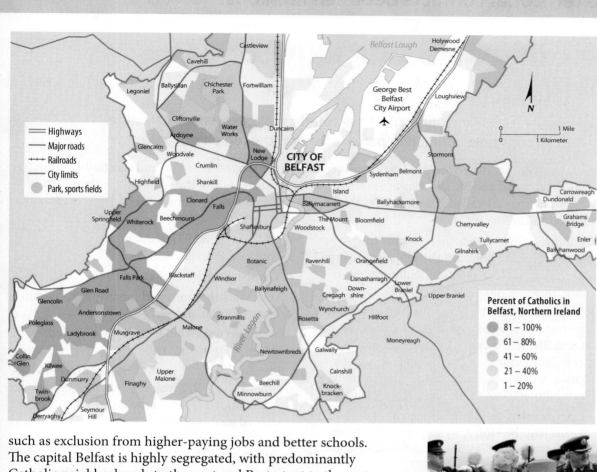

◄ 6.8.3 **DISTRIBUTION OF ROMAN CATHOLICS IN BELFAST, NORTHERN IRELAND**

Percent of Catholics in Belfast, Northern Ireland

- 81 – 100%
- 61 – 80%
- 41 – 60%
- 21 – 40%
- 1 – 20%

such as exclusion from higher-paying jobs and better schools. The capital Belfast is highly segregated, with predominantly Catholic neighborhoods to the west and Protestant to the east (Figure 6.8.3). Demonstrations by Roman Catholics protesting discrimination began in 1968, especially in areas along the boundary between the two religions. Since then, more than 3,000 have been killed in Northern Ireland—both Protestants and Roman Catholics—in a never-ending cycle of killings and reprisals.

Although the overwhelming majority of Northern Ireland's Roman Catholics and Protestants are willing to live peacefully with the other religious group, extremists disrupt daily life for everyone (Figure 6.8.4). As long as most Protestants are firmly committed to remaining in the United Kingdom and most Roman Catholics are equally committed to union with the Republic of Ireland, peaceful settlement appears difficult. Peace agreements implemented in 1999 provided for the sharing of power, but the British government has suspended the arrangement several times because of violations.

◄▼ 6.8.4 **QUEEN OF THE UNITED KINGDOM VISITS IRELAND, 2011** Most Irish welcomed the first visit by a British monarch in more than a century, but some protested.

6.9 Religious Conflicts: The Middle East

▶ **Jews, Muslims, and Christians have fought to control Israel/Palestine.**
▶ **The groups hold conflicting perspectives on the region's geography.**

Religious conflict in the Middle East is among the world's longest standing and most intractable. Jews, Christians, and Muslims have fought for 2,000 years to control the same small strip of land, which the Romans called Palestine after the Philistines, seafaring invaders who occupied the area in the twelfth century B.C.

All three groups trace their origins to Abraham in the Bible, but the religions diverge in ways that have made it difficult for them to share the same territory.

- **Judaism.** As an ethnic religion, Judaism makes a special claim to the territory it calls the Promised Land. The major events in the development of Judaism took place there, and the religion's customs and rituals acquire meaning from the agricultural life of the ancient Hebrew tribe.

- **Christianity.** Palestine is the Holy Land and Jerusalem the Holy City because the major events in Jesus's life, death, and Resurrection were concentrated there.

- **Islam.** Jerusalem is their third holy city, after Makkah and Madinah, because it is the place from which Muhammad is thought to have ascended to heaven.

Palestine was incorporated into a succession of empires, culminating with the British after World War I. In 1947, the United Nations partitioned Palestine into:

- A Jewish-controlled state of Israel

- Arab Muslim-controlled territories turned over to Jordan and Egypt.

- Jerusalem to be controlled by the United Nations (Figure 6.9.1).

Immediately after the British withdrew in 1948, neighboring Arab Muslim states attacked Israel in an attempt to prevent the creation of a Jewish-controlled state, but Israel survived. Israel's boundaries were extended beyond the UN partition, and Jerusalem was divided between Israel and Jordan.

Israel won three more wars with its neighbors, in 1956, 1967, and 1973. Especially important was the 1967 Six-Day War, when Israel captured territory from its neighbors. Israel returned the Sinai Peninsula to Egypt in exchange for a peace treaty in 1979. The West Bank (formerly part of Jordan) and Gaza (formerly part of Egypt) have been joined to create what is now known as Palestine, with its own Arab Muslim government but under Israeli military control. Israel has retained the Golan Heights (captured from Syria), as well as the Old City of Jerusalem (captured from Jordan, see next section).

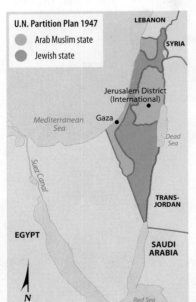

▲ 6.9.1 **BOUNDARY CHANGES IN PALESTINE/ISRAEL**
(left) The 1947 United Nations partition plan, (center) Israel after the 1948–1949 war, (right) The Middle East since the 1967 war.

PALESTINIAN PERSPECTIVES

Palestinians emerged as Israel's principal opponent after the 1973 war. Egypt and Jordan renounced their claims to Gaza and the West Bank, respectively, and recognized the Palestinians as the legitimate rulers of these territories.

Five groups of people consider themselves Palestinians:

- People living in the territories captured by Israel in 1967.
- Muslim citizens of Israel.
- People who fled from Israel after Israel was created in 1948.
- People who fled from the occupied territories after the 1967 war.
- Citizens of other countries who identify themselves as Palestinians.

Palestinians see repeated efforts by Jewish settlers to increase the territory under their control. Hostility increased after the 1967 war, when Israel occupied portions of neighboring countries, and then permitted some of its citizens to build settlements in the occupied territories (Figure 6.9.2).

Some Palestinians are willing to recognize Israel with its Jewish majority in exchange for return of all territory taken in the 1967 war. Others still do not recognize the right of Israel to exist and want to continue fighting for control of the entire territory between the Jordan River and the Mediterranean Sea.

ISRAELI PERSPECTIVES

Israel sees itself as a very small country—20,000 square kilometers (8,000 square miles)—with a Jewish majority surrounded by a region of hostile Muslim Arabs encompassing more than 25 million square kilometers (10 million square miles).

Repeated attacks by its neighbors and by Palestinians have led Israel to construct a barrier near its borders (Figure 6.9.3). The barrier is controversial because it places on Israel's side around 10 percent of the West Bank, home to 49,400 Palestinians according to a UN estimate (Figure 6.9.4). The Israeli Supreme Court has twice declared portions of the route illegal because some Palestinians could not reach their fields, water sources, and places of work. Israeli statistics show that it has drastically reduced suicide bombings and other attacks on Israeli civilians. As a result, the barrier has strong support among the Israeli public.

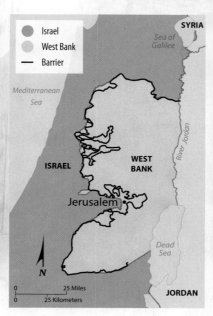

▼ 6.9.2 **ISRAELI SETTLEMENT IN THE WEST BANK**

▲▶ 6.9.3 **ISRAEL'S SEPARATION FENCE**

Israel

West Bank

— Barrier

Mediterranean Sea

SYRIA

Sea of Galilee

River Jordan

ISRAEL

WEST BANK

Jerusalem

Dead Sea

N

0   25 Miles
0   25 Kilometers

JORDAN

▲ 6.9.4 **PALESTINIAN VIOLENCE**
Palestinians attack Israeli police In the West Bank.

6.10 Jerusalem: Contested Space

▶ Places holy to Jews, Muslims, and Christians are clustered in Jerusalem.
▶ The spatial arrangement of holy places within Jerusalem makes peace especially difficult.

The geography of Jerusalem makes it difficult if not impossible to settle the long-standing religious conflicts. The difficulty is that the most sacred space in Jerusalem for Muslims was literally built on top of the most sacred space for Jews (Figure 6.10.1).

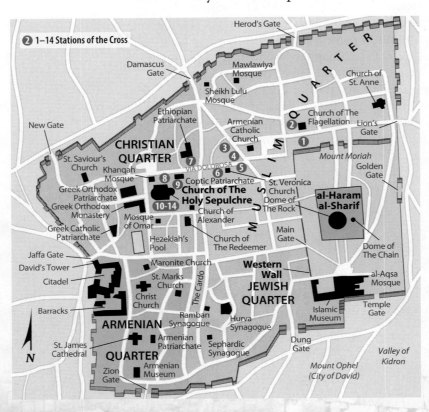

▲ 6.10.1 OLD CITY OF JERUSALEM

JUDAISM'S JERUSALEM

Jerusalem is especially holy to Jews as the location of the Temple, their center of worship in ancient times. The First Temple, built by King Solomon in approximately 960 B.C. was destroyed by the Babylonians in 586 B.C. After the Persian Empire, led by Cyrus the Great, gained control of Jerusalem in 614 B.C., Jews were allowed to build a Second Temple in 516 BC. The Romans destroyed the Jewish Second Temple in A.D. 70. The Western Wall of the Temple survives as a site for daily prayers by observant Jews (Figure 6.10.2).

Christians and Muslims call the Western Wall the Wailing Wall, because for many centuries Jews were allowed to visit the surviving Western Wall only once a year to lament the Temple's destruction. After Israel captured the entire city of Jerusalem during the 1967 Six-Day War, it removed the barriers that had prevented Jews from visiting and living in the Old City of Jerusalem, including the Western Wall. The Western Wall soon became a site for daily prayers by observant Jews.

▼ 6.10.2 JEWS PRAYING AT THE WESTERN WALL

ISLAM'S JERUSALEM

The most important Muslim structure in Jerusalem is the Dome of the Rock, built in A.D. 691 (Figure 6.10.3). Muslims believe that the large rock beneath the building's dome is the place from which Muhammad ascended to heaven, as well as the altar on which Abraham prepared to sacrifice his son Isaac. Immediately south of the Dome of the Rock is the al-Aqsa Mosque, finished in A.D. 705.

The challenge facing Jews and Muslims is that al-Aqsa Mosque was built on the site of the ruins of the Jewish Second Temple. Israel allows Muslims unlimited access to that religion's holy structures in Jerusalem and some control over them. Through a complex arrangement of ramps and passages patrolled by Palestinian guards, Muslims access the Dome of the Rock and the al-Aqsa Mosque without having to walk in front of the Western Wall where Jews are praying. But with holy Muslim structures sitting literally on top of holy Jewish structures, the two cannot be logically divided by a line on a map (Figure 6.10.4).

▲ 6.10.3 **DOME OF THE ROCK**

▼ 6.10.4 **WESTERN WALL AND DOME OF THE ROCK**
A crowd of Jews are praying at the Western Wall (lower right), situated immediately below the mount containing Islam's Dome of the Rock (top left) and al-Aqsa Mosque (top right).

The Middle East is one of many regions of the world with the potential for conflict resulting from cultural diversity. In the modern world of global economics and culture, the diversity of religions continues to play strong roles in people's lives.

Key Questions

Where are religions distributed?

► A religion can be classified as universalizing or ethnic.
► Universalizing religions can be divided into branches, denominations, and sects.
► Universalizing religions have more widespread distribution than do ethnic religions.

How do religions shape landscapes?

► Universalizing religions revere places of importance in the lives of their founders.
► Ethnic religions are shaped by the physical geography and agriculture of its hearth.

Where are territorial conflicts between religions?

► Long-standing conflicts among religious groups can be found in a number of regions.
► Religious conflicts in the Middle East have been especially long-standing and intractable.

▼ 6.CR.1 **PEOPLE PRAYING AT THE FRIDAY PRAYER IN THE DITIB-MERKEZ MOSQUE, DUISBURG-MARXLOH, NORTH RHINE-WESTPHALIA, GERMANY, EUROPE**

Thinking Geographically

Sharp demographic differences, such as NIR, CBR, and net migration, can be seen among Jews, Christians, and Muslims in the Middle East.

1. How might demographic differences affect future relationships among the religious groups in the region?

Islam seems strange and threatening to some people in predominantly Christian countries (Figure 6.CR.1).

2. To what extent is this attitude shaped by knowledge of the teachings of Muhammad and the Quran, and to what extent is it based on lack of knowledge of the religion?

People carry their religious beliefs with them when they migrate. Over time, change occurs in the regions from which most U.S. immigrants originate and in the U.S. regions where they settle.

3. How has the distribution of U.S. religious groups been affected by these changes?

On the Internet

Statistics on the number of adherents to religions, branches, and denominations are at **www.adherents.com** or by scanning the QR on the opening page of this chapter.

Glenmary Research Center, which is affiliated with the Roman Catholic Church, provides maps of U.S. religions at **www.glenmary.org**. Glenmary has a map of Americans not affiliated with any religion (high percentage in red).

Interactive Mapping

FORCED MIGRATION IN SOUTH ASIA

Millions of people were forced to migrate after South Asia gained independence from the United Kingdom in 1947.

Launch Mapmaster South Asia in
Mastering**GEOGRAPHY**™

Select: *Religions* from the *Cultural* menu, then *Ethnic Division* from the *Population* menu, then *Countries and States* from the *Political* menu.

What accounts for the migration pattern?

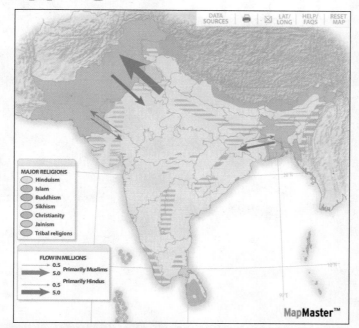

Explore

MAKKAH, SAUDI ARABIA

Use Google Earth to explore Masjid al-Haram, Islam's largest mosque in Makkah, Saudi Arabia.
Millions of Muslims make a pilgrimage to Makkah each year and gather at Masjid al-Haram Mosque.

Fly to: *Masjid al-Haram Mosque, Makkah, Saudi Arabia.*

Drag to: *Enter Street View* to the square in the middle of the mosque

Click to look around so that North is at the bottom.

Click 3D buildings.

Continue to look around to see the tall building with the clock tower immediately south of the Mosque.

1. What is in the tall building?

2. Why would this building be located immediately next to the mosque?

Key Terms

Animism
Belief that objects, such as plants and stones, or natural events, like thunderstorms and earthquakes, have a discrete spirit and conscious life.

Branch (of a religion)
A large and fundamental division within a religion.

Cosmogony
A set of religious beliefs concerning the origin of the universe.

Denomination (of a religion)
A division of a branch that unites a number of local congregations in a single legal and administrative body.

Ethnic religion
A religion with a relatively concentrated spatial distribution whose principles are likely to be based on the physical characteristics of the particular location in which its adherents are concentrated.

Fundamentalism
A literal interpretation and a strict and intense adherence to basic principles of a religion.

Missionary
An individual who helps to diffuse a universalizing religion.

Monotheism
The doctrine or belief of the existence of only one god.

Pilgrimage
A journey to a place considered sacred for religious purposes.

Polytheism
Belief in or worship of more than one god.

Sect (of a religion)
A relatively small group that has broken away from an established denomination.

Universalizing religion
A religion that attempts to appeal to all people, not just those living in a particular location.

► LOOKING AHEAD

The next chapter continues our look at the world's cultural patterns by examining ethnic diversity at several scales.

7 Ethnicity

Each of us belongs to one or more ethnic groups with which we share important attributes. Ethnicity is an especially important element of culture, because our ethnic identity is irrefutable. We can deny or suppress our ethnicity, but we cannot choose to change it in the same way we can choose to speak a different language or practice a different religion. If our parents come from two ethnic groups or our grandparents from four, our ethnic identity may be extremely diluted, but it never completely disappears.

Ethnic identity is a source of pride to people, a link to the experiences of ancestors and to cultural traditions, such as food and music preferences. Ethnicity also matters in places with a history of discrimination by one ethnic group against another. Even without discriminatory practices, ethnic groups may vary according to life expectancy, infant mortality, and other important measures.

Where are ethnicities and races distributed?

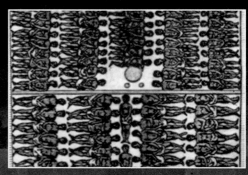

EUROF

APARTHEID MUSEUM,
JOHANNESBURG,
SOUTH AFRICA

Where are ethnicities and nationalities distributed?

SCAN TO ACCESS U.S. CENSUS DATA ON ETHNICITY AND RACE

Where do ethnicities face conflict?

S ONLY

7.1 Race and Ethnicity

▶ **Ethnicity and race are often confused.**
▶ **In the past, races have been spatially segregated by legal discrimination.**

Ethnicity and race are two important characteristics of a group of people:

• **Ethnicity** is identity with a group of people who share the cultural traditions of a particular homeland or hearth.

• **Race** is identity with a group of people who share a biological ancestor.

The two concepts are often confused. Ethnicity is the concept of particular interest to geographers, because characteristics of ethnicity are tied to a place. Race differs from ethnicity because characteristics of race are tied to biology, not location.

ETHNICITY

The complexity of ethnic identity in the United States is clearly illustrated by Barack Obama's ethnicity (Figure 7.1.1):

• President Obama's father, Barack Obama Sr., was born in the village of Kanyadhiang, Kenya. He was a member of Kenya's third largest ethnic group, known as the Luo.

• President Obama's mother, Ann Dunham, was born in Kansas. Most of her ancestors migrated to the United States from England in the nineteenth century.

• President Obama's stepfather—his mother's second husband, Lolo Soetoro—was born in the village of Yogyakarta, Indonesia. He was a member of Indonesia's largest ethnic group, known as the Javanese.

The two most numerous ethnicities in the United States are Hispanics (or Latinos), at 15 percent of the total population, and African Americans at 13 percent. In addition, about 5 percent are Asian American and 1 percent American Indian.

The U.S. Census defines Hispanic as a person of Cuban, Mexican, Puerto Rican, South or Central American, or other Spanish culture or origin regardless of race. What is significant about the definition is that it refers to places in the world as the basis for distinguishing the ethnicity. The term Hispanic was chosen by the U.S. government in 1973 to describe the ethnicity because it was an inoffensive label that could be applied to all people from Spanish-speaking countries. Some Americans of Latin American descent have instead adopted the terms Latinos (males) and Latinas (females). A 1995 U.S. Census Bureau survey found that 58 percent of Americans of Latin American descent preferred the term Hispanic and 12 percent Latino/Latina.

Mexicans are sometimes called Chicanos (males) or Chicanas (females). Originally the term was considered insulting, but in the 1960s Mexican American youths in Los Angeles began to call themselves Chicanos and Chicanas with pride (Figure 7.1.2).

▶ 7.1.1 **ETHNIC DIVERSITY: PRESIDENT OBAMA'S FAMILY**
Barack Obama with his mother (right), his father (far right), and his stepfather, mother, and stepsister (below).

▶ 7.1.2 **MEXICAN INDEPENDENCE DAY PARADE**
Each year, people gather in cities across the United States (here, New York is shown) to celebrate Mexican independence.

◄ 7.1.3 **CHARACTERISTIC OF RACE: LACTOSE INTOLERANCE**
Lactose intolerance varies among races.

RACE

The traits that characterize race are those that can be transmitted genetically from parents to children. For example, lactose intolerance affects 95 percent of Asian Americans, 65 percent of African Americans and Native Americans, and 50 percent of Hispanics, compared to only 15 percent of Americans of European ancestry. Nearly everyone is born with the ability to produce lactase, which enables infants to digest the large amount of lactose in milk (Figure 7.1.3). Lactase production typically slackens during childhood, leaving some with difficulty in absorbing a large amount of lactose as adults. A large percentage of persons of North European descent have a genetic mutation that results in lifelong production of lactase.

According to 2010 U.S. census, 72 percent of Americans are white, 13 percent black, 5 percent Asian, and 7 percent other races. In addition, 3 percent of Americans consider themselves belonging to two or more races.

- *Asian* is recognized as a distinct race by the U.S. Bureau of the Census, so Asian as a race and Asian American as an ethnicity encompass basically the same group of people.

- *African American* and *black* are different groups, although the 2000 census combined the two. Most black Americans are descended from African immigrants and therefore also belong to an African American ethnicity. Some American blacks, however, trace their cultural heritage to Latin America, Asia, or Pacific islands.

- *Hispanic or Latino* is not considered a race by the U.S. Census Bureau, so members of the Hispanic or Latino ethnicity select whatever race they feel is most accurate on the census.

RACISM

Biological features of all humans, such as skin color, hair type and color, blood traits, and shape of body, head, and facial features, were once thought to be scientifically classifiable into a handful of world races with distinct geographical distributions. Perhaps many tens or hundreds of thousands of years ago, early humans (however they emerged as a distinct species) lived in such isolation from other early humans that they were truly distinct genetically, as well as spatially. But the degree of isolation needed to keep biological features distinct genetically vanished when the first human crossed a river or climbed a hill and fell in love with someone on the other side.

At worst, attempts to classify humans by race is the basis for **racism**, which is the belief that race is the primary determinant of human traits and capacities, and that biological differences produce an inherent superiority of a particular race (Figure 7.1.4). A **racist** is a person who subscribes to the beliefs of racism.

▼ 7.1.4 **STUDENTS IN MELBOURNE, AUSTRALIA, DEMONSTRATE AGAINST RACISM**

7.2 Distribution of Ethnicities in the United States

▶ The two most numerous U.S. ethnicities are Hispanic and African American.
▶ Ethnic groups cluster in different regions of the United States.

An ethnicity may be clustered in specific areas within a country, or the area it inhabits may match closely the boundaries of a country. Within a country, clustering of ethnicities can occur on two scales. Ethnic groups may live in particular regions of the country, and they may live in particular neighborhoods within cities. Within the United States, ethnicities are clustered at both scales.

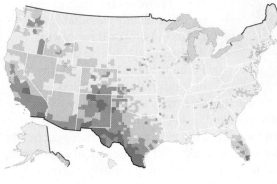

▶ **7.2.1 DISTRIBUTION OF HISPANICS IN THE UNITED STATES**

Percent Hispanic by county
- 60 and above
- 30–59
- 10–29
- below 10

▶ **7.2.2 DISTRIBUTION OF AFRICAN AMERICANS IN THE UNITED STATES**

Percent African American by county
- 60 and above
- 30–59
- 10–29
- below 10

▶ **7.2.3 DISTRIBUTION OF ASIAN AMERICANS IN THE UNITED STATES**

Percent Asian American by county
- 60 and above
- 30–59
- 10–29
- below 10

▶ **7.2.4 DISTRIBUTION OF AMERICAN INDIANS IN THE UNITED STATES**

Percent American Indian by county
- 60 and above
- 30–59
- 10–29
- below 10

REGIONAL DISTRIBUTION OF ETHNICITIES

On a regional scale, ethnicities have distinctive distributions within the United States:

- **Hispanic or Latino/Latina.** Clustered in the Southwest, Hispanics exceed one-third of the population of Arizona, New Mexico, and Texas, and one-quarter of California (Figure 7.2.1). California is home to one-third of all Hispanics, Texas one-fifth, and Florida and New York one-sixth each.

- **African Americans.** Clustered in the Southeast, African Americans comprise at least one-fourth of the population in Alabama, Georgia, Louisiana, Maryland, and South Carolina, and more than one-third in Mississippi (Figure 7.2.2). Concentrations are even higher in selected counties. At the other extreme, nine states in upper New England and the West are less than 1 percent African American.

- **Asian Americans.** Clustered in the West, Asian Americans (including native Hawaiians and other Pacific Islanders) comprise more than 49 percent of the population of Hawaii (Figure 7.2.3). One-half of all Asian Americans live in California, where they comprise 13 percent of the population. Chinese account for one-fourth of Asian Americans, Indians and Filipinos one-fifth each, and Korean and Vietnamese one-tenth each.

- **American Indians and Alaska Natives.** Within the 48 continental United States, American Indians are most numerous in the Southwest and the Plains states (Figure 7.2.4).

ETHNICITIES IN LARGE CITIES

African Americans and Hispanics are highly clustered in urban areas at two scales:

- Large cities, rather than suburbs or rural areas.
- Individual neighborhoods within large cities.

The clustering of the two ethnicities in large cities can be seen by comparing the population of a large city with that of the rest of its state. For example, African Americans comprise 85 percent of the population in the city of Detroit and only 7 percent in the rest of Michigan (Figure 7.2.5). Otherwise stated, Detroit contains less than one-tenth of Michigan's total population, but more than one-half of the state's African American population. Similarly, Chicago is one-fourth Hispanic, whereas Illinois is one-eighth Hispanic, so Chicago has one-half of the state's entire population of Hispanics.

The clustering of ethnicities is especially pronounced on the scale of neighborhoods within cities. In Chicago, for example, African Americans cluster in neighborhoods to the south and west of downtown (the "Loop"), whereas Hispanics cluster to the northwest and southwest (Figure 7.2.6).

In the early twentieth century, cities in the Midwest, including Chicago, Cleveland, and Detroit, attracted ethnic groups primarily from southern and eastern Europe to work in the rapidly growing steel, automotive, and related industries. Southern and eastern European ethnic groups clustered in newly constructed neighborhoods that were often named for their predominant ethnicities, such as Detroit's Poletown and Chicago's Pilsen (Figure 7.2.7).

The children and grandchildren of European immigrants moved out of most of the original inner-city neighborhoods during the twentieth century. For descendants of European immigrants, ethnic identity is more likely to be retained through religion, food, and other cultural traditions rather than through location of residence. A visible remnant of early twentieth-century European ethnic neighborhoods is the clustering of restaurants in such areas as Little Italy and Greektown.

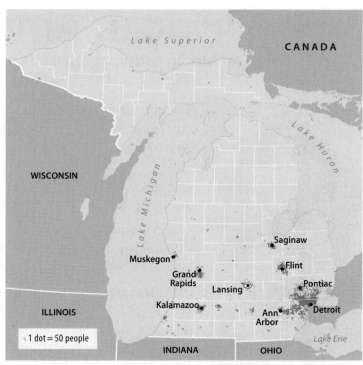

▲ 7.2.5 **DISTRIBUTION OF AFRICAN AMERICANS IN MICHIGAN**

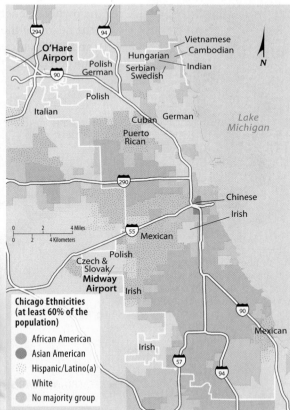

▲ 7.2.6 **DISTRIBUTION OF ETHNICITIES IN CHICAGO**

◀ 7.2.7 **ETHNIC NEIGHBORHOOD IN CHICAGO**
Chicago's Pilsen neighborhood was originally inhabited by Czech immigrants. Now it is inhabited primarily by Mexican immigrants.

7.3 African American Migration

▶ **African Americans display distinctive immigration patterns.**
▶ **The history of slavery is a major factor in the distribution of African Americans.**

The clustering of ethnicities within the United States is partly a function of the same process that helps geographers to explain the regular distribution of other cultural factors, such as language and religion—namely migration.

Three major migration flows have shaped the current distribution of African Americans within the United States:

• International forced migration: From Africa to the American colonies during the eighteenth century.

• Interregional migration: From the U.S. South to northern cities during the early twentieth century.

• Intraregional migration: From inner-city ghettos to other urban neighborhoods beginning in the second half of the twentieth century.

INTERNATIONAL FORCED MIGRATION

Most African Americans are descended from Africans forced to migrate to the Western Hemisphere as slaves (Figure 7.3.1). Slavery is a system whereby one person owns another person as a piece of property and can force that slave to work for the owner's benefit.

At the height of the slave trade between 1710 and 1810, at least 10 million Africans were uprooted from their homes and sent on European ships to the Western Hemisphere for sale in the slave market. A number of European countries adopted the **triangular slave trade**, an efficient triangular trading pattern (Figure 7.3.2). During that period, the British and Portuguese each shipped about 2 million slaves to the Western Hemisphere, with most of the British slaves going to Caribbean islands, and the Portuguese on ships to Brazil (Figure 7.3.3).

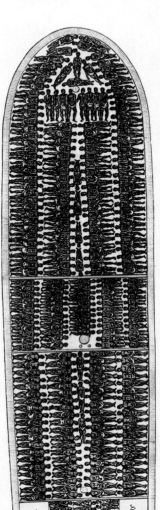

▲ 7.3.1 **SLAVE SHIP**
Africans were transported to the Western Hemisphere to be sold as slaves in extremely poor conditions. The image shows human figures packed into the hold of the ship lying next to each other with no room to move.

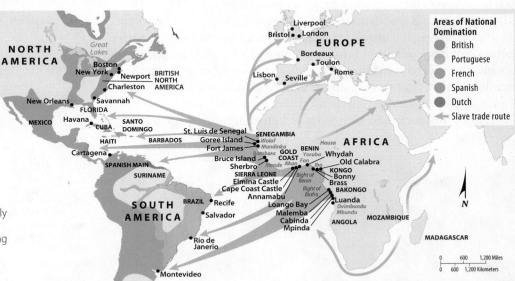

▲ 7.3.3 **ORIGIN AND DESTINATION OF SLAVES**

◀ 7.3.2 **TRIANGULAR SLAVE TRADE**
The British initiated a triangular slave trading pattern in the eighteenth century:

• Ships left Europe for Africa with cloth and other trade goods, used to buy the slaves.

• They then transported slaves and gold from Africa to the Western Hemisphere, primarily to the Caribbean islands.

• To complete the triangle, the same ships then carried sugar and molasses from the Caribbean on their return trip to Europe.

• Some ships added another step, making a rectangular trading pattern, in which molasses was carried from the Caribbean to the North American colonies, and rum from the colonies to Europe.

INTERREGIONAL MIGRATION FROM SOUTH TO NORTH

Freed from slavery during the U.S. Civil War (1861–65), most African Americans remained in the rural South during the late nineteenth century working as sharecroppers. A **sharecropper** works fields rented from a landowner and pays the rent by turning over to the landowner a share of the crops.

Sharecropping declined into the twentieth century as the introduction of farm machinery and decline in land devoted to cotton reduced demand for labor. At the same time sharecroppers were being pushed off the farms, they were being pulled to the prospect of jobs in the booming industrial cities of the North. African Americans migrated out of the South along several clearly defined channels (Figure 7.3.4).

Southern African Americans migrated north and west in two main waves, the first in the 1910s and 1920s before and after World War I and the second in the 1940s and 1950s before and after World War II. The world wars stimulated expansion of factories to produce war materiel, while the demands of the armed forces created shortages of factory workers.

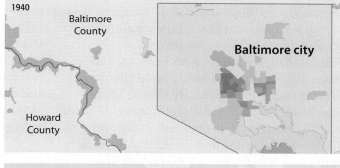

▲ 7.3.4 **AFRICAN AMERICAN INTERREGIONAL MIGRATION**
Migration followed four distinct channels:

- Northeast: From the Carolinas and other South Atlantic states north to Philadelphia, New York, and other northeastern cities, along U.S. Route 1 (parallel to present-day I-95).
- East Central: From Alabama and eastern Tennessee north to either Detroit, along U.S. Route 25 (present-day I-75), or Cleveland, along U.S. Route 21 (present-day I-77).
- West Central: From Mississippi and western Tennessee north to St. Louis and Chicago, along U.S. routes 61 and 66 (present-day I-55)
- West: From Texas west to California, along U.S. routes 80 and 90 (present-day I-10 and I-20).

INTRAREGIONAL MIGRATION: BREAKING THE GHETTO

When they reached the big cities, African American immigrants clustered in the one or two neighborhoods where the small numbers who had arrived in the nineteenth century were already living. These areas became known as ghettos, after the term for neighborhoods in which Jews were forced to live in the Middle Ages.

Densities in the ghettos were high, with 40,000 inhabitants per square kilometer (100,000 per square mile) common. Contrast that density with the current level found in typical American suburbs of 2,000 inhabitants per square kilometer (5,000 per square mile). Because of the shortage of housing in the ghettos, families were forced to live in one room. Many dwellings lacked bathrooms, kitchens, hot water, and heat.

In 1940, most of Baltimore's quarter-million African Americans lived in a 3-square-kilometer (1-square-mile) neighborhood northwest of downtown (Figure 7.3.5). In Baltimore, the African American area expanded to the west from 3 square kilometers (1 square mile) in 1940 to 25 square kilometers (10 square miles) in 1970 and to the east to a 5-square-kilometer (2-square-mile) area.

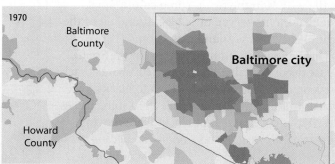

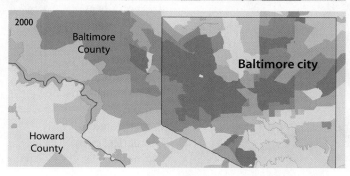

Percent African American
- 90 and above
- 60–89
- 30–59
- 10–29
- below 10

◄ 7.3.5 **EXPANSION OF AFRICAN AMERICAN POPULATION IN BALTIMORE**

7.4 Discrimination by Race

▶ In the United States, "separate but equal" rulings once permitted races to be legally segregated.

▶ In South Africa, races were once segregated under *apartheid* laws.

In explaining spatial regularities, geographers look for patterns of spatial interaction. A distinctive feature of race relations in the United States and South Africa was the strong discouragement of spatial interaction through legal means.

UNITED STATES: "SEPARATE BUT EQUAL"

The U.S. Supreme Court in 1896 upheld a Louisiana law that required black and white passengers to ride in separate railway cars. In *Plessy v. Ferguson*, the Supreme Court stated that Louisiana's law was constitutional because it provided separate but equal treatment of blacks and whites. "Equality" did not mean that whites had to mix socially with blacks.

Once the Supreme Court permitted "separate but equal" treatment of the races, southern states enacted a comprehensive set of laws to segregate blacks from whites as much as possible (Figure 7.4.1). These were called "Jim Crow" laws, named for a nineteenth-century song-and-dance act that depicted blacks offensively.

Blacks had to sit in the back of buses, and shops, restaurants, and hotels could choose to serve only whites. Separate schools were established for blacks and whites. After all, white southerners argued, the bus got blacks sitting in the rear to the destination at the same time as the whites in the front, some commercial establishments served only blacks, and all of the schools had teachers and classrooms.

Throughout the country, not just in the South, house deeds contained restrictive covenants that prevented the owners from selling to blacks, as well as to Roman Catholics or Jews in some places. Restrictive covenants kept blacks from moving into an all-white neighborhood. And because schools, especially at the elementary level, were located to serve individual neighborhoods, most were segregated in practice, even if not legally mandated.

The civil rights movement during the 1950s and 1960s staged demonstrations to eliminate laws that permitted segregation and practices that encouraged discrimination (Figure 7.4.2). The landmark Supreme Court decision *Brown v. Board of Education of Topeka, Kansas*, in 1954, found that having separate schools for blacks and whites was unconstitutional, because no matter how equivalent the facilities, racial separation branded minority children as inferior and therefore was inherently unequal. A year later the Supreme Court further ruled that schools had to be desegregated "with all deliberate speed."

The National Advisory Commission on Civil Disorders, known as the Kerner Commission, wrote in 1968 that U.S. cities were divided into two separate and unequal societies, one black and one white. Four decades later, despite serious efforts to integrate and equalize the two, segregation and inequality persist.

▲ 7.4.2 **U.S. CIVIL RIGHTS MOVEMENT**
A major event in the civil rights movement came on December 1, 1955, when Rosa Parks, an African American, was arrested in Montgomery, Alabama, for refusing to give up her seat on a bus to a white passenger. The arrest sparked demonstrations against segregation and a boycott of Montgomery's buses. The U.S. Supreme Court ruled in 1956 that segregating races on buses was illegal. In this image, Parks is riding in the front of the bus on December 21, 1956, the day that Montgomery integrated its buses in compliance with the Supreme Court ruling. The man sitting behind her is a reporter.

▼ 7.4.1 **SEGREGATION IN THE UNITED STATES** Until the 1960s in the U.S. South, whites and blacks had to use separate drinking fountains, as well as separate restrooms, bus seats, hotel rooms, and other public facilities.

FOR COLORED ONLY

SOUTH AFRICA: APARTHEID

In 1948, South Africa enacted a series of **apartheid** laws that physically separated races into different geographic areas. Under apartheid, a newborn baby was classified as being one of four races—black, white, colored (mixed white and black), or Asian. Each of the four races had a different legal status in South Africa.

The apartheid system was created by descendants of whites who arrived in South Africa from Holland in 1652. They were known either as *Boers*, from the Dutch word for *farmer*, or *Afrikaners*, from the word "Afrikaans," the name of their language, which is a dialect of Dutch. The British seized the Dutch colony in 1795, and controlled South Africa's government until 1948, when the Afrikaner-dominated Nationalist Party won elections.

The Afrikaners gained power at a time when colonial rule was being replaced in the rest of Africa by a collection of independent states run by the local black population. The Afrikaners vowed to resist pressures to turn over South Africa's government to blacks, and the Nationalist Party enacted the apartheid laws to perpetuate white dominance of the country.

The apartheid laws determined where different races could live, attend school, work, shop, travel, and own land (Figure 7.4.3). Blacks were restricted to certain occupations and were paid far lower wages than were whites for

similar work. Blacks could not vote or run for political office in national elections.

To ensure geographic isolation of different races, the Afrikaners designated ten so-called homelands for blacks (Figure 7.4.4). The Afrikaners expected every black to become a citizen of one of the homelands and to move there (Figure 7.4.5).

The white-minority government of South Africa repealed the apartheid laws in 1991. The principal anti-apartheid organization, the African National Congress, was legalized, and its leader, Nelson Mandela, was released from jail after more than 27 years of imprisonment. When all South Africans were permitted to vote in national elections for the first time, in 1994, Mandela was overwhelmingly elected the country's first black president.

Although South Africa's apartheid laws were repealed during the 1990s, it will take many years to erase the impact of past policies. South Africa's blacks have achieved political equality, but they are much poorer than white South Africans. Average income among white South Africans is about ten times higher than that of blacks.

▲ 7.4.3 **APARTHEID IN SOUTH AFRICA**
South Africa's apartheid laws spatially segregated races. Blacks and whites reached the platform at this train station in Johannesburg by walking up separate stairs. Whites waited at the front of the platform to get into cars at the head of the train, while blacks waited at the rear.

▼ 7.4.4 **HOMELANDS IN SOUTH AFRICA**
Cata-Village in the former Homeland Ciskei, Eastern Cape, South Africa. As part of its apartheid system, the government of South Africa designated ten homelands, expecting that ultimately every black would become a citizen of one of them. South Africa declared four of these homelands to be independent states, but no other country recognized the action. With the end of apartheid and the election of a black majority government, the homelands were abolished, and South Africa was reorganized into nine provinces.

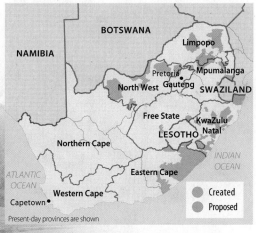

▲ 7.4.5 **SOUTH AFRICA HOMELANDS**

7.5 Ethnicities and Nationalities

► **Nationalities identify with a particular country.**
► **Loyalty to a country is instilled through nationalism.**

Ethnicity and race are distinct from nationality, another way people identify their membership with a group. **Nationality** is identity with a group of people who share legal attachment and personal allegiance to a particular country.

Nationality and ethnicity are similar concepts in that both involve identification with a place. In principle, the cultural values shared with others of the same ethnicity derive from religion, language, and folk culture, whereas those shared with others of the same nationality derive from voting, obtaining a passport, and performing civic duties.

NATIONALITIES IN NORTH AMERICA

In the United States, nationality is generally kept reasonably distinct from ethnicity in common usage:

- The American *nationality* identifies citizens of the United States of America, including those born in the country and those who immigrated and became citizens.

- *Ethnicity* in the United States identifies groups with distinct ancestry and cultural traditions, such as African Americans, Hispanic Americans, Chinese Americans, and Polish Americans.

The United States forged a nationality in the late eighteenth century through sharing the values expressed in the Declaration of Independence, the U.S. Constitution, and the Bill of Rights. To be American meant believing in the "unalienable rights" of "life, liberty, and the pursuit of happiness," and electing a President rather than submitting to a hereditary monarch (Figure 7.5.1). Initially, the last part was only true if you were a white male: African Americans weren't considered full citizens until the nineteenth century, and women weren't allowed to vote for president until the twentieth century.

Canadian is also a nationality (Figure 7.5.2). Within Canada, the Québécois are clearly distinct from other Canadians in language, religion, and other cultural traditions. But do the Québécois form a distinct ethnicity within the Canadian nationality or a second nationality separate altogether from Anglo-Canadian? The distinction is critical, because if Québécois is recognized as a separate nationality from Anglo-Canadian, the Québec government would have a much stronger justification for breaking away from Canada to form an independent country (refer to section 5.8).

Outside North America, distinctions between ethnicity and nationality are even muddier. We have already seen in this chapter that ethnic and racial discrimination can lead to segregation and inequality. Issues between ethnicity and nationality can also lead to conflict.

▼ 7.5.1 **NATIONALITY IN THE UNITED STATES** Independence Day parade in Rhode Island.

▼ 7.5.2 **NATIONALITY IN CANADA** Canada Day (July 1) celebration in Ottawa.

► 7.5.3 **NATIONALITY AND ETHNICITY IN LATIN AMERICA**

Select MapMaster Latin America in Mastering **GEOGRAPHY**

Select *Political* then *Countries*.

Select *Geopolitical* then *Shifting Political Boundaries – 1830*.

Select *Cultural* then *Dominant Ethnic Group*.

1. **Which countries in Latin America have boundaries today that closely match those at the time of independence?**

2. **Which of these countries appears to have one ethnicity occupying all or nearly all of the territory of the state?**

NATIONALISM

Nationalism is loyalty and devotion to a nationality (Figure 7.5.3). Nationalism typically promotes a sense of national consciousness that exalts one nationality above all others and emphasizes its culture and interests as opposed to those of other nationalities. People display nationalism by supporting a state that preserves and enhances the culture and attitudes of their nationality.

Nationalism is an important example of a **centripetal force**, which is an attitude that tends to unify people and enhance support for a state. (The word centripetal means "directed toward the center"; it is the opposite of centrifugal, which means "to spread out from the center.") Most states find that the best way to achieve citizen support is to emphasize shared attitudes that unify the people.

States foster nationalism by promoting symbols such as flags and songs. The symbol of the hammer and sickle on a field of red was long synonymous with the beliefs of communism (Figure 7.5.4). After the fall of communism, one of the first acts in several countries was to redesign a flag without the hammer and sickle (Figure 7.5.5).

Nationalism can have a negative impact. The sense of unity within a nationality is sometimes achieved through the creation of negative images of other nationalities. Travelers in southeastern Europe during the twentieth century found that jokes directed by one nationality against another recurred in the same form throughout the region, with only the name of the target changed. For example, "How many [fill in the name of a nationality] are needed to change a lightbulb?" Such jokes seemed harmless, but in hindsight reflected the intense dislike for other nationalities that led to conflict and breakup of countries.

DATES OF INDEPENDENCE
- Bolivia, 1825
- Brazil, 1822
- Chile, 1817
- Gran Colombia, 1819–1830
- Mexico, 1821
- Paraguay, 1811
- Peru, 1821
- United Provinces of Central America, 1823–1839
- United Provinces of La Plata, 1816
- Uruguay, 1828

▲ 7.5.4 **NATIONALISM IN UKRAINE UNDER COMMUNISM**
Under communism, Ukraine observed Revolution Day (November 7), when the Communists declared victory in 1917. As part of the Soviet Union, Ukraine's flag included symbols of communism, including the hammer and sickle and a partially red field.

► 7.5.5 **NATIONALISM IN UKRAINE AFTER COMMUNISM**
After the fall of communism in 1991, Ukraine changed its day of national celebration to August 24, when it became independent of the Soviet Union. Ukraine also changed its flag to one it used before it became part of the Soviet Union in 1922.

7.6 Combining and Dividing Ethnicities

▶ **Some nationalities peacefully embrace multiple ethnicities, and others do not.**
▶ **Some ethnicities have been divided among multiple nationalities.**

Few ethnicities inhabit an area that matches the territory of a nationality. Many nationalities have peacefully combined more than one ethnicity—but not all.

PEACE IN COMBINING ETHNICITIES: THE UNITED KINGDOM

The United Kingdom contains four main groups—English, Welsh, Scots, and Irish (Figure 7.6.1). The four have had different historical experiences.

- **English** The English are descendents of Germanic tribes who crossed the North Sea and invaded the country in the fifth century (see section 5.4).

- **Welsh** The Welsh were Celtic people conquered by England in 1282 and formally united with England through the Act of Union of 1536. Welsh laws were abolished, and Wales became a local government unit.

- **Scots** The Scots were Celtic people who had an independent country for nearly a thousand years, until 1603 when Scotland's King James VI also became King James I of England, thereby uniting the two countries. The Act of Union in 1707 formally merged the two governments, although Scotland was allowed to retain its own systems of education and local laws. England, Wales,

and Scotland together comprise Great Britain, and the term British refers to the combined nationality of the three groups.

- **Irish** Northern Ireland, along with the rest of Ireland, was ruled by the British until the 1920s. The 1801 Act of Union created the United Kingdom of Great Britain and Ireland. During the 1920s most of Ireland became a separate country, but the northern portion—with a majority of Protestants—remained under British control. The official name of the country was changed to the United Kingdom of Great Britain and Northern Ireland.

Today the strongest element of ethnic identity comes from sports. England, Scotland, Wales, and Northern Ireland field their own soccer and rugby teams and compete separately in major international tournaments, such as the World Cup (soccer) and the Six Nations' Championship (rugby).

▲ 7.6.1 **UNITED KINGDOM**

DIVIDING AN ETHNICITY: KURDS

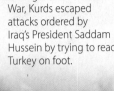

▼ 7.6.2 **KURDS ESCAPING ATTACK** During the 1991 Gulf War, Kurds escaped attacks ordered by Iraq's President Saddam Hussein by trying to reach Turkey on foot.

The Kurds are Sunni Muslims who speak a language in the Iranian group of the Indo-Iranian branch of Indo-European and have distinctive literature, dress, and other cultural traditions. The approximately 35 million Kurds are split among several countries, approximately one-half in Turkey and most of the remainder split among Iran, Iraq, and Syria (refer to Figure 7.7.2). Kurds comprise one-fourth of the population in Turkey and one-fifth in Iraq.

When the victorious European allies carved up the Ottoman Empire after World War I, they created an independent state of Kurdistan to the south and west of Van Gölü (Lake Van) under the 1920 Treaty of Sèvres. Before the treaty was ratified, however, the Turks, under the leadership of Mustafa Kemal (later known as Kemal Ataturk), fought successfully to expand

the territory under their control beyond the small area the allies had allocated to them.

Kurds lived in an independent nation-state called Kurdistan during the early 1920s, but Kurdistan became part of Turkey in 1923. To foster the development of a Turkish nationality, the Turks have tried repeatedly to suppress Kurdish culture. Use of the Kurdish language was illegal in Turkey until 1991, and laws banning its use in broadcasts and classrooms remain in force. Kurdish nationalists, for their part, have waged a guerrilla war since 1984 against the Turkish army.

Kurds in other countries have fared just as poorly as those in Turkey. Iran's Kurds secured an independent republic in 1946, but it lasted less than a year. Iraq's Kurds have made several unsuccessful attempts to gain independence, most recently after the 1991 Gulf War (Figure 7.6.2).

CONFLICT IN COMBINING ETHNICITIES: LEBANON

Lebanon is divided between around 60 percent Muslims and 39 percent Christians. The precise distribution of religions in Lebanon is unknown, because no census has been taken since 1932. Lebanon's most numerous Christian sects are Maronites and Greek Orthodox. Most of Lebanon's Muslims belong to one of several Shiite sects. Lebanon also has an important community of Druze, who were once considered a separate religion but now consider themselves Muslim.

Lebanon's diversity appears to be religious, not ethnic. But most of Lebanon's Christians consider themselves ethnically descended from the ancient Phoenicians who once occupied present-day Lebanon. In this way, Lebanon's Christians differentiate themselves from the country's Muslims, who are considered Arabs.

Lebanon's religious groups have tended to live in different regions of the country (Figure 7.6.3). Maronites are concentrated in the west central part, Sunnis in the northwest, and Shiites in the south and east. Beirut, the capital and largest city, has been divided between an eastern Christian zone and a western Muslim zone.

When Lebanon became independent in 1943, the constitution required that each religion be represented in the Chamber of Deputies according to its percentage in the 1932 census. At first, Christians constituted a majority and controlled the country's main businesses, but as the Muslims became the majority they demanded political and economic equality. Lebanon's government was unable to deal with changing social and economic conditions. A civil war broke out in 1975, and each religious group formed a private army or militia to guard its territory.

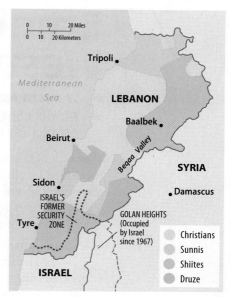

▲ 7.6.3 **ETHNICITIES IN LEBANON**

CONFLICT IN COMBINING ETHNICITIES: SRI LANKA

Sri Lanka (formerly Ceylon), an island country of 20 million inhabitants off the Indian coast, is inhabited principally by two ethnicities known as Sinhalese and Tamil (Figure 7.6.4). War between the two ethnicities erupted in 1983 and continued until 2009. During that period, 80,000 died in the conflict.

Sinhalese, who comprise 82 percent of Sri Lanka's population, migrated from northern India in the fifth century B.C., occupying the southern portion of the island. Three hundred years later the Sinhalese were converted to Buddhism, and Sri Lanka became one of that religion's world centers. Sinhalese is an Indo-European language, in the Indo-Iranian branch.

Tamils—14 percent of Sri Lanka's population— migrated across the narrow 80-kilometer-wide (50-mile-wide) Palk Strait from India beginning in the third century B.C. and occupied the northern part of the island. Tamils are Hindus, and the Tamil language, in the Dravidian family, is also spoken by 60 million people in India.

The dispute between the two ethnicities extends back more than 2,000 years but was suppressed during 300 years of European control. Since independence in 1948, Sinhalese have dominated the government, military, and most of the commerce. Tamils feel that they suffer from discrimination at the hands of the Sinhalese-dominated government and received support for the rebellion that began in 1983 from Tamils living in other countries. The long war between the two ethnicities ended in 2009 with the defeat of the Tamils.

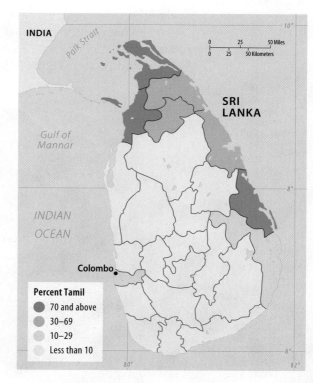

► 7.6.4 **ETHNICITIES IN SRI LANKA, 1976** When the ethnic conflict ended in 2009 with the defeat of the Tamils, the Sinhalese took control of most of the country.

Percent Tamil
- 70 and above
- 30–69
- 10–29
- Less than 10

7.7 Ethnic Diversity in Western Asia

▶ **Western Asia is a complex area of nationalities and ethnicities.**

▶ **Ethnic conflict in Western Asia has resulted in part from a mismatch between ethnicities and nationalities.**

The lack of correspondence between the territory occupied by ethnicities and nationalities is especially severe in Western Asia. Dozens of ethnicities inhabit the region, allocated among seven nationalities (Figure 7.7.1):

- Iraqi nationality. The most numerous ethnicity is Arab. The major ethnicities are divided into numerous tribes and clans. Most Iraqis actually have stronger loyalty to a tribe or clan than to the nationality or a major ethnicity (Figure 7.7.2).

- Armenian nationality. Armenian is both an ethnicity and a nationality (Figure 7.7.3).

- Azerbaijani nationality. Most numerous is Azeri, but Armenians represent an important minority (refer to Figure 7.7.3).

- Georgian nationality. Most numerous is Georgian (refer to Figure 7.7.3).

- Afghan nationality. The most numerous ethnicities are Pashtun, Tajik, and Hazara (Figure 7.7.4).

- Iranian nationality. The most numerous is Persian, but Azeri and Baluchi represent important minorities (Figure 7.7.5).

- Pakistani nationality. The most numerous are Punjabi, but the border area with Afghanistan is principally Baluchi and Pashtun (Figure 7.7.6).

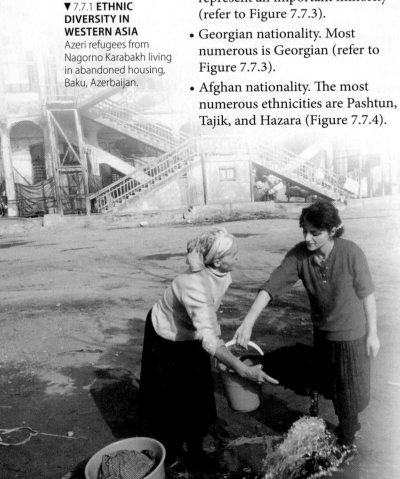

▼ 7.7.1 ETHNIC DIVERSITY IN WESTERN ASIA
Azeri refugees from Nagorno Karabakh living in abandoned housing, Baku, Azerbaijan.

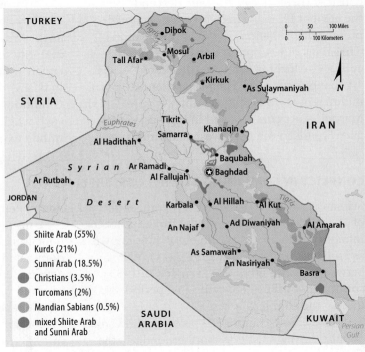

Legend:
- Shiite Arab (55%)
- Kurds (21%)
- Sunni Arab (18.5%)
- Christians (3.5%)
- Turcomans (2%)
- Mandian Sabians (0.5%)
- mixed Shiite Arab and Sunni Arab

▲ 7.7.2 ETHNICITIES IN IRAQ

The United States led an attack against Iraq in 2003 that resulted in the removal and death of the country's longtime president, Saddam Hussein. U.S. officials justified removing Hussein because he ran a brutal dictatorship, created weapons of mass destruction, and allegedly had close links with terrorists (see Chapter 8). Having invaded Iraq and removed Hussein from power, the United States expected an enthusiastic welcome from the Iraqi nation. Instead, the United States became embroiled in a complex and violent struggle among ethnic groups.

- Kurds welcomed the United States because they gained more security and autonomy than they had under Hussein.
- Sunni Muslim Arabs opposed the U.S.-led attack, because they feared loss of power and privilege given to them by Hussein, who was a Sunni.
- Shiite Muslim Arabs also opposed the U.S. presence. Although they had been treated poorly by Hussein and controlled Iraq's post-Hussein government, Shiites shared a long-standing hostility toward the United States with their neighbors in Shiite-controlled Iran.

Most Iraqis have stronger loyalty to a tribe or clan than to the nationality or major ethnicity. A tribe (ashira) is divided into several clans (fukhdhs), which in turn encompass several houses (beit), which in turn include several extended families (kham). Tribes are grouped into more than a dozen federations (qabila).

7.7.3 ETHNICITIES IN ARMENIA, AZERBAIJAN, AND GEORGIA

These nationalities became independent of the Soviet Union in 1991 (see section 8.3).

- Armenians once controlled an extensive empire, but more than one million were massacred by the Turks during the late nineteenth and early twentieth centuries.
- Azeris trace their roots to Turkish invaders who migrated from Central Asia in the eighth and ninth centuries and merged with the existing Persian population.
- Armenians and Azeris have clashed several times over control of Nagorno-Karabakh, an enclave within Azerbaijan inhabited primarily by Armenians (refer to Figure 7.7.1).
- Georgia is a more diverse country. Ossetians and Abkhazians have both attempted to leave Georgia and set up independent countries, with support from nearby Russia.

7.7.4 ETHNICITIES IN AFGHANISTAN

The current unrest among Afghanistan's ethnicities dates from 1979, with the start of a rebellion by several ethnic groups against the government, which was being defended by more than 100,000 troops from the Soviet Union. Unable to subdue the rebellion, the Soviet Union withdrew its troops in 1989, and the Soviet-installed government in Afghanistan collapsed in 1992. After several years of infighting among ethnicities, a faction of the Pashtun called the Taliban (which means "religious students") gained control over most of the country in 1995. The Taliban imposed very harsh, strict laws on Afghanistan, according to Islamic values as the Taliban interpreted them. The United States invaded Afghanistan in 2001 and overthrew the Taliban-led government, because it was harboring terrorists (see Chapter 8). Removal of the Taliban unleashed a new struggle for control of Afghanistan among the country's many ethnic groups, including the Taliban.

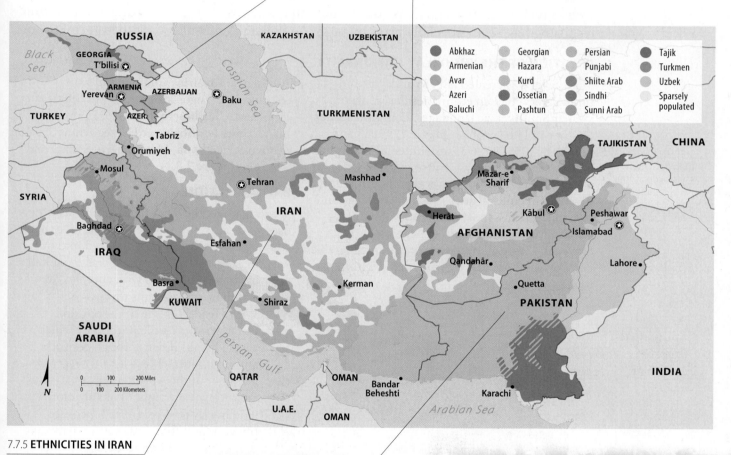

7.7.5 ETHNICITIES IN IRAN

Persians constitute the world's largest ethnic group that adheres to Shiite Islam. Persians are believed to be descendents of the Indo-European tribes that began migrating from Central Asia into what is now Iran several thousand years ago (see Chapter 5). The Persian Empire extended from present-day Iran west as far as Egypt during the fifth and fourth centuries B.C. After the Muslim army conquered Persia in the seventh century, most Persians converted to Sunni Islam. The conversion to Shiite Islam came primarily in the fifteenth century.

7.7.6 ETHNICITIES IN PAKISTAN

The Punjabi have been the most numerous ethnicity since ancient times in what is now Pakistan. As with the neighboring Pashtun, the Punjabi converted to Islam after they were conquered by the Muslim army in the seventh century. The Punjabi remained Sunni Muslims rather than convert to Shiite Islam like their neighbors the Pashtun, who comprise Pakistan's second largest ethnicity, especially along the border with Afghanistan. (right) Fighting between Pakistan's army and supporters of the Taliban forced Pakistanis to leave their homes and move into camps, where they were fed by international relief organizations.

7.8 Ethnic Cleansing in the Balkans

▶ **Ethnic cleansing is the forcible removal of an ethnic group by a more powerful one.**

▶ **Southeastern Europe has suffered as a result of ethnic cleansing in recent years.**

Ethnic cleansing is a process in which a more powerful ethnic group forcibly removes a less powerful one in order to create an ethnically homogeneous region. Ethnic cleansing is undertaken to rid an area of an entire ethnicity so that the surviving ethnic group can be the sole inhabitants. Rather than a clash between armies of male soldiers, ethnic cleansing involves the removal of every member of the less powerful ethnicity—women as well as men, children as well as adults, the frail elderly as well as the strong youth. Ethnic cleansing has been especially prominent in the Balkan Peninsula of southeastern Europe.

CREATION OF THE YUGOSLAV NATIONALITY

Yugoslavia was created after World War I to unite several Balkan ethnicities that spoke similar South Slavic languages. Longtime leader Josip Broz Tito (prime minister 1943–63 and president 1953–80) was instrumental in forging a Yugoslav nationality. Central to Tito's vision of a Yugoslav nationality was acceptance of ethnic diversity in cultural areas, such as language and religion. The five most numerous ethnicities—Croats, Macedonians, Montenegrins, Serbs, Slovenes—were allowed to exercise considerable control over the areas they inhabited within Yugoslavia. Rivalries among ethnicities resurfaced in Yugoslavia during the 1980s after Tito's death, leading to its breakup into seven small countries: Bosnia & Herzegovina, Croatia, Kosovo, Macedonia, Montenegro, Serbia, and Slovenia (Figure 7.8.1).

BALKANIZATION

A century ago, the term Balkanized was widely used to describe a small geographic area that could not successfully be organized into one or more stable states because it was inhabited by many ethnicities with complex, long-standing antagonisms toward each other. World leaders at the time regarded **Balkanization**—the process by which a state breaks down through conflicts among its ethnicities—as a threat to peace throughout the world, not just in a small area. They were right: Balkanization led directly to World War I, because the various nationalities in the Balkans dragged into the war the larger powers with which they had alliances.

After two world wars and the rise and fall of communism during the twentieth century, the Balkans has once again become Balkanized in the twenty-first century. Peace has come to the Balkans in a tragic way, through the "success" of ethnic cleansing. Millions of people were rounded up and killed or forced to migrate because they constituted ethnic minorities.

▼ **7.8.1 ETHNICITIES IN FORMER YUGOSLAVIA** Until its breakup in 1992, Yugoslavia comprised six republics (Bosnia & Herzegovina, Croatia, Macedonia, Montenegro, Serbia, and Slovenia), plus two autonomous regions (Kosovo and Vojvodina).

Legend:
- Albanians
- Croats
- Macedonians
- Muslims
- Slovenes
- Bulgarians
- Hungarians
- Montenegrins
- Serbs
- No predominant majority

◄ 7.8.2 **ETHNIC CLEANSING IN BOSNIA & HERZEGOVINA**
The Stari Most (old bridge), built by the Turks in 1566 across the Neretva River, was an important symbol and tourist attraction in the city of Mostar. (left) The bridge was blown up by Serbs in 1993 in an attempt to demoralize Bosnian Muslims as part of ethnic cleansing. (right) With the end of the war in Bosnia & Herzegovina, the bridge was rebuilt in 2004.

BOSNIA & HERZEGOVINA

At the time of Yugoslavia's breakup, Bosnia & Herzegovina was a mix of three ethnicities: 48 percent Bosnian Muslim, 37 percent Serb, and 14 percent Croat. Rather than live in an independent country with a Muslim plurality, Bosnia & Herzegovina's Serbs and Croats fought to unite the portions of the republic that they inhabited with neighboring Serbia and Croatia, respectively.

To strengthen their cases for breaking away from Bosnia & Herzegovina, Serbs and Croats engaged in ethnic cleansing of Bosnian Muslims. Ethnic cleansing by Bosnian Serbs against Bosnian Muslims was especially severe, because much of the territory inhabited by Bosnian Serbs was separated from Serbia by areas with Bosnian Muslim majorities (Figure 7.8.2). By ethnically cleansing Bosnian Muslims from intervening areas, Bosnian Serbs created one continuous area of Bosnian Serb domination rather than several discontinuous ones (Figure 7.8.3).

Accords reached in Dayton, Ohio, in 1996 by leaders of the three ethnicities divided Bosnia & Herzegovina into three regions, one each dominated, respectively, by the Bosnian Croats, Muslims, and Serbs. Because of their successful ethnic cleansing, Bosnian Serbs and Croats received more land than their share of the population warranted.

BOSNIA & HERZEGOVINA

► 7.8.3 **BOSNIA AFTER ETHNIC CLEANSING**
Compare the current distribution of ethnicities to Figure 7.8.1, which shows the distribution before ethnic cleansing.

● Predominantly Croat
● Predominantly Bosnian
● Predominantly Serb
● Bosnian-Croat mix

KOSOVO

The population of Kosovo is more than 90 percent ethnic Albanian. At the same time, Serbs consider Kosovo an essential place in the formation of the Serb ethnicity, because they fought an important—though losing—battle against the Ottoman Empire there in 1389.

As part of Yugoslavia, Kosovo had been an autonomous province. With the breakup of Yugoslavia, Serbia took direct control of Kosovo and launched a campaign of ethnic cleansing of the Albanian majority. At its peak in 1999, Serb ethnic cleansing had forced 750,000 of Kosovo's 2 million ethnic Albanian residents from their homes, mostly to camps in Albania (Figure 7.8.4).

Outraged by the ethnic cleansing, the United States and western European countries, operating through the North Atlantic Treaty Organization (NATO), launched an air attack against Serbia. The bombing campaign ended when Serbia agreed to withdraw all of its soldiers and police from Kosovo.

Kosovo declared independence from Serbia in 2008. The United States and most European countries have recognized the independence, but countries allied with Serbia, including China and Russia, oppose it.

GLODANE VILLAGE, KOSOVO

CIVILIAN VEHICLES

INTERNALLY DISPLACED PERSONS

ARMORED VEHICLES

◄ 7.8.4 **ETHNIC CLEANSING IN KOSOVO**
In this photo taken by NATO air reconnaissance in 1999, the village of Glodane is on the west (left) side of the road. The villagers and their vehicles have been rounded up and placed in the field east of the road. The red circles show the locations of Serb armored vehicles.

7.9 Ethnic Competition and Genocide in Africa

► Genocide is the mass killing of a population by another group.
► Genocide has been practiced in several areas of sub-Saharan Africa.

Ethnicities compete in many places to dominate territory and control the defining of a nationality. This competition can lead to war and ethnic cleansing, as discussed in previous sections. In a handful of the most extreme cases, competition can lead to the most extreme action, which is genocide.

Genocide is the mass killing of a group of people in an attempt to eliminate the entire group from existence. Sub-Saharan Africa has been plagued by conflicts among ethnic groups that have resulted in genocide in recent years, especially in Sudan and in central Africa.

ETHNIC COMPETITION AND GENOCIDE IN SUDAN

Sudan, a country of 42 million inhabitants, has had several civil wars in recent years (Figure 7.9.1).

• **South Sudan.** Black Christian and animist ethnicities in the south resisted attempts by the Arab Muslim–dominated government forces in the north to impose a unified nationality based on fundamentalist Muslim principles, including harsh repression of women. A north-south war between 1983 and 2005 resulted in the death of an estimated 1.9 million Sudanese, mostly civilians. The war ended with the establishment of South Sudan as an independent state in 2011. However, fighting resumed as the governments of Sudan and South Sudan could not agree on boundaries between the two countries.

• **Darfur.** As Sudan's religion-based civil war was winding down, an ethnic war erupted in Sudan's westernmost Darfur region. Resenting discrimination and neglect by the national government, Darfur's black Africans launched a rebellion in 2003. Marauding Arab nomads, known as janjaweed, with the support of the Sudanese government, crushed Darfur's black population, made up mainly of settled farmers. 480,000 have been killed and another 2.8 million have been living in dire conditions in refugee camps in the harsh desert environment of Darfur. Actions of Sudan's government troops, including mass murders and rape of civilians, have been termed genocide by many other countries, and charges of war crimes have been filed against Sudan's leaders (Figure 7.9.2).

• **Eastern Front.** Ethnicities in the east fought Sudanese government forces between 2004 and 2006 with the support of neighboring Eritrea. At issue was disbursement of profits from oil.

▼ 7.9.1 **SUDAN AND SOUTH SUDAN**

▼ 7.9.2 **DARFUR**
Sudanese police stand guard in the 4 sq km Abu Shouk refugee camp in Al Fasher, North Darfur, Sudan.

GENOCIDE IN CENTRAL AFRICA

Long-standing conflicts between two ethnic groups, the Hutus and Tutsis, lie at the heart of genocide in central Africa.

- Hutus were settled farmers, growing crops in the fertile hills and valleys of present-day Rwanda and Burundi, known as the Great Lakes region of central Africa.

- Tutsis were cattle herders who migrated to present-day Rwanda and Burundi from the Rift Valley of western Kenya beginning 400 years ago.

Relations between settled farmers and herders are often uneasy—this is also an element of the ethnic cleansing in Darfur discussed earlier. Genocide has been most severe in Rwanda and the Congo:

- **Rwanda.** Genocide in Rwanda in 1994 involved Hutus murdering hundreds of thousands of Tutsis (as well as Hutus sympathetic to the Tutsis). Hutus constituted a majority of the population of Rwanda historically, but Tutsis controlled the kingdom of Rwanda for several hundred years and had turned the Hutu into their serfs. As a colony of Germany and then Belgium during the first half of the twentieth century, Tutsis were given more privileges than the Hutus. Shortly before Rwanda gained its independence in 1962, Hutus killed or ethnically cleansed many Tutsis out of fear that the Tutsis would seize control of the newly independent country. After an airplane carrying the presidents of Rwanda and Burundi was shot down in 1994, probably by a Tutsi, the genocide began (Figure 7.9.3).

- **Congo.** The conflict between Hutus and Tutsis spilled into neighboring countries, especially the Democratic Republic of the Congo. Several million have died in the Congo in a war that began in 1998 and is the world's deadliest since World War II. The war started after Tutsis helped to overthrow the Congo's longtime president, Joseph Mobutu. Mobutu had amassed a several-billion-dollar personal fortune from the sale of minerals while impoverishing the rest of the country. After succeeding Mobutu as president, Laurent Kabila relied heavily on Tutsis and permitted them to kill some of the Hutus who had been responsible for atrocities against Tutsis back in the early 1990s. But Kabila soon split with the Tutsis, and the Tutsis once again found themselves offering support to rebels seeking to overthrow Congo's government. Kabila turned for support to Hutus, and armies from neighboring countries came to Kabila's aid. Kabila was assassinated in 2001 and succeeded by his son, who negotiated an accord with rebels the following year.

▼ 7.9.3 **RWANDA**
Thousands of Rwandan Hutu refugees from Gisenyi, Rwanda, cross the border into Goma, in the Democratic Republic of the Congo.

For many ethnicities, sharing space with other ethnicities is difficult, if not impossible. Grievances real and imagined, extending back hundreds of years, prevent peaceful coexistence. Even in countries like the United States, where ethnic diversity is a central feature of the shaping of the American nationality, discriminatory practices cast a long shadow over American history.

Key Questions

Where are ethnicities and races distributed?

► Ethnicity is identity with a group of people who share the cultural traditions of a particular homeland or hearth.

► Race is identity with a group of people who share a biological ancestor.

► Major ethnicities in the United States include African Americans, Hispanic Americans, Asian Americans, and Native Americans.

► Ethnic groups are clustered in regions of the country and within urban neighborhoods.

► African Americans have a distinctive history of forced migration for slavery.

Where are ethnicities and nationalities distributed?

► Nationality is identity with a group of people who share legal attachment and personal allegiance to a particular country.

► A nationality combines an ethnic group's language, religion, and artistic expressions with a country's particular independence movement, history, and patriotism.

Where do ethnicities face conflicts?

► The territory of a nationality rarely matches that inhabited by only one ethnicity.

► Ethnicities compete in many places to dominate territory and control the defining of a nationality.

► Ethnic cleansing is a process in which a more powerful ethnic group forcibly removes a less powerful one in order to create an ethnically homogeneous region.

► Genocide is the mass killing of a group of people in an attempt to eliminate the entire group out of existence.

On the Internet

The U.S. Bureau of the Census provides the most detailed information on the distribution by race and ethnicity in the United States at **www.census.gov**, or scan the QR at the beginning of the chapter.

Thinking Geographically

The U.S. Census permits people to identify themselves as being of more than one race, in recognition that several million American children have parents of two races.

1. What are the merits and difficulties of permitting people to choose more than one race.

Sarajevo, capital of Bosnia & Herzegovina, once contained concentrations of many ethnic groups. In retaliation for ethnic cleansing by the Serbs and Croats, the Bosnian Muslims now in control of Sarajevo have been forcing other ethnic groups to leave the city, and Sarajevo is now inhabited overwhelmingly by Bosnian Muslims (Figure 7.CR.1).

2. What are the challenges in restoring Sarajevo as a city that multiple ethnicities could inhabit?

A century ago European immigrants to the United States had much stronger ethnic ties than today, including clustering in specific neighborhoods..

3. What is the rationale for retaining strong ethnic identity in the United States as opposed to full assimilation into the American nationality?

▼ 7.CR.1 **SARAJEVO WAR GRAVES**

Interactive Mapping

ETHNICITIES AND NATIONALITIES IN SOUTHEAST ASIA

Matching the territory of a nationality to a single ethnicity is rare in the world.

Launch Mapmaster Southeast Asia in Mastering**GEOGRAPHY**

Select: *Cultural* then *Religions*. Select *Cutural* then *Languages* Select *Political* then *Countries*

Can you find an example of a nationality that almost entire encompasses a single ethnicity?

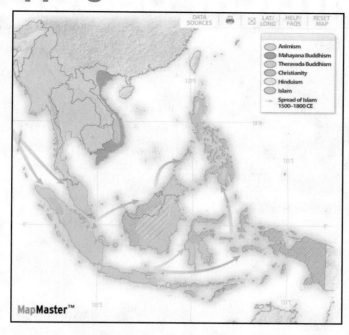

Key Terms

Apartheid
Laws (no longer in effect) in South Africa that physically separated different races into different geographic areas.

Balkanization
Process by which a state breaks down through conflicts among its ethnicities.

Centripetal force
An attitude that tends to unify people and enhance support for a state.

Ethnic cleansing
Process in which a more powerful ethnic group forcibly removes a less powerful one in order to create an ethnically homogeneous region.

Ethnicity
Identity with a group of people who share the cultural traditions of a particular homeland or hearth.

Genocide
The mass killing of a group of people in an attempt to eliminate the entire group from existence.

Nationalism
Loyalty and devotion to a particular nationality.

Nationality
Identity with a group of people who share legal attachment and personal allegiance to a particular place as a result of being born there.

Race
Identity with a group of people who share a biological ancestor.

Racism
Belief that race is the primary determinant of human traits and capacities and that racial differences produce an inherent superiority of a particular race.

Racist
A person who subscribes to the beliefs of racism.

Sharecropper
A person who works fields rented from a landowner and pays the rent and repays loans by turning over to the landowner a share of the crops.

Triangular slave trade
A practice, primarily during the eighteenth century, in which European ships transported slaves from Africa to Caribbean islands, molasses from the Caribbean to Europe, and trade goods from Europe to Africa.

Explore

MUSEUMS IN DETROIT
Use Google Earth to explore major museums in Detroit that represent ethnic traditions.

Fly to: *Charles H. Wright Museum of African American History, Detroit*

Click 3D Buildings

Drag to: *Enter Street View* in front of the museum.

Exit *Ground Level View* and zoom out until the street and buildings one block to the west are visible.

Click on the Wright museum to see a description of its collection.

Click on the large building in the front left to see what's inside.

How would you compare the collections of the two museums?

▶ LOOKING AHEAD

Ethnicities aspire to political control over areas of Earth through the creation of nation-states, discussed in the next chapter.

8 Political Geography

How many countries can you name? Old-style geography sometimes required memorization of countries and their capitals. One of Earth's most fundamental cultural characteristics—one that we take for granted—is the division of our planet's surface into countries.

In recent years, we have repeatedly experienced military conflicts and revolutionary changes in once obscure places. No one can predict where the next war will erupt, but political geography helps to explain the cultural and physical factors that underlie political unrest in the world. And you still need to know the locations of countries. Without such knowledge, it would be like translating an article in a foreign language by looking up each word in a dictionary.

What is a state?

HONG KONG'S BORDER BEFORE IT WAS UNIFIED WITH CHINA IN 1997

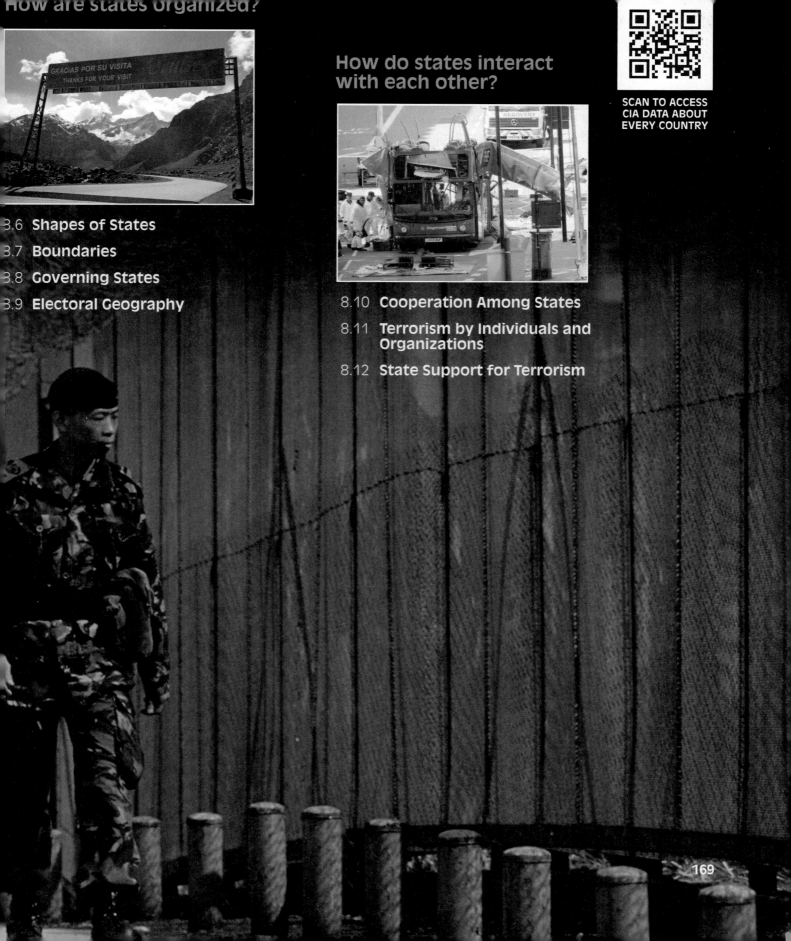

How are states organized?

How do states interact with each other?

SCAN TO ACCESS
CIA DATA ABOUT
EVERY COUNTRY

8.1 A World of States

► **The world is divided into nearly 200 states.**
► **All but a handful of states belong to the United Nations.**

A **state** is an area organized into a political unit and ruled by an established government that has control over its internal and foreign affairs. A state occupies a defined territory on Earth's surface and contains a permanent population. A state has **sovereignty**, which means control of its internal affairs without interference by other states. Because the entire area of a state is managed by its national government, laws, army, and leaders, it is a good example of a formal or uniform region. The term *country* is a synonym for state.

The term *state*, as used in political geography, does not refer to local governments, such as those inside the United States. The 50 "states" that comprise the United States are subdivisions within a single state—the United States of America.

A map of the world shows that nearly all states belong to the United Nations (Figure 8.1.1). When it was founded in 1945, only around 50 states were members of the UN (Figure 8.1.2). Membership grew to 193 states in 2011. The two most populous states not in the United Nations in 2011 were Kosovo (Figure 8.1.3) and Taiwan (Figure 8.1.4).

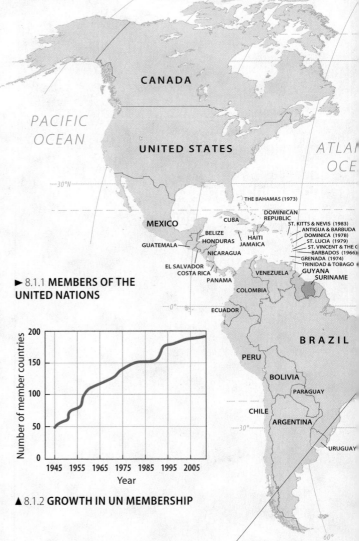

► 8.1.1 **MEMBERS OF THE UNITED NATIONS**

▲ 8.1.2 **GROWTH IN UN MEMBERSHIP**

◄ 8.1.3 **KOSOVO: A SOVEREIGN STATE?**
(left) The Republic of Kosovo declared its independence from Serbia in 2008, following ethnic cleansing and war crimes by some Serb leaders (refer to section 7.8). The United States and most European countries recognize Kosovo as an independent sovereign state, but Serbia, Russia, and most countries of Africa and Asia do not. (far left) Pristina, capital of Kosovo.

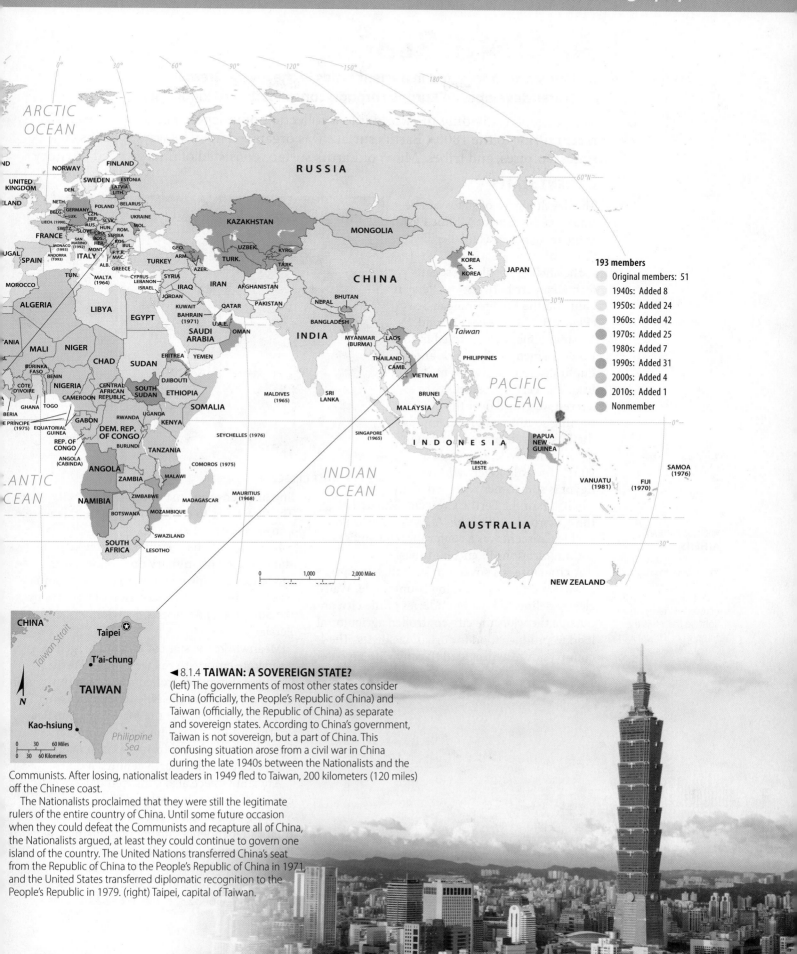

193 members

Original members: 51
1940s: Added 8
1950s: Added 24
1960s: Added 42
1970s: Added 25
1980s: Added 7
1990s: Added 31
2000s: Added 4
2010s: Added 1
Nonmember

◄ 8.1.4 **TAIWAN: A SOVEREIGN STATE?**
(left) The governments of most other states consider China (officially, the People's Republic of China) and Taiwan (officially, the Republic of China) as separate and sovereign states. According to China's government, Taiwan is not sovereign, but a part of China. This confusing situation arose from a civil war in China during the late 1940s between the Nationalists and the Communists. After losing, nationalist leaders in 1949 fled to Taiwan, 200 kilometers (120 miles) off the Chinese coast.

The Nationalists proclaimed that they were still the legitimate rulers of the entire country of China. Until some future occasion when they could defeat the Communists and recapture all of China, the Nationalists argued, at least they could continue to govern one island of the country. The United Nations transferred China's seat from the Republic of China to the People's Republic of China in 1971, and the United States transferred diplomatic recognition to the People's Republic in 1979. (right) Taipei, capital of Taiwan.

8.2 Ancient States

▶ **City-states originated in ancient times in the Fertile Crescent.**
▶ **States developed in Europe through consolidation of kingdoms.**

The concept of dividing the world into a collection of independent states is relatively recent. Prior to the 1800s, Earth's surface was organized in other ways, such as city-states, empires, and tribes. Much of Earth's surface consisted of unorganized territory.

ANCIENT STATES

The development of states can be traced to the ancient Middle East, in an area known as the Fertile Crescent.

The ancient Fertile Crescent formed an arc between the Persian Gulf and the Mediterranean Sea (Figure 8.2.1). The eastern end, Mesopotamia, was centered in the valley formed by the Tigris and Euphrates rivers, in present-day Iraq. The Fertile Crescent then curved westward over the desert, turning southward to encompass the Mediterranean coast through present-day Syria, Lebanon, and Israel. The Nile River valley of Egypt is sometimes regarded as an extension of the Fertile Crescent. Situated at the crossroads of Europe, Asia, and Africa, the Fertile Crescent was a center for land and sea communications in ancient times.

A **city-state** is a sovereign state that comprises a town and the surrounding countryside. Walls clearly delineated the boundaries of the city, and outside the walls the city controlled agricultural land to produce food for urban residents. The countryside also provided the city with an outer

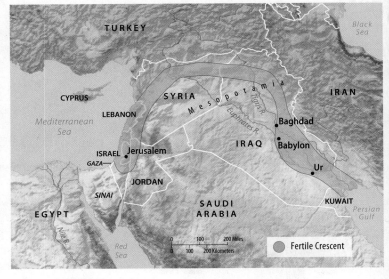

▲ 8.2.1 **FERTILE CRESCENT**

line of defense against attack by other city-states. The first states to evolve in Mesopotamia were known as city-states.

In Mesopotamia, periodically, one city-state would gain military dominance over the others and form an empire. Mesopotamia was organized into a succession of empires by the Sumerians, Assyrians, Babylonians, and Persians.

Meanwhile, the state of Egypt emerged as a separate empire to the west of the Fertile Crescent. Egypt controlled a long, narrow region along the banks of the Nile River, extending from the Nile Delta at the Mediterranean Sea southward for several hundred kilometers. Egypt's empire lasted from approximately 3000 B.C. until the fourth century B.C.

Ancient Greece also consisted of a collection city-states, including Athens, Corinth, and Sparta (Figure 8.2.2). The Greek city-states lost their independence during the fourth century B.C., when they were ruled by Macedonian kings, beginning with Philip II (382–336, ruled 359–336) and his son Alexander III ("Alexander the Great" 356–323, ruled 336–323).

▼ 8.2.2 **ANCIENT ATHENS**
The Parthenon, a temple to the goddess Athena, patron of the Athens city-state, is on the hilltop Acropolis (citadel) to the right. To the left is the Temple of Hephastaeus, the god of technology.

▲ 8.2.3 **ANCIENT ROME**
The most prominent building is the Temple of Jupiter, dedicated to the king of the ancient gods.

EUROPEAN STATES

Political unity in the ancient world reached its height with the establishment of the Roman Empire (Figure 8.2.3). The Roman Empire controlled most of Europe, North Africa, and Southwest Asia, from modern-day Spain to Iran and from Egypt to England (Figure 8.2.4). At its maximum extent, the empire comprised 38 provinces, each using the same set of laws that were created in Rome. Massive walls helped the Roman army defend many of the empire's frontiers (Figure 8.2.5).

The Roman Empire collapsed in the fifth century after a series of attacks by people living on its frontiers and because of internal disputes. The European portion of the Roman Empire was fragmented into a large number of estates owned by competing kings, dukes, barons, and other nobles. Victorious nobles seized control of defeated rivals' estates, and after these nobles died, others fought to take possession of their

▼ 8.2.5 **HADRIAN'S WALL.**
The Roman army built the wall beginning in A.D. 122 in northern Britain, possibly to prevent invasion or to control immigration.

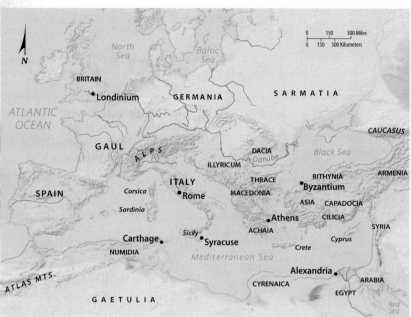

▲ 8.2.4 **ROMAN EMPIRE IN A.D. 100**

land. Meanwhile, most people were forced to live on an estate, working and fighting for the benefit of the noble.

A handful of powerful kings emerged as rulers over large numbers of estates beginning about the year 1100. The consolidation of neighboring estates under the unified control of a king formed the basis for the development of such modern European states as England, France, and Spain. However, much of central Europe—notably present-day Germany and Italy—remained fragmented into a large number of estates that were not consolidated into states until the nineteenth century (Figure 8.2.6).

▼ 8.2.6 **EUROPE IN 1300**

8.3 Nation-states and Multinational States

▶ In the modern world, many states have been created to encompass nationalities.
▶ A multinational state has more than one ethnicity recognized as distinct nationalities.

Many ethnic groups hold strong desires for **self-determination**, which is the right to govern themselves within sovereign states. A **nation-state** is a state whose territory corresponds to that occupied by a particular ethnicity that has been transformed into a nationality. Through the creation of nation-states, the aspiration of many ethnic groups for self-determination has been realized.

NATION-STATES IN EUROPE

Europe was transformed during the nineteenth and twentieth centuries from a fragmented collection of kingdoms, principalities, and empires (Figure 8.3.1, top) into nation-states (Figure 8.3.1, second). Boundaries between states were fixed to conform as closely as possible to those of leading ethnic groups.

Denmark is a fairly good example of a nation-state, because the territory occupied by the Danish ethnicity closely corresponds to the state of Denmark. But even Denmark is not a perfect example of a nation-state. The country's 80-kilometer (50-mile) southern boundary with Germany does not divide Danish and German ethnic groups precisely. To dilute the concept of a nation-state further, Denmark controls two territories in the Atlantic Ocean that do not share Danish cultural characteristics—the Faeroe Islands and Greenland (Figure 8.3.2).

Creating a German nation-state has proved especially challenging. Central Europe was a patchwork of hundreds of small states until the most powerful of them—Prussia—forged a German Empire in 1871. The boundaries of Germany were altered drastically twice during the twentieth century after losses in World War I (1914–18) and World War II (1939–45).

During the 1930s, German National Socialists (Nazis) claimed that all German-speaking parts of Europe constituted one nationality and should be unified into one state. They pursued this goal forcefully, and other European powers did not attempt to stop the Germans from taking over Austria and the German-speaking portion of Czechoslovakia, known as the Sudetenland. Not until the Germans invaded Poland (clearly not a German-speaking country) in 1939 did England and France try to stop them, marking the start of World War II.

After it was defeated in World War II, Germany was divided into two countries (Figure 8.3.1, third). Two Germanys existed from 1949 until 1990. With the collapse of communism in Europe, the German Democratic Republic ceased to exist, and its territory became part of the German Federal Republic (Figure 8.3.1, bottom).

▲ 8.3.1 **NATION-STATES IN EUROPE**

▲ 8.3.2 **DENMARK**

MULTINATIONAL STATES

A **multinational state** contains two or more ethnic groups with traditions of self-determination. Relationships among nationalities vary in different multinational states. In some states, one nationality tries to dominate another, especially if one of the nationalities greatly outnumbers the other, whereas in other states nationalities coexist peacefully.

The Union of Soviet Socialist Republics (U.S.S.R.) was an especially prominent example of a multinational state until its collapse in 1991 (Figure 8.3.3). The Soviet Union's 15 republics were based on its 15 largest ethnicities. The 15 largest ethnicities of the former Soviet Union are now independent countries that represent varying degrees of nation-states:

- **Three Baltic states: Estonia, Latvia, and Lithuania.** These three small neighbors have differences in language and religion and distinct historical traditions. They had been independent until annexed to the Soviet Union in 1940.

- **Three European states: Belarus, Moldova, Ukraine.** Belarusians and Ukrainians became distinctive ethnicities because they were isolated from the main body of Eastern Slavs—the Russians—between the thirteenth and eighteenth centuries. Moldovans are ethnically indistinguishable from Romanians.

- **Five Central Asian states: Kazakhstan, Kyrgyzstan, Tajikistan, Turkmenistan, and Uzbekistan.** The "stans" are predominantly Muslim and speak Altaic languages (except for Tajiks who speak a language similar to Persian).

- **Three Caucasus states: Armenia, Azerbaijan, and Georgia.** Armenians are Eastern Orthodox Christians who speak a separate branch of Indo-European. Azeris (or Azerbaijanis) are Muslims who speak an Altaic language. The two nation-states have clashed over their shared boundary. Georgians are Eastern Orthodox Christians. Two ethnicities within Georgia, the Ossetians and Abkhazianas, are fighting for autonomy and possible reunification with Russia.

- **Russia: Now the world's largest multinational state.** Russia identifies 21 national republics that are supposed to be the homes of its largest ethnicities, but the government recognizes in some way at least 170 ethnicities (Figure 8.3.4). Overall, 20 percent of the country's population is non-Russian. Particularly troublesome for the Russians are the ethnicities bordering the Caucasus states, especially the Chechens and Ossetians.

▲ 8.3.3 **STATES IN THE FORMER U.S.S.R.**

◀ 8.3.4 **ETHNICITIES IN FORMER U.S.S.R**

Slavic Peoples
- Russians
- Ukrainians
- Belorussians

Caucasian Peoples
- Georgians, Chechens, Ingush, peoples of Dagestan

Other Indo-European Peoples
- Lithuanians, Latvians, Armenians, Moldavians, Tadzhiks, Ossetians
- X Germans
- ▲ Jews

Turkic Peoples
- Tatars, Bashkirs, Kazakhs, Kirgiz
- Uzbeks
- Turkmen, Azerbaidzhani
- Other Turkic peoples

Paleo-Siberian Peoples
- Chukchi, Koryaks, Nivkhi
- Eskimos
- Uninhabited or sparsely settled

Other Uralic and Altaic Peoples
- Estonians, Karelians, Mari, Komi, Mordvins, Udmurts, Mansi, Khanty, Nentsy, Buryats, Kalmyks, Evenki, Eveny, Nganasany

8.4 Challenges in Defining States

▶ **The sovereignty of some land area is disputed.**
▶ **International treaties cover possession of polar and coastal regions.**

Most of the world has been allocated to sovereign states. A handful of places test the definition of sovereignty.

KOREA: ONE STATE OR TWO?

A colony of Japan for many years, Korea was divided into two occupation zones by the United States and the former Soviet Union after they defeated Japan in World War II (Figure 8.4.1). The division of these zones became permanent in the late 1940s, when the two superpowers established separate governments and withdrew their armies. The new government of the Democratic People's Republic of Korea (North Korea) then invaded the Republic of Korea (South Korea) in 1950, touching off a 3-year war that ended with a cease-fire line near the 38th parallel.

Both Korean governments are committed to reuniting the country into one sovereign state. However, progress toward reconciliation has been hindered by North Korea's decision to build nuclear weapons, even though the country has lacked the ability to provide its citizens with food, electricity, and other basic needs. Meanwhile, in 1992, North Korea and South Korea were admitted to the United Nations as separate countries.

▲ 8.4.1 **NORTH AND SOUTH KOREA**
A nighttime satellite image recorded by the U.S. Air Force Defense Meteorological Satellite Program shows the illumination of electric lights in South Korea, whereas North Korea has virtually no electric lights, a measure of its poverty and limited economic activity.

WESTERN SAHARA (SAHRAWI REPUBLIC)

The Sahrawi Arab Democratic Republic, also known as Western Sahara, is considered by most African countries as a sovereign state. Morocco, however, claims the territory and to prove it has built a 2,700-kilometer sand wall (known as a berm) around the territory to keep out rebels (Figure 8.4.2).

Spain controlled the territory on the continent's west coast between Morocco and Mauritania until withdrawing in 1976. An independent Sahrawi Republic was declared by the Polisario Front and recognized by most African countries, but Morocco and Mauritania annexed the northern and southern portions, respectively. Three years later Mauritania withdrew, and Morocco claimed the entire territory.

Morocco controls most of the populated area, but the Polisario Front operates in the vast, sparsely inhabited deserts, especially the one-fifth of the territory that lies east of Morocco's wall. The United Nations has tried but failed to reach a resolution between the parties.

▼ 8.4.2 **WESTERN SAHARA**
Morocco built a 2,700-kilometer-long wall to bolster its claim on the Western Sahara.

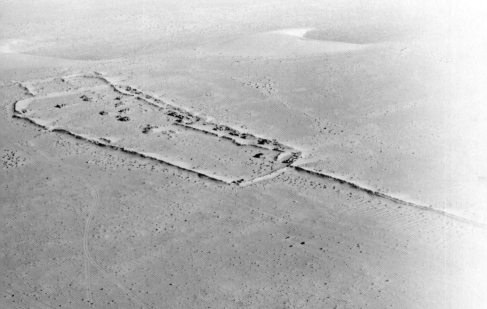

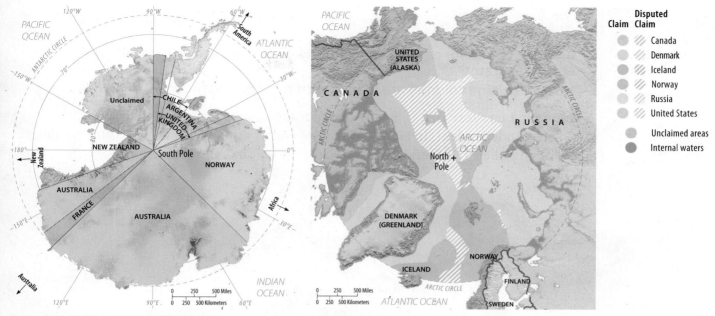

▲ 8.4.3 **NATIONAL CLAIMS TO ANTARCTICA**

▲ 8.4.4 **NATIONAL CLAIMS TO THE ARCTIC**

Legend:

Claim	Disputed Claim	
		Canada
		Denmark
		Iceland
		Norway
		Russia
		United States
		Unclaimed areas
		Internal waters

POLAR REGIONS: MANY CLAIMS

Antarctica is the only large land mass on Earth's surface that is not part of a state. Several states, including Argentina, Australia, Chile, France, New Zealand, Norway, and the United Kingdom, claim portions of Antarctica (Figure 8.4.3). Argentina, Chile, and the United Kingdom have made conflicting, overlapping claims. The United States, Russia, and a number of other states do not recognize the claims of any country to Antarctica. The Antarctic Treaty, signed in 1959, provides a legal framework for managing Antarctica. States may establish research stations there for scientific investigations, but no military activities are permitted. The treaty has been signed by 47 states.

As for the Arctic, the 1982 United Nations Convention on the Law of the Sea permitted countries to submit claims inside the Arctic Circle by 2009 (Figure 8.4.4). The Arctic region is thought to be rich in energy resources.

THE LAW OF THE SEA

The United Nations Convention on the Law of the Sea, signed by 158 countries, has defined waters extending various distances from the coastlines of states (Figure 8.4.5). Disputes can be taken to a Tribunal for the Law of the Sea or to the International Court of Justice.

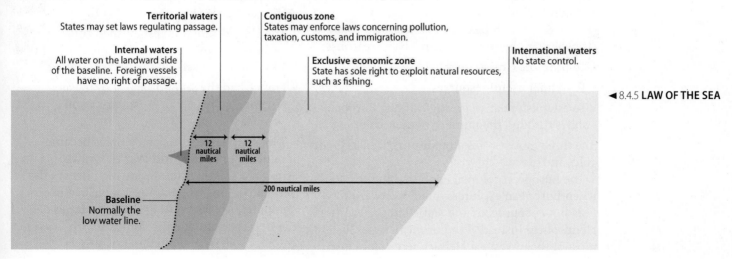

Territorial waters
States may set laws regulating passage.

Internal waters
All water on the landward side of the baseline. Foreign vessels have no right of passage.

Contiguous zone
States may enforce laws concerning pollution, taxation, customs, and immigration.

Exclusive economic zone
State has sole right to exploit natural resources, such as fishing.

International waters
No state control.

12 nautical miles
12 nautical miles
200 nautical miles

Baseline
Normally the low water line.

◄ 8.4.5 **LAW OF THE SEA**

8.5 Colonies

▶ **Until the twentieth century, much of the world consisted of colonies of European states.**

▶ **Most remaining colonies are islands with small populations.**

A **colony** is a territory that is legally tied to a sovereign state rather than being completely independent. In some cases, a sovereign state runs only the colony's military and foreign policy. In others, it also controls the colony's internal affairs.

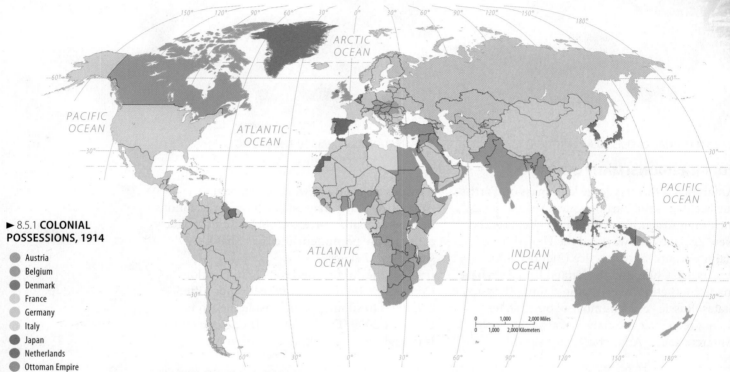

▶ 8.5.1 **COLONIAL POSSESSIONS, 1914**

- Austria
- Belgium
- Denmark
- France
- Germany
- Italy
- Japan
- Netherlands
- Ottoman Empire
- Portugal
- Russia
- Spain
- United Kingdom
- United States

EUROPEAN COLONIES

European states came to control much of the world through **colonialism**, which is the effort by one country to establish settlements in a territory and to impose its political, economic, and cultural principles on that territory (Figure 8.5.1). European states established colonies elsewhere in the world for three basic reasons:

- To promote Christianity.
- To extract useful resources.
- To establish relative prestige among European states through the number of their colonies.

The three motives could be summarized as God, gold, and glory.

The European colonial era began in the 1400s, when European explorers sailed westward for Asia but encountered and settled in the Western Hemisphere instead. The European states lost most of their Western Hemisphere colonies after independence was declared in 1776 by the United States and by most Latin American states between 1800 and 1824.

European states then turned their attention to Africa and Asia (Figure 8.5.2).

- The United Kingdom established colonies in every region of the world, and proclaimed that "the Sun never sets on the British Empire."

- France had the second-largest overseas territory, primarily in West Africa and Southeast Asia.

Most African and Asian colonies became independent after World War II. Only 15 African and Asian states were members of the United Nations when it was established in 1945, compared to 106 in 2011. The boundaries of the new states frequently coincide with former colonial provinces, although not always.

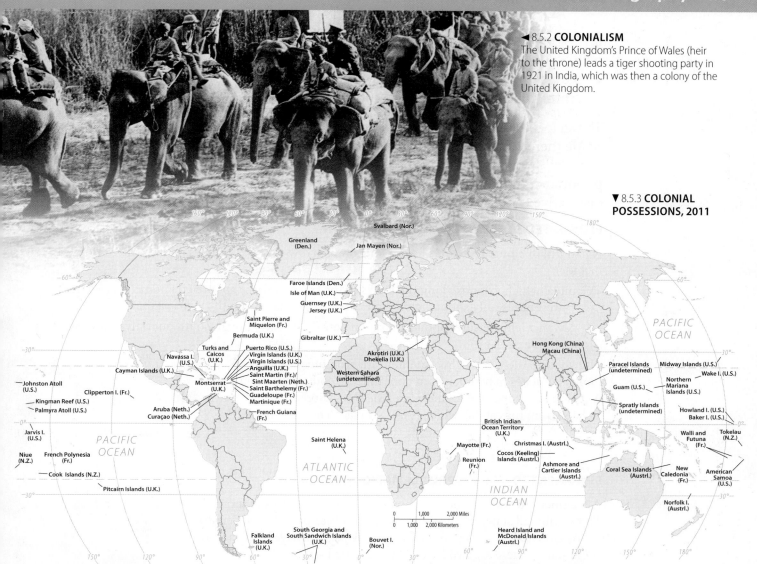

◀ 8.5.2 **COLONIALISM**
The United Kingdom's Prince of Wales (heir to the throne) leads a tiger shooting party in 1921 in India, which was then a colony of the United Kingdom.

▼ 8.5.3 **COLONIAL POSSESSIONS, 2011**

REMAINING COLONIES

The U.S. Department of State lists 68 places in the world that it calls dependencies and areas of special sovereignty (Figure 8.5.3). Most are islands in the Pacific Ocean or Caribbean Sea. The list includes 43 with indigenous populations and 25 with no permanent population.

The State Department list includes several entities that others do not classify as colonies:

• Greenland. Part of Denmark, it has a high degree of autonomy and self-rule and even makes independent foreign policy decisions.

• Hong Kong and Macao (Figure 8.5.4). Special Administrative Regions of China, with autonomy in economic matters but not in foreign and military affairs. Hong Kong was a colony of the United Kingdom until 1997, and Macao of Portugal until 1999.

On the other hand, the State Department list does not include several inhabited islands considered by other sources to be colonies, including Australia's Lord Howe Island, Britain's Ascension Island, and Chile's Easter Island.

▼ 8.5.4 **FLAGS OF HONG KONG**
Special Administrive Region (lower left) and People's Republic of China.

8.6 Shapes of States

▶ **States have one of five basic shapes.**
▶ **States that have no water boundary are landlocked.**

The shape of a state controls the length of its boundaries with other states. The shape therefore affects the potential for communication and conflict with neighbors. Countries have five basic shapes—compact, prorupted, elongated, fragmented, and perforated. Examples of each can be seen in sub-Saharan Africa. Each shape displays distinctive characteristics and challenges.

ELONGATED STATES: POTENTIAL ISOLATION

A handful of **elongated states** have a long and narrow shape. Examples in sub-Saharan Africa include :

• Gambia, which extends along the banks of the Gambia River about 500 kilometers (300 miles) east–west but is only about 25 kilometers (15 miles) north–south (Figure 8.6.1).

• Malawi, which measures about 850 kilometers (530 miles) north–south but only 100 kilometers (60 miles) east–west.

Elsewhere in the world, Chile and Italy are prominent examples. Elongated states may suffer from poor internal communications. A region located at an extreme end of the elongation might be isolated from the capital, which is usually placed near the center.

▲ 8.6.1 **GAMBIA: AN ELONGATED STATE**

FRAGMENTED STATES: PROBLEMATIC

A **fragmented state** includes several discontinuous pieces of territory. Technically, all states that have offshore islands as part of their territory are fragmented. However, fragmentation is particularly significant for some states. There are two kinds of fragmented states:

▼ 8.6.3 **TANZANIA: A FRAGMENTED STATE** Unguja (Zanzibar Island), part of Tanzania, includes Zanzibar City. Stone Town, shown here, is the old part of the city.

• Fragmented states separated by an intervening state. An example in sub-Saharan Africa is Angola, which is divided into two fragments by the Congo Democratic Republic. An independence movement is trying to detach Cabinda as a separate state from Angola, with the justification that its population belongs to distinct ethnic groups (Figure 8.6.2).

▲ 8.6.2 **ANGOLA: A FRAGMENTED STATE**

• Fragmented states separated by water. An example in sub-Saharan Africa is Tanzania, which was created in 1964 as a union of the island of Zanzibar with the mainland territory of Tanganyika (Figure 8.6.3). Although home to different ethnic groups, the two entities agreed to join together because they shared common development goals and political priorities.

Prominent examples of fragmented states elsewhere in the world include Russia (which has a fragment called Kaliningrad) and Indonesia (which comprises 13,677 islands).

PRORUPTED STATES: ACCESS OR DISRUPTION

An otherwise compact state with a large projecting extension is a **prorupted state**. Proruptions are created for two principal reasons:

1. To provide a state with access to a resource, such as water. For example, in southern Africa, Congo has a 500-kilometer (300-mile) proruption to the west along the Zaire (Congo) River. The Belgians created the proruption to give their colony access to the Atlantic (Figure 8.6.4).

2. To separate two states that otherwise would share a boundary. For example, in southern Africa, Namibia has a 500-kilometer (300-mile) proruption to the east called the Caprivi Strip. When Namibia was a colony of Germany, the proruption disrupted communications among the British colonies of southern Africa. It also provided the Germans with access to the Zambezi, one of Africa's most important rivers.

▲ 8.6.4 **CONGO AND NAMIBIA: PRORUPTED STATES**

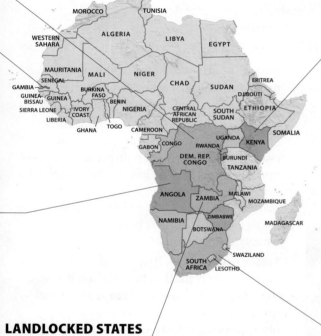

COMPACT STATES: EFFICIENT

In a **compact state**, the distance from the center to any boundary does not vary significantly. Compactness facilitates establishing good communications to all regions, especially if the capital is located near the center. Examples of compact states in sub-Saharan Africa include Burundi, Kenya, Rwanda, and Uganda (Figure 8.6.5). Compactness does not necessarily mean peacefulness, as compact states are just as likely as others to experience civil wars and ethnic rivalries.

▲ 8.6.5 **SUB-SAHARAN AFRICA: SEVERAL COMPACT STATES**

LANDLOCKED STATES

A **landlocked state** lacks a direct outlet to the sea because it is completely surrounded by other countries (only one country in the case of Lesotho). Landlocked states are especially common in sub-Saharan Africa (Figure 8.6.6). The prevalence of landlocked states in Africa is a remnant of the colonial era, when the United Kingdom and France held much of the region as colonies. As independent countries, landlocked states had to cooperate with neighboring coastal states in order to bring in supplies and ship out minerals. Railroads built by the European powers became critical in connecting landlocked states with seaports in neighboring states.

▲ 8.6.6 **SUB-SAHARAN AFRICA: SEVERAL LANDLOCKED STATES**

PERFORATED STATES: COMPLETELY SURROUNDING

A state that completely surrounds another one is a **perforated state**. For example, South Africa completely surrounds Lesotho (Figure 8.6.7). Lesotho must depend almost entirely on South Africa for the import and export of goods. Dependency on South Africa was especially difficult for Lesotho when South Africa had a government controlled by whites who discriminated against the black majority population. Italy is another prominent example, as it surrounds the Holy See (the Vatican) and San Marino.

▲ 8.6.7 **SOUTH AFRICA: A PERFORATED STATE**

8.7 Boundaries

▶ **Physical boundaries include mountains, deserts, and bodies of water.**
▶ **Cultural boundaries include geometric and ethnic boundaries.**

A state is separated from its neighbors by a **boundary**, an invisible line marking the extent of a state's territory. When looking at satellite images of Earth, we see physical features like mountains and oceans, but not boundaries between countries. Boundary lines are not painted on Earth, but they might as well be, because for many people they are more meaningful than natural features.

Boundaries are of two types:

• Physical boundaries coincide with significant features of the natural landscape.

• Cultural boundaries follow the distribution of cultural characteristics.

Neither type of boundary is better or more "natural," and many boundaries are a combination of both types.

PHYSICAL BOUNDARIES

Important physical features on Earth's surface can make good boundaries because they are easily seen, both on a map and on the ground. Three types of physical elements serve as boundaries between states (Figure 8.7.1):

• **Desert Boundaries.** Deserts make effective boundaries because they are hard to cross and sparsely inhabited. In North Africa, the Sahara has generally proved to be a stable boundary separating Algeria, Libya, and Egypt on the north from Mauritania, Mali, Niger, Chad, and the Sudan on the south.

• **Mountain Boundaries.** Mountains can be effective boundaries if they are difficult to cross. Contact between nationalities living on opposite sides may be limited, or completely impossible if passes are closed by winter storms. Mountains are also useful boundaries because they are rather permanent and are usually sparsely inhabited.

• **Water Boundaries.** Rivers, lakes, and oceans are commonly used as boundaries, because they are readily visible on maps and aerial imagery. Historically, water boundaries offered good protection against attack from another state, because an invading state had to transport its troops by ship and secure a landing spot in the country being attacked. The state being invaded could concentrate its defense at the landing point.

▲ ▶ 8.7.1 **PHYSICAL BOUNDARIES**
(above) Desert boundary between Libya and Chad. (right) Mountain boundary between Argentina and Chile. (far right) Water boundary between Germany and France.

CULTURAL BOUNDARIES

Two types of cultural boundaries are common—geometric and ethnic. Geometric boundaries are simply straight lines drawn on a map. Ethnic boundaries between states coincide with differences in ethnicity, as well as language and religion.

- **Geometric Boundaries.** Part of the northern U.S. boundary with Canada is a 2,100-kilometer (1,300-mile) straight line (more precisely, an arc) along 49° north latitude, running from Lake of the Woods between Minnesota and Manitoba to the Strait of Georgia between Washington State and British Columbia (Figure 8.7.2). This boundary was established in 1846 by a treaty between the United States and the United Kingdom, which then controlled Canada. The two countries share an additional 1,100-kilometer (700-mile) geometric boundary between Alaska and the Yukon Territory along the north–south arc of 141° west longitude.

- **Ethnic Boundaries.** Boundaries between countries have been placed where possible to separate ethnic groups. Language is also an important cultural characteristic for drawing boundaries, especially in Europe. Religious differences often coincide with boundaries between states, but in only a few cases has religion been used to select the actual boundary line (Figure 8.7.3).

▲ 8.7.2 **GEOMETRIC BOUNDARY: UNITED STATES AND CANADA** International Peace Park between North Dakota and Manitoba.

▲ 8.7.3 **ETHNIC BOUNDARY: GREEK AND TURKISH CYPRUS**
Cyprus, the third-largest island in the Mediterranean Sea, contains two nationalities—Greek and Turkish. Several Greek Cypriot military officers who favored unification of Cyprus with Greece seized control of the government in 1974. Shortly after, Turkey invaded Cyprus to protect the Turkish Cypriot minority, and the portion of the island controlled by Turkey declared itself the independent Turkish Republic of Northern Cyprus in 1983.

FRONTIERS

A **frontier** is a zone where no state exercises complete political control. A frontier is an area often many kilometers wide that is either uninhabited or sparsely settled. Historically, frontiers rather than boundaries separated many states (Figure 8.7.4). Almost universally, frontiers between states have been replaced by boundaries. Modern communications systems permit countries to monitor and guard boundaries effectively, even in previously inaccessible locations. Once-remote frontier regions have become more attractive for agriculture and mining.

◄ 8.7.4 **FRONTIERS: ARABIAN PENINSULA**

8.8 Governing States

▶ **Some governments are more democratic than others.**

▶ **Two types of government structures are unitary states and federal states.**

A state has two types of government—a national government and local governments. At the national scale, a government can be more or less democratic. At the local scale, the national government can determine how much power to allocate to local governments.

NATIONAL GOVERNMENT REGIMES

National governments can be classified as democratic, autocratic, or anocratic (Figure 8.8.1). An **autocracy** is a country that is run according to the interests of the ruler rather than the people. An **anocracy** is a country that is not fully democratic or fully autocratic, but rather displays a mix of the two types. According to the Center for Systemic Peace, a democracy and an autocracy differ in three essential elements (Figure 8.8.2).

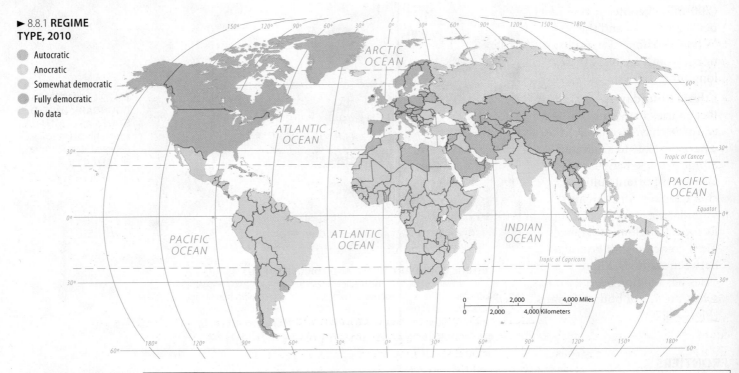

▶ 8.8.1 **REGIME TYPE, 2010**

- Autocratic
- Anocratic
- Somewhat democratic
- Fully democratic
- No data

▶ 8.8.2 **DIFFERENCES BETWEEN DEMOCRACY AND AUTOCRACY**

Element	Democracy	Autocracy
Selection of leaders	Institutions and procedures through which citizens can express effective preferences about alternative policies and leaders.	Leaders are selected according to clearly defined (usually hereditary) rules of succession from within the established political elite.
Citizen participation	Institutionalized constraints on the exercise of power by the executive.	Citizens' participation is sharply restricted or suppressed.
Checks and balances	Guarantee of civil liberties to all citizens in their daily lives and in acts of political participation.	Leaders exercise power with no meaningful checks from legislative, judicial, or civil society institutions.

TREND TOWARDS DEMOCRACY

In general, the world has become more democratic (Figure 8.8.3). The Center for Systemic Peace cites three reasons:

- The replacement of increasingly irrelevant and out-of-touch monarchies with elected governments that are able to regulate, tax, and mobilize citizens in exchange for broadening individual rights and liberties.
- The widening of participation in policy making to all citizens through universal rights to vote and to serve in government (Figure 8.8.4).
- The diffusion of democratic government structures created in Europe and North America to other regions of the world.

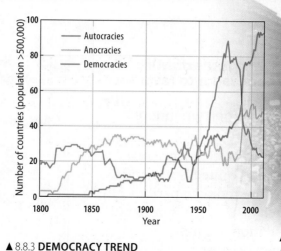

▲ 8.8.3 **DEMOCRACY TREND**

▲ 8.8.4 **DEMOCRACY**
Anti-Communist demonstration in Prague, Czechoslovakia, in 1990, just before the country's Communist government was replaced with a democratic one. Czechoslovakia split into two countries (Czech Republic and Slovakia) in 1993.

LOCAL GOVERNMENT: UNITARY STATE

The governments of states are organized according to one of two approaches: unitary and federal. The **unitary state** allocates most power to the national government, and local governments have relatively few powers. In principle, the unitary government system works best in nation-states characterized by few internal cultural differences and a strong sense of national unity. Because the unitary system requires effective communications with all regions of the country, smaller states are more likely to adopt it. Unitary states are especially common in Europe (Figure 8.8.5).

Some multinational states have adopted unitary systems, so that the values of one nationality can be imposed on others. In Kenya and Rwanda, for instance, the mechanisms of a unitary state have enabled one ethnic group to extend dominance over weaker groups. When Communist parties controlled the governments, most Eastern European states had unitary systems so as to promote the diffusion of Communist values.

▲ 8.8.5 **UNITARY STATE**
Monaco.

LOCAL GOVERNMENT: FEDERAL STATE

In a **federal state**, strong power is allocated to units of local government within the country. In a federal state, such as the United States, local governments possess more authority to adopt their own laws. Multinational states may adopt a federal system of government to empower different nationalities, especially if they live in separate regions of the country. Under a federal system, local government boundaries can be drawn to correspond with regions inhabited by different ethnicities.

The federal system is also more suitable for very large states because the national capital may be too remote to provide effective control over isolated regions. Most of the world's largest states are federal, including Russia (as was the former Soviet Union), Canada, the United States, Brazil, and India. However, the size of the state is not always an accurate predictor of the form of government: tiny Belgium is a federal state (to accommodate the two main cultural groups, the Flemish and the Waloons, as discussed in Chapter 5), whereas China is a unitary state (to promote Communist values).

In recent years there has been a strong global trend toward federal government. Unitary systems have been sharply curtailed in a number of countries and scrapped altogether in others (Figure 8.8.6).

▼ 8.8.6 **FEDERAL STATE**
Town hall meeting in Florida.

8.9 Electoral Geography

▶ **Gerrymandering is the drawing of legislative boundaries to favor the party in power.**

▶ **Some U.S. states gerrymandered electoral districts.**

The boundaries separating legislative districts within the United States and other countries are redrawn periodically to ensure that each district has approximately the same population. Boundaries must be redrawn because migration inevitably results in some districts gaining population, whereas others are losing. The districts of the 435 U.S. House of Representatives are redrawn every 10 years following the release of official population figures by the Census Bureau.

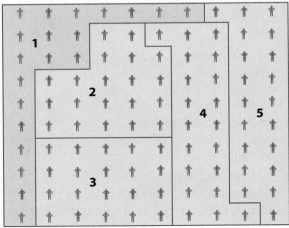

▲ 8.9.2 **"WASTED VOTE" GERRYMANDERING**
"Wasted vote" spreads opposition supporters across many districts as a minority. If the Blue Party controls the redistricting process, it could do a "wasted vote" gerrymander by creating four districts with a slender majority of Blue Party voters and one district (#1) with a strong majority of Red Party voters.

The process of redrawing legislative boundaries for the purpose of benefiting the party in power is called **gerrymandering**. The term gerrymandering was named for Elbridge Gerry (1744–1814), governor of Massachusetts (1810–12) and vice president of the United States (1813–14). As governor, Gerry signed a bill that redistricted the state to benefit his party. An opponent observed that an oddly shaped new district looked like a "salamander," whereupon another opponent responded that it was a "gerrymander." A newspaper subsequently printed an editorial cartoon of a monster named "gerrymander" with a body shaped like the district (Figure 8.9.1).

Gerrymandering works like this: suppose a community has 100 voters to be allocated among five districts of 20 voters each. The Blue Party has 52 supporters or 52 percent of the total, and the Red Party has 48 supporters or 48 percent. Gerrymandering takes three forms: "wasted vote" (Figure 8.9.2), "excess vote" (Figure 8.9.3), or "stacked vote" (Figure 8.9.4).

The job of redrawing boundaries in most European countries is entrusted to independent commissions. Commissions typically try to create compact homogeneous districts without regard for voting preferences or incumbents. A couple of U.S. states, including Iowa and Washington, also use independent or bipartisan commissions (Figure 8.9.5), but in most U.S. states the job of redrawing boundaries is entrusted to the state legislature. The political party in control of the state legislature naturally attempts to redraw boundaries to improve the chances of its supporters to win seats.

The U.S. Supreme Court ruled gerrymandering illegal in 1985 but did not require dismantling of existing oddly shaped districts, and a 2001 ruling allowed North Carolina to add another oddly shaped district that ensured the election of an African American Democrat. Through gerrymandering, only about one-tenth of Congressional seats are competitive, making a shift of more than a few seats unlikely from one election to another in the United States except in unusual circumstances.

Boundaries must be redrawn every ten years after release of census data to assure that the population is the same in each district. Political parties may offer competing plans designed to favor their candidates (Figure 8.9.6).

◀ 8.9.1 **THE ORIGINAL GERRYMANDER CARTOON**
It was drawn in 1812 by Elkanah Tinsdale.

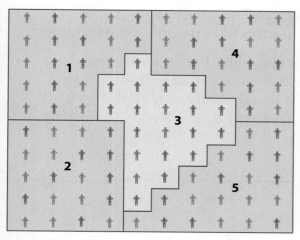

▲ 8.9.3 **"EXCESS VOTE" GERRYMANDERING**
"Excess vote" concentrates opposition supporters into a few districts. If the Red Party controls the redistricting process, it could do an "excess vote" gerrymander by creating four districts with a slender majority Red Party voters and one district (#3) with an overwhelming majority of Blue Party voters.

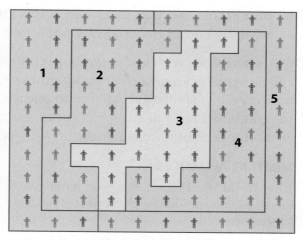

▲ 8.9.4 **"STACKED VOTE" GERRYMANDERING**
A "stacked vote" links distant areas of like-minded voters through oddly shaped boundaries. In this example, Red Party controls redistricting and creates five oddly shaped districts, four with a slender majority Red Party voters and one (#3) with an overwhelming majority of Blue Party voters.

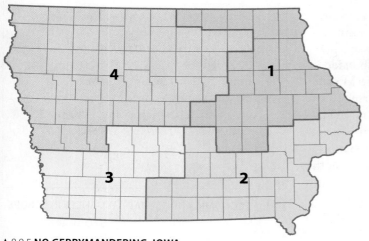

▲ 8.9.5 **NO GERRYMANDERING: IOWA**
Iowa does not have gerrymandered congressional districts. Each district is relatively compact, and boundaries coincide with county boundaries.

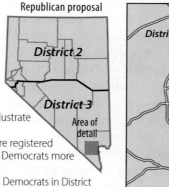

Democratic proposal

Republican proposal

Registered voters:
○ Majority Democratic
● Majority Republican

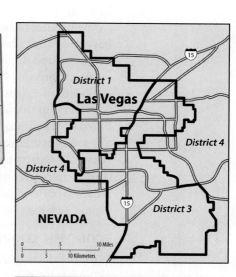

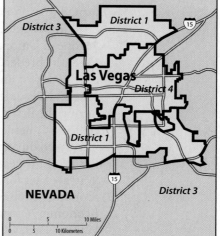

► 8.9.6 **GERRYMANDERING NEVADA: TWO PROPOSALS**
Competing proposals to draw boundaries for Nevada's four congressional districts illustrate all three forms of gerrymandering.
(top right) "Wasted vote" gerrymander. Although Nevada as a whole has slightly more registered Democrats than Republicans (43 percent to 37 percent), the Democratic plan made Democrats more numerous than Republicans in three of the four districts.
(bottom) "Excess vote" gerrymander. By clustering a large share of the state's registered Democrats in District 4, the Republican plan gave Republicans the majority of registered voters in two of the four districts.
(both) "Stacked vote" gerrymander. In the Republican plan (right), District 4 has a majority Hispanic population, and is surrounded by a "C" shaped District 1. The Democratic plan created a long, narrow District 3.

8.10 Cooperation Among States

▶ **During the Cold War, European states joined military alliances.**
▶ **With the end of the Cold War, economic alliances have become more important.**

States cooperate with each other for economic and military reasons. An economic alliance enlarges markets for goods and services produced in an individual state. A military alliance offers protection to one state through the threat of retaliation by the combined force of allies. European states have been especially active in creating economic and military alliances.

MILITARY ALLIANCES

After World War II, most European states joined one of two military alliances dominated by the superpowers:

• North Atlantic Treaty Organization (NATO): The United States, 14 Western European allies, and Canada.

• Warsaw Pact: The Soviet Union and six Eastern European allies.

In a Europe no longer dominated by military confrontation between two blocs, the Warsaw Pact and NATO became obsolete. The number of troops under NATO command was sharply reduced, and the Warsaw Pact was disbanded. Rather than disbanding, NATO expanded its membership to include most of the former Warsaw Pact countries. Membership in NATO offers eastern European countries an important sense of security against any future Russian threat, no matter how remote that appears at the moment, as well as participation in a common united Europe (Figure 8.10.1).

ECONOMIC COOPERATION

With the decline in the military-oriented alliances, European states increasingly have turned to economic cooperation. Europe's most important economic organization is the European Union. When it was established in 1958, the predecessor to the European Union included six countries. It has expanded to 12 countries during the 1980s and 27 countries during the first decade of the twenty-first century. Others hope to join.

In 1949, during the Cold War, the seven Eastern European Communist states in the Warsaw Pact formed an organization for economic cooperation, the Council for Mutual Economic Assistance (COMECON). Like the Warsaw Pact, COMECON disbanded in the

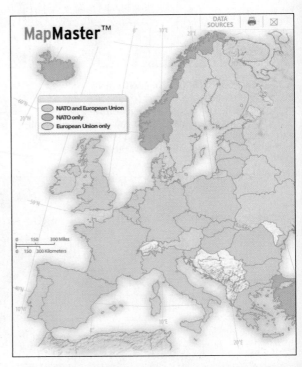

▲ 8.10.1 **ECONOMIC AND MILITARY ALLIANCES IN EUROPE**
Launch MapMaster Europe in Mastering**GEOGRAPHY**
Select *Geopolitical,* then *Economic and Military Alliances.*
Select *Political,* then *Countries.*
Select *Geopolitical,* then *Geopolitical Issues.*

Which current members of NATO and the European Union were once members of the Communist-oriented Warsaw Pact?

early 1990s after the fall of communism in Eastern Europe.

The European Union has removed most barriers to free trade. With a few exceptions, goods, services, capital, and people can move freely through Europe. A European Parliament is elected by the people in each of the member states simultaneously. Subsidies are provided to Europe's most economically depressed regions.

SUPERPOWERS

Balance of power is a condition of roughly equal strength between opposing forces. During the Cold War era (late 1940s until early 1990s), the balance of power was maintained by two superpowers—the United States and the Soviet Union (Figure 8.10.2). With the end of the Cold War, military alliances in the twenty-first century are less clearly defined (Figures 8.10.3 and 8.10.4).

▲ 8.10.3 **U. S. MILITARY VEHICLES AND AIRCRAFT LINED UP ON THE TAXIWAY AT CAMP SPEICHER, IRAQ**

▲ 8.10.2 **COLD WAR: CUBAN MISSILE CRISIS**

A major confrontation during the Cold War between the United States and Soviet Union came in 1962 when the Soviet Union secretly began to construct missile launching sites in Cuba, less than 150 kilometers (90 miles) from U.S. territory. President Kennedy went on national television to demand that the missiles be removed and ordered a naval blockade to prevent further Soviet material from reaching Cuba.

The U.S. Department of Defense took aerial photographs to show the Soviet buildup in Cuba. (top) Three Soviet ships with missile equipment are being unloaded at Mariel naval port in Cuba. Within the outline box (enlarged below and rotated 90° clockwise) are Soviet missile transporters, fuel trailers, and oxider trailers (used to support the combustion of missile fuel).

At the United Nations, immediately after Soviet Ambassador Valerian Zorin denied that his country had placed missiles in Cuba, U.S. Ambassador Adlai Stevenson dramatically revealed aerial photographs taken by the U.S. Department of Defense clearly showing them. Faced with irrefutable evidence that the missiles existed, the Soviet Union ended the crisis by dismantling them.

▲ 8.10.4 **POST-COLD WAR: IRAQ'S ALLEGED WEAPONS**

U.S. Secretary of State Colin Powell spoke at the United Nations in 2003. The speech was supposed to present irrefutable evidence that military action against Iraq by the United States and its allies was justified. Recalling the Cuban missile crisis, Powell displayed a series of aerial photos designed to prove that Iraq possessed weapons of mass destruction. Powell first showed an image of 15 munitions bunkers at Taji, Iraq (top). He also showed close-ups of some of the bunkers (bottom).

Unlike the Cuban missile crisis in 1962, the United States could not make a convincing argument using aerial photos. As a result, the United States went to war against Iraq without the support of the United Nations. A subsequent U.S. State Department analysis found many inaccuracies in the interpretation of aerial photos presented by Powell. For example, the "decontamination vehicle" in the bottom left photo turned out to be a water truck. Two years later, Powell himself said that the 2003 speech had been a "blot" on his record.

8.11 Terrorism by Individuals and Organizations

► **Terrorists have attacked the United States several times.**
► **Al-Qaeda justifies terrorism as a holy war.**

Terrorism is the systematic use of violence by a group in order to intimidate a population or coerce a government into granting its demands. Terrorists attempt to achieve their objectives through organized acts that spread fear and anxiety among the population, such as bombing, kidnapping, hijacking, taking of hostages, and assassination. They consider violence necessary as a means of bringing widespread publicity to goals and grievances that are not being addressed through peaceful means. Belief in their cause is so strong that terrorists do not hesitate to strike despite knowing they will probably die in the act.

Distinguishing terrorism from other acts of political violence can be difficult. For example, if a Palestinian suicide bomber kills several dozen Israeli teenagers in a Jerusalem restaurant, is that an act of terrorism or wartime retaliation against Israeli government policies and army actions? Competing arguments are made: Israel's sympathizers denounce the act as a terrorist threat to the country's existence, whereas advocates of the Palestinian cause argue that long-standing injustices and Israeli army attacks on Palestinian civilians provoked the act.

▲ 8.11.1 **SEPTEMBER 11, 2001 ATTACKS**

TERRORISM AGAINST AMERICANS

The most dramatic terrorist attack against the United States came on September 11, 2001. The tallest buildings in the United States, the 110-story twin towers of the World Trade Center in New York City were destroyed, and the Pentagon in Washington, D.C., was damaged (Figure 8.11.1). The attacks resulted in nearly 3,000 fatalities.

Prior to the 9/11 attacks, the United States had suffered several terrorist attacks during the late twentieth century (Figure 8.11.2). Some were by American citizens operating alone or with a handful of others.

- Theodore J. Kaczynski, known as the Unabomber, was convicted of killing 3 people and injuring 23 others by sending bombs through the mail during a 17-year period. His targets were mainly academics in technological disciplines and executives in businesses whose actions he considered to be adversely affecting the environment.

- Timothy J. McVeigh was convicted and executed for the Oklahoma City bombing, and for assisting him Terry I. Nichols was convicted of conspiracy and involuntary manslaughter. McVeigh claimed he had been provoked by U.S. government actions including the FBI's 51-day siege of the Branch Davidian religious compound near Waco, Texas, culminating with an attack on April 19, 1993, that resulted in 80 deaths.

February 26, 1993: A car bomb parked in the underground garage damaged New York's World Trade Center, killing 6 and injuring about 1,000.

April 19, 1995: A car bomb killed 168 people in the Alfred P. Murrah Federal Building in Oklahoma City.

December 21, 1988: A terrorist bomb destroyed Pan Am Flight 103 over Lockerbie, Scotland, killing all 259 aboard, plus 11 on the ground.

June 25, 1996: A truck bomb blew up an apartment complex in Dhahran, Saudi Arabia, killing 19 U.S. soldiers who lived there and injuring more than 100 people.

September 11, 2001: Airplanes crash into the World Trade Center in New York and the Pentagon near Washington, killing 3,000.

October 12, 2000: The USS *Cole* was bombed while in the port of Aden, Yemen, killing 17 U.S. service personnel.

August 7, 1998: U.S. embassies in Kenya and Tanzania were bombed, killing 190 and wounding nearly 5,000.

▲ 8.11.2 **TERRORISM AGAINST AMERICANS** 1993–2001.

▲ 8.11.4 AL-QAEDA TERRORISM, LONDON

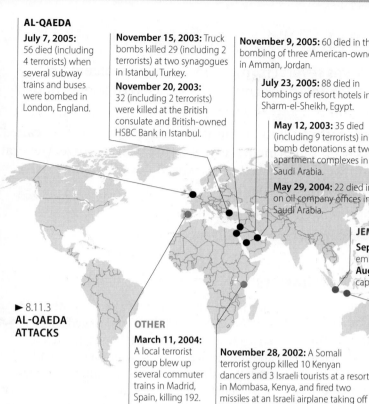

AL-QAEDA

July 7, 2005: 56 died (including 4 terrorists) when several subway trains and buses were bombed in London, England.

November 15, 2003: Truck bombs killed 29 (including 2 terrorists) at two synagogues in Istanbul, Turkey.

November 20, 2003: 32 (including 2 terrorists) were killed at the British consulate and British-owned HSBC Bank in Istanbul.

November 9, 2005: 60 died in the bombing of three American-owned hotels in Amman, Jordan.

July 23, 2005: 88 died in bombings of resort hotels in Sharm-el-Sheikh, Egypt.

May 12, 2003: 35 died (including 9 terrorists) in car bomb detonations at two apartment complexes in Riyadh, Saudi Arabia.

May 29, 2004: 22 died in attacks on oil company offices in Khobar, Saudi Arabia.

JEMAAH ISLAMIYAH

September 9, 2004: Car bombs killed 9 to 11 at the Australian embassy, in Jakarta.

August 5, 2003: Car bombs killed 12 at a Marriott hotel in the capital Jakarta.

October 12, 2002: A nightclub in the resort town of Kuta on the island of Bali was bombed, killing 202.

October 1, 2005: Attacks on a downtown square in Kuta as well as a food court in Jimbaran, Bali, killed 23 (including 3 terrorists).

► 8.11.3 AL-QAEDA ATTACKS

OTHER

March 11, 2004: A local terrorist group blew up several commuter trains in Madrid, Spain, killing 192.

November 28, 2002: A Somali terrorist group killed 10 Kenyan dancers and 3 Israeli tourists at a resort in Mombasa, Kenya, and fired two missiles at an Israeli airplane taking off from the Mombasa airport.

AL-QAEDA

Responsible or implicated in most of the anti-U.S. terrorism in Figure 8.11.2, including the September 11, 2001, attack, was the al-Qaeda network (Figure 8.11.3). Al-Qaeda (an Arabic word meaning "the foundation" or "the base") has been implicated in several bombings since 9/11 (Figure 8.11.4).

Al-Qaeda's founder Osama bin Laden (1957–2011) issued a declaration of war against the United States in 1996 because of U.S. support for Saudi Arabia and Israel. In a 1998 fatwa ("religious decree"), bin Laden argued that Muslims had a duty to wage a holy war against U.S. citizens because the United States was responsible for maintaining the Saud royal family as rulers of Saudi Arabia and a state of Israel dominated by Jews. Destruction of the Saudi monarchy and the Jewish state of Israel would liberate from their control Islam's three holiest sites of Makkah (Mecca), Madinah, and Jerusalem.

In some respects, al-Qaeda operates like a business. A leadership council sets policy and oversees committees that specialize in such areas as finance, military, media, and religious policy. The organization keeps records and reimburses its members for expenses, such as purchasing bomb-making equipment. After U.S. Navy SEALS killed bin Laden in 2011, the al-Qaeda council replaced him as commander with his deputy Ayman al-Zawahiri.

Al-Qaeda is not a single unified organization. In addition to the original organization responsible for the World Trade Center attack, al-Qaeda also encompasses local franchises concerned with country-specific issues, as well as imitators and emulators ideologically aligned with al-Qaeda but not financially tied to it. For example, Jemaah Islamiyah, an al-Qaeda franchise trying to create fundamentalist Islamic governments in Southeast Asia, launches attacks in the world's most populous Muslim country, Indonesia.

Al-Qaeda's use of religion to justify attacks has posed challenges to Muslims and non-Muslims alike. For many Muslims, the challenge has been to express disagreement with the policies of governments in the United States and Europe yet disavow the use of terrorism. For many Americans and Europeans, the challenge has been to distinguish between the peaceful but unfamiliar principles and practices of the world's 1.3 billion Muslims and the misuse and abuse of Islam by a handful of terrorists.

8.12 State Support for Terrorism

▶ **State support for terrorism takes several forms of increasing involvement.**

▶ **The U.S. war on terrorism has led to attacks on states accused of supporting terrorism.**

After the 9/11 attacks, the United States and other countries launched what they called the War on Terror. Al-Qaeda has been the principal target of the war. However, several states in Central, South, and Southwest Asia have been accused of state-sponsored terrorism, at three increasing levels of involvement:

- Providing sanctuary for terrorists wanted by other countries.
- Supplying terrorists with weapons, money, and intelligence.
- Planning attacks using terrorists.

STATE-SPONSORED SANCTUARY FOR TERRORISTS

Countries known to provide sanctuary for terrorists include Afghanistan and Pakistan. The United States with the cooperation of several other countries attacked Afghanistan in 2001 when its leaders, known as the Taliban, sheltered al-Qaeda leaders including bin Laden after 9/11. Removing the Taliban from power was considered a necessary step before going after al-Qaeda leaders, who were living in rugged mountains near Afghanistan's border with Pakistan.

The Taliban (Arabic for "students of Muslim religious schools") had gained power in Afghanistan in 1995 and had imposed strict Islamic fundamentalist law on the population. Afghanistan's Taliban leadership treated women especially harshly. Women were prohibited from attending school, working outside the home, seeking health care, or driving a car. They were permitted to leave home only if fully covered by clothing and escorted by a male relative.

Removal of the Taliban unleashed a new struggle for control of Afghanistan among the country's many ethnic groups. When U.S. attention shifted to Iraq and Iran, the Taliban were able to regroup and resume an insurgency against the U.S.-backed Afghanistan government. The United States committed more than 30,000 troops to Afghanistan to keep the Taliban from regaining control of the entire country.

After the U.S.-led attack in eastern Afghanistan, al-Qaeda's leaders, including bin Laden, were able to escape across the border into Pakistan. After searching without success for nearly a decade, U.S. intelligence finally tracked bin Laden to a house in Abbottabad, Pakistan, where he was killed in 2011 (Figure 8.12.1). The extent to which Pakistan's government and military may have sheltered bin Laden for nearly a decade is not clear.

◀ 8.12.1 **SANCTUARY FOR TERRORISTS: BIN LADEN'S COMPOUND**

Navy SEALS killed al-Qaeda leader Osama bin Laden in this compound near the city of Abbottabad, Pakistan.

Fly to: *Osama bin Laden's hideout compound, Abbottabad, Pakistan.*

Deselect 3D Buildings. Click the time slider. Click the left arrow to go back in time.

Between which two dates was the compound constructed? How does this compare to the date of the failed U.S. attack on bin Laden in Tora Bora, Afghanistan?

Remove time slider, then click 3D Buildings. Drag to enter street view, then exit street view to get an overview of bin Laden's compound.

◀ 8.12.3 **IRAQ**
Locals flee air attack in Basra.

◀ 8.12.2 **IRAN**
Anti-U.S. propoganda on the wall of the ex-U.S. embassy in Tehran.

► 8.12.4 **LIBYA**
Rebel troups with makeshift military vehicle.

PROVIDING SUPPLIES TO TERRORISTS

Since 9/11, Iran and Iraq have both been accused by the United States of not merely sheltering terrorists but providing them with active support, including potentially arming them with weapons of mass destruction. These assertions have led to U.S. intervention in a region that is home to a complex patchwork of ethnicities (refer to section 7.7).

- **Iran.** The United States has accused Iran of trying to develop nuclear weapons that could be launched against Israel or its allies. Iran has claimed that its program was for civilian purposes. Air photos and other information gathered by intelligence sources has not provided clear proof of Iran's intentions or progress in its nuclear program. Hostility between the United States and Iran dates from 1979, when a revolution forced abdication of Iran's pro-U.S. Shah Mohammad Reza Pahlavi. Fundamentalist Shiite Muslim leader Ayatollah Ruholiah Khomeini proclaimed Iran an Islamic republic and rewrote the constitution to place final authority with the ayatollah. Militant supporters of the ayatollah seized the U.S. embassy on November 4, 1979, and held 62 Americans hostage until January 20, 1981 (Figure 8.12.2).

- **Iraq.** The United States led an attack against Iraq in 2003 in order to depose Saddam Hussein, the country's longtime president. This was the second U.S.-led war against Iraq in a dozen years. In 1991, U.S.-led Operation Desert Storm repelled Iraq's invasion of Kuwait. U.S. officials' justification for removing Hussein was that he had created biological and chemical weapons of mass destruction. These weapons could fall into the hands of terrorists, the U.S. government charged, because close links were said to exist between Iraq's government and al-Qaeda. However, UN experts concluded that Iraq had destroyed these weapons in 1991 after its Desert Storm defeat, and U.S. intelligence agencies ultimately concluded that Hussein did not have close links with al-Qaeda (Figure 8.12.3).

STATE-SPONSORED TERRORIST ATTACKS

Libya was an active sponsor of terrorist attacks. Examples include:

- A 1986 bombing of a nightclub in Berlin, Germany, popular with U.S. military personnel then stationed there, killing three (including one U.S. soldier).
- Planting of bombs on Pan Am Flight 103, which blew up over Lockerbie Scotland, in 1988, killing 270.
- Planting of bombs on UTA Flight 772, which blew up over Niger in 1989, killing 170.

Libya's long-time leader Muammar el-Qaddafi (1942–2011, ruler 1969–2011) renounced terrorism in 2003, and provided compensation for victims of Pan Am 103. But his brutal attacks on Libyan protestors in 2011 again brought most other states of the world into active opposition to Qaddafi's regime, which was ultimately overthrown (Figure 8.12.4).

In the twenty-first century, the importance of the nation-state has diminished in Europe, the world region most closely associated with development of the concept during the previous two centuries. With the end of the Cold War, military alliances have become less important than patterns of global and regional economic cooperation and competition among states. At the same time, conflict has increased among groups of people who for whatever reason are not in control of a nation-state.

Key Questions

What is a state?

- ► The world is divided into nearly 200 states, nearly all members of the United Nations.
- ► Historically, most lands belonged to empires, or were colonies of states.
- ► During the past two centuries, many nation-states have been created that attempt to match the boundaries of a nationality.
- ► Few colonies are left in the world, all but a handful with very small populations.

How are states organized?

- ► States take five types of shapes—compact, prorupted, elongated, fragmented, and perforated.
- ► A number of states are landlocked, a challenge for international trade.
- ► Either physical or cultural features can be used to set boundaries between states.
- ► States may be organized into either unitary or federal systems of local government.
- ► Boundaries within countries are delineated for elections and can be gerrymandered.

How do states interact with each other?

- ► States increasingly cooperate in regional military and economic alliances, especially in Europe.
- ► During the second half of the twentieth century, the Cold War divided countries into pro-U.S. and pro-Soviet alliances.
- ► In the twenty-first century, terrorism by individuals, groups, and states has replaced the Cold War as the principal challenge to security.

Thinking Geographically

Gerald Helman and Steven Rattner have identified countries that they call "failed nation-states," including Cambodia, Liberia, Somalia, and Sudan (Figure 8.CR.1). Helman and Rattner argued that the governments of these countries were maintained in power during the Cold War era through massive military and economic aid from the United States or the Soviet Union. With the end of the Cold War, these failed nation-states sank into civil wars, fought among groups who share language, religion, and other cultural characteristics.

1. What obligations do other countries have to restore order in failed nation-states?

States have moved towards increased local government autonomy on the one hand and increased authority for international organizations on the other.

2. What is the future of the nation-state? Have political and economic trends since the 1990s strengthened the concept of nation-state or weakened it?

A century ago the British geographer Halford J. Mackinder identified a heartland in the interior of Eurasia (Europe and Asia) that was isolated by mountain ranges and the Arctic Ocean. Surrounding the heartland was a series of fringe areas, which the geographer Nicholas Spykman later called the rimland, oriented toward the oceans. Mackinder argued that whoever controlled the heartland would control Eurasia and hence the entire world.

3. To what extent was Mackinder's theory been validated by the creation and then the dismantling of the Soviet Union?

▼ 8.CR.1 **PHNOM PENH, CAPITAL OF CAMBODIA**

Interactive Mapping

TERRITORIAL CLAIMS IN THE SOUTH PACIFIC

Microstates in the Pacific Ocean have tiny areas but they control vast areas of the sea.

Launch MapMaster Australia and Oceania in **Mastering**GEOGRAPHY

Select: *Geopolitical* then *Marine Tropical Claims.*
Select: *Political* then *Countries.*

1. **How many independent microstates are named in the region (countries in addition to Australia, New Zealand, and Papua New Guinea)?**

2. **How many states have colonies in the South Pacific?**

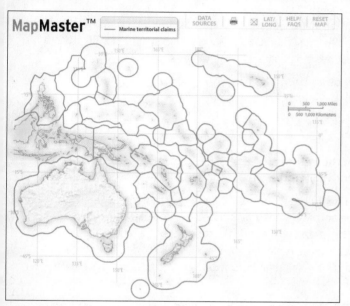

Explore

THE KREMLIN, MOSCOW, RUSSIA

Use Google Earth to explore the Kremlin, the fortified center of Moscow that has symbolized the power of the Soviet Union and now Russia.

Fly to: *The Kremlin, Moscow, Russia*

Click 3D buildings.

Drag to enter Street View in the large square in the center of the image.

Exit Ground Level View and zoom out until the walls of the complex are visible.

Click on the individual buildings.

What are the current use and history of the major buildings in the Kremlin?

Key Terms

Anocracy
A country that is not fully democratic or fully autocratic, but rather displays a mix of the two types.

Autocracy
A country that is run according to the interests of the ruler rather than the people.

Balance of power
Condition of roughly equal strength between opposing countries or alliances of countries.

Boundary
Invisible line that marks the extent of a state's territory.

City-state
A sovereign state comprising a city and its immediate hinterland.

Colonialism
Attempt by one country to establish settlements and to impose its political, economic, and cultural principles in another territory.

Colony
A territory that is legally tied to a sovereign state rather than completely independent.

Compact state
A state in which the distance from the center to any boundary does not vary significantly.

Elongated state
A state with a long, narrow shape.

Federal state
An internal organization of a state that allocates most powers to units of local government.

Fragmented state
A state that includes several discontinuous pieces of territory.

Frontier
A zone separating two states in which neither state exercises political control.

Gerrymandering
Process of redrawing legislative boundaries for the purpose of benefiting the party in power.

Landlocked state
A state that does not have a direct outlet to the sea.

Multinational state
State that contains two or more ethnic groups with traditions of self-determination that agree to coexist peacefully by recognizing each other as distinct nationalities.

Nation-state
A state whose territory corresponds to that occupied by a particular ethnicity that has been transformed into a nationality.

Perforated state
A state that completely surrounds another one.

Prorupted state
An otherwise compact state with a large projecting extension.

Self-determination
Concept that ethnicities have the right to govern themselves.

Sovereignty
Ability of a state to govern its territory free from control of its internal affairs by other states.

State
An area organized into a political unit and ruled by an established government with control over its internal and foreign affairs.

Terrorism
The systematic use of violence by a group in order to intimidate a population or coerce a government into granting it demands.

Unitary state
An internal organization of a state that places most power in the hands of central government officials.

On the Internet

The U.S. Central Intelligence Agency has a World Factbook. Select a country from the drop-down list to find background information, as well as facts and figures about the country's demography, economy, physical geography, government, and military. Maps are also available at **https://www.cia.gov/library/publications/the-world-factbook/** or scan the QR at the beginning of the chapter.

▶ LOOKING AHEAD

The second half of the book concentrates on economic elements of human geography, beginning with the division of the world into more and less developed regions.

9 Development

The world is divided into developed countries and developing countries. The one-fifth of the world's people living in developed countries consume five-sixths of the world's goods, whereas the 14 percent of the world's people who live in Africa consume about 1 percent.

The United Nations recently contrasted spending between developed and developing countries in picturesque terms: Americans spend more per year on cosmetics ($8 billion) than the cost of providing schools for the 2 billion people in the world in need of them ($6 billion).

Europeans spend more on ice cream ($11 billion) than the cost of providing a working toilet to the 2 billion people currently without one at home ($9 billion).

To reduce disparities between rich and poor countries, developing countries must develop more rapidly. This means increasing wealth and using that wealth to make more rapid improvements in people's health and well-being.

**BUILDING A NEW
ROAD, MOZAMBIQUE**

How does development vary among regions?

What are future challenges for development?

SCAN TO ACCESS THE UN'S HUMAN DEVELOPMENT REPORT

9.1 Human Development Index

► **Countries are classified as developed or developing.**

► **The Human Development Index (HDI) measures a country's level of development.**

Earth's nearly 200 countries can be classified according to their level of **development**, which is the process of improving the material conditions of people through diffusion of knowledge and technology. The development process is continuous, involving never-ending actions to constantly improve the health and prosperity of the people. Every place lies at some point along a continuum of development.

The United Nations classifies countries as developed or developing:

- A **developed country**, also known as a **more developed country (MDC)** or a **relatively developed country,** has progressed further along the development continuum. The UN considers these countries to have very high development.

- A **developing country**, also frequently called a **less developed country (LDC),** has made some progress towards development though less than developed countries. Recognizing that progress has varied widely among developing countries, the UN divides them into high, medium, and low development.

To measure the level of development of every country, the UN created the **Human Development Index (HDI)**. The UN has computed HDIs for countries every year since 1990, although it has occasionally modified the method of computation. The HDI considers development to be a function of three factors:
- A decent standard of living.
- Access to knowledge.
- A long and healthy life.

Each country gets a score for each of these three factors, which are then combined into an overall HDI (Figure 9.1.1). The highest HDI possible is 1.0, or 100 percent. These factors are discussed in more detail in sections 9.2, 9.3, and 9.4.

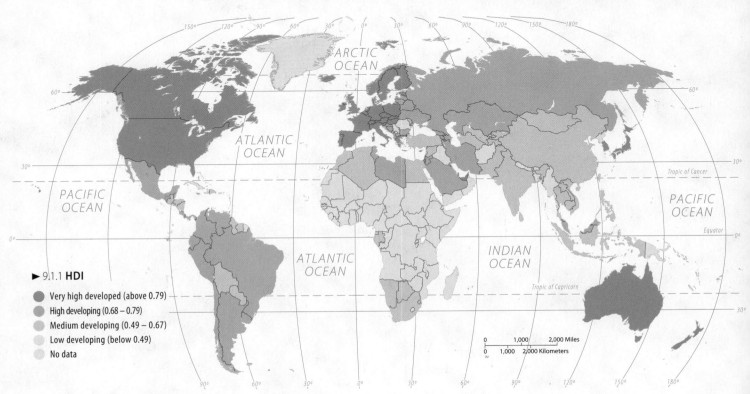

► 9.1.1 **HDI**

- Very high developed (above 0.79)
- High developing (0.68 – 0.79)
- Medium developing (0.49 – 0.67)
- Low developing (below 0.49)
- No data

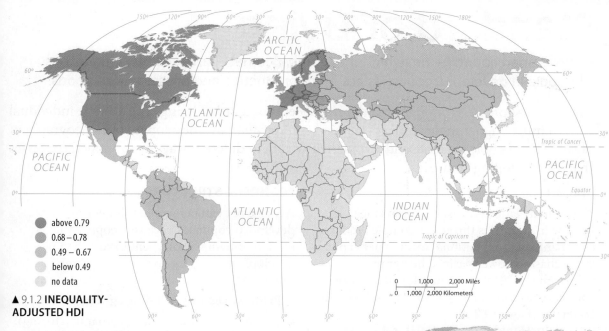

▲ 9.1.2 **INEQUALITY-ADJUSTED HDI**

Map legend:
- above 0.79
- 0.68 – 0.78
- 0.49 – 0.67
- below 0.49
- no data

INEQUALITY-ADJUSTED HDI

The United Nations believes that every person should have access to decent standards of living, knowledge, and health. The **Inequality-adjusted HDI (IHDI)** modifies the HDI to account for inequality (Figure 9.1.2).

Under perfect equality the HDI and the IHDI are the same. If the IHDI is lower than the HDI, the country has some inequality; the greater the difference in the two measures, the greater the inequality. A country where only a few people have high incomes, college degrees, and good health care would have a lower IHDI than a country where differences in income, level of education, and access to health care are minimal.

Map legend (Nine World Regions):
- Europe
- North America
- Latin America
- Southwest Asia and North Africa
- Sub-Saharan Africa
- Central Asia
- East Asia
- South Asia
- Southeast Asia
- Japan
- Russia
- South Pacific

▲ 9.1.3 **NINE WORLD REGIONS**

FOCUS ON WORLD REGIONS

Geographers divide the world into nine regions according to physical, cultural, and economic features (Figure 9.1.3). Two of the nine regions—North America and Europe—are considered developed (Figure 9.1.4). The other seven regions—Latin America, East Asia, Southwest Asia & North Africa, Southeast Asia, Central Asia, South Asia, and sub-Saharan Africa—are considered developing. In addition to these nine regions, three other distinctive areas can be identified—Japan, Russia, and South Pacific. Japan and South Pacific are grouped with the developed regions. Because of limited progress in development both under and since communism, Russia is now classified as a developing country by the United Nations. In each of the remaining nine sections of this chapter, one of the nine regions is highlighted in relation to the topic of the section.

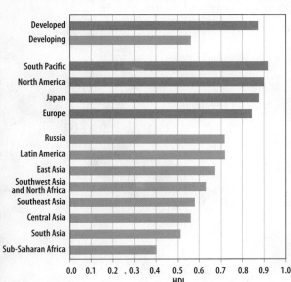

Bar chart categories (HDI by Region):
- Developed
- Developing
- South Pacific
- North America
- Japan
- Europe
- Russia
- Latin America
- East Asia
- Southwest Asia and North Africa
- Southeast Asia
- Central Asia
- South Asia
- Sub-Saharan Africa

HDI axis: 0.0 0.1 0.2 0.3 0.4 0.5 0.6 0.7 0.8 0.9 1.0
HDI

▲ 9.1.4 **HDI BY REGION**

9.2 Standard of Living

▶ **Developed countries have higher average incomes than developing countries.**
▶ **People in developed countries are more productive and possess more goods.**

Key to development is enough wealth for a decent standard of living. The average individual earns a much higher income in a developed country than in a developing one. Geographers observe that people generate and spend their wealth in different ways in developed countries than in developing countries.

INCOME

The United Nations measures the average income in countries through a complex index called annual gross national income per capita at purchasing power parity. The figure is approximately $40,000 in developed countries compared to approximately $5,000 in developing countries (Figure 9.2.1).

Gross national income (GNI) is the value of the output of goods and services produced in a country in a year, including money that leaves and enters the country. Dividing GNI by total population measures the contribution made by the average individual towards generating a country's wealth in a year. Older studies refer to **gross domestic product**, which is also the value of the output of goods and services produced in a country in a year, but it does not account for money that leaves and enters the country.

Purchasing power parity (PPP) is an adjustment made to the GNI to account for differences among countries in the cost of goods. For example, if a resident of country A has the same income as a resident in country B but must pay more for a Big Mac or a Starbucks latte, the resident of country B is better off.

ECONOMIC STRUCTURE

Average per capita income is higher in developed countries because people typically earn their living by different means than in developing countries. Jobs fall into three categories:

- **Primary sector** (including agriculture).
- **Secondary sector** (including manufacturing).
- **Tertiary sector** (including services).

Developing countries have a higher share of primary and secondary sector workers and a smaller share of tertiary sector workers than developed countries (Figure 9.2.2). The relatively low percentage of primary-sector workers in developed countries indicates that a handful of farmers produce enough food for the rest of society. Freed from the task of growing their own food, most people in a developed country can contribute to an increase in the national wealth by working in the secondary and tertiary sectors (Figure 9.2.3).

▼ 9.2.2 **FOCUS ON NORTH AMERICA: ECONOMIC STRUCTURE**
Tertiary-sector workers in Florida.

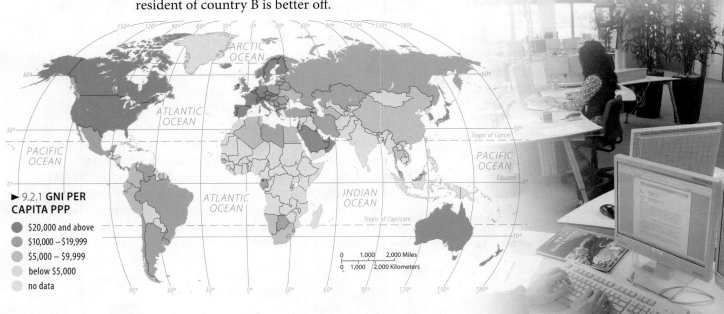

▶ 9.2.1 **GNI PER CAPITA PPP**

- $20,000 and above
- $10,000 – $19,999
- $5,000 – $9,999
- below $5,000
- no data

0   1,000   2,000 Miles
0   1,000   2,000 Kilometers

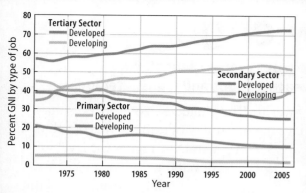

▲ 9.2.3 **PERCENT GNI CONTRIBUTED BY TYPE OF JOB**

PRODUCTIVITY

Workers in developed countries are more productive than those in developing ones. **Productivity** is the value of a particular product compared to the amount of labor needed to make it. Productivity can be measured by the value added per worker. The **value added** in manufacturing is the gross value of the product minus the costs of raw materials and energy. Workers in developed countries produce more with less effort because they have access to more machines, tools, and equipment to perform much of the work (Figure 9.2.4).

▲ 9.2.4 **FOCUS ON NORTH AMERICA: PRODUCTIVITY** Manufacturing computers in California.

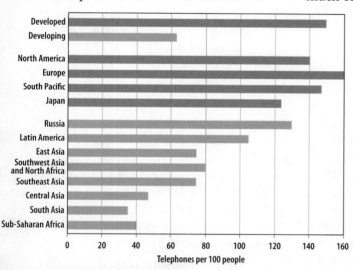

▲ 9.2.5 **TELEPHONES PER 100 PEOPLE**

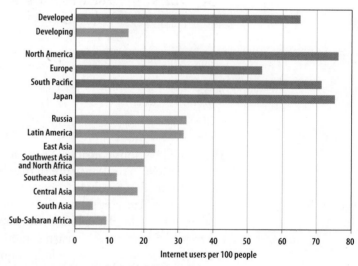

▲ 9.2.6 **INTERNET USERS PER 100 PEOPLE**

CONSUMER GOODS

Part of the wealth generated in developed countries is used to purchase goods and services. Especially vital to the economy's functioning and growth are goods and services related to communications, such as telephones and computers. Computers and telephones are not essential to people who live in the same village as their friends and relatives and work all day growing food in nearby fields.

Telephones enhance interaction with providers of raw materials and customers for goods and services (Figure 9.2.5). Computers facilitate the sharing of information with other buyers and suppliers (Figure 9.2.6). Developed countries average 150 telephones and 65 Internet users per 100 persons, compared to 60 telephones and 15 Internet users per 100 in developing countries.

FOCUS ON NORTH AMERICA

North America is the region with the world's highest per capita income. North America was once the world's major manufacturer of steel, motor vehicles, and other goods, but since the late twentieth century other regions have taken the lead. Now the region has the world's highest percentage of tertiary-sector employment, especially health care, leisure, and financial services. North Americans remain the leading consumers and the world's largest market for many products. The wealth generated in the United States and Canada enables the residents of those countries to purchase more consumer goods than in other regions.

9.3 Access to Knowledge

► **People in developed countries complete more years of school.**
► **Developed countries have lower pupil/teacher ratios and higher literacy.**

Development is about more than possession of wealth. The United Nations believes that access to knowledge is essential for people to have the possibility of leading lives of value. In general, the higher the level of development, the greater are both the quantity and the quality of a country's education. For many in developing countries, education is the ticket to better jobs and higher social status.

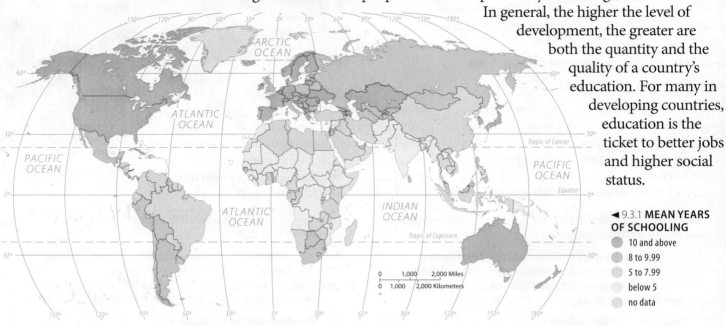

◄ 9.3.1 **MEAN YEARS OF SCHOOLING**

- 10 and above
- 8 to 9.99
- 5 to 7.99
- below 5
- no data

QUANTITY OF SCHOOLING

The United Nations considers years of schooling to be the most critical measure of the ability of an individual to gain access to knowledge needed for development. The assumption is that no matter how poor the school, the longer the pupils attend, the more likely they are to learn something.

To form the access to knowledge component of HDI, the United Nations combines two measures of quantity of schooling:

▼ 9.3.2 **EXPECTED YEARS OF SCHOOLING**

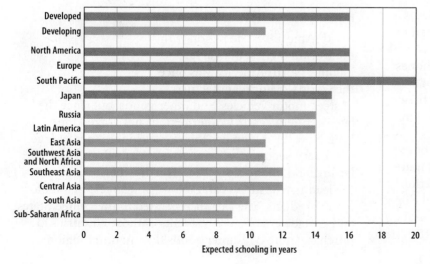

Expected schooling in years

- *Years of schooling.* The number of years that the average person aged 25 or older in a country has spent in school. The average pupil has attended school for approximately 11 years in developed countries, compared to approximately 6 years in developing countries (Figure 9.3.1).

- *Expected years of schooling.* The number of years that an average 5 year old child is expected to spend with his or her education in the future. The United Nations expects that today's 5-year-old will attend an average of 16 years of school in developed countries and 11 years in developing ones (Figure 9.3.2). Sub-Saharan Africa and South Asia are expected to lag in schooling compared to other regions.

Thus, the United Nations expects children around the world to receive an average of five years more education in the future, but the gap in education between developed and developing regions will remain high. Otherwise stated, the United Nations expects that roughly half of today's 5-year-olds will graduate from college in developed countries, whereas less than half will graduate from high school in developing ones.

QUALITY OF SCHOOLING

Two measures of quality of education include:

- *Pupil/teacher ratio.* The fewer pupils a teacher has, the more likely that each student will receive instruction. The pupil/teacher ratio is twice as high in developing countries— approximately 30 pupils per teacher— compared to only 15 in developed countries (Figure 9.3.3). Pupil/teacher ratio exceeds 40 in sub-Saharan Africa and South Asia.

- *Literacy rate.* A higher percentage of people in developed countries are able to attend school and as a result learn to read and write. The **literacy rate** is the percentage of a country's people who can read and write. It exceeds 99 percent in developed countries (Figure 9.3.4). Among developing regions, the literacy rate exceeds 90 percent in East Asia and Latin America, but is less than 70 percent in sub-Saharan Africa and South Asia.

Most books, newspapers, and magazines are published in developed countries, in part because more of their citizens read and write. Developed countries dominate scientific and nonfiction publishing worldwide—this textbook is an example. Students in developing countries must learn technical information from books that usually are not in

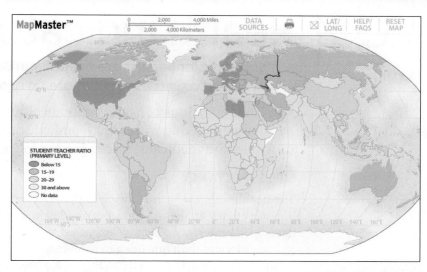

their native language but are printed in English, German, Russian, or French.

Improved education is a major goal of many developing countries, but funds are scarce. Education may receive a higher percentage of the GNI in developing countries, but their GNI is far lower to begin with, so they spend far less per pupil than do developed countries.

▲ 9.3.3 **PUPIL/?TEACHER RATIO**

Open MapMaster World in Mastering**GEOGRAPHY**

Select: *Cultural* then *Students per teacher in primary school.*
Select: *Population* then *Percentage of population under age 15.*

Are class sizes larger or smaller in countries that have a high percentage of population under age 15?

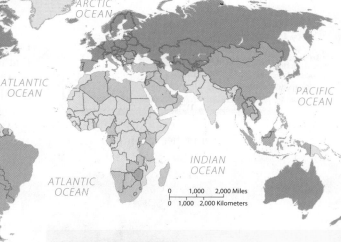

Percent literate
- 99–100
- 90–98
- 70–89
- below 70
- no data

► 9.3.4 **LITERACY RATE**

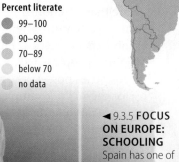

◄ 9.3.5 **FOCUS ON EUROPE: SCHOOLING**
Spain has one of the world's most favorable pupil/teacher ratios.

FOCUS ON EUROPE

Within Europe, the HDI is the world's highest in a core area that extends from southern Scandinavia to western Germany. These countries have especially high levels of schooling, favorable pupil/teacher ratios, and universal literacy (Figure 9.3.5). Europe's overall development indicators are somewhat lower because of inclusion of Eastern European countries that developed under communist rule for much of the twentieth century. Europe must import food, energy, and minerals, but can maintain its high level of development by providing high value goods and services, such as insurance, banking, and luxury motor vehicles.

9.4 Health Indicators

▶ **People live longer and are healthier in developed countries.**
▶ **Developed countries spend more on health care.**

The United Nations considers good health to be a third important measure of development, along with wealth and education. A goal of development is to provide the nutrition and medical services needed for people to lead long and healthy lives.

LIFE EXPECTANCY

The health indicator contributing to the HDI is life expectancy at birth. A baby born today in a developed region is on average expected to live ten years longer than one born in a developing region (Figure 9.4.1, and refer to Figure 2.4.3 for world map). Variation among developing regions is especially wide; life expectancy in East Asia and Latin America is comparable to the level in developed countries, but it is much lower in sub-Saharan Africa.

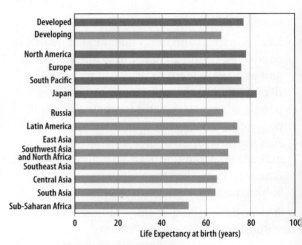

▲ 9.4.1 **LIFE EXPECTANCY BY REGION**

HEALTH CARE ACCESS

People live longer and are healthier in developed countries than in developing ones because of better access to health care. The greater wealth that is generated in developed countries is used in part to obtain health care. A healthier population in turn can be more economically productive. For example, 17 percent of children in developing countries are not immunized against measles, compared to 7 percent in developed ones. More than one-fourth of children lack measles immunization in South Asia and sub-Saharan Africa (Figure 9.4.2).

When people get sick, developed countries possess the resources to care for them. For example, developed countries on average have 50 hospital beds per 10,000 population compared to only 20 in developing countries (Figures 9.4.3 and 9.4.4).

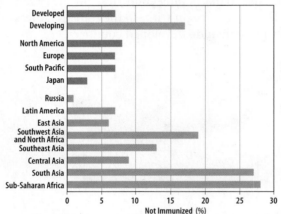

▶ 9.4.2 **CHILDREN LACKING MEASLES IMMUNIZATION**

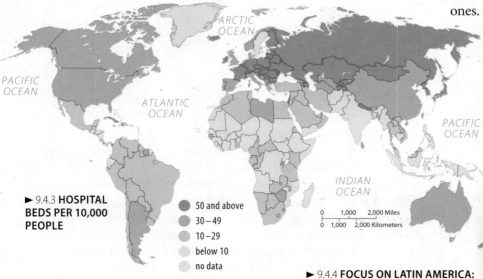

▶ 9.4.3 **HOSPITAL BEDS PER 10,000 PEOPLE**

50 and above
30 – 49
10 – 29
below 10
no data

▶ 9.4.4 **FOCUS ON LATIN AMERICA: HEALTH CARE**
Clinic in Haiti run by American missionaries.

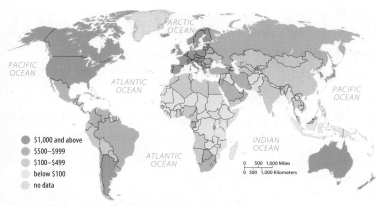

▲ 9.4.5 **HEALTH CARE EXPENDITURE PER CAPITA**

$1,000 and above
$500–$999
$100–$499
below $100
no data

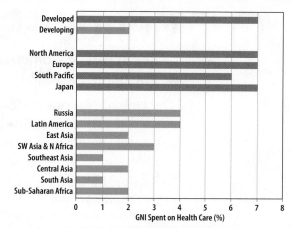

▲ 9.4.6 **HEALTH CARE EXPENDITURE AS PERCENTAGE OF GNI**

HEALTH CARE EXPENDITURES

The gap between developed and developing countries is especially high in expenditures on health care. Developed countries spend more than $4,000 per person annually on health care, compared to approximately $200 per person in developing countries (Figure 9.4.5). Hospitals, medicines, doctors—spending is much higher in developed countries.

Total expenditures on health care exceed 7 percent of GNI in developed countries, compared to 2 percent in developing ones. So not only do developed countries have much higher GNI per capita than developing countries, they spend a higher percentage of that GNI on health care (Figure 9.4.6).

In most developed countries, health care is a public service that is available at little or no cost. The government programs pay more than 70 percent of health care costs in most European countries, and private individuals pay less than 30 percent. In comparison, private individuals must pay more than half of the cost of health care in developing countries. An exception is the United States, where private individuals are required to pay 55 percent of health care, more closely resembling the pattern in developing countries.

Developed countries also use part of their wealth to protect people who, for various reasons, are unable to work. In these countries some public assistance is offered to those who are sick, elderly, poor, disabled, orphaned, veterans of wars, widows, unemployed, or single parents. European countries such as Denmark, Norway, and Sweden typically provide the highest level of public-assistance payments.

Developed countries are hard-pressed to maintain their current levels of public assistance. In the past, rapid economic growth permitted these states to finance generous programs with little hardship. But in recent years economic growth has slowed, whereas the percentage of people needing public assistance has increased. Governments have faced a choice between reducing benefits or increasing taxes to pay for them.

▼ 9.4.7 **FOCUS ON LATIN AMERICA: HEALTH CARE** Clinic in Colombia for displaced people.

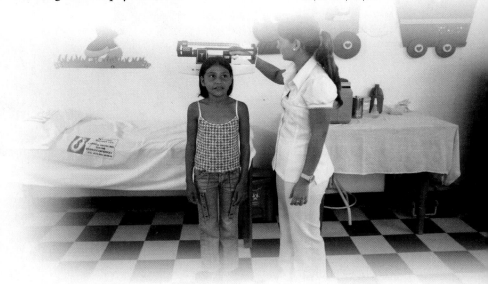

FOCUS ON LATIN AMERICA

The level of development varies sharply within Latin America. Neighborhoods within some large cities along the South Atlantic Coast enjoy a level of development comparable to that of developed countries. The coastal area as a whole has a relatively high GNI per capita. Outside the coastal area, development is lower. Among developing regions, Latin America—along with East Asia—has relatively high life expectancy, high immunization rates, more hospital beds per capita, and more money spent on health care. The levels lag, though, compared with developed regions.

9.5 Gender-Related Development

► **The status of women is lower than that of men in every country.**

► **The Gender Inequality Index (GII) measures inequality between men and women.**

The United Nations has not found a single country in the world where women are treated as well as men. At best women have achieved near equality with men in some countries, whereas in other countries the level of development of women lags far behind the level for men.

To measure the extent of each country's gender inequality, the United Nations has created the **Gender Inequality Index (GII)**. The higher the score the greater is the inequality between men and women (Figure 9.5.1). As with the other indices, the GII combines multiple measures, in this case reproductive health, empowerment, and labor.

EMPOWERMENT

The empowerment dimension is measured by two indicators:

- The percentage of seats held by women in the national legislature (Figures 9.5.2 and 9.5.3).
- The percentage of women who have completed high school.

  Both measures are lower in developing regions than in developed ones.

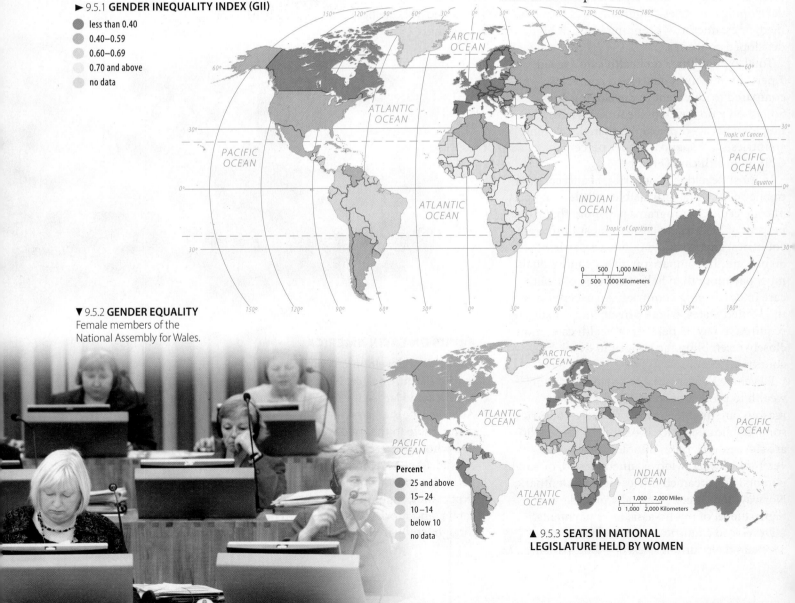

► 9.5.1 **GENDER INEQUALITY INDEX (GII)**

- less than 0.40
- 0.40–0.59
- 0.60–0.69
- 0.70 and above
- no data

▼ 9.5.2 **GENDER EQUALITY**
Female members of the National Assembly for Wales.

Percent
- 25 and above
- 15–24
- 10–14
- below 10
- no data

▲ 9.5.3 **SEATS IN NATIONAL LEGISLATURE HELD BY WOMEN**

LABOR

The labor force participation rate is the percent of women holding full-time jobs outside the home. Women in developing countries are less likely than women in developed countries to hold full-time jobs outside the home (Figure 9.5.4).

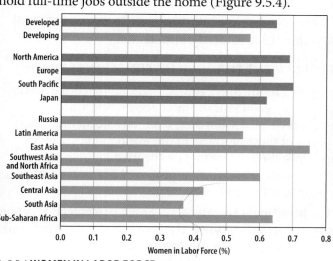

▲ 9.5.4 **WOMEN IN LABOR FORCE**

▼ 9.5.5 **ADOLESCENT FERTILITY RATE (RIGHT)**
TEENAGE MOTHER IN OHIO (BELOW)

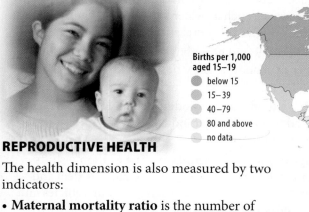

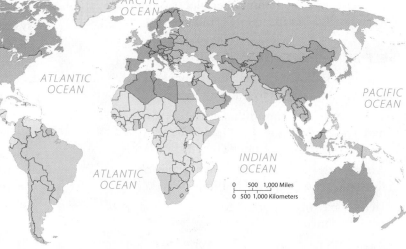

▲ 9.5.6 **FOCUS ON EAST ASIA: WOMEN IN THE LABOR FORCE**
Female workers in optical fiber factory, Ghuanzhou, China.

Births per 1,000 aged 15–19
- below 15
- 15–39
- 40–79
- 80 and above
- no data

REPRODUCTIVE HEALTH

The health dimension is also measured by two indicators:

- **Maternal mortality ratio** is the number of women who die giving birth per 100,000 births.

- **Adolescent fertility rate** is the number of births per 1,000 women age 15–19.

Women in developing regions are more likely than women in developed regions to die in childbirth and to give birth as teenagers (Figure 9.5.5).

In general, the GII is higher in developing regions than in developed ones. Sub-Saharan Africa, South Asia, Central Asia, and Southwest Asia are the developing regions with the highest levels of gender inequality. Reproductive health is the largest contributor to gender inequality in these regions. South and Southwest Asia also have relatively poor female empowerment scores. The United States ranks especially poorly in the percentage of teenagers who give birth and in the percentage of women serving in Congress.

FOCUS ON EAST ASIA

The Gender Inequality Index in East Asia is comparable to that of developed regions. Compared to other developing countries, China has high female education levels and participation in the labor force and low maternal mortality and teenage fertility rates (Figure 9.5.6). Now the world's second largest economy, behind only the United States, China accounts for one-third of total world economic growth, and GNI per capita has risen faster there than in any other country. Under communism, the government took strong control of most components of development.

9.6 Two Paths to Development

► The self-sufficiency development path erects barriers to trade.
► The international trade path allocates scarce resources to a few activities.

To promote development, developing countries typical follow one of two development models. One emphasizes self-sufficiency, the other international trade.

DEVELOPMENT THROUGH SELF-SUFFICIENCY

Self-sufficiency, or balanced growth, was the more popular of the development alternatives for most of the twentieth century. According to the self-sufficiency approach:

- Investment is spread as equally as possible across all sectors of a country's economy and in all regions.
- The pace of development may be modest, but the system is fair because residents and enterprises throughout the country share the benefits of development.
- Reducing poverty takes precedence over encouraging a few people to become wealthy consumers.
- Fledgling businesses are isolated from competition with large international corporations.
- The import of goods from other places is limited by barriers such as tariffs, quotas, and licenses.

SELF-SUFFICIENCY EXAMPLE: INDIA

India once followed the self-sufficiency model (Figure 9.6.1). India's barriers to trade included:

- To import goods into India, most foreign companies had to secure a license that had to be approved by several dozen government agencies.
- An importer with a license was severely restricted in the quantity it could sell in India.
- Heavy taxes on imported goods doubled or tripled the price to consumers.
- Indian money could not be converted to other currencies.
- Businesses required government permission to sell a new product, modernize a factory, expand production, set prices, hire or fire workers, and change the job classification of existing workers.

▼ 9.6.1 **SELF-SUFFICIENCY EXAMPLE: INDIA**
Basmati rice on sale at a market in Haryana.

DEVELOPMENT THROUGH INTERNATIONAL TRADE

According to the international trade approach, a country can develop economically by concentrating scarce resources on expansion of its distinctive local industries. The sale of these products in the world market brings funds into the country that can be used to finance other development. W. W. Rostow proposed a five-stage model of development in 1960.

- **The traditional society.** A very high percentage of people engaged in agriculture and a high percentage of national wealth allocated to what Rostow called "nonproductive" activities, such as the military and religion.
- **The preconditions for takeoff.** An elite group of well-educated leaders initiates investment in technology and infrastructure, such as water supplies and transportation systems, designed to increase productivity.
- **The takeoff.** Rapid growth is generated in a limited number of economic activities, such as textiles or food products.
- **The drive to maturity.** Modern technology, previously confined to a few takeoff industries, diffuses to a wide variety of industries.
- **The age of mass consumption.** The economy shifts from production of heavy industry, such as steel and energy, to consumer goods, such as motor vehicles and refrigerators.

INTERNATIONAL TRADE EXAMPLES

Among the first countries to adopt the international trade alternative during the twentieth century:

- **The "Four Dragons."** South Korea, Singapore, Taiwan, and the then-British colony of Hong Kong (also known as the "four little tigers" and "the gang of four") developed by producing a handful of manufactured goods, especially clothing and electronics, that depended on low labor costs.
- **Petroleum-rich Arabian Peninsula countries.** Once among the world's least developed countries, they were transformed overnight into some of the wealthiest thanks to escalating petroleum prices during the 1970s (Figure 9.6.2).

SELF-SUFFICIENCY SHORTCOMINGS

The experience of India and other developing countries revealed two major problems with self-sufficiency:

- **Self-sufficiency protected inefficient industries.** Businesses could sell all they made, at high government-controlled prices, to customers culled from long waiting lists. So they had little incentive to improve quality, lower production costs, reduce prices, or increase production. Nor did they keep abreast of rapid technological changes elsewhere.

- **A large bureaucracy was needed to administer the controls.** A complex administrative system encouraged abuse and corruption. Aspiring entrepreneurs found that struggling to produce goods or offer services was less rewarding financially than advising others how to get around the complex regulations.

INTERNATIONAL TRADE SHORTCOMINGS

Three factors have hindered countries outside the four Asian dragons and the Arabian Peninsula from developing through the international trade:

- **Local hardships.** Building up a handful of takeoff industries has forced some developing countries to cut back on production of food, clothing, and other necessities for their own people.

- **Slow market growth.** Developing countries trying to take advantage of their low-cost labor find that markets in developed countries are growing more slowly than when the "four dragons" used this strategy a generation ago.

- **Low commodity prices.** Some developing countries have raw materials sought by manufacturers and producers in developed countries. The sale of these raw materials could generate funds for developing countries to promote development. International trade worked in the Arabian Peninsula because the price of petroleum has escalated so rapidly, but other developing countries have not been so fortunate because of low prices for their commodities.

▲ 9.6.2 **INTERNATIONAL TRADE EXAMPLE: UNITED ARAB EMIRATES**
Development in Dubai, United Arab Emirates.

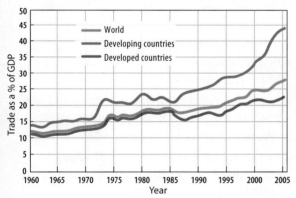

▲ 9.6.3 **WORLD TRADE AS PERCENT OF INCOME**

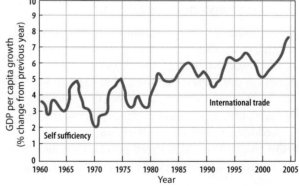

▲ 9.6.4 **GDP PER CAPITA CHANGE IN INDIA**

INTERNATIONAL TRADE TRIUMPHS

Countries have converted from self-sufficiency to international trade (Figure 9.6.3). For example, India has:

- Reduced taxes and restrictions on imports and exports
- Eliminated many monopolies
- Encouraged improvement of the quality of products

India's per capita income has increased more rapidly since conversion to international trade (Figure 9.6.4).

FOCUS ON SOUTHWEST ASIA AND NORTH AFRICA

Countries in Southwest Asia and North Africa that are oil-rich have used petroleum revenues to finance large-scale projects, such as housing, highways, airports, universities, and telecommunications networks. Imported consumer goods are readily available. However, some business practices typical of international trade are difficult to reconcile with Islamic religious principles. Women are excluded from holding many jobs and visiting some public places. All business halts several times a day when Muslims are called to prayers.

9.7 World Trade

▶ The World Trade Organization has facilitated adoption of international trade.
▶ Transnational corporations are a major source of development funds.

To promote the international trade development model, most countries have joined the World Trade Organization (WTO). Private corporations are especially eager to promote international trade.

▶ 9.7.1 **WORLD TRADE ORGANIZATION**
Open MapMaster World in
Mastering**GEOGRAPHY**

Select: *Economic* then *Gross National Income Per Capita At Purchasing Power Parity.*
Select: Geopolitical **then** World Trade Organization Members.

In what three of the nine major world regions (excluding russia) are most of the countries not members of the WTO?

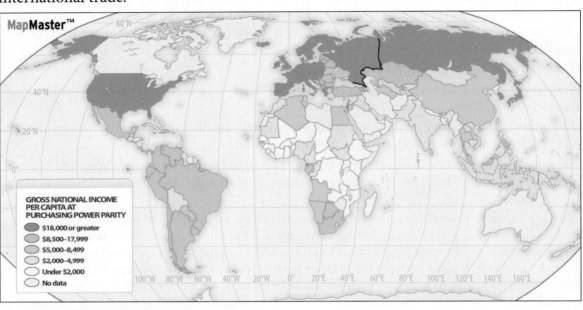

GROSS NATIONAL INCOME PER CAPITA AT PURCHASING POWER PARITY
● $18,000 or greater
● $8,500–17,999
● $5,000–8,499
● $2,000–4,999
○ Under $2,000
○ No data

WORLD TRADE ORGANIZATION

To promote the international trade development model, countries representing 97 percent of world trade established the WTO in 1995. Russia is the largest economy that has not joined the WTO (Figure 9.7.1). The WTO works to reduce barriers to trade in three principal ways:

1. Reduce or eliminate restrictions:
- On trade of manufactured goods, such as government subsidies of exports, quotas, and tariffs.
- On international movement of money by banks, corporations, and wealthy individuals.

2. Enforce agreements:
- By ruling on whether a country has violated WTO agreements.
- By ordering remedies when one country has been found to have violated the agreements.

3. Protect intellectual property:
- By hearing charges from an individual or corporation concerning copyright and patent violations in other countries.
- By ordering illegal copyright or patent activities to stop.

The WTO has been sharply attacked by critics (Figure 9.7.2). Protesters routinely gather in the streets outside high-level meetings of the WTO:

- Progressive critics charge that the WTO is antidemocratic, because decisions made behind closed doors promote the interest of large corporations rather than the poor.
- Conservative critics charge that the WTO compromises the power and sovereignty of individual countries because it can order changes in taxes and laws that it considers unfair trading practices.

▲ ▼ 9.7.2 **THE WORLD TRADE ORGANIZATION GENERATES STRONG SUPPORT AND OPPOSITION**

FOREIGN DIRECT INVESTMENT

International trade requires corporations based in a particular country to invest in other countries (Figure 9.7.3). Investment made by a foreign company in the economy of another country is known as **foreign direct investment (FDI)**. World FDI has grown from $2 trillion in 1990 to $7 trillion in 2000 and $17 trillion in 2009 (Figure 9.7.4).

FDI does not flow equally around the world. Only 30 percent of FDI in 2009 went from a developed to a developing country, whereas 70 percent moved between two developed countries. Among developing regions, more than one-fourth each was directed to East Asia and Latin America (Figure 9.7.5).

The major sources of FDI are transnational corporations (TNCs). A transnational corporation invests and operates in countries other than the one in which its headquarters are located. Of the 100 largest TNCs in 2009, 61 had headquarters in Europe, 19 in the United States, 10 in Japan, 3 in other developed countries, and only 7 in developing countries.

▲ 9.7.3 **FOREIGN DIRECT INVESTMENT**
Japanese carmakers have built several assembly plants in Thailand.

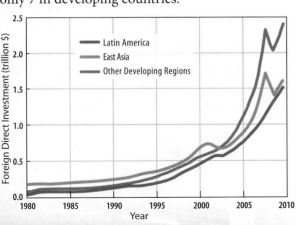

▲ 9.7.4 **GROWTH IN FDI**

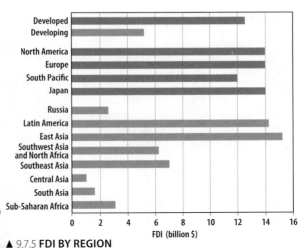

▲ 9.7.5 **FDI BY REGION**

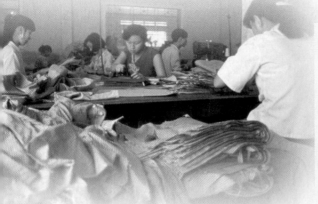

▲ 9.7.6 **FOCUS ON SOUTHEAST ASIA: INTERNATIONAL TRADE**
Child labor in clothing factory.

FOCUS ON SOUTHEAST ASIA

Southeast Asia has become a major manufacturer of textiles and clothing, taking advantage of cheap labor. Thailand has become the region's center for the manufacturing of automobiles and other consumer goods. Indonesia, the world's fourth most populous country, is a major producer of petroleum (Figure 9.7.6). Development has slowed because of painful reforms to restore confidence among international investors shaken by unwise and corrupt investments made possible by lax regulations and excessively close cooperation among manufacturers, financial institutions, and government agencies.

9.8 Financing Development

▶ **Developing countries finance some development through foreign aid and loans.**
▶ **To qualify for loans, a country may need to enact economic reforms.**

Developing countries lack the money needed to finance development. So they obtain grants and loans from governments, banks, and international organizations based in developed countries.

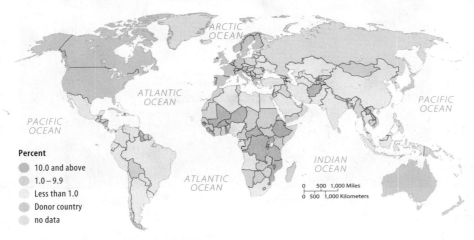

Percent
- 10.0 and above
- 1.0 – 9.9
- Less than 1.0
- Donor country
- no data

0   500   1,000 Miles
0   500   1,000 Kilometers

▲ 9.8.1 **FOREIGN AID AS PERCENT OF GNI**

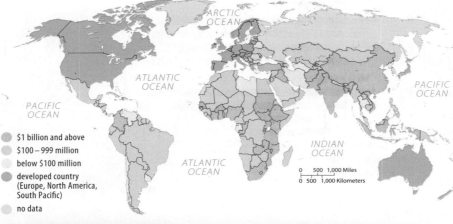

- $1 billion and above
- $100 – 999 million
- below $100 million
- developed country (Europe, North America, South Pacific)
- no data

0   500   1,000 Miles
0   500   1,000 Kilometers

▲ 9.8.2 **DEVELOPMENT ASSISTANCE**

▼ 9.8.3 **WORLD BANK INVESTMENT: THE PHILIPPINES**
Wind farm in Bangui Bay, the Philippines, financed with a World Bank loan.

FOREIGN AID

Most developing countries also receive aid directly from governments of developed countries. The U.S. government allocates approximately 0.2 percent (1/5 of 1%) of its GNI to foreign aid. European countries average a good bit more, approximately 0.5 percent (Figure 9.8.1).

LOANS

The two major international lending organizations are the World Bank and the International Monetary Fund (IMF). The World Bank and IMF were conceived in 1944 to promote development after the devastation of World War II and to avoid a repetition of the disastrous economic policies contributing to the Great Depression of the 1930s. The IMF and World Bank became specialized agencies of the United Nations when it was established in 1945. Twenty-six countries received at least $1 billion in 2009 (Figure 9.8.2).

Developing countries borrow money to build new infrastructure, such as hydroelectric dams, electric transmission lines, flood-protection systems, water supplies, roads, and hotels (Figure 9.8.3). The theory is that the new infrastructure attracts businesses, which in turn pays taxes used to repay the loans and to improve people's living conditions.

In reality, the World Bank itself judges half of the projects it has funded in Africa to be failures. Common reasons include:

- Projects do not function as intended because of faulty engineering.

- Aid is squandered, stolen, or spent on armaments by recipient nations.

- New infrastructure does not attract other investment.

STRUCTURAL ADJUSTMENT PROGRAMS

Some developing countries have had difficulty repaying their loans. The IMF, World Bank, and banks in developed countries fear that granting, canceling, or refinancing debts without strings attached would perpetuate bad habits in developing countries. Therefore before getting debt relief, a developing country is required to prepare a Policy Framework Paper (PFP) outlining a structural adjustment program.

A **structural adjustment program** includes economic "reforms" or "adjustments." Requirements placed on a developing country typically include:

- Spend only what it can afford.
- Direct benefits to the poor not just the elite.
- Divert investment from military to health and education spending.
- Invest scarce resources where they would have the most impact.
- Encourage a more productive private sector.
- Reform the government, including a more efficient civil service, more accountable fiscal management, more predictable rules and regulations, and more dissemination of information to the public.

Critics charge that poverty worsens under structural adjustment programs. By placing priority on reducing government spending and inflation, structural adjustment programs may result in:

- Cuts in health, education, and social services that benefit the poor.
- Higher unemployment.
- Loss of jobs in state enterprises and the civil service.
- Less support for those most in need, such as poor pregnant women, nursing mothers, young children, and elderly people.

In short, structural reforms allegedly punish Earth's poorest people for actions they did not commit—waste, corruption, misappropriation, military build-ups.

International organizations respond that the poor suffer more when a country does not undertake reforms. Economic growth is what benefits the poor the most in the long run. Nevertheless, in response to criticisms, the IMF

Percent
- 50 and above
- 25 – 49
- below 25
- no data

▲ 9.8.4 **DEBT AS PERCENT OF GNI**

◄ 9.8.5 **WORLD BANK INVESTMENT IN AFGHANISTAN** Use Google Earth™ to explore development aid in Afghanistan.

Fly to: *Kabul Airport, Afghanistan.*
Drag to: *Enter street view.*
Exit: *Ground level view.* Zoom out until airport is visible.

The World Bank paid for the long straight dark narrow strip.

1. **What is it?**
2. **Does it appear to be in good condition or in poor condition?**

and World Bank now encourage innovative programs to reduce poverty and corruption, and consult more with average citizens. A safety net must be included to ease short-term pain experienced by poor people. Meanwhile, in the twenty-first century, it is the developed countries that have piled up the most debt, especially in the wake of the severe recession of 2007-09 (Figure 9.8.4).

FOCUS ON CENTRAL ASIA

Within Central Asia, the level of development is relatively high in Kazakhstan and Iran. Not by coincidence, these two countries are the region's leading producers of petroleum. In Kazakhstan, rising oil revenues are being used to finance a carefully managed improvement in overall development. In Iran, a large share of the rising oil revenues has been used to maintain low consumer prices rather than to promote development.

Since coming to power in a 1979 revolution, Iran's Shiite leaders have also used oil revenues to promote revolutions elsewhere in the region and to sweep away elements of development and social customs they perceive to be influenced by Europe or North America. War-torn Afghanistan has received more development assistance than any other country in recent years (Figure 9.8.5).

9.9 Fair Trade

▶ **Fair trade is a model of development that is meant to protect small businesses and workers.**

▶ **With fair trade, a higher percentage of the sales price goes back to the producers.**

A variation of the international trade model of development is **fair trade**, in which products are made and traded following practices and standards that protect workers and small businesses in developing countries.

Two sets of standards distinguish fair trade:

- Fairtrade Labelling Organizations International (FLO) sets international standards for fair trade (Figure 9.9.1).
- Standards applied to workers on farms and in factories.

▶ 9.9.1 **FAIR TRADE CLOTHING LABEL** Fair trade label in shirt.

FAIR TRADE PRODUCER PRACTICES

Many farmers and artisans in developing countries are unable to borrow from banks the money they need to invest in their businesses. By banding together in fair trade cooperatives, they can get credit, reduce their raw material costs, and maintain higher and fairer prices for their products (Figure 9.9.2).

Cooperatives are managed democratically, so farmers and artisans learn leadership and organizational skills. The people who grow or make the products have a say in how local resources are utilized and sold. Safe and healthy working conditions can be protected. Cooperatives thus benefit the local farmers and artisans who are members, rather than absentee corporate owners interested only in maximizing profits.

For fair trade coffee, consumers pay prices comparable to those charged by gourmet brands. However, fair trade coffee producers receive a significantly higher price per pound than traditional coffee producers: around $1.20 compared to around $0.80 per pound. Through bypassing exploitative middlemen and working directly with producers, fair trade organizations are able to cut costs and return a greater percentage of the retail price to the producers.

In North America, fair trade products have been primarily craft products such as decorative home accessories, jewelry, textiles, and ceramics. Ten Thousand Villages is the largest fair trade organization in North America specializing in handicrafts. In Europe, most fair trade sales are in food, including coffee, tea, bananas, chocolate, cocoa, juice, sugar, and honey products. TransFair USA certifies the products sold in the United States that are fair trade.

◀ 9.9.2 **FAIR TRADE FOOD** Fair trade rice for export in Dehradun, India.

FAIR TRADE WORKER STANDARDS

Fair trade requires employers to:

- Pay workers fair wages (at least the country's minimum wage).
- Permit union organizing.
- Comply with minimum environmental and safety standards.

In contrast, protection of workers' rights is a low priority in the international trade development path, according to its critics:

- People in developing countries allegedly work long hours in poor conditions for low pay with minimal oversight by governments and international lending agencies.
- The workforce may include children or forced labor.

▼ 9.9.3 **FOCUS ON SOUTH ASIA: GRAMEEN BANK**

- Poor sanitation and safety may result in health problems and injuries.
- Injured, ill, or laid-off workers are not compensated.

Fair trade returns on average one-third of the price back to the producer in the developing country. The rest goes to the wholesaler who imports the item and for the retailer's rent, wages, and other expenses. On the other hand, only a tiny percentage of the price a consumer pays for a good reaches the individual in the developing country responsible for making or growing it, charge critics of international trade. A Haitian sewing clothing for the U.S. market, for example, earns less than 1 percent of the retail price, according to the National Labor Committee.

FOCUS ON SOUTH ASIA

Many would-be entrepreneurs in developing countries are too poor to qualify for regular bank loans. An alternative source of loans for development, the Grameen Bank, based in Bangladesh, has made several hundred thousand loans to women in South Asia. Only 1 percent of the borrowers have failed to make their weekly loan repayments, an extraordinarily low percentage for a bank (Figure 9.9.3). Several million loans have also been provided to women by the Bangladesh Rural Advancement Committee. For founding the bank, Muhammad Yunus was awarded the Nobel peace prize in 2006.

9.10 Millennium Development Goals

▶ By most development measures, the gap between developing and developed countries has narrowed.

▶ The United Nations has set eight goals to further reduce the gap in development.

The relationship between developed and developing countries can be depicted as one of "core" and "periphery". In an increasingly unified world economy, developed countries form an inner-core area, whereas developing countries occupy peripheral locations (Figure 9.10.1).

Developed countries account for a high percentage of the world's economic activity and wealth. Developing countries in the periphery have less access to the world centers of consumption, communications, wealth, and power. As countries like China, India, and Brazil develop, relationships between core and periphery are changing and the line may need to be redrawn.

▲ 9.10.1 **CORE AND PERIPHERY**
This unorthodox world map projection emphasizes the central role played by developed countries at the core of the world economy and the secondary role of developing countries at the periphery.

CLOSING THE GAP

Since the United Nations began measuring HDI in 1980, all but three countries have had improved HDI scores (Figure 9.10.2). The exceptions are in sub-Saharan Africa—Democratic Republic of the Congo, Zambia, Zimbabwe—and the region as a whole has improved only from 0.29 to 0.39. In contrast, East Asia's HDI has improved especially rapidly, from 0.39 to 0.65, and South Asia's has improved from 0.32 to 0.52 (Figure 9.10.3).

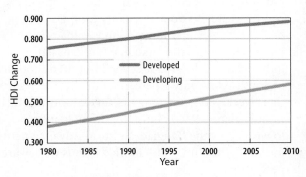

▲ 9.10.2 **HDI CHANGE, 1980–2010**

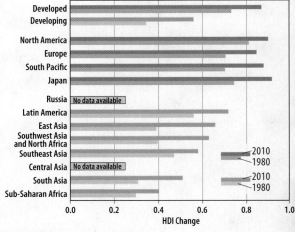

▲ 9.10.3 **HDI CHANGE BY REGION**

The gap between developed and developing countries is narrowing in health and education. For example, during the 1950s people lived on average more than two decades longer in developed countries than in developing ones. In the twenty-first century, the gap is less than ten years (Figure 9.10.4). On the other hand, the gap in wealth between developed and developing countries has widened (Figure 9.10.5).

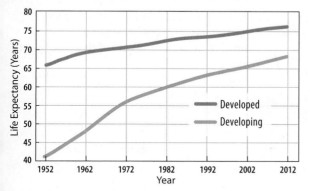

▲ 9.10.4 **CHANGE IN LIFE EXPECTANCY**

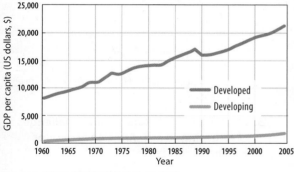

▲ 9.10.5 **CHANGE IN GDP PER CAPITA**

▼ 9.10.6 **FOCUS ON SUB-SAHARAN AFRICA: EDUCATION**
School in Kenya.

EIGHT GOALS

To reduce disparities between developed and developing countries, the United Nations has set eight Millennium Development Goals:

Goal 1: End poverty and hunger
Progress: Extreme poverty has been cut substantially in the world, primarily because of success in Asia, but it has not declined in sub-Saharan Africa.

Goal 2: Achieve universal primary (elementary school) education
Progress: The percentage of children not enrolled in school remains relatively high in South Asia and sub-Saharan Africa.

Goal 3: Promote gender equality and empower women
Progress: Gender disparities remain in all regions, as discussed in Section 9.5.

Goal 4: Reduce child mortality
Progress: Infant mortality rates have declined in most regions, except sub-Saharan Africa.

Goal 5: Improve maternal health
Progress: One-half million women die from complications during pregnancy; 99 percent of these women live in developing countries.

Goal 6: Combat HIV/AIDS, malaria, and other diseases
Progress: The number of people living with HIV remains high, especially in sub-Saharan Africa, as discussed in Chapter 5.

Goal 7: Ensure environmental sustainability
Progress: Water scarcity and quality, deforestation, and overfishing are still especially critical environmental issues, according to the United Nations.

Goal 8: Develop a global partnership for development
Progress: Aid from developed to developing countries has instead been declining.

FOCUS ON SUB-SAHARAN AFRICA

Sub-Saharan Africa has the least favorable prospect for development. The region has the world's highest percentage of people living in poverty and suffering from poor health and low education levels (Figures 9.10.6 and 9.10.7). And conditions are getting worse: the average African consumes less today than a quarter-century ago. The fundamental problem in many countries of sub-Saharan Africa is a dramatic imbalance between the number of inhabitants and the capacity of the land to feed the population.

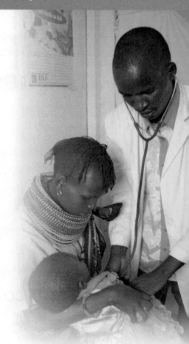

▲ 9.10.7 **FOCUS ON SUB-SAHARAN AFRICA: HEALTH**
Clinic in Kenya.

The world is divided into developed countries and developing ones. Developed and developing countries can be compared according to a number of indicators.

Key Questions

How does development vary among regions?

▶ The United Nations has created the Human Development Index to measure the level of development of every country.

▶ Gross National Income measures the standard of living in a country.

▶ Developed countries display higher levels of education and literacy.

▶ People in developed countries have a longer life expectancy.

▶ A Gender Inequality Index compares the level of development of women and men in every country.

How can countries promote development?

▶ The two principal paths to development are self-sufficiency and international trade.

▶ Self-sufficiency was the most commonly used path in the past, but most countries now follow international trade.

▶ Developing countries finance trade through loans, but may required to undertake economic reforms.

What are future challenges for development?

▶ Fair trade is an alternative approach to development through trade that provides greater benefits to the producers in developing countries.

▶ The United Nations has set Millennium Development Goals for countries to enhance their level of development.

Thinking Geographically

Review the major economic, social, and demographic characteristics that contribute to a country's level of development.

1. Which indicators can vary significantly by gender within countries and between countries at various levels of development? Why?

Some geographers have been attracted to the concepts of Immanuel Wallerstein, who argued that the modern world consists of a single entity, the capitalist world economy that is divided into three regions: the core, semi-periphery, and periphery (refer to Figure 9.10.1).

2. How have the boundaries among these three regions changed?

Opposition to international trade , as well as the severe recession of the early twenty-first century, has encouraged some countries to switch from international trade back to self-sufficiency (Figure 9.CR.1).

3. What are the advantages and challenges of returning to self-sufficiency in poor economic conditions?

On the Internet

Each year's United Nations Human Development Index Report, including numerous indicators for every country, can be accessed at **http://hdr.undp.org,** or scan QR on first page of this chapter.

Indicators cited in this chapter that are not part of the HDI can be found through the Earth Trends portion of the World Resources Institute (WRI) web site at **http://earthtrends.wri.org/.**

Several data sources, including the United Nations and the CIA, are brought together at **www.NationMaster.com.**

◀ 9.CR.1 **WTO PROTESTS**
Protesters at WTO meeting in Seattle, 1999.

Interactive Mapping

INTERNAL VARIATIONS IN DEVELOPMENT

The level of development varies within Latin America's two most populous countries, Brazil and Mexico.

Open MapMaster Latin America in Mastering**GEOGRAPHY**

Select: *Economic* then *Mapping Poverty and Prosperity.*
Select: *Population* then *Population Density.*

Use the slider tool to adjust the layer opacity.

Are high population concentrations within Brazil and Mexico found primarily in the poorer or the wealthier regions of the two countries?

Explore

BRASILIA

A number of countries have built or are considering constructing new cities to promote development in poorer regions. One example is Brasilia, which was started in the 1950s and became the capital of Brazil in 1960.

Fly to: *National Congress of Brazil, Brasilia, Brazil*
Click on box in middle of screen.

What is the predominant style of housing constructed for the residents?

Key Terms

Adolescent fertility rate
The number of births per 1,000 women age 15-19.

Developed country (more developed country or MDC)
A country that has progressed relatively far along a continuum of development.

Developing country (less developed country or LDC)
A country that is at a relatively early stage in the process of economic development.

Development
A process of improvement in the material conditions of people through diffusion of knowledge and technology.

Fair trade
Alternative to international trade that emphasizes small businesses and worker-owned and democratically run cooperatives and requires employers to pay workers fair wages, permit union organizing, and comply with minimum environmental and safety standards.

Foreign direct investment
Investment made by a foreign company in the economy of another country.

Gender Inequality Index (GII)
Indicator constructed by the United Nations to measure the extent of each country's gender inequality.

Gross domestic product (GDP)
The value of the total output of goods and services produced in a country in a year, not accounting for money that leaves and enters the country.

Gross national income (GNI)
The value of the output of goods and services produced in a country in a year, including money that leaves and enters the country.

Human Development Index (HDI)
Indicator of level of development for each country, constructed by United Nations, combining income, literacy, education, and life expectancy.

Inequality-adjusted HDI (IHDI)
Indicator of level of development for each country that modifies the HDI to account for inequality.

Literacy rate
The percentage of a country's people who can read and write.

Maternal mortality ratio
The number of women who die giving birth per 100,000 births.

Primary sector
The portion of the economy concerned with the direct extraction of materials from Earth's surface, generally through agriculture, although sometimes by mining, fishing, and forestry.

Productivity
The value of a particular product compared to the amount of labor needed to make it.

Secondary sector
The portion of the economy concerned with manufacturing useful products through processing, transforming, and assembling raw materials.

Structural adjustment program
Economic policies imposed on less developed countries by international agencies to create conditions encouraging international trade, such as raising taxes, reducing government spending, controlling inflation, selling publicly owned utilities to private corporations, and charging citizens more for services.

Tertiary sector
The portion of the economy concerned with transportation, communications, and utilities, sometimes extended to the provision of all goods and services to people in exchange for payment.

Value added
The gross value of the product minus the costs of raw materials and energy.

► LOOKING AHEAD

One of the most fundamental differences between developed and developing countries are the predominant methods of agriculture.

10 Food and Agriculture

When you buy food in the supermarket, are you reminded of a farm? Not likely. The meat is carved into pieces that no longer resemble an animal and is wrapped in paper or plastic film. Often the vegetables are canned or frozen. The milk and eggs are in cartons.

Providing food in the United States and Canada is a vast industry. Only a few people are full-time farmers, and they may be more familiar with the operation of computers and advanced machinery than the typical factory or office worker is.

The mechanized, highly productive American or Canadian farm contrasts with the subsistence farm found in much of the world. In China and India, more than half of the people are farmers who grow enough food for themselves and their families to survive, with little surplus. This sharp contrast in agricultural practices constitutes one of the most fundamental differences between the world's developed countries and developing countries.

What do people eat?

10.1 **Origin of Agriculture**

10.2 **Diet**

10.3 **Nutrition and Hunger**

ORGANIC FARM,
KASRAWAD, INDIA

No.-27
ORGANIC

How is agriculture distributed?

What challenges does agriculture face?

SCAN TO ACCESS THE UN's FOOD AND AGRICULTURE DATA

10.1 Origin of Agriculture

▶ Early humans obtained food through hunting and gathering.

▶ Agriculture originated in multiple hearths and diffused in many directions.

Agriculture is the deliberate modification of Earth's surface through cultivation of plants and rearing of animals to obtain sustenance or economic gain. Agriculture originated when humans domesticated plants and animals for their use. The word cultivate means "to care for," and a **crop** is any plant cultivated by people.

HUNTERS AND GATHERERS

Before the invention of agriculture, all humans probably obtained the food they needed for survival through hunting for animals, fishing, or gathering plants (including berries, nuts, fruits, and roots). Hunters and gatherers lived in small groups, with usually fewer than 50 persons, because a larger number would quickly exhaust the available resources within walking distance.

Typically, the men hunted game or fished, and the women collected berries, nuts, and roots. This division of labor sounds like a stereotype but is based on evidence from archaeology and anthropology, although exceptions to this pattern have been documented. They collected food often, perhaps daily. The food search might take only a short time or much of the day, depending on local conditions.

The group traveled frequently, establishing new home bases or camps. The direction and frequency of migration depended on the movement of game and the seasonal growth of plants at various locations. We can assume that groups communicated with each other concerning hunting rights, intermarriage, and other specific subjects. For the most part, they kept the peace by steering clear of each other's territory.

Today perhaps a quarter-million people still survive by hunting and gathering rather than by agriculture. Examples include the Spinifex (also known as Pila Nguru) people, who live in Australia's Great Victorian Desert; the Sentinelese people, who live in India's Andaman Islands; and the Bushmen, who live in Botswana and Namibia (Figure 10.1.1). Contemporary hunting and gathering societies are isolated groups living on the periphery of world settlement, but they provide insight into human customs that prevailed in prehistoric times, before the invention of agriculture.

▲ 10.1.1 **HUNTERS AND GATHERERS** Botswana.

CROP HEARTHS

Why did most nomadic groups convert from hunting, gathering, and fishing to agriculture? Geographers and other scientists agree that agriculture originated in multiple hearths around the world. They do not agree on when agriculture originated and diffused, or why. Early centers of crop domestication include Southwest Asia, sub-Saharan Africa, Latin America, East Asia, and Southeast Asia (Figure 10.1.2). Crop cultivation diffused from these multiple hearths:

- From Southwest Asia: west to Europe and east to Central Asia.

- From sub-Saharan Africa: south to southern Africa.

- From Latin America: north to North America and south to tropical South America.

▼ 10.1.2 **CROP HEARTHS**

Years ago
9,000 and above
7,000–9,000
3,000–7,000
Unknown

Hearth
Primary
Secondary
— Dispersal route

BARLEY
EINKORN WHEAT
EMMER WHEAT
LENTIL
OATS

RYE
BREAD WHEAT
BROAD BEAN
OLIVE

RICE
SOYBEAN
CHINESE CHESTNUT
WALNUT

ARCTIC OCEAN

Southwest Asia

East Asia

Sub-Saharan Africa

PACIFIC OCEAN

ATLANTIC OCEAN

PACIFIC OCEAN

Latin America

Southeast Asia

INDIAN OCEAN

SQUASH
PEPPER
CASSAVA
COTTON
LIMA BEAN
MAIZE
POTATO
SWEET POTATO

YAM
SORGHUM
COWPEA
AFRICAN RICE
COFFEE
FINGER MILLET

MANGO
TARO
COCONUT
PIGEONPEA
SLENDER MILLET

0   1,000   2,000 Miles
0   1,000   2,000 Kilometers

ANIMAL HEARTHS

Animals were also domesticated in multiple hearths at various dates. Southwest Asia is thought to be the hearth for the domestication of the largest number of animals that would prove to be most important for agriculture. Animals thought to be domesticated in Southwest Asia between 8,000 and 9,000 years ago include cattle, goats, pigs, and sheep. (Figure 10.1.3). The turkey is thought to have been domesticated in the Western Hemisphere (Figure 10.1.4).

Inhabitants of Southwest Asia may have been the first to integrate cultivation of crops with domestication of herd animals such as cattle, sheep, and goats. These animals were used to plow the land before planting seeds and, in turn, were fed part of the harvested crop. Other animal products, such as milk, meat, and skins, may have been exploited at a later date. This integration of plants and animals is a fundamental element of modern agriculture.

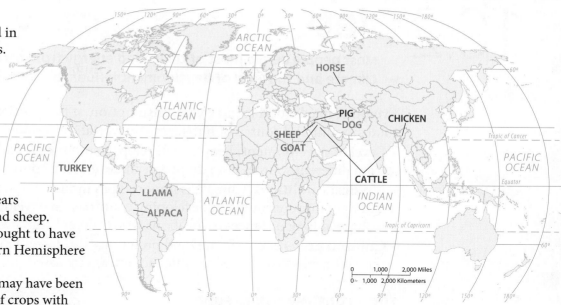

Domestication of the dog is thought to date from around 12,000 years ago, also in Southwest Asia. The horse is considered to have been domesticated in Central Asia; diffusion of the domesticated horse may have been associated with the diffusion of the Indo-European language, as discussed in Chapter 5.

▲ 10.1.3 **ANIMAL HEARTHS**

Years ago

12,000
9,000
8,000
6,000
Unknown

WHY AGRICULTURE ORIGINATED

Scientists do not agree on whether agriculture originated primarily because of environmental factors or cultural factors. Probably a combination of both factors contributed.

- **Environmental Factors.** The first domestication of crops and animals around 10,000 years ago coincides with climate change. This marked the end of the last ice age, when permanent ice cover receded from Earth's midlatitudes to polar regions, resulting in a massive redistribution of humans, other animals, and plants at that time.

- **Cultural Factors.** Preference for living in a fixed place rather than as nomads may have led hunters and gatherers to build permanent settlements and to store surplus vegetation there.

In gathering wild vegetation, people inevitably cut plants and dropped berries, fruits, and seeds. These hunters probably observed that, over time, damaged or discarded food produced new plants. They may have deliberately cut plants or dropped berries on the ground to see if they would produce new plants.

Subsequent generations learned to pour water over the site and to introduce manure and other soil improvements. Over thousands of years, plant cultivation apparently evolved from a combination of accident and deliberate experiment.

That agriculture had multiple origins means that, from earliest times, people have produced food in distinctive ways in different regions. This diversity derives from a unique legacy of wild plants, climatic conditions, and cultural preferences in each region.

▼ 10.1.4 **WILD TURKEY**
California.

10.2 Diet

▶ Most people derive most of their food energy from cereals.
▶ Climate and the level of development influence choice of food.

Everyone needs food to survive. Consumption of food varies around the world, both in total amount and source of nutrients. The variation results from a combination of:

- **Level of development.** People in developed countries tend to consume more food and from different sources than do people in developing countries.
- **Physical conditions.** Climate is important in influencing what can be most easily grown and therefore consumed in developing countries. In developed countries, though, food is shipped long distances to locations with different climates.
- **Cultural preferences.** Some food preferences and avoidances are expressed without regard for physical and economic factors, as discussed in Chapter 4.

TOTAL CONSUMPTION OF FOOD

Dietary energy consumption is the amount of food that an individual consumes. The unit of measurement of dietary energy is a kilocalorie (kcal), or Calorie in the United States. One gram (or ounce) of each food source delivers a kcal level that nutritionists can measure.

Humans derive most of their kilocalories through consumption of **cereal grain**, or simply cereal, which is a grass that yields grain for food. The three leading cereal grains—maize (corn in North America), wheat, and rice—together account for nearly 90 percent of all grain production and more than 40 percent of all dietary energy consumed worldwide.

Wheat is the principal cereal grain consumed in the developed regions of Europe and North America (Figure 10.2.1). Wheat is consumed in the form of bread, pasta, cake, and many

▲ 10.2.2 **WHEAT CONSUMPTION**
Lille, France.

other forms (Figure 10.2.2). It is also the most consumed **grain** in the developing regions of Central and Southwest Asia, where relatively dry conditions are more suitable for growing wheat than other grains.

Rice is the principal cereal grain consumed in the developing regions of East, South, and Southeast Asia (Figure 10.2.3). It is the most suitable cereal crop for production in tropical climates.

▼ 10.2.3 **RICE CONSUMPTION**
Ho Chi Minh City, Vietnam.

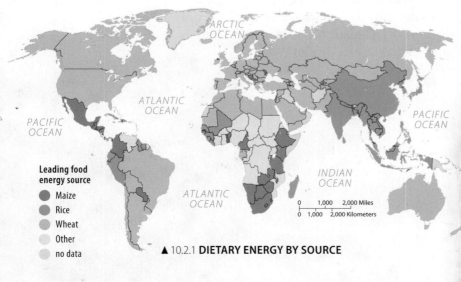

Leading food energy source
- Maize
- Rice
- Wheat
- Other
- no data

▲ 10.2.1 **DIETARY ENERGY BY SOURCE**

Maize is the leading crop in the world, though much of it is grown for purposes other than direct human consumption, especially as animal feed. It is the leading crop in some countries of sub-Saharan Africa (Figure 10.2.4).

A handful of countries obtain the largest share of dietary energy from other crops, especially in sub-Saharan Africa. These include cassava, sorghum, millet, plantains, sweet potatoes, and yams (Figure 10.2.5). Sugar is the leading source of dietary energy in several Latin American countries.

▲ 10.2.5 **YAM CONSUMPTION**
Ghana.

▲ 10.2.4 **MAIZE CONSUMPTION**
Weekly market, Madagascar.

SOURCE OF NUTRIENTS

Protein is a nutrient needed for growth and maintenance of the human body. Many food sources provide protein of varying quantity and quality. One of the most fundamental differences between developed and developing regions is the primary source of protein (Figure 10.2.6). In developed countries, the leading source of protein is meat products, including beef, pork, and poultry (Figure 10.2.7). Meat accounts for approximately one-third of all protein intake in developed countries, compared to approximately one-tenth in developing ones (Figure 10.2.8). In most developing countries, cereal grains provide the largest share of protein.

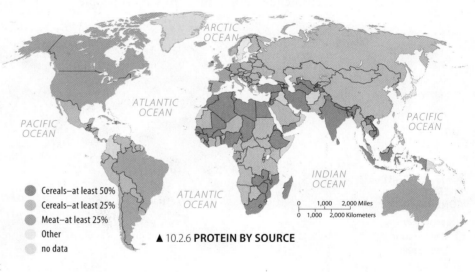

Cereals–at least 50%
Cereals–at least 25%
Meat–at least 25%
Other
no data

▲ 10.2.6 **PROTEIN BY SOURCE**

▲ 10.2.7 **MEAT CONSUMPTION**
Dublin, Ireland.

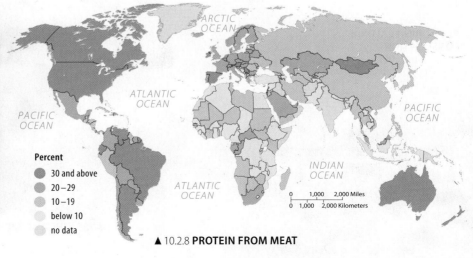

Percent

30 and above
20 – 29
10 – 19
below 10
no data

▲ 10.2.8 **PROTEIN FROM MEAT**

10.3 Nutrition and Hunger

▶ **On average, the world produces enough food to meet dietary needs.**
▶ **Some developing countries lack food security and are undernourished.**

The United Nations defines **food security** as physical, social, and economic access at all times to safe and nutritious food sufficient to meet dietary needs and food preferences for an active and healthy life. By this definition, roughly one-eighth of the world's inhabitants do not have food security.

DIETARY ENERGY NEEDS

To maintain a moderate level of physical activity, according to the United Nations Food and Agricultural Organization, an average individual needs to consume on a daily basis at least 1,800 kcal.

Average consumption worldwide is 2,780 kcal per day, or roughly 50 percent more than the recommended minimum. Thus, most people get enough food to survive. People in developed countries are consuming on average nearly twice the recommended minimum, 3,470 kcal per day (Figure 10.3.1). The United States has the world's highest consumption, 3,800 kcal per day per person. The consumption of so much food is one reason that obesity rather than hunger is more prevalent in the United States, as well as other developed countries (Figure 10.3.2).

In developing regions, average daily consumption is 2,630 kcal, still above the recommended minimum. However, the average in sub-Saharan Africa is only 2,290, an indication that a large percentage of Africans are not getting enough to eat. Diets are more likely to be deficient in countries where people have to spend a high percentage of their income to obtain food (Figure 10.3.3).

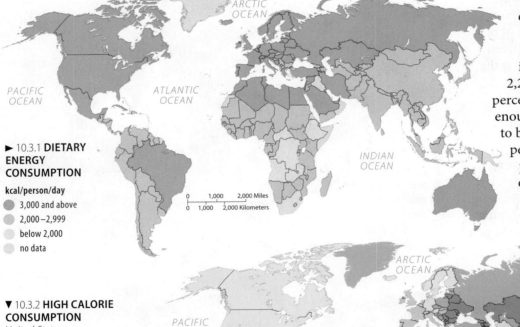

▶ 10.3.1 **DIETARY ENERGY CONSUMPTION**

kcal/person/day
- 3,000 and above
- 2,000–2,999
- below 2,000
- no data

▼ 10.3.2 **HIGH CALORIE CONSUMPTION**
United States.

Percent
- 40 and above
- 30–39
- 20–29
- below 20
- no data

▲ 10.3.3 **INCOME SPENT ON FOOD**

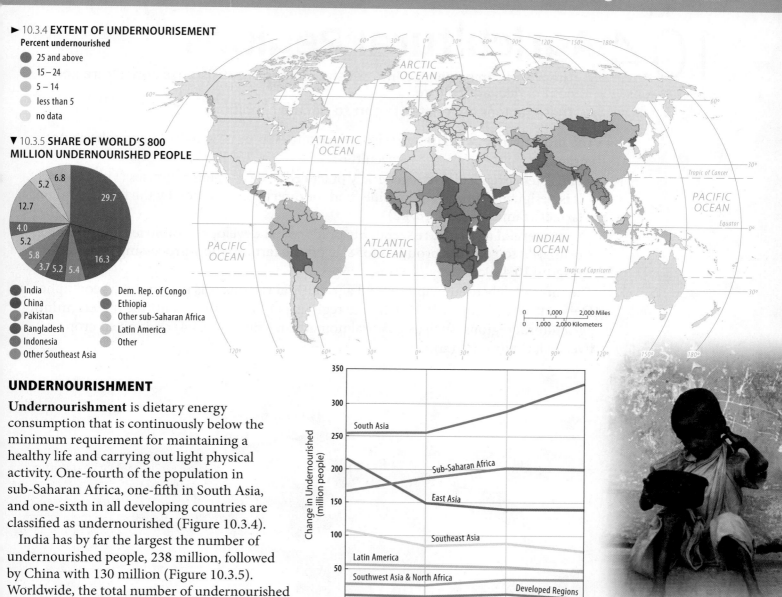

► 10.3.4 **EXTENT OF UNDERNOURISEMENT**
Percent undernourished
- 25 and above
- 15 – 24
- 5 – 14
- less than 5
- no data

▼ 10.3.5 **SHARE OF WORLD'S 800 MILLION UNDERNOURISHED PEOPLE**

- 29.7
- 6.8
- 5.2
- 12.7
- 4.0
- 5.2
- 5.8
- 3.7 5.2 5.4
- 16.3

- India
- China
- Pakistan
- Bangladesh
- Indonesia
- Other Southeast Asia
- Dem. Rep. of Congo
- Ethiopia
- Other sub-Saharan Africa
- Latin America
- Other

UNDERNOURISHMENT

Undernourishment is dietary energy consumption that is continuously below the minimum requirement for maintaining a healthy life and carrying out light physical activity. One-fourth of the population in sub-Saharan Africa, one-fifth in South Asia, and one-sixth in all developing countries are classified as undernourished (Figure 10.3.4).

India has by far the largest the number of undernourished people, 238 million, followed by China with 130 million (Figure 10.3.5). Worldwide, the total number of undernourished people has not changed much in several decades (Figure 10.3.6).

▲ 10.3.6 **CHANGE IN NUMBER UNDERNOURISHED**

(Line graph with y-axis "Change in Undernourished (million people)" ranging 0–350, x-axis "Year" from 1991 to 2006. Lines labeled: South Asia, Sub-Saharan Africa, East Asia, Southeast Asia, Latin America, Southwest Asia & North Africa, Developed Regions.)

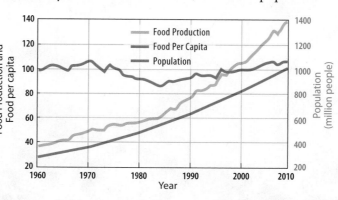

▲ 10.3.7
UNDERNOURISHMENT
Somalia.

AFRICA'S FOOD-SUPPLY STRUGGLE

Sub-Saharan Africa is struggling to keep food production ahead of population growth (Figure 10.3.7). Since 1961, food production has increased substantially in sub-Saharan Africa, but so has population (Figure 10.3.8). As a result, food production per capita has changed little in a half-century.

The threat of famine is particularly severe in the Sahel. Traditionally, this region supported limited agriculture. With rapid population growth, farmers overplanted, and herd size increased beyond the capacity of the land to support the animals. Animals overgrazed the limited vegetation and clustered at scarce water sources.

◄ 10.3.8 **POPULATION AND FOOD PRODUCTION IN AFRICA**

(Graph with left y-axis "Food Production and Food per capita" (20–140), right y-axis "Population (million people)" (200–1400), x-axis "Year" from 1960 to 2010. Legend: Food Production, Food Per Capita, Population.)

10.4 Agricultural Regions

► **The world can be divided into several regions of subsistence agriculture and commercial agriculture.**

► **These regions are related in part to climate conditions.**

The most fundamental differences in agricultural practices are between subsistence agriculture and commercial agriculture.

- **Subsistence agriculture** is generally practiced in developing countries (Figure 10.4.1). It is designed primarily to provide food for direct consumption by the farmer and the farmer's family (Figure 10.4.2).
- **Commercial agriculture,** generally practiced in developed countries, is undertaken primarily to generate products for sale off the farm to food-processing companies (Figure 10.4.3).

The most widely used map of world agricultural regions was prepared by geographer Derwent Whittlesey in 1936. Climate regions played an important role in determining agricultural regions, such as pastoral nomadism (Figure 10.4.4) and mixed crop and livestock (Figure 10.4.5).

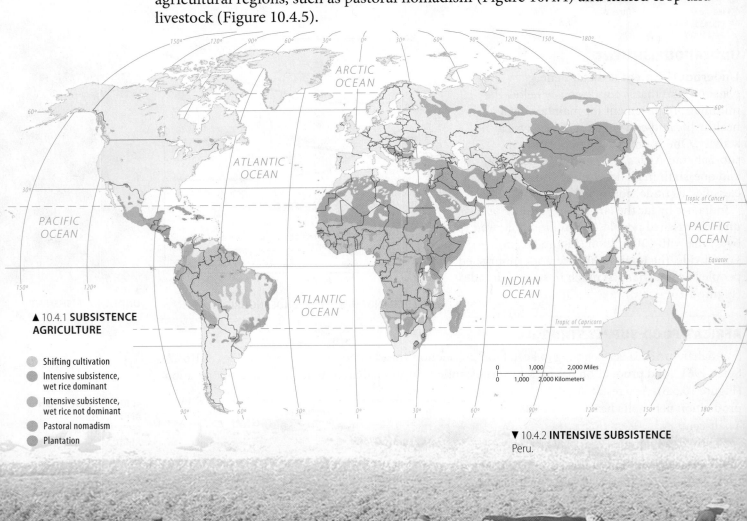

▲ 10.4.1 **SUBSISTENCE AGRICULTURE**

- Shifting cultivation
- Intensive subsistence, wet rice dominant
- Intensive subsistence, wet rice not dominant
- Pastoral nomadism
- Plantation

▼ 10.4.2 **INTENSIVE SUBSISTENCE** Peru.

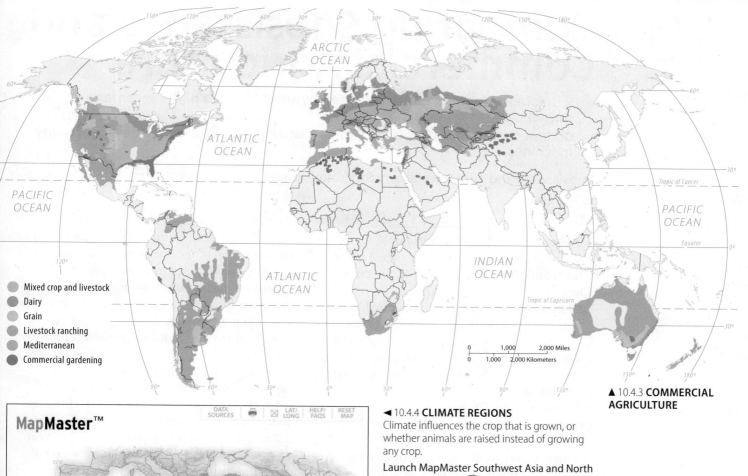

Mixed crop and livestock
Dairy
Grain
Livestock ranching
Mediterranean
Commercial gardening

▲ 10.4.3 **COMMERCIAL AGRICULTURE**

MapMaster™

DATA SOURCES | | | LAT/ LONG | HELP/ FAQS | RESET MAP

A TROPICAL AND HUMID CLIMATES
Af   Tropical wet climate
Aw   Tropical savanna climate
B DRY CLIMATES
BWh   Tropical and subtropical desert
BSh   Tropical and subtropical steppe
BSk   Midlatitude steppe
C MILD MIDLATITUDE CLIMATES
Cs   Mediterranean summer—dry
H HIGHLAND
H   Complex mountain climates

0   250   500 Miles
0   250 500 Kilometers

◀ 10.4.4 **CLIMATE REGIONS**
Climate influences the crop that is grown, or whether animals are raised instead of growing any crop.

Launch MapMaster Southwest Asia and North Africa in Mastering**GEOGRAPHY**™

Select: *Climate* from the *Physical Environment* menu, then *Agricultural Regions* from the *Economic* menu.

What climate region is correlated with pastoral nomadism?

▼ 10.4.5 **MIXED CROP AND LIVESTOCK**
France.

10.5 Comparing Subsistence and Commercial Agriculture

► **Subsistence farming is characterized by small farms, a high percentage of farmers, and few machines.**

► **Commercial farming has large farms, a small percentage of farmers, and many machines.**

Subsistence and commercial farming differ in several key ways.

FARM SIZE

The average farm size is much larger in commercial agriculture. For example, farms average about 161 hectares (418 acres) in the United States, compared to about 1 hectare in China.

Commercial agriculture is dominated by a handful of large farms. In the United States, the largest 5 percent of farms produce 75 percent of the country's total agriculture. Despite their size, most commercial farms in developed countries are family owned and operated—90 percent in the United States. Commercial farmers frequently expand their holdings by renting nearby fields.

Large size is partly a consequence of mechanization, as discussed below. Combines, pickers, and other machinery perform most efficiently at very large scales, and their considerable expense cannot be justified on a small farm. As a result of the large size and the high level of mechanization, commercial agriculture is an expensive business.

Farmers spend hundreds of thousands of dollars to buy or rent land and machinery before beginning operations. This money is frequently borrowed from a bank and repaid after the output is sold.

The United States had 13 percent more farmland in 2000 than in 1900, primarily through irrigation and reclamation. However, in the twenty-first century it has been losing 1.2 million hectares (3 million acres) per year of its 400 million hectares (1 billion acres) of farmland, primarily because of expansion of urban areas.

PERCENTAGE OF FARMERS IN SOCIETY

In developed countries around 5 percent of workers are engaged directly in farming, compared to around 50 percent in developing countries (Figure 10.5.1). The percentage of farmers is even lower in North America, only around 2 percent. Yet the small percentage of farmers in the United States and Canada produces enough food not only for themselves and the rest of the region but also a surplus to feed people elsewhere.

The number of farmers declined dramatically in developed countries during the twentieth century. The United States had 60 percent fewer farms and 85 percent fewer farmers in 2000 than in 1900. The number of farms in the United States declined from about 6 million farms in 1940 to 4 million in 1960 and 2 million in 1980. Both push and pull migration factors have been responsible for the decline: people were pushed away from farms by lack of opportunity to earn a decent income, and at the same time they were pulled to higher-paying jobs in urban areas. The number of U.S. farmers has stabilized since 1980 at around 2 million.

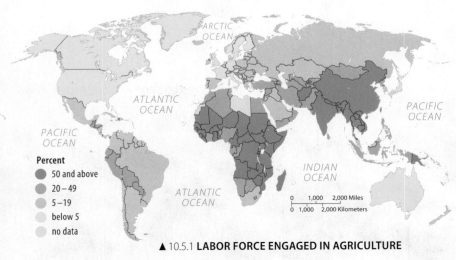

Percent
- 50 and above
- 20–49
- 5–19
- below 5
- no data

▲ 10.5.1 **LABOR FORCE ENGAGED IN AGRICULTURE**

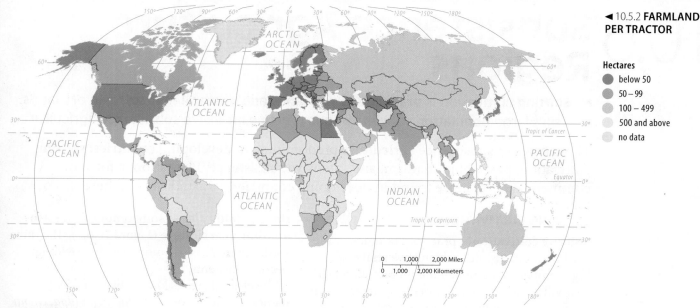

◀ 10.5.2 **FARMLAND PER TRACTOR**

Hectares
- below 50
- 50 – 99
- 100 – 499
- 500 and above
- no data

USE OF MACHINERY

In developed countries, a small number of farmers can feed many people because they rely on machinery to perform work, rather than relying on people or animals (Figure 10.5.2). In developing countries, farmers do much of the work with hand tools and animal power.

Traditionally, the farmer or local craftspeople made equipment from wood, but beginning in the late eighteenth century, factories produced farm machinery. The first all-iron plow was made in the 1770s and was followed in the nineteenth and twentieth centuries by inventions that made farming less dependent on human or animal power. Tractors, combines, corn pickers, planters, and other factory-made farm machines have replaced or supplemented manual labor (Figure 10.5.3).

Transportation improvements also aid commercial farmers. The building of railroads in the nineteenth century, and highways and trucks in the twentieth century, have enabled farmers to transport crops and livestock farther and faster. Cattle arrive at market heavier and in better condition when transported by truck or train than when driven on hoof. Crops reach markets without spoiling.

Commercial farmers use scientific advances to increase productivity. Experiments conducted in university laboratories, industry, and research organizations generate new fertilizers, herbicides, hybrid plants, animal breeds, and farming practices, which produce higher crop

yields and healthier animals. Access to other scientific information has enabled farmers to make more intelligent decisions concerning proper agricultural practices. Some farmers conduct their own on-farm research.

Electronics also aid commercial farmers. Global positioning system (GPS) units determine the precise coordinates for spreading different types and amounts of fertilizers. On large ranches, GPS is also used to monitor the location of cattle. Satellite imagery monitors crop progress. Yield monitors attached to combines determine the precise number of bushels being harvested.

▼ 10.5.3 **USE OF MACHINERY**
Combines harvest wheat, Colorado.

10.6 Subsistence Agriculture Regions

▶ Shifting cultivation is practiced in wet lands and pastoral nomadism in dry lands.
▶ Asia's large population concentrations practice intensive subsistence agriculture.

Three types of subsistence agriculture predominate in developing countries: shifting cultivation, pastoral nomadism, and intensive subsistence. Plantation, a form of commercial agriculture found in developing countries, is also discussed here.

SHIFTING CULTIVATION

Shifting cultivation is practiced in much of the world's humid tropics, which have relatively high temperatures and abundant rainfall. Each year villagers designate for planting an area near the settlement. Before planting, they remove the dense vegetation using axes and machetes.

On a windless day the debris is burned under carefully controlled conditions; consequently, shifting cultivation is sometimes called **slash-and-burn agriculture** (Figure 10.6.1). The rains wash the fresh ashes into the soil, providing needed nutrients.

The cleared area is known by a variety of names, including *swidden, ladang, milpa, chena,* and *kaingin*. The **swidden** can support crops only briefly, usually 3 years or less, before soil nutrients are depleted. Villagers then identify a new site and begin clearing it, leaving the old swidden uncropped for many years, so that it is again overrun by natural vegetation.

Shifting cultivation is being replaced by logging, cattle ranching, and cultivation of cash crops. Selling timber to builders or raising beef cattle for fast-food restaurants is a more effective development strategy than maintaining shifting cultivation. Defenders of shifting cultivation consider it a more environmentally sound approach for tropical agriculture.

▼ 10.6.1 **SHIFTING CULTIVATION** Venezuela.

PASTORAL NOMADISM

Pastoral nomadism is a form of subsistence agriculture based on the herding of domesticated animals. It is adapted to dry climates, where planting crops is impossible. Pastoral nomads live primarily in the large belt of arid and semiarid land that includes most of North Africa and Southwest Asia, and parts of Central Asia. The Bedouins of Saudi Arabia and North Africa and the Maasai of East Africa are examples of nomadic groups (Figure 10.6.2).

Pastoral nomads depend primarily on animals rather than crops for survival. The animals provide milk, and their skins and hair are used for clothing and tents. Like other subsistence farmers, though, pastoral nomads consume mostly grain rather than meat. Their animals are usually not slaughtered, although dead ones may be consumed. To nomads, the size of their herd is both an important measure of power and prestige and their main security during adverse environmental conditions.

Only about 15 million people are pastoral nomads, but they sparsely occupy about 20 percent of Earth's land area. Nomads used to be the most powerful inhabitants of the dry lands. Today, national governments control the nomadic population, using force, if necessary. Governments force groups to give up pastoral nomadism because they want the land for other uses.

▼ 10.6.2 **PASTORAL NOMADISM** Sahara Desert, Africa.

INTENSIVE SUBSISTENCE

In densely populated East, South, and Southeast Asia, most farmers practice **intensive subsistence agriculture.** Because the agricultural density—the ratio of farmers to arable land—is so high in parts of East and South Asia, families must produce enough food for their survival from a very small area of land.

Most of the work is done by hand or with animals rather than with machines, in part due to abundant labor, but largely from lack of funds to buy equipment.

The intensive agriculture region of Asia can be divided between areas where wet rice dominates and areas where it does not. The term **wet rice** refers to the practice of planting rice on dry land in a nursery and then moving the seedlings to a flooded field to promote growth. Wet rice is most easily grown on flat land, because the plants are submerged in water much of the time.

The pressure of population growth in parts of East Asia has forced expansion of areas under rice cultivation (Figure 10.6.3). One method of developing additional land suitable for growing rice is to terrace the hillsides of river valleys (Figure 10.6.4).

▲ 10.6.3 **RICE PRODUCTION**

Million metric tons
- 100.0 and above
- 10.0 – 99.9
- 1.0 – 9.9
- below 1.0
- no data

▲ 10.6.4 **INTENSIVE SUBSISTENCE FARMING**
Use Google Earth to explore rice farming in Southeast Asia.

Fly to: *Banaue, Philippines.*

Use the mouse to zoom in near the Banaue label until you see a series of brown swirling stripes.

Drag to: *street view on one of the brown swirling stripes.*

Exit ground level view.

1. Is the topography of this region flat or hilly?

2. What are the brown swirling stripes?

PLANTATION AGRICULTURE

A **plantation** is a form of commercial agriculture in developing regions that specializes in one or two crops. They are found primarily in the tropics and subtropics, especially in Latin America, sub-Saharan Africa, and Asia (Figure 10.6.5).

Although situated in developing countries, plantations are often owned or operated by Europeans or North Americans and grow crops for sale primarily in developed countries. Among the most important crops grown on plantations are cotton, sugarcane, coffee, rubber, and tobacco.

Until the Civil War, plantations were important in the U.S. South, where the principal crop was cotton, followed by tobacco and sugarcane. Slaves brought from Africa performed most of the labor until the abolition of slavery and the defeat of the South in the Civil War. Thereafter, plantations declined in the United States; they were subdivided and either sold to individual farmers or worked by tenant farmers.

▼ 10.6.5 **SUGARCANE PLANTATION**
Thailand.

10.7 Commercial Agriculture Regions

▶ **Six main types of commercial agriculture are found in developed countries.**
▶ **The type of agriculture is influenced by physical geography.**

Commercial agriculture in developed countries can be divided into six main types. Each type is predominant in distinctive regions within developed countries, depending largely on climate.

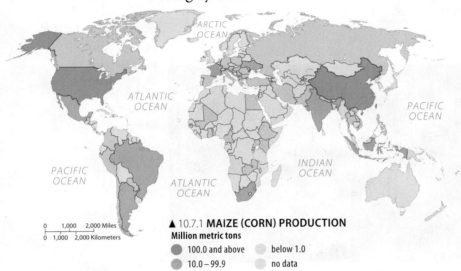

▲ 10.7.1 **MAIZE (CORN) PRODUCTION**
Million metric tons
- 100.0 and above
- 10.0 – 99.9
- below 1.0
- no data

MIXED CROP AND LIVESTOCK

The most distinctive characteristic of mixed crop and livestock farming is its integration of crops and livestock. Maize (corn) is the most commonly grown crop (Figure 10.7.1), followed by soybeans. Most of the crops are fed to animals rather than consumed directly by humans. A typical mixed commercial farm devotes nearly all land area to growing crops but derives more than three-fourths of its income from the sale of animal products, such as beef, milk, and eggs.

Mixed crop and livestock farming typically involves **crop rotation.** The farm is divided into a number of fields, and each field is planted on a planned cycle, often of several years duration.

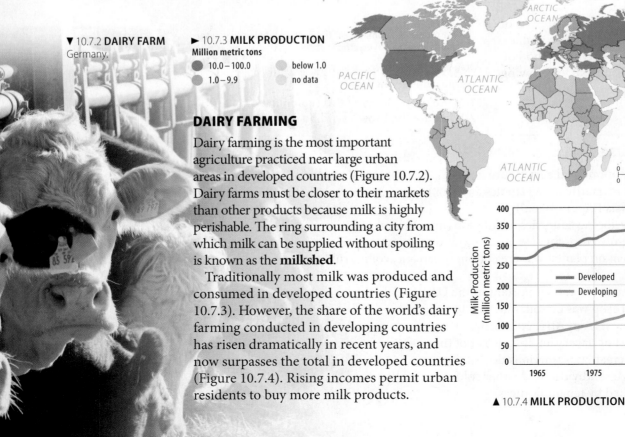

▼ 10.7.2 **DAIRY FARM** Germany.

▶ 10.7.3 **MILK PRODUCTION**
Million metric tons
- 10.0 – 100.0
- 1.0 – 9.9
- below 1.0
- no data

DAIRY FARMING

Dairy farming is the most important agriculture practiced near large urban areas in developed countries (Figure 10.7.2). Dairy farms must be closer to their markets than other products because milk is highly perishable. The ring surrounding a city from which milk can be supplied without spoiling is known as the **milkshed.**

Traditionally most milk was produced and consumed in developed countries (Figure 10.7.3). However, the share of the world's dairy farming conducted in developing countries has risen dramatically in recent years, and now surpasses the total in developed countries (Figure 10.7.4). Rising incomes permit urban residents to buy more milk products.

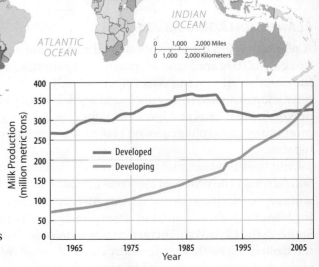

▲ 10.7.4 **MILK PRODUCTION**

GRAIN FARMING

Commercial grain farms are generally located in regions that are too dry for mixed crop and livestock farming, such as the Great Plains of North America (Figure 10.7.5). Unlike mixed crop and livestock farming, crops on a grain farm are grown primarily for consumption by humans rather than by livestock.

The most important crop grown is wheat, used to make flour. It can be stored relatively easily without spoiling and can be transported a long distance. Because wheat has a relatively high value per unit weight, it can be shipped profitably from remote farms to markets.

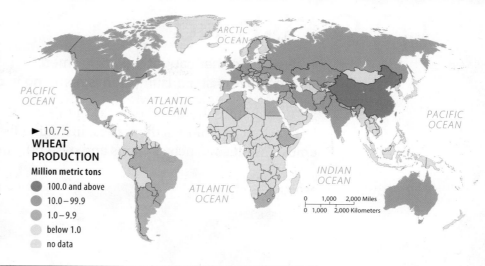

► 10.7.5
WHEAT PRODUCTION
Million metric tons
- 100.0 and above
- 10.0 – 99.9
- 1.0 – 9.9
- below 1.0
- no data

LIVESTOCK RANCHING

Ranching is the commercial grazing of livestock over an extensive area. It is practiced primarily on semiarid or arid land where the vegetation is too sparse and the soil too poor to support crops. China is the leading producer of pig meat, the United States of chicken and beef (Figure 10.7.6).

Ranching has been glamorized in novels and films, although the cattle drives and "Wild West" features of this type of farming actually lasted only a few years in the mid-nineteenth century. Contemporary ranching has become part of the meat-processing industry, rather than carried out on isolated farms.

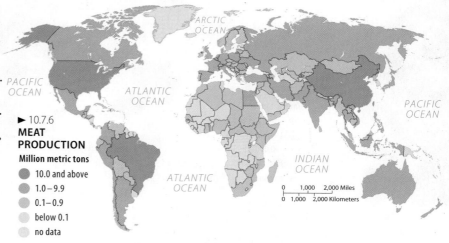

► 10.7.6
MEAT PRODUCTION
Million metric tons
- 10.0 and above
- 1.0 – 9.9
- 0.1 – 0.9
- below 0.1
- no data

COMMERCIAL GARDENING AND FRUIT FARMING

Commercial gardening and fruit farming are the predominant types of agriculture in the U.S. Southeast (Figure 10.7.7). The region has a long growing season and humid climate and is accessible to the large markets in the big cities along the East Coast. It is frequently called **truck farming**, because "truck" was a Middle English word meaning bartering or the exchange of commodities.

Truck farms grow many of the fruits and vegetables that consumers demand in developed countries, such as apples, cherries, lettuce, and tomatoes. A form of truck farming called specialty farming has spread to New England. Farmers are profitably growing crops that have limited but increasing demand among affluent consumers, such as asparagus, mushrooms, peppers, and strawberries.

MEDITERRANEAN AGRICULTURE

Mediterranean agriculture exists primarily on lands that border the Mediterranean Sea and other places that share a similar physical geography, such as California, central Chile, the southwestern part of South Africa, and southwestern Australia. Winters are moist and mild, summers hot and dry. The land is very hilly, and mountains frequently plunge directly to the sea, leaving very little flat land. The two most important crops are olives (primarily for cooking oil) and grapes (primarily for wine).

► 10.7.7 **COMMERCIAL GARDENING**
Peanut farm, Georgia, U.S.A.

10.8 Fishing

► Fish are either caught wild or farmed.

► Increasing fish consumption is resulting in overfishing.

The agriculture discussed thus far in this chapter is land-based. Humans also consume food acquired from Earth's waters, including fish, crustaceans (such as shrimp and crabs), molluscs (such as clams and oysters), and aquatic plants (such as watercress).

► 10.8.1 **FISH PRODUCTION**

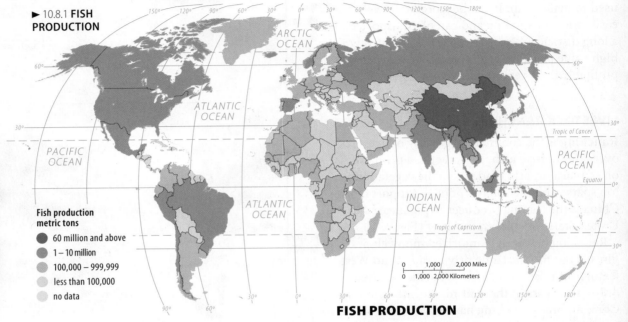

Fish production metric tons

- 60 million and above
- 1 – 10 million
- 100,000 – 999,999
- less than 100,000
- no data

▲ 10.8.2 **FISHING**
Mauritania.

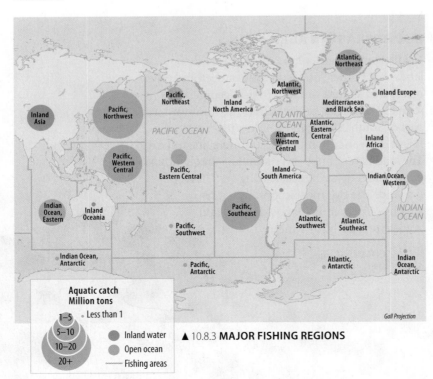

Aquatic catch Million tons

- 1–5   Less than 1
- 5–10
- 10–20   ● Inland water
- 20+   ● Open ocean
- — Fishing areas

▲ 10.8.3 **MAJOR FISHING REGIONS**

FISH PRODUCTION

Water-based food is acquired in two ways:

- Fishing, which is the capture of wild fish and other seafood living in the waters.

- **Aquaculture**, or **aquafarming**, which is the cultivation of seafood under controlled conditions.

About two-thirds of the fish caught from the ocean is consumed directly by humans, whereas the remainder is converted to fish meal and fed to poultry and hogs.

China is responsible for 40 percent of the world's yield of fish (Figure 10.8.1). The other leading countries are naturally those with extensive ocean boundaries, including Peru, Indonesia, India, Chile, Japan, and the United States.

The world's oceans are divided into 18 major fishing regions, including seven each in the Atlantic and Pacific oceans and four in the Indian Ocean (Figure 10.8.2). The three areas with the largest yield are all in the Pacific (Figure 10.8.3). Fishing is also conducted in inland waterways, such as lakes and rivers.

FISH CONSUMPTION

At first glance, increased use of food from the sea is attractive. Oceans are vast, covering nearly three-fourths of Earth's surface and lying near most population concentrations. Historically the sea has provided only a small percentage of the world food supply. Increased fish consumption was viewed as a way to meet the needs of a rapidly growing global population.

In fact, during the past half-century per capita consumption of fish has doubled worldwide, and tripled in developing countries (Figure 10.8.4). Still, fish accounts for only 6 percent of all protein consumed by humans, though a rapidly increasing source in developing countries if not in developed ones (Figure 10.8.5).

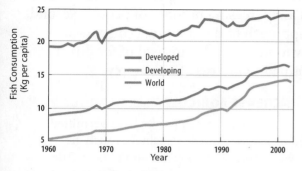

▲ 10.8.4 **FISH CONSUMPTION PER CAPITA**

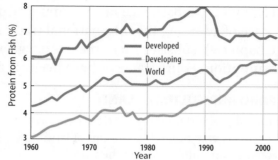

▲ 10.8.5 **PERCENT PROTEIN FROM FISH**

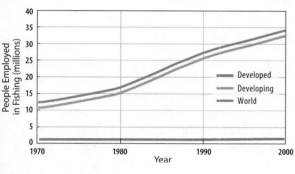

▲ 10.8.6 **EMPLOYMENT I**

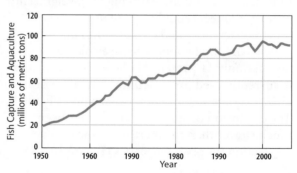

▲ 10.8.7 **WORLD FISH CAPTURE AND AQUACULTURE**

▼ 10.8.8 **AQUACULTURE**
Japan.

OVERFISHING

Worldwide, 35 million people are employed in fishing and agriculture, nearly all in developing countries (Figure 10.8.6). Production of fish is increasing worldwide (Figure 10.8.7). The growth results entirely from expansion of aquaculture (Figure 10.8.8). The capture of wild fish in the oceans and lakes has stagnated since the 1990s despite population growth and increased demand to consume fish.

The population of some fish species in the oceans and lakes has declined because of **overfishing**, which is capturing fish faster than they can reproduce. Overfishing has been particularly acute in the North Atlantic and Pacific oceans. Overfishing has reduced the population of tuna and swordfish by 90 percent in the past half-century, for example. The United Nations estimates that one-quarter of fish stocks have been overfished and one-half fully exploited, leaving only one-fourth underfished.

10.9 Subsistence Agriculture and Population Growth

► **Four strategies can increase food supply in developing countries.**
► **Increasing productivity and finding new sources are most promising.**

Two issues discussed in earlier chapters influence the challenges faced by subsistence farmers. First, because of rapid population growth in developing countries (discussed in Chapter 2), subsistence farmers must feed an increasing number of people. Second, because of adopting the international trade approach to development (discussed in Chapter 9), subsistence farmers must grow food for export instead of for direct consumption. Four strategies have been identified to increase food supply.

EXPAND AGRICULTURAL LAND

Historically, world food production increased primarily by expanding the amount of land devoted to agriculture. When the world's population increased more rapidly during the Industrial Revolution beginning in the eighteenth century, pioneers could migrate to sparsely inhabited territory and cultivate the land.

New land might appear to be available, because only 11 percent of the world's land area is currently used for agriculture. But excessive or inadequate water makes expansion difficult. The expansion of agricultural land has been much slower than the increase of the human population for several decades (Figure 10.9.1).

▼ 10.9.1
AGRICULTURAL LAND AND POPULATION GROWTH

Chart: Agricultural Land (billion hectares) and Population (billion people) vs. Year (1960–2010). Agricultural Land remains roughly flat near 4.5–5.0 billion hectares; Population rises from about 3.0 to 6.7 billion people.

▼ 10.9.2 **INTERNATIONAL RICE RESEARCH INSTITUTE, HOME OF THE "GREEN REVOLUTION"**

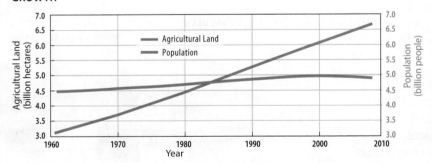

IR64680-81-2-2-1-3
BASAL   24DAT   PI
45   45   45
Kg N./ha

INCREASE AGRICULTURAL PRODUCTIVITY

New agricultural practices have permitted farmers worldwide to achieve much greater yields from the same amount of land. The invention and rapid diffusion of more productive agricultural techniques during the 1960s and 1970s is called the **green revolution**.

Scientists began experiments during the 1950s to develop a higher-yield form of wheat. A decade later, the International Rice Research Institute created a "miracle" rice seed (Figure 10.9.2). The Rockefeller and Ford foundations sponsored many of the studies, and the program's director, Dr. Norman Borlaug, won the Nobel Peace Prize in 1970. More recently, scientists have developed new high-yield maize (corn). Scientists have continued to create higher-yield hybrids that are adapted to environmental conditions in specific regions.

The green revolution was largely responsible for preventing a food crisis in developing countries during the 1970s and 1980s. The new miracle seeds were diffused rapidly around the world. India's wheat production, for example, more than doubled in 5 years. After importing 10 million tons of wheat annually in the mid-1960s, India by 1971 had a surplus of several million tons.

Will these scientific breakthroughs continue in the twenty-first century? To take full advantage of the new "miracle seeds," farmers must use more fertilizer and machinery, both of which depend on increasingly expensive fossil fuels. To maintain the green revolution, governments in developing countries must allocate scarce funds to subsidize the cost of seeds, fertilizers, and machinery.

IMPROVED FOOD SOURCES

Improved food sources could come from:

- Higher protein cereal grains. People in developing countries depend on grains that lack certain proteins. Hybrids with higher protein content could achieve better nutrition without changing food-consumption habits.

- Palatability of rarely consumed foods. Some foods are rarely consumed because of taboos, religious values, and social customs. In developed countries, consumers avoid consuming recognizable soybean products like tofu and sprouts, but could be induced to eat soybeans shaped like burgers and franks (Figure 10.9.3).

◀ 10.9.3 **SOY PRODUCT**

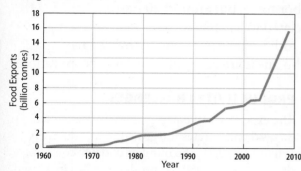

▲ 10.9.4 **WORLD FOOD EXPORTS**

EXPAND EXPORTS

Trade in food has increased rapidly, especially since 2000 (Figure 10.9.4). The three top export grains are wheat, maize (corn), and rice (Figure 10.9.5). Argentina, Brazil, the Netherlands and the United States are the four leading net exporters of agricultural products (Figure 10.9.6). Japan, China, Russia, and the United Kingdom are the leading net importers.

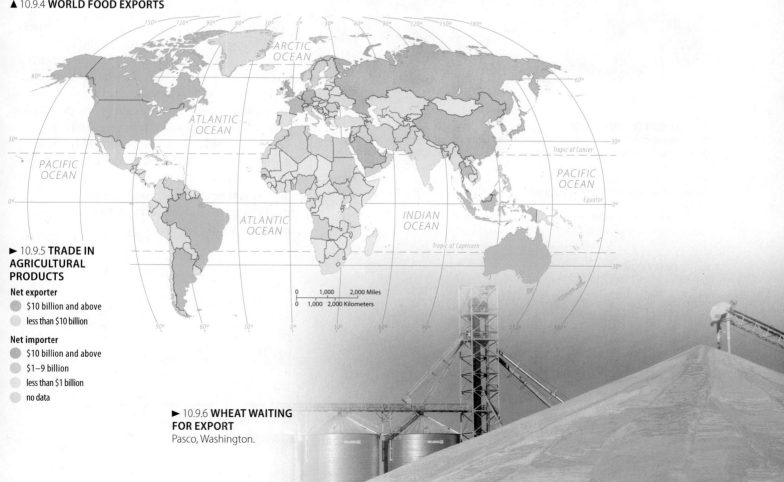

▶ 10.9.5 **TRADE IN AGRICULTURAL PRODUCTS**

Net exporter
- $10 billion and above
- less than $10 billion

Net importer
- $10 billion and above
- $1–9 billion
- less than $1 billion
- no data

▶ 10.9.6 **WHEAT WAITING FOR EXPORT**
Pasco, Washington.

10.10 Commercial Agriculture and Market Forces

▶ **Farming is part of agribusiness in developed countries.**

▶ **Because of overproduction, farmers in developed countries may receive government subsidies to reduce output.**

The system of commercial farming found in developed countries is called **agribusiness**, because the family farm is not an isolated activity but is integrated into a large food-production industry. Agribusiness encompasses such diverse enterprises as tractor manufacturing, fertilizer production, and seed distribution. This type of farming responds to market forces rather than to feeding the farmer. Geographers use the von Thünen model to help explain the importance of proximity to market in the choice of crops on commercial farms (Figure 10.10.1).

Farmers are less than 2 percent of the U.S. labor force, but around 20 percent of U.S. labor works in food production and services related to agribusiness—food processing, packaging, storing, distributing, and retailing. Although most farms are owned by individual families, many other aspects of agribusiness are controlled by large corporations.

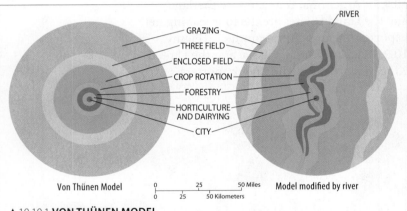

Von Thünen Model | 0 25 50 Miles | Model modified by river
0 25 50 Kilometers

▲ 10.10.1 **VON THÜNEN MODEL**
Johann Heinrich von Thünen, a farmer in northern Germany, proposed a model to explain the importance of proximity to market in the choice of crops on commercial farms. The von Thünen model was first proposed in 1826 in a book titled *The Isolated State*. According to the model, which was later modified by geographers, a commercial farmer initially considers which crops to cultivate and which animals to raise based on market location. Von Thünen based his general model of the spatial arrangement of different crops on his experiences as owner of a large estate in northern Germany. He found that specific crops were grown in different rings around the cities in the area.

PRODUCTIVITY CHALLENGES

The experience of dairy farming in the United States demonstrates the growth in productivity (Figure 10.10.2). The number of dairy cows has declined since 1960 but production has increased, because yield per cow has tripled (Figure 10.10.3).

Commercial farmers suffer from low incomes because they are capable of producing much more food than is demanded by consumers in developed countries. Although the food supply has increased in developed countries, demand has remained constant, because of low population growth and market saturation (Figure 10.10.4).

A surplus of food can be produced because of widespread adoption of efficient agricultural practices. New seeds, fertilizers, pesticides, mechanical equipment, and management practices have enabled farmers to obtain greatly increased yields per area of land.

▼ 10.10.2 **DAIRY COWS**
California.

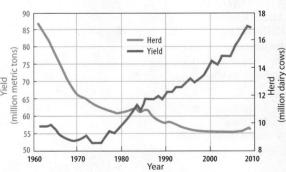

▲ 10.10.3 **U.S. DAIRY PRODUCTIVITY**

GOVERNMENT SUBSIDIES

The U.S. government has three policies that are supposed to address the problem of excess productive capacity:

- Farmers are encouraged to avoid producing crops that are in excess supply. Because soil erosion is a constant threat, the government encourages planting fallow crops, such as clover, to restore nutrients to the soil and to help hold the soil in place. These crops can be used for hay, forage for pigs, or to produce seeds for sale.

- The government pays farmers when certain commodity prices are low. The government sets a target price for the commodity and pays farmers the difference between the price they receive in the market and a target price set by the government as a fair level for the commodity. The target prices are calculated to give farmers the same price for the commodity today as in the past, when compared to other consumer goods and services.

- The government buys surplus production and sells or donates it to foreign governments. In addition, low-income Americans receive food stamps in part to stimulate their purchase of additional food.

Farming in Europe is subsidized even more than in the United States. Government policies in developed countries point out a fundamental irony in worldwide agricultural patterns. In developed countries, farmers are encouraged to grow less food, whereas some developing countries struggle to increase food production to match the rate of growth in the population.

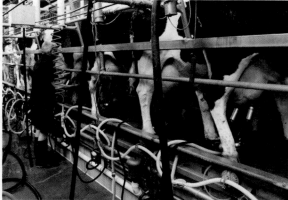

◄ 10.10.4
AGRIBUSINESS IN DAIRY FARMING
(top) Large-scale milking; (below) transportation from farm to processing; (below left) processing; (below right) bottling; and (bottom) retailing.

10.11 Sustainable Agriculture

▶ **Sustainable agriculture and organic farming rely on sensitive land management.**

▶ **Sustainable agriculture also limits the use of chemicals and integrates crops and livestock.**

Some commercial farmers are converting their operations to **sustainable agriculture**, an agricultural practice that preserves and enhances environmental quality. An increasingly popular form of sustainable agriculture is organic farming.

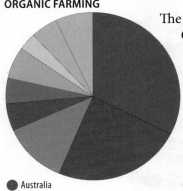

▼ 10.11.1 **SHARE OF THE WORLD'S ORGANIC FARMING**

- ● Australia
- ● Europe
- ● Argentina
- ● United States
- ● Brazil
- ● Other Latin America
- ● India
- ● China
- ● Other

The UN Food and Agriculture Organization estimates the share of agricultural land farmed through organic practices at 0.29 percent worldwide (3/10 of 1 percent). Australia is the world leader, with one-third of the world's total organic farmland (Figure 10.11.1). Europe has the highest percentage of farmland devoted to organic farming (Figure 10.11.2).

Three principal practices distinguish sustainable agriculture (and at its best, organic farming) from conventional agriculture.

SENSITIVE LAND MANAGEMENT

Sustainable agriculture protects soil in part through **ridge tillage**, which is a system of planting crops on ridge tops. Crops are planted on 10- to 20-centimeter (4- to 8-inch) ridges that are formed during cultivation or after harvest. The crop is planted on the same ridges, in the same rows, year after year. Ridge tillage is attractive for two main reasons—lower production costs and greater soil conservation.

Production costs are lower with ridge tillage in part because it requires less investment in tractors and other machinery than conventional planting. An area that would be prepared for planting under conventional farming with three to five tractors can be prepared for ridge tillage with only one or two tractors. The primary tillage tool is a row-crop cultivator that can form ridges. There is no need for a plow, or field cultivator, or a 300-horsepower four-wheel-drive tractor.

With ridge tillage, the space between rows needs to match the distance between wheels of the machinery. If 75 centimeters (30 inches) are left between rows, tractor tires will typically be on 150-centimeter (60-inch) centers and

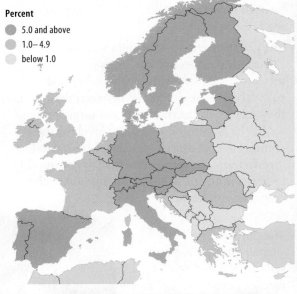

Percent
- ● 5.0 and above
- ● 1.0–4.9
- ● below 1.0

▲ 10.11.2 **FARMLAND IN ORGANIC FARMING IN EUROPE**

combine wheels on 300-centimeter (120-inch) centers. Wheel spacers are available from most manufacturers to fit the required spacing (Figure 10.11.3).

Ridge tillage features a minimum of soil disturbance from harvest to the next planting. A compaction-free zone is created under each ridge and in some row middles. Keeping the trafficked area separate from the crop-growing area improves soil properties. Over several years the soil will tend to have increased organic matter, greater water holding capacity, and more earthworms. The channels left by earthworms and decaying roots enhance drainage.

Ridge tillage compares favorably with conventional farming for yields while lowering the cost of production. Although more labor intensive than other systems, it is profitable on a per-acre basis. In Iowa, for example, ridge tillage has gained favor for production of organic and herbicide-free soybeans, which sell for more than regular soybeans.

LIMITED USE OF CHEMICALS

In conventional agriculture, seeds are often genetically modified to survive when herbicides and insecticides are sprayed on the fields to kill weeds and insects. These are known as "Roundup-Ready" seeds, because the herbicide's creator Monsanto Corp. sells it under the brand name "Roundup." Aside from adverse impacts on soil and water quality, widespread use of "Roundup-Ready" seeds is causing some weeds to become resistant to the herbicide.

Sustainable agriculture, on the other hand, involves application of limited if any herbicides to control weeds. In principle, farmers can control weeds without chemicals, although it requires additional time and expense that few farmers can afford. Researchers have found that combining mechanical weed control with some chemicals yields higher returns per acre than relying solely on one of the two methods.

Ridge tilling also promotes decreased use of chemicals, which can be applied only to the ridges and not the entire field. Combining herbicide banding—which applies chemicals in narrow bands over crop rows—with cultivating may be the best option for many farmers.

INTEGRATED CROP AND LIVESTOCK

Sustainable agriculture attempts to integrate the growing of crops and the raising of livestock as much as possible at the level of the individual farm. Animals consume crops grown on the farm and are not confined to small pens.

In conventional farming, integration between crops and livestock generally takes place through intermediaries rather than inside an individual farm. That is, many farmers in the mixed crop and livestock region actually choose to only grow crops or only raise animals. They sell their crops off the farm or purchase feed for their animals from outside suppliers.

Sustainable agriculture is sensitive to the complexities of interdependencies between crops and livestock:

- Herd size and distribution. The correct number and distribution of livestock is determined for the area based on the landscape and forage sources. Prolonged concentration of livestock in a specific location can result in permanent loss of vegetative cover, so the farmer needs to move the animals.

- Animal confinement. The moral and ethical debate regarding the welfare of confined livestock is particularly intense. From a practical perspective, manure from non-confined animals can contribute to soil fertility.

- Management in extreme weather. Herd size may need to be reduced during periods of short- and long-term droughts.

- Flexible feeding and marketing. Feed costs are the largest single variable cost in livestock operation. Feed costs can be kept to a minimum by monitoring animal condition and performance and understanding seasonal variations in feed and forage quality on the farm.

▼ 10.11.3 **ORGANIC FARMING IN EUROPE**

A country's agriculture remains one of the best measures of the level of development and standard of living. Despite major changes, agriculture in developing countries still employs a large percentage of the population, and producing food for local survival is still paramount.

Key Questions

What do people eat?

▶ Agriculture originated in multiple hearths and diffused to numerous places simultaneously.

▶ What people eat is influenced by a combination of level of development, cultural preferences, and environmental constraints.

▶ One in eight humans is undernourished.

How is agriculture distributed?

▶ Several agricultural regions can be identified based on farming practices.

▶ Subsistence agriculture, typical of developing regions, involves growing food for one's own consumption.

▶ Commercial agriculture, typical of developed countries, involves growing food to sell off the farm.

▶ Commercial agriculture involves larger farms, fewer farmers, and more mechanization than does subsistence agriculture.

What challenges does agriculture face?

▶ Subsistence agriculture faces distinctive economic challenges resulting from rapid population growth and pressure to adopt international trade strategies to promote development.

▶ Commercial agriculture faces distinct challenges resulting from access to markets and overproduction.

▶ Sustainable farming plays an increasing role in the preservation and enhancement of environmental quality.

Thinking Geographically

Assume that the United States constitutes one agricultural market centered around the largest city New York.

1. To what extent can the major agricultural regions of the United States be viewed as irregularly shaped rings around the market center, as von Thünen applied to southern Germany?

Review in Chapter 2 the concept of overpopulation: the number of people in an area exceeds the capacity of the environment to support life at a decent standard of living (Figure 10.CR.1).

2. What agricultural regions face rapid population growth but have relatively limited capacities to support intensive food production?

Compare world distributions of maize, wheat, and rice production.

3. To what extent do differences in the distribution of these crops derive from environmental conditions and to what extent from food preferences and other cultural values?

On the Internet

The United Nations Food and Agricultural Organization maintains a comprehensive database at **www.fao.org** or scan the QR on the first page of this chapter.

The principal source of data about U.S. agriculture is the U.S. Department of Agriculture's National Agricultural Statistical Service, at **www.nass.usda.gov**.

Global organic farming statistics are at the Research Institute of Organic Agriculture, at **www.organic-world.net**.

Information about sustainable agriculture is found through Sustainable Agriculture Research and Education at **www.sare.org**.

◄ 10.CR.1 **OVERPOPULATION IN MALI**
A desert region can be sparsely inhabited yet overpopulated if it has rapid population growth and limited resources, as in the case of Mali.

InteractiveMapping

AGRICULTURE AND CLIMATE REGIONS

Agriculture prcatices vary within East Asia.

Launch MapMaster East Asia in Mastering**GEOGRAPHY**

Select *Climate* from the *Physical Environment* menu.

Next select *Agricultural Regions* from the *Economic* menu.

Which practice matches most closely with which climate region?

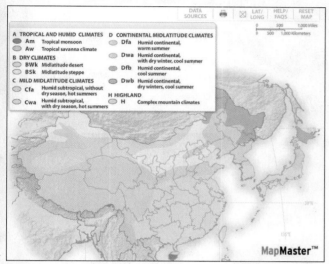

Explore

BENTON COUNTY, INDIANA

Use Google Earth to explore the agricultural landscape of Benton County, Indiana.

Fly to: *Freeland Park, Indiana*

Click to show historical imagery

Move the cursor to: *4/3/2005*, then to *8/12/2007*, then to *10/06/2009*.

Note the change in the predominant color of the fields at these three dates.

Why does the predominant color of the fields change from April to August and then to October?

Key Terms

Agribusiness
Commercial agriculture characterized by the integration of different steps in the food-processing industry, usually through ownership by large corporations.

Agriculture
The deliberate effort to modify a portion of Earth's surface through the cultivation of crops and the raising of livestock for sustenance or economic gain.

Aquaculture (or aquafarming)
The cultivation of seafood under controlled conditions.

Cereal grain
A grass yielding grain for food.

Commercial agriculture
Agriculture undertaken primarily to generate products for sale off the farm.

Crop
Grain or fruit gathered from a field as a harvest during a particular season.

Crop rotation
The practice of rotating use of different fields from crop to crop each year, to avoid exhausting the soil.

Dietary energy consumption
The amount of food that an individual consumes.

Food security
Physical, social, and economic access at all times to safe and nutritious food sufficient to meet dietary needs and food preferences for an active and healthy life.

Grain
Seed of a cereal grass.

Green revolution
Rapid diffusion of new agricultural technology, especially new high-yield seeds and fertilizers.

Intensive subsistence agriculture
A form of subsistence agriculture in which farmers must expend a relatively large amount of effort to produce the maximum feasible yield from a parcel of land.

Milkshed
The ring surrounding a city from which milk can be supplied without spoiling.

Overfishing
Capturing fish faster than they can reproduce.

Pastoral nomadism
A form of subsistence agriculture based on herding domesticated animals.

Plantation
A large farm in tropical and subtropical climates that specializes in the production of one or two crops for sale, usually to a more developed country.

Ranching
A form of commercial agriculture in which livestock graze over an extensive area.

Ridge tillage
System of planting crops on ridge tops in order to reduce farm production costs and promote greater soil conservation.

Shifting cultivation
A form of subsistence agriculture in which people shift activity from one field to another; each field is used for crops for a relatively few years and left fallow for a relatively long period.

Slash-and-burn agriculture
Another name for shifting cultivation, so named because fields are cleared by slashing the vegetation and burning the debris.

Subsistence agriculture
Agriculture designed primarily to provide food for direct consumption by the farmer and the farmer's family.

Sustainable agriculture
Farming methods that preserve long-term productivity of land and minimize pollution, typically by rotating soil-restoring crops with cash crops and reducing inputs of fertilizer and pesticides.

Swidden
A patch of land cleared for planting through slashing and burning.

Truck farming
Commercial gardening and fruit farming, so named because truck was a Middle English word meaning bartering or the exchange of commodities.

Undernourishment
Dietary energy consumption that is continuously below the minimum requirement for maintaining a healthy life and carrying out light physical activity.

Wet rice
Rice planted on dryland in a nursery and then moved to a deliberately flooded field to promote growth.

▶ LOOKING AHEAD

Agriculture is practiced throughout the inhabited world, because the need for food is universal. Industry—the manufacturing of goods in factories— is much more highly clustered in a handful of regions.

11 Industry

Manufacturing jobs are viewed as a special asset by communities around the world. They are seen as the "engine" of economic growth and prosperity. Different communities possess distinctive assets in attracting particular types of industries as well as challenges in retaining them.

A generation ago, industry was highly clustered in a handful of communities within developed countries, but industry has diffused to more communities, including some in developing countries. Meanwhile, a loss of manufacturing jobs has caused economic problems for communities in developed countries, like the United States, traditionally dependent on them.

Where is industry clustered?

11.1 **The Industrial Revolution**

11.2 **Distribution of Industry**

STEEL WORKS,
LIAONING, CHINA

246

What situation factors influence industrial location?

What site factors influence industrial location?

11.1 The Industrial Revolution

▶ **The Industrial Revolution transformed how goods are produced for society.**
▶ **The United Kingdom was home to key events in the Industrial Revolution.**

The modern concept of industry—meaning the manufacturing of goods in a factory—originated in northern England and southern Scotland during the second half of the eighteenth century. From there, industry diffused in the nineteenth century to Europe and to North America and in the twentieth century to other regions.

ORIGINS OF THE INDUSTRIAL REVOLUTION

The **Industrial Revolution** was a series of improvements in industrial technology that transformed the process of manufacturing goods. Prior to the Industrial Revolution, industry was geographically dispersed across the landscape. People made household tools and agricultural equipment in their own homes or obtained them in the local village. Home-based manufacturing was known as the **cottage industry** system (Figure 11.1.1).

The term *Industrial Revolution* is somewhat misleading:

- The transformation was far more than industrial, and it did not happen overnight.
- The Industrial Revolution resulted in new social, economic, and political inventions, not just industrial ones.

▲▼ 11.1.1 **TRANSFORMATION OF AN INDUSTRY**
(top) In the early nineteenth century, the textile industry was a cottage industry based on people spinning and weaving by hand in their homes. (bottom) By the middle of the century, the industry had become based in factories and mills. In this interior view of a cotton mill in 1835 girls and women tend carding, drawing, and roving machinery.

- The changes involved a gradual diffusion of new ideas and techniques over decades, rather than an instantaneous revolution.

Nonetheless, the term is commonly used to define the process that began in the United Kingdom in the late 1700s.

The invention most important to the development of factories was the steam engine, patented in 1769 by James Watt, a maker of mathematical instruments in Glasgow, Scotland (Figure 11.1.2). Watt built the first useful steam engine, which could pump water far more efficiently than the watermills then in common use, let alone human or animal power. The large supply of steam power available from James Watt's steam engines induced firms to concentrate all steps in a manufacturing process in one building attached to a single power source.

▲ 11.1.2 **JAMES WATT'S STEAM ENGINE**
Steam injected in a cylinder (left side of engine) pushes a piston attached to a crankshaft that drives machinery (right side of engine).

TRANSFORMATION OF KEY INDUSTRIES

Industries impacted by the Industrial Revolution included:

- **Coal:** The source of energy to operate the ovens and the steam engines. Wood, the main energy source prior to the Industrial Revolution, was becoming scarce in England because it was in heavy demand for construction of ships, buildings, and furniture, as well as for heat. Manufacturers turned to coal, which was then plentiful in England.

- **Iron:** The first industry to benefit from Watt's steam engine. The usefulness of iron had been known for centuries, but it was difficult to produce because ovens had to be constantly heated, something the steam engine could do (Figure 11.1.3).

- **Transportation:** Critical for diffusing the Industrial Revolution. First canals and then railroads enabled factories to attract large numbers of workers, bring in bulky raw materials such as iron ore and coal, and ship finished goods to consumers (Figure 11.1.4).

- **Textiles:** Transformed from a dispersed cottage industry to a concentrated factory system during the late eighteenth century, as illustrated in Figure 11.1.1. In 1768, Richard Arkwright, a barber and wigmaker in Preston, England, invented machines to untangle cotton prior to spinning. Too large to fit inside a cottage, spinning frames were placed inside factories near sources of rapidly flowing water, which supplied the power. Because the buildings resembled large watermills, they were known as mills.

- **Chemicals:** An industry created to bleach and dye cloth. In 1746, John Roebuck and Samuel Garbett established a factory to bleach cotton with sulfuric acid obtained from burning coal. When combined with various metals, sulfuric acid produced another acid called vitriol, useful for dying clothing.

- **Food processing:** Essential to feed the factory workers no longer living on farms. In 1810, French confectioner Nicholas Appert started canning food in glass bottles sterilized in boiling water.

▲ 11.1.3 **IRON ORE SMELTING**
Coalbrookdale by Night, an 1801 painting by Philip James de Loutherbourg, depicts the Coalbrookdale Company's iron ore smelter in Ironbridge, England. The painting is in London's Science Museum.

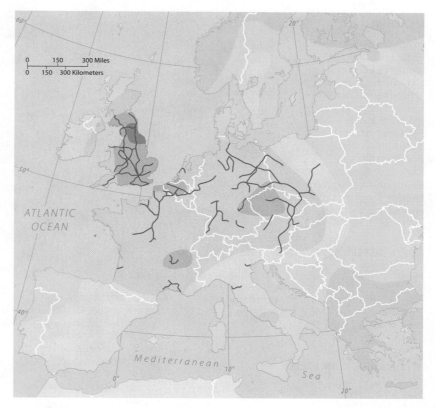

▲ 11.1.4 **DIFFUSION OF RAILROADS**
Europe's political problems retarded the diffusion of the railroad. Cooperation among small neighboring states was essential to build an efficient rail network and to raise money for constructing and operating the system. Because such cooperation could not be attained, railroads in some parts of Europe were delayed 50 years after their debut in the United Kingdom.

First railway opened by
1826 1856
1836 1876
1846 After 1876
— Rail lines constructed by 1848

11.2 Distribution of Industry

▶ **Three-fourths of the world's manufacturing is clustered in three regions.**
▶ **The major industrial regions are divided into subareas.**

Industry is concentrated in three of the nine world regions discussed in Chapter 9: Europe (Figures 11.2.1 and 11.2.2), East Asia (Figure 11.2.3), and North America (Figure 11.2.4). Each of the three regions accounts for roughly one-fourth of the world's total industrial output. Outside these three regions the leading industrial producers are Brazil and India.

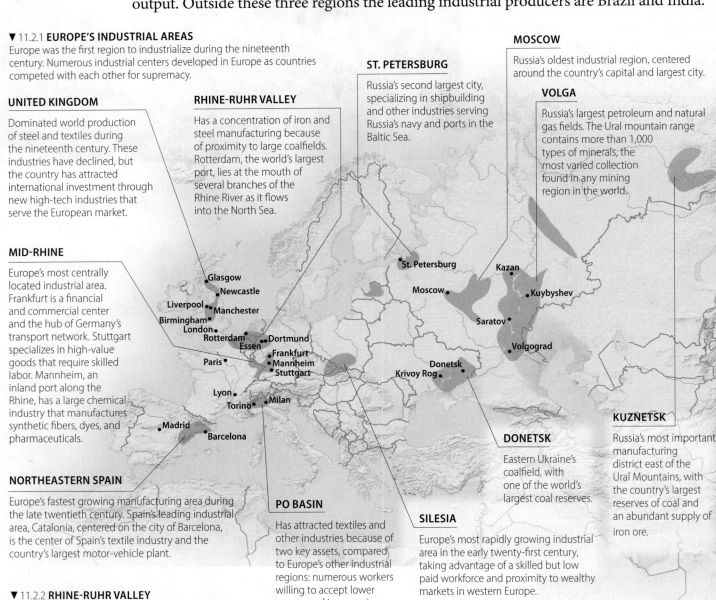

▼ 11.2.1 **EUROPE'S INDUSTRIAL AREAS**
Europe was the first region to industrialize during the nineteenth century. Numerous industrial centers developed in Europe as countries competed with each other for supremacy.

UNITED KINGDOM

Dominated world production of steel and textiles during the nineteenth century. These industries have declined, but the country has attracted international investment through new high-tech industries that serve the European market.

MID-RHINE

Europe's most centrally located industrial area. Frankfurt is a financial and commercial center and the hub of Germany's transport network. Stuttgart specializes in high-value goods that require skilled labor. Mannheim, an inland port along the Rhine, has a large chemical industry that manufactures synthetic fibers, dyes, and pharmaceuticals.

NORTHEASTERN SPAIN

Europe's fastest growing manufacturing area during the late twentieth century. Spain's leading industrial area, Catalonia, centered on the city of Barcelona, is the center of Spain's textile industry and the country's largest motor-vehicle plant.

▼ 11.2.2 **RHINE-RUHR VALLEY**

RHINE-RUHR VALLEY

Has a concentration of iron and steel manufacturing because of proximity to large coalfields. Rotterdam, the world's largest port, lies at the mouth of several branches of the Rhine River as it flows into the North Sea.

PO BASIN

Has attracted textiles and other industries because of two key assets, compared to Europe's other industrial regions: numerous workers willing to accept lower wages, and inexpensive hydroelectricity from the nearby Alps.

ST. PETERSBURG

Russia's second largest city, specializing in shipbuilding and other industries serving Russia's navy and ports in the Baltic Sea.

SILESIA

Europe's most rapidly growing industrial area in the early twenty-first century, taking advantage of a skilled but low paid workforce and proximity to wealthy markets in western Europe.

DONETSK

Eastern Ukraine's coalfield, with one of the world's largest coal reserves.

MOSCOW

Russia's oldest industrial region, centered around the country's capital and largest city.

VOLGA

Russia's largest petroleum and natural gas fields. The Ural mountain range contains more than 1,000 types of minerals, the most varied collection found in any mining region in the world.

KUZNETSK

Russia's most important manufacturing district east of the Ural Mountains, with the country's largest reserves of coal and an abundant supply of iron ore.

Cities labeled on map: Glasgow, Newcastle, Liverpool, Manchester, Birmingham, London, Rotterdam, Essen, Dortmund, Paris, Frankfurt, Mannheim, Stuttgart, Lyon, Torino, Milan, Madrid, Barcelona, St. Petersburg, Moscow, Kazan, Kuybyshev, Saratov, Volgograd, Donetsk, Krivoy Rog

▼ 11.2.3 EAST ASIA'S INDUSTRIAL AREAS

East Asia became an important industrial region in the second half of the twentieth century, beginning with Japan. In the twenty-first century, China has emerged as the world's leading manufacturing country by most measures.

CHINA

The world's largest supply of low-cost labor and the world's largest market for many consumer products. Manufacturers cluster in three areas along the east coast: near Guangdong and Hong Kong, the Yangtze River valley between Shanghai and Wuhan, and along the Gulf of Bo Hai from Tianjin and Beijing to Shenyang.

JAPAN

Became an industrial power in the 1950s and 1960s, initially by producing goods that could be sold in large quantity at cut-rate prices to consumers in other countries. Manufacturing is concentrated in the central region between Tokyo and Nagasaki.

Tianjin, Beijing & Shenyang
Shenyang
Beijing
Tianjin
Bo Hai
NORTH KOREA
SOUTH KOREA
JAPAN
Nagoya
Kyoto
Kobe
Osaka
Tokyo-Yokohama
Tokyo
Yokohama
CHINA
Nanjing
Shanghai
Wuhan
Nagasaki
Osaka-Kobe-Kyoto
Yangtze River Valley
Guangdong Province & Hong Kong
Hong Kong

▼ 11.2.4 NORTH AMERICA'S INDUSTRIAL AREAS

Industry arrived a bit later in North America than in Europe, but it grew much faster in the nineteenth century. North America's manufacturing was traditionally highly concentrated in northeastern United States and southeastern Canada. In recent years, manufacturing has relocated to the South, lured by lower wages and legislation that has made it difficult for unions to organize factory workers.

MOHAWK VALLEY

A linear industrial belt in upper New York State, taking advantage of inexpensive electricity generated at nearby Niagara Falls.

NEW ENGLAND

A cotton textile center in the early nineteenth century. Cotton was imported from southern states and finished cotton products were shipped to Europe.

SOUTHEASTERN ONTARIO

Canada's most important industrial area, central to the Canadian and U.S. markets and near the Great Lakes and Niagara Falls.

WESTERN GREAT LAKES

Centered on Chicago, the hub of the nation's transportation network, now the center of steel production.

SOUTHERN CALIFORNIA

Now the country's largest area of clothing and textile production, the second-largest furniture producer, and a major food-processing center.

MIDDLE ATLANTIC

The largest U.S. market, so the region attracts industries that need proximity to a large number of consumers and depends on foreign trade through one of this region's large ports.

PITTSBURGH-LAKE ERIE

The leading steel-producing area in the nineteenth century because of proximity to Appalachian coal and iron ore.

CANADA
NORTH AMERICA
MEXICO
San Francisco
Los Angeles
Milwaukee
Detroit
Chicago
Pittsburgh
Buffalo
Boston
New York City
Philadelphia
Baltimore

11.3 Situation Factors in Locating Industry

► **A manufacturer typically faces two geographical costs: situation and site.**
► **Situation factors involve transporting materials to and from a factory.**

Geographers explain why one location may prove more profitable for a factory than others. Situation factors are discussed in the next four sections, and site factors later in the chapter. **Situation factors** involve transporting materials to and from a factory. A firm seeks a location that minimizes the cost of transporting inputs to the factory and finished goods to consumers.

PROXIMITY TO INPUTS

Every industry uses some inputs and sells to customers. The farther something is transported, the higher the cost, so a manufacturer tries to locate its factory as close as possible to both buyers and sellers.

- If inputs are more expensive to transport than products, the optimal location for a factory is near the source of inputs.

- If the cost of transporting the product to customers exceeds the cost of transporting inputs, then the optimal plant location is as close as possible to the customer.

Every manufacturer uses some inputs. These may be resources from the physical environment (minerals, wood, or animals), or they may be parts or materials made by other companies. An industry in which the inputs weigh more than the final products is a **bulk-reducing industry**. To minimize transport costs, a bulk-reducing industry locates near the source of its inputs. An example is copper production (Figure 11.3.1). Copper ore is very heavy when mined, so mills that concentrate the copper by removing less valuable rock are located close to the mine.

▲ 11.3.1 **BULK-REDUCING INDUSTRY: COPPER**
Use Google Earth to explore Mount Isa, Australia's leading copper production center, which includes mining and smelting.

Fly to: *Parkside, Mount Isa, Australia.*

What is the large crater-like feature in the image?

Locate the plume of smoke just west of Parkside and drag the street view icon to the main road west of the Parkside label.

What type of structure is producing the smoke? Why is this structure located close to the other feature?

► 11.3.2 **BULK-GAINING INDUSTRY: BEER BOTTLING**
The two best-selling beer companies in the United States together operate 21 breweries.

Launch MapMaster North America in

Mastering**GEOGRAPHY**™

Select: *Political* then *Cities*

Select: *Economic* then *Breweries*

Select: *Population* then *Population Density*

Draw a line between Winnipeg and San Antonio.

How many of the 21 breweries are east of the line? Is population density higher or lower east of the line?

PROXIMITY TO MARKETS

For many firms, the optimal location is close to markets, where the product is sold. The cost of transporting goods to consumers is a critical location factor for three types of industries:

- **Bulk-gaining industries** make something that gains volume or weight during production. A prominent example is beverage bottling. Empty cans and bottles are brought to the bottler, filled with the soft drink or beer, and shipped to consumers. The principal input placed in the beverage container is water, which is relatively bulky, heavy, and expensive to transport (Figure 11.3.2).

- **Single-market manufacturers** make products sold primarily in one location, so they also cluster near their markets. For example, the manufacturers of parts for motor vehicles are specialized manufacturers often with only one or two customers—the major carmakers such as General Motors and Toyota (Figure 11.3.3).

- **Perishable products** must be located near their markets so their products can reach consumers as rapidly as possible (Figure 11.3.4).

▲ 11.3.3 **SINGLE-MARKET MANUFACTURER: CAR PARTS**
General Motors worker at a plant in Parma, Ohio, stamps car parts destined for GM assembly plants.

◄ 11.3.4 **PERISHABLE PRODUCT: MILK PRODUCTION**
Food producers such as bakers and milk bottlers must locate near their customers to assure rapid delivery, because people do not want stale bread or sour milk.

11.4 Changing Steel Production

▶ **Steel production has traditionally been a prominent example of a bulk-reducing industry.**

▶ **Restructuring has made steel production more sensitive to market locations.**

The two principal inputs in steel production are iron ore and coal. Steelmaking is a bulk-reducing industry that traditionally located to minimize the cost of transporting these two inputs.

U.S. STEEL MILLS

The distribution of steelmaking in the United States demonstrates that when the source of inputs or the relative importance of inputs changes, the optimal location for the industry changes:

- **Mid-nineteenth century:** The U.S. steel industry concentrated around Pittsburgh in southwestern Pennsylvania, where iron ore and coal were both mined. The area no longer has steel mills, but it remains the center for research and administration.

- **Late nineteenth century:** Steel mills were built around Lake Erie, in the Ohio cities of Cleveland, Youngstown, and Toledo, and near Detroit (Figure 11.4.1). The locational shift was largely influenced by the discovery of rich iron ore in the Mesabi Range, a series of low mountains in northern Minnesota. This area soon became the source for virtually all iron ore used in the U.S. steel industry. The ore was transported by way of Lake Superior, Lake Huron, and Lake Erie. Coal was shipped from Appalachia by train.

- **Early twentieth century:** Most new steel mills were located near the southern end of Lake Michigan. The main raw materials continued to be iron ore and coal, but changes in steelmaking required more iron ore in proportion to coal. Thus, new steel mills were built closer to the Mesabi Range to minimize transportation cost. Coal was available from nearby southern Illinois, as well as from Appalachia.

- **Mid-twentieth century:** Most large U.S. steel mills built during the first half of the twentieth century were located in communities near the East and West coasts, including Baltimore, Los Angeles, and Trenton, New Jersey. These coastal locations partly reflected further changes in transportation cost. Iron ore increasingly came from other countries, especially Canada and Venezuela, and locations near the Atlantic and Pacific oceans were more accessible to those foreign sources. Further, scrap iron and steel—widely available in the large metropolitan areas of the East and West coasts—had become an important input in the steel-production process.

- **Late twentieth century:** Many steel mills in the United States closed (Figure 11.4.2). Most of the survivors were around southern Lake Michigan and along the East Coast.

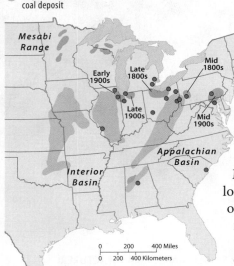

Integrated steel mills
Historical location of steel industry
Major iron ore deposit
Major bituminous coal deposit

Mesabi Range

Early 1900s
Late 1800s
Mid 1800s
Late 1900s
Mid 1900s

Appalachian Basin

Interior Basin

0   200   400 Miles
0   200   400 Kilometers

▲ 11.4.1 **INTEGRATED STEEL MILLS IN THE UNITED STATES**
Integrated steel mills are densely clustered near the southern Great Lakes, especially Lake Erie and Lake Michigan. Historically, the most critical factor in siting a steel mill was to minimize transportation cost for raw materials, especially heavy, bulky iron ore and coal. Most surviving mills are in the Midwest to maximize access to consumers.

▼ 11.4.2 **CLOSED STEEL MILL, BETHLEHEM, PENNSYLVANIA**
A large percentage of integrated steel mills in North America and Europe have closed in recent decades. Steel production has moved to less developed countries and to mini-mills.

RESTRUCTURING THE STEEL INDUSTRY

The shift of world manufacturing to new industrial regions can be seen clearly in steel production (Figure 11.4.3). World steel production doubled between 1980 and 2010, from around 700 million to around 1,400 million metric tons. China was responsible for 600 million of the 700 million increase, and other developing countries (primarily India and South Korea) for another 100 million metric tons (Figure 11.4.4). Production in developed countries remained unchanged at approximately 500 million metric tons (Figure 11.4.5).

China's steel industry has grown in part because of access to the primary inputs of iron ore and coal. However, the principal factor in recent years has been increased demand by growing industries in China that use a lot of steel, such as motor vehicles.

▲ 11.4.3 **STEEL MILL IN CHINA**
Shanxi Haixin steel mill.

1980

▶ 11.4.4 **WORLD STEEL PRODUCTION, 1980 AND 2010**

Million metric tons

- 100 and above
- 10 – 99
- 1 – 9
- below 1
- no data

1980
- Russia 14%
- Japan 10%
- United States 16%
- Other Developing 14%
- Other Developed 39%
- China 7%

2010

2010
- Japan 8%
- Other Developed 18%
- Russia 5%
- United States 6%
- Other Developing 19%
- China 44%

▲ 11.4.5 **SHARE OF GLOBAL STEEL PRODUCTION, 1980 AND 2010**

- Developed countries
- Developing countries

11.5 Changing Auto Production

▶ **Motor vehicles are bulk-gaining products that are made near their markets.**
▶ **In the United States, most carmaking operations have clustered in "auto alley".**

The motor vehicle is a prominent example of a fabricated metal product, described earlier as one of the main types of bulk-gaining industries. As a bulk-gaining industry, most motor vehicle production is concentrated near the markets for the vehicles.

GLOBAL DISTRIBUTION OF PRODUCTION

Carmakers put together vehicles at final assembly plants, using thousands of parts supplied by independent companies. Sixty percent of the world's final assembly plants are controlled by ten carmakers:

- 2 U.S.-based: Ford and GM.
- 4 Europe-based: Germany's Volkswagen, Italy's Fiat (which controls Chrysler), and France's Renault (which controls Nissan) and Peugeot.
- 4 Asia-based: Japan's Toyota, Honda, and Suzuki, and South Korea's Hyundai.

These companies operate assembly and parts plants in many countries. Nationality matters in terms of location of corporate headquarters, top managers, research facilities, and shareholders.

The world's three major industrial regions house 80 percent of the world's final assembly plants, including 40 percent in East Asia, 25 percent in Europe, and 15 percent in North America (Figure 11.5.1). Three-fourths of vehicles sold in North America are assembled in North America (Figure 11.5.2). Similarly most vehicles sold in Europe are assembled in Europe, most vehicles sold in Japan are assembled in Japan, and most vehicles sold in China are assembled in China.

Carmakers' assembly plants account for only around 30 percent of the value of the vehicles that bear their names. As a result of outsourcing, independent parts makers supply the other 70 percent of the value. Many of these parts are also made near their markets—the final assembly plants—especially the steel parts, which comprise more than half of the weight of vehicles (Figure 11.5.3).

On the other hand, many parts do not need to be manufactured close to the customer. For them, changing site factors are more important. Some locate in countries that have relatively low labor costs, such as Mexico, China, and Czech Republic.

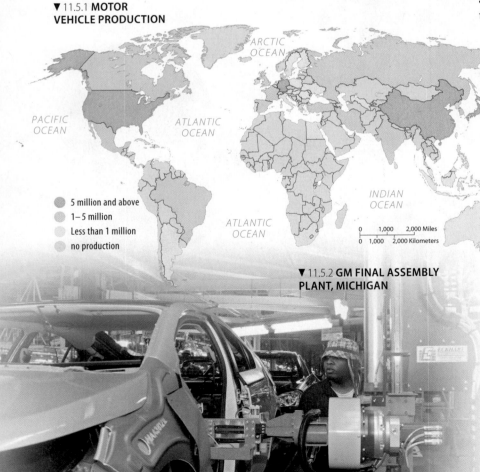

▼ 11.5.1 **MOTOR VEHICLE PRODUCTION**

ARCTIC OCEAN

PACIFIC OCEAN

ATLANTIC OCEAN

INDIAN OCEAN

ATLANTIC OCEAN

0   1,000   2,000 Miles
0   1,000   2,000 Kilometers

- 5 million and above
- 1–5 million
- Less than 1 million
- no production

▼ 11.5.2 **GM FINAL ASSEMBLY PLANT, MICHIGAN**

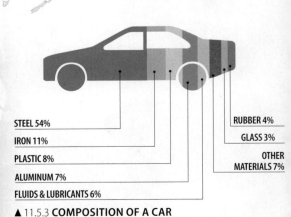

STEEL 54%
IRON 11%
PLASTIC 8%
ALUMINUM 7%
FLUIDS & LUBRICANTS 6%

RUBBER 4%
GLASS 3%
OTHER MATERIALS 7%

▲ 11.5.3 **COMPOSITION OF A CAR**

U.S. VEHICLE PRODUCTION

In the United States, vehicles are fabricated at about 50 final assembly plants, from parts made at several thousand other plants. Most of the assembly and parts plants are located in the interior of the country, between Michigan and Alabama, centered in a corridor known as "auto alley," formed by north-south interstate highways 65 and 75 (Figure 11.5.4).

For a bulk-gaining operation, such as a final assembly plant, the critical location factor is minimizing transportation to the market, in this case the 15 million North Americans who buy new vehicles each year. If a company has a product that is made at only one plant, and the critical location factor is to minimizing the cost of distribution throughout North America, then the optimal factory location is in the U.S. interior rather than on the East or West Coast.

Most parts makers also locate in auto alley to be near the final assembly plants. Seats, for example, are invariably manufactured within an hour of the final assembly plant. A seat is an especially large and bulky object, and carmakers do not want to waste valuable space in their assembly plants by piling up an inventory of them. Most engines, transmissions, and metal body parts are also produced within a couple hours of an assembly plant.

Within auto alley, U.S.-owned carmakers and suppliers have clustered in Michigan and nearby northern states, whereas foreign-owned carmakers and parts suppliers have clustered in

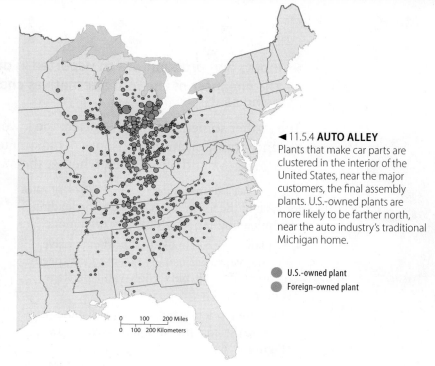

◄ 11.5.4 **AUTO ALLEY**
Plants that make car parts are clustered in the interior of the United States, near the major customers, the final assembly plants. U.S.-owned plants are more likely to be farther north, near the auto industry's traditional Michigan home.

● U.S.-owned plant
● Foreign-owned plant

the southern portion of auto alley (Figure 11.5.4). Chrysler, Ford, and General Motors are known as the Detroit 3 because their headquarters and research facilities are clustered in the Detroit area.

The share of U.S. sales accounted for by the Detroit 3 has declined from 75 percent in 1995 to 45 percent in 2010. Some "foreign" cars have turned out to have higher U.S. content than some cars sold by the Detroit 3 (Figure 11.5.5). Meanwhile, the declining fortunes of the Detroit 3 have resulted i n closure of many of the plants in the northern part of auto alley.

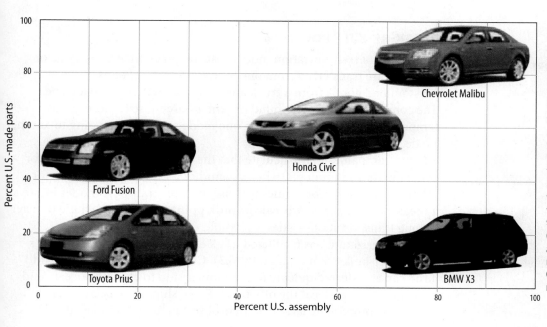

◄ 11.5.5 **"AMERICAN" AND "FOREIGN" CARS**
The x axis shows the percentage of these vehicles sold in the United States that were assembled in the United States in 2011. The y axis shows the percentage of U.S.-made parts in these vehicles. GM's Chevrolet Malibu was assembled entirely in the United States with all but a handful of U.S.-made parts. Toyota's Prius was imported from Japan with Japanese-made parts. Ford's Fusion was assembled in Mexico with about one-half U.S. parts. BMW's X3 was assembled in the United States with parts mostly imported from Germany. Some Honda Civics were assembled in the United States with mostly U.S.-made parts, and some Civics were imported from Japan with mostly Japanese-made parts.

11.6 Ship by Boat, Rail, Truck, or Air

▶ Inputs and products are transported in one of four ways: ship, rail, truck, or air.
▶ The cheapest of the four alternatives changes with the distance that goods are being sent.

The farther something is transported, the lower is the cost per kilometer (or mile). Longer-distance transportation is cheaper per kilometer in part because firms must pay workers to load goods on and off vehicles, whether the material travels 10 kilometers or 10,000.

The cost per kilometer decreases at different rates for each of the four modes, because the loading and unloading expenses differ for each mode.

- Airplanes are normally the most expensive alternative, so are usually reserved for speedy delivery of small-bulk, high-value packages (Figure 11.6.1).

- Ships are attractive for very long distances because the cost per kilometer is very low (Figure 11.6.2).

- Trains are often used to ship to destinations that take longer than one day to reach. Trains take longer than trucks to load, but once under way are not required to make daily rest stops like truck drivers.

- Trucks are most often used for short-distance delivery because they can be loaded and unloaded quickly and cheaply.

Air-cargo companies such as FedEx and UPS promise overnight delivery for most packages. They pick up packages in the afternoon and transport them by truck to the nearest airport. Late at night, planes filled with packages are flown to a central hub airport in the interior of the country, such as Memphis, Tennessee, and Louisville, Kentucky. The packages are then transferred to other planes, flown to airports nearest their destination, transferred to trucks, and delivered the next morning.

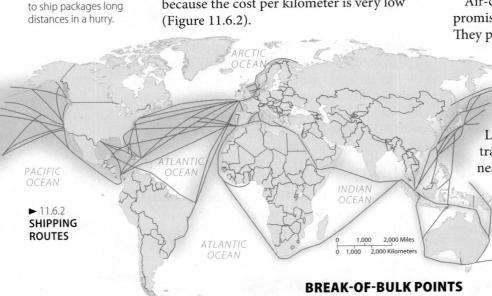

▲ 11.6.1 **SHIP BY AIR**
Air transport is used to ship packages long distances in a hurry.

▶ 11.6.2 **SHIPPING ROUTES**

BREAK-OF-BULK POINTS

Regardless of transportation mode, cost rises each time that inputs or products are transferred from one mode to another. For example, workers must unload goods from a truck and then reload them onto a plane. The company may need to build or rent a warehouse to store goods temporarily after unloading from one mode and before loading to another mode.

Some companies may calculate that the cost of one mode is lower for some inputs and products, whereas another mode may be cheaper for other goods. Many companies that use multiple transport modes locate at a break-of-bulk point. A **break-of-bulk point** is a location where transfer among transportation modes is possible.

Containerization has facilitated transfer of packages between modes at break-of-bulk points (Figure 11.6.3). Containers may be packed into a rail car, transferred quickly to a container ship to cross the ocean, and unloaded into trucks at the other end. Large ships have been specially built to accommodate large numbers of rectangular, box-like containers.

▼ 11.6.3 **BREAK-OF-BULK POINT, PORT OF LOS ANGELES**
Many goods that are shipped long distances are packed in uniformly sized containers, which can be quickly transferred between ships and trucks or trains.

JUST-IN-TIME DELIVERY

Proximity to market has long been important for many types of manufacturers, as discussed earlier in this chapter. The factor has become even more important in recent years because of the rise of just-in-time delivery.

As the name implies, **just-in-time** is shipment of parts and materials to arrive at a factory moments before they are needed. Just-in-time delivery is especially important for delivery of inputs, such as parts and raw materials, to manufacturers of fabricated products, such as cars and computers.

Under just-in-time, parts and materials arrive at a factory frequently, in many cases daily if not hourly. Suppliers of the parts and materials are told a few days in advance how much will be needed over the next week or two, and first thing each morning exactly what will be needed at precisely what time that day.

Just-in-time delivery reduces the money that a manufacturer must tie up in wasteful inventory (Figure 11.6.4). The percentage of the U.S. economy tied up in inventory has been cut in half during the past quarter-century. Manufacturers also save money through just-in-time delivery by reducing the size of the factory, because space does not have to be wasted on piling up a mountain of inventory.

To meet a tight timetable, a supplier of parts and materials must locate factories near its customers. If only an hour or two notice is given, a supplier has no choice but to locate a factory within 50 miles or so of the customer.

▲ 11.6.4 **ELIMINATING INVENTORY**
Leading computer manufacturers have cut costs in part through eliminating the need to store inventory in warehouses. These computers are being built in China only after the buyer has placed the order.

Just-in-time delivery sometimes merely shifts the burden of maintaining inventory to suppliers. Walmart, for example, holds low inventories but tells its suppliers to hold high inventories "just in case" a sudden surge in demand requires restocking on short notice.

JUST-IN-TIME DISRUPTIONS

Just-in-time delivery means that producers have less inventory to cushion against disruptions in the arrival of needed parts. Three kinds of disruptions can result from reliance on just-in-delivery:

- **Labor unrest.** A strike at one supplier plant can shut down the entire production within a couple of days. Also disrupting deliveries could be a strike in the logistics industry, such as truckers or dockworkers.

- **Traffic.** Deliveries may be delayed when traffic is slowed by accident, construction, or unusually heavy volume. Trucks and trains are both subject to these types of delays , especially crossing international borders (Figure 11.6.5).

- **Natural hazards.** Poor weather conditions can afflict deliveries anywhere in the world. Blizzards and floods can close highways and rail lines. The 2011 earthquake and tsunami in Japan put many factories and transportation lines out of service for months. Carmakers around the world had to curtail production because key parts had been made at the damaged factories.

▶ 11.6.5 **DELIVERY DISRUPTIONS**
These vehicles on a highway in Ontario are backed up trying to cross the border into Michigan.

11.7 Site Factors in Industry

▶ Site factors result from the unique characteristics of a location.
▶ The three main site factors are labor, land, and capital.

Site factors are industrial location factors related to the costs of factors of production inside the plant, notably labor, land, and capital.

LABOR

A **labor-intensive** industry is one in which wages and other compensation paid to employees constitute a high percentage of expenses. Labor costs an average of 11 percent of overall manufacturing costs in the United States, so a labor-intensive industry would have a much higher percentage than that (Figure 11.7.1).

The average annual wage paid to male workers exceeds $30,000 or $15 per hour in most developed countries, compared to less than $5,000 or $2.50 per hour in most developing countries (Figure 11.7.2). Health care, retirement pensions, and other benefits add substantially to the wage compensation in developed countries, but not in developing countries.

For some manufacturers—but not all—the difference between paying workers $2.50 and $15 per hour is critical. For example, most

▲ 11.7.1 **LABOR**
Chinese workers in a packaging factory. Around the world, approximately 150 million people are employed in manufacturing, according to the UN International Labor Organization (ILO). China has around 20 percent of the world's manufacturing workers and the United States around 10 percent.

▲ 11.7.2 **EARNED ANNUAL INCOME (MALES)**

- ● $30,000 and above
- ● $10,000 – $29,999
- ● $5,000 – $9,999
- ○ below $5,000
- ○ no data

of the cost of an iPhone is in the parts (made mostly in Japan, Germany, and South Korea) and the gross profit to Apple (based in the United States). One step in the production process is labor intensive—snapping all the parts together at an assembly plant—and this step is done in China with relative low-wage workers (Figure 11.7.3).

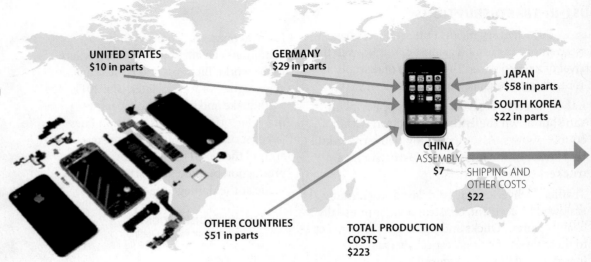

▶ 11.7.3 **COST STRUCTURE OF AN iPHONE**
The cost of manufacturing an iPhone is substantially less than the price that consumers pay.

UNITED STATES
$10 in parts

GERMANY
$29 in parts

JAPAN
$58 in parts

SOUTH KOREA
$22 in parts

CHINA
ASSEMBLY
$7

SHIPPING AND OTHER COSTS
$22

OTHER COUNTRIES
$51 in parts

TOTAL PRODUCTION COSTS
$223

LAND

In the early years of the Industrial Revolution, multistory factories were constructed in the heart of the city. Now, they are more likely to be built in suburban or rural areas, in part to provide enough space for one-story buildings.

Raw materials are typically delivered at one end and moved through the factory on conveyors or forklift trucks. Products are assembled in logical order and shipped out at the other end.

Locations on the urban periphery are also attractive for factories to facilitate delivery of inputs and shipment of products. In the past, when most material moved in and out of a factory by rail, a central location was attractive because rail lines converged there.

With trucks now responsible for transporting most inputs and products, proximity to major highways is more important for a factory. Especially attractive is the proximity to the junction of a long-distance route and the beltway or ring road that encircles most cities. Factories cluster in industrial parks located near suburban highway junctions (Figure 11.7.4).

Also, land is much cheaper in suburban or rural locations than near the center city. A hectare (or an acre) of land in the United States may cost only a few thousand dollars in a rural area, tens of thousands in a suburban location, and hundreds of thousands near the center.

▲ 11.7.4 **LAND**
Factory outside Vic, Spain.

CAPITAL

Manufacturers typically borrow capital—the funds to establish new factories or expand existing ones. One important factor in the clustering in California's Silicon Valley of high-tech industries has been availability of capital. One-fourth of all capital in the United States is spent on new industries in the Silicon Valley (Figure 11.7.5).

Banks in Silicon Valley have long been willing to provide money for new software and communications firms even though lenders elsewhere have hesitated. High-tech industries have been risky propositions—roughly two-thirds of them fail—but Silicon Valley financial institutions have continued to lend money to engineers with good ideas so that they can buy the software, communications, and networks they need to get started.

The ability to borrow money has become a critical factor in the distribution of industry in developing countries. Financial institutions in many developing countries are short of funds, so new industries must seek loans from banks in developed countries. But enterprises may not get loans if they are located in a country that is perceived to have an unstable political system, a high debt level, or ill-advised economic policies.

▼ 11.7.5 **CAPITAL**
San Jose, California, in Silicon Valley.

11.8 Textile and Apparel Production

▶ **Textile and apparel production is a prominent example of a labor-intensive industry.**

▶ **Textile and apparel production generally requires less skilled, low-wage workers.**

Production of apparel and textiles, which are woven fabrics, is a prominent example of an industry that generally requires less-skilled, low-cost workers. The textile and apparel industry accounts for 6 percent of the dollar value of world manufacturing but a much higher 14 percent of world manufacturing employment, an indicator that it is a labor-intensive industry. The percentage of the world's women employed in this type of manufacturing is even higher.

Textile and apparel production involves three principal steps. All are labor-intensive compared to other industries, but the importance of labor varies somewhat among them. As a result, their global distributions are not identical, because the three steps are not equally labor-intensive.

SPINNING OF FIBERS TO MAKE YARN

Fibers can be spun from natural or synthetic elements (Figure 11.8.1). Cotton is the principal natural fiber—three-fourths of the total—followed by wool. Historically, natural fibers were the sole source, but today synthetics account for three-fourths and natural fibers only one-fourth of world thread production. Because it is a labor-intensive industry, spinning is done primarily in low-wage countries, primarily China (Figure 11.8.2).

▲ 11.8.1 **COTTON YARN PRODUCTION, CHINA**
China produces two-thirds of the world's cotton yarn.

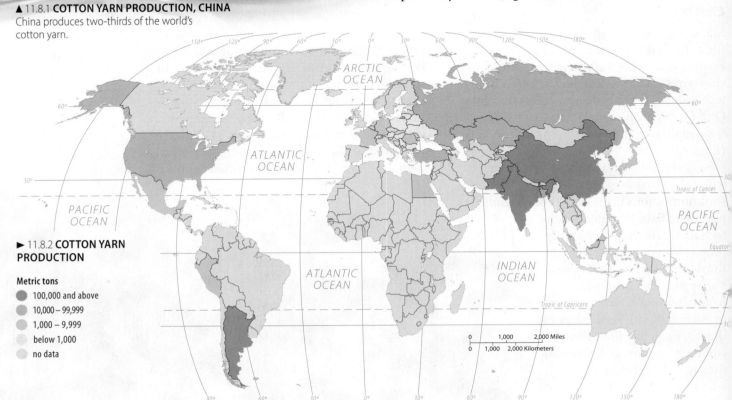

▶ 11.8.2 **COTTON YARN PRODUCTION**

Metric tons
- 100,000 and above
- 10,000 – 99,999
- 1,000 – 9,999
- below 1,000
- no data

WEAVING OR KNITTING YARN INTO FABRIC

Labor constitutes an even higher percentage of total production cost for weaving than for the spinning and assembly steps. China alone accounts for nearly 60 percent of the world's woven cotton fabric production, and India another 30 percent (Figure 11.8.3) Fabric has been woven or laced together by hand for thousands of years on a loom, which is a frame on which two sets of threads are placed at right angles to each other. Even on today's mechanized looms, a loom has one set of threads, called a warp, which is strung lengthwise. A second set of threads, called a weft, is carried in a shuttle that moves over and under the warp (Figure 11.8.4).

CUTTING AND SEWING OF FABRIC FOR ASSEMBLING INTO CLOTHING AND OTHER PRODUCTS

Textiles are assembled into four main types of products: garments, carpets, home products such as bed linens and curtains, and industrial uses such as headliners inside motor vehicles. Developed countries play a larger role in assembly than in spinning and weaving because most of the consumers of assembled products are located there. For example, two-thirds of the women's blouses sold worldwide in a year are sewn in developed countries (Figure 11.8.5). However, the percentage of clothing produced in developing countries has been increasing.

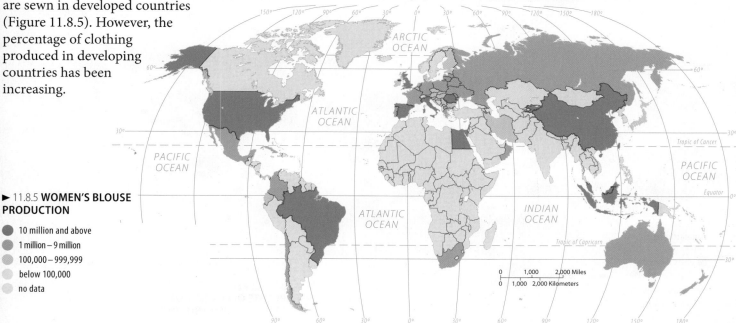

▲ 11.8.3 **WOVEN COTTON FABRIC PRODUCTION**

Square meters
- 20 billion and above
- 1 billion – 3 billion
- 0.1 billion – 1.0 billion
- below 0.1 billion
- no data

◄ 11.8.4 **WOVEN COTTON FABRIC PRODUCTION, CHINA**

► 11.8.5 **WOMEN'S BLOUSE PRODUCTION**
- 10 million and above
- 1 million – 9 million
- 100,000 – 999,999
- below 100,000
- no data

11.9 Emerging Industrial Regions

▶ Manufacturing is growing in locations not traditionally considered as industrial centers.

▶ The four BRIC countries are expected to be increasingly important industrial centers.

Industry is on the move around the world. Site factors, especially labor costs, have stimulated industrial growth in new regions, both internationally and within developed regions. Situation factors, especially proximity to growing markets, have also played a role in the emergence of new industrial regions.

INTERREGIONAL SHIFTS IN THE UNITED STATES

Manufacturing jobs have been shifting within the United States from the North and East to the South and West (Figure 11.9.1). Between 1950 and 2009, the North and East lost 6 million manufacturing jobs and the South and West gained 2 million.

The principal site factor for many manufacturers was labor-related: enactment of **right-to-work** laws by a number of states, especially in the South. A right-to-work law requires a factory to maintain a so-called "open shop" and prohibits a "closed shop."

• In a "closed shop," a company and a union agree that everyone must join the union to work in the factory.

• In an "open shop," a union and a company may not negotiate a contract that requires workers to join a union as a condition of employment.

By enacting right-to-work laws, southern states made it much more difficult for unions to organize factory workers, collect dues, and bargain with employers from a position of strength. As a result, the percentage of workers who are members of a union is much lower in the South than elsewhere in the United States. Car plants, steel, textiles, tobacco products, and furniture industries have dispersed through smaller communities in the South, many in search of a labor force willing to work for less pay than in the North and to forgo joining a union (Figure 11.9.2).

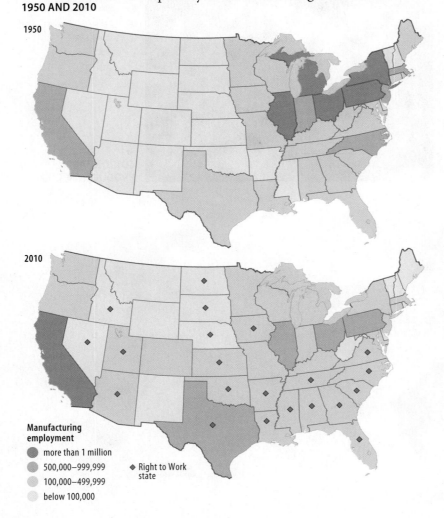

▼ 11.9.1 **CHANGING U.S. MANUFACTURING, 1950 AND 2010**

1950

2010

Manufacturing employment

- ● more than 1 million
- ● 500,000–999,999
- ● 100,000–499,999
- ○ below 100,000
- ◆ Right to Work state

▲ 11.9.2 **VEHICLE ASSEMBLY PLANTS OPEN AND CLOSED BETWEEN 1980 AND 2010**

- ● Plant opened
- ● Plant closed

CALIFORNIA

INDUSTRY IN MEXICO

Manufacturing has been increasing in Mexico. The North Atlantic Free Trade Agreement (NAFTA), effective 1994, eliminated most barriers to moving goods between Mexico and the United States.

Because it is the nearest low-wage country to the United States, Mexico attracts labor-intensive industries that also need proximity to the U.S. market. Although the average wage is higher in Mexico than in most developing countries (refer to Figure 11.7.2), the cost of shipping from Mexico to the United States is lower than from other developing countries.

Mexico City, the country's largest market, is the center for industrial production for domestic consumption (Figure 11.9.3). Other factories have located in Mexico's far north to be as close as possible to the United States.

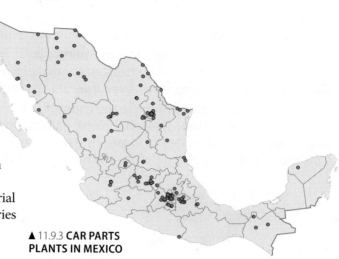

▲ 11.9.3 **CAR PARTS PLANTS IN MEXICO**

EMERGING INDUSTRIAL POWERS: THE "BRIC" COUNTRIES

Much of the world's future growth in manufacturing is expected to locate outside the principal industrial regions described earlier in section 11.2. The financial analysis firm Goldman Sachs has coined the acronym BRIC to indicate the countries it expects to dominate global manufacturing during the twenty-first century. BRIC is an acronym for four countries—Brazil, Russia, India, and China (Figure 11.9.4). They are also known as the newly emerging economies.

The four BRIC countries together currently control one-fourth of the world's land and two-fifths of the world's population, but the four combined account for only one-sixth of world GDP. All four countries have made changes to their economies in recent years, embracing international trade with varying degrees of enthusiasm. By mid-twenty-first century, the four BRIC countries, plus the United States and Mexico, are expected to have the world's six largest economies.

The four BRIC countries have different advantages for industrial location. Russia and Brazil, (Figure 11.9.5) currently classified by the United Nations as having high levels of development, are especially rich in inputs critical for industry. China and India, classified as having medium levels of development, have the two largest labor forces and potential markets for consumer goods.

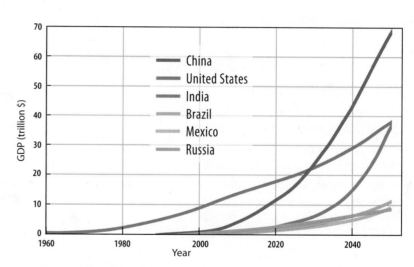

▲ 11.9.4 **GDP HISTORY AND FORECAST FOR BRIC COUNTRIES, UNITED STATES, AND MEXICO**

► 11.9.5 **COMPUTER MANUFACTURING PLANT, CURITIBA, BRAZIL**

Three recent changes in the structure of manufacturing have geographic consequences:

• Factories have become more productive through introduction of new machinery and processes. A factory may continue to operate at the same location but require fewer workers to produce the same output.

• Companies are locating production in communities where workers are willing to adopt more flexible work rules. Firms are especially attracted to smaller towns where low levels of union membership reduce vulnerability to work stoppages, even if wages are kept low and layoffs become necessary.

• By spreading production among many countries, or among many communities within one country, large corporations have increased their bargaining power with local governments and labor forces. Production can be allocated to locations where the local government is especially helpful and generous in subsidizing the costs of expansion, and the local residents are especially eager to work in the plant.

Key Questions

Where is industry clustered?

▶ The Industrial Revolution originated in the United Kingdom and diffused to Europe and North America in the twentieth century.

▶ World industry is highly clustered in three regions—Europe, North America, and East Asia.

What situation factors influence industrial location?

▶ A company tries to identify the optimal location for a factory through analyzing situation and site factors.

▶ Situation factors involve the cost of transporting both inputs into the factory and products from the factory to consumers.

▶ Steel and motor vehicle industries have traditionally located factories primarily because of situation factors.

What site factors influence industrial location?

▶ Three site factors—land, labor, and capital—control the cost of doing business at a location.

▶ Production of textiles and apparel has traditionally been located primarily because of site factors.

▶ New industrial regions are emerging because of their increased importance for site and situation factors.

Thinking Geographically

The North American Free Trade Agreement (NAFTA) among Canada, Mexico, and the United States was implemented in 1994.

1. What have been the benefits and the drawbacks to Canada, Mexico, and the United States as a result of NAFTA?

To induce Hyundai to open a plant in 2010 in West Point, Georgia, to assemble its Kia models, the state spent $36 million to buy the site and donate it to Hyundai, $61 million to build infrastructure such as roads and rail lines, $73 million to train the workers, and $90 million in tax benefits (Figure 11.CR.1).

2. Why would the state of Georgia spend $260 million to get the Kia factory? Did Georgia overpay?

Manufacturing is more dispersed than in the past, both within and among countries.

3. What are the principal manufacturers in your community or area? How have they been affected by increasing global competition?

▶ 11.CR.1 **KIA ASSEMBLY PLANT, WEST POINT, GEORGIA**

Interactive Mapping

SITUATION FACTORS AND RUSSIAN INDUSTRY

Russia's principal industrial location asset is proximity to inputs.

Launch MapMaster Russian Domain in Mastering**GEOGRAPHY**

Select *Economic* then *Industrial Regions.*

Next select *Economic* then *Major Natural resources* then *Coal and Iron only* (deslect others).

Coal and iron are the two principal inputs into steel production. Which of these inputs is close to Russia's principal industrial areas, and which must be transported relatively far?

Deselect coal and iron and instead select other natural resources to see which are near the industrial areas and which have to be transported.

What overall pattern of industrial location do you see?

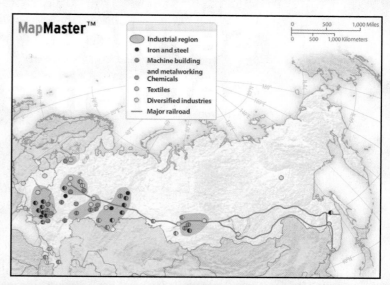

Explore

SAN ANTONIO, TEXAS

Use Google Earth to explore the changing industrial landscape in the United States.

Fly to: *1 Lone Star Pass, San Antonio, Texas, USA.*

Zoom out until the entire factory complex is visible.

Click: *Show Historical Imagery.*

Move the time line to: *9/27/2002.*

What has changed from 9/27/2002 until today?

Move the time line forward from 9/27/2002; at what date can a change in the land first be seen?

Zoom out again until the city of San Antonio is visible.

What are some advantages of 1 Lone Star Pass as an industrial location?

Key Terms

Break-of-bulk point
A location where transfer is possible from one mode of transportation to another.

Bulk-gaining industry
An industry in which the final product weighs more or comprises a greater volume than the inputs.

Bulk-reducing industry
An industry in which the final product weighs less or comprises a lower volume than the inputs.

Cottage industry
Manufacturing based in homes rather than in a factory, commonly found prior to the Industrial Revolution.

Industrial Revolution
A series of improvements in industrial technology that transformed the process of manufacturing goods.

Just-in-time delivery
Shipment of parts and materials to arrive at a factory moments before they are needed.

Labor-intensive industry
An industry for which labor costs comprise a high percentage of total expenses.

Right-to-work state
A U.S. state that has passed a law preventing a union and company from negotiating a contract that requires workers to join a union as a condition of employment.

Site factors
Location factors related to the costs of factors of production inside the plant, such as land, labor, and capital.

Situation factors
Location factors related to the transportation of materials into and from a factory.

On the Internet

Statistics on employment in manufacturing, as well as other sectors of the U.S. economy, are at the U.S. Department of Labor's Bureau of Labor Statistics website, at **www.bls.gov**, or scan the QR on the first page of this chapter.

► LOOKING AHEAD

Most of the growth in jobs in the United States and in the world are in the service (or tertiary) sector, and most service jobs are located in urban settlements.

12 Services and Settlements

Flying across the United States on a clear night, you look down on the lights of settlements, large and small. You see small clusters of lights from villages and towns, and large, brightly lit metropolitan areas. Geographers apply economic geography concepts to explain regularities in the pattern of settlements.

The regular pattern of settlements in the United States and other developed countries reflects where services are provided. Three-fourths of the workers in developed countries are employed in the service sector of the economy. These services are provided in settlements.

The regular distribution of settlements observed over developed countries is not seen in developing countries. Geographers explain that the pattern in developing countries results from having much lower percentages of workers in services.

Where are consumer services distributed?

12.1 **Types of Services**

12.2 **Central Place Theory**

12.3 **Hierarchy of Consumer Services**

12.4 **Market Area Analysis**

INTERNET CAFE, THAILAND

Where are business services distributed?

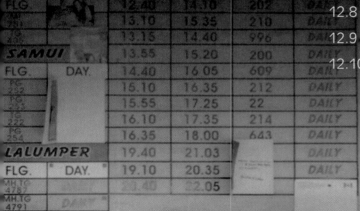

Where are settlements distributed?

12.1 Types of Services

► **Three types of services are consumer, business, and public.**
► **Employment has grown more rapidly in some services than in others.**

A **service** is any activity that fulfills a human want or need and returns money to those who provide it. Services generate more than two-thirds of GDP in most developed countries, compared to less than one-half in most developing countries (Figure 12.1.1).

► 12.1.1 **PERCENTAGE OF GDP FROM SERVICES**

Percentage of GDP from services
- 75 and above
- 50 – 74.9
- 25 – 49.9
- 0 – 24.9
- no data

CONSUMER SERVICES

The service sector of the economy is subdivided into three types—consumer services, business services, and public services. Each of these sectors is divided into several major subsectors.

Consumer services provide services to individual consumers who desire them and can afford to pay for them. Nearly one-half of all jobs in the United States are in consumer services. Four main types of consumer services are retail, education, health, and leisure (Figure 12.1.2).

▼ 12.1.2
U.S. CONSUMER SERVICES

Other U.S. Jobs

Leisure and Hospitality

About 10 percent of all U.S. jobs, primarily in restaurants and bars.

Retail and Wholesale

About 15 percent of all U.S. jobs. Department stores, grocers, and motor vehicle sales and service account for nearly one-half of these jobs. Another one-fourth are wholesalers who provide merchandise to retailers.

Education

About 7 percent of all U.S. jobs. Two-thirds of educators work in public schools, the other one-third in private schools. In Figure 12.1.5, educators at public schools are counted in public-sector employment.

Health Care

About 7 percent of all U.S. jobs, primarily hospitals, doctors' offices, and nursing homes.

BUSINESS SERVICES

Business services facilitate other businesses. One-fourth of all jobs in the United States are in business services. Professional services, financial services, and transportation services are the three main types of business services (Figure 12.1.3).

Financial Services

About 6 percent of all U.S. jobs. One-half of these jobs are in banks and other financial institutions, one-third in insurance companies, and the remainder in real estate.

▼ 12.1.3
U.S. BUSINESS SERVICES

Other U.S. Jobs

Professional Services

About 12 percent of all U.S. jobs. One-half are in technical services, including law, management, accounting, architecture, engineering, design, and consulting. The other one-half is in support services, such as clerical, secretarial, and custodial work.

Transportation and Information Services

About 5 percent of U.S. jobs. One-half are in transportation, primarily trucking. The other one-half are in information services such as publishing and broadcasting as well as utilities such as water and electricity.

PUBLIC SERVICES

Public services provide security and protection for citizens and businesses. About 16 percent of all U.S. jobs are in the public sector, 9 percent if public school employees were excluded from the total and counted instead under education (consumer) services (Figure 12.1.4). Excluding educators, one-sixth of public-sector employees work for the federal government, one-fourth for one of the 50 state governments, and three-fifths for one of the tens of thousands of local governments. When educators are counted, the percentages for state and local governments would be higher.

The distinction among services is not absolute. For example, individual consumers use business services, such as consulting lawyers and keeping money in banks, and businesses use consumer services, such as purchasing stationery and staying in hotels. A public service worker at a national park may provide the same service as a consumer service worker at Disneyland. Geographers find the classification useful, because the various types of services have different distributions, and different factors influence locational decisions.

▼ 12.1.4 **U.S. PUBLIC SERVICES**

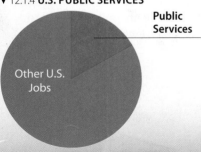

Public Services

Other U.S. Jobs

EMPLOYMENT CHANGE IN THE UNITED STATES

The growth in employment in the United States has been in services, whereas employment in primary- and secondary-sector activities has declined (Figure 12.1.5).

- **Business services:** Jobs expanded most rapidly in professional services (such as engineering, management, and law), data processing, advertising, and temporary employment agencies.

- **Consumer services** (Figure 12.1.6): The most rapid increase has been in the provision of health care, including hospital staff, clinics, nursing homes, and home health-care programs. Other large increases have been recorded in education, recreation, and entertainment.

- **Public services:** The share of employment in public services has declined during the past two decades.

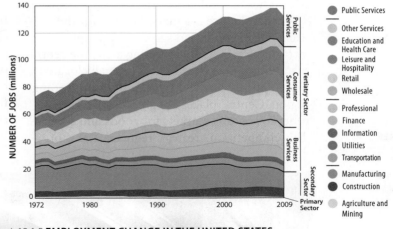

▲ 12.1.5 **EMPLOYMENT CHANGE IN THE UNITED STATES**

◄ 12.1.6 **EMPLOYMENT IN CONSUMER SERVICES**
Unemployed residents of the Detroit area lined up to apply for 200 jobs at a new Meijer store.

12.2 Central Place Theory

▶ **Central place theory explains the location of consumer services.**
▶ **A central place has a market area, range, and threshold.**

Consumer services and business services do not have the same distributions. The various types of consumer services—wholesale, retail, hospitality, education, and health care—generally follow a regular pattern based on size of settlements, with larger settlements offering more consumer services than smaller ones (Figure 12.2.1).

MARKET AREA OF A SERVICE

Selecting the right location for a new shop is probably the single most important factor in the profitability of a consumer service. **Central place theory** explains how services are distributed and why a regular pattern of settlements exists—at least in developed countries such as the United States. Central place theory was first proposed in the 1930s by German geographer Walter Christaller, based on his studies of southern Germany.

A **central place** is a market center for the exchange of goods and services by people attracted from the surrounding area. The central place is so called because it is centrally located to maximize accessibility from the surrounding region. Central places compete against each other to serve as markets for goods and services. This competition creates a regular pattern of

settlements, according to central place theory.

The area surrounding a service from which customers are attracted is the **market area** or **hinterland**. A market area is a good example of a nodal region—a region with a core where the characteristic is most intense. To establish the market area, a circle is drawn around the node of service on a map. The territory inside the circle is its market area.

Because most people prefer to get services from the nearest location, consumers near the center of the circle obtain services from local establishments. The closer to the periphery of the circle, the greater is the percentage of consumers who will choose to obtain services from other nodes. People on the circumference of the market-area circle are equally likely to use the service, or go elsewhere (Figure 12.2.2).

▶ **12.2.1 TYPES OF CONSUMER SERVICES**
Clockwise from top left
Wholesale, such as a distribution center.
Retail, such as a department store.
Health Care, such as a hospital.
Education, such as a school.
Hospitality, such as a restaurant.

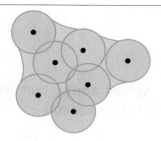

The problem with circles.
Circles are equidistant from center to edge, but they overlap or leave gaps. An arrangement of circles that leaves gaps indicates that people living in the gaps are outside the market area of any service, which is obviously not true. Overlapping circles are also unsatisfactory, for one service or another will be closer, and people will tend to patronize it.

The problem with squares.
Squares nest together without gaps, but their sides are not equidistant from the center. If the market area is a circle, the radius—the distance from the center to the edge—can be measured, because every point around a circle is the same distance from the center. But in a square the distance from the center varies among points along a square.

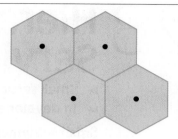

The hexagon compromise.
Geographers use hexagons to depict the market area of a good or service because hexagons offer a compromise between the geometric properties of circles and squares.

▲ 12.2.2 **WHY CENTRAL PLACE THEORY USES HEXAGONS TO DELINEATE MARKET AREAS**
Geographers use hexagons to represent market areas because of their geometric properties compared with those of circles and squares.

RANGE OF A SERVICE

The market area of every service varies. To determine the extent of a market area, geographers need two pieces of information about a service—its range and its threshold (Figure 12.2.3).

How far are you willing to drive for a pizza? To see a doctor for a serious problem? To watch a ballgame? The **range** is the maximum distance people are willing to travel to use a service. The range is the radius of the circle drawn to delineate a service's market area.

People are willing to go only a short distance for everyday consumer services, like groceries and pharmacies. But they will travel a long distance for other services, such as a major league baseball game or a concert. Thus a convenience store has a small range, whereas a stadium has a large range.

If firms at other locations compete by providing the service, the range must be modified. As a rule, people tend to go to the nearest available service: someone in the mood for a McDonald's hamburger is likely to go to the nearest McDonald's. Therefore, the range of a service must be determined from the radius of a circle that is irregularly shaped rather than perfectly round. The irregularly shaped circle takes in the territory for which the proposed site is closer than the competitors' sites.

The range must be modified further because most people think of distance in terms of time, rather than in terms of a linear measure like kilometers or miles. If you ask people how far they are willing to travel to a restaurant or a baseball game, they are more likely to answer in minutes or hours than in distance.

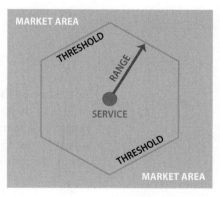

▲ 12.2.3 **MARKET AREA OF A SERVICE**
The range is the radius, and the threshold is a sufficient number of people inside the area to support the service.

THRESHOLD OF A SERVICE

The second piece of geographic information needed to compute a market area is the **threshold**, which is the minimum number of people needed to support the service. Every enterprise has a minimum number of customers required to generate enough sales to make a profit. Once the range has been determined, a service provider must determine whether a location is suitable by counting the potential customers inside the irregularly shaped circle.

How potential consumers inside the range are counted depends on the product. Convenience stores and fast-food restaurants appeal to nearly everyone, whereas other goods and services appeal primarily to certain consumer groups. Movie theaters attract younger people; chiropractors attract older folks. Poorer people are drawn to thrift stores; wealthier ones might frequent upscale department stores. Amusement parks attract families with children, but nightclubs appeal to singles. If a good or service appeals to certain customers, then only the type of good or service that appeals to them should be counted inside the range.

12.3 Hierarchy of Consumer Services

▶ **Small settlements provide services with small thresholds, ranges, and market areas.**
▶ **In developed countries, the size of settlements follows the rank-size rule.**

Small settlements are limited to consumer services that have small thresholds, short ranges, and small market areas, because too few people live in small settlements to support many services. A large department store or specialty store cannot survive in a small settlement, because the minimum number of people needed exceeds the population within range of the settlement.

Larger settlements provide consumer services having larger thresholds, ranges, and market areas. In addition, neighborhoods within large settlements also provide services having small thresholds and ranges. Services patronized by a small number of locals can coexist in a neighborhood ("mom-and-pop stores") along with services that attract many from throughout the settlement.

We spend as little time and effort as possible in obtaining consumer services and thus go to the nearest place that fulfills our needs. There is no point in traveling to a distant department store if the same merchandise is available at a nearby one. We travel greater distances only if the price is much lower or if the item is unavailable locally.

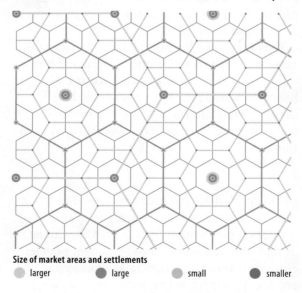

Size of market areas and settlements
⬤ larger   ⬤ large   ⬤ small   ⬤ smaller

▲ 12.3.1 **NESTING OF SETTLEMENTS AND SERVICES**
According to central place theory, market areas are arranged in a regular pattern. Larger market areas, based in large settlements, are fewer in number and farther apart from each other than smaller market areas and settlements. Larger settlements also provide services with smaller market areas; consequently larger settlements have both larger and smaller market areas drawn around them.

NESTING OF SETTLEMENTS AND SERVICES

According to central place theory, market areas across a developed country would be a series of hexagons of various sizes, unless interrupted by physical features such as mountains and bodies of water. Developed countries have numerous small settlements with small thresholds and ranges, and far fewer large settlements with large thresholds and ranges. In his original study, Walter Christaller showed that the distances between settlements in southern Germany followed a regular pattern.

The nesting pattern can be illustrated with overlapping hexagons of different sizes. Four different levels of market area—for hamlet, village, town, and city—are shown in Figure 12.3.1. Hamlets with very small market areas are represented by the smallest contiguous hexagons. Larger hexagons represent the market areas of larger settlements and are overlaid on the smaller hexagons, because consumers from smaller settlements obtain some services in larger settlements.

Across much of the interior of the United States, a regular pattern of settlements can be observed, even if not precisely the same as the generalized model shown in Figure 12.3.1. In north central North Dakota, for example, Minot—the largest city in the area, with 41,000 inhabitants—is surrounded by seven small towns with between 1,000 and 5,000 inhabitants, fifteen villages with between 100 and 999 inhabitants, and nineteen hamlets with less than 100 inhabitants (Figure 12.3.2). The small towns have average ranges of 30 kilometers (20 miles) and market areas of around 2,800 square kilometers (1,200 square miles). The hamlets have ranges of around 15 kilometers (10 miles) and market areas of around 800 square kilometers (300 square miles).

RANK-SIZE DISTRIBUTION OF SETTLEMENTS

In many developed countries, geographers observe that ranking settlements from largest to smallest (population) produces a regular pattern or hierarchy. This is the **rank-size rule**, in which the country's nth-largest settlement is 1/n the population of the largest settlement. In other words, the second-largest city is one-half the size of the largest, the fourth-largest city is one-fourth the size of the largest, and so on. When plotted on logarithmic paper, the rank-size distribution forms a fairly straight line. The distribution of settlements closely follows the rank-size rule in the United States and a handful of other countries.

If the settlement hierarchy does not graph as a straight line, then the society does not have a rank-size distribution of settlements. Several developed countries in Europe follow the rank-size distribution among smaller settlements but not among the largest ones. Instead, the largest settlement in these countries follows the **primate city rule**. According to the primate city rule, the largest settlement has more than twice as many people as the second-ranking settlement. In this distribution, the country's largest city is called the **primate city** (Figure 12.3.3).

The existence of a rank-size distribution of settlements is not merely a mathematical curiosity. It has a real impact on the quality of life for a country's inhabitants. A regular hierarchy—as in the United States—indicates that the society is sufficiently wealthy to justify the provision of goods and services to consumers throughout the country. Conversely, the primate city distribution in a developing country indicates that there is not enough wealth in the society to pay for a full variety of services (Figure 12.3.4).

▲ 12.3.2 **SETTLEMENTS IN NORTH DAKOTA** Central place theory helps to explain the distribution of settlements of varying sizes in North Dakota. Larger settlements are fewer and farther apart, whereas smaller settlements are more frequent and closer together.

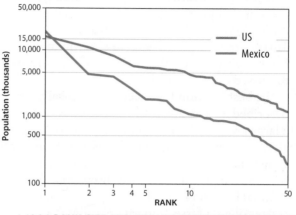

▲ 12.3.3 **RANK-SIZE AND PRIMATE CITY DISTRIBUTIONS OF SETTLEMENTS**
Mexico follows the primate city distribution. Its largest city, Mexico City, is five times larger than its second largest city, Guadalajara. The United States follows more closely the rank-size distribution, because the largest city, New York, is not that much larger than the second largest city, Los Angeles.

▶ 12.3.4 **MORELIA (above) AND BALTIMORE (right)**
Morelia and Baltimore are the twentieth largest urban settlements in Mexico and the United States, respectively. Baltimore has a population of 2.7 million compared to only 800,000 for Morelia.

12.4 Market Area Analysis

▶ Retailers determine profitability of a site by calculating the range and threshold.
▶ Site selection is facilitated through the use of GIS.

Geographers apply central place theory to create market area studies that assist service providers with opening and expanding their facilities. And in a severe economic downturn, market area analysis helps determine where to close facilities.

Service providers often say that their three most important location factors are "location, location, and location." What they actually mean is that proximity to customers is the only critical geographical factor in locating a service. This contrasts with manufacturers, who must balance a variety of site and situation factors, as discussed in Chapter 11.

The best location for a factory is typically described as a region of the world, or perhaps a large area within a region. For example, auto alley—the optimal location for most U.S. motor vehicle factories—is an area of roughly 100,000 square kilometers. For service providers, the optimal location is much more precise: one corner of an intersection can be profitable and another corner of the same intersection unprofitable.

PROFITABILITY OF A LOCATION

Would a new department store be profitable in your community (Figure 12.4.1)? The two components of central place theory described in section 12.2—range and threshold—together determine the answer. Here's how:

1. **Compute the range.** You might survey local residents and determine that people are generally willing to travel up to 15 minutes to reach a department store.

2. **Compute the threshold.** A department store typically needs roughly 250,000 people living within a 15-minute radius.

3. **Draw the market area.** Draw a circle with a 15-minute travel radius around the proposed location. Count the number of people within the circle. If more than 250,000 people are within the radius, then the threshold may be high enough to justify locating the new department store in your community. However, your store may need a larger threshold and range to attract some of the available customers if competitors are located nearby.

The threshold must also be adjusted to the fact that the further customers are from the service the less likely they are to patronize it. Geographers have adapted the gravity model from physics. The **gravity model** predicts that the optimal location of a service is directly related to the number of people in the area and inversely related to the distance people must travel to access it. The best location will be the one that minimizes the distances that all potential customers must travel to reach the service.

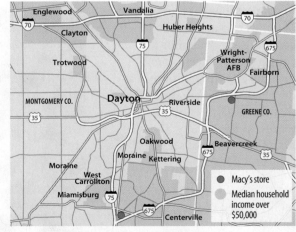

▲ 12.4.1 **MARKET AREA, RANGE, AND THRESHOLD FOR MACY'S DEPARTMENT STORES IN THE DAYTON, OHIO, METROPOLITAN AREA**

LOCATING A NEW RETAIL STORE

Major U.S. department store chains, mall developers, and other large retailers employ geographers to determine the best locations to build new stores. A large retailer has many locations to choose from when deciding to build new stores. A suitable site is one with the potential for generating enough sales to justify using the company's scarce capital to build it. Here are the steps for a large supermarket:

1. **Define market area.** The first step in forecasting sales for a proposed new retail outlet is to define the market or trade area where the store would derive most of its sales. Analysis relies heavily on the company's records of their customers' credit-card transactions at existing stores. What are the zip codes of customers who paid by credit card? The market area of a department store is typically defined as the zip codes where two-thirds to three-fourths of the customers live. Walmart locates most of its stores on the edge of the city, because that is where most of its customers live (Figure 12.4.2).

2. **Estimate range.** Based on the zip codes of credit-card customers, geographers estimate that the range for a large supermarket is about a 10-minute driving time.

3. **Estimate threshold.** The threshold for a large supermarket is about 25,000 people living within the 15-minute range with appropriate income levels. Walmart typically is attracted to areas of modest means, whereas supermarkets like Kroger, Publix, and Safeway prefer to be near higher income people. In the Dayton, Ohio, area, for example, Kroger has most of its stores in the relatively affluent south and east (Figure 12.4.3).

4. **Market share.** The proposed new supermarket will have to share customers with competitors. Geographers typically predict market share through the so-called analog method. One or more existing stores are identified in locations that the geographer judges to be comparable to the location of the proposed store. The market share of the comparable stores is applied to the proposed new store.

Information about the viability of a proposed new store is depicted through GIS. One layer of the GIS depicts the trade area of the proposed store. Other layers display characteristics of the people living in the area, such as distribution of households, average income, and competitors' stores.

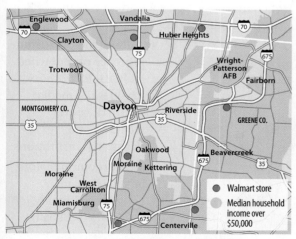

▲ 12.4.2 **MARKET AREA, RANGE, AND THRESHOLD FOR WALMART STORES IN THE DAYTON, OHIO, METROPOLITAN AREA**

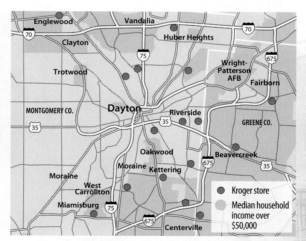

▲ 12.4.3 **MARKET AREA, RANGE, AND THRESHOLD FOR KROGER SUPERMARKETS IN THE DAYTON, OHIO, METROPOLITAN AREA**

12.5 Hierarchy of Business Services

▶ **A hierarchy of world cities can be identified based on business services.**
▶ **A hierarchy of cities also exists inside the United States.**

Every settlement provides consumer services to people in a surrounding area, but not every settlement of a given size has the same number and types of business services. Business services disproportionately cluster in a handful of settlements.

BUSINESS SERVICES IN WORLD CITIES

Geographers distinguish settlements according to their importance in the provision of business services. At the top of the hierarchy are settlements known as world cities or global cities that play an especially important role in global business services. World cities are most closely integrated into the global economic system because they are at the center of the flow of information and capital.

- Headquarters of large corporations are clustered in world cities, and shares of these corporations are bought and sold on the stock exchanges located in world cities. Obtaining information in a timely manner is essential in order to buy and sell shares at attractive prices.

- Lawyers, accountants, and other professionals cluster in world cities to provide advice to major corporations and financial institutions. Advertising agencies, marketing firms, and other services concerned with style and fashion locate in world cities to help corporations anticipate changes in taste and to help shape those changes.

- As centers for finance, world cities attract the headquarters of the major banks, insurance companies, and specialized financial institutions where corporations obtain and store funds for expansion of production.

- World cities also contain a disproportionately high share of the world's arts, culture, consumer spending on luxury goods, and political power.

Global cities are divided into three levels, called alpha, beta, and gamma. These three levels in turn are further subdivided (Figure 12.5.1). A combination of economic, political, cultural, and infrastructure factors are used to identify world cities and to distinguish among the various ranks.

- Economic factors include the number of headquarters for multinational corporations, financial institutions, and law firms that influence the world economy.

- Political factors include hosting headquarters for international organizations and capitals of countries that play a leading role in international events.

- Cultural factors include presence of renowned cultural institutions, influential media outlets, sports facilities, and educational institutions.

- Infrastructural factors include a major international airport, health-care facilities, and advanced communications systems.

▼ 12.5.1 **HIERARCHY OF WORLD CITIES**

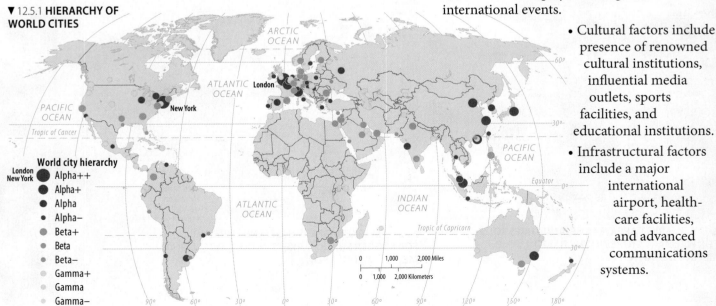

World city hierarchy
London New York ● Alpha++
● Alpha+
● Alpha
● Alpha−
● Beta+
● Beta
● Beta−
● Gamma+
● Gamma
● Gamma−

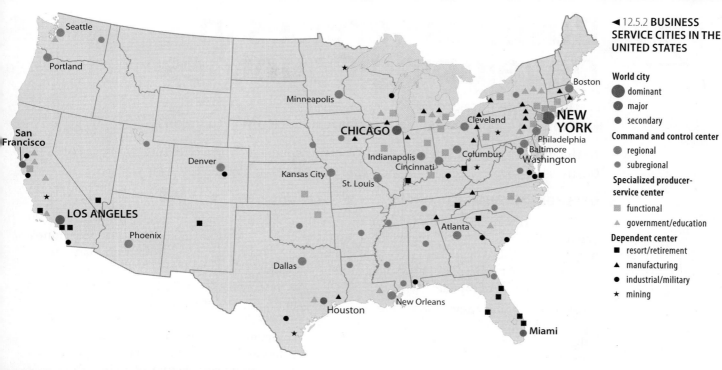

◄ 12.5.2 **BUSINESS SERVICE CITIES IN THE UNITED STATES**

World city
- 🔵 dominant
- 🔵 major
- 🔵 secondary

Command and control center
- 🔵 regional
- 🔵 subregional

Specialized producer-service center
- 🟦 functional
- 🔺 government/education

Dependent center
- ◼ resort/retirement
- ▲ manufacturing
- ● industrial/military
- ★ mining

THREE LOWER TIERS OF BUSINESS SERVICES

Below the first tier of world cities are three other tiers of settlements according to type and extent of business services. Examples of each can be seen in the United States (Figure 12.5.2). The world cities in the United States are shown in Figure 12.5.3.

Second tier: command and control centers. These contain the headquarters of many large corporations, well-developed banking facilities, and concentrations of other business services, including insurance, accounting, advertising, law, and public relations. Important educational, medical, and public institutions can be found in these command and control centers. Examples include Baltimore, Cleveland, Phoenix, and St. Louis.

Third tier: specialized producer-service centers. These offer narrower and more highly specialized services. One group of these cities specializes in the management and R&D (research and development) activities related to specific industries, such as Detroit (motor vehicles), Pittsburgh (steel), and Rochester (office equipment). A second group of these cities specializes as centers of government and education, notably state capitals that also have a major university, such as Albany, Lansing, and Madison.

Fourth tier: dependent centers. These provide relatively unskilled jobs. Four subgroups include:

- Resort, retirement, and residential centers, such as Albuquerque, Fort Lauderdale, Las Vegas, and Orlando, clustered in the South and West.

- Manufacturing centers, such as Buffalo, Chattanooga, Erie, and Rockford, clustered mostly in the old northeastern manufacturing belt.

- Military centers, such as Huntsville, Newport News, and San Diego, clustered mostly in the South and West.

- Mining and industrial centers, such as Charleston, West Virginia, and Duluth, Minnesota, located in mining areas.

► 12.5.3 **THE U.S. WORLD CITIES: LOS ANGELES (top), CHICAGO (middle), NEW YORK (bottom)**

12.6 Business Services in Developing Countries

▶ **Offshore centers provide financial services.**
▶ **Some developing countries specialize in back office functions.**

In the global economy, developing countries specialize in two distinctive types of business services: offshore financial services and back office functions.

OFFSHORE FINANCIAL SERVICES

Small countries, usually islands and microstates, exploit niches in the circulation of global capital by offering offshore financial services. Offshore centers provide two important functions in the global circulation of capital:

- **Taxes.** Taxes on income, profits, and capital gains are typically low or nonexistent in these locations. Companies incorporated in an offshore center also have tax-free status regardless of the nationality of the owners.

- **Privacy.** Bank secrecy laws help individuals and businesses evade disclosure in their home countries. People and corporations can protect their assets from lawsuits by depositing their money in offshore banks. Creditors cannot reach such assets in bankruptcy hearings. The privacy laws and low tax rates in offshore centers can also provide havens to tax dodges and other illegal schemes.

Offshore centers include dependencies of the United Kingdom and other developed countries, as well as independent countries. Many are islands (Figure 12.6.1). A prominent example is the Cayman Islands, a British Crown Colony in the Caribbean near Cuba. The Caymans have only 40,000 inhabitants, but there are 70,000 companies there, including several hundred banks and the world's four largest legal and accounting firms (Figure 12.6.2).

In the Caymans, it is a crime to discuss confidential business—defined as matters learned on the job—in public. Assets placed in an offshore center by an individual or corporation in a trust are not covered by lawsuits originating in other countries. To get at those assets, additional lawsuits would have to be filed in the offshore centers, where privacy laws would shield the individual or corporation from undesired disclosures.

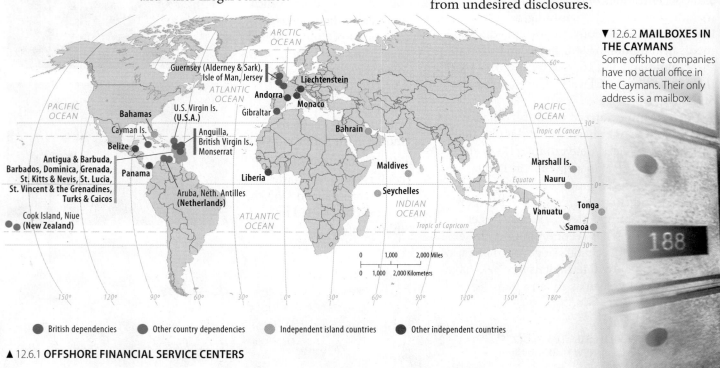

▼ 12.6.2 **MAILBOXES IN THE CAYMANS**
Some offshore companies have no actual office in the Caymans. Their only address is a mailbox.

▲ 12.6.1 **OFFSHORE FINANCIAL SERVICE CENTERS**

BACK OFFICES

Developing countries are increasingly centers for back-office functions, also known as business-process outsourcing. Typical back-office functions include processing insurance claims, payroll management, transcription work, and other routine clerical activities. Back-office work also includes centers for responding to billing inquiries related to credit cards, shipments, and claims, or technical inquiries related to installation, operation, and repair. Need to have your computer fixed? Correct a mistake on your credit card bill? Change your plane reservation? The human you have reached is probably at a call center in a developing country (Figure 12.6.3).

Traditionally, companies housed their back-office staff in the same office building as their management staff, or at least in nearby buildings. A large percentage of the employees in a downtown bank building, for example, would be responsible for sorting paper checks and deposit slips. Proximity was considered important to assure close supervision of routine office workers and rapid turnaround of information. For many business services, improved telecommunications have eliminated the need for spatial proximity.

Selective developing countries have attracted back offices for two reasons related to labor:

- **Low Wages.** Most back-office workers earn a few thousand dollars per year—higher than wages paid in most other sectors of the economy, but only one-tenth the wages paid for workers performing similar jobs in developed countries.

▲ 12.6.3 **CALL CENTER, BANGALORE, INDIA**

- **Ability to Speak English.** A handful of developing countries possess a large labor force fluent in English (Figure 12.6.4). In Asia, countries such as India, Malaysia, and the Philippines have substantial numbers of workers with English-language skills, a legacy of British and American colonial rule. The ability to communicate in English over the telephone is a strategic advantage in competing for back offices with neighboring countries, such as Indonesia and Thailand, where English is less commonly used. Familiarity with English is an advantage not only for literally answering the telephone but also for gaining a better understanding of the preferences of American consumers through exposure to English-language music, movies, and television.

▲ 12.6.4
ADVERTISEMENT, BANGALORE, INDIA

Call-center employees must be able to understand what a customer located in North America is trying to say and must be able to respond clearly in language understood by a "typical" North American. Call centers in Asia pretend that they are located in North America and are employing Americans. But in one respect, they can't escape the "tyranny" of geography. Refer to Figure 1.4.4, the map of world time zones. In the middle of the day, when most Americans are placing calls, it is the middle of the night in Asia. So call center employees in Asia typically work all night.

12.7 Economic Base

▶ **Settlements can be classified by their economic base.**
▶ **Talent is not distributed uniformly among cities.**

A settlement's distinctive economic structure derives from its **basic industries**, which export primarily to businesses and individuals outside the settlement. **Nonbasic industries** are enterprises whose customers live in the same community—essentially, consumer services. A community's unique collection of basic industries defines its **economic base**.

A settlement's economic base is important, because exporting by the basic industries brings money into the local economy, thus stimulating the provision of more nonbasic consumer services for the settlement. New basic industries attract new workers to a settlement, and they bring their families with them. The settlement then attracts additional consumer services to meet the needs of the new workers and their families. Thus a new basic industry stimulates establishment of new supermarkets, laundromats, restaurants, and other consumer services. But a new nonbasic service, such as a supermarket, will not induce construction of new basic industries.

SPECIALIZING IN SPECIFIC SERVICES

Settlements in the United States can be classified by their type of basic activity (Figure 12.7.1). Each type of basic activity has a different spatial distribution. The concept of basic industries originally referred to manufacturing. In a postindustrial society, such as the United States, increasingly the basic economic activities are in services.

 Examples of settlements specializing in business services include:

- General business: New York, Los Angeles, Chicago, and San Francisco.

- Computing and data processing services: Boston and San Jose.

- High-tech industries support services: Austin, Orlando, and Raleigh-Durham.

- Military activity support services: Albuquerque, Colorado Springs, Huntsville, Knoxville, and Norfolk.

- Management-consulting services: Washington, D.C.

Examples of settlements specializing in consumer services:

- Entertainment and recreation: Atlantic City, Las Vegas, and Reno.

- Medical services: Rochester, Minnesota.

Examples of settlements specializing in public services:

- State capitals: Sacramento and Tallahassee.

- Large universities: Tuscaloosa.

- Military: Arlington.

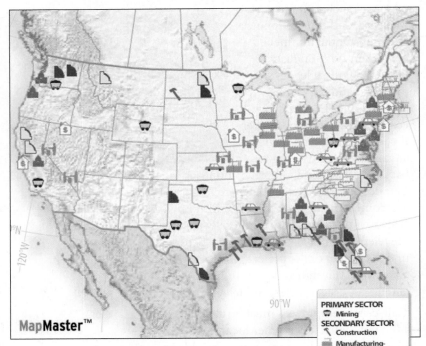

MapMaster™

▲ 12.7.1 **ECONOMIC BASE OF U.S. CITIES**
Cities have distinctive economic bases.
Launch MapMaster North America in Mastering**GEOGRAPHY**™

Select: *Economic* then *Economic base of U.S. cities*

Select: *Political* then *Cities*

What is the name of a city whose economic base is mining? Construction? Manufacturing durable goods? Manufacturing nondurable goods? Retail? Wholesale? Personal services? Finance? Transportation? Public services?

PRIMARY SECTOR
⛏ Mining
SECONDARY SECTOR
⟍ Construction
▦ Manufacturing-
Durable goods
⬯ Manufacturing-
Nondurable goods
CONSUMER SERVICES
▭ Retail trade
◣ Wholesale trade
▮▮ Personal services
BUSINESS SERVICES
Ⓢ Finance, insurance, real estate
⟺ Transportation, communication and public utilities
PUBLIC SERVICES
▲ Public Services

DISTRIBUTION OF TALENT

Individuals possessing special talents are not distributed uniformly among cities. Some cities have a higher percentage of talented individuals than others (Figure 12.7.2). Talent was measured by Richard Florida as a combination of the percentage of people in the city with college degrees, the percentage employed as scientists or engineers, and the percentage employed as professionals or technicians.

Florida found a significant positive relationship between the distribution of talent and the distribution of cultural diversity in the largest U.S. cities (Figure 12.7.3). In other words, cities with high cultural diversity tended to have relatively high percentages of talented individuals (Figure 12.7.4). Attracting talented individuals is important for a city, because these individuals are responsible for promoting economic innovation. They are likely to start new businesses and infuse the local economy with fresh ideas.

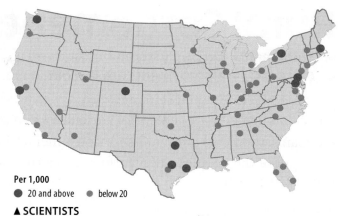

◄ 12.7.2 GEOGRAPHY OF TALENT

Per 1,000
● 20 and above ● below 20
▲ SCIENTISTS

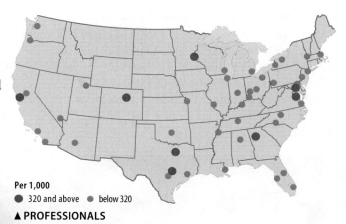

Per 1,000
● 320 and above ● below 320
▲ PROFESSIONALS

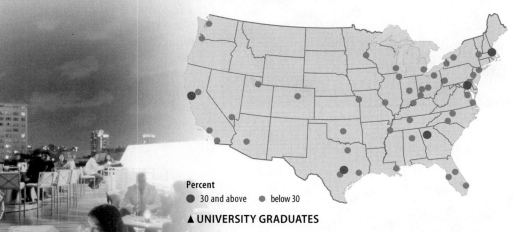

Percent
● 30 and above ● below 30
▲ UNIVERSITY GRADUATES

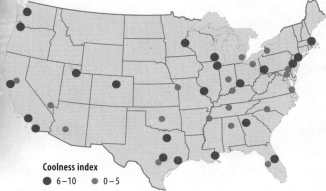

Coolness index
● 6–10 ● 0–5

◄ 12.7.4 GEOGRAPHY OF CULTURAL DIVERSITY
The map is based on a "coolness" index, developed by POV Magazine, combined the percentage of population in their 20s, the number of bars and other nightlife places per capita, and the number of art galleries per capita.

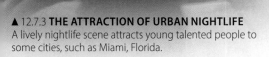

▲ 12.7.3 **THE ATTRACTION OF URBAN NIGHTLIFE**
A lively nightlife scene attracts young talented people to some cities, such as Miami, Florida.

12.8 Rural Settlements

▶ **Settlements can be clustered or dispersed.**
▶ **Clustered rural settlements are laid out in many types of patterns.**

Services are clustered in settlements.
• Rural settlements are centers for agriculture and provide a small number of services.
• Urban settlements are centers for consumer and business services.
One-half of the people in the world live in a rural settlement and the other half in an urban settlement.

DISPERSED RURAL SETTLEMENTS

A **dispersed rural settlement,** typical of the contemporary North American rural landscape, is characterized by farmers living on individual farms isolated from neighbors rather than alongside other farmers in settlements (Figure 12.8.1).

A dispersed settlement pattern originated with American colonists, primarily in the Middle Atlantic colonies. Individuals such as William Penn (Pennsylvania), Lord Baltimore (Maryland), and Sir George Carteret (the Carolinas) received large land grants by the King of England and in turn sold tracts to individual colonists. Pioneers, primarily from the Middle Atlantic colonies, crossed the Appalachian Mountains and established dispersed farms on the frontier. Land was plentiful and cheap, and people bought as much as they could manage.

◀ 12.8.1 **DISPERSED RURAL SETTLEMENT**
Use Google Earth to explore the dispersed settlement pattern in northern North Dakota.

Fly to: *Russell, North Dakota*

Zoom out until your screen begins to resemble a checkerboard.

1. **What is one personal quality a resident of this landscape would need to possess? Explain your answer.**

2. **What physical features interrupt the checkerboard pattern in the east?**

(below) Farm in northern North Dakota.

CLUSTERED RURAL SETTLEMENTS

A **clustered rural settlement** is an agricultural-based community in which a number of families live in close proximity to each other, with fields surrounding the collection of houses and farm buildings. A clustered rural settlement typically includes homes, barns, tool sheds, and other farm structures, plus consumer services, such as religious structures, schools, and shops. A handful of public and business services may also be present in the clustered rural settlement, often centered on an open area called a common.

Much of rural England was laid out in clustered settlements (Figure 12.8.2). When early English settlers reached New England they originally built clustered settlements. They typically traveled to the New World in a group and wanted to live close together to reinforce common cultural and religious values. The contemporary New England landscape contains remnants of the old clustered rural settlement pattern.

▲ 12.8.2 **CLUSTERED RURAL SETTLEMENT**
Use Google Earth to explore an English village.

Fly to: *Finchingfield, England*

Zoom in until Finchingfield occupies most of the Google Earth screen.

1. **Where is the center of Finchingfield?**
2. **How were you able to identify it?**

▲ 12.8.3 **CLUSTERED LINEAR RURAL SETTLEMENT**
Use Google Earth to explore settlement patterns along the St. Lawrence River.

Fly to: *Les Bricailles, Québec*

Drag the Street View icon west from the Les Bricailles placemark to the highway where it passes open fields and explore the landscape along the highway.

1. **How would you describe the landscape of Les Bricailles?**
Exit street view and zoom out until you can see both banks of the St. Lawrence River.

2. **Why might it be an advantage to farmers to own narrow strips of land extending far inland from the river?**

CLUSTERED LINEAR RURAL SETTLEMENTS

Clustered rural settlements are sometimes arranged in a geometric pattern. Linear rural settlements feature buildings clustered along a road or body of water to facilitate transportation and communications. The fields extend behind the buildings in long narrow strips (Figure 12.8.3). Long-lot farms can be seen today along the St. Lawrence River in Québec.

CLUSTERED CIRCULAR RURAL SETTLEMENTS

The clustered circular rural settlement consists of a central open space surrounded by structures. Von Thünen observed this circular rural pattern in Germany in his landmark agricultural studies in the early nineteenth century (refer to section 10.10). Germany's Gewandorf settlements consisted of a core of houses, barns, and churches encircled by different types of agricultural activities.

In sub-Saharan Africa, the Maasi people, who are pastoral nomads, build circular settlements known as kraal; women have the principal responsibility for constructing them. The kraal villages have enclosures for livestock in the center, surrounded by a ring of houses. Compare *kraal* to the English word *corral* (Figure 12.8.4).

▼ 12.8.4 **CLUSTERED CIRCULAR RURAL SETTLEMENT**
Maasi kraal settlement, Kenya.

12.9 Settlements in History

▶ Settlements originated in multiple hearths and diffused in multiple directions.
▶ Through history, the world's largest settlement has usually been in Southwest Asia, Egypt, or China.

Permanent settlements existed prior to the beginning of recorded history around 5,000 years ago. The earliest settlements may have been established as service centers:

- **Consumer services.** The first permanent settlements may have been places for nomads to bury and honor their dead. They were also places to house women and children while males hunted for food. Women made tools, clothing, and containers.

- **Business services.** Early settlements were places where groups could store surplus food and trade with other groups.

- **Public services.** Early settlements housed political leaders, as well as military forces to guard the residents of the settlement.

Settlements may have originated in Mesopotamia, part of the Fertile Crescent of Southwest Asia, and diffused at an early date west to Egypt and east to China and South Asia's Indus Valley. Or they may have originated independently in each of the four hearths. In any case, from these four hearths, the concept of settlements diffused to the rest of the world.

Until around 300 B.C., the world's largest settlements were in Mesopotamia and Egypt (Figure 12.9.1). Ancient Memphis, Egypt, may have been the first settlement to exceed 30,000 inhabitants around 5,000 years ago (Figure 12.9.2). Beginning around 2,400 years ago, as settlements diffused from Southwest Asia, settlements in India, China, and Europe frequently emerged as the world's largest. Constantinople (now Istanbul, Turkey) was the world's largest settlement for the longest stretch of time during the Middle Ages (Figures 12.9.3 and 12.9.4).

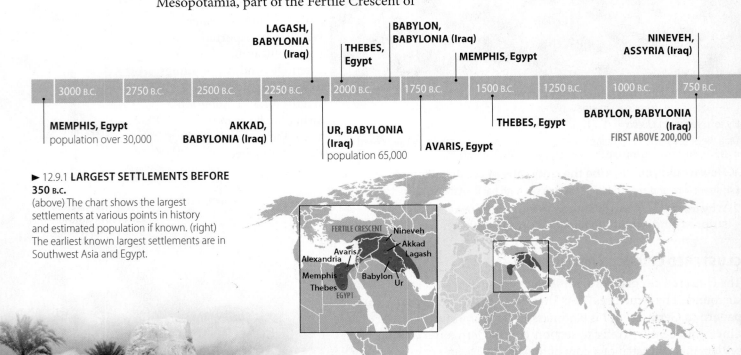

	LAGASH, BABYLONIA (Iraq)	THEBES, Egypt	BABYLON, BABYLONIA (Iraq)	MEMPHIS, Egypt		NINEVEH, ASSYRIA (Iraq)
3000 B.C.	2750 B.C.	2500 B.C.	2250 B.C.	2000 B.C.	1750 B.C.	1500 B.C.	1250 B.C.	1000 B.C.	750 B.C.

MEMPHIS, Egypt
population over 30,000

AKKAD, BABYLONIA (Iraq)

UR, BABYLONIA (Iraq)
population 65,000

AVARIS, Egypt

THEBES, Egypt

BABYLON, BABYLONIA (Iraq)
FIRST ABOVE 200,000

▶ 12.9.1 **LARGEST SETTLEMENTS BEFORE 350 B.C.**
(above) The chart shows the largest settlements at various points in history and estimated population if known. (right) The earliest known largest settlements are in Southwest Asia and Egypt.

◀ 12.9.2 **MEMPHIS, EGYPT**
The Alabaster Sphinx was constructed around 3,500 years ago near Memphis, Egypt, which at the time was probably the world's largest urban settlement.

► 12.9.3 **LARGEST SETTLEMENTS 350 B.C.–1750 A.D.**
For the past 2,000 years, the world's largest cities have been located for the most part in Asia.

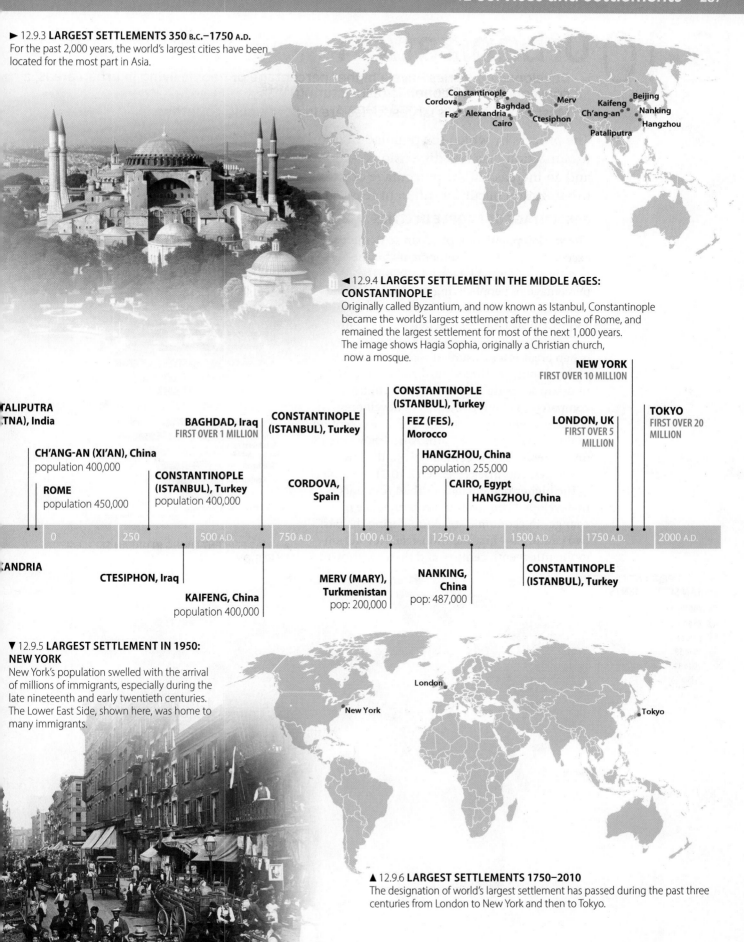

◄ 12.9.4 **LARGEST SETTLEMENT IN THE MIDDLE AGES: CONSTANTINOPLE**
Originally called Byzantium, and now known as Istanbul, Constantinople became the world's largest settlement after the decline of Rome, and remained the largest settlement for most of the next 1,000 years. The image shows Hagia Sophia, originally a Christian church, now a mosque.

TALIPUTRA (TNA), India

CH'ANG-AN (XI'AN), China
population 400,000

ROME
population 450,000

BAGHDAD, Iraq
FIRST OVER 1 MILLION

CONSTANTINOPLE (ISTANBUL), Turkey
population 400,000

CONSTANTINOPLE (ISTANBUL), Turkey

CORDOVA, Spain

CONSTANTINOPLE (ISTANBUL), Turkey

FEZ (FES), Morocco

HANGZHOU, China
population 255,000

CAIRO, Egypt

HANGZHOU, China

NEW YORK
FIRST OVER 10 MILLION

LONDON, UK
FIRST OVER 5 MILLION

TOKYO
FIRST OVER 20 MILLION

0 | 250 | 500 A.D. | 750 A.D. | 1000 A.D. | 1250 A.D. | 1500 A.D. | 1750 A.D. | 2000 A.D.

ANDRIA

CTESIPHON, Iraq

KAIFENG, China
population 400,000

MERV (MARY), Turkmenistan
pop: 200,000

NANKING, China
pop: 487,000

CONSTANTINOPLE (ISTANBUL), Turkey

▼ 12.9.5 **LARGEST SETTLEMENT IN 1950: NEW YORK**
New York's population swelled with the arrival of millions of immigrants, especially during the late nineteenth and early twentieth centuries. The Lower East Side, shown here, was home to many immigrants.

▲ 12.9.6 **LARGEST SETTLEMENTS 1750–2010**
The designation of world's largest settlement has passed during the past three centuries from London to New York and then to Tokyo.

12.10 Urbanization

▶ **Developed countries have a higher percentage of people living in urban areas, a consequence of economic restructuring.**

▶ **Most of the world's largest cities are in developing countries.**

The process by which the population of urban settlements grows, known as urbanization, has two dimensions—an increase in the number of people living in cities and an increase in the percentage of people living in cities. These two dimensions of urbanization occur for different reasons and have different global distributions.

PERCENTAGE OF PEOPLE IN CITIES

The world's population of urban settlements exceeded that of rural settlements for the first time in human history in 2008. The percentage of people living in cities increased from 3 percent in 1800 to 6 percent in 1850, 14 percent in 1900, and 30 percent in 1950.

A large percentage of people living in urban areas is a measure of a country's level of development. Three-fourths of people live in urban settlements in developed countries, compared to about two-fifths in developing countries (Figure 12.10.1). The major exception to the global pattern is Latin America, where the urban percentage is comparable to the level of developed countries (Figure 12.10.2).

The higher percentage of urban residents in developed countries is a consequence of changes in economic structure during the past two centuries—first the Industrial Revolution in the nineteenth century and then the growth

of services in the twentieth century. During the past 200 years rural residents in developed countries have migrated from the countryside to work in the factories and services that are concentrated in cities.

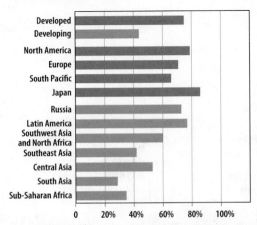

▲ 12.10.2 **PERCENT LIVING IN URBAN SETTLEMENTS BY REGION**

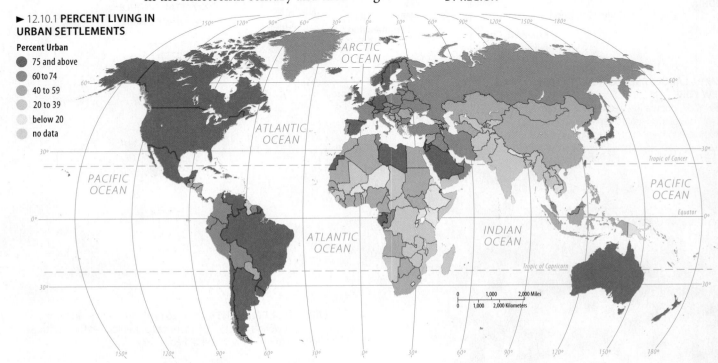

▶ 12.10.1 **PERCENT LIVING IN URBAN SETTLEMENTS**

Percent Urban
- 75 and above
- 60 to 74
- 40 to 59
- 20 to 39
- below 20
- no data

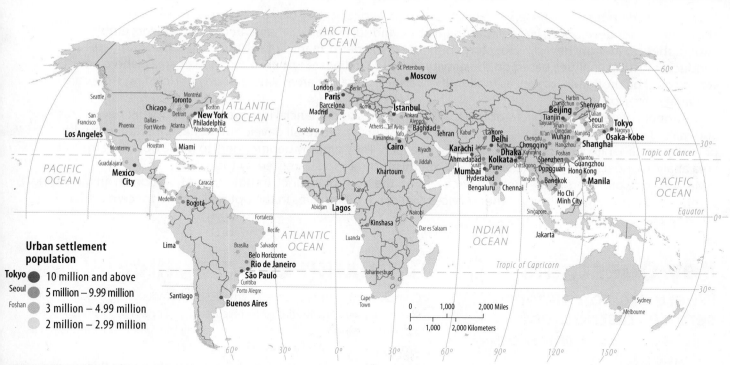

▲ 12.10.3 **URBAN SETTLEMENTS WITH AT LEAST 3 MILLION INHABITANTS**

Urban settlement population

- Tokyo — 10 million and above
- Seoul — 5 million – 9.99 million
- Foshan — 3 million – 4.99 million
- 2 million – 2.99 million

NUMBER OF PEOPLE IN CITIES

Developed countries have a higher percentage of urban residents, but developing countries have more of the very large urban settlements (Figure 12.10.3). Seven of the ten (and sixteen of the twenty) most populous cities are in developing countries.

Identifying the world's largest cities is difficult, because each country defines cities in a unique manner. *Demographia* uses maps and satellite imagery to delineate urban areas consistently regardless of country. According to *Demographia*, 171 urban areas have at least 2 million inhabitants, 105 at least 3 million, 55 at least 5 million, 22 at least 10 million, and 4 (Tokyo, Jakarta, New York, and Seoul) at least 20 million.

That developing countries dominate the list of largest urban settlements is remarkable because urbanization was once associated with economic development. In 1900, after diffusion of the Industrial Revolution from Great Britain to Europe and North America, all ten of the world's largest cities were in developed countries.

Compare the world's most populous cities to the most important business service centers (refer to Figure 12.5.1). Several of the world's most populous cities in developing countries—including Jakarta, Manila, and Mexico City—do not rank among the world's most important business service centers (Figure 12.10.4). On the other hand, cities in developed countries such as London, Paris, Chicago, and Toronto rank among the world's twenty most important settlements for business services but are not among the twenty most populous.

▼ 12.10.4 **MEXICO CITY**

Geographers do not merely observe the distribution of services; they play a major role in creating it. Shopping center developers, large department store and supermarket chains, and other retailers employ geographers to identify new sites for stores and assess the performance of existing stores. Geographers conduct statistical analyses based on the gravity model to delineate underserved market areas where new stores could be profitable, as well as to identify overserved market areas where poorly performing stores are candidates for closure.

Developers of new retail services obtain loans from banks and financial institutions to construct new stores and malls. Lending institutions want assurance that the proposed retail development has a market area with potential to generate sufficient profits to repay the loan. They employ geographers to make objective market-area analyses independent of the excessively optimistic forecasts submitted by the retailer.

Many service providers make location decisions on the basis of instinct, intuition, and tradition. In an increasingly competitive market, retailers and other services that place themselves in the optimal location secure a critical advantage.

Key Questions

Where are consumer services distributed?

► Three types of services are consumer, business, and public.

► In developed countries, the distribution of consumer services follows a regular pattern, explained through central place theory.

► Services have market areas, ranges, and thresholds that can be measured.

► Geographers apply central place theory to identify profitable locations for services.

Where are business services distributed?

► Business services are disproportionately clustered in world cities.

► Distinctive business services in developing countries include offshore financial services and back offices.

► Talented people are attracted to world cities by cultural diversity.

Where are settlements distributed?

► Outside North America, most rural settlements are clustered.

► The first settlements predate recorded history.

► Developed countries have higher percentages of urban dwellers, whereas developing countries have most of the world's largest cities.

Thinking Geographically

Consult Wikipedia's Global Cities article. Several indexes are included, with somewhat varying criteria. Some cities (such as London and Singapore) are included in the top ten global cities on all lists, whereas others (such as Sydney and Shanghai) are not (Figure 12.CR.1).

1. **Identify a city in a developed country in addition to Sydney and a city in a developing country in addition to Shanghai that do not appear among the top ten global cities on all lists. What factors have caused these two cities to be included or excluded?**

Your community's economy is expanding or contracting as a result of the performance of its basic industries. Two factors can explain the performance of your community's basic industries. One is that the sector is expanding or contracting nationally. The other is that the sector is performing much better or worse in your community than in the country as a whole.

2. **Which of the two factors better explains the performance of your community's basic industries?**

In a developed region like North America, even cities not classified as world cities are connected to the global economy.

3. **What evidence can you find in your community of economic ties to world cities located elsewhere in North America? In other regions?**

▼ 12.CR.1 **SYDNEY, AUSTRALIA**

Interactive Mapping

CITIES AND PHYSICAL FEATURES IN EAST ASIA

China's largest cities are not distributed uniformly across the country.

Launch MapMaster East Asia in

Mastering GEOGRAPHY

Select *Physical features*

Select *Cities* from *Political* menu

1. **In which physical regions are China's cities clustered?**

2. **Where are there fewer cities?**

3. **How can you explain this pattern?**

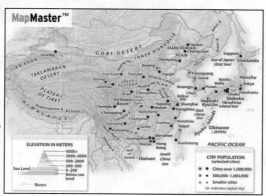

Explore

UR, IRAQ

Use Google Earth to explore one of the world's oldest cities.

Fly to: *Ur, Nassriya Iraq*

Click 3D Buildings layer in the Primary Database.

Zoom in until the runways of an airstrip appear to the northeast. Then center on the runways.

Notice the dark oval shape about 1.25 miles to the northeast. Recenter and zoom in on the oval until a 3D building appears.

1. **Measure the dimensions of the 3D building. Is it larger or smaller than your house?**

2. **What can you infer about the history of this site from the size and shape of the building and the dark, oval area around it?**

On the Internet

The population of cities organized by country can be accessed at **http://www.citypopulation.de/World.html** or scan the QR on the first page of the chapter.

An attempt to apply the same definition to measuring the population of cities everywhere has been published by *Demographia*, accessed at **www.demographia.com**. Wendell Cox, a private consultant, is the sole owner of Demographia.

Key Terms

Basic industries
Industries that sell their products or services primarily to consumers outside the settlement.

Business services
Services that primarily meet the needs of other businesses, including professional, financial, and transportation services.

Central place
A market center for the exchange of services by people attracted from the surrounding area.

Central place theory
A theory that explains the distribution of services, based on the fact that settlements serve as centers of market areas for services; larger settlements are fewer and farther apart than smaller settlements and provide services for a larger number of people who are willing to travel farther.

Clustered rural settlement
An agricultural based community in which a number of families live in close proximity to each other, with fields surrounding the collection of houses and farm buildings.

Consumer services
Businesses that provide services primarily to individual consumers, including retail services and education, health, and leisure services.

Dispersed rural settlement
A rural settlement pattern in which farmers live on individual farms isolated from neighbors.

Economic base
A community's collection of basic industries.

Gravity model
A model that holds that the potential use of a service at a particular location is directly related to the number of people in a location and inversely related to the distance people must travel to reach the service.

Market area (or hinterland)
The area surrounding a central place, from which people are attracted to use the place's goods and services.

Nonbasic industries
Industries that sell their products primarily to consumers in the community.

Primate city
The largest settlement in a country, if it has more than twice as many people as the second-ranking settlement.

Primate city rule
A pattern of settlements in a country, such that the largest settlement has more than twice as many people as the second-ranking settlement.

Public services
Services offered by the government to provide security and protection for citizens and businesses.

Range (of a service)
The maximum distance people are willing to travel to use a service.

Rank-size rule
A pattern of settlements in a country, such that the nth largest settlement is 1/n the population of the largest settlement.

Service
Any activity that fulfills a human want or need and returns money to those who provide it.

Threshold
The minimum number of people needed to support the service.

▶ LOOKING AHEAD

This chapter has looked at the distribution of cities across the world. The next chapter focuses on the distribution of people and activities within cities.

13 Urban Patterns

When you stand at the corner of Fifth Avenue and 34th Street in New York City, staring up at the Empire State Building, you know that you are in a city. When you are standing in an Iowa cornfield, you have no doubt that you are in the country. Geographers help explain what makes city and countryside different places.

A large city is stimulating and agitating, entertaining and frightening, welcoming and cold. A city has something for everyone, but a lot of those things are for people different from you. Urban geography helps to sort out the complexities of familiar and unfamiliar patterns in urban areas. Models help to explain where different people and activities are distributed within urban areas, and why those differences occur.

Where are people distributed within urban areas?

URBAN SPRAWL INTO THE DESERT, PHOENIX, ARIZONA

How are urban areas expanding?

What challenges do cities face?

SCAN FOR CENSUS
MAPS OF EVERY
U.S. CITY

13.1 The Central Business District

▶ **Downtown is known as the central business district (CBD).**
▶ **The CBD contains consumer, business, and public services.**

The best-known and most visually distinctive area of most cities is the central area, commonly called downtown and known to geographers by the more precise term **central business district (CBD)**. The CBD is usually one of the oldest districts in a city, often the original site of the settlement (Figure 13.1.1).

Consumer, business, and public services are attracted to the CBD because of its accessibility. The center is the easiest part of the city to reach from the rest of the region and is the focal point of the region's transportation network (Figure 13.1.2).

▲ 13.1.1 **LAND USES IN CBD OF WILKES-BARRE, PENNSYLVANIA**
Wilkes-Barre, a city of 40,000 inhabitants, has a downtown typical of U.S. cities, with a mix of business, consumer, and public services.

- Business services
- Consumer services
- Public and semipublic services
- Education
- Residential
- Vacant
- Park
- Parking

▼ 13.1.2 **WILKES-BARRE'S CBD**
Wilkes-Barre's CBD is situated along the south bank of the Susquehanna River.

Susquehanna River

BUSINESS SERVICES

Even with modern telecommunications, many professionals still exchange information primarily through face-to-face contact. Business services, such as advertising, banking, finance, journalism, and law, are centrally located to facilitate rapid communication of fast-breaking news (Figure 13.1.3). Face-to-face contact also helps to establish a relationship of trust based on shared professional values.

People in such businesses particularly depend on proximity to professional colleagues. Lawyers, for example, locate near government offices and courts. Services such as temporary secretarial agencies and instant printers locate downtown to be near lawyers, forming a chain of interdependency that continues to draw offices to the center city.

Extreme competition for limited building sites results in very high land values in the CBD. Because of its high value, land is used more intensively in the center than elsewhere in the city.

Compared to other parts of the city, the central area uses more space below and above ground level. Beneath most central cities runs a vast underground network of garages, loading docks, utilities, walkways, and transit lines. Demand for space in the central city has also made high-rise structures economically feasible.

▲ 13.1.3 **BUSINESS SERVICES IN WILKES-BARRE'S CBD**
Downtown office buildings house several banks.

▲ 13.1.4 **CONSUMER SERVICES IN WILKES-BARRE'S CBD**
F.M. Kirby Center for the Performing Arts.

CONSUMER SERVICES

Consumer services in the CBD serve the many people who work in the center and shop during lunch or working hours. These businesses sell office supplies, computers, and clothing, or offer shoe repair, rapid photocopying, dry cleaning, and so on.

Large department stores once clustered in the CBD, often across the street from one another, but most have relocated to suburban malls. In several CBDs, new shopping areas attract suburban shoppers as well as out-of-town tourists with unique recreation and entertainment experiences (Figure 13.1.4).

PUBLIC SERVICES

Public services typically located downtown include City Hall, courts, and libraries (Figure 13.1.5). These facilities cluster in the CBD to facilitate access for people living in all parts of town.

Sports facilities and convention centers have been constructed or expanded downtown in many cities. These structures attract a large number of people, including many suburbanites and out-of-towners. Cities place these facilities in the CBD because they hope to stimulate more business for downtown restaurants, bars, and hotels.

▼ 13.1.5 **PUBLIC SERVICES IN WILKES-BARRE'S CBD**
Much of downtown Wilkes-Barre is devoted to public services, such as Luzerne County Courthouse.

13.2 Models of Urban Structure

▶ **Three models of urban structure describe where groups typically cluster within urban areas.**

▶ **The three models demonstrate that cities grow in rings, wedges, and nodes.**

Sociologists, economists, and geographers have developed three models to help explain where different types of people tend to live in an urban area—the concentric zone, sector, and multiple nuclei models.

The three models describing the internal structure of cities were developed in Chicago. Since Chicago developed on a flat prairie, few physical features (except for Lake Michigan to the east) interrupted the growth of the city and its region. Chicago includes a central business district (CBD) known as the Loop, because elevated railway lines loop around it. Surrounding the Loop are residential areas to the south, west, and north. The three models were later applied to cities elsewhere in the United States and in other countries.

CONCENTRIC ZONE MODEL

According to the **concentric zone** model, created in 1923 by sociologist E. W. Burgess, a city grows outward from a central area in a series of five concentric rings, like the growth rings of a tree (Figure 13.2.1).

- The innermost zone is the CBD, where nonresidential activities are concentrated.

- A second ring, the zone in transition, contains industry and poorer-quality housing. Immigrants to the city first live in this zone in high-rise apartment buildings (Figure 13.2.2).

- The third ring, the zone of working-class homes, contains modest older houses occupied by stable, working-class families (Figure 13.2.3).

- The fourth zone has newer and more spacious houses for middle-class families.

- A commuters' zone beyond the continuous built-up area of the city is inhabited by people who work in the center but choose to live in "bedroom communities" for commuters.

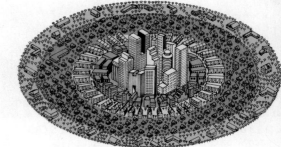

1 Central business district
2 Zone of transition
3 Zone of independent workers' homes
4 Zone of better residences
5 Commuter's zone

▲ 13.2.1 **CONCENTRIC ZONE MODEL**

▼ 13.2.2 **ZONE OF TRANSITION**
Apartments for rent in an old building, Bronx, New York.

◀ 13.2.3 **ZONE OF WORKING-CLASS HOMES**
Housing, Los Angeles, California.

SECTOR MODEL

According to the **sector** model, developed in 1939 by land economist Homer Hoyt, the city develops in a series of sectors (Figure 13.2.4). As a city grows, activities expand outward in a wedge, or sector, from the center. Hoyt mapped the highest-rent areas for a number of U.S. cities at different times and showed that the highest social-class district usually remained in the same sector, although it moved farther out along that sector over time.

Once a district with high-class housing is established, the most expensive new housing is built on the outer edge of that district, farther out from the center. The best housing is therefore found in a corridor extending from downtown to the outer edge of the city. Industrial and retailing activities develop in other sectors, usually along good transportation lines (Figure 13.2.5).

MULTIPLE NUCLEI MODEL

Geographers C. D. Harris and E. L. Ullman developed the **multiple nuclei** model in 1945 (Figure 13.2.6). According to the multiple nuclei model, a city is a complex structure that includes more than one center around which activities revolve. Examples of these nodes include a port, neighborhood business center, university, airport, and park.

The multiple nuclei theory states that some activities are attracted to particular nodes, whereas others try to avoid them. For example, a university node may attract well-educated residents, pizzerias, and bookstores (Figures 13.2.7 and 13.2.8). An airport may attract hotels and warehouses. On the other hand, incompatible land-use activities will avoid clustering in the same locations. Heavy industry and high-class housing, for example, rarely exist in the same neighborhood.

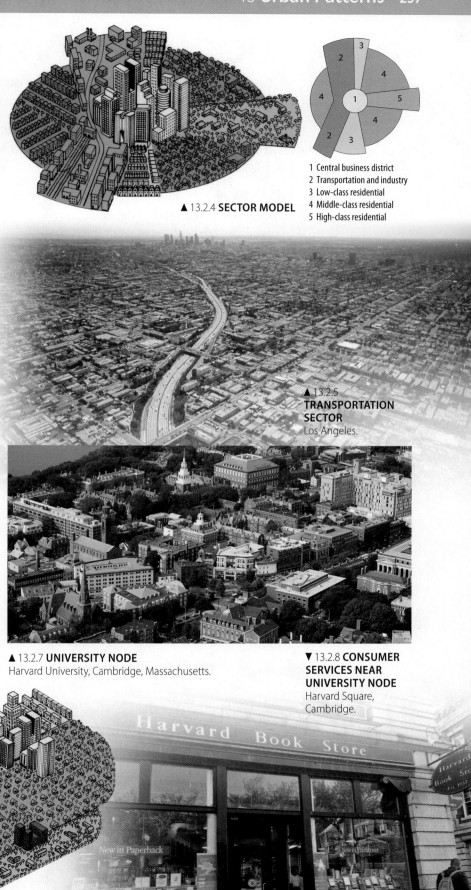

▲ 13.2.4 **SECTOR MODEL**

1 Central business district
2 Transportation and industry
3 Low-class residential
4 Middle-class residential
5 High-class residential

▲ 13.2.5 **TRANSPORTATION SECTOR**
Los Angeles.

▲ 13.2.7 **UNIVERSITY NODE**
Harvard University, Cambridge, Massachusetts.

▼ 13.2.8 **CONSUMER SERVICES NEAR UNIVERSITY NODE**
Harvard Square, Cambridge.

▼ 13.2.6 **MULTIPLE NUCLEI MODEL**

1 Central business district
2 Wholesale, light manufacturing
3 Low-class residential
4 Medium-class residential
5 High-class residential
6 Heavy manufacturing
7 Outlying business district
8 Residential suburb
9 Industrial suburb

13.3 Social Area Analysis

▶ Census data can be used to map the distribution of social characteristics.
▶ The three models together explain where people live within U.S. cities.

The three models help us understand where people with different social characteristics tend to live within an urban area. They can also help to explain why certain types of people tend to live in particular places.

THE CENSUS

Effective use of the models depends on the availability of data at the scale of individual neighborhoods. In the United States and many other countries, that information comes from a national census. Urban areas in the United States are divided into **census tracts** that contain approximately 5,000 residents and correspond, where possible, to neighborhood boundaries.

Every decade the U.S. Bureau of the Census publishes data summarizing the characteristics of the residents living in each tract. Examples of information the bureau publishes include the number of nonwhites, the median income of all families, and the percentage of adults who finished high school.

The spatial distribution of any of these social characteristics can be plotted on a map of the community's census tracts. Computers have become invaluable in this task, because they permit rapid creation of maps and storage of voluminous data about each census tract. Social scientists can compare the distributions of characteristics and create an overall picture of where various types of people tend to live. This kind of study is known as **social area analysis**.

COMBINING THE THREE MODELS

The three models taken individually do not explain why different types of people live in distinctive parts of the city. But if the models are combined rather than considered independently, they help geographers explain where different types of people live in a city, such as Dallas, Texas.

- The sector theory suggests that a family with a higher income will not live in the same sector of the city as a family with a lower income (Figures 13.3.1 and 13.3.2).
- One family owns its home, whereas the other rents. The concentric zone model suggests that the owner-occupant is much more likely to live in an outer ring and the renter in an inner ring (Figure 13.3.3).
- The multiple nuclei theory suggests that people with the same ethnic or racial background are likely to live near each other (Figure 13.3.4).

LIMITATIONS OF THE MODELS

Critics point out that the models are too simple and fail to consider the variety of reasons that lead people to select particular residential locations. Because the three models are all based on conditions that existed in U.S. cities between the two world wars, critics also question their relevance to contemporary urban patterns in the United States or in other countries.

People tend to reside in certain locations depending on their particular personal characteristics. This does not mean that everyone with the same characteristics must live in the same neighborhood, but the models say that most people prefer to live near others who have similar characteristics.

◀ 13.3.1 **DALLAS: WESTERN SECTOR**

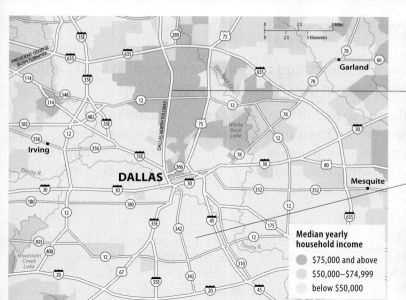

Median yearly household income
- $75,000 and above
- $50,000–$74,999
- below $50,000

◄ 13.3.2 **SECTORS IN DALLAS**
(top) High-income sector to the north.
(bottom) Low-income sector to the south.

Percent of homes owned
- 60 and above
- 30–59
- below 30

◄ 13.3.3 **CONCENTRIC ZONES IN DALLAS**
(top) Older rental housing near the center.
(bottom) Newer owner-occupied housing in the suburbs.

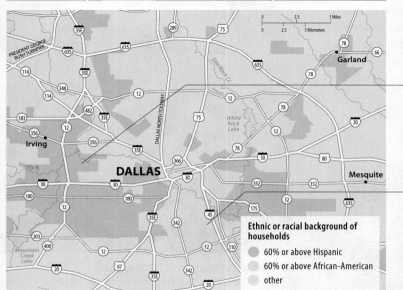

Ethnic or racial background of households
- 60% or above Hispanic
- 60% or above African-American
- other

◄ 13.3.4 **MULTIPLE NUCLEI IN DALLAS**
(top) Hispanic node to the west.
(bottom) African American node to the south.

13.4 Urban Patterns in Europe

▶ **European CBDs contain more residents and consumer services than do U.S. CBDs.**

▶ **Poor people are more likely to live in outer rings in European cities.**

The three models may describe the spatial distribution of social classes in the United States, but American urban areas differ from those elsewhere in the world. These differences do not invalidate the models, but they do point out that social groups in other countries may not have the same reasons for selecting particular neighborhoods within their cities.

EUROPE'S CBDS

More people live in the CBDs of European cities than those of the United States. Wealthy people are especially attracted to residences in European CBDs. A central location provides proximity to the region's best shops, restaurants, cafés, and cultural facilities. Wealthy people are also attracted by the opportunity to occupy elegant residences in carefully restored, beautiful old buildings.

To serve these residents, European CBDs contain consumer services, such as markets, bakeries, and butchers (Figure 13.4.1). Some European CBDs ban motor vehicles from busy streets, thus emulating one of the most attractive attributes of large shopping malls—pedestrian-only walkways (Figure 13.4.2).

On the other hand, European CBDs are less dominated by business services than U.S. CBDs. European CBDs display a legacy of low-rise structures and narrow streets, built as long ago as medieval times. The most prominent structures may be churches and former royal palaces (Figure 13.4.3). Some

European cities try to preserve their historic CBDs by limiting high-rise buildings. After several high-rise offices were permitted to be built in Paris, for example, the public outcry was so great that officials banned further ones (Figure 13.4.4).

▼ 13.4.2 **PEDESTRIAN-ONLY ZONE, PLACE GEORGES POMPIDOU, PARIS**

▼ 13.4.1 **CONSUMER SERVICES FOR RESIDENTS IN PARIS CBD**

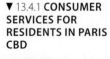

▼ 13.4.3 **LOUVRE MUSEUM, PARIS, A FORMER ROYAL PALACE**

▲ 13.4.4 **MONTPARNASSE TOWER, PARIS**
After construction of this tower, Europe's tallest, public opposition limited construction of further high-rises in Paris.

SECTOR MODEL IN EUROPEAN CITIES

As in the United States, wealthier people in European cities cluster along a sector extending out from the CBD. In Paris, for example, high-income residents moved from the royal palace at the Louvre west towards another royal palace at Versailles (Figure 13.4.5).

CONCENTRIC ZONE MODEL IN EUROPEAN CITIES

In the United States, outer rings are more likely to contain owner-occupied detached houses for families, whereas the inner rings are more likely to contain rented apartments for individuals. A similar pattern exists in European cities (Figure 13.4.6). European cities have relatively few free-standing owner-occupied houses, but to the extent that they exist they are in outer rings.

In contrast with the United States, though, outer rings of European cities also house most of the urban area's poor people. Vast suburbs containing dozens of high-rise apartment buildings house these people who were displaced from the inner city.

In the past, low-income people lived in the center of European cities. Before the invention of electricity in the nineteenth century, social segregation was vertical: wealthier people lived on the first or second floors, whereas poorer people occupied the dark, dank basements, or they climbed many flights of stairs to reach the attics. Today, low-income people are less likely to live in European inner-city neighborhoods. Poor-quality housing has been renovated for wealthy people or demolished and replaced by offices or luxury apartment buildings.

European suburban residents face the prospect of long commutes by public transportation to reach jobs and other downtown amenities. Shops, schools, and other services are worse than in inner neighborhoods, and the suburbs have high rates of crime, violence, and drug dealing. Because the housing is mostly in high-rise buildings, people lack large private yards.

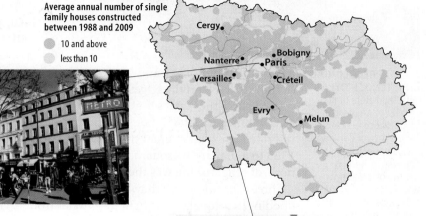

Monthly household income (euros)
- above 1,800
- 1,301 – 1,800
- 1,000 – 1,300
- less than 1,000

Average annual number of single family houses constructed between 1988 and 2009
- 10 and above
- less than 10

◄▲ 13.4.5 **SECTORS IN PARIS**
The sector to the west (left) has higher average income households than the sector to the east (above).

▲► 13.4.6 **CONCENTRIC ZONES IN PARIS**
(above) Older housing near the center. (right) Newer housing in the suburbs.

MULTIPLE NUCLEI MODEL IN EUROPEAN CITIES

European cities also show evidence of the multiple nuclei model. Many residents of the suburbs are persons of color or recent immigrants from Africa or Asia who face discrimination and prejudice by white Europeans (Figure 13.4.7).

▼ 13.4.7 **MULTIPLE NUCLEI IN PARIS**
Much of the housing for low-income minorities and immigrants is in high-rise buildings in the suburbs (top of the page). Immigrants protest in Paris against legislation aimed at limiting immigration (below).

13.5 Urban Patterns in Latin America

► **Cities in developing countries follow patterns similar to those of European cities.**
► **Cities in developing countries have been influenced by colonial rule.**

In developing countries, as in Europe, the poor tend to be accommodated in the outer rings, whereas the wealthy live near the center of cities as well as in a sector extending from the center. The similarity between cities in Europe and developing countries is not a coincidence: European colonial planning left a heavy mark on the design of cities in developing countries.

Many cities in developing countries have passed through three stages of design:

- Pre-European colonization.
- European colonial period.
- Postcolonial independence.

▲ 13.5.1 **PRECOLONIAL CITY: TENOCHTITLÁN** (left) The Aztecs built the city on an island in Lake Texcoco. (right) Templo Mayor dominated the center of the city. The twin shrines on the top of the temple were dedicated to the Aztec God of rain and agriculture (in blue) and to the Aztec God of war (in red).

PRECOLONIAL CITIES

Before the Europeans established colonies in Africa, Asia, and Latin America, most people lived in rural settlements. Cities were often laid out with a central area including marketplace, religious structures, government buildings, and homes of wealthy families. Families with less wealth and recent migrants to the city lived on the edge.

In Mexico, the Aztecs founded Mexico City—which they called Tenochtitlán—on a hill known as Chapultepec ("the hill of the grasshopper"). When forced by other people to leave the hill, they migrated a few kilometers south, near the present-day site of the University of Mexico, and then in 1325 to a marshy 10-square-kilometer (4-square-mile) island in Lake Texcoco (Figure 13.5.1). The node of religious life was the Templo Mayor (Great Temple).

Three causeways with drawbridges linked Tenochtitlán to the mainland and also helped to control flooding. An aqueduct brought fresh water from Chapultepec. Most food, merchandise, and building materials crossed from the mainland to the island by canoe, barge, or other type of boat, and the island was laced with canals to facilitate pickup and delivery of people and goods. Over the next two centuries the Aztecs conquered the neighboring peoples and extended their control through the central area of present-day Mexico. As their wealth and power grew, Tenochtitlán grew to a population of a half-million.

▼ 13.5.2 **COLONIAL CITY: MEXICO CITY ZÓCALO**
After the Spanish conquered Tenochtitlán in 1521, they destroyed the city and dispersed or killed most of the inhabitants. The city, renamed Mexico City, was rebuilt around a main square, called the Zòcalo, in the center of the island, on the site of the Aztecs' sacred precinct. The Spanish reconstructed the streets in a grid pattern extending from the Zòcalo. A Roman Catholic cathedral was built near the site of the demolished Great Temple, and the National Palace was erected on the site of the Aztec emperor Moctezuma's destroyed palace.

COLONIAL CITIES

When Europeans gained control of Africa, Asia, and Latin America, they expanded existing cities to provide colonial services, such as administration, military command, and international trade, as well as housing for Europeans who settled in the colony. Existing native towns were either left to one side or demolished because they were totally at variance with European ideas.

Colonial cities followed standardized plans. All Spanish cities in Latin America, for example, were built according to the Laws of the Indies, drafted in 1573. The laws explicitly outlined how colonial cities were to be constructed—a gridiron street plan centered on a church and central plaza, walls around individual houses, and neighborhoods built around central, smaller plazas with parish churches or monasteries (Figure 13.5.2). Compared to precolonial cities, these European districts typically contained wider streets and public squares, larger houses surrounded by gardens, and much lower densities.

CITIES SINCE INDEPENDENCE

Following independence, Latin American cities have grown in accordance with the sector and concentric zone models (Figure 13.5.3).

- **Sectors.** An elite sector forms along a narrow "spine" that contains offices, shops, and amenities attractive to wealthy people, such as restaurants, theaters, and parks. In Mexico City, the "spine" is a 14-lane, tree-lined boulevard called the Paseo de la Reforma, designed by Emperor Maximilian in the 1860s. The wealthy built imposing *palacios* (palaces) along it (Figure 13.5.4).

- **Concentric zones.** Cities in developing countries have expanded rapidly as millions of people immigrate in search of work. In Mexico City, most of Lake Texcoco was drained in 1903 to permit expansion of the city, including the airport (Figure 13.5.5). A large percentage of poor immigrants to urban areas in developing countries live in squatter settlements on the periphery, especially on hillsides (Figure 13.5.6). Squatter settlements lack such services as paved roads and sewers, because neither the city nor the residents can afford them. Electricity service may be stolen by running a wire from the nearest power line. The United Nations estimated that 1 billion people worldwide lived in squatter settlements in 2005.

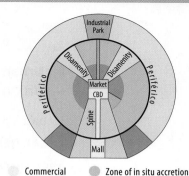

- Commercial
- Market
- Industrial
- Elite residential sector
- Zone of maturity
- Zone of in situ accretion
- Zone of peripheral squatter settlements
- Gentrification
- Middle-class residential

▲ 13.5.3 **MODEL OF A LATIN AMERICAN CITY**
Geographers Ernest Griffin and Larry Ford show that in Latin American cities wealthy people push out from the center in a well-defined elite residential sector. The poor live in the outer (Periférico) ring.

▼ 13.5.4 **SECTOR MODEL IN MEXICO CITY**
Wealthy people live in a sector along the Paseo de la Reforma, a wide boulevard to the west of downtown.

▲ 13.5.5 **CONCENTRIC ZONE MODEL IN MEXICO CITY**
Mexico City has grown rapidly. Low income areas are on the periphery, especially near the airport (top of image).

◄ 13.5.6 **MEXICO CITY SQUATTER SETTLEMENT**
Squatter settlements have developed on the hillsides surrounding Mexico City.

13.6 Defining Urban Settlements

▶ Urban settlements can be defined legally, or as urbanized or metropolitan areas.
▶ Urban growth has caused adjacent metropolitan areas to overlap.

Urban settlements can be defined in three ways.

LEGAL DEFINITION OF CITY

The term **city** defines an urban settlement that has been legally incorporated into an independent, self-governing unit. In the United States, a city surrounded by suburbs is sometimes called a **central city**.

A city has locally elected officials, the ability to raise taxes, and the responsibility for providing essential services. The boundaries of the city define the geographic area within which the local government has legal authority (Figure 13.6.1).

URBANIZED AREA

With the rapid growth of urban settlements, many urban residents live in suburbs, beyond the boundaries of the central city. In the United States, the central city and the surrounding built-up suburbs are called an **urbanized area**. Approximately 70 percent of Americans live in urbanized areas, including about 30 percent in central cities and 40 percent in surrounding jurisdictions.

Working with urbanized areas is difficult because few statistics are available about them. Most data in the United States and other countries are collected for cities, counties, and other local government units, but urbanized areas do not correspond to government boundaries.

METROPOLITAN STATISTICAL AREA

The area of influence of a city extends beyond legal boundaries and adjacent built-up jurisdictions. For example, commuters may travel a long distance to work and shop in the city or built-up suburbs. People in a wide area watch the city's television stations, read the city's newspapers, and support the city's sports teams.

The U.S. Bureau of the Census has created a method of measuring the functional area of a city, known as the **metropolitan statistical area (MSA)**. An MSA includes the following:

1. An urbanized area of at least 50,000 inhabitants.

2. The county within which the city is located.

3. Adjacent counties with a high population density and a large percentage of residents working in the central city's county.

The census designated 366 MSAs as of 2009, encompassing 84 percent of the U.S. population.

The census has also designated smaller urban areas as **micropolitan statistical areas (μSAs)**. The Greek letter μ or "mu" stands for *micro-*. These include an urbanized area of between 10,000 and 50,000 inhabitants, the county in which it is found, and adjacent counties tied to the city. The United States had 576 micropolitan statistical areas in 2009, for the most part found around southern and western communities previously considered rural in character. About 10 percent of Americans live in a micropolitan statistical area.

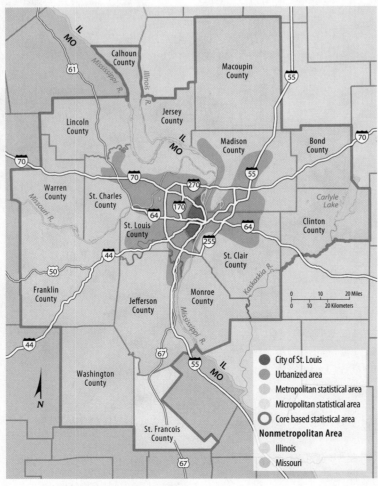

City of St. Louis
Urbanized area
Metropolitan statistical area
Micropolitan statistical area
Core based statistical area
Nonmetropolitan Area
Illinois
Missouri

▲ 13.6.1 **DEFINITIONS OF ST. LOUIS**

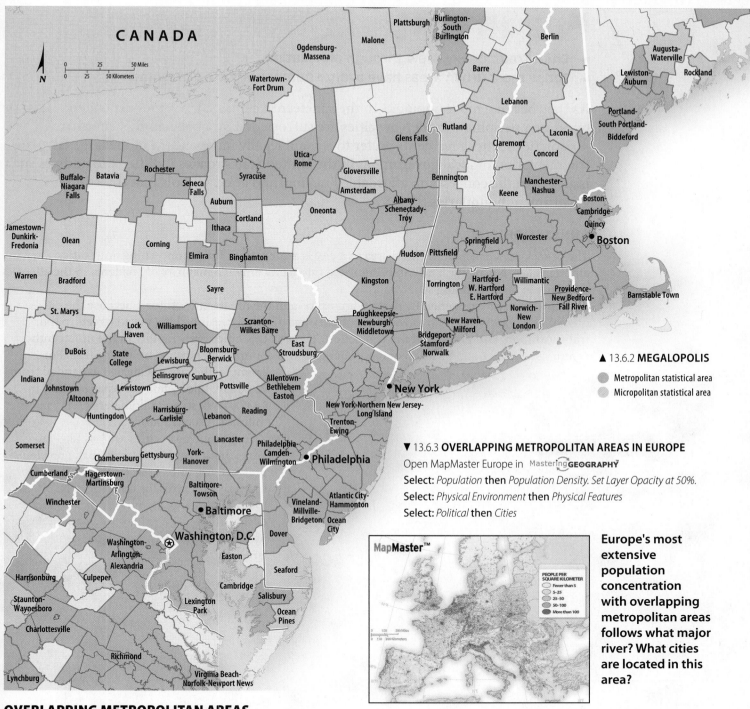

▲ 13.6.2 **MEGALOPOLIS**

- ● Metropolitan statistical area
- ○ Micropolitan statistical area

▼ 13.6.3 **OVERLAPPING METROPOLITAN AREAS IN EUROPE**

Open MapMaster Europe in   Mastering**GEOGRAPHY**

Select: *Population* then *Population Density. Set Layer Opacity at 50%.*

Select: *Physical Environment* then *Physical Features*

Select: *Political* then *Cities*

Europe's most extensive population concentration with overlapping metropolitan areas follows what major river? What cities are located in this area?

OVERLAPPING METROPOLITAN AREAS

The 366 MSAs and 576 µSAs together are known as **core based statistical areas (CBSAs)**. Recognizing that many MSAs and µSAs have close ties, the census has combined some of them into 125 **combined statistical areas (CSAs)**. A CSA is defined as two or more contiguous CBSAs tied together by commuting patterns. The 125 CSAs plus the remaining 186 MSAs and 407 µSAs together are known as **primary census statistical areas (PCSAs)**.

In the northeastern United States, metropolitan areas are so close together that they now form one continuous urban complex, extending from north of Boston to south of Washington, D.C. (Figure 13.6.2). Geographer Jean Gottmann named this region Megalopolis, a Greek word meaning "great city." Overlapping metropolitan areas exist in other developed regions, including Europe and Japan (Figure 13.6.3).

13.7 Fragmented Government

▶ **Cities traditionally grew through annexation.**
▶ **Today most urban areas have a large number of local governments.**

As they became more populous in the nineteenth century, U.S. cities expanded by adding peripheral land. Now cities are surrounded by a collection of suburban jurisdictions whose residents prefer to remain legally independent of the large city. The fragmentation of local government in the United States makes it difficult to address such issues as traffic congestion, affordable housing, and good schools that transcend local government boundaries.

ANNEXATION

The process of legally adding land area to a city is **annexation**. Rules concerning annexation vary among states. Normally, land can be annexed into a city only if a majority of residents in the affected area vote in favor of doing so.

Peripheral residents generally desired annexation in the nineteenth century, because the city offered better services, such as water supply, sewage disposal, trash pickup, paved streets, public transportation, and police and fire protection. Thus, as U.S. cities grew rapidly in the nineteenth century, the legal boundaries frequently changed to accommodate newly developed areas. For example, the city of Chicago expanded from 26 square kilometers (10 square miles) in 1837 to 492 square kilometers (190 square miles) in 1900 (Figure 13.7.1).

Today, however, cities are less likely to annex peripheral land because the residents prefer to organize their own services rather than pay city taxes for them. As a result, today's cities are surrounded by a collection of suburban jurisdictions, whose residents prefer to remain legally independent of the large city.

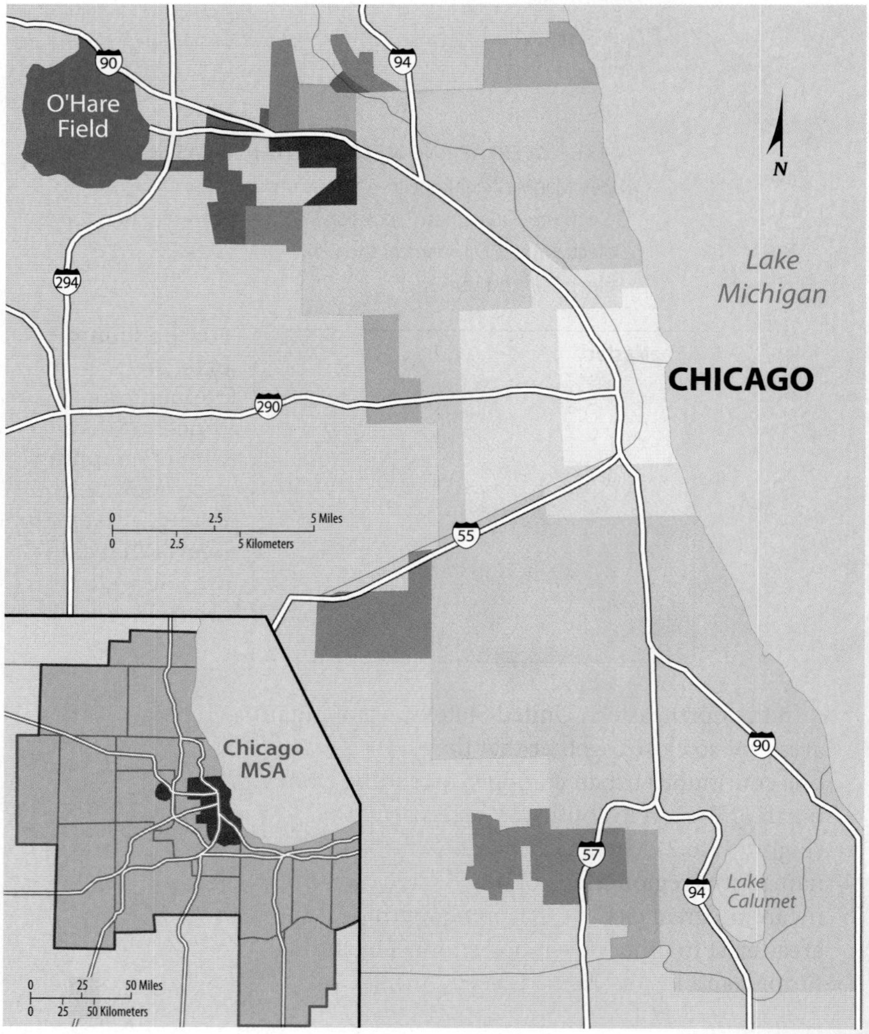

◀ 13.7.1 **ANNEXATION IN CHICAGO**

City limits in 1837
Annexed by
1870
1890
1900
1930
1960
1990

METROPOLITAN GOVERNMENT

The number of local governments exceeds 20,000 throughout the United States, including several hundred in the Detroit area alone (Figure 13.7.2). The fragmentation of local governments in the Detroit area has wealthier suburbs (Figure 13.7.3) surrounding an impoverished city of Detroit (Figure 13.7.4).

Originally, some of these peripheral jurisdictions were small, isolated towns that had a tradition of independent local government before being swallowed up by urban growth. Others are newly created communities whose residents wish to live close to the large city but not legally be part of it.

The large number of local government units has led to calls for a metropolitan government that could coordinate—if not replace—the numerous local governments in an urban area. Strong metropolitan-wide governments have been established in a few places in North America. Two kinds exist:

- **Federations.** Examples include Toronto and other large Canadian cities. Toronto's metropolitan government was created in

1953 through federation of 13 municipalities. A two-tier system existed until 1998, when the municipalities were amalgamated into a single government.

- **Consolidations of City and County Governments.** Examples include Indianapolis and Miami. The boundaries of Indianapolis were changed to match those of Marion County. Government functions that were once handled separately now are combined into a joint operation in the same office building. In Florida, the city of Miami and surrounding Dade County have combined some services, but the city boundaries have not been changed to match those of the county.

▼ 13.7.3 **WEALTHY DETROIT SUBURB**

▲ 13.7.2 **LOCAL GOVERNMENTS IN DETROIT METROPOLITAN AREA**

County boundary
Township boundary
● Village
● City
● Township

Local governments named on map have at least 50,000 inhabitants

▲ 13.7.4 **INNER-CITY DETROIT**

13.8 Decline and Renewal

► **Low-income residents concentrate in the inner-city neighborhoods in U.S. cities.**
► **Some U.S. inner-city neighborhoods have been gentrified.**

Inner cities in the United States contain concentrations of low income people who face a variety of economic, social, and physical challenges very different from those faced by suburban residents.

INNER-CITY CHALLENGES

Inner city residents are frequently referred to as a permanent underclass because they are trapped in an unending cycle of hardships:

- **Inadequate job skills.** Inner city residents are increasingly unable to compete for jobs. They lack technical skills needed for most jobs because fewer than half complete high school.

- **Culture of poverty.** Unwed mothers give birth to two-thirds of the babies in U.S. inner-city neighborhoods, and 80 percent of children in the inner city live with only one parent. Because of inadequate child-care services, single mothers may be forced to choose between working to generate income and staying at home to take care of the children.

- **Crime.** Inner-city neighborhoods have a relatively high share of a metropolitan area's serious crimes, such as murder (Figure 13.8.1).

- **Drugs.** Trapped in a hopeless environment, some inner-city residents turn to drugs. Although drug use is a problem in suburbs as well, rates of use have increased most rapidly

▲ 13.8.2 **HOMELESSNESS**
Homeless people camp under I-75 bridge across the Ohio River.

in inner cities. Some drug users obtain money through criminal activities.

- **Homelessness.** Several million people are homeless in the United States. Most people are homeless because they cannot afford housing and have no regular income. Homelessness may have been sparked by family problems or job loss (Figure 13.8.2).

- **Lack of services.** The concentration of low-income residents in inner-city neighborhoods of central cities has produced financial problems. These people require public services, but they can pay very little of the taxes to support the services. Central cities face a growing gap between the cost of needed services in inner-city neighborhoods and the availability of funds to pay for them.

- **Deteriorated housing.** Inner-city housing is subdivided by absentee landlords into apartments for low-income families, a process known as filtering. Landlords stop maintaining houses when the rent they collect becomes less than the maintenance cost. In such a case, the building soon deteriorates and grows unfit for occupancy.

▼ 13.8.1 **MURDERS IN DALLAS**
Compare with Figures 13.3.2, 13.3.3, and 13.3.4. Most of the murders in Dallas occurred in low-income minority areas, and most victims, as well as those arrested for murder in Dallas, were minorities.

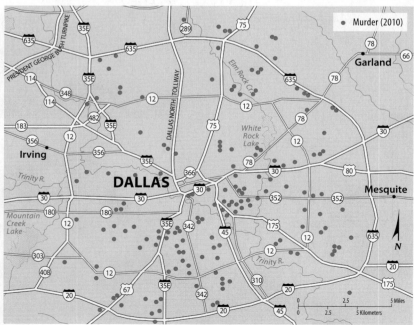

GENTRIFICATION

Gentrification is the process by which middle-class people move into deteriorated inner-city neighborhoods and renovate the housing. Most cities have at least one gentrified inner-city neighborhood. In a few cases, inner-city neighborhoods never deteriorated, because the community's social elite maintained them as enclaves of expensive property. In most cases, inner-city neighborhoods have only recently been renovated by the city and by private investors (Figure 13.8.3).

Middle-class families are attracted to deteriorated inner-city housing for a number of reasons. First, houses may be larger, more substantially constructed, yet cheaper in the inner city than in the suburbs. Inner-city houses may also possess attractive architectural details such as ornate fireplaces, cornices, high ceilings, and wood trim.

Gentrified inner-city neighborhoods also attract middle-class individuals who work downtown. Inner-city living eliminates the strain of commuting on crowded freeways or public transit. Others seek proximity to theaters, bars, restaurants, and other cultural and recreational facilities located downtown. Renovated inner-city housing appeals to single people and couples without children, who are not concerned with the quality of inner-city schools (Figure 13.8.4).

Because renovating an old inner-city house can be nearly as expensive as buying a new one in the suburbs, cities encourage the process by providing low-cost loans and tax breaks. Public expenditures for renovation have been criticized as subsidies for the middle class at the expense of people with lower incomes, who are forced to move out of the gentrified neighborhoods because the rents in the area are suddenly too high for them.

▲ 13.8.3
GENTRIFICATION
Spitalfields neighborhood in London before gentrification (left) and after gentrification (right).

▲ 13.8.4 **INNER CITY REDEVELOPMENT**
Fly to: 3600 S State St, Chicago, IL
Below is an image from 9/26/2000.
Drag to enter Street view at the corner of 45th and State St.

How does the current use of land compare to what was there in 2000? Which time period appears to provide more attractive and better living conditions?

13.9 Suburban Sprawl

▶ **Suburbs sprawl outside American cities.**

▶ **Retailing as well as housing has grown in suburbs.**

In 1950, only 20 percent of Americans lived in suburbs. After more than a half-century of rapid suburban growth, 50 percent of Americans now live in suburbs. U.S. suburbs are characterized by **sprawl**, which is the progressive spread of development over the landscape.

THE PERIPHERAL MODEL

North American urban areas follow what Chauncey Harris (creator of the multiple nuclei model) called the **peripheral model**. According to the peripheral model, an urban area consists of an inner city surrounded by large suburban residential and business areas tied together by a beltway or ring road (Figure 13.9.1).

Peripheral areas lack the severe physical, social, and economic problems of inner-city neighborhoods. But the peripheral model points to problems of sprawl and segregation that characterize many suburbs.

1 Central city
2 Suburban residential area
3 Shopping mall
4 Industrial district
5 Office park
6 Service center
7 Airport complex
8 Combined employment & shopping center

ATTRACTIONS OF SUBURBS

Public opinion polls in the United States show people's strong desire for suburban living. In most polls, more than 90 percent of respondents prefer the suburbs to the inner city. Suburban living offers many attractions:

- A detached single-family dwelling rather than a row house or apartment.
- A yard surrounding the house for children to play.
- Space to park several cars at no cost.
- A greater opportunity for home ownership.
- Protection from inner-city crime and congestion.
- Proximity to good schools.

▶ 13.9.1 **PERIPHERAL MODEL OF URBAN AREAS**

▶ 13.9.2 **SPRAWL**
Pockets of new housing are interspersed with farmland.

THE COSTS OF SPRAWL

When private developers select new housing sites, they seek cheap land that can easily be prepared for construction—land often not contiguous to the existing built-up area. Land is not transformed immediately from farms to housing developments. Instead, developers buy farms for future construction of houses by individual builders. Developers frequently reject land adjacent to built-up areas in favor of sites outside the urbanized area, depending on the price and physical attributes of the alternatives. The periphery of U.S. cities therefore looks like Swiss cheese, with pockets of development and gaps of open space (Figure 13.9.2).

Urban sprawl has some undesirable traits:

• Roads and utilities must be extended to connect isolated new developments to nearby built-up areas.

• Motorists must drive longer distances and consume more fuel.

• Agricultural land is lost to new developments, and other sites lie fallow while speculators await the most profitable time to build homes on them.

• Local governments typically spend more on services for these new developments than they collect in additional taxes.

SEGREGATION

The modern residential suburb is segregated in two ways.

• Housing in a given suburb is usually built for people of a single social class, with others excluded by virtue of the cost, size, or location of the housing. Segregation by race and ethnicity also persists in many suburbs (see Sections 7.2 and 7.3).

• Residents are separated from commercial and manufacturing activities that are confined to compact, distinct areas.

SUBURBAN RETAILING

Suburban residential growth has fostered change in the distribution of consumer services. Historically, urban residents bought food and other daily necessities at small neighborhood shops in the midst of housing areas and shopped in the CBD for other products. CBD sales have stagnated because suburban residents won't make the long journey there.

Instead, retailing has been increasingly concentrated in planned suburban shopping malls, auto-friendly strip malls, and big-box stores, surrounded by generous parking lots (Figure 13.9.3). These nodes of consumer services are called **edge cities**. Edge cities originated as suburban residences for people who worked in the central city, and then shopping malls were built to be near the residents. Edge cities now also serve as nodes of business services (Figure 13.9.4).

A shopping center is built by a developer, who buys the land, builds the structures, and leases space to individual merchants. The key to a successful large shopping center is the inclusion of one or more anchors. Most consumers go to a center to shop at an anchor and, while there, patronize the smaller shops. The anchors may be a supermarket and discount store in a smaller center or several department stores in a larger center.

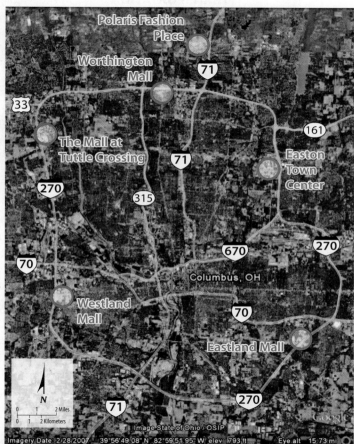

▲ 13.9.3 **SHOPPING MALLS NEAR COLUMBUS, OHIO**

▼ 13.9.4 **EDGE CITY**
Easton Town Center, outside Columbus, Ohio.

13.10 Urban Transportation

▶ **Most trips in the U.S. are by private motor vehicle.**
▶ **Public transportation has made a modest comeback in some cities.**

People do not travel aimlessly; their trips have a precise point of origin, destination, and purpose. More than half of all trips are work related. Shopping or other personal business and social journeys each account for approximately one-fourth of all trips. Sprawl makes people more dependent on motor vehicles for access to work, shopping, and social activities.

DEVELOPMENT OF URBAN TRANSPORTATION

Historically, people lived close together in cities because they had to be within walking distance of shops and places of employment. The invention of the railroad in the nineteenth century enabled people to live in suburbs and work in the central city. Cities then built street railways (called trolleys, streetcars, or trams) and underground railways (subways) to accommodate commuters. Rail and trolley lines restricted suburban development to narrow strips within walking distance of the stations.

▲ 13.10.1 **HIGHWAYS IN SAN FRANCISO**

MOTOR VEHICLES

▼ 13.10.2 **CONGESTION CHARGING IN LONDON**

Until the twentieth century, the growth of suburbs was constrained by poor transportation. Motor vehicles have permitted large-scale development of suburbs at greater distances from the center, in the gaps between the rail lines. More than 95 percent of all trips within U.S. cities are made by car.

The U.S. government has encouraged the use of cars and trucks by paying 90 percent of the cost of limited-access high-speed interstate highways, which crisscross 74,000 kilometers (46,000 miles) across the country (Figure 13.10.1). The use of motor vehicles is also supported by policies that keep the price of fuel below the level found in most other countries.

The motor vehicle is an important user of land in the city. An average city allocates about one-fourth of its land to roads and parking lots (refer to Figure 13.1.1). Valuable land is devoted to parking cars and trucks, although expensive underground and multistory parking structures can reduce the amount of ground-level space needed. Freeways cut a wide path through the heart of cities, and elaborate interchanges consume even more space.

Motor vehicles have costs beyond their purchase and operation: delays imposed on others, increased need for highway maintenance, construction of new highways, and pollution. The average American loses 36 hours per year sitting in traffic jams and wastes 55 gallons of gasoline.

Technological improvements may help traffic flow. Computers mounted on the dashboards alert drivers to traffic jams and suggest alternate routes. On freeways, vehicle speed and separation from other vehicles can be controlled automatically rather than by the driver.

Motorists can be charged for using congested roads or pay high tolls to drive on uncongested roads (Figure 13.10.2). The inevitable diffusion of such technology in the twenty-first century will reflect the continuing preference of most people to use private motor vehicles.

PUBLIC TRANSIT

In larger cities, public transportation is better suited than motor vehicles to moving large numbers of people, because each traveler takes up far less space. Public transportation is cheaper, less polluting, and more energy efficient than the automobile. It also is particularly suited to rapidly bringing a large number of people into a small area. Despite the obvious advantages of public transportation for commuting, only 5 percent of trips in U.S. cities are by public transit. Outside of big cities, public transportation is extremely rare or nonexistent.

Public transportation has been expanded in some U.S. cities to help reduce air pollution and conserve energy. New subway lines and existing systems expanded in a number of cities (Figure 13.10.3). The federal government has permitted Boston, New York, and other cities to use funds originally allocated for interstate highways to modernize rapid transit service instead. The trolley—now known by the more elegant term of light-rail transit—is making a modest comeback in North America (Figure 13.10.4). California, the state that most symbolizes the automobile-oriented American culture, is the leader in construction of new light-rail transit lines, as well as retention of historic ones (Figure 13.10.5).

Despite modest recent successes, most public transportation systems are caught in a vicious circle, because fares do not cover operating costs. As patronage declines and expenses rise, the fares are increased, which drives away passengers and leads to service reduction and still higher fares.

▲ 13.10.3 **PUBLIC TRANSIT OPTIONS IN SAN FRANCISCO: BART SUBWAY**

◄ 13.10.4 **PUBLIC TRANSIT OPTIONS IN SAN FRANCISCO: MUNI LIGHT RAIL**

▼ 13.10.5 **PUBLIC TRANSIT OPTIONS IN SAN FRANCISCO: CABLE CARS**

What is the future for cities? As shown in this chapter, contradictory trends are at work simultaneously. Why does one inner-city neighborhood become a slum and another an upper-class district? Why does one city attract new shoppers and visitors while another languishes?

The suburban lifestyle as exemplified by the detached single-family house with surrounding yard attracts most people. Yet inner-city residents may rarely venture out to suburbs. Lacking a motor vehicle, they have no access to most suburban locations. Lacking money, they do not shop in suburban malls or attend sporting events at suburban arenas. The spatial segregation of inner-city residents and suburbanites lies at the heart of the stark contrasts so immediately observed in any urban area. Several U.S. states have taken strong steps in the past few years to curb sprawl, reduce traffic congestion, and reverse inner-city decline. The goal is to produce a pattern of compact and contiguous development, while protecting rural land for agriculture, recreation, and wildlife.

Key Questions

Where are people distributed within urban areas?

▶ The Central Business District (CBD) contains a large share of a city's business and public services.

▶ The concentric zone, sector, and multiple nuclei models describe where different types of people live within urban areas.

▶ The three models together foster understanding that people live in different rings, sectors, and nodes depending on their stage in life, social status, and ethnicity.

How are urban areas expanding?

▶ Urban areas have expanded beyond the legal boundaries of cities to encompass urbanized areas and metropolitan areas that are functionally tied to the cities.

▶ With suburban growth, most metropolitan areas have been fragmented into a large number of local governments.

What challenges do cities face?

▶ Most Americans now live in suburbs that surround cities.

▶ Low-income inner-city residents face a variety of economic, social, and physical challenges.

▶ Tying together sprawling American urban areas is dependency on motor vehicles.

Thinking Geographically

Draw a sketch of your community or neighborhood. In accordance with Kevin Lynch's *The Image of the City,* place five types of information on the map—districts (homogeneous areas), edges (boundaries that separate districts), paths (lines of communication), nodes (central points of interaction), and landmarks (prominent objects on the landscape).

1. How clear an image does your community have for you?

Jane Jacobs wrote in *Death and Life of Great American Cities* that an attractive urban environment is one that is animated with an intermingling of a variety of people and activities, such as found in many New York City neighborhoods (Figure 13.CR.1).

2. What are the attractions and drawbacks to living in such environments?

Officials of rapidly growing cities in developing countries discourage the building of houses that do not meet international standards for sanitation and construction. Also discouraged are private individuals offering transportation in vehicles that lack decent tires, brakes, and other safety features. Yet the residents prefer substandard housing to no housing, and they prefer unsafe transportation to no transportation.

3. What would be the advantages and problems for a city if health and safety standards for housing, transportation, and other services were relaxed?

▶ 13.CR.1 **NEW YORK'S GREENWICH VILLAGE**

Interactive Mapping

OVERLAPPING METROPOLITAN AREAS IN NORTH AMERICA

Overlapping metropolitan areas are emerging in North America in addition to Megalopolis.

Open MapMaster North America in **Mastering** GEOGRAPHY™

Select: *Political* then *Cities*

Select: *Population* then *Population Density*.

Where in North America other than Megalopolis do there appear to be overlapping metropolitan areas?

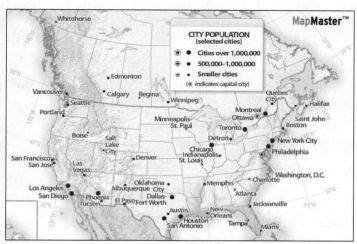

Explore

CHICAGO, ILLINOIS

Use Google Earth to explore Chicago's changing lakefront.

Fly to: *Soldier Field, Chicago*.

Drag to enter Street view on top of Soldier Field.

Exit Ground level view.

Rotate compass so that North is at the top.

Zoom out and move the image until the lakefront and green peninsula (Northerly Island Park) are visible to the east and buildings to the west.

Click Historical Imagery and slide date back to 4/23/2000

1. **What changes have occurred to the east of Soldier Field, along the lakefront?**
2. **What changes have occurred to the west of Soldier Field?**
3. **How do you think the development of this node of the city will influence people's activities?**

Key Terms

Annexation
Legally adding land area to a city in the United States.

Census tract
An area delineated by the U.S. Bureau of the Census for which statistics are published; in urbanized areas, census tracts are often delineated to correspond roughly to neighborhoods.

Central business district (CBD)
The area of a city where consumer, business, and public services are clustered.

City
An urban settlement that has been legally incorporated into an independent, self-governing unit.

Combined statistical area (CSA)
In the United States, two or more contiguous core based statistical areas tied together by commuting patterns.

Concentric zone model
A model of the internal structure of cities in which social groups are spatially arranged in a series of rings.

Core based statistical area (CBSA)
In the United States, a term referring to either a metropolitan statistical area or a micropolitan statistical area.

Edge city
A large node of office and retail activities on the edge of an urban area.

Gentrification
A process of converting an urban neighborhood from a predominantly low-income renter-occupied area to a predominantly middle-class owner-occupied area.

Metropolitan statistical area (MSA)
In the United States, a central city of at least 50,000 population, the county within which the city is located, and adjacent counties meeting one of several tests indicating a functional connection to the central city.

Micropolitan statistical area (μSA)
In the United States, an urban area of between 10,000 and 50,000 inhabitants, the county in which it is found, and adjacent counties tied to the city.

Multiple nuclei model
A model of the internal structure of cities in which social groups are arranged around a collection of nodes of activities.

Peripheral model
A model of North American urban areas consisting of an inner city surrounded by large suburban residential and business areas tied together by a beltway or ring road.

Primary census statistical area (PCSA)
In the United States, all of the combined statistical areas plus all of the remaining metropolitan statistical areas and micropolitan statistical areas.

Sector model
A model of the internal structure of cities in which social groups are arranged around a series of sectors, or wedges, radiating out from the central business district (CBD).

Social area analysis
Statistical analysis used to identify where people of similar living standards, ethnic background, and lifestyle live within an urban area.

Sprawl
Development of new housing sites at relatively low density and at locations that are not contiguous to the existing built-up area.

Squatter settlement
An area within a city in a developing country in which people illegally establish residences on land they do not own or rent and erect homemade structures.

Urbanized area
In the United States, a central city plus its contiguous built-up suburbs.

On the Internet

Social Explorer provides access to census data at all scales, including urban, at **www.socialexplorer.com**, or scan the QR at the beginning of the chapter. An interactive map enables users to choose the area of interest from among hundreds of census variables.

► LOOKING AHEAD

Our journey ends with an examination of the use, misuse, and reuse of resources.

14 Resource Issues

People transform Earth's land, water, and air for their benefit. But human actions in recent years have gone far beyond actions of the past. With less than one-fourth of the world's population, developed countries consume most of the world's energy and generate most of its pollutants. Meanwhile in developing countries, 2 billion people live without clean water or sewers, and 1 billion live in cities with unsafe sulfur dioxide levels.

Geographers study the troubled relationship between human actions and the physical environment in which we live. From the perspective of human geographers, Earth offers a large menu of resources available for people to use. The problem is that most resources are limited, and Earth has a tremendous number of consumers. Geographers observe two major misuses of resources:

- We deplete scarce resources, especially petroleum, natural gas, and coal, for energy production.

- We destroy resources through pollution of air, water, and soil.

These two misuses are the basic themes of this chapter.

NUCLEAR POWER STATION, HAMM-UENTROP, GERMANY.

How are resources being depleted?

How are resources polluted?

SCAN FOR DATA
ON ENERGY

How are resources being conserved?

14.1 Nonrenewable Energy Resources

▶ **Most energy comes from the three fossil fuels.**
▶ **Energy is consumed primarily in businesses, homes, and transportation.**

Earth offers a large menu of resources available for people to use. A **resource** is a substance in the environment that is useful to people, is economically and technologically feasible to access, and is socially acceptable to use. Resources include food, water, soil, plants, animals, and minerals.

Two kinds of resources are especially valuable—energy (discussed below and in section 14.2) and minerals (section 14.3). We depend on abundant, low-cost energy and minerals to run our industries, transport ourselves, and keep our homes comfortable. But we are depleting the global supply of some resources.

THE THREE FOSSIL FUELS

A **fossil fuel** is the residue of plants and animals that were buried millions of years ago. As sediment accumulated over these remains, intense pressure and chemical reactions slowly converted them into the fossil fuels we use today. Three fossil fuels provide five-sixths of the world's energy:

- **Coal.** Supplanted wood as the leading energy source in developed countries in the late 1800s.

- **Petroleum.** First pumped in 1859, but not an important energy source until the diffusion of motor vehicles in the twentieth century (Figure 14.1.1).

- **Natural gas.** Originally burned off as a waste product of oil drilling, but now used to heat homes.

Historically, people relied primarily on **animate power,** which is power supplied by animals or by people themselves. Animate power was supplemented by biomass fuel (such as wood, plant material, and animal waste) which is burned directly or converted to charcoal, alcohol, or methane gas.

Biomass remains the most important source of fuel in some developing countries, but during the past 200 years developed countries have converted primarily to energy from fossil fuels (Figure 14.1.2).

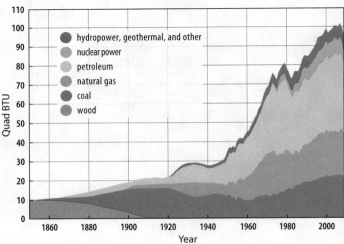

▲ 14.1.2 **U.S. ENERGY SOURCES**

Legend:
- hydropower, geothermal, and other
- nuclear power
- petroleum
- natural gas
- coal
- wood

(y-axis: Quad BTU; x-axis: Year, 1860–2000)

RENEWABLE AND NONRENEWABLE ENERGY

Earth's energy resources can be divided between those that are renewable and those that are not:

- **Renewable energy** is replaced continually, or at least within a human life span. It has an essentially unlimited supply and is not depleted when used by people. Solar energy, hydroelectric, geothermal, fusion, and wind are examples.

- **Nonrenewable energy** forms so slowly that for practical purposes the supply is finite. The fossil fuels, as well as nuclear energy, are examples.

The world faces an energy problem in part because we are rapidly depleting the remaining supply of the three fossil fuels, especially petroleum. Once the present supply of fossil fuels is consumed, it is gone, and we must look to other resources for our energy. (Technically, fossil fuels are continually being formed, but the process takes millions of years, so humans must regard the current supply as essentially finite.)

▼ 14.1.1 **PETROLEUM PRODUCTION**
Pumping petroleum in the desert.

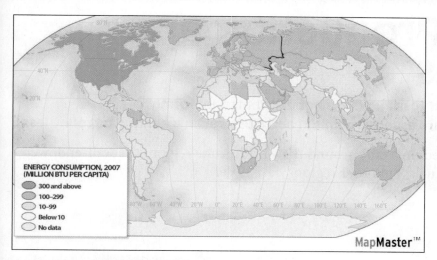

◄ 14.1.3 **ENERGY CONSUMPTION PER CAPITA**
Per capita energy consumption varies widely around the world.

Launch MapMaster World in Mastering**GEOGRAPHY**

Select: *Political then Continents and Country Borders*

Select: *Physical Environment then Energy Consumption*

Set layer opacity to 50%

Select: *Population then Arithmetic Density*

Deselect 100-199, 50-99, and Below 50

Which countries with very high arithmetic density have high per capita energy consumption, and which have low consumption?

FOSSIL FUEL CONSUMPTION

The one-sixth of the world's inhabitants who live in developed countries consume about the same amount of energy as the five-sixths who live in developing countries (Figure 14.1.3). The United States alone, with just 5 percent of the world's population, accounts for 20 percent of world energy consumption (Figure 14.1.4). This high energy consumption by a modest percentage of the world's population supports a lifestyle rich in food, goods, services, comfort, education, and travel in developed countries.

As they promote development and cope with high population growth, developing countries are consuming much more energy. China, the country with the second-largest consumption of energy—17 percent of world consumption in 2008—is expected to pass the United States in the 2010s. As a result of increased demand in developing countries, global consumption of petroleum is expected to increase by about 50 percent during the next two decades, whereas both coal and natural gas consumption are expected to double (Figure 14.1.5).

Energy is consumed in three principal places:

- **Businesses.** For U.S. businesses the main energy resource is coal, followed by natural gas and oil. Some businesses directly burn coal in their own furnaces. Others rely on electricity, mostly generated at coal-burning power plants.

- **Homes.** At home, energy is used primarily for the heating of living space and water. Natural gas is the most common source, followed by petroleum (heating oil and kerosene).

- **Transportation.** Almost all transportation systems operate on petroleum products, including automobiles, trucks, buses, airplanes,

and most railroads. Only subways, streetcars, and some trains run on coal-generated electricity.

We can use other resources for heat, fuel, and manufacturing, but they are likely to be more expensive and less convenient to use than fossil fuels. And converting from fossil fuels will likely disrupt our daily lives and cause us hardship.

Because of dwindling supplies of fossil fuels, most of the buildings in which we live, work, and study will have to be heated another way. Cars, trucks, and buses will have to operate on some other energy source. The many plastic objects that we use (because they are made from petroleum) will have to be made with other materials.

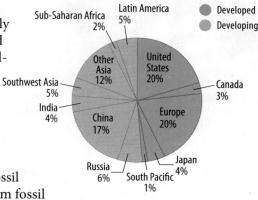

▲ 14.1.4 **SHARE OF WORLD FOSSIL FUEL CONSUMPTION**

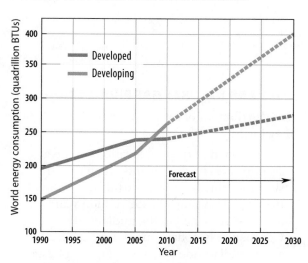

▲ 14.1.5 **FUTURE ENERGY CONSUMPTION**

14.2 Energy Production and Reserves

▶ **Remaining supplies of fossil fuels are not distributed uniformly.**

▶ **Petroleum reserves are especially limited and clustered in a handful of countries.**

Fossil fuels are distributed unevenly around the world. Some regions are well-endowed with one or more fossil fuels, but other regions have little.

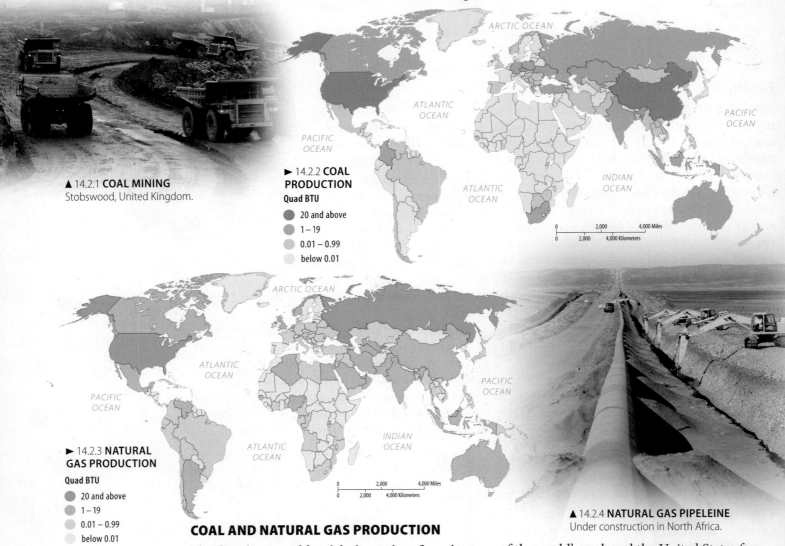

▲ 14.2.1 **COAL MINING**
Stobswood, United Kingdom.

▶ 14.2.2 **COAL PRODUCTION**
Quad BTU
- 20 and above
- 1 – 19
- 0.01 – 0.99
- below 0.01

▶ 14.2.3 **NATURAL GAS PRODUCTION**
Quad BTU
- 20 and above
- 1 – 19
- 0.01 – 0.99
- below 0.01

▲ 14.2.4 **NATURAL GAS PIPELEINE**
Under construction in North Africa.

COAL AND NATURAL GAS PRODUCTION

The distribution of fossil fuels partly reflects how they form.

- Coal formed in tropical locations, in lush, swampy areas rich in plants. Thanks to the slow movement of Earth's drifting continents, the tropical swamps of 250 million years ago have relocated to the midlatitudes. Consequently, today's main deposits of coal are in midlatitude countries (Figure 14.2.1). China is responsible for extracting 40 percent of the world's coal, and the United States for 20 percent (Figure 14.2.2).

- Natural gas formed millions of years ago from sediment deposited on the seafloor. Some still lies beneath such seas as the Persian Gulf and the North Sea, but other supplies are located beneath land that had been under water millions of years ago. Russia and the United States each account for 18 percent of current natural gas production (Figures 14.2.3 and 14.2.4).

PETROLEUM PRODUCTION

Petroleum, like natural gas, formed millions of years ago from residue deposited on the seafloor. Russia, Saudi Arabia, and the United States together account for one-third of current petroleum production (Figure 14.2.5).

The United States produced more petroleum than it consumed during the first half of the twentieth century. But beginning in the 1950s the handful of large transnational companies then in control of international petroleum distribution determined that extracting domestic petroleum was more expensive than importing it from Southwest Asia.

Several oil-producing countries, primarily in Southwest Asia, created the Organization of Petroleum Exporting Countries (OPEC) in 1960. OPEC flexed its muscles in 1973–74 by refusing to sell petroleum to states that supported Israel, including the United States. OPEC lifted the boycott in 1974 and instead raised the price of petroleum (Figure 14.2.6). The price of petroleum plummeted during the late twentieth century, leading the United States and other major consuming countries to believe that the price would remain low for some time in the twenty-first century. As in the 1970s, Americans were unprepared for the shock of steep oil price rises in the twenty-first century when supplies were disrupted in the wake of terrorist attacks and several wars in the Middle East.

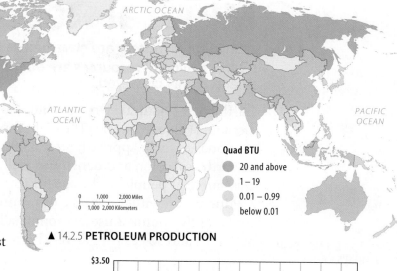

Quad BTU
- 20 and above
- 1 – 19
- 0.01 – 0.99
- below 0.01

▲ 14.2.5 **PETROLEUM PRODUCTION**

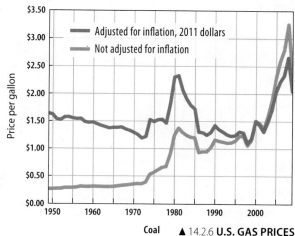

▲ 14.2.6 **U.S. GAS PRICES**

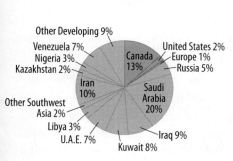

Petroleum

Other Developing 9%
Venezuela 7%
Nigeria 3%
Kazakhstan 2%
Canada 13%
United States 2%
Europe 1%
Russia 5%
Iran 10%
Saudi Arabia 20%
Other Southwest Asia 2%
Libya 3%
U.A.E. 7%
Kuwait 8%
Iraq 9%

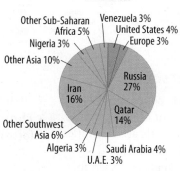

Natural Gas

Other Sub-Saharan Africa 5%
Venezuela 3%
United States 4%
Europe 3%
Nigeria 3%
Other Asia 10%
Russia 27%
Iran 16%
Qatar 14%
Other Southwest Asia 6%
Algeria 3%
Saudi Arabia 4%
U.A.E. 3%

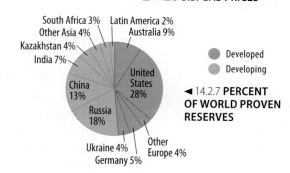

Coal

South Africa 3%
Other Asia 4%
Kazakhstan 4%
India 7%
Latin America 2%
Australia 9%
China 13%
United States 28%
Russia 18%
Ukraine 4%
Germany 5%
Other Europe 4%

- Developed
- Developing

◀ 14.2.7 **PERCENT OF WORLD PROVEN RESERVES**

FOSSIL FUEL RESERVES

How much of the fossil-fuel supply remains? The amount of energy remaining in deposits that have been discovered is called a **proven reserve**. At current rates of use, proven reserves are approximately 50 years for petroleum, 60 years for natural gas, and 175 years for coal (Figure 14.2.7).

Unless substantial new proven reserves are found—or consumption decreases sharply—the world's petroleum and natural gas reserves will be depleted sometime in the twenty-first century. However, some deposits in the world have not yet been discovered. The energy in deposits that are undiscovered but thought to exist is a **potential reserve**. Estimates of proven reserves of petroleum and natural gas vary widely, from a few years to several hundred years (Figure 14.2.8).

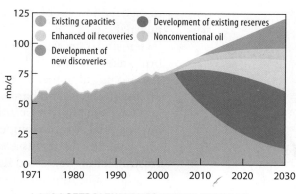

- Existing capacities
- Enhanced oil recoveries
- Development of new discoveries
- Development of existing reserves
- Nonconventional oil

▲ 14.2.8 **PETROLEUM PRODUCTION OUTLOOK**

14.3 Mineral Resources

▶ Mineral resources are classified as nonmetallic or metallic.

▶ Some mineral resources are ubiquitous and abundant, whereas others are scarce and highly clustered.

Earth has 92 natural elements, but about 99 percent of the crust is composed of eight elements (Figure 14.3.1). The eight most common elements combine with thousands of rare ones to form approximately 3,000 different minerals, all with their own properties of hardness, color, and density, as well as spatial distribution. Each mineral is potentially a resource, if people find a use for it (Figure 14.3.2).

Minerals are either metallic or nonmetallic. In weight, more than 90 percent of the minerals that humans use are nonmetallic, but metallic minerals are important for economic activities and so carry relatively high value.

▼ 14.3.1 **ELEMENTS IN EARTH'S CRUST**

▶ 14.3.2 **PRODUCTION OF IMPORTANT MINERALS**

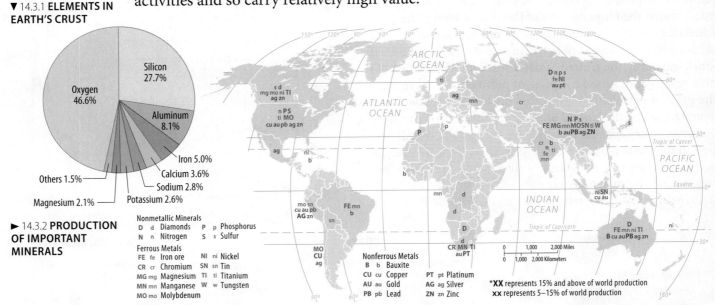

Nonmetallic Minerals			
D d	Diamonds	P p	Phosphorus
N n	Nitrogen	S s	Sulfur

Ferrous Metals			
FE fe	Iron ore	NI ni	Nickel
CR cr	Chromium	SN sn	Tin
MG mg	Magnesium	TI ti	Titanium
MN mn	Manganese	W w	Tungsten
MO mo	Molybdenum		

Nonferrous Metals			
B b	Bauxite		
CU cu	Copper	PT pt	Platinum
AU au	Gold	AG ag	Silver
PB pb	Lead	ZN zn	Zinc

*XX represents 15% and above of world production
xx represents 5–15% of world production

NONMETALLIC MINERAL RESOURCES

Building stones, such as rocks, coarse gravel, and fine sand, account for 90 percent of nonmetallic mineral extraction. These minerals are fashioned into objects of daily use, such as roads and tools. The rocks and earthen materials used for these purposes are so common that differences in distribution are of little consequence at the international scale.

Gemstones are valued for their color and brilliance when cut and polished. Diamonds are also useful in manufacturing, because they are the strongest and hardest known material and have the highest thermal conductivity of any material at room temperature. Two-thirds of the world's diamonds are currently mined in Australia, Botswana, and Russia.

Nonmetallic minerals are also used for fertilizer. Because soils are often deficient in these minerals, farmers add them. Important nonmetallic mineral sources of fertilizers include:

- **Phosphorus.** Obtained from phosphate rock (apatite), found among the marine sediments of old seabeds. Morocco possesses one-half of the world's reserves.

- **Potassium.** Obtained from the evaporation of saltwater. Principal sources include former Soviet Union countries, North America, and the Dead Sea.

- **Calcium.** Concentrated in subhumid soils such as the plains and prairies of the western United States and Canada, as well as Russia's steppes.

- **Sulfur.** Used to make insecticides and herbicides, as well as fertilizers. North America produces one-fourth of the world total (Figure 14.3.3).

- **Nitrogen.** Ubiquitous in the atmosphere but it takes a lot of energy to capture nitrogen.

METALLIC MINERALS: IRON ORE AND STEEL ALLOYS

Metallic minerals have properties that are especially valuable for fashioning machinery, vehicles, and other essential elements of contemporary society. They are to varying degrees malleable (able to be hammered into thin plates) and ductile (able to be drawn into fine wire) and are good conductors of heat and electricity. Each metal possesses these qualities in different combinations and degrees and therefore has its distinctive set of uses.

Many metals are capable of combining with other metals to form alloys with distinctive properties. Alloys are known as ferrous or nonferrous. A **ferrous** alloy contains iron, and a nonferrous one does not. The word "ferrous" comes from the Latin for iron.

Iron is extracted from iron ore, by far the world's most widely used ore. Humans began fashioning tools and weapons from iron 4,000 years ago.

Important metals used to make ferrous alloys include:

- **Chromium.** A principal component of stainless steel, extracted from chromite ore, one-half of which is mined in South Africa.

- **Manganese.** Especially vital for making steel because it imparts toughness and carries off undesirable sulfur and oxygen during the

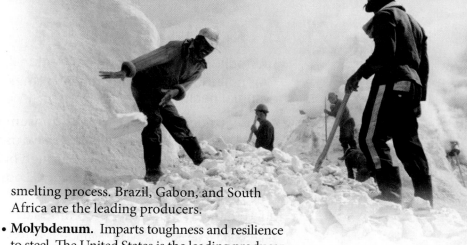

smelting process. Brazil, Gabon, and South Africa are the leading producers.

- **Molybdenum.** Imparts toughness and resilience to steel. The United States is the leading producer.

- **Nickel.** Used primarily for stainless steel and high-temperature and electrical alloys. Russia, Australia, and Canada are the leading producers.

- **Tin.** Valued for its corrosion-resistant properties, used for plating iron and steel. China is the leading producer.

- **Titanium.** A lightweight, high-strength, corrosion-resistant metal used as white pigment in paint. Australia is the leading producer, extracted primarily from the mineral ilmenite.

- **Tungsten.** Makes very hard alloys with steel and is used to manufacture tungsten carbide for cutting tools. China is responsible for 90 percent of world production.

▲ 14.3.3 **SULFUR MINING** Indonesia.

OTHER METALLIC METALS

Important metals utilized for products other than iron and steel include:

- **Aluminum.** The most abundant nonferrous metal, lighter, stronger, and more resistant to corrosion than iron and steel; obtained primarily through extraction from bauxite ore. Australia is the leading producer.

- **Copper.** Valued for its high ductility, malleability, thermal and electrical conductivity, and resistance to corrosion, used primarily in electronics and constructing buildings. Chile is the leading producer.

- **Lead.** Very corrosion-resistant, dense, ductile, and malleable, used for thousands of years, first in building materials and pipes, then in ammunition, brass, glass, and crystal, and now primarily in motor-vehicle batteries. Australia and China are the leading producers.

- **Magnesium.** Relatively light yet strong, so used to produce lightweight, corrosion-

resistant alloys, especially with aluminum to make beverage cans. China supplies three-fourths of the world's magnesium.

- **Zinc.** Primarily a coating to protect iron and steel from corrosion and as an alloy to make bronze and brass. China is the leading producer.

- **Precious metals.** Silver and gold have been prized since ancient times for their beauty and durability. Platinum is used in motor vehicles for catalytic converters and fuel cells (Figure 14.3.4).

▼ 14.3.4 **GOLD MINING** Open pit at Fort Knox mine, near Fairbanks, Alaska.

14.4 Air Pollution

▸ **Air pollution occurs at global, regional, and local scales.**

▸ **Air pollution can cause global warming, damage lakes and vegetation, and harm animal health.**

In our consideration of resources, consumption is half of the equation—waste disposal is the other half. All of the resources we use are eventually returned to the atmosphere, bodies of water, or land surface through burning, rinsing, or discarding. We rely on air, water, and land to remove and disperse our waste. Pollution occurs when more waste is added than a resource can accommodate.

At ground level, Earth's average atmosphere is made up of about 78 percent nitrogen, 21 percent oxygen, and less than 1 percent argon. The remaining 0.04 percent includes several trace gases, some of which are critical. **Air pollution** is a concentration of trace substances at a greater level than occurs in average air. Air pollution concerns geographers at three scales—global, regional, and local.

GLOBAL-SCALE AIR POLLUTION

Two global-scale issues are global warming and ozone damage:

• **Global warming.** The average temperature of Earth's surface has increased by 1° Celsius (2° Fahrenheit) during the past century (Figure 14.4.1). Human actions, especially the burning of fossil fuels (which release carbon dioxide), may have caused this (Figure 14.4.2). Global warming of only a few degrees could melt the polar ice caps and raise the level of the oceans many meters (Figure 14.4.3).

A concentration of trace gases in the atmosphere can delay the return of some of the heat leaving Earth's surface heading for space, thereby raising Earth's temperatures. When fossil fuels are burned, one of the trace gases, carbon dioxide, is discharged into the atmosphere.

Plants and oceans absorb much of the discharges, but increased fossil-fuel burning during the past 200 years has caused the level of carbon dioxide in the atmosphere to rise by more than one-fourth, according to the UN Intergovernmental Panel on Climate Change. The increase in Earth's temperature, caused by carbon dioxide trapping some of the radiation emitted by the surface, is called the **greenhouse effect**.

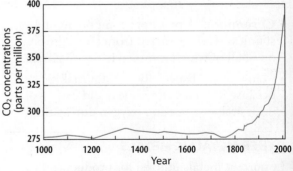

▲ 14.4.1 **GLOBAL WARMING AND CARBON DIOXIDE CONCENTRATIONS 1880–2010**

▲ 14.4.2 **CARBON DIOXIDE CONCENTRATIONS 1000–2010**

• **Global-scale ozone damage.** Earth's stratosphere—the zone between 15 and 50 kilometers (9 to 30 miles) above Earth's surface—contains a concentration of **ozone** gas. The ozone layer absorbs dangerous ultraviolet (UV) rays from the Sun. Were it not for the ozone in the stratosphere, UV rays would damage plants, cause skin cancer, and disrupt food chains.

Earth's protective ozone layer is threatened by pollutants called **chlorofluorocarbons (CFCs)**. CFCs such as freon were once widely used as coolants in refrigerators and air conditioners. When they leak from these appliances, the CFCs are carried into the stratosphere, where they break down Earth's protective layer of ozone gas. Most countries have agreed to cease using CFCs by 2020 in developed countries and by 2030 in developing countries.

▼ 14.4.3 **RECEDING NORTH POLAR ICE CAP** Between 1979 and 2005, the polar ice cap melted visibly.

REGIONAL-SCALE AIR POLLUTION

At the regional scale, air pollution may damage a region's vegetation and water supply through **acid deposition** (Figure 14.4.4). Sulfur oxides and nitrogen oxides, emitted by burning fossil fuels, enter the atmosphere, where they combine with oxygen and water. Tiny droplets of sulfuric acid and nitric acid form and return to Earth's surface as acid deposition. When dissolved in water, the acids may fall as **acid precipitation**—rain, snow, or fog. The acids can also be deposited in dust.

Geographers are particularly interested in the effects of acid precipitation because the worst damage may not be experienced at the same location as the emission of the pollutants. Before they reach the surface, these acidic droplets might be carried hundreds of kilometers (Figure 14.4.5).

LOCAL-SCALE AIR POLLUTION

At the local scale, air pollution is especially severe in places where emission sources are concentrated, such as in urban areas. The air above urban areas may be especially polluted because a large number of factories, motor vehicles, and other polluters emit residuals in a concentrated area. Weather conditions may make it difficult for the emissions to dissipate.

Urban air pollution has three basic components:

- **Carbon Monoxide.** Produced by improper combustion in power plants and vehicles.

- **Hydrocarbons.** Also produced by improper combustion, as well as from evaporation of paint solvents. Hydrocarbons and nitrogen oxides in the presence of sunlight form **photochemical smog**, which causes respiratory problems, stinging in the eyes, and an ugly haze over cities (Figure 14.4.6).

- **Particulates.** Dust and smoke particles, especially from factory smoke stacks and vehicle exhausts.

Air quality has improved in developed countries, where strict clean-air regulations are enforced on vehicles and factories. Limited emission controls in developing countries contribute to severe urban air pollution.

▲ 14.4.4 **EFFECTS OF ACID DEPOSITION**
Spruce-fir forest in North Carolina's Blue Ridge Mountains damaged by acid precipitation.

1989–1991

2001–2003

kg/ha

| 0 | 10 | 20 | 30 | 40+ |

▲ 14.4.5 **ACID DEPOSITION IN THE UNITED STATES**
Maps show the changing rate of deposition of wet sulfate, a major source of acid deposition. As a result of emissions controls, the rate declines significantly between the two periods shown on the maps.

▼ 14.4.6 **SMOG OVER LOS ANGELES**

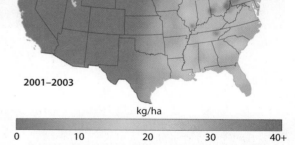

14.5 Water Pollution

▶ **Three water pollution sources are industries, sewers, and agriculture.**

▶ **Sources of water pollution are either point or nonpoint.**

Water serves many human purposes. Water must be drunk to survive. It is used for cooking and bathing. Water provides a location for boating, swimming, fishing, and other recreational activities. It is home to fish and other aquatic life.

These uses depend on fresh, clean, unpolluted water. But that is not always available, because people also use water for purposes that pollute it. Pollution is widespread, because it is easy to dump waste into a river and let the water carry it downstream where it becomes someone else's problem. Water can decompose some waste without adversely impacting other activities, but the volume exceeds the capacity of many rivers and lakes to accommodate it.

SOURCES OF WATER POLLUTION

Three main sources generate most water pollution:

- **Industries.** Industries such as steel, chemicals, paper products, and food processing are major water polluters. Each requires a large amount of water in the manufacturing process and generates a lot of wastewater. Food processors, for example, wash pesticides and chemicals from fruit and vegetables. They also use water to remove skins, stems, and other parts. Water can also be polluted by industrial accidents, such as petroleum spills from ocean tankers and leaks from underground tanks at gasoline stations (Figure 14.5.1).

- **Municipal Sewage.** In developed countries, sewers carry wastewater from sinks, bathtubs, and toilets to a municipal treatment plant, where most—but not all—of the pollutants are removed. The treated wastewater is then typically dumped back into a river or lake. In developing countries, sewer systems are rare, and wastewater usually drains untreated into rivers and lakes (Figure 14.5.2).

- **Agriculture.** Fertilizers and pesticides spread on fields to increase agricultural productivity are carried into rivers and lakes by the irrigation system or natural runoff. Expanded use of these products may help to avoid a global food crisis, yet they destroy aquatic life by polluting rivers.

▲ 14.5.1 **WATER POLLUTION SOURCE: INDUSTRY**
Tributary of the Schelde River near Antwerp, Belgium.

◀ 14.5.2 **WATER POLLUTION SOURCE: SEWAGE**
Gozo Island, Malta.

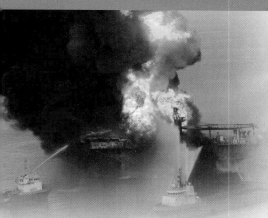

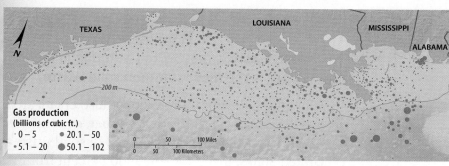

◀ 14.5.3 **DEEPWATER HORIZON OIL RIG EXPLOSION**

▲ 14.5.4 **GULF OF MEXICO OIL DRILLING SITES**

Gas production
(billions of cubic ft.)
· 0 – 5   ● 20.1 – 50
· 5.1 – 20   ● 50.1 – 102

POINT-SOURCE WATER POLLUTION

Sources of pollution can be divided into point sources and nonpoint sources. **Point-source** pollution enters a stream at a specific location. Industries and municipal sewage systems tend to pollute through point sources, such as a pipe from a wastewater treatment plant.

An especially severe example of point-source pollution resulted from the 2010 explosion of the Deepwater Horizon oil rig in the Gulf of Mexico, around 60 kilometers (40 miles) off the coast of Louisiana. The rig, owned and operated by Transocean, was drilling for oil on the seafloor, when it exploded, killing 11 workers on the platform (Figure 14.5.3). During the three months it took emergency repairers to cap the leak, 780,000 cubic meters (4.9 million barrels) of crude oil gushed into the Gulf of Mexico. The spill did extensive damage to marine plants and animals, as well as to those along the shoreline of Louisiana and neighboring states. BP, which had commissioned the rig, was ultimately assigned principal responsibility for the disaster, because it had been found to have authorized a flawed design for the rig and had rushed construction of the rig (Figure 14.5.4).

NONPOINT-SOURCE WATER POLLUTION

Nonpoint-source pollution comes from a large, diffuse area. Farmers tend to pollute through nonpoint sources, such as by permitting fertilizer to wash from a field during a storm. Deepwater Horizon notwithstanding, point-source pollutants are usually smaller in quantity and much easier to control. Nonpoint sources usually pollute in greater quantities and are much harder to control.

One of the world's most extreme instances of nonpoint-source water pollution is the Aral Sea in the former Soviet Union, now divided between the countries of Kazakhstan and Uzbekistan. The world's fourth-largest lake in 1960, the Aral has been shrinking rapidly in area and volume (Figure 14.5.5). The Aral Sea died because the Soviet Union diverted its tributary rivers, the Amu Dar'ya and the Syr Dar'ya, beginning in 1954, to irrigate cotton fields. Ironically, the cotton now is withering because winds pick up salt from the exposed lakebed and deposit it on the cotton fields.

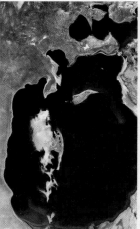
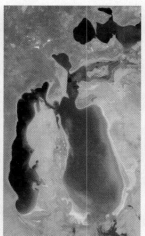
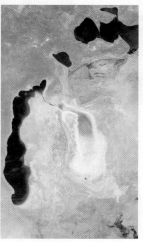

◀ 14.5.5 **THE DISAPPEARING ARAL SEA**
The Aral Sea in 1989 (left), 2003 (center), and 2009 (right). The 1989 image shows small islands forming in the sea. The 2003 image shows that the islands have grown so large that they have divided the sea. The 2009 image shows that silting has turned most of the former water area into a wasteland of salt.

14.6 Solid Waste Pollution

▶ **Solid waste is most often dumped in landfills.**

▶ **Paper is the most common solid waste.**

When we consume a product, we also create an unwanted by-product—a glass, metal, paper, or plastic box, wrapper, or container in which the product is packaged. About 2.1 kilograms (4.6 pounds) of solid waste per person is generated daily in the United States, including about 60 percent from residences and 40 percent from businesses. Disposal of solid waste is done in three ways: landfill, incineration, and recycling.

LANDFILL DISPOSAL

The **sanitary landfill** is by far the most common strategy for disposal of solid waste in the United States. More than one-half of the country's waste is trucked to landfills and buried under soil. This strategy is the opposite of our disposal of gaseous and liquid wastes: We disperse air and water pollutants into the atmosphere, rivers, and eventually the ocean, but we concentrate solid waste in thousands of landfills. Concentration would seem to eliminate solid-waste pollution, but it may only hide it—temporarily. Chemicals released by the decomposing solid waste can leak from the landfill into groundwater. This can contaminate water wells, soil, and nearby streams.

The number of landfills in the United States has declined by three-fourths since 1990. Thousands of small-town "dumps" have been closed and replaced by a small number of large regional ones (Figure 14.6.1). Better compaction methods, combined with expansion in the land area of some of the large regional dumps, have resulted in expanded landfill capacity (Figure 14.6.2).

Some communities now pay to use landfills elsewhere. New Jersey and New York are two states that regularly try to dispose of their solid waste by transporting it out of state. New York City exports 25,000 tons of trash a day to other communities. Passaic County, New Jersey, hauls waste 400 kilometers (250 miles) west to Johnstown, Pennsylvania. San Francisco trucks solid waste to Altamont, California, 100 kilometers (60 miles) away.

▼ 14.6.2 **LANDFILL, UNITED KINGDOM**

▲ 14.6.1 **SANITARY LANDFILL**
Much of the solid waste generated in Ohio, Kentucky, and Indiana is transported to this sanitary landfill near Cincinnati. Use Google Earth to see how it has increased in land area.

Fly to *3800 Struble Road, Cincinnati, OH 45251.*

Rotate image so that N is to the right (west is at the top).

Zoom out and reposition the image so that the entire landfill can be viewed.

Use the ruler to measure the area of the landfill.

Click the clock to move the image to 3/31/94. Measure the area of the landfill on that date.

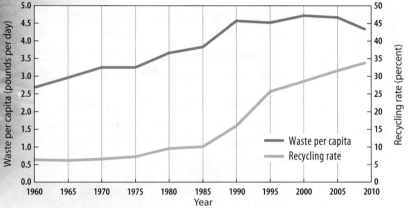

▲ 14.6.4 **RECYCLING IN THE UNITED STATES**

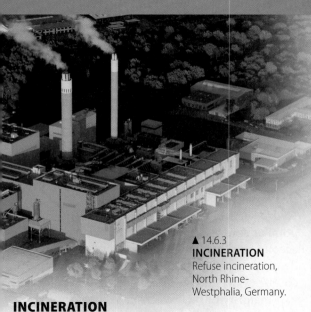

▲ 14.6.3
INCINERATION
Refuse incineration,
North Rhine-
Westphalia, Germany.

INCINERATION

Incineration reduces the bulk of the trash by about three-fourths, and the remaining ash demands far less landfill space. Incineration also provides energy—the incinerator's heat can boil water to produce steam heat or to operate a turbine that generates electricity. Given the shortage of space in landfills, the percentage of solid waste that is burned has increased rapidly during the past three decades, to one-sixth of solid waste (Figure 14.6.3). However, solid waste, a mixture of many materials, may burn inefficiently. Burning releases some toxins into the air, and some remain in the ash. Thus, solving one pollution problem may increase another.

HAZARDOUS WASTE

Disposing of hazardous waste is especially difficult. Hazardous wastes include heavy metals (including mercury, cadmium, and zinc), PCB oils from electrical equipment, cyanides, strong solvents, acids, and caustics. These may have been unwanted by-products generated in manufacturing or discarded after use. If poisonous industrial residuals are not carefully placed in protective containers, the chemicals may leach into the soil and contaminate groundwater or escape into the atmosphere. Breathing air or consuming water contaminated with toxic wastes can cause cancer, mutations, chronic ailments, and even immediate death (Figure 14.6.5).

As toxic-waste disposal sites become increasingly hard to find, some European and North American firms have tried to transport their waste to West Africa, often unscrupulously.

RECYCLING SOLID WASTE

Recycling is the separation, collection, processing, marketing, and reuse of the unwanted material. Recycling increased in the United States from 7 percent of all solid waste in 1970 to 34 percent in 2009 (Figure 14.6.4). The percentage of materials recovered by recycling varies widely by product: Two-thirds of yard trimmings and one-half of paper products are recycled, compared to only 7 percent of plastic and 3 percent of food scraps. The amount of solid waste generated by Americans increased by 122 million tons between 1970 and 2009 and the amount recycled increased by 74 million tons, so despite increased recycling, more waste went into landfills or incinerators over the period.

Some firms have signed contracts with West African countries, whereas others have found isolated locations to dump waste without official consent.

▼ 14.6.5 **MEXICO CITY'S GARBAGE PICKERS**
In Mexico City, thousands of people known as pepenadores, or garbage pickers, survive by going through rubbish. Older men make up the largest share of pepenadores. What they find is sold to companies for a small amount. In many cases, pepenadores actually live at the dump.

14.7 Renewable Resources

► Renewable energy sources provide alternatives to fossil fuels.
► Renewable energy sources include biomass, hydroelectric, wind, and solar power.

Renewable energy provides alternatives to fossil fuels. Water, wind, and the Sun provide sources of renewable energy. Nuclear power, though not renewable, has been an important alternative to fossil fuels in some places.

► 14.7.1
ELECTRICITY FROM HYDROELECTRIC POWER
Hoover Dam.

HYDROELECTRIC

Hydroelectricity is the world's second-most popular source of electricity, after coal, accounting for about one-fourth of worldwide demand (Figure 14.7.1). Many developing countries depend on hydroelectric power for the vast majority of their electricity. Hydroelectric dams may flood formerly usable land, cause erosion, and upset ecosystems. The world's largest hydroelectric river dam, China's Three Gorges Dam, spanning the Yangtze River, has been especially criticized for its effects on local ecosystems (Figure 14.7.2).

► 14.7.2 **THREE GORGES DAM, YANGTZE RIVER, CHINA**

SOLAR

The ultimate renewable resource is solar energy, supplied by the Sun. The Sun's energy is free and ubiquitous and utilizing it does not damage the environment or cause pollution. Solar energy is harnessed in two ways:

• **Passive solar energy systems**, such as heat-generating south-facing windows.

• **Active solar energy systems**, such as **photovoltaic cells**, which convert light energy to electrical energy (Figure 14.7.3).

▲ 14.7.3 **SOLAR PANELS**
Fixing sloar panels to a warehouse roof, Germany.

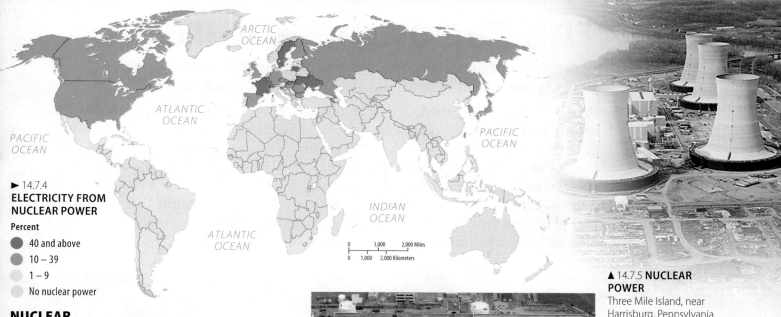

► 14.7.4
ELECTRICITY FROM NUCLEAR POWER

Percent

- 40 and above
- 10 – 39
- 1 – 9
- No nuclear power

▲ 14.7.5 **NUCLEAR POWER**
Three Mile Island, near Harrisburg, Pennsylvania, was the site of the worst nuclear power plant accident in the United States, in 1979.

◄ 14.7.6 **FUKUSHIMA DAIICHI NUCLEAR POWER PLANT, JAPAN**

NUCLEAR

Nuclear power supplies about one-sixth of the world's electricity (Figure 14.7.4). The big advantage of nuclear power is the large amount of energy released from a small amount of material. One kilogram of enriched nuclear fuel contains more than 2 million times the energy in 1 kilogram of coal. Waste from nuclear fuel is highly radioactive and lethal for thousands of years, and no one has yet devised permanent storage for it. Uranium, required for nuclear power, is a finite resource. Explosions and radiation leakage at Japan's Fukushima Daiichi nuclear power plant after an earthquake and tsunami in 2011 caused a number of countries to reduce dependency on nuclear power (Figure 14.7.6).

WIND POWER

Hundreds of wind "farms" consisting of dozens of windmills have been constructed across the United States. One-third of the country is considered windy enough to make wind power economically feasible (Figure 14.7.7). Like moving water, moving air can turn a turbine. Construction of a windmill modifies the environment much less severely than construction of a dam across a river. However, some environmentalists oppose construction of windmills because they can be noisy and lethal for birds and bats. They also can be visually blighting when constructed on mountaintops or offshore of places of outstanding beauty.

◄ 14.7.7 **AREAS SUITABLE FOR WIND POWER**

Classes of wind power density
Wind energy producing regions

- 7 (highest wind power)
- 6
- 5
- 4
- 3
- 2
- 1 (lowest wind power)

Unsuitable for wind energy production

► 14.7.8 **WINDFARM**
California.

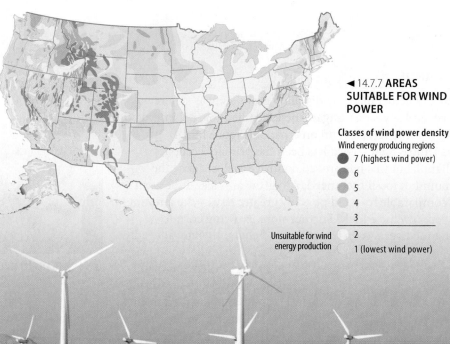

14.8 The Car of the Future

▶ Cars of the future will run on a variety of alternative power sources.
▶ The "greenest" alternative power source varies by location.

One of the greatest challenges to reducing pollution and conserving nonrenewable resources is reliance on petroleum as automotive fuel. Consumers in developed countries are reluctant to give up their motor vehicles, while demand for vehicles is soaring in developing countries. So carmakers are scrambling to bring alternative fuel vehicles to the market. Alternative technologies include diesel, biofuel, hybrid, electric, and hydrogen (Figure 14.8.1). The Department of Energy forecasts that around one-half of all new vehicles sold in the United States in 2020 will be powered by one of these alternatives to the conventional gas engine.

▼ 14.8.1
ALTERNATIVE FUEL VEHICLE TIME LINE

DIESEL

Diesel engines burn fuel more efficiently, with greater compression at a higher temperature than conventional gas engines. Most new vehicles in Europe are diesel-powered, where they are valued for zippy acceleration on crowded roads, as well as for high fuel efficiency (Figure 14.8.2). Diesels have made limited inroads in the United States, where they were identified with ponderous heavy trucks, poorly performing versions in the 1980s, and generation of more pollutants. Biodiesel fuel mixes petroleum diesel with biodiesel (typically 5 percent), which is produced from vegetable oils or recycled restaurant grease.

▲ 14.8.2 **DIESEL**
Germany.

▶ 14.8.3 **HYBRID**
Toyota Prius.

HYBRID

Sales of hybrid vehicles increased rapidly during the first decade of the twenty-first century, led by Toyota's success with the hybrid Prius (Figure 14.8.3). A gasoline engine powers the vehicle at high speeds, but at low speeds, when the gas engine is at its least efficient, an electric motor takes over. Energy that would otherwise be wasted in coasting and braking is also captured as electricity and stored until needed.

1990

2000

ETHANOL

Ethanol is fuel made by distilling crops such as sugarcane, corn, and soybeans. Sugarcane is distilled for fuel in Brazil, where most vehicles run on ethanol (Figure 14.8.4). In the United States, corn has been the principal crop for ethanol, but this has proved controversial, because the amount of fossil fuels needed to grow and distill the corn is comparable to—and possibly greater than—the amount saved in vehicle fuels. Furthermore, growing corn for ethanol diverts corn from the food chain, thereby allegedly causing higher food prices in the United States and globally. More promising is ethanol distilled from cellulosic biomass, such as trees and grasses.

▲ 14.8.5 **PLUG-IN HYBRID**
Chevrolet Volt.

PLUG-IN HYBRID

The battery supplies the power at all speeds. It can be recharged in one of two ways. While the car is moving, the battery can be recharged by a gas engine. When it is parked, the car can be recharged by plugging into an electrical outlet (Figure 14.8.5). The principal limitation of a full electric vehicle has been the short range of the battery before it needs recharging (see Figure 14.8.6). Using a gas engine to recharge the battery extends the range of the plug-in hybrid to that of a conventional gas engine.

◀ 14.8.4 **ETHANOL**
Gas station in Brazil.

PROMOÇÃO
ÁLCOOL
Comum
1.49

▲ 14.8.6 **FULL LECTRIC**
Nissan Leaf

FULL ELECTRIC

A full electric vehicle has no gas engine. When the battery is discharged, the vehicle will not run until the battery is recharged by plugging it into an outlet. Motorists can make trips in a local area and recharge the battery at night. Out-of-town trips are difficult because recharging opportunities are scarce. In large cities, a number of downtown garages and shopping malls have recharging stations, but few exist in rural areas (Figure 14.8.6).

2020

HYDROGEN FUEL CELL

Hydrogen forced through a PEM (polymer electrolyte membrane or proton exchange membrane) combines with oxygen from the air, producing an electric charge. The electricity powers an electric motor. Fuel cells are now widely used in small vehicles such as forklifts. Fuel cell vehicles are on the streets first in a handful of large East- and West-Coast cities, where hydrogen fueling stations have been constructed (Figure 14.8.7).

REGIONAL VARIATIONS IN ELECTRICITY

Electric-powered vehicles require recharging by plugging into a source of electricity such as an outlet in the garage that ultimately comes from a power plant. Though fossil fuel is not being pumped directly into the tank of the electric-powered vehicle, fossil fuel is being consumed to generate the electricity at the power plant.

In fact, the United States as a whole generates around one-half of its electricity from coal-burning power plants and another one-fifth from natural gas. An electric vehicle does reduce consumption of an increasingly scarce and expensive resource—petroleum. But if the electricity is generated by natural gas, then plugging a vehicle into the electric grid may conserve petroleum at the expense of more rapid depletion of natural gas. If electricity is generated by coal, a plug-in may cause more air pollution.

Electricity is generated differently across the fifty U.S. states. In the Pacific Northwest, where hydroelectric is the leading source of electricity, recharging electric vehicles will have much less of an impact on air quality than will be the case in the Midwest (Figure 14.8.8). States that depend on farm production may benefit from increased use of ethanol. Thus, the "greenest" alternative varies by location (Figure 14.8.9).

◄ 14.8.7 **HYDROGEN FUEL CELL**
Filling station in California.

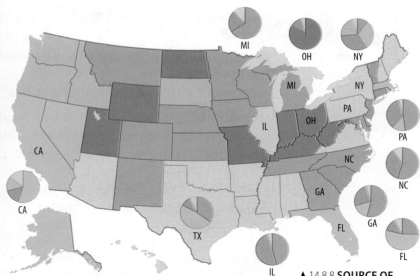

▲ 14.8.8 **SOURCE OF ELECTRICITY BY U.S. STATE**
- 75% and above coal
- 50%–74% coal
- 50% and above natural gas
- 50% and above nuclear
- 50% and above hydroelectric
- No source 50% or above

Source of electricity in the ten most populous states

▼ 14.8.9 **CONSTRUCTING POWER LINES IN VIRGINIA**

14.9 Sustainability

▶ Sustainable development utilizes resources at a rate that conserves them for the future.
▶ Biodiversity measures the number of species in an area.

Sustainability is the use of Earth's limited resources by humans in ways that do not constrain resource use by people in the future. Geographers emphasize that each resource has a distinctive capacity for accommodating human activities.

SUSTAINABLE DEVELOPMENT

Sustainable development is "development that meets the needs of the present without compromising the ability of future generations to meet their own needs," according to the United Nations. The UN definition came in the 1987 Brundtland Report, named for the World Commission on Environment and Development's chair, Gro Harlem Brundtland, former prime minister of Norway. Titled *Our Common Future*, the Brundtland Report was a landmark in recognizing sustainable development as a combination of environmental and economic elements.

The report argued that sustainable development had to recognize the importance of economic growth while conserving natural resources. Environmental protection, economic growth, and social equity are linked because economic development aimed at reducing poverty can at the same time threaten the environment (Figure 14.9.1).

A rising level of economic development generates increased pollution, at least until a country reaches a GNI of about $30,000 per person, according to the World Bank (Figure 14.9.2). In the early stages of industrialization, pollution-control devices are an unpopular luxury that makes cars and other consumer goods more expensive.

Critical to world pollution in the twenty-first century is China. The rapid economic transformation of China has resulted in rapidly rising levels of pollution. The country has 16 of the 20 most polluted cities, according to the World Bank (Figure 14.9.3).

Some environmentally oriented critics have argued that it is too late to discuss sustainability. One critic, the World Wildlife Fund (WWF), claims that the world surpassed its sustainable level around 1980. The WWF Living Planet Report calculates that humans are already using all of the productive land and none is left for future growth. Others criticize sustainability from the opposite perspective: Human activities have not exceeded Earth's capacity, they argue, because resource availability has no maximum, and Earth's resources have no absolute limit because the definition of resources changes drastically and unpredictably over time.

▼ 14.9.1 **SUSTAINABLE DEVELOPMENT**

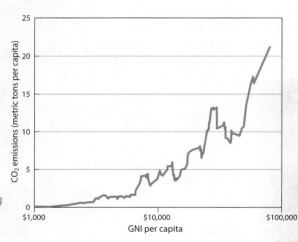

▶ 14.9.2 **POLLUTION COMPARED TO A COUNTRY'S WEALTH**
As a country's per capita income increases, its per capita carbon dioxide emissions also increase. Some of the wealthiest countries, with GNI per capita between $30,000 and $50,000, located primarily in Europe, show declines in pollution. However, the world's richest countries, including the United States and several in Southwest Asia, display the highest pollution levels.

CO_2 emissions (metric tons per capita)

25
20
15
10
5
0

$1,000 $10,000 $100,000

GNI per capita

▼ 14.9.3 **POLLUTION IN CHINA**
Children wearing smog-protection masks.

CONSERVATION AND PRESERVATION

Conservation and preservation are two different approaches to resource management

- **Conservation** is the sustainable use and management of natural resources such as wildlife, water, air, and Earth's resources to meet human needs, including food, medicine, and recreation. Renewable resources such as trees are conserved if they are consumed at a less rapid rate than they can be replaced (Figure 14.9.4). Nonrenewable resources such as fossil fuels are conserved if remaining reserves are maintained for future generations.

- **Preservation** is the maintenance of resources in their present condition, with as little human impact as possible. Preservation takes the view that the value of nature does not derive from human needs and interests, but from the fact that every plant and animal living on Earth has a right to exist and should be preserved regardless of the cost.

Preservation does not regard nature as a resource for human use. In contrast, conservation is compatible with development but only if natural resources are utilized in a careful rather than a wasteful manner.

▲ 14.9.4 **LOGGING IN IDAHO**

BIODIVERSITY

Many sustainable development initiatives aim to maintain **biodiversity**. Biological diversity, or biodiversity for short, refers to the variety of species across Earth as a whole or in a specific place. Biodiversity is an important development concept because it is a way of summing the total value of Earth's resources available for human use. Sustainable development is promoted when the biodiversity of a particular place or Earth as a whole is protected.

Species variety can be understood from several perspectives. Geographers are especially concerned with biogeographic diversity, whereas biologists are especially concerned with genetic diversity. Biodiversity is measurement of the number of species within a specific region or habitat. A community containing a large number of species is said to be species-rich, whereas an area with few species is species-poor.

Strategies to protect genetic diversity have been established on a global scale. Some endangered species have been protected by the Convention on International Trade in Endangered Species of Wild Fauna and Flora. Examples include the curtailing of logging, whaling, and taking of porpoises in tuna seines (nets). Strategies to protect biogeographic diversity vary among countries. Luxembourg protects 44 percent of its land and Ecuador 38 percent, whereas Cambodia, Iraq, and some former Soviet Union republics have no land under conservation (Figure 14.9.5).

► 14.9.5 **BIODIVERSITY**
The welcome sign at a trailhead to the Monteverde Cloud Forest Reserve, Costa Rica.

Geographers emphasize that each resource in the physical environment has a distinctive capacity for accommodating human activities. Just as a good farmer knows how many animals can be fed on a parcel of land, a geographer can explain the constraints that resources place on population density or economic development in a particular region. With knowledge of these constraints, we will be able to maintain agricultural and industrial development in the future.

Key Questions

How are resources being depleted?

► Most energy comes from three nonrenewable fossil fuels—petroleum, natural gas, and coal.
► Developed countries consume most of the fossil fuels and must import most of them from other countries.
► Petroleum reserves are especially scarce and located primarily in Southwest and Central Asia.
► Nonmetallic and metallic mineral resources of importance to humans are clustered in a handful of locations.

How are resources polluted?

► Air pollution occurs at global, regional, and local scales.
► Water is needed for human survival and is used to discharge waste, especially from industries, sewage, and agriculture.
► Solid waste is clustered in a handful of sanitary landfills.

How are resources being conserved?

► Renewable energy sources include hydroelectric, wind, and solar power.
► Several alternative fuels will be available to power future motor vehicles.
► Sustainable development conserves resources for future generations and preserves biodiversity.

On the Internet

Statistics on production, consumption, and reserves of different energy sources in the United States and worldwide can be founded at the website of the U.S. Department of Energy's Energy Information Administration, accessed at **www.eia.doe.gov**, or scan the QR at the beginning of the chapter.

The U.S. Environmental Protection Agency provides information organized by various types of pollution on its website **www.epa.gov**.

Thinking Geographically

Conservation efforts vary widely around the world (Figure 11.CR.1).

1. What steps has your community taken to recycle solid waste and to conserve energy?

A recent study compared paper and polystyrene foam drinking cups. Foam cups are made from petroleum and do not degrade in landfills. Production of a paper cup consumes 36 times more electricity and generates 580 times more wastewater compared to production of a foam cup, and as it degrades in a landfill, a paper cup releases methane gas, a contributor to the greenhouse effect.

2. Which type of cups should restaurants such as McDonald's be encouraged to use? Why?

Companies that sell motor vehicles in the United States must meet a standard for Corporate Average Fuel Economy (CAFE). This means that the average miles per gallon achieved by all of the vehicles sold in the United States by a particular company must meet a government-mandated level. If they do not, the company must pay a stiff fine.

3. What would be the benefits and challenges of raising the CAFE standard?

▼ 14.CR.1 **COMMUNITY RECYCLING** New Jersey.

Interactive Mapping

ENVIRONMENTAL ISSUES IN NORTH AMERICA

Environmental issues are not distributed uniformly across the United States and Canada.

Open MapMaster North America in   Mastering GEOGRAPHY™

Select: *Environmental Issues* from the *Physical Environment* menu.

For each environmental issue shown on the map, which region has the largest concentration?

Explore

DEFORESTATION IN THE AMAZON

Deforestation in the humid tropics, such as the Amazon region of Brazil, is one of the greatest threats to biodiversity.

Fly to: *10S 63W*

Zoom in to approximately 50,000 ft.

Click the time slider to go back to 6/1975.

How has the use of land changed? Were the changes greater prior to 2000 or after 2000?

Key Terms

Acid deposition
Sulfur oxides and nitrogen oxides, emitted by burning fossil fuels, enter the atmosphere—where they combine with oxygen and water to form sulfuric acid and nitric acid—and return to Earth's surface.

Acid precipitation
Conversion of sulfur oxides and nitrogen oxides to acids that return to Earth as rain, snow, or fog.

Active solar energy systems
Solar energy system that collects energy through the use of mechanical devices such as photovoltaic cells or flat-plate collectors.

Air pollution
Concentration of trace substances, such as carbon monoxide, sulfur dioxide, nitrogen oxides, hydrocarbons, and solid particulates, at a greater level than occurs in average air.

Animate power
Power supplied by people or animals.

Biodiversity
The number of species within a specific habitat.

Chlorofluorocarbon (CFC)
A gas used as a solvent, a propellant in aerosols, a refrigerant, and in plastic foams and fire extinguishers.

Conservation
The sustainable use and management of a natural resource, through consuming at a less rapid rate than it can be replaced.

Ferrous
Metals, including iron ore, that are utilized in the production of iron and steel.

Fossil fuel
Energy source formed from the residue of plants and animals buried millions of years ago.

Greenhouse effect
Anticipated increase in Earth's temperature, caused by carbon dioxide (emitted by burning fossil fuels) trapping some of the radiation emitted by the surface.

Nonferrous
Metals utilized to make products other than iron and steel.

Nonpoint-source pollution
Pollution that originates from a large, diffuse area.

Nonrenewable energy
A source of energy that is a finite supply capable of being exhausted.

Ozone
A gas that absorbs ultraviolet solar radiation, found in the stratosphere, a zone between 15 and 50 kilometers (9 to 30 miles) above Earth's surface.

Passive solar energy systems
Solar energy system that collects energy without the use of mechanical devices.

Photochemical smog
An atmospheric condition formed through a combination of weather conditions and pollution, especially from motor vehicle emissions.

Photovoltaic cell
Solar energy cells, usually made from silicon, that collect solar rays to generate electricity.

Point-source pollution
Pollution that enters water from a specific source.

Pollution
Addition of more waste than a resource can accommodate.

Potential reserve
The amount of energy in deposits not yet identified but thought to exist.

Preservation
Maintenance of a resource in its present condition, with as little human impact as possible.

Proven reserve
The amount of a resource remaining in discovered deposits.

Recycling
The separation, collection, processing, marketing, and reuse of unwanted material.

Renewable energy
A resource that has a theoretically unlimited supply and is not depleted when used by humans.

Resource
A substance in the environment that is useful to people, is economically and technologically feasible to access, and is socially acceptable to use.

Sanitary landfill
A place to deposit solid waste, where a layer of earth is bulldozed over garbage each day to reduce emissions of gases and odors from the decaying trash, to minimize fires, and to discourage vermin.

Sustainability
The use of Earth's limited resources by humans in ways that do not constrain resource use by people in the future.

Sustainable development
The level of development that can be maintained in a country without depleting resources to the extent that future generations will be unable to achieve a comparable level of development.

Glossary

Abiotic   A system composed of nonliving or inorganic matter.

Acid deposition   Sulfur oxides and nitrogen oxides, emitted by burning fossil fuels, enter the atmosphere—where they combine with oxygen and water to form sulfuric acid and nitric acid—and return to Earth's surface.

Acid precipitation   Conversion of sulfur oxides and nitrogen oxides to acids that return to Earth as rain, snow, or fog.

Active solar energy systems   Solar energy system that collects energy through the use of mechanical devices such as photovoltaic cells or flat-plate collectors.

Adolescent fertility rate   The number of births per 1,000 women age 15–19.

Agribusiness   Commercial agriculture characterized by the integration of different steps in the food-processing industry, usually through ownership by large corporations.

Agricultural density   The ratio of the number of farmers to the total amount of land suitable for agriculture.

Agriculture   The deliberate effort to modify a portion of Earth's surface through the cultivation of crops and the raising of livestock for sustenance or economic gain.

Air pollution   Concentration of trace substances, such as carbon monoxide, sulfur dioxide, nitrogen oxides, hydrocarbons, and solid particulates, at a greater level than occurs in average air.

Animate power   Power supplied by people or animals.

Animism   Belief that objects, such as plants and stones, or natural events, like thunderstorms and earthquakes, have a discrete spirit and conscious life.

Annexation   Legally adding land area to a city in the United States.

Anocracy   A country that is not fully democratic or fully autocratic, but rather displays a mix of the two types.

Apartheid   Laws (no longer in effect) in South Africa that physically separated different races into different geographic areas.

Aquaculture (or aquafarming)   The cultivation of seafood under controlled conditions.

Arable land   Land suited for agriculture.

Arithmetic density   The total number of people divided by the total land area.

Atmosphere   The thin layer of gases surrounding Earth.

Autocracy   A country that is run according to the interests of the ruler rather than the people.

Balance of power   Condition of roughly equal strength between opposing countries or alliances of countries.

Balkanization   Process by which a state breaks down through conflicts among its ethnicities.

Basic industries   Industries that sell their products or services primarily to consumers outside the settlement.

Biodiversity   The number of species within a specific habitat.

Biosphere   All living organisms on Earth.

Biotic   The system composed of living organisms.

Boundary   Invisible line that marks the extent of a state's territory.

Brain drain   Large-scale emigration by talented people.

Branch (of a religion)   A large and fundamental division within a religion.

Break-of-bulk point   A location where transfer is possible from one mode of transportation to another.

Bulk-gaining industry   An industry in which the final product weighs more or comprises a greater volume than the inputs.

Bulk-reducing industry   An industry in which the final product weighs less or comprises a lower volume than the inputs.

Business services   Services that primarily meet the needs of other businesses, including professional, financial, and transportation services.

Cartography   The science of making maps.

Central business district (CBD)   The area of a city where consumer, business, and public services are clustered.

Central place   A market center for the exchange of services by people attracted from the surrounding area.

Central place theory   A theory that explains the distribution of services, based on the fact that settlements serve as centers of market areas for services; larger settlements are fewer and farther apart than smaller settlements and provide services for a larger number of people who are willing to travel farther.

Census tract   An area delineated by the U.S. Bureau of the Census for which statistics are published; in urbanized areas, census tracts are often delineated to correspond roughly to neighborhoods.

Centripetal force   An attitude that tends to unify people and enhance support for a state.

Cereal grain   A grass yielding grain for food.

Chain migration   Migration of people to a specific location because relatives or members of the same nationality previously migrated there.

Chlorofluorocarbon (CFC)   A gas used as a solvent, a propellant in aerosols, a refrigerant, and in plastic foams and fire extinguishers.

City   An urban settlement that has been legally incorporated into an independent, self-governing unit.

City-state   A sovereign state comprising a city and its immediate hinterland.

Clustered rural settlement   An agricultural based community in which a number of families live in close proximity to each other, with fields surrounding the collection of houses and farm buildings.

Colonialism   Attempt by one country to establish settlements and to impose its political, economic, and cultural principles in another territory.

Colony   A territory that is legally tied to a sovereign state rather than completely independent.

Combined statistical area (CSA)   In the United States, two or more contiguous core based statistical areas tied together by commuting patterns.

Commercial agriculture   Agriculture undertaken primarily to generate products for sale off the farm.

Compact state   A state in which the distance from the center to any boundary does not vary significantly.

Concentration   The spread of something over a given area.

Concentric zone model   A model of the internal structure of cities in which social groups are spatially arranged in a series of rings.

Connection Relationships among people and objects across the barrier of space.

Conservation The sustainable use and management of a natural resource, through consuming at a less rapid rate than it can be replaced.

Consumer services Businesses that provide services primarily to individual consumers, including retail services and education, health, and leisure services.

Contagious diffusion The rapid, widespread diffusion of a feature or trend throughout a population.

Core based statistical area (CBSA) In the United States, a term referring to either a metropolitan statistical area or a micropolitan statistical area.

Cosmogony A set of religious beliefs concerning the origin of the universe.

Cottage industry Manufacturing based in homes rather than in a factory, commonly found prior to the Industrial Revolution.

Counterurbanization Net migration from urban to rural areas in more developed countries.

Creole or creolized language A language that results from the mixing of a colonizer's language with the indigenous language of the people being dominated.

Crop Grain or fruit gathered from a field as a harvest during a particular season.

Crop rotation The practice of rotating use of different fields from crop to crop each year, to avoid exhausting the soil.

Crude birth rate (CBR) The total number of live births in a year for every 1,000 people alive in the society.

Crude death rate (CDR) The total number of deaths in a year for every 1,000 people alive in the society.

Cultural ecology The geographic study of human-environment relationships.

Cultural landscape Fashioning of a natural landscape by a cultural group.

Culture The body of customary beliefs, social forms, and material traits that together constitute a group of people's distinct tradition.

Custom The frequent repetition of an act, to the extent that it becomes characteristic of the group of people performing the act.

Demographic transition The process of change in a society's population from a condition of high crude birth and death rates and low rate of natural increase to a condition of low crude birth and death rates, low rate of natural increase, and a higher total population.

Denglish Combination of German and English.

Denomination (of a religion) A division of a branch that unites a -number of local congregations in a single legal and administrative body.

Density The frequency with which something exists within a given unit of area.

Dependency ratio The number of people who are considered too young or too old to work (under age 15 or over age 64), compared to the number of people in their productive years.

Developed country (more developed country or MDC) A country that has progressed relatively far along a continuum of development.

Developing country (less developed country or LDC) A country that is at a relatively early stage in the process of economic development.

Development A process of improvement in the material conditions of people through diffusion of knowledge and technology.

Dialect A regional variety of a language distinguished by vocabulary, spelling, and pronunciation.

Dietary energy consumption The amount of food that an individual consumes.

Diffusion The process of spread of a feature or trend from one place to another over time.

Dispersed rural settlement A rural settlement pattern in which farmers live on individual farms isolated from neighbors.

Distance decay The diminishing in importance and eventual disappearance of a phenomenon with increasing distance from its origin.

Distribution The arrangement of something across Earth's surface.

Doubling time The number of years needed to double a population, assuming a constant rate of natural increase.

Ecology The scientific study of ecosystems.

Economic base A community's collection of basic industries.

Ecosystem A group of living organisms and the abiotic spheres with which they interact.

Edge city A large node of office and retail activities on the edge of an urban area.

Elderly support ratio The number of working-age people (ages 15–64) divided by the number of persons 65 or older.

Elongated state A state with a long, narrow shape.

Emigration Migration from a location.

Environmental determinism A nineteenth- and early twentieth-century approach to the study of geography that argued that the general laws sought by human geographers could be found in the physical sciences. Geography was therefore the study of how the physical environment caused human activities.

Epidemiologic transition Distinctive causes of death in each stage of the demographic transition.

Epidemiology Branch of medical science concerned with the incidence, distribution, and control of diseases that affect large numbers of people.

Ethnic cleansing Process in which a more powerful ethnic group forcibly removes a less powerful one in order to create an ethnically homogeneous region.

Ethnicity Identity with a group of people who share the cultural traditions of a particular homeland or hearth.

Ethnic religion A religion with a relatively concentrated spatial distribution whose principles are likely to be based on the physical characteristics of the particular location in which its adherents are concentrated.

Expansion diffusion The spread of a feature or trend among people from one area to another in an additive process.

Extinct language A language that was once used by people in daily activities but is no longer used.

Fair trade Alternative to international trade that emphasizes small businesses and worker-owned and democratically run cooperatives and requires employers to pay workers fair wages, permit union organizing, and comply with minimum environmental and safety standards.

Federal state An internal organization of a state that allocates most powers to units of local government.

Ferrous Metals, including iron ore, that are utilized in the production of iron and steel.

Forced migration Permanent movement compelled usually by cultural factors.

Formal region (or uniform or homogeneous region) An area in which everyone shares in one or more distinctive characteristics.

Folk culture Culture traditionally practiced by a small, homogeneous, rural group living in relative isolation from other groups.

Food security Physical, social, and economic access at all times to safe and nutritious food sufficient to meet dietary needs and food preferences for an active and healthy life.

Foreign direct investment Investment made by a foreign company in the economy of another country.

Fossil fuel Energy source formed from the residue of plants and animals buried millions of years ago.

Fragmented state A state that includes several discontinuous pieces of territory.

Franglais A term used by the French for English words that have entered the French language; a combination of *français* and *anglais,* the French words for "French" and "English," respectively.

Frontier A zone separating two states, in which neither state exercises political control.

Functional region (or nodal region) An area organized around a node or focal point.

Fundamentalism A literal interpretation and strict and intense adherence to basic principles of a religion.

Gender Inequality Index (GII) Indicator constructed by the United-Nations to measure the extent of each country's gender inequality.

Genocide The mass killing of a group of people in an attempt to -eliminate the entire group from existence.

Gentrification A process of converting an urban neighborhood from a predominantly low-income renter-occupied area to a predominantly middle-class, owner occupied area.

Geographic grid A system of imaginary arcs drawn in a grid pattern on Earth's surface.

Geographic Information Science (GIScience) The development and analysis of data about Earth acquired through satellite and other electronic information technologies.

Geographic information system (GIS) A computer system that stores, organizes, analyzes, and displays geographic data.

Gerrymandering Process of redrawing legislative boundaries for the purpose of benefiting the party in power.

Globalization Actions or processes that involve the entire world and result in making something worldwide in scope.

Global Positioning System (GPS) A system that determines the -precise position of something on Earth through a series of satellites, -tracking stations, and receivers.

Grain Seed of a cereal grass.

Gravity model A model that holds that the potential use of a service at a particular location is directly related to the number of people in a location and inversely related to the distance people must travel to reach the service.

Greenhouse effect Anticipated increase in Earth's temperature, caused by carbon dioxide (emitted by burning fossil fuels) trapping some of the radiation emitted by the surface.

Green revolution Rapid diffusion of new agricultural technology, especially new high-yield seeds and fertilizers.

Greenwich Mean Time (GMT) The time in that time zone encompassing the prime meridian, or 0° longitude.

Gross domestic product (GDP) The value of the total output of goods and services produced in a country in a year, not accounting for money that leaves and enters the country.

Gross national income (GNI) The value of the output of goods and services produced in a country in a year, including money that leaves and enters the country.

Guest worker A term once used for a worker who migrated to the developed countries of northern and western Europe, usually from southern and eastern Europe or from North Africa, in search of higher-paying jobs.

Habit A repetitive act performed by a particular individual.

Hearth The region from which innovative ideas originate.

Hierarchical diffusion The spread of a feature or trend from one key person or node of authority or power to other persons or places.

Human Development Index (HDI) Indicator of level of development for each country, constructed by United Nations, combining income, literacy, education, and life expectancy.

Hydrosphere All of the water on and near Earth's surface.

Immigration Migration to a new location.

Industrial Revolution A series of improvements in industrial technology that transformed the process of manufacturing goods.

Inequality-adjusted HDI (IHDI) Indicator of level of development for each country that modifies the HDI to account for inequality.

Infant mortality rate (IMR) The total number of deaths in a year among infants under 1 year old for every 1,000 live births in a society.

Intensive subsistence agriculture A form of subsistence agriculture in which farmers must expend a relatively large amount of effort to produce the maximum feasible yield from a parcel of land.

Internal migration Permanent movement within a particular country.

International Date Line A meridian that for the most part follows 180° longitude. When you cross the International Date Line heading east (toward America), the clock moves back 24 hours (one day), and when you go west (toward Asia), the calendar moves ahead one day.

International migration Permanent movement from one country to another.

Interregional migration Permanent movement from one region of a country to another.

Intraregional migration Permanent movement within one region of a country.

Isogloss Geographical boundary of a language feature.

Isolated language A language that is unrelated to any other languages and therefore not attached to any language family.

Just-in-time delivery Shipment of parts and materials to arrive at a factory moments before they are needed.

Labor-intensive industry An industry for which labor costs comprise a high percentage of total expenses.

Landlocked state A state that does not have a direct outlet to the sea.

Language A system of communication through the use of speech, a collection of sounds understood by a group of people to have the same meaning.

Language branch A collection of languages related through a common ancestor that existed several thousand years ago. Differences are not as extensive or as old as with language families, and archaeological evidence can confirm that the branches derived from the same family.

Language family A collection of languages related to each other through a common ancestor long before recorded history.

Language group A collection of languages within a branch that share a common origin in the relatively recent past and display many similarities in grammar and vocabulary.

Latitude   The numbering system used to indicate the location of parallels drawn on a globe and measuring distance north and south of the equator (0°).

Life expectancy   The average number of years an individual can be expected to live, given current social, economic, and medical conditions. Life expectancy at birth is the average number of years a newborn infant can expect to live.

Lingua franca   A language mutually understood and commonly used in trade by people who have different native languages.

Literacy rate   The percentage of a country's people who can read and write.

Literary tradition   A language that is written as well as spoken.

Lithosphere   Earth's crust and a portion of the upper mantle directly below the crust.

Location   The position of anything on Earth's surface.

Longitude   The numbering system used to indicate the location of meridians drawn on a globe and measuring distance east and west of the prime meridian (0°).

Map   A two-dimensional, or flat, representation of Earth's surface or a portion of it.

Map scale   The relationship between the size of an object on a map and the size of the actual feature on Earth's surface.

Market area (or hinterland)   The area surrounding a central place, from which people are attracted to use the place's goods and services.

Maternal mortality ratio   The number of women who die giving birth per 100,000 births.

Meridian   An arc drawn on a map between the North and South poles.

Metropolitan statistical area (MSA)   In the United States, a central city of at least 50,000 population, the county within which the city is located, and adjacent counties meeting one of several tests indicating a functional connection to the central city.

Micropolitan statistical area (μSA)   In the United States, an urban area of between 10,000 and 50,000 inhabitants, the county in which it is found, and adjacent counties tied to the city.

Migration   Form of relocation diffusion involving a permanent move to a new location.

Migration transition   Change in the migration pattern in a society that results from industrialization, population growth, and other social and economic changes that also produce the demographic transition.

Milkshed   The ring surrounding a city from which milk can be supplied without spoiling.

Missionary   An individual who helps to diffuse a universalizing religion.

Monotheism   The doctrine or belief of the existence of only one god.

Multinational state   State that contains two or more ethnic groups with traditions of self-determination that agree to coexist peacefully by recognizing each other as distinct nationalties.

Multiple nuclei model   A model of the internal structure of cities in which social groups are arranged around a collection of nodes of activities.

Nationalism   Loyalty and devotion to a particular nationality.

Nationality   Identity with a group of people who share legal attachment and personal allegiance to a particular place as a result of being born there.

Nation-state   A state whose territory corresponds to that occupied by a particular ethnicity that has been transformed into a nationality.

Native speakers   People for whom a particular language is their first language.

Natural increase rate (NIR)   The percentage growth of a population in a year, computed as the crude birth rate minus the crude death rate.

Net migration   The difference between the level of immigration and the level of emigration.

Nonbasic industries   Industries that sell their products primarily to consumers in the community.

Nonferrous   Metals utilized to make products other than iron and steel.

Nonpoint-source pollution   Pollution that originates from a large, diffuse area.

Nonrenewable energy   A source of energy that is a finite supply capable of being exhausted.

Official language   The language adopted for use by the government for the conduct of business and publication of documents.

Overfishing   Capturing fish faster than they can reproduce.

Overpopulation   The number of people in an area exceeds the capacity of the environment to support life at a decent standard of living.

Ozone   A gas that absorbs ultraviolet solar radiation, found in the stratosphere, a zone between 15 and 50 kilometers (9 to 30 miles) above Earth's surface.

Pandemic   Disease that occurs over a wide geographic area and affects a very high proportion of the population.

Parallel   A circle drawn around the globe parallel to the equator and at right angles to the meridians.

Passive solar energy systems   Solar energy system that collects energy without the use of mechanical devices.

Pastoral nomadism   A form of subsistence agriculture based on herding domesticated animals.

Pattern   The regular arrangement of something in a study area.

Perforated state   A state that completely surrounds another one.

Peripheral model   A model of North American urban areas consisting of an inner city surrounded by large suburban residential and business areas tied together by a beltway or ring road.

Photochemical smog   An atmospheric condition formed through a combination of weather conditions and pollution, especially from motor vehicle emissions.

Photovoltaic cell   Solar energy cells, usually made from silicon, that collect solar rays to generate electricity.

Physiological density   The number of people per unit of area of arable land, which is land suitable for agriculture.

Pidgin language   A language that mixes a simplified grammar and limited vocabulary of a lingua franca with another language.

Pilgrimage   A journey to a place considered sacred for religious purposes.

Place   A specific point on Earth distinguished by a particular characteristic.

Plantation   A large farm in tropical and subtropical climates that specializes in the production of one or two crops for sale, usually to a more developed country.

Point-source pollution   Pollution that enters water from a specific source.

Polder   Land created by the Dutch by draining water from an area.

Pollution   Addition of more waste than a resource can accommodate.

Polytheism   Belief in or worship of more than one god.

Popular culture   Culture found in a large, heterogeneous society that shares certain habits despite differences in other personal characteristics.

Population pyramid   A bar graph that displays the percentage of a place's population for each age and gender.

Possibilism   The theory that the physical environment may set limits on human actions, but people have the ability to adjust to the physical environment and choose a course of action from many alternatives.

Potential reserve   The amount of energy in deposits not yet identified but thought to exist.

Preservation   Maintenance of a resource in its present condition, with as little human impact as possible.

Primary census statistical area (PCSA)   In the United States, all of the combined statistical areas plus all of the remaining metropolitan statistical areas and micropolitan statistical areas.

Primary sector   The portion of the economy concerned with the direct extraction of materials from Earth's surface, generally through agriculture, although sometimes by mining, fishing, and forestry.

Primate city   The largest settlement in a country, if it has more than twice as many people as the second-ranking settlement.

Primate city rule   A pattern of settlements in a country, such that the largest settlement has more than twice as many people as the second-ranking settlement.

Prime meridian   The meridian, designated as 0° longitude that passes through the Royal Observatory at Greenwich, England.

Productivity   The value of a particular product compared to the amount of labor needed to make it.

Projection   The system used to transfer locations from Earth's surface to a flat map.

Prorupted state   An otherwise compact state with a large projecting extension.

Proven reserve   The amount of a resource remaining in discovered deposits.

Public services   Services offered by the government to provide security and protection for citizens and businesses.

Pull factor   Factor that induces people to move to a new location.

Push factor   Factor that induces people to leave old residences.

Quotas   In reference to migration, laws that place maximum limits on the number of people who can immigrate to a country each year.

Race   Identity with a group of people who share a biological ancestor.

Racism   Belief that race is the primary determinant of human traits and capacities and that racial differences produce an inherent superiority of a particular race.

Racist   A person who subscribes to the beliefs of racism.

Ranching   A form of commercial agriculture in which livestock graze over an extensive area.

Range (of a service)   The maximum distance people are willing to travel to use a service.

Rank-size rule   A pattern of settlements in a country, such that the nth largest settlement is 1/n the population of the largest settlement.

Recycling   The separation, collection, processing, marketing, and reuse of unwanted material.

Refugees   People who are forced to migrate from their home country and cannot return for fear of persecution because of their race, religion, nationality, membership in a social group, or political opinion.

Region   An area of Earth distinguished by a distinctive combination of cultural and physical features.

Relocation diffusion   The spread of a feature or trend through bodily movement of people from one place to another.

Remote sensing   The acquisition of data about Earth's surface from a satellite orbiting the planet or other long-distance methods.

Renewable energy   A resource that has a theoretically unlimited supply and is not depleted when used by humans.

Resource   A substance in the environment that is useful to people, is economically and technologically feasible to access, and is socially acceptable to use.

Ridge tillage   System of planting crops on ridge tops in order to reduce farm production costs and promote greater soil conservation.

Right-to-work state   A U.S. state that has passed a law preventing a union and company from negotiating a contract that requires workers to join a union as a condition of employment.

Sanitary landfill   A place to deposit solid waste, where a layer of earth is bulldozed over garbage each day to reduce emissions of gases and odors from the decaying trash, to minimize fires, and to discourage vermin.

Scale   The relationship between the portion of Earth being studied and Earth as a whole.

Secondary sector   The portion of the economy concerned with manufacturing useful products through processing, transforming, and assembling raw materials.

Sect (of a religion)   A relatively small group that has broken away from an established denomination.

Sector model   A model of the internal structure of cities in which social groups are arranged around a series of sectors, or wedges, radiating out from the central business district (CBD).

Self-determination   Concept that ethnicities have the right to govern themselves.

Service   Any activity that fulfills a human want or need and returns money to those who provide it.

Sharecropper   A person who works fields rented from a landowner and pays the rent and repays loans by turning over to the landowner a share of the crops.

Shifting cultivation   A form of subsistence agriculture in which people shift activity from one field to another; each field is used for crops for a relatively few years and left fallow for a relatively long period.

Site   The physical character of a place.

Site factors   Location factors related to the costs of factors of production inside the plant, such as land, labor, and capital.

Situation   The location of a place relative to other places.

Situation factors   Location factors related to the transportation of materials into and from a factory.

Slash-and-burn agriculture   Another name for shifting cultivation, so named because fields are cleared by slashing the vegetation and burning the debris.

Social area analysis   Statistical analysis used to identify where people of similar living standards, ethnic background, and lifestyle live within an urban area.

Sovereignty   Ability of a state to govern its territory free from control of its internal affairs by other states.

Space   The physical gap or interval between two objects.

Space-time compression   The reduction in the time it takes to diffuse something to a distant place, as a result of improved communications and transportation systems.

Spanglish   Combination of Spanish and English, spoken by Hispanic Americans.

Spatial interaction   The movement of physical processes, human activities, and ideas within and among regions.

Sprawl   Development of new housing sites at relatively low density and at locations that are not contiguous to the existing built-up area.

Squatter settlement An area within a city in a developing country in which people illegally establish residences on land they do not own or rent and erect homemade structures.

State An area organized into a political unit and ruled by an established government with control over its internal and foreign affairs.

Stimulus diffusion The spread of an underlying principle, even though a specific characteristic is rejected.

Structural adjustment program Economic policies imposed on less developed countries by international agencies to create conditions encouraging international trade, such as raising taxes, reducing government spending, controlling inflation, selling publicly owned utilities to private corporations, and charging citizens more for services.

Subsistence agriculture Agriculture designed primarily to provide food for direct consumption by the farmer and the farmer's family.

Sustainability The use of Earth's limited resources by humans in ways that do not constrain resource use by people in the future.

Sustainable agriculture Farming methods that preserve long-term productivity of land and minimize pollution, typically by rotating soil-restoring crops with cash crops and reducing inputs of fertilizer and pesticides.

Sustainable development The level of development that can be maintained in a country without depleting resources to the extent that future generations will be unable to achieve a comparable level of development.

Swidden A patch of land cleared for planting through slashing and burning.

Taboo A restriction on behavior imposed by social custom.

Terroir The contribution of a location's distinctive physical features to the way food tastes.

Terrorism The systematic use of violence by a group in order to intimidate a population or coerce a government into granting it demands.

Tertiary sector The portion of the economy concerned with transportation, communications, and utilities, sometimes extended to the provision of all goods and services to people in exchange for payment.

Threshold The minimum number of people needed to support the service.

Toponym The name given to a portion of Earth's surface.

Total fertility rate (TFR) The average number of children a woman will have throughout her childbearing years.

Transnational corporation A company that conducts research, operates factories, and sells products in many countries, not just where its headquarters or shareholders are located.

Triangular slave trade A practice, primarily during the eighteenth century, in which European ships transported slaves from Africa to Caribbean islands, molasses from the Caribbean to Europe, and trade goods from Europe to Africa.

Truck farming Commercial gardening and fruit farming, so named because truck was a Middle English word meaning bartering or the exchange of commodities.

Unauthorized (or undocumented) immigrants People who enter a country without proper documents.

Undernourishment Dietary energy consumption that is continuously below the minimum requirement for maintaining a healthy life and carrying out light physical activity.

Unitary state An internal organization of a state that places most power in the hands of central government officials.

Universalizing religion A religion that attempts to appeal to all people, not just those living in a particular location.

Urbanized area In the United States, a central city plus its contiguous built-up suburbs.

Value added The gross value of the product minus the costs of raw materials and energy.

Vernacular region (or perceptual region) An area that people believe exists as part of their cultural identity.

Wet rice Rice planted on dryland in a nursery and then moved to a deliberately flooded field to promote growth.

Credits

FM Half Title Page ASP/YPP/agefotostock Title Page Axiom Photographic Agency/agefotostock

Chapter 1 1.CO.MAIN Blaine Harrington III/Alamy 1.CO.B Google, Inc. 1.CO.D Jocelyn Augustino/Photoshot 1.1.1 Blaine Harrington III/Alamy 1.1.2 Jon Arnold/Alamy 1.1.5 Jenny Matthews/Alamy 1.1.7 jeremy sutton-hibbert/Alamy 1.2.1A Image & Stories/Alamy 1.2.1B blickwinkel/Alamy 1.2.2 North Wind Picture Archives/Alamy 1.2.3 World History Archive/Alamy 1.2.1C Courtesy of James Mellaart 1.2.4 Courtesy of The Library of Congress 1.2.5 Interfoto/History/Alamy 1.5.2 Dennis MacDonald/Alamy 1.5.1 Google, Inc. 1.5.4 Google, Inc. 1.6.1 Robert Spencer/Redux Pictures 1.6.2 Jelle van der Wolf/Alamy 1.6.4 Google, Inc. 1.8.1 Ron Yue/Alamy 1.8.3A Kevin Foy/Alamy 1.8.3B Christoph Papsch/Alamy 1.8.3C Michael Jenner/Alamy 1.8.3D Andrew Woodley/Alamy 1.8.3E Alison Wright/Alamy 1.8.3F Andrew Melbourne/Alamy 1.9.3A Chen Xiaobo/Alamy 1.9.3B Jeremy Hoare/Alamy 1.10.4 Christoph Papsch/Alamy 1.11.1 Astrofoto/Alamy 1.11.2 Norbert Probst/Alamy 1.11.3 T. Dressler/Specialist Stock 1.11.5 Balthasar Thomass/Alamy 1.12.1 jochem wijnands/Alamy 1.12.2 Jocelyn Augustino/Photoshot 1.CR.1 Worldspec/NASA/Alamy 1.CR.2 Pearson 1.CR.3 Google, Inc. 1.CR.4 Google, Inc. 1.EOC.MAIN ERproductions Ltd/photolibrary.com

Chapter 2 2.CO.MAIN ERproductions Ltd/photolibrary.com 2.CO.A Bertrand Rieger/Photoshot 2.CO.B David R. Frazier/Alamy 2.CO.C jeremy sutton-hibbert/Alamy 2.1.1 Sue Cunningham/Alamy 2.1.2 Frans Lemmens/Alamy 2.2.2 Bertrand Rieger/Photoshot 2.2.4 Pearson 2.3.3 Penny Tweedie/Alamy 2.5.1 Jake Lyell/Alamy 2.5.STAGE 2 Renato Bordoni/Alamy 2.5.STAGE 3 David R. Frazier/Alamy 2.5.STAGE 4 Holger Leue/Alamy 2.6.4 jeremy sutton-hibbert/Alamy 2.7.4 Helene Rogers/Alamy 2.7.5 Alain Le Garsmeur/Photolibrary.com 2.8.1 Neil Emmerson/Photolibrary.com 2.8.3 Yvan Travert/Photolibrary.com 2.9.1 Wissam Al-Okaili/Getty Images 2.9.2 Liba Taylor/Alamy 2.9.3B Google, Inc. 2.CR.1 Bertand Rieger/Photoshot 2.CR.2 Pearson 2.CR.3 Google, Inc. 2.EOC.MAIN Yvan TRAVERT/Photolibrary.com

Chapter 3 3.CO.MAIN Yvan TRAVERT/Photolibrary.com 3.1 Mark Peterson/Photolibrary.com 3.1.3 JULIO ETCHART/Photolibrary.com 3.2.2 World History Archive/Alamy 3.2.3 Courtesy of the Library of Congress 3.2.4 David Grossman/Alamy 3.3.3 TravelStockCollection - Homer Sykes/Alamy 3.3.4 Cesario da Fonseca/Photolibrary.com 3.4.1 Sean Sprague/Photolibrary.com 3.5.2 Boris Heger/Photolibrary.com 3.5.4 Ian Dagnall/Alamy 3.5.5 Terry North/iStockPhoto.com 3.6.2 Alain Le Bot/Photononstop/Photolibrary.com 3.6.5 Balthasar Thomass/Alamy 3.7.2 Jim West/Alamy 3.7.1 Jim West/Photolibrary.com 3.7.3 David Grossman/Alamy 3.7.4 Jim West/Alamy 3.8.3 Aerial Archives/Alamy 3.8.4 Pearson 3.8.5 Robert Harding Picture Library Ltd/Alamy 3.8.6 Jim Wark/Photolibrary.com

3.8.7 Sean Sprague/Photolibrary.com 3.9.1 Wayne J Grundy/Alamy 3.9.2 Gordon M. Grant/Alamy 3.9.3 A. Farnsworth/Photolibrary.com 3.9.4 Homer Sykes Archive/Alamy 3.CR.1 wendy connett/Alamy 3.CO.1 Terry North/IStockPhoto.com 3.CO.2 David Grossman/Alamy 3.CO.3 Sean Sprague/Photolibrary.com 3.EOC.MAIN NobleIMAGES/Alamy

Chapter 4 4.CO.MAIN NobleIMAGES/Alamy 4.CO.1 Arco Images GmbH/Alamy 4.CO.2 Amar and Isabelle Guillen - Guillen Photography/Alamy 4.CO.3 Alan Copson/photolibrary.com 4.1.1 Tao Gan/photolibrary.com 4.1.2 Felipe Rodriguez/photolibrary.com 4.1.3 Imago stock&people/Newscom 4.1.4 Blair Seltz/photolibrary.com 4.1.5 Chris Willson/Alamy 4.2.1 Cathrine Wessel/CORBIS 4.2.2 HOANG DINH NAM/Getty Images 4.2.3 Lou Linwei/Alamy 4.2.4 "The Landscape of Music." Reprinted with Permission of AT&T Labs. All Rights Reserved. 4.3.1A Amar and Isabelle Guillen - Guillen Photography/Alamy 4.3.1B imagebroker/Alamy 4.3.1C Eric Nathan/Alamy 4.3.3 Megapress/Alamy 4.3.4 David Morgan/Alamy 4.3.5 Gunter Marx/Alamy 4.4.1a John Burke/photolibrary.com 4.4.1b Nyttend 4.4.1c Library of Congress 4.5.1 Arco Images GmbH/Alamy 4.5.4a Cephas Picture Library/Alamy 4.5.4b Scott Kemper/Alamy 4.6.1a zhanna ocheret/Shutterstock.com 4.6.1b Visions of America, LLC/Alamy 4.6.1c Jacek Kadaj/Shutterstock.com 4.6.2 REUTERS/Jean-Paul Pelissier 4.6.3a Alan Gignoux/Alamy 4.6.3b Charles O. Cecil/Alamy 4.6.3c Tim Graham/Alamy 4.7 Tim Caddick/Alamy 4.7.3 Pearson 4.8.1a Giorgio Fochesato/iStockphoto.com 4.8.1b tao jiarong/iStockphoto.com 4.8.1c RENE DROUYER/iStockphoto .com 4.8.1d Aman Khan/iStockphoto.com 4.8.3 Google, Inc. 4.8.4 Ron Niebrugge/Alamy 4.9.1 Hemis/Alamy 4.9.3 Manor Photography/Alamy 4.9.4 Alan Copson/photolibrary.com 4.9.5 Courtesy of Brenda Alvarez 4.CR.1 Robert Voets/CBS/ZUMA Press/Newscom 4.EOC.1 Google, Inc. 4.EOC.2 Pearson 4.EOC.3 Pearson 4.EOC.4 Pearson 4.EOC.5 Pearson 4.EOC.MAIN REUTERS/Nguyen Huy Kham

Chapter 5 5.CO.B Picture Contact BV/Alamy 5.CO.C Erwin Gavic 5.2.2 INSADCO Photography/Alamy 5.3.3 Kasia Nowak/Alamy 5.4.1 Courtesy of Pearson 5.5.3 Drive Images/Alamy 5.6.3 CNS/photolibrary.com 5.7.1 Eye Ubiquitous/photolibrary.com 5.7.2 Picture Contact BV/Alamy 5.7.3 Jeff Morgan/Alamy 5.8.1 Andre Jenny/Alamy 5.8.4 David R. Frazier/Alamy 5.8.5 CulturalEyes-AusSoc/Alamy 5.9.3 swissworld.org 5.9.5 Stephen Rees/iStockphoto.com 5.CR.1 Mathieu Belanger/Reuters Pictures 5.EOC Courtesy of Ethnologue.com 5.CO.MAIN REUTERS/Nguyen Huy Kham 5.EOC.MAIN Joshua Haviv/Shutterstock.com

Chapter 6 6.CO.MAIN Joshua Haviv/Shutterstock.com 6.CO.2 Pearson 6.CO.3 Jim Zuckerman/Alamy 6.CO.4 Ryan Rodrick Beiler/Alamy 6.1.3 Ray Roberts/Alamy 6.1.4 Michael Ventura/Alamy 6.2.1a David Lyons/Alamy 6.2.1b Peter Barritt/Alamy 6.2.1c

FALKENSTEINFOTO/Alamy 6.2.2a luminous/Alamy 6.2.2b Peter M. Wilson/Alamy 6.2.3 Jim Zuckerman/Alamy 6.2.4a Alan Novelli/Alamy 6.2.4b imagebroker/Alamy 6.3.1 Raymond Forbes/photolibrary.com 6.3.3 Pearson 6.3.4 Dennis MacDonald/photolibrary.com 6.4.1 Aurora Photos/Alamy 6.4.2 VojtechVlk/Shutterstock.com 6.4.3 JTB Photo/photolibrary.com 6.4.4 JTB Photo/photolibrary.com 6.5.2 Stephen Frink Collection/Alamy 6.5.3 Pearson 6.5.4 Iain Lowson/Alamy 6.6.1 Library of Congress 6.6.2 JTB Photo/photolibrary.com 6.6.3 Dallas and John Heaton/photolibrary.com 6.6.4b Linda Whitwam/Dorling Kindersley 6.6.5 Dinodia Photos/Alamy 6.7.1 Peter Arnold, Inc./Alamy 6.7.2 Zou Yanju/photolibrary.com 6.7.3 Robert Estall photo agency/Alamy 6.7.4 Chris Cheadle/photolibrary.com 6.8.2 Purcell Team/Alamy 6.8.4a BRYAN O'BRIEN /POOL/Photoshot 6.8.4b Enda Doran/Photoshot 6.9.2 dbimages/Alamy 6.9.3a Ryan Rodrick Beiler/Alamy 6.9.4 Nir Alon/Alamy 6.10.2 Robert Harding Picture Library Ltd/Alamy 6.10.3 Israel images/Alamy 6.CR.1 Jochen Tack/photolibrary.com 6.EOC.1 Courtesy of adherents.com 6.EOC.2 Courtesy of glenmary.org 6.EOC.3 Pearson 6.EOC.4 Google, Inc. 6.EOC.MAIN TOMASZ TOMASZEWSKI/National Geographic Stock

Chapter 7 7.CO.MAIN TOMASZ TOMASZEWSKI/National Geographic Stock 7.CO.2 Library of Congress 7.CO.3 Garry Black/Alamy 7.CO.4 Wim van Cappellen/photolibrary.com 7.1.1A REUTERS/Ho New 7.1.1B REUTERS/Ho New 7.1.1C OBAMA PRESS OFFICE/UPI/Newscom 7.1.2 FRANCES M. ROBERTS/Newscom 7.1.3 Corbis Flirt/Alamy 7.1.4 REUTERS/Will Burgess 7.2.7 Kim Karpeles/Alamy 7.3.1 Library of Congress 7.4.1 Bettmann/CORBIS 7.4.2 Bettmann/CORBIS 7.4.3A William Campbell/Corbis Images 7.4.3B William Campbell/Corbis Images 7.4.4 Florian Kopp/photolibrary.com 7.5.1 Robert Francis/photolibrary .com 7.5.2 Garry Black/Alamy 7.5.3 Pearson 7.5.4 Mike Goldwater/Alamy 7.5.5 Gavin Hellier/photolibrary .com 7.6.2 Trinity Mirror/Mirrorpix/Alamy 7.7.1 Imagestate Media Partners Limited - Impact Photos/Alamy 7.7.6 Picture Contact BV/Alamy 7.8.2a Nigel Chandler/Sygma/Corbis Images 7.8.2b PCL/Alamy 7.8.4 U.S. Department of Defense Visual Information Center 7.9.2 RichardBakerSudan/Alamy 7.9.3 Wim van Cappellen/photolibrary.com 7.CR.1 Graham Lawrence/photolibrary.com 7.EOC.1 Pearson 7.EOC.2 Google, Inc. 7.EOC.MAIN Mark Henley/agefotostock.com

Chapter 8 8.CO.MAIN Mark Henley/agefotostock .com 8.CO.2 North Wind Picture Archives/Alamy 8.CO.3 David R. Frazier Photolibrary, Inc./Alamy 8.CO.4 Trinity Mirror/Mirrorpix/Alamy 8.1.3a Walter Bibikow/photolibrary.com 8.1.4b Ulana Switucha/photolibrary.com 8.2.3 North Wind Picture Archives/Alamy 8.2.2 North Wind Picture Archives/Alamy 8.2.5 Robert Estall photo agency/Alamy 8.4.2 National Geographic Image Collection/Alamy 8.5.2 The Print Collector/

Index

World States

ARCTIC OCEAN
Queen Elizabeth Islands
GREE (Den

Beaufort Sea

RUSSIA
ALASKA (U.S.)

Baffin Island

Bering Sea
Gulf of Alaska

Hudson Bay

CANADA
Canadian Shield
Newfoundland

Aleutian Islands

60°N

40°N

SIERRA NEVADA
ROCKY MOUNTAINS

Great Lakes

UNITED STATES
APPALACHIAN MTS.

ATLANTIC OCEAN

PACIFIC OCEAN

Tropic of Cancer

SIERRA MADRE

Gulf of Mexico

THE BAHAMAS

Baja California

CUBA

DOMINICAN REPUBLIC

20°N

HAWAII (U.S.)

MEXICO
BELIZE

HAITI
JAMAICA
ST. KITTS & NEVIS

ANTIGUA & BARBUDA
DOMINICA
ST. LUCIA
BARBADOS

GUATEMALA
HONDURAS
EL SALVADOR
NICARAGUA
COSTA RICA
PANAMA

GRENADA
ST. VINCENT & THE GRENADINES
TRINIDAD & TOBAGO

MARSHALL ISLANDS

VENEZUELA
COLOMBIA

GUYANA
SURINAME
FRENCH GUIANA (France)

Guiana Highlands

P O L Y N E S I A

0°

NAURU

K I R I B A T I

Equator

Galápagos Islands

ECUADOR

AMAZON BASIN

TUVALU

BRAZIL

SOLOMON IS.

VANUATU
FIJI

SAMOA

PERU
ANDES MOUNTAINS
BOLIVIA

Brazilian Highlands

20°S

TONGA

Tropic of Capricorn

Atacama Desert

PARAGUAY

NEW ZEALAND

PACIFIC OCEAN

CHILE

URUGUAY
Pampa
ARGENTINA

40°S

Patagonia

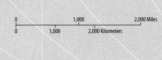

Falkland Islands

Strait of Magellan
Cape Horn

Tierra del Fuego
40°

180°W 160°W 140°W 120°W 100°W 80°W 60°S 60°W

Antarctic Circle